THE COLLECTED WORKS OF
SAMUEL TAYLOR COLERIDGE · 5

LECTURES 1808–1819
ON LITERATURE

General Editor: KATHLEEN COBURN
Associate Editor: BART WINER

THE COLLECTED WORKS

1. LECTURES 1795: ON POLITICS AND RELIGION

2. THE WATCHMAN

3. ESSAYS ON HIS TIMES

4. THE FRIEND

5. LECTURES 1808–1819: ON LITERATURE

6. LAY SERMONS

7. BIOGRAPHIA LITERARIA

8. LECTURES 1818–1819: ON THE HISTORY OF PHILOSOPHY

9. AIDS TO REFLECTION

10. ON THE CONSTITUTION OF THE CHURCH AND STATE

11. SHORTER WORKS AND FRAGMENTS

12. MARGINALIA

13. LOGIC

14. TABLE TALK

15. OPUS MAXIMUM

16. POETICAL WORKS

Mr. COLERIDGE

Informs the former Attendants at his Lectures, and his Friends in general, that being now recovered from his severe and protracted Illness, he proposes to give

Six Lectures,

ON THE FOLLOWING SUBJECTS AND IN THE FOLLOWING ORDER,

ON TUESDAY AND THURSDAY EVENINGS,

SEVEN o'Clock,

AT THE WHITE LION,

In BROAD STREET.

1st.—On the LIFE, CHARACTER, and PROSE WRITINGS of MILTON.

2nd.—On the MINOR POEMS of MILTON.

3rd and 4th.—On the PLAN, METRE, CHARACTERS, and distinguishing BEAUTIES of the PARADISE LOST.

5th.—On the Means of acquiring a just and austere POETIC TASTE, and its close connection with religious and moral feelings.—And

6th.—(By particular desire) a PHILOSOPHIC ANALYSIS of the DON QUIXOTE of Cervantes.

It is intended to give the first Lecture on TUESDAY next, the 5th of April 1814.—The Subscription for the Course, ONE GUINEA: Single Tickets, FOUR SHILLINGS.

Names received, and Tickets either for the Course or single Lectures to be had at Messrs. NORTON and SONS, and at Mr. SHEPPARD's, Booksellers ; at Mr. GUTCH's Printing Office ; or from Mr. COLERIDGE, at No. 2, QUEEN's SQUARE ; and at the Bar of the WHITE LION.

P.S. Mr. COLERIDGE has been desired by several highly respectable Ladies, to carry into effect a Plan of giving one or two LECTURES, in the MORNING, on the Subject of FEMALE EDUCATION, of a nature altogether practical, and explaining the whole machinery of a School organised on rational Principles, from the earliest Age to the completion of female education, with a list of the books recommended, &c. so as to evolve gradually into utility and domestic happiness the powers and qualities of womanhood. Should a sufficient number of Ladies and Gentlemen express their design to patronize this plan, Mr. COLERIDGE will hold himself ready to realize it, at such time as may be found most convenient to his auditors.

J. M. Gutch, Printer.

1. Prospectus issued for Coleridge's lectures on Milton and Cervantes at Bristol in 1814; this was preserved by Joseph Cottle, who inserted it in a copy of his *Early Recollections; Chiefly Relating to the Late Samuel Taylor Coleridge* (2 vols 1837).
The Houghton Library, Harvard University
reproduced by kind permission

THE COLLECTED WORKS OF

Samuel Taylor Coleridge

Lectures 1808–1819

On Literature

II

EDITED BY

R. A. Foakes

ROUTLEDGE & KEGAN PAUL

BOLLINGEN SERIES LXXV
PRINCETON UNIVERSITY PRESS

The Collected Works, sponsored by Bollingen Foundation,
is published in Great Britain
by Routledge & Kegan Paul Ltd
14 Leicester Square, London WC2H 7PH
ISBN 0–7100–9382–9
and in the United States of America
by Princeton University Press, 41 William Street
Princeton, New Jersey
ISBN 0–691–09872–7
LCC 85–43198
The Collected Works constitutes
the seventy-fifth publication in Bollingen Series

The present work, number 5 of the Collected Works,
is in 2 volumes, this being 5: II

Printed in the United States of America
by Princeton University Press

THIS EDITION
OF THE WORKS OF
SAMUEL TAYLOR COLERIDGE
IS DEDICATED
IN GRATITUDE TO
THE FAMILY EDITORS
IN EACH GENERATION

CONTENTS

━━━━━━ II ━━━━━━

LIST OF ILLUSTRATIONS

II

1814
LECTURES ON MILTON
AND CERVANTES
(WHITE LION, BRISTOL)

INTRODUCTION

When Coleridge arrived in Bristol in October 1813 he was full of energy and in good spirits; he set about raising money and help for the Morgans and applied himself to giving lectures in Bristol and in Clifton during the following month. In spite of the poor attendance at his Clifton lectures, he could say at the end: "I have made Friends of them all, even by my sarcastic observations on the contrast between Bristol & Clifton Patronage".[1] His health was good, except for a brief spell of sickness that began in drinking too much wine, and the care of the Morgans, with whom he had been living for eighteen months, had checked his reliance on opium.[2] At the end of the final lecture, the eighth, on 23 November, he announced his intention, according to the report in the *Bristol Gazette*, of offering another course in a fortnight's time, to consist of two lectures on "the Epic and Romantic of Shakespeare, not yet spoken of" and four on Milton.[3] Evidently he had hoped to persuade Mrs Morgan and Charlotte Brent to move from London to Bristol, where he thought they would find assistance in their financial difficulties and where he could exploit his success in lecturing by giving more courses and even setting up an academy.[4] However, Mrs Morgan refused to transfer to Bristol, and on 24 November Coleridge travelled to London, with the idea of carrying out the promise he made in a letter of 18 November when he wrote to her: "if your feelings are insurmountable, I will take leave of my Bristolian Friends, & instantly go off with you to Keswick".[5] In fact, Mrs Morgan and her sister went to live in Ashley, near Bath, and Coleridge accompanied them there, leaving London on 30 November. They halted at Reading on the way and travelled slowly, so that Coleridge left them at their lodgings on Sunday, 5 December, and walked in foul wintry conditions to Bath, where he found accommodation at the Greyhound Inn. According to a letter addressed on 8 December to his friend Josiah Wade, with whom he had been staying in Bristol, he already had a "violent cold" when

---

[1] To Mrs Morgan [20 Nov 1813]: *CL* III 459–60.
[2] See *CL* III 453 and *CN* III 4293 and n.
[3] See above, Lect 8 of the 1813 lectures (last paragraph of report). The reporter seems to have misrepresented what

C said; his prospectus refers to the "Poetic and Romantic character" of Shakespeare (see paragraph below).
[4] *CL* III 458.
[5] *CL* III 457.

3

he set out to walk to Bath, and there he fell ill, and had been confined to his bedroom ever since.[6] He was still in Bath on 19 December, having been seriously ill there. In late December he went to Bristol, expecting to lecture there in January, but could not do so. He was not able to start lecturing again until April 1814.

Before leaving Bristol for London on 24 November, Coleridge must have arranged for the printing of the prospectus of a course he intended to begin on Tuesday, 7 December. A copy of this is now in the Berg Collection of the New York Public Library, and the text printed here is taken from this; it has no indication of a printer, no heading, and no date, but runs as follows.

WITH grateful acknowledgements of the kindness with which he has been honored by his Auditors, Mr. COLERIDGE proposes to give a SECOND Course of LECTURES, TWO on those Plays of SHAKESPEAR which were not referred to in the former Course, and illustrative of the Poetic and Romantic character of our great Dramatist, namely, *The Tempest, Midsummer-Night's Dream, Merchant of Venice, As You Like It, Twelfth Night,* &c. and FOUR on the PARADISE LOST, and the Character of MILTON as a Man and a Poet; with an examination of Doctor JOHNSON's Preface to Shakespear, and his life of Milton.

The lectures to commence on TUESDAY, 7th December 1813, at the WHITE LION, Broad-Street, at Seven o'clock in the evening.

Subscription-Ticket, One Guinea.

Admission to the single Lecture, 5s.

Ladies and Gentlemen who propose to honor the Lectures with their attendance, are requested to leave their names at the Commercial Room, Mr. SHEPPARD's, on the Exchange, or at Mr. J. WADE's, No. 2, Queen-Square.
Bristol, Nov. 25, 1813.[7]

The text of this prospectus must have provided the copy for the advertisements that appeared in the *Bristol Mercury* on 29 November, *Felix Farley's Bristol Journal* on 4 December, and the *Bristol Mercury* on 6 December, all of which follow the prospectus with minor variants and include the date, "Nov. 25", at the foot. During this period Coleridge was away from Bristol, and was taken ill in Bath on his journey back from London on 5 December, so that he was not able to give the lectures as announced. He had recovered sufficiently by late December to think of offering the same course to begin on Tuesday, 4 January 1814, and accordingly he placed the following notice in the *Bristol Gazette* on 30 December, in *Felix Farley's Bristol Journal* and the *Bristol Mirror* on 1 January, and in the *Bristol Mercury* on 3 January:

---

[6] To Wade [8 Dec 1813]: *CL* III 462.
[7] The Berg ms is a single sheet, measuring 7″ x 4 ½″, apparently torn from a larger sheet that had been folded in two; if so, there may have been a heading on the missing half.

MR. COLERIDGE having been surprised and confined by sudden and severe illness at his arrival at Bath, six days before the promised commencement of his Second course, 7th December 1813, respectfully informs his Friends that this Second Course will commence on TUESDAY 4th January, 1814 at the WHITE LION; two Lectures on the remaining Plays of SHAKESPEAR, and four on the PARADISE LOST, and the Character of MILTON as a Man and a Poet . . . [the rest as in the prospectus, quoted above].

A letter written to Charlotte Brent a few days before 4 January shows that Coleridge expected to ''recommence on Tuesday Evening'',[8] but in it he complains of being still ''very far from well'', and since there is no other mention of lectures in January in the press or in other records, it seems certain that he had once again to cancel or postpone this course.

The next few months are a blank in Coleridge's history; no letters survive from this period, and apart from the publication in *Felix Farley's Bristol Journal* on 19 February of his poem *Tranquillity*,[9] nothing is heard of him until the spring of 1814, when he issued an undated prospectus announcing his intention to give six lectures on Milton and Cervantes beginning on 5 April;[10] this runs as follows:

Mr. COLERIDGE

Informs the former Attendants at his Lectures, and his Friends in general, that being now recovered from his severe and protracted Illness, he proposes to give

Six Lectures,

ON THE FOLLOWING SUBJECTS AND IN THE FOLLOWING ORDER,

ON TUESDAY AND THURSDAY EVENINGS,

SEVEN o'Clock,

AT THE WHITE LION,

In BROAD STREET.

1st.—On the LIFE, CHARACTER, and PROSE WRITINGS of MILTON.
2nd.—On the MINOR POEMS of MILTON.
3rd and 4th.—On the PLAN, METRE, CHARACTERS, and distinguishing BEAUTIES of the PARADISE LOST.
5th.—On the Means of acquiring a just and austere POETIC TASTE, and its close connection with religious and moral feelings.—And
6th.—(By particular desire) a PHILOSOPHIC ANALYSIS of the DON QUIXOTE of Cervantes.

[8] *CL* III 465.
[9] *PW* (EHC) I 361–2. As *Ode to Tranquillity* the poem was first published in the *M Post* in Dec 1801; it was reprinted in Jun 1809 in *The Friend* No 1 (*CC*) II 14.
[10] A copy of this, from which the text given here is reprinted, is in the Houghton Library at Harvard University. It is a single sheet approximately 9″ x 7½″, and the printer's name, J. M. Gutch, is given in the lower left-hand corner. The proprietor and publisher of *Felix Farley's Bristol Journal*, Gutch was later to be involved with the printing of *BL*.

It is intended to give the first Lecture on TUESDAY next, the 5th of April 1814.—The Subscription for the Course, ONE GUINEA: Single Tickets, FOUR SHILLINGS.

Names received, and Tickets either for the Course or single Lectures to be had at Messrs. NORTON and SONS, and at Mr. SHEPPARD's, Booksellers; at Mr. GUTCH's Printing Office; or from Mr. COLERIDGE, at No. 2, QUEEN'S SQUARE; and at the Bar of the WHITE LION.

P.S. Mr. COLERIDGE has been desired by several highly respectable Ladies, to carry into effect a Plan of giving one or two LECTURES, in the MORNING, on the Subject of FEMALE EDUCATION, of a nature altogether practical, and explaining the whole machinery of a School organised on rational Principles, from the earliest Age to the completion of female education, with a list of the books recommended, &c. so as to evolve gradually into utility and domestic happiness the powers and qualities of womanhood. Should a sufficient number of Ladies and Gentlemen express their design to patronize this plan, Mr. COLE-RIDGE will hold himself ready to realize it, at such time as may be found most convenient to his auditors.

The text of this prospectus was printed as an advertisement in the *Bristol Mirror* and *Felix Farley's Bristol Journal* on 2 April and in the *Bristol Mercury* on 4 April. It lists Coleridge's address as 2, Queen Square, showing that he was living once more, as in the previous autumn, at the house of his friend Josiah Wade; it is possible that this faithful and *"inexhaustibly patient* Friend"[11] had taken care of him throughout his long illness. The course of six lectures was delivered more or less as advertised. The *Bristol Gazette* carried a separate advertisement for the second lecture on Thursday, 7 April, and for the fourth on 14 April, promising in this one not only to comment, as stated in the prospectus, on *Paradise Lost*, but also to offer an ''Analytic Character'' of Napoleon, who had abdicated on 6 April and whose name was much in the news at this time. Lectures 3 and 4 in this series were also advertised jointly in the other three Bristol newspapers, and a brief review of his remarks on Napoleon in the conclusion of Lecture 4 appeared in *Felix Farley's Bristol Journal* on 16 April and was reprinted in the *Bristol Mercury* on 18 April. The last two lectures were not advertised further, but it is clear from his remarks in a letter to Cottle dated 24 April that he completed the course, even though, as he says, ''An erysipelatous complaint, of an alarming nature, has rendered me barely able to attend, & go thro' with, my Lectures—the Receipts of which have *almost* paid the expences of the Room, Advertisements, &c.''[12]

Nothing much is known about the content of these lectures, and no identifiable notes for them survive. Coleridge had lectured on Milton, but not so extensively, in 1808 and 1811. *Don Quixote* was the subject

[11] *CL* III 491.   [12] *CL* III 474.

of Lecture 8 in the 1818 series, so that the topics of all these lectures were matters of continuing interest to Coleridge. In his second lecture he referred to Satan as a *"sceptical Socinian"*,[13] giving offence to at least one eminent citizen of Bristol, the Unitarian minister John Prior Estlin, whom he had known and respected for many years. The day after delivering this lecture, Coleridge wrote an explanatory letter to Estlin, apologising for what may have seemed "improper Levity" in the use of the objectionable phrase, but defending his basic position, that Satan denied the divinity of Christ.[14] Estlin did not attend the lecture and must have heard from others what Coleridge said; but it seems from the comment of Coleridge's acquaintance Le Breton immediately after the lecture that the phrase had some special significance for Estlin, who was still "raising the city" of Bristol against Coleridge more than a fortnight later.[15]

The general advertisement and prospectus for the course ended with an offer of two lectures on female education if enough people expressed a desire to patronise them; presumably Coleridge had insufficient assurance of support when the course ended, for on 24 April he wrote:

the two far, far more important Lectures, for which I have been long preparing myself and have given more thought to than to any other Subject, viz. those on female Education from Infancy to Womanhood, practically systematized, I shall be (God permitting) ready to give, the latter end of the Week after next—[16]

Nothing more is heard of them, and there is no evidence to suggest that they were in fact delivered. Although Coleridge managed to give one further lecture in Bristol, the first of a proposed series of three on the French Revolution, he was too ill to continue those. He remained in Bristol with his friend Josiah Wade until September 1814, and his letters show that he consulted several doctors and that with Wade's help he was making a determined effort in May to overcome the heavy dependence on opium that had no doubt been a major contributing factor in the postponement or cancellation of courses since the previous December.

---

[13] To J. P. Estlin 9 Apr 1814: *CL* III 471.
[14] *CL* III 472.
[15] To Cottle 26 Apr 1814: *CL* III 477.
[16] To Cottle: *CL* III 474.

LECTURES 1–6

As so little information is available for this series delivered at the White Lion in Bristol, a commentary on the individual lectures is presented in a summary form.

LECTURE 1

DATE. Tuesday, 5 April 1814.

SUBJECT. "On the LIFE, CHARACTER, and PROSE WRITINGS of MILTON."

The subject is known only from the prospectus and general advertisement for the course. No separate advertisement was issued, and no reports of it were published. No notes by C can be certainly related to this lecture. On the day of delivery, C wrote a complimentary letter to the Unitarian minister John Prior Estlin, enclosing a ticket of admission; see the note on Lect 2, below.

LECTURE 2

DATE. Thursday, 7 April 1814.

SUBJECT. "On the MINOR POEMS of MILTON", including *Paradise Regained.*

The subject as announced in the prospectus and general advertisement, the minor poems of Milton, was confirmed in a separate advertisement for this lecture that appeared in the *Bristol Gazette* 7 Apr, giving the date, presumably in error, as "to-morrow evening", i.e. Fri, 8 Apr. No reports of it were published, and no notes by C can certainly be assigned to it. However, C must have included in the minor poems *Paradise Regained*, for a remark he made in the lecture was reported to Estlin, who took offence and, more than a fortnight later, was still angry about it (*CL* III 477). C had sent a ticket of admission to his lectures, presumably the whole course, to Estlin on 5 Apr. But Estlin did not attend Lect 2, as C's account of the affair, in an apologetic letter to him written on 9 Apr makes clear: "I have this very moment returned home: and on eagerly opening your note was, as it were, thunder-struck: and I have no reason to believe that I should have guessed the cause, had it not been for an accidental Speech of Mr Le Breton's to me, after my Lecture—'At a certain phrase of your's, (said he) I looked round to see whether Dr E. was there'—I instantly replied to him—Would to Heaven, he had been! the very sight of Him would have made it impossible that so foolish an expression should have entered into my mind, much less have been uttered by me.—And (I continued) yet I solemnly declare, that to the best of my Belief I should have been just as likely to have used it, being in a similar tone of mind, at the time that I was myself a most sincere & fervent Unitarian.—

"First, dear Sir! let me entreat you to consider that my Lectures, with

11

exception only of the general Plan & leading Thoughts, are literally & strictly *extempore*—the words of the moment! Next, let me hope that the expression used by me has not been represented with all the palliating Circumstances. Whoever was your Informer, can likewise tell you that the immediately preceding part of the Lecture had been of a (*for me*) unusually cheerful & even mirth-exciting nature—& in speaking of a sublime Invention of Milton, unsupported by the natural and obvious Sense of the Text (for had it been a mere quotation, like that of 'Let there be Light! &c' where had been *his* Sublimity?) I said in previous explanation these very words—'*for Milton has been pleased to represent Satan as a sceptical Socinian*'—

"Now had I said, that Milton had represented Satan as convinced of the prophetic & Messianic Character of Christ, but sceptical concerning any higher claims—I should have stated the mere matter of fact—& can I think it possible, that you should for ever withhold your affection & esteem from me merely because most incautiously & with improper Levity, I confess & with unfeigned Sorrow, I conveyed the very same thought or fact in a foolish Phrase?—" *CL* III 471–2. In a letter to Cottle on 26 Apr, C again defended himself as having said no more than was true in calling Satan a Socinian, because he denied the divinity of Christ; C claimed that without making this point he could not have explained the "sublimest single Passage" in all Milton's writings, referring Cottle to *Paradise Regained* IV 196ff and 500ff. *CL* III 477–8.

LECTURE 3

DATE. Tuesday, 12 April 1814.

SUBJECT. *Paradise Lost.*

The prospectus and general advertisement announced that Lects 3 and 4 would be "On the PLAN, METRE, CHARACTERS, and distinguishing BEAUTIES of the PARADISE LOST". The separate advertisement for Lect 2 in the *Bristol Gazette* 7 Apr also advertised Lect 3 as "on the Paradise Lost, with illustrative Readings". An advertisement for Lects 3 and 4, repeating the wording of the prospectus and general advertisement, also appeared in *Felix Farley's Bristol Journal* and the *Bristol Mirror* Sat, 9 Apr, and in the *Bristol Mercury* Mon, 11 Apr. No reports of this lecture were published, and no notes by C can be related to it with any certainty.

LECTURE 4

DATE. Thursday, 14 April 1814.

SUBJECT. *Paradise Lost*, leading into an account of the character of Napoleon.

The advertisements for Lects 3 and 4 that appeared in three Bristol newspapers 9 and 11 Apr simply repeated the wording of the prospectus and general advertisement, announcing the subject of this lecture as *Paradise Lost*. However, C placed a separate advertisement for Lect 4 in the *Bristol Gazette* Thurs, 14 Apr, the day on which he was scheduled to speak, as follows: "TO-MORROW EVENING, Seven o'Clock, at the WHITE LION, Mr. COLERIDGE will give his FOURTH LECTURE, Namely—1st. On the Metre of the Paradise Lost. 2nd. On the Construction of the Periods. 3rd. On the Characters, principally those of Adam and Eve, and of Satan; and he will conclude with a full Analytic Character of the late *'French Emperor'*, so entitled by the opprest Continent and ———; but who, thank Heaven! has never been for *Britons*, or by acknowledgement of Great Britain, other than Napoleon Bonaparte, the cowardly Corsican Usurper, Rebel and Assassin." Once again, as for Lect 2, the advertisement in the *Bristol Gazette* Thurs announced the date of it as "TO-MORROW EVENING", but it is clear from the brief report of this one printed in *Felix Farley's Bristol Journal* Sat, 16 Apr, and reprinted in the *Bristol Mercury* Mon, 18 Apr, that the lecture was in fact given on Thurs, not Fri. This report is not very informative and begins by quoting the advertisement. Most of it was reprinted in *Sh C* II 209 (257); it is reprinted below in full from *Felix Farley's Bristol Journal*, in which it was printed without a heading amongst other Bristol news:

"Mr. Coleridge's Lectures upon MILTON have been attended by those numerous and respectable audiences, which the splendid talents of this Gentleman cannot fail to attract and draw together. He concluded his 4th Lecture on Thursday last with a full Analytic Character of the late *'French Emperor'*, so entitled by the opprest Continent and ———; but who, thank Heaven! has never been for *Britons*, or by acknowledgment of Great Britain, other than Napoleon Buonaparte, the cowardly Corsican Usurper, Rebel and Assassin,— We are only performing an act of justice to inform our readers, that it was Mr. Coleridge, who wrote those essays and leading paragraphs in the Morning Post during the treacherous Peace of Amiens, which procured for all the English Newspapers, except the *Morning Chronicle*, the honour of exclusion from France; and which, as Mr. Fox asserted, produced the war with France, that war which has liberated Europe and human nature. Since that time Mr. C. has not ceased to fight the same good fight; and as he informed us in his lectures, in consequence, when he was on the Continent, his life was hunted for by the blood-thirsty Tyrant, an order for his arrest was sent express to Rome, and he escaped only by the providential favour of a noble Italian."

On 6 Apr Napoleon abdicated and retired to Elba. News of this event prompted C to conclude Lect 4 with an analysis of the French emperor, and presumably his character was linked with that of Satan, for, according to the report, C referred to Napoleon as a "blood-thirsty Tyrant". This was an appropriate moment to triumph in the fall of Napoleon, but C's attitude to him was varying and complex, and although he wrote elsewhere describing him as the "genuine offspring of the old serpent" (*Friend—CC*—I 232), and earlier in 1802 had written hostile essays on him for the *M Post* (*EOT—CC*—I 311–44), he also recognised Napoleon's abilities and stature, as many scattered comments in his writings and letters show. The report also indicates that C told a version of the story of his narrow escape from arrest at the orders of Napoleon when he was at Rome in 1806. It is difficult to discover how far C was exaggerating in telling an anecdote that probably had some foundation in actual events; a more detailed account of it is to be found in *BL* ch 10 (*CC*) I 216, and a comment on the various versions in *CN* II 2785n should be consulted; see also *EOT (CC)* I 226n–8. C's departure from the Rome area in May 1806 seems to have been arranged in too leisurely a fashion to allow credence to the notion that he was "hunted for".

LECTURE 5

DATE. Tuesday, 19 April 1814.

SUBJECT. "On the Means of acquiring a just and austere POETIC TASTE, and its close connection with religious and moral feelings."

The subject of this lecture is known only from the prospectus and general advertisement; no separate advertisement was issued, and no reports of it were published. The subject was one to which C returned again and again, and variant forms of it were the concern of Lect 1 in the 1808 series, Lect 2 of the 1811–12 series, and Lect 1 of the 1812–13 series. No notes by C can be certainly related to this lecture of 1814, but later in the year, on 13, 20, 27 Aug and 10 Sept, C published three essays, the last divided into two parts, "On the Principles of Genial Criticism Concerning the Fine Arts", and these may have had a connexion with his previous lectures on such matters as defining terms like beauty and describing what he meant by taste; these essays may be found in *BL* (1907) II 219–46.

LECTURE 6

DATE. Thursday, 21 April 1814.

SUBJECT. A "PHILOSOPHIC ANALYSIS of the DON QUIXOTE of Cervantes".

The subject of this lecture is known only from the prospectus and general advertisement. No separate advertisement was published, and no reports of it have been found. No notes by C can be related to this lecture with any certainty. He lectured again on *Don Quixote* in 1818 (Lect 8) and in 1819 (Lect 7) and may have used old materials for these. According to a letter he wrote on 24 Apr, he was ill and ''barely able'' to complete this course (*CL* III 474), but at least this shows that he did give the full number of six lectures, as promised in the prospectus.

1814
LECTURES ON THE FRENCH REVOLUTION
(WHITE LION, BRISTOL)

In late April 1814 the newspapers were full of reports and comments on the entry of the allies into Paris and the abdication of Napoleon. Coleridge had already seized the opportunity to talk about Napoleon in the series on Milton he completed on 21 April, and the general excitement occasioned by current events no doubt encouraged him, as he wrote in a letter of Sunday, 24 April, to "make another Trial, by advertising 3 Lectures, on the Rise, & Progress, & Conclusion of the French Revolution, with a critique on the proposed Constitution; but unless 50 names are procured, not a Lecture give I".[1] The advertisement had appeared the previous day in *Felix Farley's Bristol Journal*, as follows:

MR. COLERIDGE proposes to deliver THREE LECTURES in the Great Room at the WHITE LION, in Broad-Street, in this City—The first, on the RISE and CAUSES; the second, on the PROGRESS; and the third, on the CONCLUSION of the FRENCH REVOLUTION, with Remarks on the present Constitution accepted by Louis the Eighteenth.

The first lecture on Tuesday Evening on the 26th April, the second on Friday the 29th, and the last on Tuesday the 3rd of May.

Tickets of admission, 4s. each, to be had of Messrs. NORTON and Sons, Mr. SHEPPARD, Mr. GUTCH, and of Mr. COLERIDGE, No. 2 Queen's Square; also at the Bar of the White-Lion.

This advertisement was printed also in the *Bristol Mirror* Saturday, 23 April, and in the *Bristol Mercury* Monday, 25 April. Since admission was to be by ticket, not subscription, it is not clear how Coleridge hoped to procure fifty names, unless by private soliciting. A brief notice of the first lecture was published in *Felix Farley's Bristol Journal* Saturday, 30 April, indicating that Coleridge attracted a good audience:

Mr. COLERIDGE's Lecture, on Tuesday evening last, upon the rise & causes of the French Revolution was most numerously and respectably attended; but we lament to add, as must have been evident to every auditor, that Mr. C. from severe indisposition, was compelled abruptly to close his lecture, and he has since continued so indisposed that he was last night also obliged to postpone his second lecture, which if his health permits, he hopes to deliver on Tuesday evening in the ensuing week.

It seems that Coleridge at least intended to give the second, for he broke off a letter written probably on 27 or 28 April with the words, "I have to prepare my Lecture—O! with how *blank* a spirit!"[2] The blankness

---

[1] To Cottle: *CL* III 474. [2] To Cottle: *CL* III 480.

of spirit was caused partly by ill-health, but more by his sense of guilt and self-disgust in relation to a renewal of an excessive dependence on opium. His letters at this time record his agonies of body and mind, when he thought of placing himself under restraint in a madhouse; he had to endure the unsympathetic response of Cottle and Southey, who thought a mere effort of will would release him from his addiction, but by mid-May he had made a considerable recovery through the care of Josiah Wade, who had been away from Bristol when Coleridge was in his lowest state. Evidently Coleridge was, in the event, quite unable to give the second and third lectures, and the last mention of them occurs in the *Bristol Mercury* Monday, 2 May, with the announcement that, "Mr. COLERIDGE still continuing unwell, the lectures on the French Revolution are unavoidably postponed until further notice."[3]

---

[3] It is noted amongst other local news on p 3 col 4. No similar announcements in other Bristol newspapers have been found.

1818
LECTURES ON THE PRINCIPLES OF JUDGEMENT, CULTURE, AND EUROPEAN LITERATURE
(LONDON PHILOSOPHICAL SOCIETY)

INTRODUCTION

When he went to live with the Gillmans in Highgate in April 1816, Coleridge found a haven where he could begin a new and settled life and give the lie to the common image of him as "the wild eccentric Genius that has published nothing but fragments & splendid Tirades".[1] In the next two years he published *Christabel, The Statesman's Manual* (1816), *A Lay Sermon, Biographia Literaria*, his unperformed play *Zapolya* (all three in 1817), and his Introduction to *The Encyclopaedia Metropolitana* (January 1818). He also redesigned, largely rewrote, and prepared for the press the three-volume edition of *The Friend*, which appeared in November 1818. This hectic period of writing did not bring the financial returns he had hoped for. He made a bad mistake in deciding to deal with the publishing firm of Gale and Curtis rather than the larger and better known John Murray, though his reasons for doing so were high-minded: "I have a high opinion of Mr. Gale and Curtis's *principles*; and I prefer forming a connection with a religious house".[2] In fact, Thomas Curtis, who had recently taken orders and had nominally retired from the company, which became known as Gale and Fenner, proved to be quite unprincipled and, with his new partner Fenner, not only cheated Coleridge, but succeeded in poisoning his relations with Murray.[3] In 1819 Gale and Fenner were declared bankrupt, and Coleridge not only lost the profits he might have expected on the sale of his own books, but was forced, so he said, to purchase the stock of his own books and the half copyright in them held by the publisher.[4] Long before this, in July 1817, he was expressing frustration and anger at the double-dealing of Curtis and Fenner over *The Encyclopaedia Metropolitana*.[5] In addition to these troubles and anxieties, he had to endure the sneeringly hostile and malicious reviews of his *Lay Sermons* and *Biographia Literaria* by Hazlitt ("Till he can do something better, we would rather hear no more of him") and John Wilson or "Christopher North" ("the work is most execrable"), which had a "sudden and not to be mistaken influence" on the sale of his works.[6]

In the course of a letter to Crabb Robinson dated 3 December 1817,

[1] *SM (CC)* xxix, 114n.
[2] To Rest Fenner 22 Sept 1816: *CL* IV 680.
[3] *CL* IV 703, 709.
[4] *CL* IV 954.
[5] *CL* IV 755.
[6] See *CH*, especially pp 322, 328; to HCR 3 Dec 1817: *CL* IV 785.

in which he was considering bringing an action for libel against William Blackwood, publisher of the *Edinburgh Monthly Magazine*, in which Wilson's review had appeared, Coleridge went on to outline his financial commitments, providing for an insurance policy to benefit his wife, paying Hartley's expenses during vacations from Oxford, and saving in the hope of providing for Derwent, his younger son, to be with him.[7] In addition, he had commitments to the Gillmans, with whom he lodged. It was in these circumstances, "in bad health and worse mind", as Charles Lamb said,[8] that Coleridge began, towards the end of 1817, to think of a new course of lectures as a way of raising money. In early January he wrote to his old friend John Morgan:

> As I cannot starve, and yet cannot with ease to my own feelings engage in any work that would interfere with my Days' Work, till the MSS of the third Volume of the Friend is out of my hands, I have been able to hit on [no] mode of reconciling the difficulties, but by attempting a course of Lectures . . .[9]

By 10 January 1818 he was able to send a few prospectuses, announcing fourteen lectures to begin on 27 January, to Francis Wrangham in Yorkshire, evidently hoping his friends would help him to "procure a decent number of Subscribers".[10] In his elaborate Prospectus, which is reprinted in full at the end of this headnote, Coleridge explained his design in the lectures as being to convey "rules and principles of sound judgment, with a kind and degree of connected information, such as the hearers, generally speaking, cannot be supposed likely to form, collect, and arrange for themselves, by their own unassisted studies". The topics to be discussed would be "*various*, rather than *miscellaneous*", and were planned to help auditors take "an intelligent interest" in general conversation.

The general intention is reflected in the wide range of subjects: three lectures on early European history and literature; three on Shakespeare; three more on major authors including Cervantes and Rabelais; and at the end a sequence of four lectures on themes dear to Coleridge, the best books to use in the education of children, apparitions and ghosts, the definition of the arts, and English prose style. The lectures were to be given in the "Great Room" of the London Philosophical Society, near Fleet Street, where he had lectured in 1811–12.[11] The Prospectus gives the address as "Fleur-de-Luce Court", which is an extension of Crane Court, the address given in the 1811 Prospectus, off Fetter Lane.

---

[7] *CL* IV 786.
[8] In a letter to John Payne Collier 10 Dec 1817: *LL* II 220.
[9] *CL* IV 796.

[10] *CL* IV 803.
[11] See the Introduction to the 1811–12 series (at nn 33–5).

The London Philosophical Society was founded in 1810 by the surgeon T. J. Pettigrew and various friends of his;[12] he became treasurer and secretary of the Society, and the *Philosophical Magazine and Journal* in 1817 recorded an anniversary meeting at which officers and a council were elected for the following year, and "many excellent addresses" were made by various people ranging from the Duke of Sussex, who was in the chair, to "Messrs. Coleridge, Pettigrew, &c. &c.".[13] Evidently Coleridge was at this time a well-known member of the Society, which aimed to promote subjects for lectures and discussions to embrace "all those included in Literature and Science, excepting Theology and Politics", at weekly meetings.[14] Soon after the end in March of Coleridge's course of lectures, a quarrel involving Pettigrew and a Mr Lemaitre over financial issues led to a motion for the expulsion of the latter on 27 May 1818, and when this was defeated, a majority of the members of the Society, including Coleridge, resigned from it.[15]

Perhaps Coleridge had in mind the interests of members of the Society in planning such a wide-ranging course. At the same time he exerted himself in an attempt to publicise it, enlisting the aid of old friends like Crabb Robinson and Charles Lamb in distributing prospectuses.[16] He also advertised widely, placing announcements about the course in the *New Times* (21 and 22 January), the *Courier* (24 January), the *Times* (23 January), the *Morning Chronicle* (23 January), and the *Morning Post* (26 January). Coleridge had contributed essays on political and other topics to the *Courier* over a long period, but this evening newspaper paid relatively little attention to literature as long as T. G. Street was in control of it. Late in 1817 a new editor, William Mudford, took over, who was friendly towards Coleridge, and who was perhaps anxious to retain his services for the newspaper at a time when Coleridge was contemplating the possibility of writing instead for the *Morning Chronicle*.[17] Mudford not only encouraged some attention to literary matters in the *Courier*, but went out of his way to publicise Coleridge's new course of lectures, making over for this purpose some of the very limited space available in a four-page newspaper, much of it used for adver-

---

[12] For an account of C's relations with him, see *CN* III 4407 and n.

[13] *Philosophical Magazine and Journal* XLIX (Jan–Jun 1817) 461.

[14] George Nicholas Rankin *Reply to a Pamphlet Purporting to Be a "Report of the Council and Committee of the Philosophical Society of London, Presented to a Special General Meeting of the So-* *ciety, Held at the Crown and Anchor Tavern, Strand, on Tuesday, the 1st of December, 1818 . . .* " (1819) 1.

[15] Rankin p 7; *CL* IV 865. See also Fanny E. Ratchford "S. T. Coleridge and the London Philosophical Society" *MLR* XX (1925) 76–80.

[16] *CL* IV 812.

[17] *CL* IV 814–15.

tisements.[18] On 16 January the *Courier* reprinted the Prospectus, and on Saturday, 24 January, the newspaper carried not only a general advertisement on p 1 for the course placed by Coleridge but also an editorial puff on p 3, as follows:

We take pleasure in drawing the public attention to Mr. COLERIDGE's Lectures. It is a proof of extensive reading joined to a reflecting and original mind, that subjects so various and interesting should be brought to bear on one common point. We believe, too, that few conversations of topics of general interest in mixed society can occur, in which an attentive auditor of these Lectures would not find himself qualified to join with an intelligent interest.

Coleridge was also helped by John Stoddart, who in 1803 had invited him to go to Malta, where Stoddart was King's Advocate from 1803 to 1807.[19] More recently Stoddart had been involved in revising Coleridge's Introduction to *The Encyclopaedia Metropolitana*,[20] and it was perhaps out of regard for him that Stoddart's newspaper, the *New Times*, also gave editorial space to promoting the lectures. Most of the preliminary advertisements simply announced the date of the commencement of the course (27 January 1818) and where prospectuses or tickets could be obtained. The advertisement Coleridge inserted in the *New Times* on 21 January was a little more elaborate, beginning:

MR. COLERIDGE's LECTURES, on the Topics of Conversation in General Society, relative to the Productions of Genius in Literature and the Fine Arts, from the Eighth Century to the present time, will COMMENCE, by permission of the London Philosophical Society, at their Great Room . . . on TUESDAY EVENING, Jan. 27, 1818, and will be continued on the Friday and Tuesday evenings following. . . .

This was repeated on the front page of the issue of 22 January, which also contained, on p 3 among the editorial matter, a long prefatory statement followed by a reprinting of the "Syllabus of the Course" as it had been presented in the Prospectus. This statement incorporates towards the end two passages from Coleridge's preface to the Prospectus, one being the opening sentence, and the other consisting of sentences drawn from the third and fifth paragraphs rearranged; in other words, it is an editorial statement worked up from a reading of the Prospectus, and it reads as follows:

PUBLIC LECTURES
Among the various modes which are employed in the present day, to communicate information of a scientific, literary or miscellaneous character, to the

[18] For a full account of C's relations with Mudford and the *Courier*, see *EOT (CC)* I clxxiv–clxxv; also *Friend (CC)* I lxxxiii–lxxxv and *CL* IV 723–5.
[19] *CL* II 977.
[20] *CL* IV 821.

higher and middle classes of society, there is none which is more used, or abused, than Public Lecturing. We certainly find many shallow pretenders to learning, and many men whose talents have been warped, and rendered worse than useless by passions and prejudices of the lowest kind, coming before respectable audiences as Lecturers; but, on the other hand, we have occasionally seen this function no less usefully than honourably discharged by some of the most distinguished characters in the literary and scientific world. When, there-fore, we observe an individual of distinguished talent and of sound principle, coming forward to discuss, in this manner, topics of general interest and concern, we cannot but feel it a duty to call the attention of the Public to his undertaking. Such is the case at present with Mr. Coleridge, whose name is sufficiently known in the republic of letters, to render any specific praise of ours superfluous. It is only proper for us to observe, that this Gentleman's attainments are not of the superficial kind too frequent in the present day. His published Works shew, that to great originality of genius, he adds classical attainments of the highest degree, that his reading has been no less profound, than extensive, and that he has manifestly cultivated an intimate acquaintance as well with the best productions of German and Italian, as of Grecian and Roman literature.

It is perhaps to be lamented by the friends of Mr. Coleridge, that his studies have been so miscellaneous; and that his great talents have not been concentrated on some one large and important work; but this circumstance renders him eminently fit for the task, which he appears, by the Advertisement in our first page, to have undertaken, and which is developed in the curious and interesting Syllabus of his lectures. From this latter document it will be seen, that his attempt, which is in a great measure novel, is to convey, in a form best fitted to render them impressive at the time, and remembered afterwards, rules and principles of sound judgment, with a kind and degree of connected information, such as hearers, generally speaking, cannot be supposed likely to form, collect and arrange for themselves, by their own unassisted studies. The subjects of the lectures are indeed very *different*, but not (in the strict sense of the term) *diverse*: they are *various* rather than *miscellaneous*. There is this bond of con-nexion common to them all,—that the mental pleasure which they are calculated to excite is not dependent on accidents of fashion, place, or age, or the events or the customs of the day; but commensurate with the good sense, taste, and feeling, to the cultivation of which they themselves contribute, as being all in *kind*, though not all in the same *degree*, productions of Genius.

There are few families, at present, in the higher and middle classes of English society, in which literary topics and the productions of the Fine Arts, in some one or other of their various forms, do not occasionally take their turn in contributing to the entertainment of the social board, and the amusement of the circle at the fire-side; there are, therefore, few to whom these lectures may not offer, together with the charm of novelty, matter for useful and entertaining reflection for subsequent discussion. They may contribute to bestow even on conversation and casual study, a degree of consistency and consequent impor-tance.

Perhaps Coleridge was singing his own praises in this laudatory an-nouncement, but whether he or Stoddart wrote it, two newspapers, in effect, were giving free publicity to his Prospectus and Syllabus. He also received what was probably unexpected help from the radical *Champion*, which generally devoted itself to praising the lectures on the English poets that Hazlitt was giving at the Surrey Institution during this period (the course began on 13 January 1818) and the lectures the editor, John Thelwall, was giving on Shakespeare. In the issue of Sunday, 25 January, and repeated 26 January, following on a report praising Hazlitt's opening lectures, there appeared the following comment:

Mr. Coleridge too has announced a similar Intention; and whatever difference may exist between us we heartily congratulate the public on it. "The topics of conversation in general society" is not we trust a very explanatory title, or the subject must be wretchedly commonplace. But the truth is that the Literature, Philosophy &c. of the dark ages, the Tales and Metrical Romances of the fifteenth century, Chaucer, Spencer, Ariosto, Shakespear, Ben Jonson, Milton, &c. are not comprehended in his title, although they form a principal feature in his syllabus. Few men are better qualified for such an undertaking, and we had rather listen to him for a whole twelvemonth, on such subjects, than prose for one hour over his promised volume on the Logos.

This passage reflects Thelwall's ambivalent attitude to Coleridge as an old friend who had betrayed his early radical sympathies, and anticipates his more extended commentary in the report he wrote of Lecture 1 in the 1818–19 series.[21] Finally, and rather belatedly, a brief editorial announcement of the course was printed in the *Monthly Magazine* issued on 1 February.[22]

All this advance publicity, and the regular advertising of each lecture in daily newspapers, must have contributed to the success of a course that, if James Gillman's account can be trusted, was the most profitable of all those Coleridge gave.[23] As so often at the start of a course, he was anxious and depressed, the more so because he had been trudging about daily "in all weathers" to publicise the lectures, "solicit subscriptions", and complete his arrangements for giving them, and as a result had developed an alarming cold and hoarseness of voice.[24] Dr Gillman advised Coleridge to stay indoors all day on 26 and 27 January,[25] and this enforced rest seems to have had a beneficial effect, for although "a few minutes before the Lecture" his spirits were "sadly agitated"[26] because of his continuing hoarseness, he was able to go

---

[21] See his report in the *Champion* of 21 Dec 1818, reprinted under Lect 1 of the 1818–19 series.

[22] *M Mag* XLV (1 Feb 1818) 68. The announcement runs: "Mr. COLERIDGE intends to give a course of literary Lectures, which, if filled up according to his outlines, cannot fail of being, to a large portion of society, of considerable interest and attraction."

[23] *C Life* (G) 335.

[24] *CL* IV 816, 818, 823.

[25] *CL* IV 819.

[26] To Thomas Allsop 28 Jan 1818: *CL* IV 819.

through with it. Crabb Robinson, who attended it, noted that Coleridge had a bad cold and said his voice was "scarcely audible".[27] After this, Coleridge seems to have recovered his health and his voice steadily, and the remaining lectures were all given according to plan. On 9 February he wrote to H. F. Cary on the blank last page of a copy of the Prospectus, adding comments written against the printed announcements in the Syllabus of the first four lectures. His comment on the first reads, "Tho' I was dreadfully hoarse, it went off famously",[28] and his sense of triumph at a lecture attended, according to Crabb Robinson, by "a large and respectable audience", no doubt gave him confidence. The second lecture he regarded as a failure because he attempted too much in it, but the third he noted was "*very* popular", and the fourth "went off well". In other notes written on the day of the fourth lecture, 6 February, Coleridge said, "My Lectures are very respectably and very respectfully attended: and tho' not as yet very numerously, yet sufficiently so as to make them *answer* pecuniarily."[29]

Most of the lectures of this course were advertised in elaborate announcements that often expanded on, or varied, the description given in the Syllabus. According to this, Lecture 2 was to include selections translated from Swedish, Danish, and German by Coleridge, a proposal dropped from the advertisements of the lecture. However, he had promised some "recitations", and found he had no time to include them in the lecture, so he inserted a letter in the *Courier* (3 February) and the *New Times* (4 February) announcing his intention to offer "a supernumerary Lecture, at the end of the course, given gratis, and composed wholly of poetic translations, in chronological order, and concluding with an original Poem".[30] These were further described as extracts from English romances and "metrical translations" he had himself made from romances "of the northern languages". In the advertisements for Lecture 2, Coleridge had also promised that, "The First Lecture will be published in a few days, with additional illustrations and proofs".[31] His notes for Lecture 2 begin with a statement that his introductory lecture is "jam sub prelo", i.e. already in the press, and the letter he published on 3 and 4 February (he gave Lecture 3 on 3 February) includes a notice of intention to publish "the two first Lectures . . . with the examples from *our own* Romances, &c. in an inexpensive form, in order to avoid the necessity of all recurrences and repetition in the following Lectures . . . and as an act of justice and respect to

[27] *CRB* I 218.
[28] *CL* IV 834.
[29] To Cary 6 Feb 1818: *CL* IV 833.
[30] *CL* IV 826.
[31] See Lect 2 headnote: Advertisements.

my subscribers: whose goodness will palliate an error which arose wholly from my desire of doing the utmost.''[32] Coleridge was still confidently assuming they would be published on 9 February, when he promised to send Cary a copy,[33] but on 19 February he was more cautious, committing himself only to the conditional "if in the mean time I can make such an arrangement concerning the publication of my two first Lectures, greatly enlarged, under the Title of 'Portrait of the Middle or (so called) Dark Ages' ''.[34] Only sketchy memoranda have been found for the first lecture, but Coleridge may have been assuming he could rely on notes taken by his friend and disciple J. H. Green;[35] more elaborate notes for Lecture 2 survive, but they would have needed a lot of revision and expansion to make them suitable for publication. The available evidence suggests that Coleridge was unable to make arrangements for the publication of the lectures and thus lacked the incentive that might have driven him to work on them; at any rate, they were never published.

The only tangible by-product of these first two lectures was the publication in the *New Times* on 31 January of a poem Coleridge read in Lecture 2 (delivered 30 January), headed "Imitation of one of the Minnesinger of the Thirteenth Century".[36] This is a variant version of the last three stanzas of what was included in C's collected poems as *The Blossoming of the Solitary Date-Tree. A Lament*; there it has six stanzas, the first two in rough draft only, and Coleridge added a prefatory note linking the subject of the poem with "Hebrew writers" and the title with Linnaeus.[37] The only connexion with the Minnesinger seems to lie in the stanza form and rhyme-scheme. What happened about Coleridge's promised supernumerary lecture is not altogether clear; after the course finished on 13 March he was busy writing under pressure and stirring up others on behalf of Peel's Factory Bill, designed to protect children employed in cotton mills,[38] which came to a vote in the House of Commons on 27 April, and he did nothing about the lecture until May. He was planning on 9 May to spend the following week in preparing it,[39] and he advertised it in the *New Times* on Thursday, 21 May, in *The Times* on 22 May, and the *Courier* on 23 May as to be delivered on Tuesday, 26 May. The wording of the advertisement varies slightly, but the sense is the same in all three; that in the *New Times* runs as follows:

[32] *CL* IV 826–7.
[33] *CL* IV 835.
[34] To Thomas Boosey Jr: *CL* IV 841.
[35] See *CN* III 4383 and n.

[36] Reprinted, below, under Lect 2.
[37] *PW* (EHC) I 395.
[38] See *EOT (CC)* I clxxvi, II 483–9.
[39] *CL* IV 859.

MR. COLERIDGE'S SUPERNUMERARY LECTURE will be delivered on TUESDAY EVENING NEXT, May 26, at a quarter past Eight,—In Flower-de-luce-court, Fleet-street, with free admission to Subscribers and to those who have received Tickets.—The Lecture will consist of free Translation of the Northern Poets of the middle ages, woven into a Poem, descriptive of the Manners, Opinions, &c. of the same. Mr. C. regrets the delay, the occasion of which will be explained.

On Saturday, 23 May, he wrote giving directions to Hugh Rose about the location of the lecture-room,[40] so there is plenty of evidence to show that he fully intended to be there, but in the event, it seems he did not attend, but sent a message of apology: some months later, Mrs Clarkson wrote to Crabb Robinson to say:

You heard perhaps what an ungracious leave he took of his auditory last spring, calling them together to hear a gratuitous lecture, causing them to be told he was too ill to meet them, but as soon as he recovered they should be sure of the lecture. Either he never recovered, or he forgot his promise . . .[41]

Otherwise the course proceeded as planned. The Syllabus announced Lectures 4, 5, and 6 as enlarging Coleridge's previous courses on Shakespeare, but the newspaper advertisements provided more elaborate descriptions, showing that Coleridge intended to divide the plays into "three great classes", meaning the "Comedies and romantic Dramas" in Lecture 4, the history plays in Lecture 5, and the tragedies in Lecture 6,[42] which was in fact mainly on *Hamlet* and possibly *Othello*. Lecture 7 was announced in the Syllabus as touching on "Shirley and Otway", but none of the advertisements mentions Shirley, and not all of them include Otway; the lecture seems to have been devoted entirely to Ben Jonson, Beaumont and Fletcher, and Massinger, but this was the first of Coleridge's lectures to deal at length with these authors, and he seems to have attached importance to it, for the advertisements in the *New Times* and *Courier* were both printed on p 3 among editorial matter and with an introductory sentence, "The subject of Mr. Coleridge's Lecture for this evening is peculiarly interesting". Coleridge had lectured on *Don Quixote* at Bristol in 1814, but he evidently felt that Lecture 8 on Cervantes would be original in London and "new to the Audience",[43] and he arranged for the *Courier* and the *New Times* to carry an advertisement in the form of an editorial puff, announcing that the lecture "excites much curiosity and expectation". His optimism was justified, for Crabb Robinson found the lecture-room fuller than at any previous

---

[40] *CL* IV 862.
[41] Morley p 100.
[42] See below, Lect 4 (headnote: Advertisements).
[43] To Mudford [18 Feb 1818]: *CL* IV 839.

lecture,[44] and a report of it was published in the *New Times* a few days later. The remaining lectures were all on subjects new for Coleridge as a lecturer. Lecture 10 included comments on Milton, but in relation to Dante, a comparison Coleridge is not known to have made previously in his lectures. Newspaper reports have been found only of Lectures 4 and 8 in this course, but in 1831 an anonymous contributor supplied accounts of Lectures 9 and 14 to the *Tatler*, a short-lived periodical issued between 1830 and 1832.[45]

Before the start of the course Coleridge wrote to Crabb Robinson, ''I shall have written every Lecture . . . but shall deliver them without book.''[46] This was perhaps written to reassure an old friend who had suspected him of laziness in preparing his lectures,[47] but it also sums up the method Coleridge claimed to find best for producing ''order in the matter and animation in the manner''. The elaborate notes that survive for most of the lectures of this course, together with the reports of a number of them in newspapers, or made by J. H. Green, H. H. Carwardine, and William Hammond, show that Coleridge worked hard to prepare these lectures, with the possible exception of those on Shakespeare, which may have echoed his 1813 lectures. As for other courses, he did not write out the lectures in full, but usually prepared an introduction in a form in which it could be read, and notes to supplement this, which might include references to quotations from books or annotations in copies of books he possessed. Much of the material for this course was new, and he was gathering information and ideas for it from a variety of sources. He borrowed from A. W. Schlegel again in Lectures 1 and 3, and the influence of Jean Paul Richter (Lecture 9) and Schelling or Schiller (Lecture 13) can be traced. An important new source for the first three lectures, and used again by Coleridge in 1819, is Friedrich Schlegel's *Geschichte der alten und neuen Litteratur* (2 vols Vienna 1815), which was translated into English in 1818 under the title *Lectures on the History of Literature, Ancient and Modern*. This translation has many errors and omissions, which provide proof that Coleridge was using the German text.[48] For Lectures 2 and 3 he

---

[44] *CRB* I 219.

[45] See below, Lect 9 (headnote: Report).

[46] [17] Jan 1818: *CL* IV 812.

[47] See his comments on the 1811–12 series, under General Comments and Reports (HCR's letter of 16 Dec 1811 to his brother Thomas).

[48] An error in the case of a single word makes the point; the translation of a passage in Lect 6 reads, ''Gothic heroic poems were already sung in the time of Attila'' (*Lectures*—1818—I 253); the German text has ''In Atilla's Zelt wurden gothische Heldenlieder gesungen'', which C correctly renders in his notes ''Gothic heroic lays sung in the tent of Attila'' (*Geschichte* I 215; and see Lect 2, paragraph containing n 18). The translator confused *Zeit* and *Zelt*.

also used Ritson's *Ancient Engleish Metrical Romancëes* (3 vols 1802), buying a set in March 1818.[49]

For other lectures Coleridge tried to borrow or buy the works of Cervantes, and certainly borrowed copies of Sterne and Swift, from the bookseller Thomas Boosey,[50] and he made detailed notes on several books relating to witchcraft for Lecture 12. He was especially pleased with his lecture on Dante,[51] which enabled him to draw attention to Cary's translation. He had met Cary in the autumn of 1817, and this led to his reading Cary's translation of Dante, which had been published in 1814 but had not sold. In late January, while giving his opening lectures, Coleridge was successfully negotiating with Taylor and Hessey the publishers to issue under their imprint the remaining thousand or so unsold copies of the 1814 edition.[52] He gave his Dante lecture on 27 February, and Taylor and Hessey published Cary's Dante on 3 March; Coleridge's lecture, in which he almost certainly, as in 1819, praised Cary, may well have promoted sales of this new issue, for it sold out, and a new edition appeared in 1819. Coleridge referred to many other works in the course of these lectures, and the last one included something of an anthology of quotations from his favourite English prose writers.

While Hazlitt was lecturing on English poets, Coleridge's lectures ranged into European history and literature, a significant innovation at a time when, three years after Waterloo, a peaceful Europe was open once again.[53] In relating Spenser to Ariosto, Rabelais to Swift, and Dante to Milton, Coleridge also helped to establish the comparative study of literature in Britain. All these factors probably contributed to make this course attractive to audiences, and there is other evidence to support Gillman's testimony to its success. After Lecture 7, Charles Lamb wrote in his usual joking way to Mrs Wordsworth, presenting himself as being pestered by people asking questions on such matters as what Coleridge said at last night's lecture. If this need not be taken too seriously, he went on to report dining with Coleridge at the Gillmans, and noted, "S. T. C. is lecturing with success".[54] Samuel Rogers, who attended Lecture 10, reported that "there were about a hundred and twenty persons in the room".[55] Attendance evidently varied, since the room seems to have been unusually crowded for the Cervantes lecture, and possibly the figure for the Dante lecture was closer to the average.

[49] *CL* IV 846.
[50] *CL* IV 841, 844.
[51] *CL* IV 827.
[52] See below, Lect 10 headnote (Background and Circumstances, second and third paragraphs).

[53] See below, ibid (fourth paragraph).
[54] *LL* II 225, 227.
[55] *Recollections of the Table-Talk of the Late Samuel Rogers* ed A. Dyce (1887) 285.

All this suggests that Crabb Robinson's comments on the first ten lectures (he went on circuit then and so missed the last four) should not be taken too seriously.[56] His long acquaintance and frequent conversations with Coleridge had made him familiar with Coleridge's reading and ways of thinking, and he found in some of the lectures only a repetition of what he knew as Coleridge's "favourite ideas".[57] He was bored by the lecture on Cervantes, which moved the reporter of the *New Times* and was applauded by the audience, but to him Coleridge's remarks on *Don Quixote* were "old and . . . oft repeated",[58] whereas no London audience had heard them before. In any case, Coleridge's notes and the reports of these lectures show that for the most part he was working up his material freshly for the occasion or doing quite new things; and even though Crabb Robinson's long acquaintance with Coleridge, and reading in the German background to some of Coleridge's basic ways of thinking in Kant, Schiller, Schlegel, etc, made him an unusually knowledgeable auditor, he may be regarded as a prejudiced witness. The course succeeded well enough for Coleridge to contemplate another series on Shakespeare in May. On the blank half torn from a letter addressed to him, bearing the date stamp 19 May 1818, Coleridge drafted an announcement, as follows:

Mr C has been ~~particulary~~ requested to give six lectures of particular and practical Criticism,[59] taking ⟨some⟩ one play of Shakespear's, scene by ~~act~~ scene, as the subject of each Lecture. The Plays proposed *at present*, ~~but which with the exception of the first will be submitted to the alterable at the expressed wish of his auditors~~ are 1. Richard the Second, 2 Lear, 3 Macbeth, 4 Antony and Cleopatra, 5 some of his Comedies, and 6th the reasons for doubting the two gentlemen of Verona, and a large proportion of the three parts of Henry the 6, and some scenes of Richard the third, as Shakespear's—illustrated from Pericles, Titus Andronicus, and some extraordinary scenes of an Old Drama.

As this ~~Lectures~~ course must commence almost immediately, if at all, the Friends of the Plan will confer an obligation on Mr Coleridge by signifying their intention either by letter (*post* paid) to himself at Highgate, or by leaving their names at Messrs Hookham's, Bond Street; Taylor and Hesse, Fleet Street, or Boosey and Sons, Broad Street.[60]

A slightly different version of this was added as a "P.S." to the advertisement for the supernumerary lecture that appeared in the *New*

[56] As they were e.g. by R. W. Armour and R. F. Howes in *C Talker* 52–5.

[57] *CRB* I 218.

[58] *CRB* I 219.

[59] C gave currency to this phrase—cf *BL* ch 15 (*CC*) II 19; it was adopted by I. A. Richards in his book *Practical Crit-* icism (1929) and has passed into common usage. Here it marks the change in C's approach to lecturing since his first course in 1808, when his primary concern was theoretical, to illustrate the "Principles of Poetry".

[60] Folger MS W.a. 143.

Times on 21 May and then in *The Times* and the *Courier*.[61] "Particular and practical Criticism" became "particular and continuous Criticism"; and the subjects for Lectures 5 and 6 were changed to, "Fifth, Twelfth Night.—And for the Sixth, Critical doubts concerning Sundry Plays and parts of Plays attributed to Shakspeare, supported by an examination of Henry VI and Richard III."[62] Coleridge was thinking of such a course by 12 May,[63] but advertising towards the end of May meant that it could hardly have begun before June, and a weekly series would have run into July. So it would not be surprising if response to the advertisements was poor; at any rate by some date early in June Coleridge wrote, "After due advice and consideration I have abandoned all thought of giving any further Lectures for the present season."[64]

[61] See above, extract following n 39.

[62] So in the *Courier; The Times* has the addition, "and illustrated from Pericles &c".

[63] *CL* IV 860.

[64] To unknown correspondent: *CL* IV 865.

PROSPECTUS

PROSPECTUS

OF

A COURSE OF LECTURES

BY S. T. COLERIDGE.

THERE are few families, at present, in the higher and middle classes of English society, in which literary topics and the productions of the Fine Arts, in some one or other of their various forms, do not occasionally take their turn in contributing to the entertainment of the social board, and the amusement of the circle at the fire-side. The acquisitions and attainments of the intellect ought, indeed, to hold a very inferior rank in our estimation, opposed to moral worth, or even to professional and specific skill, prudence, and industry. But why should they be *opposed,* when they may be made subservient merely by being *subordinated?* It can rarely happen that a man of social disposition, altogether a stranger to subjects of taste (almost the only ones on which persons of both sexes can converse with a common interest), should pass through the world without at times feeling dissatisfied with himself. The best proof of this is to be found in the marked anxiety which men who have succeeded in life without the aid of these accomplishments shew in securing them to their children. A young man of ingenuous mind will not wilfully deprive himself of any species of respect. He will wish to feel himself on a level with the average of the society in which he lives, though he may be ambitious of *distinguishing* himself only in his own immediate pursuit or occupation.

Under this conviction, the following Course of Lectures was planned. The several titles will best explain the particular subjects and purposes of each; but the main objects proposed, as the result of all, are the two following:—

I. To convey, in a form best fitted to render them impressive at the time, and remembered afterwards, rules and principles of sound judgment, with a kind and degree of connected information, such as the hearers, generally speaking, cannot be supposed likely to form, collect, and arrange for themselves, by their own unassisted studies. It might be presumption to say, that any important part of these Lectures could not be derived from books; but none, I trust, in supposing, that the

39

same information could not be so surely or conveniently acquired from such books as are of commonest occurrence, or with that quantity of time and attention which can be reasonably expected, or even wisely desired, of men engaged in business and the active duties of the world.

II. Under a strong persuasion that little of real value is derived by persons in general from a wide and various reading; but still more deeply convinced as to the actual *mischief* of unconnected and promiscuous reading, and that it is sure, in a greater or less degree, to enervate even where it does not likewise inflate; I hope to satisfy many an ingenuous mind, seriously interested in its own development and cultivation, how moderate a number of volumes, if only they be judiciously chosen, will suffice for the attainment of every wise and desirable purpose: that is, *in addition* to those which he studies for specific and professional purposes. It is saying less than the truth to affirm, that an excellent book (and the remark holds almost equally good of a Raphael as of a Milton) is like a well-chosen and well-tended fruit-tree. Its fruits are not of one season only. With the due and natural intervals, we may recur to it year after year, and it will supply the same nourishment and the same gratification, if only we ourselves return with the same healthful appetite.

The subjects of the Lectures are indeed very *different,* but not (in the strict sense of the term) *diverse:* they are *various,* rather than *miscellaneous.* There is this bond of connexion common to them all,—that the mental pleasure which they are calculated to excite is not dependent on accidents of fashion, place, or age, or the events or the customs of the day; but commensurate with the good sense, taste, and feeling, to the cultivation of which they themselves so largely contribute, as being all in *kind,* though not all in the same *degree,* productions of GENIUS.

What it would be arrogant to promise, I may yet be permitted to hope,—that the execution will prove correspondent and adequate to the plan. Assuredly, my best efforts have not been wanting so to select and prepare the materials, that, at the conclusion of the Lectures, an attentive auditor, who should consent to aid his future recollection by a few notes taken either during each Lecture or soon after, would rarely feel himself, for the time to come, excluded from taking an intelligent interest in any general conversation likely to occur in mixed society.

S. T. COLERIDGE.

SYLLABUS OF THE COURSE.

LECTURE I. *Tuesday Evening, January* 27, 1818.—On the Manners, Morals, Literature, Philosophy, Religion, and the State of Society in

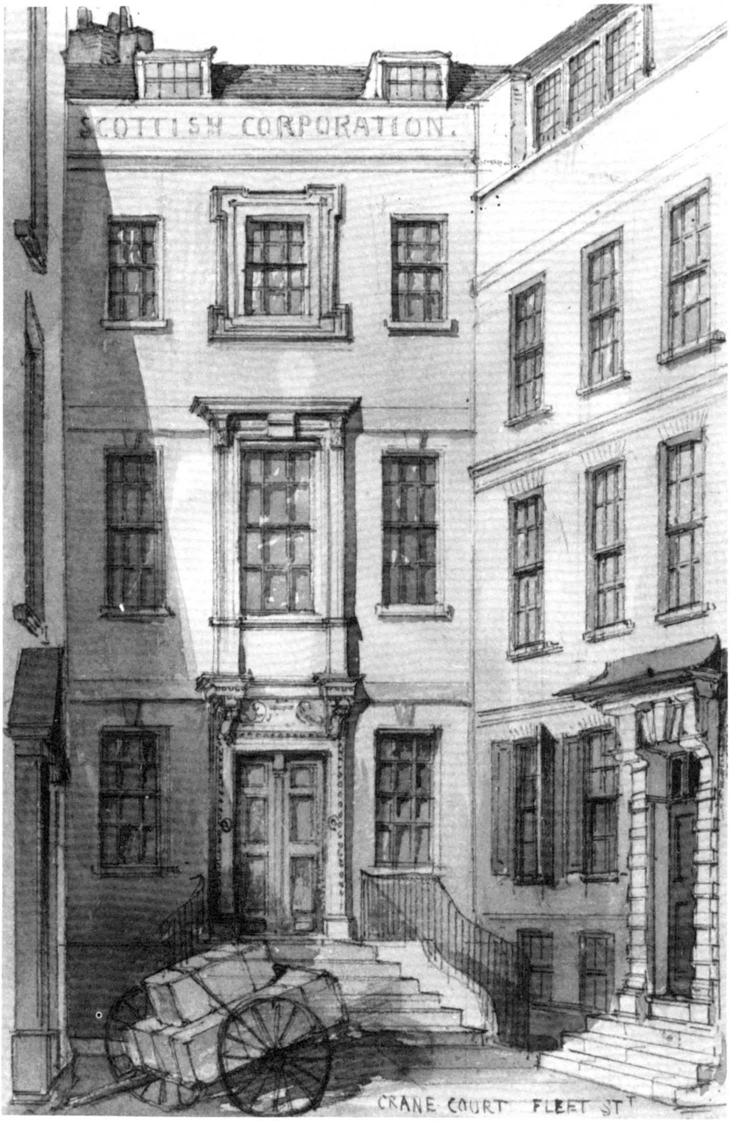
SCOTTISH CORPORATION.
CRANE COURT FLEET STT

2. The Crane Court entrance to the Scottish Corporation Hall,
rented by the London Philosophical Society, and used by Coleridge
for his courses of lectures in 1811–12 and 1818.
He complained that the entrance was "disagreeable
even to foot-comers, and far more so to carriages,
from the narrowness and bendings of the lane". *CL* III 349.
From a sketch by T. C. Dibdin, the Guildhall Library, London
reproduced by kind permission

general, in European Christendom, from the eighth to the fifteenth Century (that is, from A.D. 700 to A.D. 1400), more particularly in reference to England, France, Italy, and Germany: in other words, a portrait of the (so called) Dark Ages of Europe.

LECTURE II. *Friday Evening, January* 30.—On the Tales and Metrical Romances common, for the most part, to England, Germany, and the North of France; and on the English Songs and Ballads; continued to the Reign of Charles the First.—A few Selections will be made from the Swedish, Danish, and German Languages, translated for the purpose by the Lecturer.

LECTURE III. *Tuesday Evening, February* 3.—Chaucer and Spenser; of Petrarch; of Ariosto, Pulci, and Boiardo.

LECTURES IV. V. and VI. on *Friday Evening, February* 6; on *Tuesday Evening, February* 10; and on *Friday Evening, February* 13.—On the Dramatic Works of SHAKSPEARE. In these Lectures will be comprised the substance of Mr. Coleridge's former Courses on the same subject, enlarged and varied by subsequent study and reflection.

LECTURE VII. *Tuesday Evening, February* 17.—On Ben Jonson, Beaumont and Fletcher, and Massinger; with the probable Causes of the Cessation of Dramatic *Poetry* in England with Shirley and Otway, soon after the Restoration of Charles the Second.

LECTURE VIII. *Friday Evening, February* 20.—Of the Life and *all* the Works of CERVANTES, but chiefly of his Don Quixote. The Ridicule of Knight-Errantry shewn to have been but a secondary Object in the Mind of the Author, and not the principal Cause of the Delight which the Work continues to give in all Nations, and under all the Revolutions of Manners and Opinions.

LECTURE IX. *Tuesday Evening, February* 24.—On Rabelais, Swift, and Sterne: on the Nature and Constituents of genuine Humour, and on the Distinctions of the Humourous from the Witty, the Fanciful, the Droll, the Odd, &c.

LECTURE X. *Friday Evening, February* 27.—Of Donne, Dante, and Milton.

LECTURE XI. *Tuesday Evening, March* 3.—On the Arabian Nights Entertainments, and on the *romantic* Use of the Supernatural in Poetry, and in Works of Fiction not poetical. On the Conditions and Regulations under which such Books may be employed advantageously in the earlier Periods of Education.

LECTURE XII. *Friday Evening, March* 6.—On Tales of Witches, Apparitions, &c. as distinguished from the Magic and Magicians of Asiatic Origin. The probable Sources of the former, and of the Belief in them in certain Ages and Classes of Men. Criteria by which mistaken and exaggerated Facts may be distinguished from absolute Falsehood and Imposture. Lastly, the Causes of the Terror and Interest which Stories of Ghosts and Witches inspire, in early Life at least, whether believed or not.

LECTURE XIII. *Tuesday Evening, March* 10.—On Colour, Sound, and Form, in Nature, as connected with POESY: the word "Poesy" used as the *generic* or class term, including Poetry, Music, Painting, Statuary, and ideal Architecture, as its Species. The reciprocal Relations of Poetry and Philosophy to each other; and of both to Religion, and the Moral Sense.

LECTURE XIV. *Friday Evening, March* 13.—On the Corruptions of the English Language since the Reign of Queen Anne, in our Style of writing Prose. A few easy Rules for the Attainment of a manly, unaffected, and pure Language, in our genuine Mother-Tongue, whether for the purposes of Writing, Oratory, or Conversation. Concluding Address.

By Permission of the PHILOSOPHICAL SOCIETY of London, the Lectures will be delivered at their Great Room, Fleur-de-Luce Court, Fleet-Street; and will commence on each Evening at a Quarter after Eight precisely.

Single Subscription Tickets for the whole Course, *Two Guineas* each: and Tickets admitting a Gentleman and Lady, *Three Guineas* each; may be procured at Messrs. TAYLOR and HESSEY, 93, Fleet-Street; HOOKHAM and SONS, Old Bond-Street; BOOSEY and SONS, New Broad-Street; and at the Society's Rooms, on the Lecture Nights.

Admission to the Single Lecture, *Five Shillings.*

LECTURE 1

DATE AND PLACE OF DELIVERY. Tuesday, 27 January 1818, in the Great Room of the London Philosophical Society, Fleur-de-Luce Court, Fleet Street.

SUBJECT. C spoke on the subject promised in the Syllabus, "On the Manners, Morals, Literature, Philosophy, Religion, and the State of Society in general, in European Christendom, from the eighth to the fifteenth century (that is, from A.D. 700 to A.D. 1400), more particularly in reference to England, France, Italy, and Germany: in other words, a portrait of the (so called) Dark Ages of Europe."

ADVERTISEMENTS. *M Post*, Mon, 26 Jan: "MR. COLERIDGE's COURSE of LECTURES will commence at Eight o'clock TO-MORROW EVENING, 27th January, at the Great Room of the London Philosophical Society, Fleur-de-luce-court, Fleet-street, with a portrait of the (so-called) Dark Ages, on their Arts, Literature, and Manners. The Second lecture, on Metrical Romances, Ballads, and National Songs, on the Friday Evening following. Prospectuses and Tickets may be procured at Messrs. Hookham's, Bond-street, Taylor and Hessey, Fleet-street; and Bousey and sons, Broad-street; or at the Rooms, on the Lecture Evenings. Single Tickets, for the Course (of fourteen lectures), two guineas; double ticket, three guineas; admission to any single lecture, five shillings." *The Times* Tues, 27 Jan: "MR. COLERIDGE's COURSE of LECTURES will commence at 8 o'clock THIS EVENING, at the Great Room of the London Philosophical Society, Flower de luce-court, Fleet-street, with 'A Portrait of the (so called) Dark Ages', or of the arts, literature, and manners of Christian Europe, from the 8th to the 14th century; the second lecture on metrical Romances, Ballads, and National songs, on the Friday evening following." (The rest as in the advertisement of 26 Jan in the *M Post*.) *M Chron* Tues, 27 Jan: as in *The Times* of this date, with minor variants. This lecture was also advertised in general notices about the course in the *Courier* Sat, 24 Jan; *New Times* Wed, 21 Jan; the *Champion* Sun, 25 Jan, and in *The Times* and *M Chron* Fri, 23 Jan.

TEXT. Some notes by C in N 21½ relate very closely to the subject of the lecture and to the reports by Green and Carwardine. As Kathleen Coburn has pointed out in her presentation of these notes in *CN* III 4378–4379, a good deal of the material in the longer of these notes, *CN* III 4378, was redeployed in Lect 8 of the lectures on the history of philosophy delivered on 15 Feb 1819, and both read more like "memoranda-taking than lecture preparation". At the same time, they appear to have been written in connexion with C's thinking about Lect 1 of the 1818 series and are accordingly reprinted below. The text is based on that of *CN*, omitting cancellations. If these served as an introduction, then another set of notes, now BM MS Egerton 2801 ff 26–31ᵛ, would seem to be a development of the brief outline of migrations of tribes at the end of the notebook entry. These are printed here as representing materials probably prepared for the lecture; C dealt with the "origin of nations" also in his philosophical lectures, but in relation to the history of philosophy; see *P Lects* (1949) 254–7.

REPORTS. A brief report of this lecture, prepared from notes taken at it by Joseph Henry Green, under the title "General Character of the Gothic Mind in the Middle Ages", was printed by HNC in *LR* I 67–9 and reprinted in *Misc C* 6–8. The title was presumably invented by HNC, who in *LR* gave each lecture of this series a title that does not always coincide with the outline given in C's Syllabus: in the case of Lect 1 this title corresponds to what Green registered as the dominant theme of the lecture. Notes at this lecture were also taken by H. H. Carwardine and were published for the first time by his nephew Charles Probert in *N&Q* series IV vol V (1870) 335; these were included in *Misc C* 8– 10. Carwardine's ms, a small unbound notebook of twenty-four pages, is now in the Essex County Record Office, where it is listed as MS D/D Pr 549. The notes for this lecture, which occupy the first five and a half pages, the rest of f 6 being blank, are reprinted below. The notes are in ink and contain some cancellations and words interlined and also comments in square brackets by Carwardine himself, so that it looks as though he were copying and perhaps expanding rough notes taken at the lecture or possibly transcribing from short-hand.

BACKGROUND AND CIRCUMSTANCES. The extended outlines of lectures in C's Syllabus for this course show how seriously he planned it. In a letter to HCR of 17 Jan, asking him to "scatter a few Prospectuses advantageously", C went on to say that he would "have *written* every Lecture", as if he had intended to read them, but would deliver them "without book—which plan will, I trust, answer all purposes—that of order in the matter, and of animation in the manner". *CL* IV 812. This may have been written partly to persuade HCR that C intended to stick to his Syllabus, but his notes relating to Lect 2 in N 29 are prefaced by the statement "the introductory lecture jam sub prelo", already in the press. Also, the advertisement placed for the second lecture in the *Courier* on 29 Jan announced, "The First Lecture will be published in a few days". Early in February he was still talking of publishing the first two lectures (*CL* IV 826), and although this proved to be another scheme never fulfilled, C must have been confident that the material for the first two lectures was substantial and important enough to warrant bringing them out in print. N 29 contains some extended notes for Lect 2, but the memoranda in N 21½ relating to Lect 1 read like thoughts for an introduction, and the notes in MS Egerton 2801 appear to be a rough draft, with numerous cancellations or false starts, for a continuation. It is possible that C knew that his friend Green would be taking notes at the lecture and that he could use these, but if C did prepare his first one carefully with publication in mind, then possibly a more finished set of notes has been lost.

C was suffering from a bad cold on the day of the lecture, brought on as he thought from tramping about in foul winter weather soliciting subscriptions and making arrangements for the course, and on 30 Jan he wrote to H. F. Cary: "I got such a hoarseness (now only a little better) that I was obliged to deliver the first Lecture with a voice that sounded throughout to my own ears, as a Batrachomyomachia or battle between the Croaks & Squeaks". *CL* IV 824. He was conscious that he spoke at a disadvantage, and this is confirmed by HCR, who attended the lecture, and commented on it as follows in his Diary: ". . . I went to a lecture by Coleridge in Fleur de Luce Court, Fleet Street. I was gratified unexpectedly by finding a large and respectable audience—generally of very superior looking persons—in physiognomy rather than dress. But the lecture was heavy. Coleridge treated of the origin of poetry and of Oriental Works, but he was little animated, and an exceedingly bad cold rendered his voice scarcely audible." *CRB* I 218.

About a fortnight later C sent Cary a letter written on a copy of the Prospectus and annotated the announcement of Lect 1 there with the comment, "Tho' I was dreadfully hoarse, it went off famously". *CL* IV 834. The report by Green at least gives the impression that it was a coherent lecture. On 19 Feb C was still thinking of publishing his first two lectures, "greatly enlarged, under the Title of 'Portrait of the Middle or (so called) Dark Ages' ". *CL* IV 841. The lecture was certainly different from Lect 1 of the 1812 series (first course), which was developed largely from Lect 1 of A. W. Schlegel's *Ueber dramatische Kunst und Litteratur* (see headnote to that lecture: Background and Circumstances), for now C was able to use Friedrich Schlegel's *Geschichte der alten und neuen Litteratur* (2 vols Vienna 1815). Although much of his information about the dark ages came from this work, C took what materials he needed from several lectures by Schlegel, rearranged them to suit his own purposes, and mixed in references to other works and ideas of his own. Nevertheless, his reliance on Schlegel may have been what deterred him from publication. An anonymous translation, a free one with numerous errors and omissions, was published in 1818 as *Lectures on the History of Literature Ancient and Modern*, but there is nothing to show whether C knew of this, and he certainly used the German text; see e.g. Lect 2 nn 13, 19 etc, below.

LECTURE 1

RECORDS OF THE LECTURE

(1) COLERIDGE'S DRAFT MEMORANDA
CN III 4378–4379

*a*To shew the best means of leading the mind to Science, that is, to its true Object there are two ways—the one strictly scientific, and therefore requiring a degree of attention not to be expected in a numerous Audience, and a frequent recurrence to precedent proofs, in aid of the memory, which is not possible except in private/ this is, the proof from an analysis of the human mind in itself, in its component forms and faculties—. the other, not less efficacious, and more suited to the present occasion, is from History. What *has been* [the]*b* Ladder, what have been the various Rounds by which what may be called the continuously successive portions of the Human Race, have ascended to the present Height. From this we may abstract perhaps, and certainly in this we may exemplify, the principles, by which we may arrive at our desired end—namely, that of preparing the mind of the Individual for the acquirement of Truth, and in that course, for the Progress of Knowlege in general, as effected by the efforts of Individuals.—If, I thought, I can point out how it pleased Providence to educate the earliest period of the Human Race, then its Youth, and lastly if not its Manhood yet the preparation for its Manhood, I shall derive a lesson applicable to particular states and even to Individuals—for as the Instincts, by which Providence works, so are the correspondent Objects and Results—The Butterfly is not led in vain for a purpose unknown to itself & unconnected with any existing desire or want, to lay its eggs on the particular Sort of Leaf that is fitted to sustain the Caterpillar[1]—and is it in Man, the sole magnificent Temple in the world of visible Existence, and is it in

a CN III 4378
b Word supplied by the editor; C cancelled "the Road", substituting "Ladder"

[1] A favourite image used by C in various ways from as early as 1794; a version of it occurs in a letter to RS of 21 Oct 1794 (*CL* I 115). See *CN* III 3290 f 13ᵛn.

the Holy of Holies of this Temple, that is, in the moral & rational part of Humanity, that Nature tells her first and only Lie?[2]—Impossible.

Therefore I attempted to represent the periods of the human Race hitherto, as a Line with two opposite Poles—the patriarchal Period, best represented and longest preserved in the Hebrew nation as the primary or mid point from which both were produced, the Greeks as the Ideal Pole, and the Romans as the Real—and I observed that the synthesis or Union of Both was in Christendom.[3]—From this point therefore I now take up the Disquisition—It is but a simile, and no Simile is expected to be compleat in all points—Else it would not be a Simile, but an Instance—I have said, that the Greeks succeeded just so far & no further, than as they acted upon the stores which the mind found within itself, awakened indeed by excitement from external objects, but not afforded by them/ and instanced it, in Poetry, the other Fine Others,[c] pure Mathematics, and Universal Logic—and that the Romans, adding nothing to these, yet were the instruments of realizing, of fixing them, and of preparing a soil properly cleared and fenced for their after growth & ramification by War, Empire, and Law—I have now to add, that the first influences that followed this period, were to neutralize.—The World during the existence of the Roman Empire presents at large (not Individuals: for as is always the case in periods of preparation, these were many & most illustrious—but in the World at large) a state in which Christianity was still held in check, & incapable of shewing itself in its full influences upon Society by Paganism, and Paganism reduced to a Caput Mortuum[4] by Christianity. This I should characterize as our fourth point—that of Indifference/ At length, in the destruction of the Roman Empire the intermedium was furnished, in the stern and austere habits, and more indefinite and imaginative Superstitions of the Gothic Nations—and the fifth Point, or Period, that of the Union of the Ideal and Real by combination, in which each power acts but in harmony with the other, began—and in an advanced part of this period we ourselves are now living—

Thus we have accompanied the Race first through its boyhood, then thro' its Youth, and lastly in the preparation of making the practical use of its acquirements/—Palestine, Greece, and Rome (*observe* here

---

[c] A slip for "other Fine Arts"

[2] C asked the same question in slightly different terms in Lect 8 of the lectures on the history of philosophy given in Feb 1819; see *P Lects* (1949) 249.
[3] For a polished development of this argument, see *Friend (CC)* I 504–6.

[4] Literally "death's head", the old chemical term for the inert residue left after distillation. C liked the phrase and used it elsewhere, as in *SM (CC)* 77 and *CN* III 3972 f 134[v].

as to smallness of the 2 former & of 3 orig.) But as between our quitting the universities, and final Establishment there intervenes a period of Travel and Excursions, or what is called the Grand Tour; even so with the Human Race—Travels almost guideless into the world within us, and into the external World—A Great Revolution had taken place— consisting chiefly in this—that in the elder world the Infinite was hidden in the Finite[5]—Every Stream had its Naiad—the Earth its Cybele, the Ocean its Neptune/ the upper Air was Jupiter, the lower Juno[6]—Fire was Vesta, as the fixive, preservative Power—and the artificial technical Fire Neptune[7]—all was reduced to the Finite—The Ages, we call the Dark, were the counterpart—

Lord Bacon—his true Principles—he had to attack Schoolmen—and Alchemists—but as the former were the most to be feared against those he chiefly directed his attacks—hence aided by Commerce his Philosophy has been perhaps injurious by being but half understood/

[d]*Gothic* Architecture, rightly so named—⚵ the Greek and Græco-roman, for their effect on the Climates of the North.[8]—Take for instance a rainy windy day, or sleet, or a fall of Snow, or an icicle-hanging Frost— and then compare the total and the partile effect of the South-European roundnesses and smooth perpendicular Surface with the angles and meeting lines of the N. European or Gothic.

Of the Iapetidæ the Descendents of Iavan, the Ioaones (Javan being pronounced Ion by the Greeks) pushed downwards and onwards S.W. to the Peloponnesus, the Archipelago, and the Southern half of Italy— the Descendants of (Gog?) to the North West, thro' North Germany into Denmark & Sweden[9]—Of their final re-union European Christen-

[d] *CN* III 4379

[5] Cf C's remarks on the Bible in *SM (CC)* 49: "each of its Elements is at the same time a living GERM, in which the Present involves the Future, and in the Finite the Infinite exists potentially".

[6] Cf *P Lects* (1949) 68, 249–50, in which C says he found this related by one of the "Eclectic Philosophers", i.e. the late Alexandrian philosophers who sought to "set up a pseudo-Platonic polytheism against Christianity".

[7] An error for Vulcan.

[8] Perhaps an echo of A. W. Schlegel, who in Lect 1 drew a contrast between Greek and Roman architecture on the one hand and Gothic on the other in relation to climate. *DKL* I 15–16 (Black I 9–10).

[9] This is based on Gen 10, in which the descendants of Noah and his sons Ham, Shem, and Japeth are listed, and it is said "by these were the nations divided in the earth after the flood". Gen 10.32. Javan and Magog were sons of Japeth, and Javan settled the "isles of the Gentiles". Gen 10.5. Cf *CM (CC)* II 578 and n 1, C's annotation on Faber. Japetus was also, in Greek mythology, the son of Earth and Heaven, and Ion was the reputed ancestor of all Ionians and a son of Apollo. A more elaborate version of all this is contained in the notes for Lect 2 (paragraphs following n 2) and in Lect 8 of the lectures on the history of philosophy of 1819. See *P Lects* (1949) 254–5.

dom is the result, and the Centuries from A.D. 600 to 1400 contain the history. The Gothic Tribes fought their way down Southward; the Romans upward North—met in collision—which ended in a chemical Union.

$$\left.\begin{array}{l} \text{Goths} \\ \\ \text{Feudal Europe} \\ \\ \text{Greek + Roman} \end{array}\right.$$

(2) COLERIDGE'S DRAFT NOTES
BM MS EGERTON 2801 FF 26–31ᵛ

ᵉAs Sacred History is almost exclusively confined to ⟨two of ⟨the⟩ three original Branches of Noah: namely to⟩ the Descendants of Shem, and ~~of~~ among the different Semitic nations chiefly to the posterity of Heber through Abraham

Of the three great primary Branches from the Noetic Stem the sacred records have respect almost exclusively to the descendants of Shem, and to those of Ham, ~~and Canaan sometimes the Vassals, sometimes the Conquerors, but always the enemies of the former,~~ the Father of Canaan; while the volumes of profane History are filled with the fates and fortunes of the Iapetidæ, or the widely-spread Posterity of Japhet.[10] And as among the different Semitic tribes, of whose ~~common~~ original brotherhood the proof and monument still exists in the close affinity of the Semitic Languages, the Hebrew, Syriac, Chaldaic, and Arabic, the inspired ~~Historian~~ Annals are chiefly occupied by the History of the posterity of Heber thro' Abraham, and with the ⟨other⟩ nations sprung either from Shem or Canaan, only as far as theyir ~~were~~ history is interwoven with that of the Hebrew Tribes:[11] so with the earliest dawn of profane History, and soon after the commencement of the so called Heroic Age which answers to the period from Joshua to Samuel, or that of the Judges of Israel,[12] is our attention ~~pre~~-eminently attracted to a race of men strongly distinguished and peculiarized personally, in-

ᵉ f 26

[10] C repeated more briefly and coherently in Lect 2 the history of tribal migrations outlined in this paragraph; see below, at nn 3ff. On the posterity of Japhet, Noah's third son, see Gen 10.2ff and last paragraph of C's draft memoranda, above.

[11] Their lineage is to be found in Gen 10 and 11; Heber, or Eber (hence "Hebrew"), descended from Shem (10.21), and Abraham from Heber 11.27).

[12] Joshua succeeded Moses as lawgiver and leader of the Israelites (Deut. 31.14, 23), and Samuel ended the period of the judges and made Saul the first king (1 Sam 8–11).

tellectually, and morally by their predominant powers and tendencies, by ~~their attempt to combine the passion for Liberty with a reverential Love of established Law~~ a peculiar logical character in the groundwork and grammatical forms of their various dialects, the ~~strongest~~ surest mark of a thoughtful Race, disposed to notice and retain the relations and connections of things; by their being the only race (for the Jews by their long repugnancy to the Laws ~~commanded moved~~ miraculously given and enforced by miracles present a confirmation of the rule rather than an exception to it)—by their being, I repeat, the only race who at different times, and in different states at the same *ᶠ*time, ~~tried a~~ attempted experimentally to combine Liberty ~~and fixed~~ with a system of Laws ~~in the form of a~~ under constitutional governments; ~~and lastly, in for passing by many other striking peculiarities~~ *ᵍ*by being the only Race in which the sense of Beauty and the love of formal Truth, each for its own sake, appear to have been fully developed, in the forms of Philosophy and the Fine Arts;*ʰ* by the direction, in which as by a divine impulse, the various ~~tribes~~ families of this Race spread out and settled themselves, some northward, some southward, but all toward the west, and all within the temperate Zone; lastly, ~~and as bearing more particularly (not only) on the subject of this present~~ and as not only having a particular Bearing on the subject of the present lecture, but as forming likewise the groundwork of the whole course, the common principle, which each of its various subjects will present anew to my Auditors as the same characteristic quality manifested in a different shape, the Race, of which I am speaking, has been distinguished by the promptness and facility with ~~the more northerly and the more south~~ ⟨with*ⁱ* its⟩ two main divisions, tha~~n~~t part namely which in successive colonies moved onward and expanded to the ~~Northward~~ West-ward and North west, and that which ~~settled in more favored genial climates~~ destined by providence to an earlier developement were impelled to more genial climates under more auspicious circumstances, ~~have been found~~ by the facility with which they have been found to re-unite, and like ~~the~~ opposite forces of the same power, to combine in a third ~~and~~ more permanent form whatever ~~of fair, or~~ of good, and useful the difference ~~of~~ and even contrariety of circumstances and situations had called forth in either.—If we admit the almost universal opinion of the learned, that Africa was peopled by the posterity of Ham, and that the Celtic tribes, as the still remaining

ᶠ f 26ᵛ
ᵍ·ʰ C marked this passage, written lower on the sheet, for insertion here,
adding "by the direction &c" after "Fine Arts";
ⁱ A slip for "which"

resemblances of their different dialects, together with their customs and traditions make highly probable, had their origin in a greater or less intermixture of the descendants of Shem with those of Ham or Canaan: and then contemplate the third distinct race, ~~first as the~~ by one offset ~~occupyantsing~~ of the Peloponnesus, the ~~Grecian~~eek Islands, and the coasts of Asia Minor ~~the~~ by another ~~of~~ penetrating thro' the forests of Germany, and becoming the ancestors of the Swedes, Danes, *ʲ*Anglo-saxons, and of the most conspicuous and influencive of the different German Confederacies; while between both, and destined to be the point and the means of their re-union, the Colony who in the remotest æra of profane History formed the rudiments of ~~the~~ a mighty Empire in Italy, and the ancestral stock of the Roman Republic; ~~infidelity itself, methinks~~ we cannot but be struck with—nay, infidelity itself, methinks, could scarcely refrain from adverting with reverence to the prophetic words of Noah—and to the prophecy in the following Chapter—God shall enlarge Japhet, and he shall dwell in the Tents of Shem: and Canaan shall be his Servant.[13]—By the sons of Javan, the Son of Japhet, shall the Islands of the Gentiles be divided in their lands; every one after his Tongue, after their families, in their nations.[14]—/ In this description we find all the main distinguishing characters of the Gothic Race, in all its genuine branches, ~~Ionian~~ Teutonic or Ionian, for the Ἰωαονες, or Descendants of Ion, is but the greek softening of the Oriental, Jawan or Javan)[15]—the tendency namely to individualize, yet so as to confederate—the tendency to form independent nations, and a common Christendom.—

I have regarded the Greeks and Romans as originally Gothic; but so different were the climate & circumstances in which they rose & flourished, and so ~~variously~~ mightily were the former and thro' them the latter modified ~~to~~ in the two great influences of mankind, religion & language, by importations from the Egyptians, and Phœnicians,[16] that

ʲ f 27

[13] Referring to Gen 9.25–7 and quoting verse 27.

[14] Referring to Gen 10.1–5, which list the "generations of Noah, Shem, Ham and Japhet" in verses 1–4, and continue in verse 5, quoted by C, "By these were the isles of the Gentiles divided in their lands . . .".

[15] Named in Gen 10.2 and 10.4; see above, last paragraph of C's draft memoranda, also Lect 2, below, from nn 4ff.

[16] This was suggested by a passage in Lect 1 of F. Schlegel's *Geschichte*: "Zwar haben auch die Griechen nach ihrem eignen Zeugniss die Schrift von der Phöniziern enlernt, die Anfänge der bildenden Kunst und der Mathematik, manche einzelne Ideen der Philosophen und viele Künste des Lebens von der Ägyptern oder von andern asiatischen Nationen entlehnt" (tr "Indeed the Greeks by their own testimony acquired their script from the Phoenicians, and borrowed the elements of the fine arts and mathematics,

we may advantageously considered them as an intermediaum between their ruder Brethren, who emigrated Northward, and the Oriental Nations—and we shall understand ~~our own an~~[k] the character of our ancestors & therein our own character more fully, by a brief discrimination of the three—By the oriental nations I here mean, those who either remained in their original home or spread to the East & South—earliest developed and soonest decayed [l]as living bodies by disorganization pass back into the universal & bear only a testimony that they have been, so in the East is all individuality lost—the will of all subjected to the will of one—whether on the Throne, or in the Haram[17]—Master and Slave—so is it now, so has it ever been—It seems destined to represent the Past—

In early Greece and Rome the contrary spirit prevails—instead of the will of one over all, we have the will of all over each—and this in forms ⟨so oppressive⟩ that as soon as temporary stimuli, of defence or conquest were removed, they yielded to a sort of modified despotism that ended in their fall—with regard to Slavery and the treatment of Women they stand midway—. While they continued, in Arts & public enjoyment of Life, they seem (especially the Greeks) to give us the feeling of the *Present*. Enjoyment and transiency is their characteristic—

In the third each man is sacred to himself and others—and the government of one or of a few is preferred if only it leave there untouched the domestic & individual independence—The sacred monogamy—the frowning Castle—the Cap a pie[18] Armour—even the power of the Hierarchy as given to it by the individualest part of each individual's nature, by Conscience—

[m]From the ~~old~~ Greek & Roman World the Middle ages received a common Language, Logic, Geometry and partly directly, and partly indirectly thro' the Arabians in Spain, Chemistry, Medicine, and Astronomy[19]—such as they were—

[k] "an" not deleted in ms
[l] f 27[v]
[m] f 28

---

various individual ideas of philosophers, and many of the arts of life from the Egyptians or from other asiatic nations"). *Geschichte* I 22 (Bohn 12).

[17] Formerly a common, and etymologically correct, spelling of "harem" derived from the Arabic *haram*, that which is prohibited, hence a sacred place, and so what a man defends, the women's part of the house. *OED*.

[18] Head to foot; echoing *Hamlet* I ii

200.

[19] In his Lect 10 F. Schlegel surveyed the history of philosophy, briefly commenting that the Arabs introduced the knowledge of mathematics, chemistry, and medicine ("So bekamen sie von den Arabern, nebst den mathematischen, chemischen und medicinischen Kenntnisse . . .".), but that these were overlaid by astrology and alchemy. *Geschichte* II 63–4 (Bohn 230).

From the Northern Nations the reverence of freedom, dignity attached to the character of every free man as a man—reverence for the female Sex[20] (quote Ottfried[21][)][n]—the ~~foundation~~ peerage or equality of Free men, that with increase of population & decrease of vassalage necessarily introduced *representation*—and imaginations accustomed by their priests and the peculiar nature of their Mythology to the Indefinite—.

Then as both were gradually blended by Christianity, so as to form a fit and lasting base for its all-harmonizing Spirit to combine with— Whatever was evil, it restrained & moderated, where it could not remove—as the propensity to War—Whatever was excellent, as the dignity of man as man, and the moral equality of women, it substantiated by the doctrines of immortality, ⟨and a future Judgement,⟩ and the exclusion of Polygamy & lawless Divorce—

Symbolical Architecture,[22] for which as it is evidently neither Moorish nor Roman, I still can find no fitter word than Gothic—.

Finally, as the common spirit of the Middle ages, recognizable in all the great works of the different nations of Christendom—the distinguishing yet ~~soon~~ combining Spirit, that excludes nothing yet harmonizes all—and in which as [o]its distinctive character, the finite derives its effect ~~as the~~ from being the symbol or, were ~~ever~~ it even by contrast, the remembrancer of the infinite / / N.b. not the immense; but that which in its nature is incapable of a representable bound—/—

[p]Nearly about the time when the Northern Nations, the process of whose combination with the Laws and Language of Rome, and with the arts and literature of Grecian ~~institutes~~ forms the ~~true import and~~

---

[n] Closing bracket supplied by the editor
[o] f 29; f 28ᵛ is blank   [p] f 30; f 29ᵛ is blank

[20] In this passage C was recalling A. W. Schlegel's Lect 1, in which he spoke of the reverence for women inspired by the cult of the Virgin Mary in the Middle Ages among the Germanic peoples. *DKL* I 20 (Black II 13).

[21] In Lect 6 F. Schlegel spoke of the fondness of the Germanic peoples for poetry, referring to Ottfried as the Christian bard who adopted the style of the old heroic lays. *Geschichte* I 228–9 (Bohn 156). Otfrid von Weissenburg (c 800– 70), an Alsatian monk, is the earliest German poet known by name, and is credited with introducing end-rhymes in his *Evangelienbuch*, a long discursive poem in couplets, based on the gospels, and arranged in five books, one on each of the senses. C no doubt intended to quote from his translation of Otfrid's "metrical paraphrase of the gospel", probably the same passage, on the Virgin Mary with the babe, quoted in *BL* ch 10 (*CC*) I 208n (and see 208–9.)

[22] C had in mind both A. W. Schlegel's enthusiasm for Gothic architecture in his Lect 1 and F. Schlegel's comment in Lect 8: "Symbolisch muss daher alle Baukunst seyn, und mehr als jede andere ist es diese christliche des deutschen Mittelalters" (tr "All architecture therefore is symbolic, and the Christian architecture of mediaeval Germany more so than any other"). *DKL* I 16 (Black I 10), *Geschichte* I 292–3 (Bohn 191).

most important, the generally and permanently interesting portion of the records of the (so called Dark Ages)—constitutes the true *philosophy* of their History: the Greeks,[23] their elder and more favored Brethren, had already completed the task appointed them by Providence. They had discovered the principles ~~and exemplified~~ of Legislation, and exemplified all the forms of free government, ~~that could exist~~ compatible with the existing nature of Property, and with the absence of that precious discovery of modern Europe, representative Legislatures—they had discovered the elements of all the pure sciences,—and as far as they went, ~~exhibited models~~ produced works that approached near to perfection—in History and the fine Arts of Statuary; and[q] Architecture they still remain our masters—in Poetry, ~~it is enough, if on the whole~~[r] as far as the difference of the kinds will admit of any comparison, our equals—in Painting and in instrumental music probably our inferiors— above all, they had perfected ⟨their Logic, their Rhetoric, & their all-expressing⟩ their inimitable Language, which remained the common language of the civilized world even as low as the fifth Century after Christ.—These they had communicated to their Roman Conquerors, who adopted what it was in the genius of that People to ~~adopt~~ receive, and reduced to practice whatever was practical, and realized ~~what~~ for the world what the Greeks had but made experiments of in their tumultuary republics.—But there was one and that the most important point, which the Greeks themselves did not ~~poss~~ actually possess, ~~and to whi~~ tho' ~~their~~ various Scholars of Socrates must be regarded as its Heralds & Pioneers—a Religion for mankind—.—Causes of the insufficiency of Polytheism for the Roman Empire[24] as soon as it became extensive—/ The Greek mythology too complex ~~&, too trifling~~ its personages too numerous—and in all its very trifles too definite/—the Gothic Mythology—of which the elder Edda[25] is a genuine relique— distinguished by a lofty unity of Purpose—

[q] A slip for "in"   [r] "if on the" not deleted in ms

[23] Behind this paragraph lies C's reading of F. Schlegel's Lect 3, on the influence of the Greeks on the Romans, and Lect 6, in which he spoke of the indebtedness of mediaeval Europe to the Greeks and the Romans. But C's argument differs from that of Schlegel, who attributed the introduction of a sound legislative system to the Romans, not the Greeks. See *Geschichte* I 205 (Bohn 139).

[24] In Lect 6 F. Schlegel dealt with the influence of Christianity on the language and literature of Rome, and C probably had this in mind. *Geschichte* I 199ff (Bohn 135ff). See also *P Lects* (1949) 230–1.

[25] Here C was referring to Lect 6, in which Schlegel said that Greek mythology was too rich to be capable of being apprehended as a unified whole, and contrasted with this the Elder Edda, which in its most notable parts, he said, breathed the pure spirit of the northern mythology, which was distinguished from the Greek by its lofty unity of purpose ("ihre

⁵Remains of the old religion, with the mysteries, as those mentioned by Tacitus, of Hertha²⁶—and the refugees from Paganism, among whom combinations that must be regarded as degeneracies of the Samothracian²⁷—passed on one hand into mere *superstition* as Faeries, good neighbours,²⁸ Cobolts,²⁹ *Schomen*³⁰—and on the other hand into a mystical Alchemy and Theosophy—the dying echoes of which Paracelsus appears evidently to have collected³¹

Theodoric,³² the Goth—Alfred—Charlemagne All proposed to cultivate both the Latin—& the mother-tongue—the latter for poetry, especially religious—

Edda—Unity of purpose—and perfect charm—while the Greek passed too gradually from the Gods to the Heroes and from the Heroes to

⁵ f 30ᵛ

---

hohe Einheit''). *Geschichte* I 226 (Bohn 154). The Elder Edda, a collection of Old Norse poems on mythological subjects, dating from the ninth century or earlier, was known to C in the original and in Latin translation; see *CN* I 170n.

²⁶ In Lect 6 Schlegel spoke of the secret rites of Hertha, which Tacitus depicted as a kind of mystery (". . . jenes geheimnissvollen Dienstes der Hertha, welche uns Tacitus allerdings als eine Art von Mysterien schildert''). *Geschichte* I 223 (Bohn 152). Tacitus in *Germania* 40 (LCL pp 320–1) describes the ceremonies of the tribes who worshipped Nerthus, identified as Mother Earth. See also Lect 2, below (paragraph after n 12, and n 13).

²⁷ C meditated for years on early religious beliefs, and especially at this time on the Samothracian or Cabiric mysteries. Schelling (see Lect 2 n 25, below) had made this connexion between the Cabiri and the supernatural beings of modern folklore; for which cf *P Lects* Lect 11 (1949) 321–2.

²⁸ Witches or fairies; an obsolete Scottish phrase, according to *OED*, which records no example later than 1605, but cf *P Lects* (1949), "the *bonae societae*, the good members, which is still a name for the dairies in Scotland".

²⁹ Kobolds, goblins of the mines from

which cobalt (hence the word) was extracted in the Harz or Erzgebirge areas of Germany; cf *P Lects* (1949) 322, 449.

³⁰ Probably C meant *Schemen*, German for "phantom" or delusion", and italicised as a foreign term.

³¹ Paracelsus (1493–1541), the most famous chemist and alchemist of his age, had a mystical conception of the world as filled with theorgic spirits. C had taken down abstracts from his works in 1809 (*CN* III 3616–18), but here the reference is general.

³² This passage is derived from Schlegel's Lect 6: ". . . des gothischen Theodorich, Karls des Grossen, und Alfreds: eines Theils die ganze Erbschaft, aller der in der lateinischen Sprache überkommenen Kenntnisse, unversehrt zu erhalten und allgemein nussbar anzuwenden, und andern Theils die eigne Volkssprache, und durch sie auch den Geist der Nation zu bilden, die dichterischen Denkmahle zu erhalten . . .'' (tr "Theodoric the Goth, Charlemagne, and Alfred [had two aims], one to preserve intact the whole legacy, all the learning handed down in Latin, and the other, to maintain the native language, and by this means to mould the spirit of the nation, and preserve its poetic memorials . . .''). *Geschichte* I 206 (Bohn 139). See also Lect 2, below (at nn 18ff).

historic realities—. All in the Gothic Mythology a grand progressive
Poem or Tragedy—From the bones of the ossified Giants rose the ~~Ash~~
holy Ash, Igdrasyl, the tree of Life, with its roots in the abyss and its
branches over the Earth—the Powers of Light and the Heroes animated
[b]y*ᵗ* them fight against and partially conquer the Giant Powers of Darkness—but finally all must submit, that is finite, Gods and Heroes to
destruction before the unknown Destroyer—[33]

ᵘ~~From~~ About this time the Romans ~~ha~~ formed a closer acquaintance
with ~~theire~~ German Tribes:[34] tho' it was not till after the conquest of
Gaul by Cæsar, and the subjugation of the intermediate Celtic Tribes,
that they fully understood the ~~character~~ powers and dispositions of their
destined Conquerors—and already in the time of Seneca they had foreseen their danger—and such was the ~~eh~~ number & such the character
of the Slaves ~~who~~ obtained in their wars with the Germans that Seneca/[35]
do not let them know their number—. Morals, Courage, superior—in

ᵗ Letter supplied by the editor
ᵘ f 31

[33] See n 25, above; C returned here to
Geschichte ɪ 227 (Bohn 154), in which
Schlegel said: "Die Götter- und Heldenwelt der Griechen verliehrt sich allmäh-
lig in die Menschenwelt; die Poesie in
die Prosa und Wirklichkeit. Die nor-
dische Götterlehre erhält durch die letzte
Katastrophe, auf die als prophetisch
hindeutet, einen vollkommnen Schluss.
Es ist das Ganze wie ein einziges fort-
gehendes Gedicht, ein Trauerspiel. Von
dem ersten Anfang, wie die Welt und die
Erde aus den Gebeinen des erstarrten
Riesen entsteht, bis dann glücklichere
Zeiten kommen, über dem alten Abgrunde
die heilige Esche, Ygdrasill, aufgrünt;
der Baum des Lebens, der seine Wurzeln
durch alle Tiefen, und seine Zweige über
das Weltall ausbreitet; wie dann kühne
Helden und gutgesinnte lichte Geister die
Macht der Riesen, und die alten Kräfte
der Finsterniss, in manchen Kämpfen
besiegen; bis zu dem bevorstehenden
Untergang der Götter . . . ist alles ein
zusammenhängendes, grosses Natur- und
Heldengedicht. Das Wesentliche, wor-
auf alles hinzielt, ist abermahls wie in
den meisten alten Dichtersagen der Untergang einer herrlichen Heldenwelt" (tr

"The world of the Greek gods and heroes is gradually absorbed into that of
human beings, as poetry gives way to
prose and reality. The northern mythology, through its final catastrophe, to which
everything prophetically points, achieves
a perfect close. It is all like a single,
continuous poem, a tragedy. At the first
beginning, the universe and the earth arose
from the bones of the ossified giant, until
the coming of happier times, when the
holy ash-tree, Ygdrasil, burst into leaf
over the ancient abyss, the tree of life,
spreading its roots through the depths,
and its branches over the world. Heroes
and friendly spirits of light in many battles overcame the power of giants, and
the ancient forces of darkness . . .").

[34] C perhaps found a hint for this passage in *Geschichte* ɪ 205–6 (Bohn 138),
in which Schlegel said that the new world
of the Middle Ages developed from the
combination of the characteristics of Roman civilisation and the free spirit of the
Germans ("Freyheitsgeiste der germa-
nischen Völker"), but Schlegel did not
mention Seneca in this context.

[35] C may have been thinking of Seneca's comments in "Of Anger" *Moral*

intellect, more than equal—with our discipline they must be our conquerors—/

The Christian religion preceded by attempts to introduce the Persian,
Egyptian, & even the Jewish[36]—Rome lasted long enough to lend its
power & legislative genius to the formation of an Hierarchy, indispensable to the progress of Europe in the middle ages—& to which we
owe only not every thing—

ᵛOnly one Copy of Aristotle's works in the time of Cicero among
the ancients[37]—The middle ages not to be accused of Barbarism on this
account—Wars in all ages, & neglect in all ages, have produced the
same effects—nor while the battle was still hot, should we be too severe
on the destruction of Poems which however costly as works of art, were
detrimental to morals and religion—.—Constantinople[38] was not sacked
by the Goths—yet before its capture by the Turks how scanty had the
catalogue of Greek writers become—

ᵛ f 31ᵛ

Essays 1.11 (LCL I 133–4), in which he said that no men were more courageous than the Germans, who only needed discipline and reason to be a match for the Romans; see also below, at n 40.

[36] Schlegel said in Lect 6 that in commenting on the battle between oriental systems of thought (in relation to the great conflict between the ancient and the Christian worlds), he had to speak of nations whose entire literature is lost to us, like the Egyptians, others, like the ancient Persians, from whom we have only the reworkings of later times, and the Hebrews, whose holy scriptures constitute at the same time the essence of their literature and poetry ("Ich musste . . . von Nationen reden, deren Litteratur ganz für uns untergegangen ist, wie die Aegypter; anderen, von denen nur Umarbeitungen aus später Zeit vorhanden sind, wie die alten Perser; von den Hebräern, deren heilige Schriften aller- · dings zugleich den Inbegriff ihrer Litteratur und Dichtkunst ausmachen . . ."). *Geschichte* I 200 (Bohn 135).

[37] Cf Schlegel's Lect 7: "wie von den Werken des Aristoteles . . . bey den Al-

ten selbst nur eine einzige Abschrift übrig geblieben war . . ." (tr "of the words of Aristotle . . . only one single transcript was preserved by the ancients . . ."). *Geschichte* I 241 (Bohn 163). Schlegel does not mention Cicero in this context.

[38] This passage is derived from Schlegel's Lect 7: "Konstantinopel ist nie durch die Gothen erobert, noch von sogenannten Barbaren überschwemmt worden, bis auf die Kreuzzüge und Türkenzeit. Gleichwohl ist dessen, was wir durch die Byzantiner von der alten griechischen Litteratur erhalten haben, im Verhältniss mit dem unermesslichen Reichthum der alten Zeit, ungleich weniger, als was sich von der ursprünglich gar nicht sehr reichen und ungleich ärmern lateinischen Litteratur erhalten hat" (tr "Constantinople was not conquered by the Goths, or overrun by so-called Barbarians, up to the period of the Crusades and the Turks. But yet the ancient Greek literature preserved for us by the Byzantines was very much less, in proportion to the immense riches of ancient times, than has survived of the much feebler Latin literature, which

REPORTS
(1) NOTES TAKEN AT THE LECTURE BY
JOSEPH HENRY GREEN
(AS PRINTED IN *LR* I 67–9)

Mr. Coleridge began by treating of the races of mankind as descended from Shem, Ham, and Japhet,[39] and therein of the early condition of man in his antique form. He then dwelt on the pre-eminence of the Greeks in Art and Philosophy, and noticed the suitableness of polytheism to small insulated states, in which patriotism acted as a substitute for religion, in destroying or suspending self. Afterwards, in consequence of the extension of the Roman Empire, some universal or common spirit became necessary for the conservation of the vast body, and this common spirit was, in fact, produced in Christianity. The causes of the decline of the Roman empire were in operation long before the time of the actual overthrow; that overthrow had been foreseen by many eminent Romans, especially by Seneca.[40] In fact, there was under the empire an Italian and a German party in Rome, and in the end the latter prevailed.

He then proceeded to describe the generic character of the Northern nations, and defined it as an independence of the whole in the freedom of the individual, noticing their respect for women and their consequent chivalrous spirit in war; and how evidently the participation in the general council laid the foundation of the representative form of government, the only rational mode of preserving individual liberty in opposition to the licentious democracy of the ancient republics.[41]

He called our attention to the peculiarity of their art, and showed how it entirely depended on a symbolical expression of the infinite,— which is not vastness, nor immensity, nor perfection, but whatever cannot be circumscribed within the limits of actual sensuous being. In the ancient art, on the contrary, every thing was finite and material. Accordingly, sculpture was not attempted by the Gothic races till the ancient specimens were discovered, whilst painting and architecture were of native growth amongst them. In the earliest specimens of the

---

originally was nothing like as copious"). *Geschichte* I 242 (Bohn 163).

[39] The sons of Noah, according to Gen 10.1. F. Schlegel in Lect 4 of the *Geschichte* (I 149) gives an account of the origin of human races in three distinct families, without mentioning the sons of Noah, whose names, curiously, were

added in the Bohn translation p 89.

[40] C was probably thinking of Seneca's treatise on mercy addressed to Nero in A.D. 55 or 56, which envisages the possible collapse of Rome if the emperor loses the support of the people. *De clementia* 1.4.1–2.

[41] See below (at n 49).

paintings of modern ages, as in those of Giotto and his associates in the cemetery at Pisa,[42] this complexity, variety, and symbolical character are evident, and are more fully developed in the mightier works of Michel Angelo and Raffael.[43] The contemplation of the works of antique art excites a feeling of elevated beauty, and exalted notions of the human self; but the Gothic architecture impresses the beholder with a sense of self-annihilation;[44] he becomes, as it were, a part of the work contemplated. An endless complexity and variety are united into one whole, the plan of which is not distinct from the execution. A Gothic cathedral is the petrifaction of our religion. The only work of truly modern sculpture is the Moses of Michel Angelo.[45]

The northern nations were prepared by their own previous religion for Christianity; they, for the most part, received it gladly, and it took root as in a native soil. The deference to woman, characteristic of the Gothic races, combined itself with devotion in the idea of the Virgin Mother, and gave rise to many beautiful associations.

Mr. C. remarked how Gothic an instrument in origin and character the organ was.[46]

He also enlarged on the influence of female character on our education, the first impressions of our childhood being derived from women. Amongst oriental nations, he said, the only distinction was between lord and slave. With the antique Greeks, the will of every one conflicting with the will of all, produced licentiousness;[47] with the modern descendants from the northern stocks, both these extremes were shut out, to reappear mixed and condensed into this principle or temper;—sub-

---

[42] C visited Pisa in 1806 and was especially impressed by the frescoes in the Campo Santo there. At the time he jotted down the names of seven artists (*CN* II 2856–2857), perhaps from a guide or guidebook; the list included Giotto, who is now known not to have painted any of them. C associated them with Giotto also in *TT* 25 Jun 1830.

[43] For C's coupling of these two artists as representatives of the greatest in painting, "the true Ideal" (*CN* II 2828), see Lect 2 (at n 27) and Lect 3 (at n 10) of the 1811–12 series.

[44] The term had religious connotations for C, who had used "self-annihilated" in *Religious Musings* line 43, with reference to the soul being absorbed into God. *PW* (EHC) I 110.

[45] C saw this when he visited Rome in 1806, and recorded an anecdote about it in *BL* ch 21 (*CC*) II 116–17.

[46] In Lect 6 of his *Geschichte*, F. Schlegel said that ancient music was put to new use for Christian worship and "ascended from the organ in peals of exquisite melody". I 213 (Bohn 146).

[47] In Lect 2 of his *Geschichte* F. Schlegel says that the Greeks imitated oriental peoples in their treatment of women, and a deterioration of manners "and unnatural depravity attended the degradation of the sex" ("auch die entschiedenste Unsittlichkeit und Unnatur hatte jene Herabwürdigung des weiblichen Geschlechts zur Folge"). *Geschichte* I 50 (Bohn 31–2).

mission, but with free choice,—illustrated in chivalrous devotion to women as such, in attachment to the sovereign, &c.

(2) NOTES TAKEN AT THE LECTURE
BY H. H. CARWARDINE
ESSEX COUNTY RECORD OFFICE
MS D/D PR 549 FF 1–3ᵛ

ʷ1818

Jany 27   Attended Mʳ Coleridges first Lectʳ on the Manners, Morals, Literature Philosophy, Religion, and state of Society in general, in European Christendom from the 8ᵗʰ to the 15ᵗʰ Century—more particularly in reference to England, France, Italy and Germany:

Mʳ C— contended that the irruption of the Barbarians, as they have been called, and the downfall of Rome was by no means so sudden & unexpected an event as has been imagined—that it was long foreseen and often foretold by many of the Romans themselves long before it happened ⟨cited Seneca—⟩⁴⁸ —and that there was a German party in Rome who aided their northern countrymen, ⟨& that Rome did not fall till after long & repeated struggles⟩—Observed that the Germans of that day had a higher moral Character than the Romans ⟨whom they conquered⟩—that their feelings were elevated by that respectful and chivalrous feeling towards women, which was perfected by the influence ˣof Christianity—made a beautiful Eulogium on the influence of female affection⁴⁹ (particularly in the maternal care & instruction when we first [become]ʸ susceptible of impressions ⟨& imbibe instruction⟩) in forming our character, in repressing all our evil tendencies and encouraging every good and amiable sentiment and making us what we are in after life—Spoke of our superiority in this respect over the ancients which he attributed to the institution of Marriage which had given woman her proper rank & station in the scale of society—& contrasted it with the licentiousness & polygamy of the antients

ʷ f 1   ˣ f 1ᵛ
ʸ Word supplied by the editor

⁴⁸ See above (at n 40).

⁴⁹ F. Schlegel, especially in Lects 6 and 7, traced the development of mediaeval Europe as springing from the union of Christianity, derived from Rome, with the free spirit of the North, and argued that the Germans were not barbarians. He also emphasised the growth of chivalry and love-songs, and, like A. W. Schlegel in Lect 1 of *DKL*, emphasised the reverence of the German tribes for women. See esp *Geschichte* I 262–3 (Bohn 174–5).

Spoke of the Romans as [z]perfecting (in many things) what the Greeks had begun

[P [50] q[d] as to the truth of this of which I think he failed to adduce any very clear & satisfactory evidence][a]

Spoke of the Greeks as our superiors in Sculpture—History—Rhetoric Logic—equals in Poetry & Architecture—inferiors in music & painting—

Spoke of the inferior excitement of his own feelings produced by view of a fine specimen of ancient architecture, compared to the intensity of the emotions which had been produced by a view of the cathedral at York and the interior of King's Coll Chapel[51]—[Perhaps[b] the gothic architecture is more particularly adapted to religious buildings but I hardly think that good taste as it influences the feelings of the majority will prefer the [c]gothic for all—or even the majority of public or national buildings—and certainly there was a good deal of fustian and wandering out of the road of common sense in the enthusiasm with which M[r] C— expressed his feelings on this occasion—they were ⟨also⟩ evidently associated with feelings of religion—such feelings & associations are pardonable & even amiable and in a Poet we have no business to expect that he should always address himself to the cold & sober reason of a mere Philosopher—Our Poet was more happy in one of his flights upon Painting when he described a picture [d]of the Triumph of Death by Giotto (or some such name) a very early painter which he saw at the Cemetery at Pisa[52]—a rude drawing & poorly coloured—but so grandly composed, & happily designed as to have produced a marvellous effect upon the poet which can be adequately described only in his own language— Death is seen of a livid white—"killing the air with the swiftness of his motion"[53]—groups of figures are seen flying in all directions with

[z] f 2
[a] Carwardine's brackets
[b] Carwardine's bracket
[c] f 2[v]
[d] f 3

[50] Unidentified; presumably the initial of someone who questioned what C said, either at the lecture or in conversation later.

[51] Cf a note made in 1810: "Then to speak of the incomparable superiority of a grand Gothic Cathedral to the Pantheon & finest Temples of Greece or Rome, & the analogy of both to the several Religions . . .". *CN* III 4021. C found in

F. Schlegel's lectures, delivered in 1812 and published in 1815, a strong reinforcement of such ideas; but see Lect 1 of the 1813 series (n 20, also second sentence after n 21).

[52] See above (at n 42). This fresco of *The Triumph of Death* in the Campo Santo at Pisa is now attributed to Francesco Traini.

[53] Untraced.

actions & features characteristic of their station conduct & dread of the great destroyer—while 5 poor Beggars are alone seen prostrate on their knees with uplifted *e*hands & eyes to welcome his arrival—]*f* [54]

[M*r* C— has a solemn and pompous mode of delivery which he applies indiscriminately to the elevated and the familiar—and he reads poetry, I think as ill as any Man I ever heard]*g*

---

e f 3*v*
f Carwardine's bracket
g Carwardine's brackets

[54] C described this painting again in Lect 4 of the lectures on the history of philosophy, changing the sex of Death, which became a "dreadful Goddess descending with a kind of air-chilling white". *P Lects* (1949) 167.

LECTURE 2

DATE AND PLACE OF DELIVERY. Friday, 30 January 1818, in the Great Room of the London Philosophical Society, Fleur-de-Luce Court, Fleet Street.

SUBJECT. The Syllabus promised more than C could do, and he had to omit the promised translations, but the subject was basically as announced: "On the Tales and Metrical Romances common, for the most part, to England, Germany, and the North of France; and on the English Songs and Ballads; continued to the Reign of Charles the First.—A few Selections will be made from the Swedish, Danish, and German Languages, translated for the purpose by the Lecturer."

ADVERTISEMENTS. *The Times* Thurs, 29 Jan: "MR. COLERIDGE'S SECOND LEC-TURE, at 8 o'clock TO-MORROW EVENING, Friday, Jan. 30, on the METRICAL ROMANCES, English, French, and German, Characteristic of the Poetry, Chivalry, and Customs of the 12th, 13th, and 14th Centuries: and on National Songs and Ballads, continued to the reign of Charles the First, at the Great Room of the London Philosophical Society, Flower-de-luce-court, Fleet-street. Admission 5s. Prospectuses and tickets for the course (transferable), with the abatement for those who attended the first lecture, may be procured at Messrs. Hookham's, Bond-street; Taylor and Hessey's, Fleet-street; and at Boosey and Son's, Broad-street. The Lecture commences at half after 8 precisely. The First Lecture will be published in a few days, with additional illustrations and proofs." *Courier* Thurs, 29 Jan: as in *The Times*, with minor variations and the alteration of the lecture time to "a Quarter after Eight precisely". *M Chron* Fri, 30 Jan: as in *The Times*, but with a different opening: "This evening, Mr. Coleridge delivers his Second Lecture, on the Metrical Romances . . .". *New Times* Fri, 30 Jan: as in the *M Chron*.

TEXT. In N 29 C wrote in bold fashion, "Heads of the Lectures from 27 Jany to 13 March, 1818". The first or introductory lecture is mentioned as in the press ("jam sub prelo"; see Lect 1 headnote: Background and Circumstances), and then, under the heading "Second Lecture", C wrote extensive notes for it. After apologising for his croaky delivery in the first lecture, he went on to draft in full, with quite a few cancellations and false starts, the first part of the lecture, continuing with notes largely in the form of headings for the rest of it. The text printed below is based on Kathleen Coburn's presentation of it in *CN* III 4383–4384, omitting cancelled passages and incorporating into the text the detached notes C keyed in by using asterisks, etc. On the day following the lecture, the *New Times* printed a poem recited by C during the lecture, as an imitation of a minnesinger of the thirteenth century, and this is also reprinted here. A variant version of this poem was included by C in *PW* (1828), in which it formed the last three stanzas of *The Blossoming of the Solitary Date-tree*, a poem there related in a prefatory note to a tale found in a compilation by "Hebrew writers". This can be found in *PW* (EHC) I 395–7, ascribed to 1805.

REPORTS. C's own notes may be compared with the report made on the lecture by William Hammond printed first in *LR* I 70–8; this was included in *Misc C* 11–17 and is reprinted below.

BACKGROUND AND CIRCUMSTANCES. The hoarseness from which C suffered in delivering his first lecture was now "only a little better", according to a letter addressed to H. F. Cary on 30 Jan (*CL* IV 824). Nevertheless, this second lecture seems to have been a success, and HCR noted in his Diary (*CRB* I 218): "It was much more brilliant than the first and seemed to give general satisfaction." In preparing for it, C had difficulty in finding a copy of Joseph Ritson's *Ancient Engleish Metrical Romancëes* (3 vols 1802) and wrote to Godwin the day before the lecture, 29 Jan, requesting him to procure a loan of the volumes "till tomorrow night, post lecturam" (*CL* IV 822). He succeeded in obtaining at any rate the first volume, for he summarised the tale of "Ywaine and Gawin" from it (see Hammond's report, below, at n 35). He seems to have read the "Dissertation on Romance and Minstrelsy", which forms the long introduction to Vol I, and his praise of Alfred the Great is no doubt drawn from this. Many of C's own notes for the lecture are developed from Friedrich Schlegel's *Geschichte der alten und neuen Litteratur, Vorlesungen gehalten zu Wien im Jahre 1812* (2 vols Vienna 1815), freely translated, with numerous errors and omissions, as *Lectures on the History of Literature, Ancient and Modern* in 1818. C seems to have used the German text, and the links with this are developed in Kathleen Coburn's notes in *CN* III. The lecture notes also echo some of A.W. Schlegel's distinctions between classical and romantic art in the first lecture of his *Ueber dramatische Kunst und Litteratur*. In the course of the lecture C told stories from a play by Hans Sachs, *Die ungleichen Kinder Eve, wie sie Got der Herr anredt*. He had read this play when in Germany in 1798–9, and may have referred to it in Lect 2 in the 1808 series (see n 19). It was closely linked in his memories with the study he made at the same time of early German poetry, as is shown in his account of his visit to Germany in *BL* ch 10 (*CC*) I 209. He there says he "read with sedulous accuracy the MINNESINGER (or singers of love, the provençal poets of the Swabian court)", and on the day after he gave Lect 2, the *New Times* printed, on p 3 under the heading "Fashionable Mirror", an "Imitation of one of the Minnesinger of the Thirteenth Century" recited by C in the course of the lecture. The poem is not mentioned in his notes for the lecture. The form of the poem, three stanzas of seven lines each, and the rhyme-scheme, ABABCCC, provide a link with the love-poems of the Minnesinger, in which similar forms can be found, but the subject of the poem is C's own, and, as noted above, the version published in *PW* (1828) was associated by C with a Hebrew rather than a German tradition.

This poem was the only part of his first two lectures C is known to have published, although he announced his intention of bringing out both of them, "with the examples from *our own* Romances, &c" that he had been unable to quote in the time available. In the same letter to the editors of the *Courier* (printed 3 Feb) and the *New Times* (printed 4 Feb), in which he proposed publication of the lectures, he also offered to give an extra lecture free after the end of the course, to consist wholly of readings: "The subjects announced for the second Lecture, including all the recitations, which I had prepared, as extracts from our English metrical Romances and Ballads, and as metrical translations made by myself from those of the northern languages, had occasioned a space which it was impossible to deliver in the utmost time allotted to a Lecture. As the least of two evils, therefore, I solicited, and now solicit, the attendance of all who had or shall have attended me, to a supernumerary Lecture, at the end of the course, given gratis, and composed wholly of poetic translations, in chronological order, and concluding with an original Poem."

CL IV 826. This supernumerary lecture of readings was advertised to take place on 26 May 1818 (*CL* IV 862), but C did not in fact deliver it. (See the Introduction to this series, paragraph following n 29.) It would be interesting to know if the poem he published in the *New Times* was what he had in mind as the "original Poem" designed to round off his extra lecture. Although HCR found the lecture "brilliant", C seems to have felt that it suffered from the necessary omission of much of the material he said he had prepared, and in a letter to Cary written on 9 Feb on a copy of the Prospectus, he noted against the printed announcement of Lect 2: "I failed by attempting too much". *CL* IV 834.

LECTURE 2

RECORDS OF THE LECTURE

COLERIDGE'S NOTES

CN III 4383–4384

*a*Heads of   from 27 Jan*y* to 13 March, 1818.
the Lectures
(the introductory lecture jam sub prelo)

Second Lecture
Friday Night, 30 January—on
the Metrical Romances
Ballads and nation-
al Songs of the
Middle
Age.

*b*Heads
of
Lecture the Second

1. Batrachomyomachia, or battle between the Croaks and Squeaks.—[1]

2. In the Address of this evening my Object is twofold—first, to exemplify the positions of my last Lecture ⟨concerning the morals, manners, & specific genius of the Mid. Ages⟩ from the old Tales, Songs, and Metrical Romances that appear to have been equally popular in England, Norman France, and the North of Europe generally. For in these we possess not only the most amusing illustrations, but actually the fairest and least objectionable proofs, of the true character of the Times, in which they were written. For they are at once Portrait-painters,

a CN III 4383
b CN III 4384

---

[1] C began with an apology for his hoarseness during Lect 1, when he had a cold; he made the same joking refer- ence to the mock epic "Battle Between the Frogs and the Mice" in a letter to H. F. Cary of 30 Jan: *CL* IV 824.

and themselves portraits—and are prominent figures in the great Family Piece, ⟨of⟩ which they are the Painters.—Secondly, as the result of both Lectures to discover those principles, to fix that true point of view, by and from which we may ⟨most clearly understand,⟩ most rightly appreciate, most fully enjoy these immortal works which are to form the subjects of the following Lectures, and of all which ⟨both the Soil and⟩ the Germs the ⟨true⟩ solution, and the justifying scheme, purpose, and principle are ⟨only⟩ to be found in the character of the middle ages— works as various in their kinds as they are different or even opposite in their kinds as they are different or even opposite in their purposes, and agreeing in one point only that they are alike the legitimate offspring of Genius, with this best credential of their backward parentage, that they continued to give delight to mankind in all times & countries in proportion to the power of receiving it.—For it should never be forgotten, that Rules are ⟨are in all cases⟩ but Means to Ends—that therefore the end, the nature, the Idea of a work must be first known and appreciated, before we can discover, much more apply, the Rules, according to which we are to judge of its merits or defects.—To apply the same technical criticism to a Virgil and a Dante, or to a Shakespear and a Sophocles is scarcely less absurd, than to demand in a Pointer the form & proportions of a Greyhound.—[2]

Such are the Objects of this evening's address; but in order to make its content intelligible throughout to the Audience at large, I must in a few sentences re-state the main position of the Lecture Preceding.— With the commencement of profane History (about the time of the Judges in the sacred Writings)[3] a race of man, whom taken collectively we may distinguish by the common name, Japetidæ, or descendants of Japhet, diverged from their native Asia, and, as far at least, as concerns our present question, into two main branches[4]—The one, who as the posterity of Yahaun, or in our pronunciation, Javan (one of the sons of Japhet) are called by the Greek Writers, Ιωαονες, proceeded downward S.W., took possession of Greece, and the Greek Isles, and then colonized the coasts of Asia Minor—and thus by a literal fulfilment of

---

[2] In a marginal note in Richard Baxter's *Reliquiae Baxterianae*, C compared himself to a pointer and RS to a greyhound; see *CM (CC)* I 331. Cf also "Southey once said to me: You are nosing every nettle along the Hedge, while the Greyhound (meaning himself, I presume) wants only to get sight of the Hare, and Flash—strait as a line! he has it in his mouth!" *IS* 143.

[3] The book of Judges in the Old Testament begins with the conquest and settlement of the Israelites in Canaan.

[4] See Lect 1 (at n 9), above, and cf *P Lects* Lect 8 (1949) 254–5. See also *CN* III 4384n, in which C's wide reading on the subject of racial migrations is described.

the Noetic prediction, dwelt in the Tents of Shem/[5] while others at a somewhat later perhaps but still very remote period adventured still farther West, colonized the southern half of Italy, and became the founders of Rome.

The former (the Grecian I mean) bright, ample, and impetuous as the mighty stream was as long as it continued distinct, Sooner however reached the end of its historic Course, and ran, as the Missouri into the Mississippi, by various channels into the latter branch, and became part of the Roman Empire.

The other Branch, who are best known by the name of Goths, or the Gothic Nations, the Getæ and Massagetæ of the classics,[6] pressed onward North-West, thro' the North of Germany & thro' Holstein into Denmark and Sweden—and to those the name of Germans in ancient History exclusively belongs.—But as the name has since acquired a much more extensive and promiscuous application, I shall use the words, Goths and Gothic, for the whole of this North-Westward Branch: while the whole of the Southwestward I shall name the Romans tacitly including the Greeks, except when I am speaking distinctively of the latter in relation to Philosophy, Science, Poetry, and the Fine Arts.—

Between these two mighty Brotherhoods, the Gothic and the Roman, lay the Celtic Tribes: who appear from their customs, their dialects, and their mythology to have had another origin in an intermixture of the descendants of Shem with those of Ham and Canaan: a misalliance which was prevented in the posterity of Heber and Abraham by a miraculous ⟨interference⟩ and in the descendants of Ishmael, ⟨or the Arabians,⟩ by a natural yet equally providential dispensation.[7] All the other Semitic Nations (If we except those who intermarrying with the descendants of and N.b. Madai,[8] the Son of Japhet, and probably with

[5] Gen 9.27.

[6] According to Strabo *Geography* 7.3.4.11 and 11.8.2, the Getae were a tribe inhabiting lands north of Thrace, i. e. to the north of Greece and bordering on Germany; the Massagetae inhabited lands to the east of the Caspian Sea (see also Herodotus 1.215 and 2.93). Strabo describes the Getae as establishing a great empire. It was by a false etymology that they, and the more obscure Massagetae, were linked with the Goths in later times.

[7] Eber and Abraham were descendants of Shem, and Ishmael was a son of Abraham, whereas Canaan was Ham's son (so Gen 11.16, 27; 1 Chron 1.8, 28–9).

The "miraculous interference" that kept apart the descendants of Shem and Ham was presumably a reference to Gen 12.1–2, in which God speaks to Abraham and tells him to go away; the text reads: "out of thy country, and from thy kindred, and from thy father's house, unto a land that I will shew thee". In Lect 8 of the lectures on the history of philosophy of 1819, C said that " the children of Ham seem by Providence to have been impelled south", to become the inhabitants of Africa; see *P Lects* (1949) 255.

[8] Mentioned in Gen 10.2 and 1 Chron 1.5 as son of Japhet, the name is an eponym of Media, hence C's stress on

others of the elder Brothers of Javan, became the Ancestors of the Medes and of the Persians, who are to this day happily characterized as the Europeans of Asia, and the groundwork of whose language has a still perceptible affinity with that of the Gothic or oldest German) all the other Semitic nations more or less transgressed the command—and the descendants of these mixt marriages appeared to have spread out due East and West, and in the latter direction peopled the vast interspace that for a series of ages divided and estranged the Goths, and the Romans from each other.—The most famous and important nations, however, that sprung from the union of the posterity of Ham and of Canaan with the descendants of Shem, were those that were least removed from the patriarchal center, the Egyptians and the Phœnicians—while on the contrary the mere and least mixed descendants of Ham passed Southward into Africa, there alas! to fulfil the dread prediction of the patriarch by a fate, the alleviation of which commenced by ⟨Granville Sharp, by⟩ Clarkson, ⟨& by⟩ Wilberforce,[9] whose names being mentioned all other panegyric becomes superfluous, as it has, I trust, received its final seal, and security with the Treaty with Spain, just now made public,[10] and the perusal of which (gloomy as the morning was & with the rain clattering on the windows) seemed to me for the moment to fill the room with sunshine.—You have forgiven me this digression—and permit me to prolong it a few moments for the sake of a curious fact which cannot but at least amuse you—. The resemblance of the Welsh and the Irish Languages with the Hebrew is at once explained by their still greater affinity with the Phœnician and Punic or Carthaginian Languages, and it is more than probable that the latter is a Semitic Dialect, for the Hebrew, Syriac, Chaldean and Arabic are happily classed as the Semitic Languages, the term, Oriental, being far too vague and comprehensive/—it is more than probable, I say, that the Phœnician and Carthaginian are a compound of the Semitic Dialect and the Libyan, or original African.—Now during my residence in Malta ⟨Admiral⟩ Sir Alexander Ball,[11] whose accuracy and sound judgement were as con-

---

it in relation to Persia, Media being an ancient area in what is now Iran.

[9] Three notable early abolitionists of slavery, also mentioned as a group in *Friend (CC)* I 102. C reviewed Clarkson's *History of the . . . Abolition of the African Slave-Trade* in 1808; see Lect 12A headnote (sentence following n 20).

[10] The articles of this treaty, signed 23 Sept 1817 at Madrid, were published in *The Times* 29 Jan 1818, on the same page as the advertisement of C's lecture. The treaty provided for the abolition of traffic in slaves by Spanish or British ships from May 1820 and for Britain to compensate Spanish shipowners for losses resulting from this.

[11] While he was in Malta in 1804–6, C served as Public Secretary to Sir Alexander Ball, Governor, whom he regarded

spicuous as his veracity was above all suspicion, informed me then
when the Ship, he commanded, was off Goree, on the coast of Africa,
there were on board of her several companies of the 75ᵗʰ Regiment,
composed entirely of Welshmen, few of whom could speak English
with any fluency—that a party of them being on shore, and talking
Welsh to each other while they were bargaining for some trifles with
some Negroes from the interior, they found themselves understood by
the Negroes—and enough to carry on a mutually intelligible, tho' broken, conversation with each other. On their return on shipboard some
of the Negroes accompanied them—the discovery was announced—and
Sir Alex. Ball selected from those ⟨of the Welsh Soldiers⟩ who had not
gone on Shore, those whom he had noticed as the most intelligent and
sober men, who in his presence talked with the natives—and the experiment lasted for more than an hour—and both the men selected and
their comrades who stood eagerly, and by their looks & ejaculations
sufficiently shewed their wonder & exultation assured Sir Alex. that
tho' it was not altogether Welsh, yet it was a sort of Welsh, and one
of them declared, that he understood what they said better than he had
understood a man who talked Irish even—. The curiosity of the fact
and its bearing so close on my subject, will, I hope, be thought to
compensate for this delay.—for what in writing would come in without
inconvenience as Notes, become digressions in a Lecture. I hasten
therefore to compleat the Statement.—[12]

The Celtic Tribes, that by a wide interspace separated the Roman
Might from the Gothic, were attacked and finally conquered on both
sides: tho' chiefly by the disciplined valour & the policy of Rome,—
and after the reduction of Gaul into a roman province, and the Roman
Eagle had ⟨even⟩ alighted on the banks of the Rhine, the Shock and the
Collision took place—the struggle commenced and continued as long
as it was the strife of courage with skill. But generation after generation,
the hardy German learnt more and more of the arts and discipline of
Rome: while the corrupt Roman was more ready to purchase, than to
imitate the free spirit, contempt of death, and simple habits of the
German,—And when a large portion of the latter had received Christianity, the result was no longer doubtful,—the German Party became

as "the abstract Idea of a wise & good
governor". *CL* ii 1141. See also *Friend*
(CC) i 532–8. This anecdote C recorded
in a more abbreviated form in *CN* ii 2138
in Jul 1804. Gorée is a small island just
off Dakar in Senegal, West Africa, and
was one of the earliest European settle-

ments there.
[12] It may be that this long paragraph,
recapitulating, with additional material,
things said in Lect 1, was abbreviated or
largely omitted in delivery, if the report
by Hammond can be trusted.

predominant in Rome itself, and throughout the North of Italy—her eastern and Asiatic empire indeed was reprieved to a slow decay & a more dishonorable extinction—but the West fell to the might of the stronger, under different arrangements that were not ill proportioned to the remaining virtues of the Natives—Thus in Spain the Lands appeared to have been divided between the Conquerors and the Conquered, the language of the latter was modified rather than changed, and both soon blended with few other distinctions but those of Heraldry and Family Pride, while elsewhere the Victors granted to the Inhabitants no other tenure but that of Vassalage—in one form or other however the Roman Provinces became Gothic Kingdoms, and the Western Empire our modern Christendom: and the *process* of the Re-union constitutes the History and the philosophy of the History of the Dark or Middle Ages. Place before your eyes the Palace of the imperial Goth the great Theodoric, frowning opposite to the Christian Temple, ⟨that alone overlooks it,⟩ the Magnificence of Greek and Roman Art, and the sole remaining Object of Reverence and willing Submission—and you have the commencement of this æra presented to you in a symbol.[13] Imagine the temple too removed, and with it all its Greek and Roman Associations— and instead of it is a Cathedral, of ⟨York, of⟩ Milan or of Strasburg, with all its many Chapels, its pillared stem and leaf-work Roof,[14] as if some sacred Grove of Hertha, the mysterious Deity of their pagan Ancestors, had been awed into stone at the approach of the true divinity, and thus dignified by permanence into a symbol of the everlasting Gospel, while the choral thanksgiving rolled in peals through its silence, or the chaunt of penitence and holy pity ⟨from consecrated Virgins⟩ sobbed and died away in its dark recesses—among strange grotesques as strangely and yet harmoniously combined with the Images of Saints and the brazen Tombs of Warriors—and perhaps still soaring Heavenward, as if indefatigible in devotion and aspiration, the vast Dome

[13] C was putting together and developing in his own way bits of information culled from F. Schlegel's lectures. Schlegel speaks in Lect 6 of the time of Theodoric the Goth (c 454–526) marking the transition from antiquity to the Middle Ages and goes on to instance the Church of St Sophia in Constantinople as showing how a Christian style of architecture developed from Greek forms. *Geschichte* I 213 (Bohn 145). Later on, in Lect 9, he mentions the cathedral of Milan in a rhapsodic celebration of Gothic church architecture (*Geschichte* I 291;

Bohn 190) and, in another passage in Lect 6, refers to the "secret worship of Hertha, which Tacitus describes as a kind of mystery" (*Geschichte* I 223; Bohn 152). Hertha, or Nerthus, was a goddess of the earth, or fertility, mentioned by Tacitus as worshipped in Germany. The palace of Theodoric, ruler of Italy from 493 to 526, faced his church of St. Apollinare Nuovo, at Ravenna; the church still stands, but the palace is a ruin.

[14] C was developing a contrast drawn in Lect 1 (at n 51).

seemed a temple for unseen Angels that hovered over the adoring multitude and re-echoed their adorations—and behold at the high Altar the warrior Monarch kneeling with bowed and bared head, he and his attendant Peers, and with child-like awe receiving from the aged Bishop or mitred Abbot the precepts, the blessing, and the sacramental Pledge of Peace and Mercy,—and in this assemblage thus collected before your imagination you will see and recognize the completion of the Æra—. a marvellous compound, in which the philosophy and the loveliness of Grecian Genius, the legislatorial and ordonnant[15] Mind of civilizing Rome joined with the deep feelings, the high imagination, the chivalrous courtesies, and strong breathings after immortality of the Goths had produced the Base, and Christianity the all-combining, all-penetrating, all-transforming Spirit of union and ennoblement—.

⟨History of any country begins with the Gothic—Anglo-saxons in England/⟩

During the interval between these two epochs, and vividly characterizing the imperfections, the progress and the interruptions and Prechristian accompaniments of the Process, were the Poems composed of which I am to treat—

Few mistakes more common, but scarce any more groundless than the notion that at any one time there was a dark Age of *Europe*[16]— each country indeed had its eclipses, but in very different times—in England, for instance, it took place just when the Fountain of ancient Learning began to play again out of all its pipes—[17]

Theodoric Amaler (origin of our Royal Family)[18] the Goth, collected German Poems—Charlemagne did the same afterwards—And ALFRED[19]— conceive him, by his midnight lamp translating the Scriptures, the ecclesiastic History of his own Subjects—& framing Hymns to the Madonna—to the Harp of his Ancestors—Gothic Heroic lays sung in the Tent of Attila (Latin Epic Poems of the Goth tribes)

---

[15] I. e. that arranges in order; a word C seems to have coined. The only use recorded in *OED* is from *LR* III 32, a marginal note in Hooker's *Laws of Ecclesiastical Polity*; see *CM (CC)* II 1146.

[16] The main argument of the first part of F. Schlegel's Lect 7 is a defence of the Middle Ages against the charge of barbarism, or that this period was a kind of void space between antiquity and modern times (see esp Bohn 158–60). But C had spoken in this way about the "dark ages" long before Schlegel's lectures were published; see e.g. Lect 5 of

the 1811–12 series (paragraph containing n 12).

[17] In other words, in the fifteenth century, a period virtually ignored by C in his lectures, as perhaps more truly a dark age.

[18] Theodoric was descended from a King Amal, and F. Schlegel twice says that the praises of the Amaler line were sung in Gothic heroic lays. *Geschichte* I 216, 217 (Bohn 147, 148). Schlegel says nothing about a connexion with the British royal family.

[19] In Lect 6 Schlegel twice groups to-

The Goths preserved from Hero Worship—for I dare say that tho' in one instance the confusion of the names of the God, Odin, with that of a famous Chieftain who probably had introduced the mysteries from Asia[20]—&c—. Ill effects on the Greeks—

the public undomestic Habits of the Greeks, whose hearts and affections were in the Courts & Assemblies of the People—

The consequence of the intense domesticity of the German—a craving for and belief of the marvellous—

It had good effects indeed[21]—they early learnt the lessons of Art—Beauty and proportion—by the production of works in which the comprehensible Total was formed by the subordination of the Parts ⟨to the Whole⟩ and their co-ordination with each—so that both the Whole as a Whole, and the Parts, as its components, should be clearly and simultaneously perceived. Complacency[22]—compleat satisfaction—the result.—

But they produced them by a severe separation of whatever was heterogeneous—this even in their political Constitutions—and in their treatment of women/

Contrast of the Middle Ages—

On the other hand, an inwardness, a deeper reflection in the German Nations   The Song of Roland sung by the Normans—yet Charlemagne was unfortunate—but they *died for Christ*—.[23] This a contrast

gether Theodoric, Charlemagne, and Alfred, first as educators and preservers of the poetry of the past (*Geschichte* I 206; Bohn 139) and later in relation to the sponsoring and collecting of poetry (*Geschichte* I 215–16; Bohn 147–8). C's comments on Alfred are his own, but he then quotes from Schlegel (*Geschichte* I 215; Bohn 147): "Gothic heroic poems were sung in the tent of Attila" ("In Attila's Zelt wurden gothische Heldenlieder gesungen"), and briefly notes Schlegel's next comment, that even Latin writers cited legendary history from German poems. Hammond's report shows that C expanded his comments on Alfred considerably; see below (paragraph containing nn 33 and 34).

[20] In Lect 6 Schlegel went on to say that the songs collected by Charlemagne were not in praise of Odin or ancient pagan heroes, but were Christianised. He

then commented at some length on the existence of more than one Odin, one being a historic chieftain whose tribal territories extended to the bounds of Asia and who revived the mysteries of the North. *Geschichte* I 217–21 (Bohn 148–51).

[21] I. e. on the Greeks.

[22] C was evidently using it in the sense of "tranquil pleasure or satisfaction", as the Hammond report makes clear; see below (paragraph following n 29).

[23] C was abstracting material from the close of Schlegel's Lect 7, in which he says that the *Song of Roland* was used as a war-song by Norman soldiers, that Charlemagne was unfortunate ("unglückliche") in the defeat at Roncesvalles, and that the knights who died there did so like heroes for the cause of God ("für die Sache Gottes"). *Geschichte* I 265–6 (Bohn 176–7).

to the Greeks & Romans[24] but not to the Pagan Goths—

When the Greeks and Romans could no longer keep things separate and insulated, they *fused*—and ran in like figures on blotting paper into despotism.

The fools and the mixture of Comic in the dark ages—

The Superstitions, distinct from Religion—illustrate from the Cabiric Mysteries—[25]

Allegorical Spirit—on the Sᵗ Graal—[26]

The influence of Arabian Poetry over-rated—Had we the Milesian Tales of the Greeks:—these Arabian Tales originally old Persian[27]—Sons of Madai—[28]

POEM BY COLERIDGE CITED IN
THE LECTURE, PRINTED IN THE *NEW TIMES*
SATURDAY, 31 JANUARY 1818

Later published in a variant version as the last three stanzas of *The Blossoming of the Solitary Date-tree: PW* (EHC) I 395. The most notable variants are ''Death'' for ''chance'' and ''Hear man!'' for ''Dear Maid'' in the final stanza.

---

[24] The Hammond report makes C's point clear, that the Greeks and Romans would not have recorded in heroic verse the defeat of their countrymen; see below (sentence following n 32).

[25] C read widely on the subject of Samothracian or Cabiric mysteries. He annotated a copy of G. S. Faber's *A Dissertation on the Mysteries of the Cabiri* (2 vols Oxford 1803), now in the Berg Collection in NYPL; he also used and annotated a copy of Schelling's *Über die Gottheiten von Samothrace* (Stuttgart and Tübingen 1815), now in the BM. In *CN* III 4322 he quoted from William Warburton's *Divine Legation of Moses Demonstrated* (2 vols 1738–41), which has a long essay, bk II sect 4, on the mysteries, arguing that they taught ''the Error of Polytheism'' and the ''Unity of the Godhead'' (I 152, 150). Probably C was arguing in this lecture along similar lines, about the way in which superstition and polytheism were superseded. See also *Misc C* 191–3, a passage from *LR* linked by HNC with Lect 11 of this series, and

P Lects Lects 2, 11 (1949) 89–90, 320–3.

[26] Schlegel says in Lect 8 that the name of the St Graal refers to a series of allegorical poems of chivalry, but does not mention any specific examples. *Geschichte* I 273 (Bohn 179).

[27] In Lect 8 Schlegel said that the origin of the fabulous and fairy-tale parts of the ''Arabian Tales'' or *Thousand and One Nights* was Persian. *Geschichte* I 275 (Bohn 180–2). See also Lect 11, below (C's notes *a*).

[28] On Madai see n 8, above. The general idea of the paragraph is from Schlegel's Lect 8, in which he says that the influence of oriental poetry on Europe through the Crusades was less than was often supposed and was Persian rather than Arabian. The reference to ''Milesian Tales'' may be from Ritson, who says, ''The Milesian Tales of Aristides, so famous in their day, though none of them now remain, must have been some kind of romancëes, whether in prose or verse.'' *Ancient Engleish Metrical Romancëes* I viii. Aristides of Miletus wrote

IMITATION OF ONE OF THE MINNESINGER
OF THE THIRTEENTH CENTURY.
INTRODUCED BY MR. COLERIDGE IN HIS LECTURE ON
THE LITERATURE OF THE MIDDLE AGES.

O! ever as the gladness stirs my heart
    All tim'rously beginning to rejoice,
Like a blind Arab, that from sleep doth start,
    In lonesome tent, I listen for thy voice:
Beloved! 'tis not thine! thou art not there!
Then melts the bubble into idle air:
And wishing without hope, I restlessly despair.

The mother, with anticipated glee,
    Smiles o'er the child, which, standing by her chair,
And pressing its round cheek upon her knee,
    Looks up, and doth its little lips prepare,
To mock the coming sounds—at that sweet sight
She hears her *own* voice with a new delight:
And if the babe perchance should lisp the notes aright,

Then is she tenfold gladder than before:
    But should Disease, or Death, the darling take,
What then avail these songs, which, sweet of yore,
    Were only sweet for their sweet echo's sake?
Hear man! no prattler, at a mother's knee,
Was e'er so dearly prized, as I prize thee—
Why was I made for love, and love denied to me?

                            S. T. C.

NOTES TAKEN BY WILLIAM HAMMOND
(AS PRINTED IN *LR* I 70–8)

In my last lecture I stated that the descendants of Japhet and Shem peopled Europe and Asia, fulfilling in their distribution the prophecies of Scripture, while the descendants of Ham passed into Africa, there also actually verifying the interdiction pronounced against them. The Keltic and Teutonic nations occupied that part of Europe, which is now France, Britain, Germany, Sweden, Denmark, &c. They were in general a hardy race, possessing great fortitude, and capable of great endurance.

---

or collected these tales about 100 B.C.; they were translated into Latin a century later and served as models for Petronius in *Satyricon* and Apuleius in *The Golden Ass*. C seems to have argued here, as in Lect 11 (C's notes *a*), that the Greek empire established by Alexander in the fourth century B.C. made a deep cultural impression on Persian literature, which in turn influenced later European literature. See also *TT* 9 May 1830.

The Romans slowly conquered the more southerly portion of their tribes, and succeeded only by their superior arts, their policy, and better discipline. After a time, when the Goths,—to use the name of the noblest and most historical of the Teutonic tribes,—had acquired some knowledge of these arts from mixing with their conquerors, they invaded the Roman territories. The hardy habits, the steady perseverance, the better faith of the enduring Goth rendered him too formidable an enemy for the corrupt Roman, who was more inclined to purchase the subjection of his enemy, than to go through the suffering necessary to secure it. The conquest of the Romans gave to the Goths the Christian religion as it was then existing in Italy; and the light and graceful building of Grecian, or Roman–Greek order, became singularly combined with the massy architecture of the Goths, as wild and varied as the forest vegetation which it resembled. The Greek art is beautiful. When I enter a Greek church, my eye is charmed, and my mind elated; I feel exalted, and proud that I am a man. But the Gothic art is sublime. On entering a cathedral, I am filled with devotion and with awe; I am lost to the actualities that surround me, and my whole being expands into the infinite; earth and air, nature and art, all swell up into eternity, and the only sensible impression left, is, "that I am nothing!" This religion, while it tended to soften the manners of the Northern tribes, was at the same time highly congenial to their nature. The Goths are free from the stain of hero worship.[29] Gazing on their rugged mountains, surrounded by impassable forests, accustomed to gloomy seasons, they lived in the bosom of nature, and worshipped an invisible and unknown deity. Firm in his faith, domestic in his habits, the life of the Goth was simple and dignified, yet tender and affectionate.

The Greeks were remarkable for complacency and completion; they delighted in whatever pleased the eye; to them it was not enough to have merely the idea of a divinity, they must have it placed before them, shaped in the most perfect symmetry, and presented with the nicest judgment; and if we look upon any Greek production of art, the beauty of its parts, and the harmony of their union, the complete and complacent effect of the whole, are the striking characteristics. It is the same in their poetry. In Homer you have a poem perfect in its form,[30]

---

[29] See above (conclusion of paragraph containing n 15). In Lect 6 Schlegel comments on the softening and refinement of Germanic races and their poetry under the influence of Christianity. *Geschichte* I 215 (Bohn 147).

[30] C was probably recalling A. W. Schlegel's Lect 1 and F. Schlegel's Lects 1 and 3, in which he would have found comments on the harmony and serenity of Greek life and art, and, in the latter, some extensive commentary on Homer.

whether originally so, or from the labour of after critics, I know not; his descriptions are pictures brought vividly before you, and as far as the eye and understanding arc concerned, I am indeed gratified. But if I wish my feelings to be affected, if I wish my heart to be touched, if I wish to melt into sentiment and tenderness, I must turn to the heroic songs of the Goths, to the poetry of the middle ages. The worship of statues in Greece had, in a civil sense, its advantage, and disadvantage; advantage, in promoting statuary and the arts; disadvantage, in bringing their gods too much on a level with human beings, and thence depriving them of their dignity, and gradually giving rise to scepticism and ridicule. But no statue, no artificial emblem, could satisfy the Northman's mind; the dark wild imagery of nature, which surrounded him, and the freedom of his life, gave his mind a tendency to the infinite, so that he found rest in that which presented no end, and derived satisfaction from that which was indistinct.

We have few and uncertain vestiges of Gothic literature till the time of Theodoric, who encouraged his subjects to write, and who made a collection of their poems. These consisted chiefly of heroic songs, sung at the Court; for at that time this was the custom. Charlemagne, in the beginning of the ninth century, greatly encouraged letters, and made a further collection of the poems of his time,[31] among which were several epic poems of great merit; or rather in strictness there was a vast cycle of heroic poems, or minstrelsies, from and out of which separate poems were composed. The form of poetry was, however, for the most part, the metrical romance and heroic tale. Charlemagne's army, or a large division of it, was utterly destroyed in the Pyrenees, when returning from a successful attack on the Arabs of Navarre and Arragon; yet the name of Roncesvalles became famous in the songs of the Gothic poets.[32] The Greeks and Romans would not have done this; they would not have recorded in heroic verse the death and defeat of their fellow-countrymen. But the Goths, firm in their faith, with a constancy not to be shaken, celebrated those brave men who died for their religion and their country! What, though they had been defeated, they died without fear, as they had lived without reproach; they left no stain on their names, for they fell fighting for their God, their liberty, and their rights; and the song that sang that day's reverse animated them to future victory and certain vengeance.

[31] C is borrowing from F. Schlegel's Lect 6; see above (at n 19).

[32] This is based on F. Schlegel, who at the end of Lect 7 refers to the total defeat of Charlemagne's army and ar-gues that the battle of Roncesvalles was celebrated as heroic in spite of the defeat because it was regarded as another crusade against the Arabs. *Geschichte* I 266–8 (Bohn 176–7).

I must now turn to our great monarch, Alfred, one of the most august characters that any age has ever produced; and when I picture him after the toils of government and the dangers of battle, seated by a solitary lamp, translating the holy scriptures into the Saxon tongue,[33]—when I reflect on his moderation in success, on his fortitude and perseverance in difficulty and defeat, and on the wisdom and extensive nature of his legislation, I am really at a loss which part of this great man's character most to admire. Yet above all, I see the grandeur, the freedom, the mildness, the domestic unity, the universal character of the middle ages condensed into Alfred's glorious institution of the trial by jury.[34] I gaze upon it as the immortal symbol of that age;—an age called indeed dark;—but how could that age be considered dark, which solved the difficult problem of universal liberty, freed man from the shackles of tyranny, and subjected his actions to the decision of twelve of his fellow countrymen? The liberty of the Greeks was a phenomenon, a meteor, which blazed for a short time, and then sank into eternal darkness. It was a combination of most opposite materials, slavery and liberty. Such can neither be happy nor lasting. The Goths on the other hand said, You shall be our Emperor; but we must be Princes on our own estates, and over them you shall have no power! The Vassals said to their Prince, We will serve you in your wars, and defend your castle; but we must have liberty in our own circle, our cottage, our cattle, our proportion of land. The Cities said, We acknowledge you for our Emperor; but we must have our walls and our strong holds, and be governed by our own laws. Thus all combined, yet all were separate; all served, yet all were free. Such a government could not exist in a dark age. Our ancestors may not indeed have been deep in the metaphysics of the schools; they may not have shone in the fine arts; but much knowledge of human nature, much practical wisdom must have existed amongst them, when this admirable constitution was formed; and I believe it is a decided truth, though certainly an awful lesson, that nations are not the most happy at the time when literature and the arts flourish the most among them.

The translations I had promised in my syllabus I shall defer to the

[33] Here C is echoing what he had written in *The Friend* No 8 of 5 Oct 1809 about Luther writing and translating the New Testament: "Methinks I see him sitting, the heroic Student, in his chamber in the Warteburg, with his midnight Lamp before him . . .". See *Friend (CC)* II 119.

[34] C's admiration for Alfred the Great is expressed also in *Friend (CC)* I 91 and in *P Lects* Lect 9 (1949) 269. The institution of trial by jury is traditionally ascribed to Alfred, as is a translation of a number of the Psalms. Alfred was deeply interested in theology, translated Boethius and Pope Gregory I's *Pastoral Care*, but is not known to have translated the Scriptures.

end of the course, when I shall give a single lecture of recitations illustrative of the different ages of poetry. There is one Northern tale I will relate, as it is one from which Shakespeare derived that strongly marked and extraordinary scene between Richard III. and the Lady Anne.[35] It may not be equal to that in strength and genius, but it is, undoubtedly, superior in decorum and delicacy.

A Knight had slain a Prince, the lord of a strong castle, in combat. He aferwards contrived to get into the castle, where he obtained an interview with the Princess's attendant, whose life he had saved in some encounter; he told her of his love for her mistress, and won her to his interest. She then slowly and gradually worked on her mistress's mind, spoke of the beauty of his person, the fire of his eyes, the sweetness of his voice, his valour in the field, his gentleness in the court; in short, by watching her opportunities, she at last filled the Princess's soul with this one image; she became restless; sleep forsook her; her curiosity to see this Knight became strong; but her maid still deferred the interview, till at length she confessed she was in love with him;—the Knight is then introduced, and the nuptials are quickly celebrated.

In this age there was a tendency in writers to the droll and the grotesque, and in the little dramas which at that time existed, there were singular instances of these. It was the disease of the age. It is a remarkable fact that Luther and Melancthon, the great religious reformers of that day, should have strongly recommended for the education of children, dramas which at present would be considered highly indecorous, if not bordering on a deeper sin.[36] From one which they particularly recommended, I will give a few extracts; more I should not

[35] Raysor suggested that C had in mind the story of "Ywaine and Gawin", the first in Joseph Ritson's collection of *Ancient Engleish Metrical Romancëes* I 1–169, and the tale C told does correspond roughly with the first 1250 lines of this romance, in which the knight Ywaine slays a lord and falls in love with his widow, the Lady Alundyne. Her maid, who was once helped by Ywaine when she was at court, now helps him by persuading her lady that she would do well to remarry to protect her lands, and Ywaine is to hand, and a prince, and so their marriage takes place. For other possible uses of Ritson, see Lect 3, below (nn 1 and 2). C linked this with Richard's successful wooing of Anne after killing her husband, Edward, Prince of Wales, in *Richard III* I ii.

[36] In *Unterricht der Visitatoren* (1528), or "Instructions for the Visitors of Parish Pastors", a work written by Melanchthon but embodying Luther's ideas and issued with a preface by him, the final section deals with the education of children. This recommends training them to study and speak in Latin and that they should be given the plays of Terence to be learned by heart and then some of the comedies of Plautus. Luther and Melanchthon did not recommend plays by Hans Sachs, or any German drama, but specifically urged schoolmasters to teach only Latin, in order to lighten the burden for children who had hitherto been taught several languages simultaneously.

think it right to do.[37] The play opens with Adam and Eve washing and dressing their children to appear before the Lord, who is coming from heaven to hear them repeat the Lord's Prayer, Belief, &c. In the next scene the Lord appears seated like a schoolmaster, with the children standing round, when Cain, who is behind hand, and a sad pickle, comes running in with a bloody nose and his hat on. Adam says, "What, with your hat on!" Cain then goes up to shake hands with the Almighty, when Adam says (giving him a cuff), "Ah, would you give your left hand to the Lord?"[38] At length Cain takes his place in the class, and it becomes his turn to say the Lord's Prayer. At this time the Devil (a constant attendant at that time) makes his appearance, and getting behind Cain, whispers in his ear; instead of the Lord's Prayer, Cain gives it so changed by the transposition of the words, that the meaning is reversed; yet this is so artfully done by the author, that it is exactly as an obstinate child would answer, who knows his lesson, yet does not choose to say it.[39] In the last scene, horses in rich trappings and carriages covered with gold are introduced, and the good children are to ride in them and be Lord Mayors, Lords, &c;[40] Cain and the bad ones are to be made cobblers and tinkers, and only to associate with such.

This, with numberless others, was written by Hans Sachs. Our simple ancestors, firm in their faith, and pure in their morals, were only amused by these pleasantries, as they seemed to them, and neither they nor the reformers feared their having any influence hostile to religion. When I was many years back in the north of Germany, there were several innocent superstitions in practice. Among others at Christmas, presents used to be given to the children by the parents, and they were delivered

---

[37] The play was *Die ungleichen Kinder Eve, wie sie Got der Herr anredt*, or "The Dissimilar Children of Eve, and How God the Father Spoke to Them". This comedy in five acts was printed in the set of works by Hans Sachs that C borrowed from the library of the University of Göttingen when he was in Germany in 1799: *Sehr Herrliche Schöne und warhaffte Gedicht* (5 vols Nuremberg 1558–79) I 10–19. See Alice Snyder in *MP* xxv (1928) 379 and *RX* (rev ed 1951) 542–4. In *BL* ch 10 *(CC)* I 209 C recalled the "five folio volumes with double columns" of the Göttingen set. He also told the story of the play in conversation with Clement Carlyon, who was in Germany at the same time as C; see Carlyon I 93–4. He was recalling the play inaccurately from memory, and God in fact first appears in Act III, when he enters with two angels to meet Eve's six obedient and six disobedient children. In connexion with this play see also Lect 2 of the 1808 series (n 19).

[38] It is in fact Eve who rebukes Cain in Act III:

Ey, reicht ir denn an diesem End
Unserm Hergott die lincken Hend?

She also tells him to take his hat off. *Gedicht* I 14.

[39] This takes place in Act IV.

[40] This is not from the play by Sachs, in which, after the murder of Abel, God announces his reward in heaven and the damnation of Cain, after which a Herald points the moral in a long epilogue.

on Christmas day by a person who personated, and was supposed by the children to be, Christ: early on Christmas morning he called, knocking loudly at the door, and (having received his instructions) left presents for the good and a rod for the bad.[41] Those who have since been in Germany have found this custom relinquished; it was considered profane and irrational. Yet they have not found the children better, nor the mothers more careful of their offspring; they have not found their devotion more fervent, their faith more strong, nor their morality more pure.

[41] HNC directed attention to *The Friend* No 19 of 28 Dec 1809, which includes a charming and much fuller account of this Christmas custom as witnessed by C at Ratzeburg, where he spent the winter of 1798–9; see *Friend (CC)* II 256–7.

LECTURE 3

DATE AND PLACE OF DELIVERY. Tuesday, 3 February 1818, in the Great Room of the London Philosophical Society, Fleur-de-Luce Court, Fleet Street.

SUBJECT. "Chaucer and Spenser; of Petrarch; of Ariosto, Pulci, and Bioardo", according to the Syllabus. C's notes for this lecture suggest that it was devoted mainly to Italian poetry, and it is not certain that he spoke on either Chaucer or Spenser in the course of it.

ADVERTISEMENT. *Courier* Mon, 2 Feb: "Mr. COLERIDGE's Third Lecture, Eight o'Clock, To-morrow Evening, 3d February, at the Great Room of the Longon Philosophical Society, Fleur-de-luce-court, Fleet-street—on CHAUCER, SPENSER, and ARIOSTO. Admission five shillings." A letter survives from C to William Mudford, editor of the *Courier*, asking him to print an enclosed advertisement in the *Courier* of "to day", being "Monday", or failing that in the Tuesday issue (*CL* IV 825). Possibly he applied to no other journal, and this note reflects a late realisation that he had forgotten to advertise. At any rate, the advertisement in the *Courier* seems to have been the only printed announcement of this lecture.

TEXT. The story is a complicated one. Various bits and pieces, which defeated HNC's ability to link material together, were printed in *LR* I 79–97. This includes an edited version of C's notes as written out in N 29, under "Heads of Lecture the third", and continuing from the notes for Lect 2; but HNC also printed some marginalia on Petrarch and some critical remarks on Spenser drawn from an unidentified source. All this material was reproduced in *Misc C* 18–39, but Raysor added further items in the form of some marginalia on Spenser and three passages from BM MS Egerton 2800. The first of these, from f 41, begins, "Ladies and Gentlemen", refers to "two preceding lectures", and its theme, the origin of romance, is appropriate to this lecture. The second, from f 50, clearly belongs with the lecture notes, since it refers to and quotes from C's introductory paragraphs in N 29. The third, from ff 48–9, consists of an essay on allegory, which breaks off in the middle of a reference to Spenser's *Faerie Queene*. Although it is related to the subject of the lecture, there is no clear evidence that it was written for this series or used in it. Lastly, at one point in his notes in N 29, C reminded himself that he should "turn over the leaf of the black book", which Kathleen Coburn identifies as N 15, in which there is a relevant comment in a note on Boccaccio.

The materials for the text of this lecture thus raise some problems of coherence and of authenticity. Here are reprinted: (1) a transcript of BM MS Egerton 2800 ff 41 and 50. The sheet f 41 is headed with the numeral "2", which Raysor ignored, but as the fragment of f 50 is numbered "3", and the initial phrase completes the unfinished sentence at the foot of f 41, these two pages are printed consecutively. There is little doubt that they form C's revised introduction to the lecture, written after he had drafted the "Heads of Lecture the third" in N 29, for they refer to the "Lecture Book" twice, once to remind himself to interpolate the opening page or so from the notes there, and then, at the end, to return to it for the rest of the lecture. In the first of these references, C directed himself to read from the "Lecture Book" down to the phrase "toilsome Scholar", and the passage following this in N 29 is cancelled by a vertical stroke drawn through it, indicating that it was to be replaced by the revised version of it in BM MS Egerton 2800 f 50. The verso of f 50 is blank, except for the words "Italian Poet", written in pencil and not in C's hand. I have not traced a leaf headed "1" in this series, and there is no obvious need for one. Raysor took f 50, headed "3", to refer to Lect 3 and printed the notes on it accordingly in *Misc C* 23, but it plainly belongs with the notes for Lect 2. (2) A version of the draft notes in N 29, based on Kathleen Coburn's presentation in *CN* III 4388–4389, but omitting cancelled passages, including the long passage revised by C on BM MS Egerton 2800 f 50. The first entry, *CN* III 4388, represents C's first draft of his introduction for the lecture, but it ends with abbreviated notes for development on Petrarch and the phrase "This leads to Ariosto". The next entry, *CN* III 4389, is devoted wholly to Pulci. It would seem probable that C had somewhere made preparatory notes on "darling Ariosto", whom he regarded as the greatest of Italian narrative poets and on whose work he contemplated writing a critical study (*CN* II App A pp 401–3), but if so, they have not been traced. (3) The entry in N 15, made in 1805, on the confusion of pagan and Christian mythology in poets of the fifteenth century, which fits in well with the argument C was making. Accordingly this passage, from *CN* II 2670, is also reprinted below. These various notes by C have been arranged consecutively in the order in which he used them, which means that a passage from N 29 is incorporated into BM MS Egerton 2800 f 50, and the entry from N 15 is inserted, following C's indications, into the introduction in N 29.

Besides the notes on BM MS Egerton 2800 ff 41 and 50, C also wrote, on paper from the same stock, two drafts of an introduction, on the subject of allegory, to part of a lecture on Spenser. Although there is no evidence to show that C spoke on Spenser in Lect 3, he advertised it as on Chaucer, Spenser, and Ariosto, and it seems certain that the notes were prepared for this lecture. Not only are the drafts, BM MS Egerton 2800 ff 48–9, on two sheets from the stock of paper he used to make notes for several lectures in this course, bearing the watermark "RUSE & TURNERS 1817", but in them he promises to comment on Milton in a later lecture, as he did in Lect 10 of the 1818 course. The drafts cannot have been made, therefore, for the Spenser lecture of the 1819 series, since that one, Lect 6, followed after a lecture on Milton (Lect 4). It is possible that C used the notes on both occasions or on neither, but they record his thinking for the 1818 lecture. The second draft is a revision of the first, and C marked his intention to include passages from the first into the second, without actually writing them into the revised draft. The revision breaks off in mid-sentence at the foot of 49 with a reference to *The Faerie Queene*, and the continuation is lost. The first draft ends in the middle of f 48ᵛ, the rest of which is blank. Raysor combined the two drafts into one and printed this version in *Misc C* 28–32. Below, both are printed from the mss as C wrote them. The other notes on Spenser printed in *Misc C* in association with this lecture belong rather to Lect 6 of the 1819 series, in which they are included in this edition.

REPORTS. H. H. Carwardine, who wrote reports of Lects 1 and 4 in an unbound notebook, now Essex County Record Office MS D/D Pr 549, also added later on the last leaf, ff 12ᵛ–12, a brief note dated 8 Feb 1818, but referring to the subject-matter of Lect 3, which he also must have attended. This has not been published hitherto, and a transcript from the ms is printed below. J. H. Green may also have been present at the lecture, for HNC printed a paragraph on Chaucer "from Mr. Green's note" in *LR* I 88–9, which could be an edited version of a passage from it, and this is printed below; it was included in *Misc C* 27–8.

BACKGROUND AND CIRCUMSTANCES. As in the preceding lecture, C borrowed ideas from F. Schlegel's *Geschichte der alten und neuen Litteratur* and from A. W. Schegel's *Ueber dramatische Kunst und Litteratur*, combining and developing them in his own way. The notes on Pulci draw heavily, as Kathleen Coburn points out in her commentary in *CN* III, on the introduction to an edition of *Il Morgante Maggiore* published in Florence in 1732; C once owned a copy of it, which cannot now be traced. The revised introduction for the lecture in BM MS Egerton 2800 ff 41 and 50 shows the influence of Joseph Ritson, whose essay on romance and minstrelsy in Vol I of *Ancient Engleish Metrical Romancëes* C had apparently read when preparing for Lect 2 (see n 35). So e.g. C follows Ritson in assigning erroneously the first publication of Chaucer's *Canterbury Tales* to 1380.

C was pleased with his performance at this lecture and wrote on the Prospectus he sent to H. F. Cary: "This was *very* popular". *CL* IV 834. HCR also enjoyed it, noting: "Coleridge lectured on Dante, Ariosto, etc., more entertainment than instruction; splendid irregularities throughout." *CRB* I 218. C's lack of moral sympathy with early Italian literature, and his insensitivity to its humour, may partly account for HCR's comment. Italian was a language C began to study seriously not long before he went to Malta in 1804, and he was never thoroughly at home in it; see *CN* II App A "Coleridge's Knowledge of Italian" pp 397–404.

LECTURE 3

RECORDS OF THE LECTURE

COLERIDGE'S NOTES
(1) BM MS EGERTON 2800 FF 41, 50;
CN III 4388–4389; *CN* II 2670 (IN THE
ORDER USED IN THE LECTURE)

*a*Ladies and Gentlemaen

The ⟨final⟩ re-union of the Goths and the Romans, as the N.W. and S.W. Branches of the same original Stock, and the character of the Compounds ~~formed~~ produced by this re-union according as the ~~one~~ one or the other of the two component parts predominated, formed the subject of my two preceding Lectures. From this same union arose the Romance or Romantic Language,[1] in which the Soul (if I may dare so express myself) was Gothic, but the outward forms and the etymology of ~~a great~~ the far greater portion of the words were *Roman*: by which term I mean the ~~language~~ Latin actually spoken in Italy and ~~the~~ Roman Europe; and which was by no means so different from the ~~Ita~~ present Spanish and Italian, as the Latin of the Classics, ~~which~~ in which the Roman Nobles, Gentry & men of letters, ~~and the highly educated Ro~~ wrote and conversed. If ~~þ~~ we take the Roman at the one extreme, and the Teutonic Languages ⟨i.e.⟩ the Norse, Danish, Swedish, and German,

---

a Egerton 2800 f 41

[1] In this passage C was probably drawing in memory on a variety of sources. Both A. W. Schlegel, in Lect 1 of *DKL*, and F. Schlegel, in Lect 6 of *Geschichte*, comment on the origin of Romance languages. In Lect 7 F. Schlegel says that Provençal was the first of the Romance languages to develop and English the last. But C had spoken of a Romance (or Romaunt) language in Lect 5 of the 1812 series, first course (at n 3) and in Lect 1 of the 1813 series (at n 27), and there, as here, a more likely source seems to be Ritson I xii–xv, in which the decline of Latin, "gradually intermix'd" with the "jargons of the different northern nations", is described as leading to the growth of a "new dialect call'd the *Roman* or *Romance*, a mixture, it would seem, of Latin, Frankish, and Celtick". Ritson goes on to tell a story of Lewis, King of Germany, making an alliance with Charles the Bald of France, one speaking "in the *Roman* tongue", the other in the "*Teutonick* tongue". See also the next n, below.

as ~~being a~~ modifications of the Gothic, at the other, as the two rings or staples of a Chain, ~~we shall have~~ the chain ~~is~~ will commence at the Southern Roman end with the ~~Provencal~~ Romance or Romantic, or the language in which the Troubadours or Love-singers of Provence and the ~~North~~ neighboring districts wrote or sang: and at the ~~Gothic~~ other end, namely the German, it ends with the English from 1280, the date when Robert of Gloucester finished his ~~rom~~ Chronicle in rhyme, to 1380, in which the year the Canterbury Tales of Chaucer were first made public:[2] and as the intermediate Link between the Romance, ~~with the (old) Spanish and Italian included~~ and the English, we have the Norman French, or Language of the Trouveurs ~~and R~~ as more Gothic than the Romance, including the elder Italian and Spanish, and more Romanized than the English, in the generation before Chaucer—which is the more striking because the old metrical Romances of the English Minstrels ~~fol~~ were most of them translations from the ⟨Norman⟩ Trouveurs or Inventors, ~~of Normandy~~ a name which they amply merited—

Great however as the merits of the Trouveurs were ~~and wonderful as manifold as our obligations are~~ and wonderfully as they had combined ~~the~~ whatever had been inherited from the North ~~and with~~ with all that the Crusaders had imported from the East, they yet left no successors in their own Country; but bequeathed their Genius first to the [b]Italian Poets from Boccaccio to Tasso, and then thro' these to the English ~~Giants of the Reign of Elizabe~~ —first to Chaucer, then after the distracting Interval of the civil wars between York and Lancaster, the true Dark Age of England, to Spenser and the giants of our Elizabeth's reign and that of her successor.—THEN TURN TO THE LECTURE BOOK—as then my last Lecture was allotted &c—down to "toilsome Scholar".

[c]Heads of Lecture the third.

The last Lecture was allotted to an investigation into the origin and character of a species of Poetry, the least influenced by the literature of Greece and Rome, that in which the portion contributed by the Gothic

---

[b] f 50
[c] *CN* III 4388 f 147

[2] Here C may have been relying on Ritson, who locates the beginning of English poetry in "the year 1278, when Robert of Gloucester completeëd his rimeing chronicle", and later refers to "the year 1380, when *The Canterbury tales* are generally suppose'd to have been publish'd". I lxxiv, xcv. Warton in his *History of English Poetry* I 48 says that Robert of Gloucester's poem "appears to have been composed about the year 1280". The chronicle was first printed in 1724 and reissued in 1810 in vols I–II of *The Works of Thomas Hearne* (4 vols 1810).

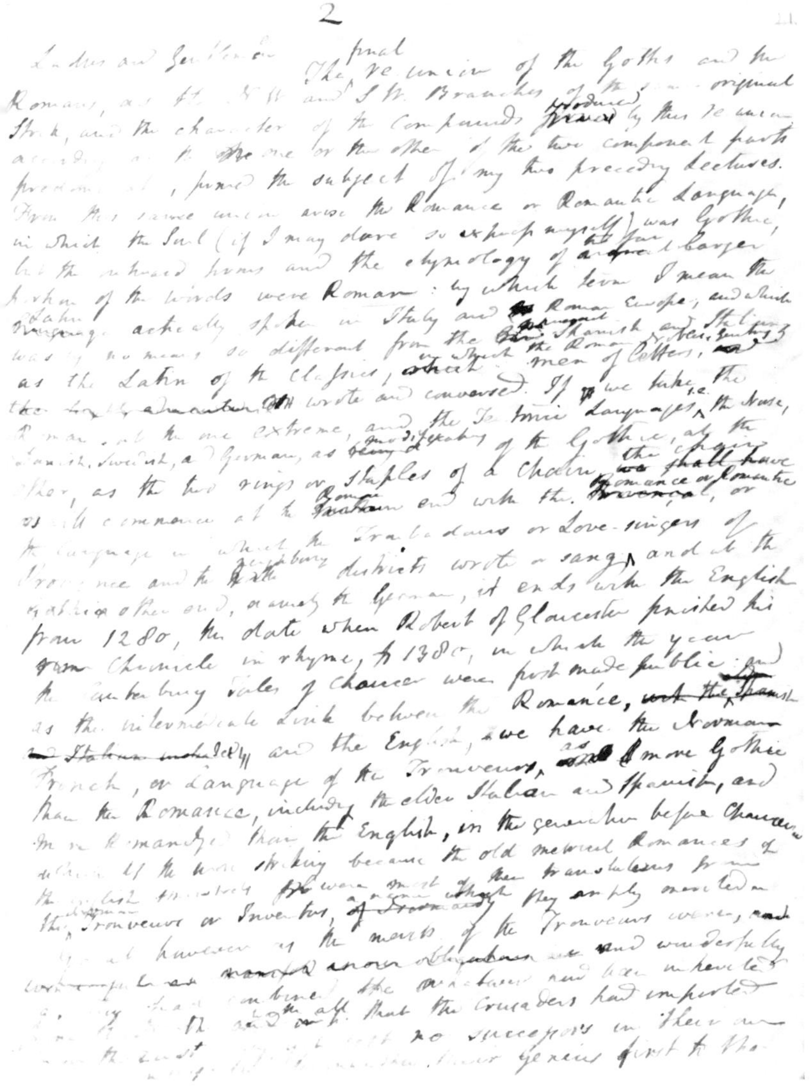

3. A page from Coleridge's notes for Lecture 3 of the 1818 series. Although this looks like a beginning, it is headed "2", perhaps because Coleridge opened with his first draft for the start of this lecture in Notebook 29. BM MS Egerton 2800 f 41. The British Library reproduced by kind permission

Conquerors, the predilections and general tone or habit of Thought and feeling which our remote ancestors brought with them from the Forests of Germany, or the deep dells and rocky mountains of Norway, are most prominent. In the present I must introduce you to a species of Poetry, which had its birth-place near the centre of Roman Glory, and in which, as might be anticipated, the influences of the Greek and Roman Muse are far more conspicuous—as great indeed, as the efforts of intentional imitation on the part of the Poets themselves could render them. But happily for us and for their own fame the intention of the Writers as men is often at compleat variance with the genius of the same men as Poets. To force of their intention we owe their mythological ornaments, and the greater definiteness of their imagery: and their passion for the Beautiful, the Voluptuous, and the Artificial, we must in part attribute to the same intention but in part likewise to their natural dispositions and taste: for the same climate and many of the same circumstances were acting on them, which had acted on the great Classics whom they were endeavoring to imitate. But the Love of the Marvellous, the deeper sensibility, the higher reverence for Womanhood,[3] the characteristic spirit of Sentiment and Courtesy, these were the Heirlooms of Nature, that still retained the ascendant whenever the use of their living Mother-language enabled the inspired Poet to appear instead of the toilsome Scholar.—

[d]Yet so strong was the prejudice in favor of classical learning, than[e] Dante is said to have hesitated whether he should not rather compose his immortal Poem in Latin[4]—the same we are certain, that Ariosto had not only at one time intended to have composed the Orlando Furioso in Latin—and that the Italian Sonnets and Canzons which alone have preserved and which endear the name of Petrarch, were considered by the Author as unworthy trifles, while his own expectations of fame and glory were grounded by him on his Latin works, but chiefly on a huge Latin Epic Poem in Latin Hexameters, entitled Africa, & having Scipio for its Hero[5]—a poem, in which the rudeness of the Latinity, and spite

[d] Egerton 2800 f 50, beginning seven lines down the page
[e] A slip for "that"

[3] As Kathleen Coburn notes in *CN* III 4388n, C borrowed here from F. Schlegel's Lect 7, in which, commenting particularly on the *Minnegesang* and German poetry, he speaks of the poetic belief in the marvellous ("der poetische Glaube an das Wunderbare") and of the reverence for women originally characteristic of the Germans ("Aus der den Deutschen ursprünglich eignen Achtung vor den Frauen"); but C relates these traits to all Romance poetry. *Geschichte* I 259–63 (Bohn 172–5).

[4] F. Schlegel, Lect 9, says that Dante at first intended to write his poem in Latin. *Geschichte* II 4 (Bohn 197).

[5] F. Schlegel in Lect 7 says that Petrarch rested his hopes of fame and glory

of the endless centos and ends of lines from Virgil, Ovid, and Statius the harshness & yet feebleness of the versification are the least defects— for some years ago I ~~had the pu~~ imposed on myself the perusal of the whole, and as I may safely believe that I am almost the only Englishman who ever levied so heavy a subsidy on his own time and patience, I can inform them for their satisfaction, that it is almost the only ~~work~~ poem of ~~the~~ nearly the same length in which I could discover no one beautiful Passage, or not one striking thought or novel Image—and this from a writer, in whose Italian Poems, even in the most indifferent of them, and when is there no other merit, there is yet always a fascinating delicacy in the choice and position of the words and the flow of the metre: so heavily did the Sehackles which were sought as more than regal ornaments by the prejudices of the Scholar, press on the genius of the Poet—

Then turn to the Lecture Book.

/My object in adverting to the Italian Poets is not so much for their own sakes, in which point of view Ariosto alone would have required a separate Lecture, but for the elucidation of the merits of our Country-men, as to what extent we must consider them as fortunate Imitators of their Italian Predecessors, and in which points they have the higher claims of original Genius/. Of Dante I am to speak elsewhere.[6] ⟨Of⟩ Boccaccio, who has little interest as a metrical Poet in any respect, and none for our present purpose, it will be sufficient to say—that we owe to him the Subjects of so many poems, in his famous Tales—the happy art of narration—and the still greater merit of a depth and fineness in the workings of the Passions, ⟨in⟩ which last excellence as likewise in the wild and imaginative character of the situations his almost neglected Romances appear to me greatly to excel his far famed Decamerone[7]—

^f *CN* III 4388 ff 147–146^v

on a Latin poem on Scipio that has long been forgotten. *Geschichte* I 237–8 (Bohn 161). C read, and cited in his notebooks and elsewhere, Latin works by Petrarch, and he used Petrarch *Opera quae extant omnia* (Basle 1581), which includes *Africa* in pt 3. See *CN* III 3360 and n. But his comment here is the only evidence found of his reading of Petrarch's epic.

    [6] In Lect 10, below.

    [7] C had a copy of Boccaccio's *Opere* and made two notes in it on *Il Filocopo*, his early prose romance. *CM (CC)* I 543–

4. Later on in this lecture C refers to the *Teseida*, the source of Chaucer's "Knight's Tale" (sentence containing n 23). Warton remarked of this that it was "so scarce, and so little known, even in Italy", as to have denied Boccaccio a reputation as a poet (I 344–5). F. Schlegel in Lect 9 merely praises his romances in general terms. *Geschichte* II 18 (Bohn 204). In 1814–15 C had thought of translating Boccaccio's prose works other than the *Decameron*, but nothing came of this. *CL* III 529, IV 562, 570.

to him too we owe the more doubtful merit of having introduced into the Italian Prose, and by the Authority of his name and the influence of his Example, more or less throughout Europe, the long inwoven Periods, which arose from the very nature of their language in the Greek Writers, but which already in the Latin Orators and Historians betrayed a something of effort, a foreign something that had been superinduced on the language instead of growing out of it[8]—but far, far too alien from that individualizing and tho' confederating yet not blending character of the North, to be permanent—tho' the magnificence & stateliness &c yet it diminished the controll over the feelings of men—made too great a chasm between Books and Life—hence abandoned by Luther—. But lastly to Boccaccio's sanction we must trace a large portion of the mythological pedantry and incongruous paganisms which for so long a period deformed the poetry even of the truest Poets—To such an extravagance did Boccaccio himself carry this folly, that in a Romance of Chivalry he has uniformly styled Jehovah Jupiter, our Saviour Apollo, and the Evil Being Pluto[9]—and Ariosto (the *black* book)—[10]

[8]a striking instance of this gross confusion of this Paganizing of Christianity, Jehovah : V. Mary :: Jupiter to Leda, or Mars to the Mother of Romulus—in the *first Canzone* of the darling Ariosto—5th Stanza or paragraph of it/

> Nè il dì, nè l'anno tacerò, nè il loco
> Dove io fui preso: e insieme

[8] *CN* II 2670 f 80ᵛ

[8] Kathleen Coburn notes that C here seems to be bringing together recollections of two passages from different parts of F. Schlegel's lectures, one from Lect 6, on the elaborate interweaving of periods in Greek prose being foreign to Latin, but adopted by many Latin writers in an effort to resemble Greek; the other, from Lect 9, on Boccaccio's adoption of an artificial style based on the manner of Livy and Cicero. *Geschichte* I 208, II 5 (Bohn 143, 197).

[9] More or less quoting from F. Schlegel *Geschichte* II 5 (Bohn 197–8): "Many of his works include an unsuccessful attempt to interweave the mythology of the ancients into Christian histories, or to express Christian ideas in the language and mythology of the ancients; as, for example, where it appears remarkably out of place, he introduces God the Father by the name of Jupiter; our Saviour,

by that of Apollo; and gives the Prince of Hell the name Pluto.'' So *CN* III 4388n. The romance C refers to is *Il Filocopo*, in which the ancient deities help the hero, Florio, to win Biancafiore; see *CN* II 2670n. At the end of his first note in his copy of Boccaccio (see n 7, above), C added, "Quote p. 8", possibly a direction to himself for this lecture. The passage, as translated in *CM (CC)* I 543, relates that Jupiter, ruler in heaven, "gave Pluto and his followers the twilight regions of Dis, set in stygian marshes, and condemned them to perpetual exile from his own pleasant and gracious kingdom".

[10] I.e. N 15 (so Kathleen Coburn in *CN* III 4388n); the relevant entry, from *CN* II 2670, is included here. This notebook C used when he was in Malta and Italy in 1804–6, and the entry is dated 15 Sept 1805.

Dirò gli altri trofei, ch'allora aveste,
Tal che appo loro il vincer me fu poco.
Dico, *da che il suo seme*
Mandò nel chiuso ventre il Re celeste,
Avean le ruote preste
Dell' Omicida lucido d'Achille
Rifatto il Giorno mille
E cinquecento tredici fiate
Sacro al Battista, in mezo de la estate.[11]

[h]But for this there might be some excuse pleaded (turn over the leaf of the black book)

[i]Among the numerous examples of confusion of Heathen & Christian Mythology in the Poets of the 15th Century (pleasing inasmuch as they prove how intimately the works of Homer & Virgil &c were *worked* in & *scripturalized*[12] in their *minds*—1. was taught this hour, the other the next—or both together & by the same man with the same countenance, with the same seriousness and zeal, at the same early age—& in a time when Authority was all in all—and what was publickly *taught* of Aristotle, was individually & perhaps more generally, *felt of Homer/* in the various broken reflections of him throughout the Latin Poets & all men of Education/ & in the original & the echoing series of the other Greek Poets to the Politians,[13] &c &c,/—indeed, it requires a strong imagination as well as an accurate psycho-analytical[14] understanding in order to be able to conceive the *possibility*, & to picture out the reality, of the *passion* of those Times for Jupiter, Apollo &c/ & the nature of the *Faith* (for a Faith it was—it vanished indeed at the Cock-crowing of a deliberate Question, in *most* men; but in the ordinary unchecked stream of Thought it moved on, as naturally as Contraband

[h] *CN* III 4388 f 146[v]
[i] *CN* II 2670 ff 79[v]–80

[11] Tr (from *CN* II 2670n): "I shall conceal neither the year nor the place where I was captured: and at the same time I shall speak of the other trophies which you took then, such that in comparison your conquest of me was a trifle. I say that since the celestial King had sent his seed into the closed womb, the swift steeds of Achilles's bright Slayer had one thousand five hundred and thirteen times renewed that Day in midsummer sacred to the Baptist."

[12] C's coinage; the first recorded use in *OED* is dated 1858.

[13] Angelo Poliziano (1454–94), humanist, poet, and classical scholar, patronised by Lorenzo the Magnificent, in whose *Life* by William Roscoe (2 vols Liverpool 1795) C may have first learned about him.

[14] The first use of this term recorded in *OED* is dated 1906. Cf C's use of "psychological" in 1800 (*EOT—CC*—I 98) and again in the Introduction to *EM* (1818), in which he added an apology for introducing an unfamiliar term "to express the philosophy of the human mind". See *Sh C* (1930) II 348 and n.

& Legal Goods in the same Vessel, when no Revenue Officers are on the Track.)

*j*we dare make[15] none for the gross and disgusting licentiousness, the daring profaneness of both together, which rendered the Decamerone of Boccace, as the Parent of an hundred worse children, fit to be classed amg the enemies of the human Race—which poisons Ariosto (for that I may not speak oftener than necessary of so odious a subject, I mention it here) intermingles a painful mixture with the humor of Chaucer—and which has once or twice seduced even our pure-minded Spenser to a grossity as heterogeneous from the Spirit of his Poem as it was alien to the delicacy of his morals—

—Petrarch—the final blossom & perfection of the Troubadours—quote from the Literary Life[16]—The Chivalry of the North, the genuine Chivalry, less felt in Italy[17] than in any other part of Europe—and on the contrary, the importations from the East by the Crusaders far more/ This leads to Ariosto—[18]

*k*Pulci/ of one of the Noblest Florentine Families—reputed to have been one of those Frankish stocks who remained in Florence after the depart. of Charlemagne—Verino de illustrat. urb. Flor. lib. 3. v. 118—[19]

j *CN* III 4388 f 146ᵛ

k *CN* III 4389

[15] C means "no excuse", picking up the linking comment he made just before citing the passage from N 15; see above (sentence after n 11).

[16] HNC thought that C was here referring to a passage in *BL* ch 15 on poets of the fifteenth and sixteenth centuries, but it is more likely that he meant to turn to the following from ch 18: "Yet when the torch of ancient learning was re-kindled, so cheering were its beams, that our eldest poets, cut off by christianity from all *accredited* machinery, and deprived of all *acknowledged* guardians and symbols of the great objects of nature, were naturally induced to adopt, as a *poetic* language, those fabulous personages, those forms of the supernatural in nature, which had given them such dear delight in the poems of their great masters. Nay, even at this day what scholar of genial taste will not so far sympathize with them, as to read with pleasure in PETRARCH, CHAUCER, or SPENSER, what

he would perhaps condemn as puerile in a modern poet?" See *BL (CC)* II 33, 75–6.

[17] From F. Schlegel's Lect 9: "The spirit of chivalry and chivalric poetry attained least sway and influence in Italy." *Geschichte* II 4 (Bohn 197). C repeated this remark in Lect 5 in 1819 (at n 1).

[18] If C had some lecture-notes on Ariosto to use at this point, they have not been traced.

[19] The *Green SC* (1880) included a copy of Luigi Pulci *Il Morgante Maggiore* (3 vols Florence 1732), which was reissued in London and Paris in 1768. C drew heavily on the "life" of Pulci, which serves as an introduction, and took his references from this. Ugolino Verino's work on the city of Florence is cited in I iii, tr "The Pulci family, of Gallic stock, descended upon a city famous indeed in war and not inhospitable to the sacred Muses." So Kathleen Coburn, *CN* III 4389n.

> Pulcia Gallorum suboles descendit in urbem,
> Clara quidem bello, sacris nec inhospita Musis

The family 5 times elected to the Priorate, the second honor of the Republic.—Luigi Pulci, born in Florence, 15 August, 1432, had two Brothers, and one of their wives, Antonia, Poets—[20]

> Carminibus patriis notissima Pulcia proles.
> Qui non hanc urbem Musarum dicat amicam,
> Si tres producat fratres domus una poetas?
> Verino. 1. 2. v. 241.[21]

Married Lucrezia di Uberto, of the Albizi family; intimate with the great men of his time but more especially with Angelo Politian and Lorenzo the Magnificent[22]—his Morgante attributed in part at least to the assistance of Marsilius Ficinus, and by others the whole to Politian—the first utterly improbable—and the last possible from its licentiousness but with no direct grounds—. It is the first proper Romance—tho' perhaps he had Boccaccio's Theseide before him/—The story is taken from the fabulous History of Turpin—and if the Author had any distinct object, it seems to be that of making himself merry with the absurdities of the old Romances[23]—sometimes we think of Rabelais[24]—the copia of Mother Florentine tongue, and the easiness of style afterwards brought to perfection by Berni, his chief merit—the heartless spirit of Jest & Buffoonery its chief demerit[25]—Sovereigns & Courtiers flattered by degradation of Nature, or *impossibilifications*[26] of pretended Virtue—[27]

---

[20] From Pulci I iii, xvi–xvii.

[21] From Verino's *De illustratione urbis Florentiae*; tr "The descendants of Pulci, well known for songs in their native tongue. Who would deny that this city is a friend of the Muses, if one house produces three brothers who are poets?" Cited in Pulci I xv.

[22] From C's (or Green's) copy of Pulci I xvii, xix (the reference to Poliziano), xviii (Lorenzo de' Medici), and xix again (Ficino).

[23] Based on the introduction to Pulci I xxi, xxv–xxvi, xxiii–xxiv. Turpin, abp of Reims (d c 800), was credited with a Latin chronicle on the life and adventures of Charlemagne. The author of the introduction refers to it as "Il Romanzo di Turpino"; he says that he does not believe Pulci borrowed from Boccaccio.

[24] C's own comment; he was to speak on Rabelais later in the course; see Lect 9, below (paragraph containing nn 29–31).

[25] The introduction to Pulci twice compares him with Francesco Berni, firstly, on I xxv–xxvi, as the father of comic poetry, saying the *Morgante* is "del genere faceto, e burlesco" (of the facetious and comic kind), and then, on I xxxiii, as the source of the grace, urbanity, and sweetness shown by Berni.

[26] C's coinage; *OED* cites this passage (from *LR* I 88).

[27] Kathleen Coburn added here her conjectural reading of a "very small and slurred" phrase at the bottom of the page: "? not as Corneille." An allusion to Pierre Corneille's plays, like *Le Cid* (1636-7), in which love is opposed to honour and virtue, would not have been out of place, but C does not seem to refer elsewhere to Corneille.

The very first stanza of the Morg. Magg.—is a sufficient of the lawless sometimes motiveless, sometimes apparently mockful, jumble of sacred truths and the most absurd fables—

> In principio era il Verbo appresso a Dio
> Ed era Iddio il Verbo, e il Verbo lui
> Quest' era nel principio, il PARER MIO   !!
> E nulla si può far sanza costui—
> Però, giusto Signor, benigno e pio
> *Mandami solo un degli angeli tui*
> Che m'accompagni, e rechimi a memoria
> Una famosa, antica, e degna storia.[28]

2

> An address to the Virgin
> E tu Vergine, figlia e madre e sposa
> Di quel signor che ti dette la chiave
> Del cielo, e del Abisso, e di ogni cosa
> Quel di che Gabriel tuo ti disse *ave/*[29]

to assist the verses with dolce rime e style grato e soave.—[30]

3

A jumble of Heathen Mythology to tell the time (namely sunset)[31]

4

When he schemed his poem—because—E stata questa istoria, a quel ch' io veggio Di Carlo male intesa e scritta peggio.—[32]

---

[28] All the Italian quotations are from canto I of Pulci's *Morgante Maggiore*, and, following Kathleen Coburn in *CN* III 4389n, the translations given here are from Byron's version, finished c 1820, too late for C to have used it for this lecture. St 1:

In the beginning was the Word next God;
God was the Word, the Word no less was He:
This was in the beginning, to my mode
Of thinking, and without Him nought could be:
Therefore, just Lord! from out thy high abode,
Benign and pious, bid an angel flee,
One only, to be my companion, who
Shall help my famous, worthy, old song through.
[29] St 2:

And thou, oh Virgin! daughter, mother, bride,
Of the same Lord, who gave to you each key
Of Heaven, and Hell, and every thing beside,
The day thy Gabriel said "All hail!" to thee.
[30] I.e. with sweet rhymes and a smooth and pleasant style.
[31] This describes st 3, in which the sunset is imaged in Phaeton's car sinking below the horizon, but which also refers to Philomel and Tithonus.
[32] C quotes the last two lines of st 4, but refers to the whole:

When I prepared my bark first to obey,
As it should still obey, the helm, my mind,
And carry prose or rhyme, and this my lay
Of Charles the Emperor, whom you

5 (very good)

Diceva già Leonardo Aretino Che s'egli avessi avuto scrittor degno Com'egli ebbe un Ormanno il suo Pipino Che avessi diligenzia avuto e ingegno. Sarebbe Carlo Magno un uom divino Però ch'egli ebbe Gran vittorie e regno E fece per la Chiesa e per la Fede *Certo assai più che non si dice o crede.*[33]

Charles at his camp with all his Paladins listens to Gano's insinuations concerning Orlando who after an attempt to kill the Traitor goes off in dudgeon in Pagania—arriving at an Abbey on the Confines, near to the Castle of the Three Giants—and stanza 25, part of the Abbot Chiaromonte's complaint, is a good specimen of the Jokes cut on scripture/

> Gli antichi padri nostri nel deserto,
> Se le lor opre sante erano e giuste
> Del ben servir da Dio n'avean buon merto:
> *Né creder, sol vivessin di locuste.*
> *Piovea dal ciel la mann, questo e certo*
> *Ma qui convien, che spesso assaggi e guste*
> *Sassi che piovon di sopra quel Monte*
> Che gettano Alabastro e Passamonte.[34]

26

> E'l terzo, ch'è Morgante, assai più fiero,
> Isveglie i pini &c

While talking un sasso venni da', alto da giganti—[35]

---

will find
By several pens already praised; but they
    Who to diffuse his glory were inclined,
For all that I can see in prose and verse,
Have understood Charles badly, and wrote worse.

[33] St 5:

Leonardo Aretino said already,
    That if, like Pepin, Charles had had a writer
Of genius quick, and diligently steady,
    No hero would in history look brighter;
He in the cabinet being always ready,
    And in the field a most victorious fighter,
Who for the church and Christian faith had wrought,
Certes, far more than yet is said or thought.

[34] St 25:

Our ancient fathers, living the desert in,
    For just and holy works were duly fed;
Think not they lived on locusts sole, 'tis certain
    That manna was rained down from heaven instead;
But here 'tis fit we keep on the alert in
    Our bounds, or taste the stones showered down for bread,
From off yon mountain daily raining faster,
And flung by Passamont and Alabaster.

[35] St 26:

The third, Morgante, 's savagest by far; he
    Plucks up pines, beeches, poplar-

27

Tirati drento, Cavalier, per Dio,
Disse l'Abate, *che la Manna casca.*[36]

(2) BM MS EGERTON 2800 FF 48–49

These sheets contain two drafts on the same subject, Allegory, which are printed below in sequence.

[l]Allegory, = αλλο αγοϱᾶν— to talk of one thing, but so as purposely to convey another.[37] This however would include Irony: the word therefore is too wide for its exclusive meaning. ~~We may therefore define Allegory~~

[m]~~If we take from allegory~~ as the employment ~~and connection~~ of one set of images ~~and correspondent~~ with actions or accompaniments correspondent so as ~~to re~~ at once to disguise and yet convey either ~~general truths,~~ qualities conceptions of the mind that in themselves are not objects of the senses, or persons,[n]   .

We ~~may~~ust seek therefore in the thing ~~for~~ what we cannot find in the term: and ~~the best definition, I can offer is the I can~~ we shall not err in any material point if we define allegoric ~~writing~~ composition as the employment of one set of ⟨agents and⟩ images with actions and accompaniments correspondent, so as to convey, while we disguise, either moral qualities or ~~men~~ conceptions of the mind that are not in themselves objects of the Senses, or other ⟨images,⟩ agents, ~~images,~~ actions, fortunes and circumstances, so that the difference is every where presented to the eye or imagination while the Likeness is suggested to the mind: and ~~with such a connection of the Parts to a~~ this connectedly so that the Parts combine to form a consistent Whole. The last sentence is

[l] f 48
[m-n] C cancelled this paragraph with lines drawn through it

---

trees, and oaks . . .
While thus they parley in the cemetery,
   A stone from one of their gigantic strokes,
Which nearly crushed Rondell, came tumbling over,
So that he took a long leap under cover.
   [36] St 27 lines 1–2:

"For God-sake, Cavalier, come in with speed;
   The manna's falling now,'' the Abbot cried.
   [37] C's interest in allegory was of long standing, and these notes relate to a notebook entry of 1807–8 (*CN* ii 3203) in which he recorded a desire to ''trace the origin, historical & metaphysical, of Allegory''.

necessary to distinguish allegory from metaphor. For ⟨a metaphor is but the fragment of an allegory: even⟩ as a simile passes into a metaphor by ~~mere omission of the~~ substituting ~~instead of adjoining it~~ it for the thing, it resembles, instead of adjoining it. ~~(as for instance~~ Thus: if in speaking of the Duke of Wellington's ~~in his~~ campaign in Portugal against Massena[38] we should say—At length he left his mountain strongholds, and fell on the rear of the retreating army, as a Cloud from the Hill Tops, ~~and~~ it is a simile:—if more briefly we say—at length the Cloud descended from its hill and discharged itself in thunder and lightning on the Plain,[39] it becomes a metaphor—. ~~a and a metaphor is the fragment of an Allegory~~ But will not this definition apply to a Fable as well as to an Allegory? It does: and I confess my inability to define either so as to distinguish it from the other, except by ~~making~~ using allegory ~~the term of the class and Fable the a species~~ in two senses, now for the *kind*, including Fable—and then as a specific term, ~~from specified~~ made specific simply by excluding it—just as we are obliged to do in distinguished*ᵒ* a Shrub from a Tree. A Shrub ~~is~~ we should explain as a smaller ~~sor of~~ and shorter sort of Tree: and as there is no chance of mistaking any other vegetable form for a Tree except a Shrub, or for a Shrub except a tree, we are content to say—A smaller sort of Trees are called Shrubs—all other Trees are called Trees. So a Fable is ~~a shorter an~~ the shortest and simplest form of *ᵖ*Allegory: ~~A~~ tho' perhaps it might be justly said, that in a Fable no ~~agent or all~~ allegoric agent or Image should be used, which has not had some one paramount quality universally attributed to it beforehand—while in an allegory the resemblance may have been presented for the first time by the writer. This is the true cause, why Animals, the Heathen Gods, and Trees the properties of which are recalled by their very names, are ~~the~~ almost the only proper dramatis personæ of a Fable/ A Bear, a Fox, a Tyger, a Lion, ~~Minerva, Mars~~ Diana, an Oak, a Willow are *every man's* Metaphors for clumsiness, cunning, ferocious or magnanimous Courage, Chastity, unbendingness, and flexibility—and it would be a safe rule that what would not be ~~obvious~~ at once and generally intelligible in a metaphor ~~ought~~ may be introduced in a ~~good~~ Allegory, but ought not

ᵒ A slip for "distinguishing"

ᵖ f 48ᵛ

[38] C had contributed essays to the *Courier* on Wellington's campaign in 1810–11 against Marshal André Mas-séna, whose French army was forced to retreat into Spain in the spring of 1811; see *EOT (CC)* II 151–6.

[39] Cf C's comment on Wellington and Masséna ("the modern Hannibal") in the *Courier* 11 May 1811: "it was confi-dently anticipated in almost every Paper . . . that 'the cloud would descend from the hill', and fall in thunder and lightning on the backs of the modern Hannibal and his miscellaneous conscripts . . .". See *EOT (CC)* II 138.

to be in a Fable./ ~~It is~~ This however is one of the conditions of a good Fable rather than a definition of a Fable generally/~~much less a position~~ and fortunately the difficulty of defining a thing or term is almost always in ~~an~~ inverse proportion to the necessity—Linnæus found no difficulty in ~~d~~ establishing discriminating characters of the different Tribes of Apes;[40] but very great in scientific contra-distinctions between the genera, Man and Ape; but it is to be hoped, that he had not met with many individuals of either kind, that had produced any practical hesitation in determining his judgement.—.[q]

[r]Substitute a simile for the thing, it resembles, instead of annexing it, and it becomes a metaphor:—thus D. of W.[41]—and a metaphor is a fragment of an Allegory. But if it be asked, how do you define an Allegory so as to distinguish it from a Fable, I ~~confess must~~ can reply only by a confession of my ignorance or inability—. ~~un~~ The fact is, that Allegory must be used in two senses—the one includ~~esing, and~~ while the other is defined by excluding Fable. Fable is a shorter and simpler ~~k~~ sort of Allegory—this is the first sense—and again whatever of this kind is not a Fable, not only is but is called, an Allegory. So a pony is a ⟨smaller⟩ sort of Horse: and Horses, that are not Ponies, are called ~~a~~ Horses. ~~as~~ A Shrub is a smaller sort of Tree: and we are in no risk of being misunderstood when we say, the Laurel is but a Shrub in this Country, but in the South of Europe it is a Tree. It may indeed be justly said, that in a Fable &c—[42]
We may then safely define allegoric writing, as—

and then add—whatever composition answering to this definition is not a Fable, is entitled an Allegory—of which may be called Picture Allegories ~~as the Tablet of Ceres, or the Choice~~ or real or supposed Pictures interpreted and moralized, and satirical Allegories, we have several instances among the classics—as the Tablet of Cebes, the Choice of Hercules, and Simonides's origin of women[43]—but of narrative or epic allegories scarce any, the multiplicity of their Gods and Goddesses precluding it—unless we choose rather to say, that all the machinery

[q] The text occupies rather more than half the page, the rest of which is blank
[r] f 49

[40] Carolus Linnaeus, or Carl von Linné (1707–78), Swedish botanist. His *Systema naturae* (1735) had been translated and enlarged ''by the improvements and discoveries of later naturalists'' by W. Turton: *A General System of Nature, Through the Three Grand Kingdoms of Animals* (7 vols 1802–6).

[41] Referring to the passage on the Duke of Wellington, above (at n 38).

[42] Referring back to his earlier definition of a fable (sentences after n 39).

[43] The *Tablet of Cebes*, written c A.D. 100, but often wrongly attributed to that

of their Poets is allegorical—A̶ Of a People, who raised Altars to Fever, to Sport, to Fright, &c it is impossible to determine, how far they meant a personal power, or a̶n̶ ̶i̶m̶ personification of a Power. This only is certain, that the introduction of these agents could not have the same unmixed effect, as the same agents used allegorically w̶o̶u̶l̶d̶ ̶m̶a̶k̶e̶ produce on our minds—but something more nearly resembling the effect produced by the introduction of characteristic Saints in the roman catholic poets, or of Moloch, Belial, and Mammon in the second Book of Paradise Lost compared with his Sin and Death.—. The most beautiful Allegory ever composed, the Tale of Cupid and Psyche, tho' composed by an Heathen, was subsequent to ⟨the general spread of Christianity⟩ Christianity, & written by a̶ ̶P̶l̶a̶t̶o̶n̶i̶c̶ ̶a̶ ̶p̶a̶r̶t̶i̶z̶a̶n̶ ̶o̶f̶ one of those Philosophers, who attempted to christianized*[s] a sort of oriental '[t]and Egyptian Platonism enough to set it up against Christianity;[44] but the first Allegory compleatly modern in its form is the Psychomachia or B̶a̶ Battle of the Soul, by Prudentius, a Christian Poet of the 5th Century[45]—facts that fully explain both the origin and nature of narrative Allegory, as a substitute for the i̶m̶a̶g̶e̶r̶y̶ ̶o̶f̶ mythological imagery of Polytheism, and differing from it only in the g̶r̶e̶a̶ more obvious and intentional disjunction of the a̶ sense from the symbol, and the d̶i̶s̶i̶n̶t̶e̶r̶e̶s̶t̶e̶d̶ known unreality of the latter—so as to be a kind of intermediate step between Actual Person, and mere Personification—. But for this very cause it is incapable of exciting any lively interest for any length of t̶h̶e̶m̶ time— for if the allegoric personage be strongly individualized so as to interest us, we n̶o̶ cease to think of it as allegory—and if it does not interest

*[s] So in ms; C's slip for "christianize"
'[t] f 49ᵛ

disciple of Socrates, presents an allegorical picture of human life. C had read and annotated the translation by Jeremy Collier, *The Mythological Picture of Cebes the Theban*, added to his translation of Marcus Aurelius, *The Emperor Marcus Antoninus His Conversation with Himself* (1701). See *CM (CC)* I 182–5. The other references are to the allegory of Hercules at the crossroads, set forth in Xenophon's *Memorabilia* 2, much used in emblem-books and analysed in Edgar Wind *Pagan Mysteries in the Renaissance* (1958) 78–88; and to the fragment of a creation myth by Simonides or Semonides of Amorgos, a poet of the seventh century B.C., consisting of brief accounts of how various kinds of women were created by the gods out of animals (a translation by Hugh Lloyd-Jones is contained in *Females of the Species. Semonides on Women*, 1974).

[44] The story is told in *The Golden Ass* by Lucius Apuleius, who was born in Madaura in Africa early in the second century A.D. and who later studied Platonic philosophy in Athens. C referred to it again in Lect 11; see below (sentences after n 1).

[45] Prudentius (348–c 410) was the first important Christian poet to write in Latin; his *Psychomachia* turns great battles of pre-Christian epics into allegories of the war between good and evil for the soul of man. Cf *TT* 2 Sept 1833.

us, it had better be away.— The ~~mos~~ dullest and most defective parts of Spenser are those in which ~~you~~ we are compelled to think of his agents as allegories—and how far the Sin and Death of Milton are exceptions to this censure, is a delicate ~~question~~ problem which I shall attempt to solve in another lecture[46]—but in that admirable Allegory, the first Part of Pilgrim's Progress, which ~~interests~~ delights every one, the interest is so great that spite of all the writer's attempts to force the allegoric purpose on the Reader's mind by his strange names—Old Stupidity of the Tower of Honesty, &c &c[47]—his ~~own genius~~ piety was baffled by his Genius, and the Bunyan of Parnassus had the better of Bunyan of the Conventicle—and with the same illusion as we read any tale known to be fictitious, as a Novel—we go on with his characters as real persons, who had been ~~so~~ nicknamed by their neighbours.—. But the most ~~striking~~ decisive verdict against narrative Allegory is to be found in Tasso's own account of what he would have the reader understand by the persons and events of his Jerusalem/[48]Apollo be praised! not a thought like it would ever enter of its own accord into any mortal mind—and what is an additional good feature, when put there, it will not stay.—having the very opposite quality that Snakes have—they come out of their Holes into open view at the sound of sweet music, while the allegoric meaning slinks off at the very first notes—and lurks in~~t~~ murkiest oblivion—and utter invisibility—/and in the Faery[u][49]

NOTES TAKEN AT THE LECTURE
BY H. H. CARWARDINE
ESSEX COUNTY RECORD OFFICE
MS D/D PR 549 FF 12^{v}–12

[v]Coleridge
observed th[at][w] Boccatchi—Chaucer Pulci &c and all the early Romantic poets were supposed to give artificial characters—which they

[u] The text breaks off at the foot of the page

[v] f 12^{v}

[w] Word completed by the editor

[46] C spoke on Milton in Lect 10, the notes for which are lost, unless they are the same as those remaining for Lect 4 of the 1819 series, when he did comment on Sin and Death in relation to allegory (at n 18). Cf also Lect 7 of the 1811–12 series (at n 21).

[47] C was confusing in memory the account in Bunyan's *Pilgrim's Progress* pt 2 of the encounter of Great-heart and the pilgrims with "Old Honest" who comes from "the Town of Stupidity".

[48] Tasso's own explanation of the allegory of his *Gerusalemme liberata*, frequently printed in editions of his long poem, was appended by Edward Fairfax to his well-known translation first published in 1600.

[49] This is the last word on the page, and the continuation is lost; evidently C went on with a comment on Spenser's *Faerie Queene*.

did in a sort of sarcastic, Burlesque manner—for example when they described a character of great virtue or excellence, the poet steps forward in his own person—with "Thus I am told", "thus I have been informed but I do not vouch for it" or "nevertheless I would not put my finger in the fire for it" implying that though there may be so much virtue yet they do not believe it & are not called to any pledge of the truth of it—their great efforts were employed upon characters combining a mixture of vice & folly pleasant drolls &c vide Chaucers Canterbury Tales— Boccaccio, Pulci &c &c Spencer in England & Tasso in Italy were the *x*first poets who dared to write Truth, or what they truly felt then*y* were not Burlesque writers and how much more delightful [to]*z* us with true sentiment—perhaps none superior to our own Spencer

Translated to us the comment of Pulci—begins with saying in the beginning was god &c &c ⟨Virgin Mary—⟩[50] in a little sort of parenthesis says in his own person "at least so I am informed"—gave us many other points & turns of this kind which reminded me strong[ly]*a* of the witty sarcastic turn so often brought into play by Voltaire when treating upon sacred subjects—

8 Feby 1818—

NOTE BY JOSEPH HENRY GREEN

FROM *LR* 88–9

Chaucer must be read with an eye to the Norman-French Trouveres, of whom he is the best representative in English. He had great powers of invention. As in Shakespeare, his characters represent classes, but in a different manner; Shakespeare's characters are the representatives of the interior nature of humanity, in which some element has become so

x f 12
y An error for "they"
z Word supplied by the editor
a Word completed by the editor

[50] In his note on this passage EHC said that C "seems to have read a translation of the opening stanzas of Pulci's *Morgante Maggiore*", adding that Byron's translation was not yet written, but that specimens of a translation by J. H. Merivale had appeared in the *M Mag*. These were published anonymously, in a series of essays paraphrasing the poem, between 1 May 1806 and 30 Jul 1807. The account of the beginning of the poem in vol XXI pt 1 (1806) 511–15 included translations of canto I sts 39–41, of seven stanzas from the end of canto I and beginning of canto II, and of sixteen stanzas from canto II sts 18ff. Byron's translation of canto I appeared in 1822.

predominant as to destroy the health of the mind; whereas Chaucer's are rather representatives of classes of manners. He is therefore more led to individualize in a mere personal sense. Observe Chaucer's love of nature; and how happily the subject of his main work is chosen. When you reflect that the company in the Decameron have retired to a place of safety from the raging of a pestilence, their mirth provokes a sense of their unfeelingness; whereas in Chaucer nothing of this sort occurs, and the scheme of a party on a pilgrimage, with different ends and occupations, aptly allows for the greatest variety of expression in the tales.

LECTURE 4

DATE AND PLACE OF DELIVERY. Friday, 6 February 1818, in the Great Room of the London Philosophical Society, Fleur-de-Luce Court, Fleet Street.

SUBJECT. Shakespeare's comedies and romantic plays, chiefly *Love's Labour's Lost* and *The Tempest*. The Syllabus announced "LECTURES IV. V. and VI . . . On the Dramatic Works of SHAKESPEARE. In these Lectures will be comprised the substance of Mr. Coleridge's former Courses on the same subject, enlarged and varied by subsequent study and reflection."

ADVERTISEMENTS AND ANNOUNCEMENTS. *Courier* Thurs, 5 Feb (announcement): "MR. COLERIDGE'S LECTURES.—To-morrow evening, Feb. 6, quarter after eight *precisely*, Mr. COLERIDGE will commence his Lectures on the Plays of SHAKESPEAR, divided into three great classes, at the Great Room of the London Philosophical Society, Fleur-de-luce-court, Fleet-street. The second and third Lectures on SHAKESPEAR (being the 5th and 6th of the Course) on the following Tuesday and Friday Evenings. Admission Five Shillings— Prospectuses and Tickets for the Course, with allowances for the former Lectures, at the Lecture-room . . .". *New Times* Thurs, 5 Feb (advertisement): substantially as in the *Courier*, but giving the time of the lecture as "Half past Eight o'clock". *M Chron* Fri, 6 Feb (advertisement): substantially as in the *Courier*, but with the addition: "The first Lecture on Shakespear will comprise the Comedies and romantic Dramas; the second the Historical Plays; and the third the great Tragedies—Hamlet, Othello, Macbeth, etc." *The Times* Fri, 6 Feb (advertisement): substantially as in the *New Times*.

TEXT. Among miscellaneous fragmentary notes in *Sh C* I 214–17, Raysor included a transcript of BM MS Egerton 2800 ff 42–4, identified as C's notes for his introduction to this lecture. Raysor seems to have ignored f 45, printing only one sentence from it as a detached footnote (*Sh C* I 202), yet f 44 is numbered "2", and f 45 "3", indicating a continuation. In another set of mss, BM Add MS 34225 ff 49–51, Raysor found some further notes on Shakespeare, parts of which he printed as separate fragments in *Sh C* I 83–4, 89, 118, 200– 1 (92–3, 99, 131, 226–7) as unrelated to each other. One fragment, on *Love's Labour's Lost*, appears among other material on that play (*Sh C* I 83–4); a paragraph on *The Tempest* is printed among other comments on that play (I 118); a brief note on *Two Gentlemen of Verona* is printed on its own (I 89); and two paragraphs of more general comment are joined to an account of the characteristics of Shakespeare (I 200–1), in accordance with the treatment of them by HNC in *LR* II 81–2. In fact, all these mss are linked: BM MS Egerton 2800 f 44 is numbered "2", f 45 "3", and BM Add MS 34225 f 49 "4"; moreover, at the top of Egerton 2800 f 45 the text begins "His advantages— 1. . . .", and this run of numbers continues with "2", "3", and "4" on Add MS 34225 f 49, running over on to f 51, with "5" and "6". In other words, the notes on these two mss appear to form a consecutive, if somewhat disjointed, series of notes for this lecture, and they are printed below in sequence.

Raysor's failure to note a connexion between these documents is understandable, for not only are they bound up in separate volumes, but they are from different stocks of paper. In the Egerton mss, ff 42–3 appear to be formed from a single sheet that has been cut along the length and the two halves pasted together. C's notes are written down the inner side, so that f 42 and f 42ᵛ are blank. The whole measures approximately 412 × 265 mm and has an undated watermark of a crown and shield with the letter "B". The other sheet, of a similar size but a different stock of paper, has been torn in two to form ff 44 and 45; f 44 is watermarked "J BUDGEN", has notes on the recto and the quotation from Phineas Fletcher on the verso, whereas f 45 is watermarked with the date "1815" and has a blank verso. Both measure roughly 265 × 205 mm. The documents in Add MS consist of a single sheet folded once (ff 49–50) and a half-sheet (f 51), giving a page measuring roughly 225 × 185 mm. The whole sheet is watermarked "RUSE & TURNERS 1817"; the half-sheet has no watermark but appears to be of the same stock. The notes begin with "Love's labor lost—" on f 49 and continue on f 50 and f 51. The versos of ff 49 and 51 are blank, and f 50ᵛ has "*Shakspear*" written on it, not in C's hand. The notes for this lecture were thus written on sheets from three different stocks of paper, of different sizes and watermarks, and are now catalogued in two separate collections. The evidence from the text, however, seems to show conclusively that the notes are connected and form the basic outline from which the lecture developed.

REPORTS. The lecture was attended by H. H. Carwardine, whose ms notes of it form ff 4–11 of a small unbound notebook now MS D/D Pr 549 in the Essex County Record Office in Chelmsford. The notes end in the middle of f 11, the lower half of which is blank. On f 11ᵛ is written: "Notes of some Lectures delivered by S. T. Coleridge in 1818—made by the late Henry Holgate Carwardine Esq of Colne Priory Essex and found by me amongst his papers in Aug⸱ 1867—M⸱ Carwardine was personally acquainted with Coleridge thro' his friends the Gilmans of Highgate. Chas: K: Probert   Newport. Essex". The notes were first published by Probert, Carwardine's nephew, in *N&Q* ser ɪv vol v (1870) 335–6 and were included in *Sh C* ɪɪ 250—3 (312–16). The text printed below is based on a fresh transcript of the ms. For this and several other lectures in the series the *Courier* printed an announcement, thus giving C useful publicity, and C wrote to the editor, William Mudford, on 18 Feb to express his gratitude for the "favorable notice taken of" his lectures in this newspaper (*CL* ɪv 839). The *Courier* also printed a brief report of Lect 4, which is reprinted below. This was also included in *Sh C* ɪɪ 249 (311).

BACKGROUND AND CIRCUMSTANCES. Although C announced in the Syllabus that the three Shakespeare lectures in this course would cover the "substance" of his previous courses on the same subject, the surviving notes for the first of them show that he prepared it as a new lecture and was not content merely to repeat himself. The page-references in the notes are apparently to C's copy of *Sh* (Ayscough), and he may have used some of the marginalia in those two volumes in the lecture, though the notes on *The Tempest* written on blank leaves adjacent to the printed text of the play seem to have been prepared for the first lecture in the 1819 series and are printed there.

The prospect of lecturing again on Shakespeare revived C's resentment against the charge that he had borrowed the "general principles" of his lectures from Schlegel, and he wrote to James Perry on 5 Feb to claim that he had arrived at them independently, in the lectures given at the RI in 1808; he went on to comment, "nay, Mr Hazlitt in answer to the charge that I had borrowed my opinions from Schlegel had openly said—'That must be a Lie: for I myself heard Coleridge give the very same theory before he went to Germany and when he did not even understand a word of German.' " *CL* IV 831. In this letter C complained of "Hazlitt's rancor" and his refusal to acknowledge C's priority (in the review he wrote of John Black's translation of Schlegel's lectures for the *Ed Rev* in Feb 1816). The controversy re-emerged in connexion with the series of lectures C began in Dec 1818; see Lect 1 of the 1818–19 series (headnote: Reports).

Ironically, Hazlitt saw the report of this lecture in the *Courier*, in which C is said to have referred to Caliban as "an original and caricature of Jacobinism", and used it as an occasion for an amusing but abusive attack on C's politics. In this piece, published in the *Yellow Dwarf* 14 Feb 1818 (*H Works* XIX 206–10), Hazlitt, claiming that Caliban was really the legitimate sovereign of the island in *The Tempest*, said that C shuffled out of his principles and in any case went beyond his brief to include matters of religion and politics in literary lectures. He also told an anecdote concerning one of C's lectures, when "Mr. C. was interrupted in a tirade upon this favourite topic, on which he was led out of pure generosity to enlighten the grown gentlemen who came to hear him, by a person calling out in good broad Scotch, 'But you once praised that Revolution, Mr. Coleridge!' " Hazlitt's venom was directed at the *Courier* itself as much as at C.

In his Diary HCR noted that he attended this lecture, which, he wrote, "was like his other lectures in most particulars, but rather less interesting. He treated of Shakespeare, and dwelt on mere accidents which served to bring out some of his favourite ideas, which after a certain number of repetitions becomes tiresome." *CRB* I 218. C himself was reasonably satisfied with it, and wrote on the Prospectus he sent to Cary, "Went off well—but the general opinion was, that it was more instructive than, but not so splendid as the 3rd." *CL* IV 834. The report in the *Courier*, usually sympathetic to C, suggests a more brilliant occasion, ending with "a thunder of applause".

LECTURE 4

RECORDS OF THE LECTURE

COLERIDGE'S NOTES
BM MS EGERTON 2800 FF 42ᵛ–45,
CONTINUING ON BM ADD MS 34225 FF 49–51

*In my last   Poets of the Italian and English School, who like fair and stately ~~Bran~~ Plants, each with a ~~vital and individualizing~~ living principle of its own taking up into itself and diversely organizing the nutriment derived from the peculiar soil in which they[y]ᵇ grew—or rather like various fruit branches engrafted on the same tree; each a different sort but all the same kind and drawing the sap from one trunk and a common root—and that root the allegorical, chivalrous, and ⟨at once individualizing yet⟩ amalgamating Genius of the middle ages—or the arts and philosophy of the South superinduced ~~the~~ on the deeper sensibility, the wilder imagination, ~~and more robust morals~~ in one word, the greater Inwardness of the North,—and combined into one complex Whole, ~~by the~~ fixed and concreted ~~and~~ by the vital air of ~~reli~~ a common Faith. ~~This evening a different, and far higher phænomenon demands my bes truest efforts—and these ⟨again⟩ at their happiest height, will require your candid allowances   All these however In proportion to these vigor of their Genius and the elevation of their moral Being~~ These Poets, and our own Spenser more than his predecessors, English or Italian, had ~~forced the surrounding aliments into surrounding and~~ indeed ~~modified the aliments~~ by the alchemy of ~~their~~ Genius modified and transmuted the aliments, ~~amid which they~~ offered by the Soil in which they ~~were planted~~ grew; but yet in all their ~~forms~~ hues and qualities ⟨they⟩ ~~bore~~ear witness to their birth-place and the accidents and conditions of their ~~outer~~ inward growth and outward expansion.—

ᶜOn this evening a different and far mo~~re~~ ~~wonderful~~ complex Phænomenon forms the Problem, to be solved— ~~a solution problem, to~~

---

a Egerton 2800 f 42ᵛ; f 42 is blank
b Word completed by the editor
c–d C cancelled this passage with a vertical line

the solution of which but but Powers tenfold greater than mine would be incommensurate to the solution, which its nearest approach, its most adventurous Parhelion,[1] must still leave a wide chasm, which our Love and Wonder alone can fill up. Be mine then the effort; but let your a candid allowances be proportioned to the difficulty of keep pace with them—The praises of our illustrious benefactor are not the less delightful will not want an interest with you—feeble as the voice may be proclaims them, and superflous as all eulogy praise must be when all hearts or a greatness which all   Feeble would every will my voice be that would to my own ears, while I speak of SHAKESPEAR: and superflous must all praises be of the myriad-minded man[2] whom all English Hearts feel to be above praise.[d]

> [e]Great Son of Memory! dear Heir of Fame
> Thou need'st not &c—[3]

A Not so the poet, whose mighty mind demands my utmost efforts scarcely more, than these efforts will require your utmost allowances—. Weigh however but the difficulty of the attempt, and But I shall hope for your rely on a pardon from your candor, and hope for encouragement from your sympathy; if only your the interest of the subject find its counterweight in your sense of the its difficulty. For to what shall I compare an immortal ever-living Dramatist? To the self-sustaining Pine the Monarch of some Norwegian Precipice mourns, soul-like now mourning with a sea like almost soul-like voice, and now copes with the swell as if the Spirit of the calm were wooing the breezes in its branches, and now with imperium copes with the swell of the Tempest—or with the grand Yew, that has cleft itself a way and a rooting-space out of the bare Rock, owinges no service to no homage of maintenance to soil, or no subscription [to][f] culture, but feeds itself from the invisible

---

[d] See [c–d], above   [e] f 43
[f] Word supplied by the editor

[1] Literally a spot on a solar halo giving the impression of a mock-sun. C seems to mean that at best he can provide a faint image or reflection of the great sun that is Shakespeare.

[2] The Greek source of this term was cited by C in *CN* I 1070, and in her note to that entry Kathleen Coburn gives a detailed account of how C seized on one phrase from an absurdly inflated eulogy by one Naucratius of his master, Theodorus, abbot of a monastery in Constantinople, who died in 826. C found the passage in William Cave *Scriptorum ecclesiasticorum historia literaria* (2 vols 1688–9) I 509 and was translating the Greek μυριόνους. See also *BL* ch 15 *(CC)* II 19.

[3] Misquoting lines 5–6 from Milton's sonnet *On Shakespear* (1630):

Dear son of memory, great heir of fame,
What need'st thou such weak witness of thy name?

elements, that tells not its age ~~and own~~ and owns not the change of
seasons

> "beneath whose sable Branches ghostly Shapes
> May meet at noon-tide—Fear and trembling Hope,
> Silence and Foresight—Death, the Skeleton,
> And Time, the Shadow—there to celebrate
> United worship—?"[4]

Or if our Thoughts turn rather to the expense and endless opulence,
⟨and incessant reproduction⟩ of his genius, may we not compare it to
that Tree, itself a forest—

> The Tree which t at this day to Indians known
> In Malabar or Decan spreads her Arms
> Branching so broad and long, that in the ground
> The bended twigs take root, and daughters grow
> About the mother tree, a pillar'd shade
> [g]High-overarched, and echoing walks between—[5]

and in its innumerous[6] boughs we will imagine all the gay plumages ~~of
Fancy~~ and all the sweet Warblers of Fancy[7]—and lower down the ~~nimble
Harlequins and~~ urchin shews, the nimble ⟨Harlequins &⟩ living Grotesques of Nature, that in ~~a~~ strange discords as strangely resolved into
~~harm~~ the total Harmony ~~mouthe~~ and chatter[8] at the brooding Faquir ~~and
lively~~ or meditative Humorist ~~in the Shade below~~ that sits at the root—
or mock the group of dancing Girls, ~~or~~ annoy the simple Shepherd that

> Shelters in cool and tends his pastring herds
> At loop-holes cut thro' t deepest shade—[9]

[g] f 44; f 43ᵛ is blank

[4] WW *Yew-trees* (published in *Poems*—1815) lines 23–31 (var, with omissions). In *BL* ch 22 C cited a longer passage from the poem, including these lines, as an example to illustrate his claim that "in imaginative power" WW stood "nearest of all modern writers to Shake-spear and Milton". *BL (CC)* II 151–2. See also n 5, below.

[5] Milton *Paradise Lost* IX 1102–7, with var first line, which should read: "But such as at this day . . .". The tree is the banyan, which perhaps led C to the im-age of the "brooding Faquir". He quoted these lines in a longer passage from the poem in *BL* ch 22 to show how the "Poet should paint to the imagination, not to the fancy". *BL (CC)* II 127–8. See also

n 4, above.

[6] A Miltonic word; see *Paradise Lost* VII 455.

[7] Probably an echo of Milton in *L'Al-legro* lines 133–4:

Or sweetest Shakespeare, fancy's child,
Warble his native wood-notes wild.

[8] C is recalling Caliban's speech in *The Tempest* II ii 1–9, in which he speaks of Prospero's spirits as frightening him with "urchin-shows", or apparitions like hedgehogs, and as appearing "like apes that mow and chatter at me". To "moe" or "mow" means to make faces.

[9] *Paradise Lost* IX 1109–10 (var). These lines were included in the passage

That a such a mind ~~could dwell~~ evolved itself in the narrow bounds of a human form is a Problem ~~which Nature~~ indeed—Powers tenfold greater than mine would be incommensurate to its Solution, which in its nearest ~~approach~~ and most adventurous Approach must still leave a wide chasm which our Love and Admiration alone can fill up. Feeble will my words sound to my own ears while I speak of SHAKESPEAR, and superfluous must all praises be of the myriad-minded man,[10] whom every English Heart feels to be above Praise—

~~Great~~ Dear Son of Memory, Great Heir of Fame &c[11]

—Least of all poets colored in any particulars by the spirit or customs of his Age—that ~~only which~~ the spirit of all that it had pronounced intrinsically and permanently good ~~had~~ concentrated and perfected itself in his mind. Thus we have neither the chivalry of the North, nothing indeed in any peculiar sense of the word, chivalrous ⟨and as little of the genii and winged Griffins of the Earth⟩[12] in an age of religious and political Heats nothing sectarian in Religion or Politics—in an age of Misers so flagrant in all the Dramas of his Contemporaries and Successors no miser-characters[13]—in an age of Witchcraft ⟨and Astrology⟩ no Witches (for we must [not][h] be deluded by stage-directions)[14] or few but the female character—the craving for foresight (Macbeth)—all that must ever be elements of the social State—/ &c—

> [i]Witness our Colin whom tho' all the Graces
> And all the Muses nurs'd; whose well-taught song
> Parnassus' self and Glorian embraces
> And all the learn'd, and all the Shepherd Throng—
> Yet all his hopes were cross'd, all suits deny'd

[h] Word supplied by the editor
[i] f 44[v]

C cited in *BL* ch 22, with the correct reading, "thickest shade", in the second line. See n 5, above.

[10] C's coinage, explained in *BL* ch 15 as "borrowed from a Greek monk". See n 2, above.

[11] Quoting from Milton's sonnet on Shakespeare line 5; see n 3, above.

[12] Referring to topics of Lects 2 and 3, Gothic romances, and the "Love of the Marvellous" associated with Ariosto. But C seems to have forgotten that in Lect 2 he cited a "Northern tale" because of its connexion with Shakespeare's *Richard III* (at n 35). The Carwardine report (sentences after n 34) perhaps illustrates better what C actually said at this point.

[13] So C had argued in Lect 7 of the 1811–12 series (paragraph containing n 35). Carwardine's notes show that C developed this point in relation to Shylock; see below (at n 35).

[14] In the Folio text of *Macbeth* the Weird Sisters are called Witches only in stage-directions, never in the text. C thought of them as "awful beings" who "blended in themselves the Fates and Furies of the ancients with the sorceresses of Gothic and popular superstition"; see Lect 2 of the 1813 series (at n 16).

Discouraged, scorn'd, his writings vilified—
Poorly, poor man! he liv'd, poorly, poor Man, he died!

And had not [that]ʲ great Hart, whose honor'd head
Ah! lies full low, pity'd thy woful plight,
There had'st thou lain unwept, unburied,
Unbless'd nor grac'd with any common rite,
Yet shalt thou live when thy great Foe shall sink
Beneath his mountain tomb, whose fame shall stink
And Tim~~e~~me his blacker name shall blur with blackest ink.

O let th' Iambic Muse avenge that wrong
Which can not slumber in thy sheet of lead—

O may that Man that hath the muses scorn'd
Alive nor dead be ever of a Muse adorn'd—

                                P. F.—[15]

ᵏHis advantages—

1. Compared with the tragic opera of the Greeks[16]—Imitation not *Copy* essential to all works of art[17]—Shakspeare took an apparently larger quantum of resemblance—but every where ever men idealized by Language &c—
The want of Scenery on the Stage—

The vigor ~~and~~ that was then fashionable in conversation, and the search for felicities in language—and yet if you met a paragraph of Sh. in a wilderness, you would know it—

Characteristic qualities—
Meditation, and Observation as its vehicle—chiefly used to bring enough external individualities to balance the internal *character*—and the general Truths, the ~~passion for wh~~ predominance of which in his mind from the earliest period all his earliest works attest—(quote from the LIT. LIFE.).—[18]

ʲ Word supplied by the editor
ᵏ f 45

[15] Citing canto I sts 19–21 (var) of Phineas Fletcher's *The Purple Island* (1633), but omitting the middle three lines of the last stanza. The text is close to that in Chalmers *English Poets* (1810) VI 84, from which C probably copied this extract, but he may have used *B Poets* IV 384. "Colin" is Edmund Spenser.

[16] See below (at n 37).

[17] This was a vital point to C, the cor-nerstone of his theory of dramatic illusion; see e.g. Lect 4 of the 1808 series (at n 30).

[18] As Carwardine's report indicates, C probably quoted from the final pages of *BL* ch 15, in which he celebrates Shakespeare's depth and energy of thought: "No man was ever yet a great poet, without being at the same time a profound philosopher. For poetry is the blossom

Of The order in which his works were written, having no outward evidence[19]—for even if we knew the time in which they were acted this would be no proof (for confidence will increase) therefore internal testimony—

By this rule I should not hesitate to place Love's Labor lost as the first—And All's Well that ends Well—the second/ originally Love's Labor ⟨to which, after probably no great interval, he looked back with some parental fondness—⟩[20]

The first *all intellect*—with little other observation than such a country town might have afforded to a Shakespear—

Instances, p. 148. 174[l] [21]

[m]Love's labor lost—

2 The germs of characters afterwards seen fully developed—His Costard the ground-work of his Tapster in Measure for measure, and ⟨Dull⟩ his Dogberry, BYRON, of Benedict in the Much Ado about Nothing, and of Mercutio in Romeo and Juliet. Both pre-existent in p. 156.[22]

3. His unceasing war against Pedantry—⟨in⟩ Holofernes   Polonius contrast as far [as][n] the forms of words were concerned & in Costard's remuneration (156) and the ridicule of antithetic writing which is by no means superannuated, p. 164—.[23]

---

[l] The text ends at the foot of the page
[m] Add MS 34225 f 49
[n] Word supplied by the editor

---

and the fragrancy of all human knowledge, human thoughts, human passions, emotions, language. In Shakespeare's *poems* the creative power, and the intellectual energy wrestle as in a war embrace. . . ." *BL (CC)* II 25–6. C repeatedly stressed that Shakespeare's characters were not drawn merely from observation. For the importance of this point and its relation to his distinction between copy and imitation, see Lect 6 of the 1811–12 series (at n 14).

[19] See Lect 4 of the 1811–12 series (at nn 1 and 21). The chronology of Shakespeare's plays was largely a matter of guesswork at this time.

[20] C repeatedly argued that *Love's Labour's Lost* must have been Shakespeare's first play, most elaborately in

Lect 5 of the 1811–12 series (C's notes, opening sentences), but does not appear on previous occasions to have linked it with *All's Well That Ends Well* as *Love's Labour's Won.*

[21] The references are to C's copy of *Sh* (Ayscough): I 148 refers to *Love's Labour's Lost* I i, probably to the passage about spring and winter, "He weeds the corn . . ." and the "frost | That bites the first-born infants of the spring" (lines 96–101); I 174 refers to the songs that end the play, "When daisies pied . . ." and "When icicles hang by the wall".

[22] *Sh* (Ayscough) I 156, the exchange between Costard and Berowne on the subject of "remuneration" at III i 136ff; see below (at n 42).

[23] *Sh* (Ayscough) I 164, the opening

4. The exquisite beauty of his blank verse, in his very earliest works—while yet the tendency to rhyme was strong—causes of his blank verse and importance of ~~th~~ it in certain of his plays—.

Then to take the plays as they come—i.e. the Comedies or romantic Dramas.—For to the illustration of Shakespear's characteristics it is almost indifferent which—and as the two next lectures will be more on particular ~~Plays~~ merits and contradistinctions of particular plays & characters &c—. Introduction, remarks on the haply*o* titles—

Tempest—(Ariel &c as well as Caliban for themselves—Prospero no *Magician* in our feeling; all by human feelings—[)]*p*

1. Exquisite Judgement—first the noise & confusion—then the silence of a deserted Island—and Prospero and Miranda—I have often thought of Shakespear as the mighty wizard himself introducing as the first ⟨and favorite⟩ pledge of his so potent art, the female character in all its charms, as if conscious that he first had represented womanhood/, as a dramatist—.

The management of the first scene—

The character of Caliban—how *poetical*—for tho' a misshaped creature he suggests a child of Nature—11th page—[24]

*q*Nothing more impressive than the comic Scene, or more novel than Trinculo with Caliban—but Trinculo's self-complacency in his growing contempt of Caliban, the excessive weakness that delights itself or prides itself by comparison—Stephano's ambition—and (Shakespear's prophetic powers and therefore inexhaustible ~~nay terrible~~ applicability[)]*r*—Caliban's revolutionary Freedom—

Sh two gentlemen of Verona—p. 36.[25] Likeness of Launce to Launcelot in Merchant of Venice—(and Wi~~t~~s passing into humor.)

Merry Wives of Windsor.—

---

o A slip for "happy"

p Closing bracket supplied by the editor; the passage in brackets was probably squeezed in as an afterthought

q f 50; f 49v is blank

r Closing bracket supplied by the editor

---

of v i, in which Holofernes displays his pedantry in his analysis of Armado's way of speaking, and Nathaniel speaks in antitheses, "Your reasons at dinner have been sharp and sententious, pleasant without scurrility, witty without affection, audacious without impudency, learned without opinion, and strange without heresy . . .".

[24] *Sh* (Ayscough) I 11: *The Tempest* II ii 36ff, in which Trinculo creeps under Caliban's "gaberdine" and Stephano enters with his bottle of wine.

[25] *Sh* (Ayscough) I 36, Launce's comments on the catalogue of the virtues of the milkmaid he loves, as recited by Speed: *The Two Gentlemen of Verona* III i 301ff.

Welch—and broken French English—[26]
Comedy of Errors—*France* in the old cause.—[27]
Much ado about Nothing—change in Beatrice's Character, p. 139—[28]
Midsummer Night's Dream/[s]

'5. the interfusion of the Lyrical, of that which in its very essence is poetical, not only with the Dramatic, as in the Plays of Metastasio where at the end of the Scene comes the Aria, as the Exit speech of the Character[29]—Now Songs in Shakespear are introduced as *Songs*, ~~are~~ and just as Songs are in real Life—beautifully as they are often made characteristic of the person who has called for them—Desdemona—& the Count in As you like it[30]—~~but I mean~~ not only with the Dramatic, but as a part of the Dramatic—The whole *midsummer Night's Dream* is one continued Specimen of the Lyrical dramatized—but take the beginning of the III[d] Act of F. P. of Henry IV—represent the Hotspur "Marry, and I'm glad on't with all my heart" and then Mortimer—"I understand thy looks—" p. 458.[31]

6. closely connected with this is that Sh's Characters are like those in life to be *inferred* by the reader, not *told to him*. Of this excellence I know no other instance—and it has one mark of real life—that Sh's Characters have been as generally misunderstood and from precisely the same causes—. If you take what his friends say, you may be deceived—still more so, if his Enemies; and the character himself sees himself thro' the medium of his character, not exactly as it is   but the

---

[s] The text ends halfway down the page
[t] f 51; f 50[v] is blank except for the word *"Shakspear"*, not in C's hand

[26] Referring to Sir Hugh Evans, the Welsh parson, and Dr Caius, the French physician, in *The Merry Wives of Windsor*.

[27] *The Comedy of Errors* III ii 123–5, in which Dromio's punning line about France, "armed and reverted, making war against her heir" is thought to relate to the French civil wars involving the "old cause" of the Protestant Henry of Navarre, who became Henry IV of France in 1593.

[28] *Sh* (Ayscough) I 139, referring to *Much Ado About Nothing* IV i 255ff, in which Beatrice admits she loves Benedick and bids him "kill Claudio".

[29] C made this same point about the aria at the end of the scene in *BL* ch 22 (*CC*) II 122. He had read plays and letters by Pietro Metastasio (1698–1782) when he was in Malta and Italy in 1804–6 and also heard some of his operas; see *CN* II 2184, 2224, 3190 and n.

[30] Referring to *Othello* IV iii 40ff, "The poor soul sat sighing by a sycamore tree", and *As You Like It* II vii 174ff, in which the Duke Senior calls on Amiens to sing "Blow, blow, thou winter wind".

[31] Both lines are on *Sh* (Ayscough) I 458. The first is from Hotspur's speech rejecting songs and "mincing poetry" (III i 125ff), the second from Mortimer's lines in praise of Welsh spoken by his wife, which sounds "as sweet as ditties highly penn'd" (III i 198ff); these contrasting speeches "represent" the two characters.

Clown or the Fool will suggest a shrewd hint—and take all together—
& the impression is right—and all have it—and it may be given as
~~deduced from~~ soon as the true Idea is given—and then all the speeches
receive ~~the~~ light and attest by reflecting it—."[32]

NOTES TAKEN AT THE LECTURE
BY H. H. CARWARDINE
ESSEX COUNTY RECORD OFFICE
MS D/D PR 549 FF 4–11

[v]Coleridge 6 Feby
On Shakespear

His predecessors ⟨the Poets of Italy France England &c⟩ drew their
aliment from the soil. There was a nationality—they were of a country
of a genus—grafted with the chivalrous spirit & sentiment of the North—
and with the wild magic imported from the East. Not so Shakspear—
He bore no obvious witness of the soil from whence he grew—compare
him with mountain Pine[33]

Self-sustained—deriving his genius immediately from heaven—independent of all earthly or national influence

That such a mind involved itself in a human form is a problem indeed
which my feeble powers may witness with admiration but cannot explain. My words are indeed feeble when I speak of that myriad minded
man who all artists feel above all praise—[34]

Least of all poets antients or modern does shakespear appear to be
coloured or affected by the [w]age in which he lived—he was of all times—
& countries. true to the great & enduring eternal of our nature

North the chivalrous of the North art was a mere accident, a sub-
ordin[ate][x] to his genius

& nothing ⟨of⟩ the importation of the East—

He drew from the eternal of our nature—

When misers were most common in his age—yet he has drawn no

---

[u] The text ends two inches from the foot of the page
[v] f 4
[w] f 4[v]
[x] Word completed by the editor

---

[32] Cf Lect 7, below (at n 4), in which
C developed a similar argument about
characterisation in Shakespeare. If Carwardine reported the whole of the lecture, C did not use his notes here, and
in this case would not in Lect 7 have
been repeating himself.

[33] For C's reference to "the self-sustaining Pine" see above (fourth sentence
after n 3).

[34] See above (at nn 2 and 10).

such character—and why because it was a mere transitory Character—Shylock no miser not the great feature of his Character[35]

In an age of political & religious heat—yet there is no sectarian character of Politician or religion:

In an Age of superstition when witchcraft was the passion [y]of the monarch[36]—yet he has never introduced such characters For the wierd Sisters are as different as possible

Judgement and Genius are as much one as the fount & the stream that flows from it—and I must dwell on the Judgement of Shaksp[r]

When astrolog: predictions had possession of the mind he has no such character it was a transient folly merely of the time & therefore it did not belong to Shaksp—in company with Homer & Milton & whatever is great on Earth—he invented the Drama—The Greek Tragedy [z]was tragic opera[37]—differing only in this that in Greek the scenery & Music &c were subserv[t] to the poetry in mod[n] opera the poetry is subserv[t] to the Music & decoration—

A *mere* copy never delights us in any thing[38]—Why do we go to a Tragedy to witness the representation of the woe which we may daily witness

Ancients confined the Tragedies confined their subjects to gods & heroes & traditional people

Shak—a more difficult task in drawing not only from nature but from the times as well as things before him & so [a]true to nature—that you never can conceive his characters could speak otherwise than they do in the situation in which they are placed

—Common expressions—''How natural Shakespear is''—and yet so peculiar that if you read but a few detached lines you immediately say this must be Shakespear—

Such peculiar propriety & excellence & truth to nature that there is no thing in any man at all like him

---

[y] f 5   [z] f 5[v]   [a] f 6

[35] Here Carwardine's notes show how C developed his own general note about misers; see above (at n 13).

[36] This phrase amplifies C's notes, which have no reference to James I; see above (phrase after n 13).

[37] Voltaire gave currency to this idea in his *Dissertation sur la tragédie ancienne et moderne* (1749), in which he said that an image of ancient Greek tragedy on the stage could be found in modern Italian operas like those of Meta-

stasio: "Où trouver un spectacle qui nous donne une image de la scène grecque? C'est peut-être dans vos tragédies, nommées opéras, que cette image subsiste." *Œuvres complètes* (Paris 1877–85) IV 489. C had made a similar comparison in Lect 2 of the 1812 series, first course (at n 8).

[38] See n 17, above. Carwardine's report goes on here to show how C developed the headings in his notes, above (after n 17).

—a research for that felicity of language current in the Courts of Eliz.ᵗʰ & James—but so was Massinger B Johnson ᵇBeaumont & Fletcher &c but yet they are not like Shaks Language

Divide his Works into 3 great Classes—no division[s]ᶜ can be made that apply to Tragedy & Comedy, for Nature acknowleges none of those distinct sharp Lines & Shakespr is the Poet of nature—pourtraying things as they exist—He has as it were prophesied what each man in his different passions would have produced

ᵈ1.ˢᵗ his Comedies & Romantic Dramas

2 his Historical plays

3 his great Tragedies

There is a C⟨h⟩aracter of observation—a happiness of noticing whatever is external and arranging them like a gallery of pictures[39]—represent⁸ Passions which no man appropriates to himself & yet acknowl[edg]esᵉ his share

Character of his mind depth & Energy of Thought—No Man was ever a great poet without being a great Philosopher   in thisᶠ earlyest poems the ⁸poet & philosopher are perpetually struggling with each other—till found unified when they were blended & flowed in sweetest harmony & strength[40]

Loves labour Lost, I affirm must have been the 1ˢᵗ of his play[s]ʰ 1ˢᵗ it has the least observation & the characters merely such [as]ⁱ a young Man of genius might have made out himself—But it has other marks it is all intellect—there is little to interest as a Dramatic representation— yet affording infinite matter of beautiful quotation—

King & Biron—light seekg light blinds us—[41]

ᵇ f 6ᵛ
ᶜ Final letter supplied by the editor
ᵈ f 7
ᵉ Missing letters supplied by the editor
ᶠ So in ms   ⁸ f 7ᵛ
ʰ Carwardine wrote "play"
ⁱ Word supplied by the editor

[39] Cf C's comment, perhaps made with John Boydell's Shakespeare Gallery in mind: "It is Shakespeare's peculiar excellence, that throughout the whole of his splendid picture gallery (the reader will excuse the confest inadequacy of this metaphor), we find individuality every where, mere portrait no where." See *Friend (CC)* I 457 and n.

[40] See n 18, above. This is additional evidence that C planned to quote from *BL* ch 15.

[41] The reference is to *Love's Labour's Lost* I i 75–7, in which Berowne says to the King:

while truth the while
Doth falsely blind the eyesight of his look.
Light seeking light doth light of light beguile.

Sh (Ayscough) I 148.

no instance in which the [j]same thought so happily expressed—

In the Character of Byron he has the germ of Benedict & of Mercurtio—it was the 1.st rough draught which he afterwards finished into Ben: & Merc:

In Holofernes the sketch of Polonius[42]—he never on any occasion spares pedantry

—remuneration

Nathanal[k]—"I praise god for you sir" &c—[43]

Much of this wordiness (here ridiculed) shewn in modern poetry, words nicely balanced till you come to seek the meaning when you are surprised to find none—

[l]His Blank verse, has nothing equal to it but that of Milton such fullness of thought, gives an involution of metre so natural to the expression of passion—it is this excitement of passions which fills & elevates the mind and gives general truths in full free & poetic language

Lear—Macbeth &c—

Shakespear the only one who has made passion the vehicle of general Truth   As in his Comedy he has made even folly itself the vehicle of philosophy

[m]Each speech is what every man feels to be latent in his nature— what he would have said in that situation if he had had the ability & readiness to do it—and these are multiplied and individuallized with the most extraordinary minuteness & truth—

Of the exquisite judgement of Sh

1.st must conceive a stage without scenery—acting a poor recitation— he frequently speaks to his audience—if says he, ⟨you⟩ will listen to me with your minds—& not with your eyes to scene & [n]assist me with your imagination I will do so & so—[44]

Characteristic of his Comedy & Romantic Drama

1.st his Characters never introduced for the sake of his plot, but his plot arises out of his Characters   Nor are all those involved in them—

[j] f 8
[k] So in ms
[l] f 8[v]
[m] f 9   [n] f 9[v]

[42] This echoes, with variations, a point made by C in Lect 5 of the 1811–12 series (at n 32) and Lect 4 of the 1812 series, first course (at n 14). Cf also C's notes for this lecture, above (at n 22).

[43] Referring to the play on Armado's offer of "remuneration" by Costard in *Love's Labour's Lost* III i 131ff and to Nathaniel's enthusiasm at IV ii 73 for Holofernes, who has just delivered his absurdly pedantic "'extemporal epitaph'" on the death of the deer or "'pricket'" killed by the Princess.

[44] Recalling the Prologue to *Henry V* line 23, "Piece out our imperfections with your thoughts", and the Chorus to III 35, "And eke out our performance with your mind".

You meet people who meet & speak to you as in real[i]ty[o] life interesting you differently—having some distinctive peculiarity which interests you & thus the story is introduced which you appear casually made [p]acquainted with—yet still you feel that it excites an interest—you feel that there is something that is applicable to certain situation[s][q] &c

Again his Characters have something more than a mere amusing property

Example in the Tempest   The delight of Trinculo at finding something more sottish than himself,[45] and that honors him—the characteristic of base & vulgar minds which Shakespear is fond of lashing & placing in a ridiculous light—[read scene between Trinculo & Caliban][r]

[s]but Shakespear can make even rude vulgarity the vehicle of profound truths & thoughts—Prospero—the mighty wizard whose potent art could not only call up all the spirits of the deep[46]—but the characters as they were, & are, & will be &c Seems a portrait of ⟨the bard⟩ himself.[47] No magicians or magic in the proper sense of the word—a being to excite either fear or wonder. Nothing in common with such Characters as were brought from the East—

If there be any imitation [t]in Shak—of what is it imitation—what so earthly as Calliban—so aerial as Ariel[48]—so fanciful so exquisitely light—yet some striving of thought—of an undeveloped power

I know no ⟨Character in Shak to which he has given a⟩ propensity to sneer or scoff or listen ⟨or express contempt⟩ but he has made that man a *Villain*[49]

REPORT IN THE *COURIER*
MONDAY, 9 FEBRUARY 1818

LECTURES ON SHAKSPEARE

On Friday evening Mr. Coleridge gave his first Lecture on Shakspeare to a numerous and genteel audience. He stated the permanent objects

[o] Letter supplied by the editor
[p] f 10
[q] Final letter supplied by the editor
[r] Carwardine's brackets
[s] f 10[v]   [t] f 11

[45] Trinculo's discovery of Caliban in II ii.
[46] Cf *1 Henry IV* III i 52.
[47] Echoing C's notes, above (fourth paragraph after n 23), in which, however, his description of Prospero is related to the introduction of Miranda.
[48] See Lect 9 of the 1811–12 series (at

n 44), in which this contrast is developed more fully. The idea is drawn from A. W. Schlegel's lectures: *DKL* II ii 129 (Black II 180).
[49] If C's lecture ended at this point, he did not use all his notes, which continue with comments on other comedies; see above (from n 25 onwards).

Shakspeare had in view in drawing his characters, and how obviously he disregarded those that were of a transitory nature. The character of Caliban, as an original and caricature of Jacobinism,[50] so fully illustrated at Paris during the French Revolution, he described in a vigorous and lively manner, exciting repeated bursts of applause. He commenced an inquiry into the order of succession in which Shakspeare wrote his plays, and decided that "Love's Labour Lost" must have been the first, as there are so many allusions in it such as a youth would make, few or none resulting from an experience of the world. That play and "*The Tempest*" were the chief objects of his discourse, into which, however, he introduced a great variety of new and striking remarks, not confined to any particular play. As, for instance, he said, wherever Shakspeare had drawn a character addicted to sneering, and contempt for the merits of others, that character was sure to be a villain. Vanity, envy, and malice, were its certain accompaniments: too prudent to praise itself, it fed its concentrated egotism by sarcasm and lowering others. This is but a poor description of the very glowing language, ample detail, and profound thought Mr. Coleridge displayed on this topic which produced a thunder of applause.

[50] C evidently went well beyond his lecture notes at this point, provoking an attack on him by Hazlitt; see headnote to this lecture (Background and Circumstances).

LECTURE 5

DATE AND PLACE OF DELIVERY. Tuesday, 10 February 1818, in the Great Room of the London Philosophical Society, Fleur-de-Luce Court, Fleet Street.

SUBJECT. Shakespeare's history plays, especially the characters of Richard III and Falstaff. The Syllabus merely announced that Lects 4, 5, and 6 would be "On the Dramatic Works of SHAKSPEARE".

ADVERTISEMENTS AND ANNOUNCEMENTS. *Courier* Mon, 9 Feb (announcement): "To-morrow evening, Feb. 10, at a quarter after Eight precisely, Mr. COLERIDGE will commence his second Lecture on SHAKESPEAR, including the characters of *Richard the Third* and *Falstaff*, at the Great Room of the London Philosophical Society, Fleur-de-luce-court, Fleet-street—Admission, Five Shillings." *M Post* Tues, 10 Feb (advertisement): "THIS EVENING, February 10, at a Quarter after Eight precisely, Mr. COLERIDGE will COMMENCE his SECOND LECTURE on SHAKESPEAR . . ." (the rest as in the *Courier*). *The Times* and the *M Chron* Tues, 10 Feb: advertisements substantially the same as that in the *M Post*.

TEXT. The evidence seems to indicate that C used some notes numbered 1 to 4 on BM MS Egerton 2800 f 40 for the beginning of this lecture. This single sheet of paper has writing on both sides, ending about 20 mm from the bottom of f 40ᵛ, with a short line that may mark the end of the numbered notes. In *LR* II 77–81 HNC linked these notes with the report of C's first lecture in Bristol, which appeared in the *Bristol Gazette* 4 Nov 1813; following him, Raysor also assigned them to 1813—*Sh C* I 199–200 (225–6)—and specifically related them to Lect 1 of that series. He also associated them with the notes on BM Add MS 34225 f 51, which in fact were written for Lect 4 of the 1818 series (see headnote: Text). The notes on BM MS Egerton 2800 f 40 appear to be self-contained, and the partial watermark "WM: RUSE & T" is the same as that on paper C used for lectures in 1818; the full watermark, as on Egerton 2800 ff 48 and 50, contains the date 1817, and these sheets were used for Lect 3 in the 1818 course. All the other sheets with this watermark used by C contain notes for Lects 3, 4, and 6 of the 1818 course, which are pretty well documented. Little, however, is known about Lect 5 in this series, which was advertised as on "SHAKESPEAR, including the characters of *Richard the Third* and *Falstaff*'. The other two Shakespeare lectures in this course both begin with a general introduction on Shakespeare, and it would fit the pattern of the series if C had done the same again in Lect 5. The notes on Egerton 2800 f 40 constitute such an introduction and are accordingly printed below. Corroboration that they relate to this lecture is provided by C's note, "For Tues", written in a large hand on the verso with the sheet turned sideways. It looks as though he wrote this at the top edge of the blank lower half of the verso after completing note 3, and added note 4 later, since this fills most of the lower part of the page, continuing around "For Tues", which is boxed in on the left side. Tuesday was the day of the week on which this lecture was given.

The lectures of 1818 on Shakespeare correspond roughly in plan, though not in order, with those of the 1813 series at Bristol. There C's sixth lecture was chiefly concerned with Richard III and Falstaff, as the report on it in the *Bristol Gazette* shows. Some notes by C for that lecture survive in a transcript by EHC from a lost notebook, and they end with two comments, one on Falstaff and one on Richard, which apparently were written at a different time from the other notes copied by EHC, for they contain page-references to C's copy of *Sh* (Ayscough) and not, like the rest of the notes for that series, to his set of *Sh* (Rann). It is impossible to guess from EHC's transcript how these notes were set out by C, and whether he linked them with the 1813 notes, but it is conceivable that C expanded his Bristol material for use again in Lect 5, for he seems to have returned to them in preparing for Lect 6 (see the headnote to this lecture). The use of *Sh* (Ayscough) is a feature of the 1818 course, and it seems appropriate therefore to include these two notes here.

REPORTS. No reports of this lecture have been found.

BACKGROUND AND CIRCUMSTANCES. The advertisement of 6 Feb relating primarily to Lect 4 also announced the subject of the next lecture as "the Historical Plays" of Shakespeare. The advertisements for Lect 5 narrow this down to the characters of Richard III and Falstaff. HCR attended the lecture, noting in his Diary: "Coleridge's lecture, on Shakespeare and as usual; but he was apparently ill." *CRB* I 219. On the day before he gave this lecture C wrote cheerfully to Cary, and there is no mention in this or later letters of illness at this time. HCR may simply have been indicating that in his opinion C gave a poor performance.

LECTURE 5

RECORDS OF THE LECTURE

COLERIDGE'S NOTES
BM MS EGERTON 2800 FF 40–40ᵛ

*ᵃ*1. Expectation in preference to surprize—God said, let there be LIGHT: and there was LIGHT.[1] not there *was* Light. As the feeling with which we startle at a shooting star, compared with that of watching the Sunrise at the pre-established moment, such and so low is Surprize Comp. with Expect.—

2. Signal adherence to the great Law of ~~hu~~ nature, that opposites tend to attract and temper each other. Passion ~~moralizes   and Passion exclusively~~ in Shakespear displays, Libertinism involves, Morality—the *exceptions* characteristic, independent of the intrinsic value/ as the farewell Precepts of ~~na~~ the Parent, & having some end ~~on the way~~ beyond even the parental relation—thus the Countess's beautiful Precepts to Bertram by elevating her character elevates that of Helena,[2] her favorite, & ~~rei~~ softens down the parent in her which Shakespear does not mean ~~to hide~~ us not to see but to see & forgive and at length to justify. ~~hence the P~~ So Polonius,[3] who is the personified *Memory* of wisdom no longer actually possessed—

~~To m~~ So again Folly, Dullness itself, the vehicles of Wisdom—.[4] As all the Deities of Sparta were in armour, even Venus &c—so all in Shakespear strong—. No difficulty in ~~ma~~ being a Fool to imitate a fool—but to be, remain, and speak like a wise man, and yet so as [to]*ᵇ* give a vivid representation of a fool—hic labor, hoc opus[5]—Dogberry—&c

ᵃ f 40
ᵇ Word supplied by the editor

[1] Gen 1.3.
[2] *All's Well That Ends Well* I i 61ff.
[3] C sums up here what he said about Polonius in Lect 1 of the 1813 series (paragraph containing n 31).
[4] Here C passed on to *Much Ado About Nothing* and was thinking of Dogberry.
[5] Virgil *Aeneid* 6.129, "Hoc opus, hic labor est''; tr ''This is the difficulty, this the toil''.

3. Independence of the Interest on the ~~story~~ Plot—The plot interests us on account of the characters, not vice versa—it is the canvass only—Justification of the same stratagem in Benedict & Beatrice—same vanity—&c—ᶜtake away ~~the~~ from Much ado about nothing all that which is indispensable to the Plot, either as having little to do ~~it~~ with it, or at best, like Dogberry & his Comrades, forced into the service when any other less ingeniously absurd Watchmen & Night-Constables would have answered—take away Benedict, Beatrice, Dogberry & the reaction of the former on the character of Hero—& what will remain?—In other writers the main agent of the Plot is always the prominent Character/ In Shakespear so or not so, as the Character is in itself calculated or not calculated to form the plot—So Don John, the main spring of the Plot, is merely shewn and withdrawn—

4. Independence of the Interest in *the Story* as the ground-work of the Plot—Hence Sh. did not take the trouble of inventing Stories—It was enough for him to select from those that had been invented[d] or recorded—such as had one or other, or both, of two recommendations, namely, ~~capability~~ suitableness to his purposes—and 2. there being already parts of popular tradition— ~~old acquaintances~~ names we had often heard of, and of their fortunes—and we should like to see the *man* himself/ It is the man himself that *Sh* for the first time makes us acquainted with. Lear—(omit the first scene, yet all remains)—so Shylock/

COLERIDGE'S NOTES, AS TRANSCRIBED
BY ERNEST HARTLEY COLERIDGE
VCL MS BT 8 F 61

Shakesp (Stockdale)[e] p. 443[6]—The first introduction of Falstaff the consciousness intentionality of his wit—so that when it does not flow of its own accord its absence is felt, and effort visibly employed to recall it—and the pride gratified in the power of influencing a prince of the Blood, the heir apparent by means of it—his dislike grounded on this to the Duke of Lancaster—first expressing his over-rating of wit, and his mortification whenever his own failed.

ᶜ f 40ᵛ

[d] Beginning here, five lines are indented where C wrote "For Tues" up the left edge of the ms
ᵉ EHC wrote "(I took date)"

[6] *1 Henry IV* I ii. The page-reference is to *Sh* (Ayscough), printed for John Stockdale, vol I.

p. 497—L—Fare[f] you well, Falstaff—[I] in[g] my condition
      Shall better speak of you than you deserve—
F. I would you had but the wit— it were better than your Dukedom
  Good faith, this same young [sober-][h] blooded Boy doth not love me
nor a man cannot make him laugh.[7]

---

[f] EHC inadvertently wrote ''Farewell''

[g] EHC omitted ''I'' and wrote ''In''

[h] Word supplied by the editor; EHC left a space marked by a dash

[7] *2 Henry IV* IV iii 84–9; Prince John of Lancaster (''L'') speaks the first
two lines.

LECTURE 6

DATE AND PLACE OF DELIVERY. Friday, 13 February 1818, in the Great Room of the London Philosophical Society, Fleur-de-Luce Court, Fleet Street.

SUBJECT. *Hamlet* and *Othello*. The Syllabus merely announced that Lects 4, 5, and 6 would be "On the Dramatic Works of SHAKSPEARE".

ADVERTISEMENTS. *The Times* Fri, 13 Feb: "THIS EVENING, a quarter after 8, at the Great Room of the London Philosophical Society, Fleur-de-Lis Court, Fleet-street, Mr. COLERIDGE will deliver his LECTURE on the characters of HAMLET and OTHELLO. On the Tuesday following, on Jonson, Beaumont and Fletcher, Massinger, and the Causes of the Decline of Dramatic Poetry, after the Restoration. Admission 5s." *New Times* Fri, 13 Feb: as in *The Times*, with minor variants. *M Post* Fri 13 Feb: "THIS EVENING, February 13, at a Quarter after Eight precisely . . . Mr. COLERIDGE'S LECTURE on the characters of HAMLET and OTHELLO. On Tuesday Evening, on Ben Jonson, Beaumont and Fletcher, and Massinger—Admission 5s." *M Chron* Fri, 13 Feb: as in the *M Post*, with minor variants.

TEXT. Some autograph notes for this lecture survive in BM MS Egerton 2800 ff 28–36. They are headed "Lecture VI", and C amused himself on ff 28ᵛ–30 by jotting down a mock-advertisement, which at least ties the notes firmly to this series. It runs as follows, after a heading half-deleted: "For Tuesday morning's Chronicle":
"~~Tomorrow~~ Friday Evening 13 Febʸ 1818. by permission of the London Philosophical Society, at their Great Room, Fleur de Luce Court, Fetter Lane or Fleet Street: for this Fleur de Luce, like its Goddess Godmother, Iris, has ⟨both⟩ its Exit and its Entrance Hole; but which is not so easy to divine, the one being never wiped nor the other rinsed: so that (sit, domine, reverentia!)

> The Nose of Hound and Eye of Tarsol
> Might blunder twixt its μαυθ ανδ ἄρσωλ.''

C was playing on the name of the court in which the lectures were held, the fleur-de-luce being the iris; the "Tarsol" is presumably a tercel, or hawk, and there is no need to restore the obscene joke transliterated into Greek at the end.

These notes seem to be written on odd scraps of paper, none of which bears a complete watermark. They vary a little in size, but all are small and typically measure about 110 × 95 mm; ff 28–9 are formed from one sheet folded once to give four pages of this size. The first page, f 28, has on it the title "*Hamlet*" and the letters "AG", both in the hand of Anne Gillman, wife of James Gillman, the doctor in whose house C lived from 1816 to his death. The mock-advertisement begins on f 28ᵛ and runs over on to f 30 (f 29 is blank), which also has on it the title "*Hamlet*", again in Anne Gillman's hand. The notes begin on f 31 under the heading "Lecture VI" and continue on f 31ᵛ and so through to f 36, on which they end in the middle of the page. As is the case with so many of C's notes, each page is scored through with a single line in ink running vertically down the page, perhaps made by HNC when he used these notes in *LR* II 207–13, in which they are broken up and linked with various other fragments to form a continuous sequence. The notes deal only with the opening scene of *Hamlet* and do not touch upon *Othello*, which, according to the advertisements, was also to be discussed in this lecture. However, they begin with an introduction on the significance of the titles of Shakespeare's plays, which echoes the opening remarks of Lect 4 of the series given at Bristol in 1813. That lecture was on *The Winter's Tale* and *Othello*. Lect 3 of the 1813 series was on the character of Hamlet, and this could have formed a continuation for a new introduction. The notes in BM MS Egerton 2800 ff 28–36 analyse the first scene, before the entry of Hamlet himself, whereas those for Lect 3 of the 1813 series are concerned with the development of the character of Hamlet. The scheme for the three lectures on Shakespeare announced in the advertisements for Lect 4 of the 1818 series, on the comedies, the histories, and the tragedies, roughly parallels the plan of the Bristol course, and C may well have had this in mind in constructing his Syllabus in 1818. The text printed below is based on the ms; Raysor printed the notes in *Sh C* I 37–40 (41–4).

REPORTS. No reports of this lecture have been found.

BACKGROUND AND CIRCUMSTANCES. There is no mention of this lecture in C's letters, and HCR, who attended it, says only that it "was as usual interesting". *CRB* I 219. Although C seems to have taken trouble to advertise Lects 5 and 6, the last two of the announced group of three Shakespeare lectures, it is likely that they were largely reworkings of old material and, as noted above, were based on the series given at Bristol in 1813. As the Shakespeare lectures were preceded by a letter showing a revival of his concern about Schlegel (see Lect 4 headnote: Background and Circumstances), so they were followed by another letter, addressed to William Mudford, editor of the *Courier*, on 18 Feb, again claiming priority over Schlegel in the proof that "Shakespear's Judgement was if possible still more wonderful than his Genius". *CL* IV 839. C also said in this letter that what seemed "startling Paradoxes" in his 1808 lectures on Shakespeare had since been adopted and indeed "produced as their own legitimate children" by those who most criticised him initially. Perhaps this reflects a sense on his part that he was going over ideas by now familiar to many in his audience.

LECTURE 6

RECORD OF THE LECTURE

COLERIDGE'S NOTES
BM MS EGERTON 2800 FF 31–36

*a*Lecture VI.

1. The significancy of the names of Shakespear's Plays,[1] the Twelfth Night, Midsummers Night's Dream, As you like it, Winter's Tale, when the total effect is produced by a co-ordination of the Characters, by a wreath of Flowers: but Coriolanus, Lear, Romeo and Juliet, Hamlet, Othello, Moor of Venice, when the effect arises from the subordination of all to ~~a~~ one, either as the prominent person or the principal Object. Cymbeline is the only exception and even that has its advantages ~~by~~ and prepar~~inge~~s the audience for the chaos of Time, Place, and Costume by throwing the date back into a King Olim's Reign—

*b*2. But as of more importance, so more striking is the Judgement displayed by our truly *dramatic* Poet as well as *Poet* of the Drama in the management of his first Scenes.[2]—⟨With the single exception of Cymbeline they⟩ ~~which~~ either place before ~~the~~ us ~~the causes of that which is to come in some lively effect of~~ in one glance both the Past and the Future in some effect which implies the continuance & full agency of its cause, as in the feuds and party spirit of the servants of the two Houses in the first scene of Romeo and Juliet, or in the ~~unthinking~~ *c*~~excessive~~ degrading passion ⟨of the Roman P⟩ for shews and public spectacles, and the~~ir~~ overwhelming attachment for the newest ~~or Favorite~~ successful War-chief in the Roman People already become a Populace[3] contrasted with the Jealousy ~~and and~~ of the Nobles ~~an~~ in

a f 31   *b* 31ᵛ   *c* f 32

[1] This helps to clarify C's notes on the titles of the plays made for Lect 4 (at n 2) and Lect 6 (at n 3) of the 1813 Bristol series.

[2] Here C expounds most interestingly a point he liked to stress, as in Lect 5 of the Bristol series in 1813 (sentence after n 2 and paragraph after n 20).

[3] For this distinction see *CL* III 137 and *EOT (CC)* II 432–3, in which, in an essay of 1816, C wrote of a truth being "forced on the higher and middle classes—say rather on the people at large as distinguished from mere populace . . .". See also *Friend (CC)* I 439.

Julius Caesar; or they at once commence the action so as to excite a curiosity for the explanation in the following, as in the storm of the Wind, the Waves, and the Boatswain in the Tempest, instead of antic-ipating ~~rather~~ our ~~curiou~~iosity as in most other first scenes & in too many other First *Acts*; or they act by contrast of diction suited to the characters at once to heighten the effect and yet to give a *d*naturalness to the language and rhythm of the principal characters, ~~as of Prospero and~~ either as that of Prospero and Miranda in the last instance by the appropriate lowness of the Style or as in King John by the equally appropriate stateliness of state harangue or ~~st~~ official narration, so that the after blank verse seems to belong to the rank and quality of the Speakers and not to the Poet; or they strike at once the key-note, ~~of~~ give the predominant ~~character~~ spirit of the Play, as in the Twelfth Night and in Macbeth; or the~~y compri~~ first scene comprizes all these advan-tages at once, as in Hamlet.

*e*In all the best attested stories of Ghosts and visions, as in that of Brutus, of Archbishop Cranmer, that of Benvenuto Cellini ~~as~~ recorded by himself and the vision of Galileo communicated by him to his favorite Pupil Torricelli,[4] the Ghost-seers were in a state of Cold or chilling Damp ~~under~~ from without and of anxiety inwardly—It has been with all of them as with Francesco or his Guard— ~~they were~~ alone, ~~at deep night,~~ in the depth and silence of the Night/ twas bitter cold and they were sick at heart—and not a mouse *f*stirring.[5] The attention to minute sounds, naturally associated with the recollection of minute Objects, and the more familiar and trifling they ~~become~~ the more impressive from the unusualness of their producing any impression/ at all— ~~give~~ gives a philosophic pertinency to this last image/ but it has likewise its dramatic use and purpose/ for its commonness ~~could~~ in ordinary con-versation tends to produce the sense of *reality*, and at once ~~precludes the~~ hides the Poet and yet ~~places~~ approximates the Reader or Spectator

d f 32ᵛ   *e* f 33   *f* f 33ᵛ

[4] Before the battle at Philippi Brutus saw a monstrous apparition in a dream, according to Plutarch *Lives* "Brutus" 36, 48 (LCL vi 207, 235). In his autobiog-raphy Cellini recounts his dream of a wonderful being like Christ, which helped him to avoid suicide while in prison. *The Life of Benvenuto Cellini* bk ii ch 13 tr Thomas Nugent (2 vols 1771) i 484–5, 492–500. In his life of Galileo, Vincenzo Viviani (1622–1703), his pupil and biog-rapher, reports Galileo dreaming that Copernicus stood before him when he was held in Rome by the Inquisition. C probably came across this story in J. J. Engel's "Traum des Galilei" in *Schrif-ten* (6 vols Berlin 1801–3) i 239–58, in which it is correctly attributed to Vivi-ani. C seems to have confused him with Galileo's other distinguished pupil, Evangelista Torricelli (1608–47). The vision of Thomas Cranmer, abp of Can-terbury (1489–1556), has not been traced.

[5] *Hamlet* i i 8–10.

i̶n̶ to that state in which [g]the highest poetry will appear, and in its component parts tho' not in whole composition really is, the language of Nature. I̶f̶ ̶n̶o̶w̶ If I should not speak it, I̶ I feel that I should be thinking it—the voice only is the Poet's, the words are my own—.— That Shakespear s̶u̶p̶p̶l̶i̶e̶d̶ ̶a̶ ̶b̶e̶a̶u̶t̶y̶ ̶t̶o̶ ̶t̶h̶e̶ ̶a̶c̶t̶o̶r̶ ̶i̶n̶ ̶t̶h̶e̶ meant to put an *effect* in the Actor's power in the very first words—*Who's there*—is evident from the n̶e̶x̶t̶ ̶w̶o̶r̶d̶s̶—N̶a̶y̶ impatience expressed in the words that follow—

Nay, answer me: stand and unfold yourself.[6] A brave man is never so peremptory, as when he fears that he is afraid. [h]The gradual transition from the silence—and the t̶h̶e̶ recent habit of listening in Francesco's— I think, I hear them[7]—and the more chearful call out, which a good actor would observe, in the, stand, ho! Who is there[8]—Barnardo's En-quiry after Horatio, and the repetition of his name, ⟨and in his own presence, *respect* or eagerness alike,⟩ that p̶r̶e̶p̶a̶r̶e̶s̶ implies a̶n̶d̶ ̶p̶r̶e̶p̶a̶r̶e̶s̶ f̶o̶r̶ him as one of the persons who are to appear in the fore-ground— and h̶i̶s̶ ̶o̶p̶i̶n̶i̶o̶n̶ the scepticism attributed to him—Horatio says, I̶t̶ tis but our phantasy and will not let belief take hold of him[9]—preparing us for Hamlet's after eulogy on him w̶h̶ as one whose blood and judge-ment were happily commingled—the indefiniteness of the first opening out [i]of the occasion of this anxiety

              gladness   courtesy
        WELCOME, Horatio!—welcome, good Marcellus—
        M. What has *this thing &c*[10]

rising with the next speech into Touching this dreaded Sight, twice seen of us—.[11] Horatio's confirmation of his Disbelief—and the silence with which the Scene opened again restored by the narration—the solemnity of it and the exquisite proof of the narrator's deep feeling of what he is himself about to relate by his turning off from it as from a something that is forcing him too deep into himself to the outward objects, the realities of nature that had accompanied it—Last night of all &c[12]— [j]seem to contradict t̶h̶e̶ the critical law that what is told makes a faint impression compared with what is p̶r̶e̶s̶e̶n̶t̶e̶d̶ ̶t̶o̶ ̶t̶h̶e̶ ̶E̶y̶e̶s̶ beheld, and does indeed convey t̶h̶r̶o̶ to the mind more than the eye can see/ and the interruption of the narration at the very moment, when we are most

---

                    [g] f 34   [h] f 34[v]   [i] f 35
                              [j] f 35[v]

[6] *Hamlet* I i 2.   [10] *Hamlet* I i 20–1.
[7] *Hamlet* I i 14.   [11] *Hamlet* I i 25.
[8] Ibid.   [12] *Hamlet* I i 35ff.
[9] *Hamlet* I i 23–4.

intensively listening for the sequel, and have ~~been~~ our thoughts diverted from the dreaded Sight in expectation of the desired yet almost dreaded Tale—thus giving all the suddenness, and surprize of the original appearance/—

Peace, break thee off!—look where it comes again![13]
The *k*judgement in having two of the persons present ~~who had~~ as having seen it twice before—hence naturally confirming their former opinions—/ while the Sceptic is silent—and after twice been addressed by his friends, answers with two hasty syllables—Most like—and confession of horror—*l*[14]

l The text ends halfway down the page, the rest of which is blank

[13] *Hamlet* I i 40.   It harrows me with fear and wonder.''
[14] *Hamlet* I i 44, Horatio's ''Most like.

LECTURE 7

DATE AND PLACE OF DELIVERY. Tuesday, 17 February 1818, in the Great Room of the London Philosophical Society, Fleur-de-Luce Court, Fleet Street.

SUBJECT. Ben Jonson, Beaumont and Fletcher, and Massinger considered in relation to Shakespeare. The Syllabus promised a lecture "On Ben Jonson, Beaumont and Fletcher, and Massinger; with the probable Causes of the Cessation of Dramatic *Poetry* in England with Shirley and Otway, soon after the Restoration of Charles the Second", but there is no evidence that C proceeded beyond Massinger.

ADVERTISEMENTS AND ANNOUNCEMENTS. *Courier* Tues, 17 Feb (announcement): "The subject of Mr. Coleridge's Lecture for this evening is peculiarly interesting. He proposes to consider the kind and degree of SHAKSPEARE's dramatic excellencies, compared with those of BEN JONSON, BEAUMONT and FLETCHER, MASSINGER, OTWAY, etc. These lectures, our Readers are aware, are delivered at the Great Room of the London Philosophical Society . . . the best entrance for carriages is from Fetter-lane. The price of admission is five shillings and the time of commencement precisely a quarter past *Eight*." *New Times* Tues, 17 Feb (announcement): as in the *Courier. The Times* Tues, 17 Feb (advertisement): "THIS EVENING, quarter after 8, at the Great Room of the London Philosophical Society . . . Mr COLERIDGE's SEVENTH LECTURE, on the kind and degree of Shakespeare's merits as a Dramatist, Compared with those of his contemporaries and immediate successors, Ben Jonson, Beaumont and Fletcher, Massinger, etc. Admission 5s."

TEXT. Extensive autograph notes for this lecture survive in BM Add MS 34225 ff 57–67. These are headed simply with the word "Beginning" and concern chiefly Beaumont and Fletcher and Massinger. They contain several references to Ben Jonson, which may be enough to account for HCR's reporting that C "spoke of Ben Jonson, Beaumont, and Fletcher, etc.". *CRB* I 219. C's notes are written on odd leaves of paper, all roughly the same size, but varying from 107 to 120 mm in width and from 180 to 204 mm in length, and drawn from several stocks of paper. C began on f 57, headed "Beginning", and wrote a page and a third, ending on f 57ᵛ, the rest of which is blank. He continued, with a small overlap in sense, on f 58 and so through ff 59, 60, 61, and 62, with one note on f 58ᵛ keyed by a mark into the end of a paragraph on f 59. At the end of f 62 he returned to f 61ᵛ, continuing on f 62ᵛ, the bottom third of this page being blank. He then seems to have completed the notes for a broad comparison of Shakespeare and his later contemporaries on f 63. The rest of the notes consist of a numbered sequence on Massinger, which begin on f 67ᵛ (§§ 1 to 4), proceed via f 66ᵛ, which has an addition to § 4 on it, to f 67 (headed "1. 2. 3. and 4 overleaf"), to f 65ᵛ (§§ 6 to 9), and to f 64ᵛ (§ 10). C used Gifford's edition of Massinger (1805 or 1813) for this lecture, and the notes end with a page of commentary, f 66, relating to this; the relationship of this page to the rest of C's notes for this lecture is uncertain, and he may not have intended these comments on Gifford for the lecture-room. On f 63ᵛ are some jottings that appear to be unrelated to the lecture, but belong to Lect 9.

The notes contain some cancellations, but not enough to make them difficult to use; however, C would have had to shuffle the sheets around in the lecture-room to find the right sequence. If he made separate sets of notes on Beaumont and Fletcher or Ben Jonson, these cannot now be traced. When he edited C's notes for this lecture in *LR* I 97–113, HNC incorporated into them a comment on Ben Jonson "From Mr. Green's note"; Raysor printed it after the other notes in *Misc C* 40–7. There is no reason to doubt the authenticity of Green's report, which implies that C was addressing an audience and which relates very well to the announced subject of this lecture. It is accordingly reprinted below, after C's own notes; the text of these is based on a fresh transcript of the ms.

REPORTS. No newspaper reports of this lecture have been found. For Green's report, see directly above.

BACKGROUND AND CIRCUMSTANCES. There is no mention of this lecture in C's letters. In his Diary HCR reports that C spoke of the "impurity" of Jonson and Beaumont and Fletcher, "as he had done before, and further convinced me that his circle of favourite ideas he is confined within as much as any man, and that his speculations have ceased to be living thoughts, in which he is making progress". *CRB* I 219. This comment is less than fair to C in respect of this particular lecture, for he gives more attention to Shakespeare's fellow-dramatists for their own sake than ever previously, and this is the first time, as far as is known, that he lectured primarily on them. His earlier comments in lectures (see e.g. Lect 6 of 1811–12 series) tend to be brief, and designed merely to illustrate the superiority of Shakespeare. C had borrowed the edition of Massinger ed John Monck Mason (1779) from the Bristol Library in 1797–8 (*Bristol LB* 95) and used William Gifford's edition in 1808–9, when he read and quoted from Gifford's introduction (*CN* III 3445), citing it again in Lect 6 in the 1811–12 series (at n 27). In 1806 he was reading Beaumont and Fletcher (*CN* II 2926, 2931), in 1811 he borrowed Lamb's copy of the 1679 folio of their works, and later he owned a set of *The Dramatic Works of Ben Jonson and Beaumont and Fletcher* ed Peter Whalley and George Colman (4 vols 1811) and printed for John Stockdale, marking the front flyleaf of each volume with the date of purchase, 29 Mar 1815. In the 1818 lectures, he again cited Gifford, whose edition of Massinger was reissued in 1813, and referred to Henry Weber's edition of the works of Beaumont and Fletcher (14 vols Edinburgh 1812). In other words, C had been reading in these dramatists from time to time for many years. In a letter written to Sir George Beaumont in Feb 1804 he outlined a plan to read "not carelessly tho' of course with far less care" the plays of Jonson, Beaumont and Fletcher, and Massinger "so as to see & to be able to prove what of Shakspere belonged to his Age, & was common to all the *first-rate* men of that true Saeculum aureum of English Poetry, and what is his own, & his only" (*CL* II 1054), and this may have been the main interest in his early reading of these dramatists. His lecture on them in 1818 shows that he had thought deeply about them, as is further shown by his extensive annotations— on five plays in Lamb's 1679 folio of Beaumont and Fletcher, on twenty-seven plays by these authors in his own Stockdale ed (*CM—CC*—I 362–408), and on eleven plays by Ben Jonson in this same set (*CM—CC*—III). There are no known marginalia on Massinger, but his lecture notes show that C studied a number of his plays with care. His annotations in his Stockdale set of Jonson and Beaumont and Fletcher show how thoroughly he read or re-read many of their plays, but there is little connexion between his comments there and the lecture notes printed below.

LECTURE 7

RECORDS OF THE LECTURE

COLERIDGE'S NOTES
BM ADD MS 34225 FF 57–67

*a*Beginning

A contemporary is rather an ambiguous Term, when applied to Authors.—It may simply mean that one man lived, and wrote while another was yet alive—tho' one the former should owe the better half of however deeply the former may have been indebted to the latter model as his model. There have been instances in the literary world that might remind one of a Botanist of a singular sort of parasite Plant, which rises above ground, independent and unsupported, an apparent original; but trace its roots and you will find then their fibres all terminating in the root of a⟨nother⟩ plant at an unspuspected distance—which perhaps from want of sun and general soil, and the loss of sap, has scarcely been able to peep above ground.—Or it may mean whose compositions were contemporaneous in such a sense as to preclude all likeli[hood]*b* of the one having beenorrowed from the other.—In this latter sense I shall call Ben Jonson a contemporary of Shakespear, tho' he long survived him—while I should prefer the phrase of immediate Successors for Massinger, & B. & F.—tho' these too were Shakes' Contemps in the former sense.

*c*Mr Weber, to whomse we owe the the last taste, industry, and appropriate Erudition we owe the I will [not]*d* say the best: for that would say little/ but a really good Edition of Beaumont and Fletcher, has compliment[ed]*e* the Philaster, which he himself speaks of ⟨as⟩ inferior to the Maid's Tragedy by the same writers, as but little inferior

---

a f 57; at the top, in pencil, not in C's hand: "Mr H Coleridge has had this"
b The end of the word is obscured by a smudge
c f 57v
d Word supplied by the editor
e Word completed by the editor

145

to the noblest of Shakespear's, The Lear, and Macbeth—consequently implying the equality at least of the Maid's Tragedy[1]—and another ~~still more~~ living Critic of deserved eminence &c[f]

[g]An eminent living Critic, who ~~has produced the best credentials of office in his own in his Works published in his~~ in his original works and in the manly wit, strong sterling sense, and robust Style had presented the best possible credentials of office, as chargé d'affaires of Literature in general; and who by his Edition of Massenger, a work in which there was more for an Editor to do, and in which more was actually done and well done, than in any similar work within my knowlege, has proved an especial right of authority in the appreciation of dramatic poetry, and hath, in its effect, potentially a double voice ~~in the critical Synod~~ with the public as well as in the critical Synod where as princeps senatus he possesses it by his prerogative—has affirmed that ~~in~~ Shakespear's superiority to his Contemporaries rests on his superior Wit alone, while in all the other ~~species of~~ and as I should deem higher excellences of the Drama, Character, Pathos, Depth of Thought, &c he is equalled by ~~his~~ B. & F. B. J. and Massinger/[2]

Of Wit I am engaged to treat in my IXth Lecture—it is a genus of many species—and at present I shall only say, that the Species, which is predominant in Shakespear, is so compleatly Shakespearian, and in its essence so interwoven with all his other characteristic excellencyes that I am equally incapable of comprehending, both how [h]it can be detached from his other Powers and how being disparate in kind from the wit of ~~his~~ contemporary Dramatists, it can be compared ~~with~~ with them in degree. ~~that~~ Again, ~~if~~ supposing ⟨both⟩ th~~i~~se detachment and

[f] This paragraph occupies less than half of f 57[v], the rest of which is blank

[g] f 58

[h] f 59

[1] Henry Weber's edition of *The Works of Beaumont and Fletcher* (14 vols Edinburgh) appeared in 1812. In the Introduction he says (I xiv), ''Macbeth, Lear, Julius Caesar, and Volpone, had appeared shortly before, and, though Philaster possesses excellencies little inferior to those of the plays just enumerated, they are not of so prominent and striking a nature''. He goes on to comment on the ''great excellence'' of *The Maid's Tragedy* (I xv), but does not compare the two plays.

[2] William Gifford, in his Introduction to *The Plays of Philip Massinger* (4 vols 1805, 2nd ed 1813), says: ''nor do I think it either wise or just to hold him [Shakespeare] forth as supereminent in every quality which constitutes genius; Beaumont is as sublime, Fletcher as pathetick, and Jonson as nervous . . . Indeed, if I were asked for the discriminating quality of Shakspeare's mind, that by which he is raised above all competition, above all prospect of rivalry, I should say it was WIT.'' Ed 1805 I li. C had registered his shock at this comment in Lect 6 of the 1811–12 series (at n 27); see also *CN* III 3445, in which he quotes this passage from Gifford.

then comparison practicable, I should, I confess, be rather inclined to concede the contrary: and in the most common species of wit, and in the ordinary application of the term, to yield the palm to Beaumont and Fletcher:[i] [j]whom here and henceforward I ~~men~~ take as one Poet, with two names—leaving undivided what a rare Love and still rarer congeniality had united/ ~~the Genius, which was but one in both~~ at least, I have never been able to ~~detect either~~ distinguish the presence of Fletcher ~~as distinguished from~~ during the life of ~~the latter~~ Beaumont, nor the absence of Beaumont ~~in the works of Fletcher~~ during the survival of Fletcher—

[k]But waiving, or rather deferring, this question, I protest against the remainder of the position in toto—and while I shall not, I trust, shew myself blind to the various merits of ~~of~~ Jonson, ~~Beaumont and~~ Fletcher, [l]and Massinger, or insensible of the greatness of the ~~specific~~ merits which the[y][m] possess in common, or of the specific excellences which give to each of the three ~~(for as I take B. and Fletcher but as one)~~ a worth of his own; but I confess, that one main object of this Lecture was to prove that Shakespear's eminence is his own, and his age's— as the Pine Apple, ~~and~~ the Melon, and the Gourd may grow in the same bed—nay, the same circumstances of warmth and soil may be necessary to their full developement—but does not account for the golden hue, the ambrosial flavor, the perfect shape of the Pine Apple, or the tufted Crown on its head—Would that those who would twist it off could but promise us in this instance to make it the germ of an equal Successor—

[n]What had a grammatical and logical consistency for the Ear, what could be put together and represented to the Eye, these Poets took from the Ear and Eye/ unchecked by any intuition of an inward impossibility—just as a man might ~~put~~ fit together a quarter of an orange, a quarter of an Apple, and the like of a Lemon and of a Pomegranate, and make it look like one round diverse colored fruit—but Nature who works from within, ~~who forms and not shapes,~~[3] by evolution and assimilation according to a Law, cannot do it—nor could Shakespear: for he too worked in the spirit of Nature, by evolving the Germ within by the imaginative Power according to an Idea—: for as the power of Seeing

---

[i] C marked this with a dagger to key in a passage written on f 58[v]

[j] Marked with a dagger, this passage is written at the foot of f 58[v]

[k] Returning to f 59

[l] f 60

[m] Word completed by the editor

[n] f 61

[3] C developed the "Difference of Form as proceeding and Shape as superinduced" in Lect 13 (at n 26).

is to Light, so is an Idea ⟨in Mind⟩ to a Law in Nature[4]—they are correlatives that suppose each other.—Doubtless, from mere observation, or from the occasional similarity of the writer's own ᵒcharacter, more or less will happen to be in correspondence with nature, and still more in apparent compatibility—but yet the false source is always discoverable, first by the ⟨gross⟩ contradictions to Nature in so many other parts, and secondly by the want of the impression, which Shakespear makes, that the thing said not only might have been said but that nothing else could be substituted ~~with~~ to excite the same sense of its exquisite propriety—illustrated from Iago when brought into Othello's sight—[5]

Hence Massinger and Ben Jonson both more perfect in their kind than Beaumont & Fletcher—the former more to story & affecting incidents, the ~~rat~~ latter more to manners and peculiarities & whims in language & ⟨vanities of⟩ appearance—

ᵖBut there is a diversity of the most dangerous kind here. S. shaped his characters out of the Nature within—but we cannot so safely say, out of *his own* Nature, as an *individual person.*—No! this latter is itself but a *natura naturata*[6]—an effect, a product, not a *power.* It was S's prerogative to have the *universal* which is potentially in each *particular*, opened out to him—the *homme generale*[7] not as an abstraction of observation ⟨from a variety of men;⟩ but as the Substance capable of endless modifications of which his own personal Existence was but one—& to use *this one* as the eye that beheld the other, and as the Tongue that could convey the discovery—No greater or more common vice in Dramatic Writers than to draw out of themselves—how *I* alone & in the self-sufficiency of my study as all men are apt to be proud in their

---

ᵒ f 62   ᵖ f 61ᵛ

[4] Here C developed at greater length an argument about characterisation similar to that in notes for Lect 4; but see that lecture, above (at n 32).

[5] Referring to the confrontation between Othello and Iago after the death of Desdemona; C was probably thinking of Iago's response to Othello (v ii 301–4):

> Will you, I pray, demand that demi-devil
> Why he hath thus ensnared my soul and body?
>
> *Iago.* Demand me nothing. What you know, you know.
> From this time forth I never will speak word.

[6] C defined *natura naturata* in Lect 13 of the lectures on the history of philosophy as "the aggregate of phenomena . . . nature in the passive sense", the objective world as opposed to *natura naturans*, or nature as subject, "nature in the active sense". *P Lects* (1949) 370. This distinction, central in C's thinking, is developed further in Lect 13; see below (at n 11).

[7] In *Friend* (1818) C wrote that he was adopting "the bold but happy phrase of a late ingenious French writer" (Rousseau) in contrasting "the homme *particuliere*" with "l'homme *generale*". See *Friend (CC)* I 490, also *P Lects* Lect 11 (1949) 332.

*q*Dreams, should *like* to be talking—King?—I am the King who would bully the Kings—*Tut!*—Shakespear in composing had no *I* but the I representative.—Bertoldo in Massinger &c &c—[8]

*r*B. & F.—The fair maid of the Inn!—!
Thierry & Theodoret—An other!—a *Case* for a Mad-doctor—[9]
*s*I ~~will~~ can with less pain admit a fault in Shakespear, than beg an excuse for it. I will not therefore attempt to palliate the grossness that actually exists by the ~~manners~~ customs of his age or by the far greater coarseness of all his Contemporaries—excepting Spencer who is himself not wholly blameless tho' nearly so[10]—for I have placed his merits in being of no Age. But I would clear away what is clearly not his (as the Porter in Macbeth)[11]—what is [his]*r* in manners only—& what is derived from association with *crimes* (foul thoughts & sentiments)[12]

*u*1 Massinger—Vein of *Satire* on the *Times*—i.e. not as in Shakespear the Natures evolving themselves according to their incidental dispro-

q f 62v
r This is written an inch below the line above, and the bottom two inches of the page are blank
s f 63
t Word supplied by the editor
u f 67v

[8] In *The Maid of Honour* Bertoldo is the impatient and overbearing natural brother of Roberto, King of Sicily, and the play opens with his bullying the King into allowing his subjects to make war on behalf of the Duke of Urbino. C expands this reference in his § 3, below.

[9] The references here are to Fletcher's tragicomedy *The Fair Maid of the Inn* and tragedy *Thierry and Theodoret*. The latter play is a "*Case* for a Mad-doctor" because of the extravagant behaviour of some of the main characters; the action turns on the attempts by two brothers, both kings, to restrain the vices of their mother, whose "Gallant", Protaldye, stabs Theodoret before she poisons Thierry. Cf C's marginal note on the Preface to Peter Whalley's ed (1811) of Ben Jonson: "Jonson's Personæ are too often not Characters but Derangements: the hopeless Patients of a Mad-doctor . . .". *CM (CC)* III. See also Lect 6 of the 1811–12 series (at n 27).

[10] Cf Lect 8 of the 1811–12 series, in

which C said that only Shakespeare and Sidney among their contemporaries "entertained a just conception of the female character" (sentence before n 5). In his 1856 ed Collier added a note that "in conversing on this very point at a subsequent period . . . Coleridge made a willing exception in favour of Spenser". *Sh C* II 113n (149n). But Collier may have been recalling this lecture; see n 11, below.

[11] Cf C's annotation in his set of *Sh* (Theobald) VI 310–11: "This low Porter Soliloquy I believe written for the Mob by some other Hand . . .". *CM (CC)* IV. Collier heard this lecture and says that C "admitted there was something of Shakespeare in 'the primrose way to the everlasting bonfire' ". *The Works of William Shakespeare* (8 vols 1842–4) VII 96.

[12] A point C repeatedly stressed; see Lect 6 of the 1811–12 series, in which he developed a distinction between manners and morals.

portions, from excess, deficiency, or mislocation of ~~the component~~ one or more of ~~the component~~ elements—but what is attributed to them by others.—

2 His excellent metre—a better model for Dramatists in general (even tho' a dramatic Taste existed in the Frequenters of the Stage, and could be gratified in the present size and management ~~of our~~ (or rather [mis]management)^v of our two patent Theatres.[)]$^{w\,13}$

3 Impropriety, indecorum of Demeanor in his favorite Characters: as in Bertoldo, who is a *swaggerer*—who talks to his Sovereign what no sovereign could endure, & to gentlemen what no gentleman would answer but by pulling his nose—[14]

4. Shakespear's Sir Andrew Ague-Cheek & Osric displayed by others—in the course of social intercourse, as by the mode of their performing some office in which they are employed—but Massinger SYLLI comes forward to declare himself a fool, ad arbitrium Authoris,[15] and so the diction always needs the subintelligitur[16] (the man looks *as if he thought so & so*) expressed in the language of the satirist not of the man himself—Ex. gr. V. 3 p. 29. ASTUTIO. So FULGENTIO. The Author mixes his own feelings & judgements concerning him—but the man himself, till mad, fights up against them & betrays by the attempt to modify.—[17]

^{x}Add to N° 4.

An activity & copiousness of thought, Image and expression which belongs not to Sylli but to a man of wit making himself merry with his character

^{y}1. 2. 3. and 4 overleaf

^{v} C inadvertently omitted the first syllable
^{w} Closing bracket supplied by the editor
^{x} This addition is written at the top of f 66^v, the rest of which is blank
^{y} f 67

[13] Drury Lane and Covent Garden, which operated under letters patent granted by Charles II in 1662.

[14] See n 8, above.

[15] Sylli is a foolish lover in *The Maid of Honour*, who is made to display his folly on his first entry in I ii, "as the decision of the Author".

[16] "An unexpressed or implied addition to a statement". *OED*. See also *BL* ch 12 (*CC*) I 267. C means that Massinger has to provide pointers in his own voice to indicate how dialogue is to be understood rather than in the language appropriate to the character. He gives as an example vol III r p 29 of Gifford's edi-

tion, i.e. *The Maid of Honour* II i 33–6, in which he takes Astutio to be speaking in the author's voice in the heavy irony of his lines agreeing with the King that perjury is allowable. In an annotation on Ben Jonson C similarly objected to the playwright speaking in the character's voice, calling it "ventriloquism": "Ventriloquism, because Sejanus is a Puppet out of wch the Poet makes his own voice appear to come.—" *CM (CC)* III. See also Lect 9 of the 1811–12 series (at n 18).

[17] C returns to the character of Sylli, who is "mad" only in the sense of being "desperate" at IV v 27.

5. Utter want of *preparation*—as in Camiola, the Maid of Honor[18]—Why? because the Dramatis Personæ were all planned, *each by itself*—but in Sh.—the Play is a *syngenesia*,[19] each has indeed a life of its own & is an individuum of itself; but yet an organ to the whole—as the Heart & the Brain—&c/. *The* Heart &c of *that* particular Whole.—S. a comparative Anatomist.

Hence Massinger & all indeed but Sh. take a dislike to their own characters, and spite themselves upon them by making them talk like *fools* or *monsters*—So Fulgentio in his visit to CAMIOLA.[20] Hence too the continued *Flings* at Kings, Courtiers, and all the favorites of Fortune, like one who had enough of intellect to see the *disproportion* & injustice of his own inferiority in the share of the good things of life, but not genius enough to rise above it & forget himself—envy democratic. B. and F. the same vice in the opposite Pole—Servility of Sentiment—partizanship of the monarchical Faction—[21]

˙6. From the want of Character, of a guiding Point, in Massinger's Character[s]*ᵃ* you never know what they are about.

7. Soliloquies = with all the connections and arrangements that have no other purpose but ~~that of ea~~ our fear lest the person to whom we speak should ~~mis~~ not understand us.

8.—Neither a one effect produced by the spirit of the whole, as in "as you like it"—nor by any one indisputably prominent as [in]*ᵇ* in the Hamlet—"Which you like, Gentlemen!"—[22]

9 Unnaturally irrational passions that deprive the Reader of all sound interest in the Character, as in Mathias in the Picture—[23]

˙ f 65ᵛ

ᵃ The end of the word is obscured where the leaf is tipped in
ᵇ Word supplied by the editor

[18] C is thinking perhaps of her sudden reversal in III iii. In Act I she refuses to marry Bertoldo, in spite of her love for him, but then he is taken prisoner, and she determines "to ransome him, and receive him | Into my bosom, as my lawful husband". III iii 199–200.

[19] C explains his meaning; the word "syngenesia" is a term from botany, referring in the system of Linnaeus to the class of plants in which the stamens are coherent with the anthers, or pollen-bearing elements.

[20] In II ii Fulgentio attempts to win Camiola, the maid of honour, by threats and, when she rejects him, goes off saying he will proclaim her a whore.

[21] See Lect 1 of the 1818–19 series (at n 25). Cf also C's note in his copy of the Stockdale ed of Beaumont and Fletcher (1811): "Massinger was a Democrat, B + F. the most servile jure divino Royalist". *CM (CC)* I 380; cf I 389.

[22] Perhaps C was thinking of I v in *Hamlet*, in which Hamlet, in his "wild and whirling words" after seeing the Ghost, twice addresses his companions as "gentlemen", though not with this phrase.

[23] *The Picture* follows *The Maid of Honour* in vol III of Gifford's ed. In Act IV Mathias, the hero, suddenly abandons his devotion to his wife Sophia merely

*c*10 The comic Scenes in Massinger not only do not harmonize with the tragic, not only interrupt the feeling, but degrade the characters that are to form ~~in the~~ any Part in the action of the Piece so as to render them unfit for any *tragic interest*—as when a gentleman is insulted by a mere Black-guard—it is the same as if any other accident of nature had occurred, as if a Pig had run made his horse throw him/—*d*

*e*Have I not over-rated Gifford's Edition of Massinger?—*Not* if I have, as but just is, main reference to the restitution of the Text; but *yes* perhaps, if I were talking of the *Notes*. These are more often wrong than right. So Vol. 3. p. 6. "A Gentleman yet no Lord." G. supposes a transposition of the Press for No Gentleman yet a Lord.—But this would have no connection with what follows—and we have only to recollect, that Lord means a Lord of Lands—to see that the after lines are explanatory—He is a man of high birth, but no ~~Estate~~ landed Property/ as to [the]*f* former, he is a distant branch of the Blood Royal—as to the latter, his whole Estate lies "In a narrow compass, the King's Ear"—[24]

P. 11.*g* My *ear* deceives me if Mason's "initiation" be not the right word.[25] In short, imitation is utterly impertinent to all that follows— he tells Antonio that he had been initiated into manners suited to the Court by two or three sound beatings—& that a similar experience would be equally useful for his initiation into the Camp.—Not a word of his imitation.

c f 64ᵛ
d This paragraph ends 2½″ from the foot of the page, the rest of which is blank
e f 66
f Word supplied by the editor
g Change of pen; C perhaps added this paragraph at the foot of f 66 later

upon the report that she is false in "consent and wishes" (IV i 38), though not in fact, and transfers his affections to Honoria, whom he has hitherto spurned.

[24] C refers to a note by Gifford relating to *The Maid of Honour* I i 23–6; the relevant lines are

A gentleman, yet no lord. He hath some drops
Of the king's blood running in his veins, derived
Some ten degrees off. His revenue lies
In a narrow compass, the king's ear . . .

[25] This refers to Gifford's vol III p 11, *The Maid of Honour* I i 88–92; the rel-

evant lines are:

Gasparo.   I must tell you
In private, as you are my princely friend,
I do not like such fiddlers.
Bertoldo.   No! they are useful
For your imitation; I remember you,
When you came first to the court . . .

"Initiation", first suggested by John Monck Mason in his ed of Massinger (1779), is the reading adopted by Massinger's latest editors, P. W. Edwards and Colin Gibson (5 vols Oxford 1976) I 124.

REPORT BY JOSEPH HENRY GREEN
FROM *LR* I 98–100

It cannot be proved that this relates to Lect 7, but C is not known to have lectured on Ben Jonson on any other occasion.

Ben Jonson is original;[26] he is, indeed, the only one of the great dramatists of that day who was not either directly produced, or very greatly modified, by Shakspeare. In truth, he differs from our great master in every thing—in form and in substance—and betrays no tokens of his proximity. He is not original in the same way as Shakspeare is original; but after a fashion of his own, Ben Jonson is most truly original.

The characters in his plays are, in the strictest sense of the term, abstractions. Some very prominent feature is taken from the whole man, and that single feature or humour[27] is made the basis upon which the entire character is built up. Ben Jonson's *dramatis personæ* are almost as fixed as the masks of the ancient actors; you know from the first scene—sometimes from the list of names—exactly what every one of them is to be. He was a very accurately observing man; but he cared only to observe what was external or open to, and likely to impress, the senses. He individualizes, not so much, if at all, by the exhibition of moral or intellectual differences, as by the varieties and contrasts of manners, modes of speech and tricks of temper; as in such characters as Puntarvolo, Bobadill, etc.[28]

I believe there is not one whim or affectation in common life noted in any memoir of that age which may not be found drawn and framed in some corner or other of Ben Jonson's dramas; and they have this merit, in common with Hogarth's prints,[29] that not a single circumstance

[26] Most of C's earlier comments on dramatists of this period were designed to show "the immense Superiority of Shakespear over his contemporaries". Marginal note on *The Fall of Sejanus*: Jonson *Dramatic Works* (1811) I 200–1: *CM (CC)* III. This is the first lecture in which he examined Jonson in some detail; but see Lect 5 of the 1811–12 series (at n 29) and Lect 6 of the 1813 series at Bristol (at n 6).

[27] C does not seem to have developed here the historical account of the origin of the term "humour" he gave in Lect

6 of the 1813 series (sentence after n 6).

[28] Puntarvolo is the vainglorious Knight in *Every Man Out of His Humour* (acted 1599, printed 1600), and Bobadil the braggart captain in *Every Man in His Humour* (acted 1598, printed 1601). Cf Lect 5 of the 1811–12 series (at n 29).

[29] C greatly admired Hogarth as one of England's "great men", so this is praise indeed of Jonson; see *CM (CC)* I 366 (an annotation on Beaumont and Fletcher) and II 816 (an annotation on Thomas Fuller *The Worthies of England*).

is introduced in them which does not play upon, and help to bring out, the dominant humour or humours of the piece. Indeed I ought very particularly to call your attention to the extraordinary skill shown by Ben Jonson in contriving situations for the display of his characters. In fact, his care and anxiety in this matter led him to do what scarcely any of the dramatists of that age did—that is, invent his plots. It is not a first perusal that suffices for the full perception of the elaborate artifice of the plots of the Alchemist and the Silent Woman;—that of the former is absolute perfection for a necessary entanglement, and an unexpected, yet natural, evolution.[30]

Ben Jonson exhibits a sterling English diction, and he has with great skill contrived varieties of construction; but his style is rarely sweet or harmonious, in consequence of his labour at point and strength being so evident. In all his works, in verse or prose, there is an extraordinary opulence of thought; but it is the produce of an amassing power in the author, and not of a growth from within. Indeed a large proportion of Ben Jonson's thoughts may be traced to classic or obscure modern writers, by those who are learned and curious enough to follow the steps of this robust, surly, and observing dramatist.

[30] C may have had Aristotle *Poetics* ch 18 in mind, in which it is said that every tragedy has a complication and an unravelling (δέσις and λύσις); if so, his terms provide a better correspondence with the Greek than most English translations.

LECTURE 8

DATE AND PLACE OF DELIVERY. Friday, 20 February 1818, in the Great
Room of the London Philosophical Society, Fleur-de-Luce Court, Fleet Street.

SUBJECT. Cervantes and *Don Quixote*. This was more or less in accordance
with the Syllabus, which promised an account "Of the Life and *all* the Works
of CERVANTES, but chiefly of his Don Quixote. The Ridicule of Knight-Errantry
shewn to have been but a secondary Object in the Mind of the Author, and not
the principal Cause of the Delight which the Work continues to give in all
Nations, and under all the Revolutions of Manners and Opinions."

ADVERTISEMENTS AND ANNOUNCEMENTS. *Courier* Thurs, 19 Feb (announcement): "Mr. Coleridge's Friday Evening's Lecture excites much curiosity and expectation, from the peculiar interest of the subject, namely the *Life*
of the great CERVANTES, a critical account of *all* his works, but chiefly of his
Don Quixote. Mr COLERIDGE has already avowed his opinion, that the ridicule
of Knight errantry was but a very secondary object with the author, and very
far from being the principal cause or true Solution of the delight which the *Don
Quixote* gives and has given in all nations and under all the revolutions of
manners and opinions. The lecture will commence at a quarter after Eight
precisely, at the Great Room, in Fleur-de-luce-court, Fleet-street." *New Times*
Fri, 20 Feb (announcement): substantially as in the *Courier*, with minor variants
and one addition at the beginning of the second sentence: "Mr. COLERIDGE has
already, as our Readers may recollect, from the Prospectus of the Course,
announced his opinion . . .". *The Times* Fri, 20 Feb (advertisement): "THIS
EVENING, Mr. COLERIDGE'S LECTURE on the LIFE and ALL the WORKS OF
CERVANTES . . ." (the rest as in the Syllabus, with the addition of the place
of delivery and the admission charge of 5s). *M Chron* Fri, 20 Feb (advertisement): "THIS EVENING, Mr COLERIDGE'S LECTURE on the LIFE of the GREAT
CERVANTES, on ALL his Writings, but chiefly on the Don Quixote, and the true
cause of the delight which this immortal work gives and has given in all countries
and languages. At the Great Room of the London Philosophical Society . . .".

TEXT. No autograph notes for this lecture have been found. HNC included in
LR I 113–31 a substantial text for this lecture, which was reprinted in *Misc C*
98–110. This appears to be based partly on notes prepared for it, partly on
marginalia, and partly on C's notes for Lect 7 of the 1819 series written in N
29 (*CN* III 4503; see headnote to Lect 7: Text). The very full report of this
lecture in the *New Times* provides confirmation that the "observations on particular passages" printed in *LR* I 121–30 (*Misc C* 103–10) and the brief "Summary on Cervantes" that follows (*LR* I 130–1, *Misc C* 110) did not form part
of the lecture, and these are not reprinted here. The passages HNC incorporated
from notes for Lect 7 of the 1819 course have also been omitted, and what
remains from *LR* I 113–14, 115–21 (*Misc C* 98, 99–103) may with some
confidence be linked with the 1818 series.

REPORTS. The *New Times* Mon, 23 Feb, published a full and sympathetic
report of this lecture, headed "From a Correspondent", and this is reprinted
below. The lecture was also noticed briefly in the *M Post* Sat, 21 Feb, as
follows: "Mr. COLERIDGE'S LECTURES.—Last night Mr. COLERIDGE delivered
his eighth Lecture to a very crowded audience. The subject was the genius of

Cervantes and the object which that greatest ornament of Spanish literature had in view when he wrote *Don Quixote*.''

BACKGROUND AND CIRCUMSTANCES. A letter is extant, written Wed, 18 Feb, to William Mudford, editor of the *Courier*, in which C solicited ''the insertion of rather a more circumstantial paragraph'' (*CL* IV 840) concerning his lecture on Cervantes. He went on to supply the wording of the notice, which duly appeared among other announcements on p 3 of the *Courier* the day before he gave the lecture. Presumably C wrote in similar terms to John Stoddart of the *New Times*, since an announcement in similar terms appeared in that newspaper on the day of the lecture. C seemed to be particularly confident about the novelty of what he was going to say and commented in the letter to Mudford: ''My next Friday's Lecture will, if I do not grossly *flatter-blind* myself, be interesting and the points of view not only original, but new to the Audience.'' *CL* IV 839. On the day before he was due to lecture, C wrote to Thomas Boosey, Jr, the bookseller, to beg the loan of a set of the complete works of Cervantes in Spanish; he went on: ''I mean to purchase the Work—which indeed I shall be little afraid to do at a moderate price, should my tomorrow's Lecture make the impression which (my hopes flatter me) it will''. *CL* IV 841. There is no evidence to show whether C was successful in his application to Boosey, but he may have been seeking to prepare himself for the fulfilment of his announced intention to lecture on ''*all* the Works'' of Cervantes. Although the lecture was mainly on *Don Quixote*, the newspaper report shows that he commented also on the story *Persilis and Sigismunda*. C was using for his commentary on *Don Quixote* the translation by Charles Jarvis (4 vols 1809), which he also used for Lect 7 in the series he gave in 1819. The notes in N 29 for that lecture were prepared for the occasion, since they are headed with the date 25 Mar 1819, but other entries in this notebook relate to the 1818 lectures (see the headnote, under Text, to Lect 3, above, and *CN* III 4501 and n). This may have encouraged HNC, who in *LR* made no reference to the 1819 lectures, to incorporate passages from notes for the 1819 lecture into the material he printed as relating to Lect 8 of the 1818 series. He may also have done it to swell out notes that could only have related to a part of the lecture and that C must have expanded in the lecture-room.

The report in the *New Times* is laudatory and suggests that C's lecture had quite an impact on, at any rate, some members of his audience. HCR seems to have found it dull and unoriginal, but long acquaintance had made C's ideas familiar to him. Also the comments of the party sitting in front of him may have made it difficult for him to give all his attention to it. He wrote in his diary (*CRB* I 219): ''We found the lecture-room fuller than I had ever seen it, and were forced to take back seats, but it was a pleasure to Mrs. Pattison to sit behind Sir James Mackintosh. He was with Serjeant Bosanquet and Rolland and some genteel woman. The party was, however, in a satirical mood, and made sneering remarks, as it seemed, throughout the lecture. Indeed, Coleridge was not in one of his happiest moods to-night. His subject was Cervantes, but he was more than usually prosing, and his tone peculiarly drawling. His digressions on the nature of insanity were carried too far, and his remarks on the book but old and by him often repeated.'' HCR's comments show that two eminent lawyers, Sir James Mackintosh, who was acquainted with C, and attended lectures by him in 1812 and 1818–19, and John, later Sir John Bosanquet, who became Serjeant-at-Law in 1814, were present, as was Mrs. William Pattison, a friend of HCR's. "Rolland" is mentioned nowhere else by HCR and has not been identified. It may well be a slip for "Holland", for John Holland, editor of the *New Monthly Magazine*, had very recently asked C to contribute to it; C's letter of acknowledgement is dated 14 Feb (*CL* IV 838; and see also *CN* III 4464 and n), and Holland's attendance at one or two of C's lectures could have been one result of their exchange of courtesies. The report in the *New Times* suggests that C prepared carefully for this lecture and earned the applause he received; this testimony, and C's own claim to be saying something new, may perhaps be trusted on this occasion rather than HCR's comment. It is notable that the attendance was high at this lecture, but whether this was owing to C's exertions in advertising it or because of the popularity of the subject is not clear. C had lectured previously on *Don Quixote* in his first course at Bristol in 1814, but nothing is known of what he said on that occasion; see Lect 6 of that series.

LECTURE 8

RECORDS OF THE LECTURE

COLERIDGE'S NOTES, AS EDITED BY
HENRY NELSON COLERIDGE
FROM *LR* I 113–14, 115-21

DON QUIXOTE.
CERVANTES.

Born at Madrid, 1547;—Shakespeare, 1564; both put off mortality on the same day, the 23rd of April, 1616,—the one in the sixty-ninth, the other in the fifty-second, year of his life. The resemblance in their physiognomies is striking, but with a predominance of acuteness in Cervantes, and of reflection in Shakspeare, which is the specific difference between the Spanish and English characters of mind.[1] . . .

Cervantes's own preface to Don Quixote is a perfect model of the gentle, every where intelligible, irony in the best essays of the Tatler and the Spectator.[2] Equally natural and easy, Cervantes is more spirited than Addison; whilst he blends with the terseness of Swift, an exquisite flow and music of style, and above all, contrasts with the latter by the sweet temper of a superior mind, which saw the follies of mankind, and was even at the moment suffering severely under hard mistreatment; and yet seems every where to have but one thought as the undersong— "Brethren! with all your faults I love you still!"—or as a mother that chides the child she loves, with one hand holds up the rod, and with the other wipes off each tear as it drops!

Don Quixote was neither fettered to the earth by want, nor holden

---

[1] A comparison suggested probably by the "Life of Cervantes" prefixed to Jarvis's translation of *Don Quixote*, which gives the dates of Cervantes' birth and death, "being then in his 69th year", and describes Cervantes as "eagle-faced, his forehead smooth and open, his eyes lively, nose hooked . . . He wore his mustachios very large, and his beard very thick" (I xvii).

[2] Included in Jarvis, I xix–xxvii, and well described by C, this preface is on the difficulty of writing prefaces and why no lists of authorities are provided, etc.

in its embraces by wealth;—of which, with the temperance natural to his country, as a Spaniard, he had both far too little, and somewhat too much, to be under any necessity of thinking about it. His age too, fifty, may be well supposed to prevent his mind from being tempted out of itself by any of the lower passions;—while his habits, as a very early riser and a keen sportsman, were such as kept his spare body in serviceable subjection to his will,[3] and yet by the play of hope that accompanies pursuit, not only permitted, but assisted, his fancy in shaping what it would. Nor must we omit his meagerness and entire featureliness, face and frame, which Cervantes gives us at once: "It is said that his surname was *Quixada* or *Quesada*", &c.[4]—even in this trifle showing an exquisite judgment;—just once insinuating the association of *lantern-jaws* into the reader's mind,[5] yet not retaining it obtrusively like the names in old farces and in the Pilgrim's Progress—but taking for the regular appellative one which had the no meaning of a proper name in real life, and which yet was capable of recalling a number of very different, but all pertinent, recollections, as old armour, the precious metals hidden in the ore, &c.[6] Don Quixote's leanness and featureliness are happy exponents of the excess of the formative or imaginative in him, contrasted with Sancho's plump rotundity, and recipiency of external impression.

He has no knowledge of the sciences or scientific arts which give to the meanest portions of matter an intellectual interest, and which enable the mind to decypher in the world of the senses the invisible agency—that alone, of which the world's phenomena are the effects and manifestations,—and thus, as in a mirror, to contemplate its own reflex, its life in the powers, its imagination in the symbolic forms, its moral instincts in the final causes, and its reason in the laws of material nature: but—estranged from all the motives to observation from self-interest—the persons that surround him too few and too familiar to enter into any connection with his thoughts, or to require any adaptation of his conduct to their particular characters or relations to himself—his judgment lies fallow, with nothing to excite, nothing to employ it. Yet,—and here is the point, where genius even of the most perfect kind, allotted but to few in the course of many ages, does not preclude the necessity in part,

[3] *Don Quixote* pt 1 ch 1 tr Jarvis (1809) I 2, "The age of our gentleman bordered upon fifty years. He was of a robust constitution, spare-bodied, of a meagre visage, a very early riser, and a keen sportsman."

[4] Citing Jarvis's tr I 2.

[5] This is from Jarvis's note, I 283: " 'Quixana'. derived from the Spanish word Quixas, *lantern-jaws*".

[6] C was thinking of the Spanish *quijote*, or thigh-armour, and *quilate*, meaning the degree of purity of gold, from *quilatar*, "to assay gold or silver".

and in part counterbalance the craving by sanity of judgment, without which genius either cannot be, or cannot at least manifest itself,—the dependency of our nature asks for some confirmation from without, though it be only from the shadows of other men's fictions.

Too uninformed, and with too narrow a sphere of power and opportunity to rise into the scientific artist, or to be himself a patron of art, and with too deep a principle and too much innocence to become a mere projector, Don Quixote has recourse to romances:—

His curiosity and extravagant fondness herein arrived at that pitch, that he sold many acres of arable land to purchase books of knight-errantry, and carried home all he could lay hands on of that kind! C. 1.[7]

The more remote these romances were from the language of common life, the more akin on that very account were they to the shapeless dreams and strivings of his own mind;—a mind, which possessed not the highest order of genius which lives in an atmosphere of power over mankind, but that minor kind which, in its restlessness, seeks for a vivid representative of its own wishes, and substitutes the movements of that objective puppet for an exercise of actual power in and by itself. The more wild and improbable these romances were, the more were they akin to his will, which had been in the habit of acting as an unlimited monarch over the creations of his fancy! Hence observe how the startling of the remaining common sense, like a glimmering before its death, in the notice of the impossible-improbable of Don Belianis, is dismissed by Don Quixote as impertinent:—

He had some doubt as to the dreadful wounds which Don Belianis gave and received: for he imagined, that notwithstanding the most expert surgeons had cured him, his face and whole body must still be full of seams and scars. *Nevertheless* he commended in his author the concluding his book with a promise of that unfinishable adventure! C. 1.[8]

Hence also his first intention to turn author; but who, with such a restless struggle within him, could content himself with writing in a remote village among apathists and ignorants? During his colloquies with the village priest and the barber surgeon,[9] in which the fervour of critical controversy feeds the passion and gives reality to its object— what more natural than that the mental striving should become an eddy?— madness may perhaps be defined as the circling in a stream which should be progressive and adaptive: Don Quixote grows at length to be a man

[7] Jarvis's tr I 2 (var).
[8] Ibid I 3; the italics are C's. Don Quixote at this point is reading the romances of Feliciano de Silva, in which

he finds the story of Don Belianis.
[9] These take place in ch 1, I 3–4; Don Quixote has "quite lost his wits" on p 4.

out of his wits; his understanding is deranged; and hence without the least deviation from the truth of nature, without losing the least trait of personal individuality, he becomes a substantial living allegory, or personification of the reason and the moral sense, divested of the judgment and the understanding. Sancho is the converse. He is the common sense without reason or imagination; and Cervantes not only shows the excellence and power of reason in Don Quixote, but in both him and Sancho the mischiefs resulting from a severance of the two main constituents of sound intellectual and moral action. Put him and his master together, and they form a perfect intellect; but they are separated and without cement; and hence each having a need of the other for its own completeness, each has at times a mastery over the other. For the common sense, although it may see the practical inapplicability of the dictates of the imagination or abstract reason, yet cannot help submitting to them. These two characters possess the world, alternately and interchangeably the cheater and the cheated. To impersonate them, and to combine the permanent with the individual, is one of the highest creations of genius, and has been achieved by Cervantes and Shakspeare, almost alone.

REPORT IN THE *NEW TIMES* MONDAY,
23 FEBRUARY 1818, HEADED
''FROM A CORRESPONDENT''

I can claim little merit and little singularity in having ever been an admirer of the immortal work of Cervantes. When, therefore, I learnt, that a public lecture was to be given on the works of this admired genius, in the course of a series delivered by Mr. Coleridge, it is needless to say that my curiosity was considerably excited by the celebrity both of the author and of the lecturer. I attended this exhibition on Friday evening; and if your columns afford room for my observations on it, I shall be happy to lay them before your readers.

The professed object of the lecturer was to shew that in the *Don Quixote*, the ridicule of Knight Errantry was but a secondary object in the mind of the author, and not the principal cause of the delight, which this work continues to give, in all nations, and under all the revolutions of manners and opinions. Some people might have thought this a paradox. I own, I did not: and I presume that men of great genius and talents thought it at least a paradox incapable of ingenious illustration; for among the company present, I noticed several distinguished literary characters, such as the author of *The Pleasures of Memory*, the author of *Mandeville*, etc. etc.[10]

Every nation, as well as every individual, has certain distinct privileges in the society of mankind, to infringe on which would be a breach of the laws that bind them together. In the learned, as well as in the other classes which compose this great union, these laws, which may be unknown to the other parts of the society, must not be broken in upon by any author, however great his fame, who would not have the literary republic in arms against him. To present the character of *Don Quixote* in a new light, 200 years after the death of its author, to treat this work as it were with an innovating spirit unknown to the country in which it is indigenous, seemed an attempt pregnant with danger, yet, at the same time, interesting to curiosity; nor was this latter feeling ungratified. Mr. Coleridge commenced his lecture with a striking comparison between our great countryman, Shakespeare, and the extraordinary Castilian. The similarity of their features, as delivered down to us by sculpture and painting—the age in which they lived—the difficulties under which they laboured—their birth within a few years of each other—the heaven-gifted mental powers which each enjoyed, their union in death as well as in merit, struck me powerfully. Both relinquished a world which they delighted on the same day in the same year, 23rd of April, 1616. The life of the Spanish writer, as Mr. C. well expressed it, is covered with clouds, like those of the other writers of that time. But in the description of Cervantes and his studies, his entrance from necessity into the army, his transcendent valour in the glorious battle of Lepanto, his subsequent captivity, and his release from the slavery of Algiers, Mr. C. gave much pleasure.[11] Of the Comedies, which the same cruel fate that compelled Dryden to relinquish the noble heroic poem of which he had formed the outline,[12] obliged the impoverished Cervantes to present to his country, as the

[10] Samuel Rogers, whose poem *The Pleasures of Memory* first appeared in 1792, and William Godwin, who published the novel *Mandeville* in 1817.

[11] The "Life of Cervantes" in Jarvis's tr I iii–xviii, describes his military career, how he was wounded at the Battle of Lepanto, remained a soldier for some years, was taken captive by Moors in 1575, and was released from slavery in "Argel" in 1580 at the intercession of his mother and sister, so C may have

based his account on this.

[12] In "A Discourse Concerning the Original and Progress of Satire" (1693) Dryden said that he had intended to make his life's work an epic on the theme of King Arthur or Edward the Black Prince, but "being encouraged only with fair words by King Charles II", and with his "little salary ill paid, and no prospect of a future subsistence", he abandoned the project. See *Essays of John Dryden* ed Ker II 38.

first fruits of his genius, but little mention was made. On *Persilis* and *Sigismunda*,[13] Mr. C. made an excellent observation, when he offered to the view Cervantes himself as the hero of the poem, and the lady to whom he afterwards was united as the heroine, and declared that in the feelings of the Spanish cavalier, and of his enamoured fair, were described the sensations of the author.

But these were but preliminary observations: the great question remained to be solved. Was the *Don Quixote* a mere ridicule of Knight Errantry? Certainly not, said the Lecturer, for a very simple reason. A great genius would not direct his powers against a thing which never had any existence. Knight Errantry is a mere fiction; it is unknown to real history.

But was not this work a ridicule of the books of Knight Errantry? To a certain degree it was. Cervantes saw that the rage which his countrymen had for the reading of these books, took them off from all sober study, and created in them a wild and objectless spirit of adventure, of which they to this day rue the consequences; and he accordingly exposed, with great force of wit and humour, the extravagant style and absurd subjects of many of those works. Yet it is clear that he did not wish to annihilate, but only to *weed out* these works, rooting up the "things rank and gross in nature",[14] and suffering the beauteous plants and lovely flowers to remain.

Yet, if even this had been his sole object, how would it have interested us, who know little of Amadis de Gaul beyond his name, and never read a page of the works of Feliciano de Silva?[15] *Don Quixote* must have something else to recommend him to our sympathies: and truly so he has: he is a symbol and exponant of human nature under the perversion of one of its chief faculties, the judgment, yet retaining what is most aimiable and interesting in its moral characteristics; in short, *Don Quixote*, in spite of his absolute madness, which is at the most only ludicrous, claims our love and respect, because he is truly aimiable, and a perfect gentleman.

Here the lecturer entered into some curious remarks on madness,[16]

[13] *Persilis y Sigismunda*, the last work of Cervantes, was published posthumously in 1617; it was translated into English in 1619 and again in 1741.

[14] Shakespeare *Hamlet* I ii 136.

[15] The authorship of the first four books of the Spanish romance *Amadis de Gaula*, published 1508, remains uncertain. Feliciano de Silva (d 1560) wrote bks 7, 9, 10, and 11 of the continuation of the romance, which RS translated in an abridged version in 1803. C is thinking of *Don Quixote* bk 1 ch 1, in which the hero reads above all in the books of knight-errantry written by de Silva because, as Cervantes makes clear by the examples Don Quixote quotes, their style was inflated and absurd.

[16] See Lect 7 of the 1819 series (sentences following n 1).

which he distinguished into four species:—1st, Frenzy, wherein the whole physical and mental organisation is disturbed—2d. Hypochondriasis, wherein a man is *out of his senses*, feeling as if he were made of glass, or as if his nose were too big to enter a door, etc.—3d, Fatuity, where a man *loses his reason*, and can no more argue on causes and consequences than an infant—And, 4thly, such madness as that of *Don Quixote*, where the senses are perfect, and the reasoning faculty is accurate enough; but the man is totally mistaken in his judgment. Grant him but one assumption and everything that he does is not only reasonable, but admirable. Admit that *Don Quixote* really lived in an age of Knight Errantry, that the Inn was a Castle, and the Windmill a Giant: and Alexander or Julius Caesar could not have behaved with more true courage, or more noble magnanimity.

The characters of Shakespeare are at once individual and general. So it is with those of Cervantes. They stand cut in the pictures of the imagination. We know *Don Quixote*, as we do Hamlet: and yet they both partake so much of the *permanent* part of human nature that they are as fresh, and as probable, and as interesting, now in the 19th century, as they were, when they were first delineated, in the sixteenth. As the melancholy traits of *Hamlet*, too, are relieved, by the coarse humour, and low-bred common-sense of the grave-diggers; so is *Don Quixote* relieved by Sancho; and in the exquisite contrasts, which these two characters bring out, we constantly see the superiority of moral refinement over the mixture of good humor and low cunning, which constitute genuine vulgarity.

Mr. Coleridge justly lamented, that the English reader of *Don Quixote* was precluded from enjoying one great source of delight—the happy appropriation of style to the respective characters. In our translations of this admirable work there is a sameness, and, in general, a flatness of style; in the Spanish, where the Knight himself is the speaker, and where he indulges, as he often does, in moral reflection, there is a rhythm and beauty in the prose almost equal to the cadence of well-constructed verse, yet not so approaching to it as to appear inflated and bombastic.

I have not time to enter into the minute remarks of the Lecturer on the various scenes of the Romance, the Knight's preparation of his armour, his watching it previously to his being dubbed by the innkeeper, his resolute attack on the lions, his descent into the cave of Montesinos, etc. etc.,[17] suffice it to say, that in all these Scenes, Mr. Coleridge,

---

[17] These "various scenes" occur respectively in pt 1 chs 1 and 3; pt 2 ch 17; pt 2 ch 23.

with great taste and judgment, pointed out the elevated and honourable feelings of *Don Quixote*, which, even in the midst of insanity, constantly attach to him the admiration and esteem of the reader.

The conclusion of the lecturer was to me, I own, its most affecting part: and I sincerely joined in the applause which arose at the concluding passage—Cervantes felt, said Mr. Coleridge, that there was no other way to close his narrative in an impressive manner, but by the death of the Knight; and that to contemplate a death of madness would be painful and revolting to the reader. The unfortunate Quixote, therefore, on the verge of the grave regards the exercise of his judgment; and as that judgment could not but impress him in so awful a moment with the deep sense of humility, he dies with the resignation of a man, and the penitence of a Christian, imputing to his own transgression the wanderings of his judgment. " 'Twas pride", says he, "that caused my fall; 'twas in labouring to be great, that I became little. I must now be humble, that I may become great."[18]

---

[18] These are C's words, not Don Quixote's—he repents and acknowledges his folly in the final chapter (Jarvis tr IV 317), but does not speak of becoming humble.

LECTURE 9

DATE AND PLACE OF DELIVERY. Tuesday, 24 February 1818, in the Great Room of the London Philosophical Society, Fleur-de-Luce Court, Fleet Street.

SUBJECT. In accordance with the Syllabus, "On Rabelais, Swift, and Sterne: on the Nature and Constituents of genuine Humour, and on the Distinctions of the Humourous from the Witty, the Fanciful, the Droll, the Odd, &c."

ADVERTISEMENTS AND ANNOUNCEMENTS. *Courier* Mon, 23 Feb (announcement): "To-morrow Evening, Mr. COLERIDGE follows up his CERVANTES by a Lecture on RABELAIS, SWIFT, and STERNE, in which he is to establish the nature and constituents of genuine *Humour*; wherein the Humorous is distinguished from the Droll, the Fanciful and the Odd; the difference between Humor and Wit: and the various sorts of the latter, illustrated by appropriate instances and anecdotes. At the Great Room, Fleur-de-luce-court, Fleet-street, at a quarter after Eight precisely. Admission five shillings." *The Times* Tues, 24 Feb (advertisement): "THIS EVENING, Mr. COLERIDGE follows up the Don Quixote by a LECTURE on RABELAIS, SWIFT, and STERNE, on Humour as different from Wit, and on the various sorts of Wit, the Shaksperian, the French, etc., illustrated by appropriate instances and anecdotes . . .". *New Times* Tues, 24 Feb (advertisement): as in *The Times*, with some variation of phrasing, as follows: ". . . on the nature of genuine Humour as distinguished from Wit; and on the various species of Wit, as the Shaksperian, the French, the Italian, etc . . .". *M Chron* Tues, 24 Feb (advertisement): as in *The Times*, with the variant: "on Humour as distinguished from Wit, and on the various sorts of Wit, as the Shakespearian, the Voltairian, etc . . .".

TEXT. C's notes for part of this lecture were written on thirteen small leaves of paper varying from 84 to 109 mm in width and from 108 to 183 mm in length, now BM Add MS 34225 ff 68–80. None of them has a dated watermark, and they are not all from the same stock of paper, though some leaves, ff 75 and 76, for instance, which between them complete the watermark "J BUDGEN", appear to have been cut from the same sheet. They are similar to the leaves C used for his notes relating to Lect 7, and the newspaper report of Lect 9 in the *Tatler* shows that he prefaced the lecture with some examples of wit that he jotted down on the blank verso of a page of his notes for the earlier lecture, Add MS 34225 f 63ᵛ. The rest of the notes fall into two groups, one, ff 74–80, concerned with wit and humour in general, the other, ff 68–73, leading into a specific critique of Sterne's *Tristram Shandy*. The newspaper report shows that C spoke on Sterne in the later part of the lecture and on wit in more general terms in the first part. His notes are accordingly printed below in the order in which he appears to have used them, namely, f 63ᵛ, followed by ff 74–80, followed in turn by ff 68–73. For the most part C used only one side of each leaf, but he added additional material on four versos. On f 69ᵛ there is a passage keyed into the notes on f 70 by a cross, and on f 70ᵛ he added to § 3 on f 71, heading the addition also with the number "3". He did not indicate where the other two extra passages, on ff 68ᵛ and 76ᵛ, fitted into the text, and Raysor placed them respectively before the notes on ff 69 and 77. It seems more probable that they were afterthoughts to what C wrote on these pages, and this is how they are presented below, though the proper location of them in the sequence of C's notes remains uncertain, especially as f 76 is blank.

168

The notes were first printed by HNC, who wove into them additional material and freely reworked them, in *LR* I 131–48. Some of his interpolations and additions may be from C's marginalia or from lost notes, notably the opening paragraph, with its comments on the wit of Shakespeare with reference to Falstaff. The report in the *Tatler* shows that C commented on Falstaff, and the passage from *LR* is appended below as a footnote to this report, to enable comparison to be made. Other passages in *LR* seem to be indebted to Richter's *Vorschule der Aesthetik*, which C used in the lecture, citing it in his ms notes, and may be authentic. However, HNC edited his material very heavily, without indicating his sources, and the text he presented for Lect 9 is a patchwork of fragments, partly drawn from C's ms notes, partly from elsewhere, and partly also made up by HNC to effect smooth transitions. The material he added may be based on lost notes or marginalia, but since its connexion with the lecture is uncertain, and is not directly supported by the newspaper report, it is not reprinted here. Raysor published C's ms notes in *Misc C* 117–26, printing the general notes on wit first (ff 74–80), then the instances of wit on f 63ᵛ, then two additional examples of wit taken from *LR* I 147–8, which seem to have no connexion with the lecture, and then the notes on Sterne (ff 68–73). He also reprinted HNC's version of notes for this lecture in an Appendix in *Misc C* 440–6. The newspaper report shows that C commented on Shakespeare, Rabelais, and Swift, as promised in the advertisements, but the ms notes do not relate to these parts of his lecture.

REPORT. A substantial report of this lecture was published in the *Tatler* II No 225 (24 May 1831) 897–8, under the heading "Recollections of Another of Mr. Coleridge's Lectures". It followed a report of Lect 14 in the issue of the previous day (see Lect 14 headnote: Report). The *Tatler*, a short-lived periodical, ran from 1830 to 1832, and the name of the correspondent who contributed these reports is not known. The report of 24 May corresponds sufficiently well with C's ms notes for Lect 9 to establish its authenticity, and it is reprinted below. It was reprinted for the first time in *Misc C* 111–17. Raysor also included in *Misc C* 128 a note on Swift supplied, according to HNC, by J. H. Green and first printed in *LR* I 140. This relates closely to the comment on Swift included in the *Tatler* report and is also reprinted below. Green wrote a report of Lect 1 in this series and, as a friend and admirer of C, probably attended the rest of the course, but it is possible that his note on Swift was derived from C's conversation.

BACKGROUND AND CIRCUMSTANCES. On 25 Feb, the day after the lecture was given, C returned the copies of "Sterne with the two Vol. of Swift" he had borrowed from the bookseller, Thomas Boosey, Jr. *CL* IV 844; VI 1045. The report in the *Tatler* shows that C commented on Swift, but no notes have been found relating to this part of the lecture. HCR attended the lecture and commented in his Diary on it: "The lecture was on Wit and Humour, and the great writers of wit and humour. There was much obscurity and metaphysics in the long introduction and not a little cant and commonplace in the short criticisms. I fear that Coleridge will not on the whole add to his reputation by these lectures." *CRB* I 220. HCR's attitude to this series seems to have been rather sour, and perhaps his comments on Lect 9 were as prejudiced as his reaction to Lect 8 seems to have been (see Introduction to this 1818 series, at nn 56–8).

LECTURE 9

RECORDS OF THE LECTURE

COLERIDGE'S NOTES
BM ADD MS 34225 FF 63ᵛ, 74–80, 68–73

*a*Why are you reading *Romances* at your Age—. Why—I used to be fond of History—but I have given it up, it was so grossly improbable— Pray, *Sir*! do it—altho' you have promised me—¹

Spartan Mother—Return with or ~~without~~ on thy Shield— or the short sword—a step forwarder—²

The Gasconade/—I believe you, sir! but you will excuse my repeating it on account of my provincial accent/

*b*The pure unmixed Ludicrous or Laughable belongs exclusively to the Understanding and the senses of Eye and Ear—thence to the Fancy. Not to the Reason or the moral Sense³—Out of time and place (the positive) *without danger* (the negative.—)⁴

Neither the understanding without the Object of the Senses (as an

a f 63ᵛ
b f 74

¹ The report in the *Tatler* shows that C began with these and other examples of wit, and it helps to explain what he meant by them; see below (first paragraph of the report). A "Gasconade" was an example of extravagant boasting, for which natives of Gascony had a reputation, and C's example, taken from Richter *Vorschule* § 48 pp 366–7 (*Werke* v 181), shows how to respond wittily to it. The example of the Spartan mother is also from Richter § 44 p 348 (*Werke* v 173). See also below (paragraph following n 24).

² See below, *Tatler* report (first paragraph).
³ C was echoing Richter here: § 28 pp 197–8 and § 26 p 181 (*Werke* v 109, 91), in which Aristotle's definition of the laughable is referred to. This C must have known anyway. In his expansion of these notes in *LR* I 132–3 HNC quoted from the *Poetics* ch 5, which underlies the concept of the comic as affording no pain or danger.
⁴ Cf Richter *Vorschule* § 26 p 181 (*Werke* v 91).

error, or idiotcy) nor any external Object unless as attributed to the Understanding, poetically laughable—.[5] Nay, in ridiculous positions laughed at by the vulgar, there is a subtle personification going on/—something symbolical—. Hence the imperfect and awkward effect of comic stories of ~~animals~~ Animals:[6] the *Understanding* is satisfied ~~with by~~ with the allegory;/ but the *senses* are not.—

[c]Hence too, that the Laughable is its *own end*. When serious Satire commences or satire that is felt as serious however comically drest, the ⟨*free*⟩ Laughter ceases—it becomes Sardonic. Felt in Young's Satire—not uninstanced in Butler—the truly Comic is the *Blossom of the Nettle*[7]

In the simply Laughable,[d] there is a mere disproportion between a definite act and a definite purpose or end—or a disproportion of the end itself to the rank ~~end~~ &c of the definite person—but when we contemplate a finite in reference to the Infinite, consciously or unconsciously, *Humor*. (So says Jean Paul Richter)[8]

[e]That there is something in this is evident: for you cannot conceive a humorous man who does not give some disproportionate *generality* universality to his hobby-horse/ as M[r] Shandy—or at least, an absence of any interest but what arise[s][f] from the Humor itself, as in Uncle Toby—there is *the idea* of the Soul with its undefined capacity and dignity, that gives the sting to any absorption of it by any one pursuit—and this not as a member of society for any particular however mistaken Interest, but as Man. Hence in Humor the Little is made great and the

---

[c] f 75
[d] C wrote "Laughable simply" and marked the words for transposing
[e] f 77
[f] C omitted the final *s*

---

[5] Cf Richter § 28 pp 197–8 (*Werke* v 109).

[6] Richter § 28 p 208 (*Werke* v 113) says that to be laughable a creature must have a semblance of freedom, and hence we laugh only at clever animals, to which we grant some form of personification.

[7] Putting together sentences from Richter § 29 p 214 (*Werke* v 116): "Der Scherz kennt kein anderes Ziel als sein eignes Daseyn. Die poetische Blüte seiner Nesseln sticht nicht . . . Werke, worin der satirische Unwille und der lachende Scherz . . . in einander gemengt und verwirret sind, z. B. Youngs Satiren und Pope's Dunciade, quälen mit dem gleichzeitigen Genusse entgegengesetzter Tonarten"; tr: "Humour knows no other aim than its own existence. The poetic blossoms of its nettles do not sting . . . Works in which satiric indignation and laughing humour are mixed and confused, such as Young's *Satires* and Pope's *Dunciad*, annoy with the simultaneous sense of pleasure and its opposite." Edward Young (1683–1765) wrote *The Love of Fame or the Universal Passion* (1725), and Samuel Butler (1612–80) was the author of *Hudibras*, published in three parts between 1663 and 1678.

[8] In the passage paraphrased in the *Tatler* report (at n 27).

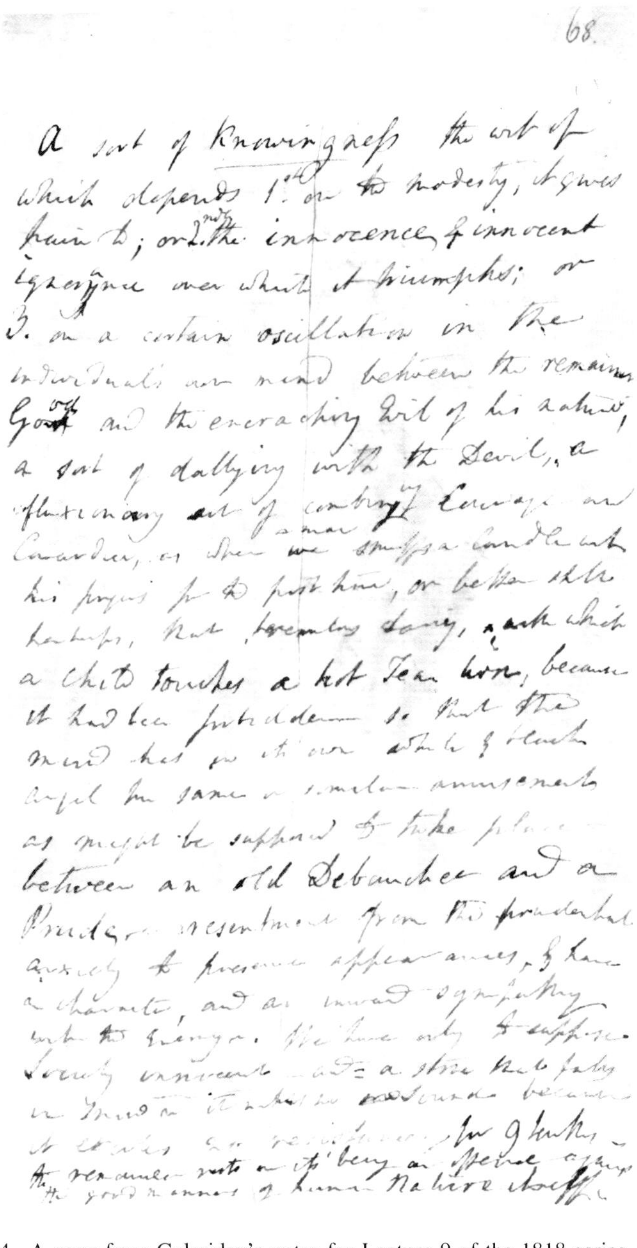

[Manuscript page in Coleridge's hand — largely illegible cursive notes.]

4. A page from Coleridge's notes for Lecture 9 of the 1818 series,
from BM Additional MS 34225 f 68. The British Library
reproduced by kind permission

great Little in order to destroy both: because all is equal in contrast with the Infinite—[9]

*g*Humorous Writers therefore, as Sterne in particular, delight to end in nothing—or a direct contradiction/.[10]

*h*Hence the tender feeling connected with the *Humors* or Hobby horses of a man 1 Respect: for there is absence of any Interest as the ground-work, tho' the imagination of *a[n]i Interest* by the Humorist may exist—as if a remarkably simple hearted Man should pride himself on his knowlege of the World, & how well he can manage it—

2. acknowlegement of the hollowness & farce of the world, and its disproportion to the Godlike within us—

*j*Hence when particular *Acts* having reference to particular *selfish* motives, the Humoristous bursts into the *Indignant* & Abhorring—All follies *not selfish* it pardons or palliates—the *danger* of this exemplified in Sterne/

A seriousness in Humor—Spain & England/—Irony Italy—Wit, France.[11]

The ancients little or no Humor—. The Devil, the Vice of the Mysteries, characterize the modern *Humor* in its elements—it is a Spirit measured by dispro[po]rtionate*k* Finites. The Devil *l*not humorous, only because he is the Extreme of Humor—

Of all the ancients Socrates or at least Plato under his name gives the idea of Humor, in the Banquet—where he ~~derives~~ gave to Comedy and Tragedy the same ground/*m*[12]

---

g This sentence at the head of f 76ᵛ seems to belong here; the rest of f 76ᵛ and all of
f 76 are blank
h f 78   *i* C wrote "a"   *j* f 79
k C scribbled the word, missing out several letters
l f 80
m The text occupies less than half the page, the rest of which is blank

[9] The idea comes from *Vorschule* § 32 pp 238–9 (*Werke* v 125–6). Richter says that the humourist takes some folly general to mankind, because this moves the heart or soul ("sein Inneres bewegt"), and Uncle Toby's campaigns do not make him or Louis xiv laughable, but are rather allegories of all men's hobbyhorses.

[10] In his *Vorschule* § 33 p 253 (*Werke* v 131), Richter says that humour pleases often by its contradiction and impossibility, and thence comes another agreeable form of humour that issues in noth-ing ("Daher kommt dem Humor jene Liebe zum leersten Ausgange''); he instances Sterne's habit of presenting long and weighty accounts of events and then saying not a word of them is true.

[11] In *Vorschule* § 29 pp 216–20 (*Werke* v 117–18) Richter says that the serious British and Spaniards have produced more comedies than the French and Italians put together and associates Paris with courtly wit.

[12] Largely based on *Vorschule* § 33 pp 249–50 (*Werke* v 129–30). Richter says

*n*A sort of *knowingness* the wit of which depends 1st on the modesty, it gives pain to; or 2^ndly the innocence & innocent ignoryance over which it triumphs; or 3. on a certain oscillation in the individual's own mind between the remaining Godod and the encr[o]aching*o* Evil of his nature, a sort of dallying with the Devil, a fluxionary act of combinging Courage and Cowardice, as when we a man snuffs a Candle with his fingers for the first time, or better still perhaps, that tremulous daring, with which a Child touches a hot Tea Urn, because it had been forbidden—so that the mind has in its own white & black angel the same or similar amusements as might be supposed to take place between an old Debauchee and a Prude—resentment from the prudential anxiety to preserve appearances, & have a character, and an inward sympathy with the Enemy—. We have only to suppose Society *innocent*—and = a stone that falls in snow—it makes no noi sound because it excites no resistance—for 9 tenths—the remainder rests on its being an offence against the good manners of human Nature itself—

*p*Asympatheia[13]—in the closet devotions, alone with a bottle of Wine—with or without a book?—

This source, unworthy as it is, may doubtless be combined with the wit, drollery, fancy, and even humor—and we have only to regret the mesalliance/ but that the latter are quite distinct from the former may be made evident by abstracting in our imagination the *characters* of Mr Shandy my Uncle Toby, and Trim/ which are all *antagonists* to this wit—& suppose instead of them two or three callous Debauchees/ & the result will be pure disgust.—Sterne cannot be too severely censured for this—for he makes the best dispositions of our nature the pandars & Condiments for the basest.

*q*The vile comments and aidances offensive & defensive of Pope's Lust thro' some gentle strainers well refined Is Love[14]—contrasted with

n f 68
o Letter supplied by the editor
p f 69
q f 68^v

that he can regard the Devil as the greatest humourist and "whimsical man", but his laughter has too much pain in it ("kann ich mir leicht als den grössten Humoristen und *whimsical man* gedenken . . . denn sein Lachen hätte zu viel Pein"). The reference to Plato is also in the same passage in Richter, but C knew it well, as it was cited by A. W. Schlegel, and C had commented on *Symposium* 223 in

Lect 4 of the 1812 series, first course (at n 1).

[13] Transliterated from the Greek; tr "want of fellow-feeling". It is not in *OED*, and C's point here is obscure—is this the ultimate image of "selfish motives", a "knowingness" showing a want of sympathy?

[14] From Pope *Essay on Man* II 189–90:

Shakespear, & even with the dogmata of B. and F., M. &c—Hence Sterne a favorite with the French/[15]

The unfairness of this—because they cannot be answered where ~~the~~ an answer would be most desirable, from the painful nature of one part of the Position—but this very pain a demonstration of the False-hood/—[r]

[s]Excellences

1 The bringing forward into distinct consciousness those minutiæ of thought and feeling which appear trifles, ~~to an or~~ have an importance for the moment/ and yet almost every man feels in one way or other.— Thus it has the novelty of an individual peculiarity, and yet the interest of a something that belongs to our common nature—. In short, to seize happily on those points, in which every man is more or less a *Humorist*,[t] and the propensity to notice these things ~~is~~ does itself ~~chara~~ constitute a Humorist, and the ⟨superadded⟩ power of so presenting them to men in general gives us the man of Humor.—Hence the difference of the Man of Humor, ~~but~~ the effect of whose portraits does not depend on the felt presence of himself as a Humorist, as Cervantes and Shake-spear—nay, Rabelais—and those in which the effect is in the Humorist's own oddity—Sterne—& *? Swift?*

[r] This paragraph ends just over halfway down the page, the rest of which is blank

[s] f 70

[t] Linked by a cross to the passage on f 69[v], which is inserted here

---

Lust, through some certain strainers well refined
Is gentle love, and charms all woman-kind.

C echoes here a notebook entry of 1809 in which he quoted this passage, with the comment, "Either therefore we must brutalize our notions with Pope . . . or dissolve & thaw away all bonds of morality by the inevitable Shocks of an irresistible Sensibility with Sterne." *CN* III 3562.

It is not clear what C meant by "comments and aidances"; possibly he was thinking of Warburton's commentary on the poem, printed with it in editions like that of William Lisle Bowles (10 vols 1806); the note on these lines relating to the "ruling passion" (II 138) reads: "Its *Moral* use is to ingraft our ruling Virtue upon it; and by that means to enable us to promote our own good, by turning the exorbitancy of the *ruling Passion* into its neighbouring Virtue . . . The Wisdom of the Divine Artist is, as the Poet finely observes, very illustrious in this contrivance." This looks like a justification of and "aidance" to debauchery.

[15] In the wake of the worst excesses of the French Revolution C came to associate the French with sensuality; see *CL* I 395–8 and *EOT (CC)* I 210n, II 98 and n. According to the report of this lecture in the *Tatler*, C spoke of Sterne's "degradation of the passion of Love" (sentence after n 33), and was probably referring to the affair of Uncle Toby and Widow Wadman in *Tristram Shandy* bks III and IX, which he called "disgusting" in *TT* 18 Aug 1833. (See also Lect 8 of the 1811–12 series, at n 29.) "B. and F., M." = Beaumont and Fletcher, Massinger.

[u]2. Traits of *human* nature, which so easily assume a particular cast and color from individual character, hence this and the pathos connected with it, quickly passes into *humor*—and forms the ground of it.—

P. 46. 117.[16] or the Story of the Fly—Character by a delicacy & higher degree of a good quality—

[v]3. In M[r] Shandy's character as of all M[r] Shandy; a craving for sympathy in exact proportion to the oddity & unsympathizability—next to this to be at least disputed with—or rather both in one, dispute and yet agree—but worst of all, to acquiesce without either resistance or sympathy—most happily conceived—

[w]3—Contrasts sometimes increasing the Love between the Brothers— and always either balanced or remedied/

Drollery in Obadiah[x][17]

[y]4. No writer so happy as Sterne in the unexaggerated & truly natural representation of that species of Slander, which consists in gossiping about our neighbors, as *whetstones* of our moral discrimination/ as if they were Conscience-blocks which we used in our apprenticeship not to waste such precious materials as our own consciences in the trimming & shaping of by self-examination—p. 47.[18]

[z]5. p. 53.[19]—When you have secured a man's liking—and prejudices in your favor, you may then safely appeal to his impartial Judgement— = acute sense in ironical wit—but now add *Life* to it & character— and it becomes *dramatic*—as on p. 53.

6. The physiognomic fact common in very different degrees indeed

---

[u] The text continues here on f 70
[v] f 71
[w] C wrote this addition to note 3 at the top of f 70
[x] This phrase is written an inch below the previous entry; the rest of the page is blank except for some jottings of numbers for addition
[y] The text continues here on f 71
[z] f 72

---

[16] The references identify the edition C was using as *The Works of Laurence Sterne* (4 vols 1815): I 46 refers to Mrs Shandy's determination to use the midwife rather than Dr Slop, as an example of "greatness of soul" (bk I ch 18); I 117 to the episode in which Uncle Toby, rather than kill a fly that has been tormenting him, opens the window and lets it escape (bk II ch 12).

[17] C was probably thinking of bk II ch 9, in which Obadiah, sent to fetch Dr Slop, carefully pulls his cap off twice in salute to him, even as his horse is splashing the doctor with mud. In *Works* (1815) I 110.

[18] I 47 is a reference to bk I ch 18, in which Mr Shandy torments himself in his anxiety over his wife's lying-in in the country, conscious that if anything goes wrong, "the world judged by events, and would add to his afflictions in such misfortune, by loading him with the whole blame of it".

[19] C quoted here from bk I ch 19, as is shown by the report in the *Tatler*, below (at n 33), which printed a passage from it. In *Works* (1815) I 53–4.

to us all, gratified in Dr Slop—and in general, all that happiest use of Drapery & Attitude which at once gives the *reality* ~~of~~ by individualizing, and the vividiness of unusual yet probable combinations—108.[20]

^{a}7 More *Humor* in the single remark—Learned Men, Brother Toby, do not write dialogues on long noses for nothing,[21] than in the whole Slawkenburghian Tale that follows—which is ~~however~~ oddity interspersed with Drollery—

8. The moral *good* of Sterne in the characters of Trim &c—as contrasted with Jacobinism—*p. 393.*[22]

9. Each part by right of Humoristic Universality a Whole—hence the Digressi~~onsv~~e Spirit not wantonness, but the *very form* of his genius—. The connection is given by the continuity of the Characters/^{b}

REPORT IN THE *TATLER* II NO 225
(24 MAY 1831) 897–8

Recollections of Another of Mr Coleridge's Lectures;
Namely, on Rabelais, Swift, Sterne, &c. No account
of which has been published

In a few prefatory observations on the nature of wit, the Lecturer stated that surprise in the hearers was one of its most common effects. He proceeded to illustrate his meaning by some remarkable sayings of the ancients:—for example, the answer made to one who complained of the shortness of his sword,—"It is but to advance a step further;" and the remark of Cato, "That he would rather be asked, Why no statue of him was erected, than why there was one."[23] These instances may with

^{a} f 73
^{b} The text ends at the foot of the page

[20] Bk II ch 9, in which Dr Slop is described: "Imagine to yourself a little squat, uncourtly figure of a Doctor Slop, of about four feet and a half perpendicular height, with a breadth of back, and a sesquipedality of belly, which might have done honour to a serjeant in the horse-guards. . . ." *Works* (1815) I 108.

[21] C was quoting from bk III ch 37: *Works* (1815) I 243 (var). The tale of Slawkenbergius comes a little further on and occupies the long first chapter of bk IV.

[22] The reference I 393 is to bk v ch 9,

in which Trim delights in living "in the service of two of the best of masters" and boasts of his previous service to King William III; hence a contrast with the ultra-democratic principles of Jacobinism.

[23] This was Cato's response to those who expressed amazement that other famous men had statues while he had none, as reported in Plutarch *Lives* "Marcus Cato" 19.4. The illustration comes from Richter *Vorschule* § 47 p 364 (*Werke* v 186).

propriety come under the denomination of wit, from the deep meaning which they involve, and the surprise they occasion.

The character of *Falstaff*, as drawn by Shakspeare, may be described as one of wit, rather than of humour. The speeches of *Falstaff* and *Prince Henry* would, for the most part, be equally proper in the mouth of either, and might indeed, with undiminished effect, proceed from any person. This is owing to their being composed almost wholly of wit, which is impersonal, and not of humour, which always more or less partakes of the character of the speaker. The Character of *Parson Evans*, on the other hand, is one of humour throughout.[24]

The wit of the Italians is of a mixed kind, something mid-way between what we understand by wit and humour. It is generally tinged with irony, and partakes of the character of the speaker. There is something sardonic about it. The three instances following are illustrative of French wit. "An old man reading a romance was asked the reason of his partiality for that species of writing. He answered,—In my younger days I read a great deal of History; but to confess the truth I am obliged to discontinue it, *I found it so very improbable.*" The second is the address of a suitor to a French minister, from whom he had received many promises, and as many disappointments:—"I entreat you, sir, to grant me the favour *although you have promised me so many times.*" The third is of two Gascons, one of whom related an incredible story, of which the other shewed his disbelief by his gestures. The relator, perceiving this, indignantly demands, "Do you not believe me, sir?" The other answers, "Certainly, I believe you; but you'll excuse my repeating the story, lest I should injure it by my provincial accent."

It may be remarked, that real wit always appeals to the understanding, and does not necessarily produce laughter. Error and idiotcy are not proper subjects of laughter.[25]

The satires of Young are witty, but they are little productive of pleasure. Even Butler, when describing Hudibras as a sectary and a persecutor, ceases to give that pleasure which is afforded by his representations of his hero in love.[26]

The origin of the word humour may be traced to the science of Pathology. The ancients were unacquainted with its present meaning. They considered the human body as the repository of four humours, viz., blood, phlegm, bile or gall, and the black bile, and according to

---

[24] Sir Hugh Evans, in *The Merry Wives of Windsor*.

[25] Based on Richter *Vorschule* § 28 pp 196–8 (*Werke* v 109). C's "idiotcy"

corresponds to Richter's "Verstandeslosigkeit".

[26] See above (at n 7).

the predominance of either of these they believed the character to be sanguine, phlegmatic, choleric, or melancholy. When these distinctions ceased to be regarded, the word was still retained, and one of its applications was to persons engaged in pursuits of no abstract utility, but which had the limited effect of making happy those engaged in them. Sterne's Uncle Toby is of this kind. The fortifications on which he employed himself in his garden are represented as a source of unceasing delight to him, totally abstracted from the remotest idea of utility. Humour is also displayed in the comparison of finite things with those which our imaginations cannot bound; such as make our great appear little and our little great; or, rather, which reduces to a common littleness both the great and the little, when compared with infinity.[27]

Plato, in his dialogues, gives the first true idea of humour in theory, when describing the effects at times produced on us by Tragedy and Comedy.[28]

Humour and pathos are generally found together. In Sterne, they are admirably blended, so as to serve as reliefs to each other.

Mr Coleridge next considered separately the humourist and the man of humour.

The humourist is one who erroneously supposes himself calculated for certain things which occupy his mind, and whose deficiencies, in the very particulars on which he prides himself, are obvious to all about him. I knew, said Mr C., a man of this description. He was fond of giving advice as to the best way of addressing the great, and of escaping the arts of the designing. He was one of the most simple-hearted men in the world, one of the most undesigning and disinterested, and much less fitted to contend with the subtleties of mankind than to become himself their dupe. The man of humour is one skilled in the representation of the peculiarities of others.

Rabelais next engaged the Lecturer's notice. He considered it unaccountable how a man of genius should disfigure his works by so much sheer ribaldry. He conjectured that the ribaldry of Rabelais was merely a disguise, like the idiotcy of Brutus.[29] Under this disguise he attacked boldly, but still with great peril, the vices of the priesthood and of the court of Francis the First. In perusing his writings therefore (an occu-

---

[27] A free rendering of a passage in Richter § 32 pp 237–8 (*Werke* v 125); see above (at n 8).

[28] See above (at n 12).

[29] Lucius Junius Brutus, who feigned lunacy to ensure his safety from the tyranny of the Tarquins; see Plutarch *Lives* "Publicola" 3.4. In an annotation on *The Works of Rabelais* (4 vols 1784) C wrote: "His buffoonery was not merely Brutus's rough stick that contained a rod of gold. It was necessary as an Amulet against the Monks & Bigots." Annotation on I flyleaf: *CM (CC)* IV.

pation perhaps only proper to scholars) his remarks should be considered, beyond a certain point, as so many words of no meaning, such as are made use of in those cyphers which pass between governments and their agents, to deceive those who are not in possession of the explanatory key. Mr C. here read two extracts from the character of Panurge.[30] One of them related to the adventure of the sheep and Dingdong.[31] Rabelais loses by the attempts made to particularize his characters. Their beauty consists in their truth to general nature. The writings of Swift and Rochefoucauld do not evince an accurate knowledge of mankind; they contain representations only of the dark side of things. The writings of Swift are also censurable for the vast quantity of physical dirt with which they abound; and not merely on that account, but for their moral dirt.

Gulliver's Travels is Swift's greatest work. The unimportance of mere exterior is well illustrated in the adventures of Gulliver among the great and little people. Adverting to absurd reports which are suffered to remain uncontradicted because they excite only the contempt of the parties attacked, but, owing to their circumstantiality, are believed by some, who ask—If these reports are unfounded, why are they not contradicted?—Mr C. quoted the following passage from Gulliver's Voyage to Lilliput, relative to the Lilliputian sheep:—

> I shall not trouble the reader with a particular account of this voyage, which was very prosperous for the most part. We arrived in the Downs on the 13th of April 1702. I had only one misfortune, that the rats on board carried away one of my sheep; I found her bones in a hole, picked clean from the flesh. The rest of my cattle I got safe ashore, and set them a-grazing in a bowling-green at Greenwich, where the fineness of the grass made them feed very heartily, though I had always feared the contrary: neither could I possibly have preserved them in so long a voyage, if the captain had not allowed me some of his best biscuit, which, rubbed to powder, and mingled with water, was their constant food. The short time I continued in England, I made a considerable profit by

---

[30] C's annotations on Rabelais includes a characterisation of Panurge: he "is throughout the παvουϱγια,—the Wisdom, no, Cunning of the Human Animal—the Understanding, as the faculty of means to purposes without ultimate ends, in the most comprehensive sense, and including Art, sensuous Fancy, & all the passions of the Understanding". One of the passages C read was probably from bk III ch 9, in which Panurge seeks Pantagruel's advice about marrying; C wrote another annotation on this, as "an exquisite satire on the spirit, in which

people commonly ask advice". Annotations on II back flyleaf, II 258–61: *CM (CC)* IV.

[31] In *Gargantua and Pantagruel* bk IV chs 5–8, in which Panurge, insulted on shipboard by a sheepdrover named Dingdong, persuades him to sell a sheep, paying well over its value; the triumph of the drover is short-lived, for Panurge throws the ram into the sea, whereupon the whole herd follow, and in trying to save his best ram, Dingdong is pulled overboard and drowned.

showing my cattle to many persons of quality and others: and before I began my second voyage, I sold them for six hundred pounds. Since my last return, I find the breed is considerably increased, especially the sheep, which I hope will prove much to the advantage of the woollen manufacture, by the fineness of the fleeces.[32]

In further illustration of Sterne, Mr C. adduced as a happy specimen of his talents, Mr Shandy's address to a friend on the importance of Christian names.

My father's opinion in this matter, was, that there was a strange kind of magic bias, which good or bad names, as he called them, irresistibly impressed upon our characters and conduct.

The hero of Cervantes argued not the point with more seriousness,—nor had he more faith,—or more to say on the powers of necromancy in dishonouring his deeds, or on Dulcinea's name, in shedding lustre upon them, than my father had on those of Trismegistus or Archimedes, on the one hand—or of Nyky and Simpkin on the other. How many Caesars and Pompeys, he would say, by mere inspiration of the names, have been rendered worthy of them? And how many, he would add, are there, who might have done exceeding well in the world, had not their characters and spirits been totally depressed and Nicodemus'd into nothing?

I see plainly, Sir, by your looks, (or as the case happened) my father would say,—that you do not heartily subscribe to this opinion of mine,—which, to those, he would add, who have not carefully sifted it to the bottom,—I own has an air more of fancy than of solid reasoning in it; and yet, my dear Sir, if I may presume to know your character, I am morally assured, I should hazard little in stating a case to you, not as a party in the dispute,—but as a judge, and trusting my appeal upon it to your own good sense and candid disquisition in this matter;—you are a person free from as many narrow prejudices of education as most men;—and, if I may presume to penetrate farther into you— of a liberality of genius above bearing down an opinion merely because it wants friends. Your son—your dear son,—from whose sweet and open temper you have so much to expect;—your Billy, Sir!—would you for the world have called him Judas?—Would you, my dear Sir, he would say, laying his hand upon his breast, with the genteelest address,—and in that soft irresistible *piano* of voice, which the nature of the *argumentum ad hominem* absolutely requires;—Would you, Sir, if a *Jew* of a god-father had proposed the name of your child, had offered you his purse along with it, would you have consented to such a desecration of him?—O my God!—he would say, looking up,—if I know your temper right, Sir, you are incapable of it;—you would have trampled upon the offer;—you would have thrown the temptation at the tempter's head with abhorrence.

Your greatness of mind in this action, which I admire, with that generous contempt of money which you shew me in the whole transaction, is really noble;—the workings of a parent's love upon the truth and conviction of this very hypothesis, namely, that was your son called Judas, the sordid and treach-

[32] "A Voyage to Lilliput" ch 8 in *Gulliver's Travels* ed H. Davis (Oxford 1959) 79–80.

erous idea, so inseperable from the name, would have accompanied him through life like his shadow, and, in the end, made a miser and a rascal of him,—in spite, Sir, of your example.[33]

He next passed to the faults of Sterne, whom he severely censured for his indecency, his degradation of the passion of Love, and his affected sensibility. In conclusion, he expressed his opinion that the works of Sterne had been productive of much more evil than good.[34]

NOTE BY JOSEPH HENRY GREEN
FROM *LR* I 140

In Swift's writings there is a false misanthropy grounded upon an exclusive contemplation of the vices and follies of mankind, and this misanthropic tone is also disfigured or brutalized by his obtrusion of physical dirt and coarseness. I think Gulliver's Travels the great work of Swift. In the voyages to Lilliput and Brobdingnag he displays the littleness and moral contemptibility of human nature; in that to the Houyhnhnms he represents the disgusting spectacle of man with the understanding only, without the reason or the moral feeling, and in his horse he gives the misanthropic ideal of man—that is, a being virtuous from rule and duty, but untouched by the principle of love.

[33] Citing from *Tristram Shandy* bk I ch 19; see also above (at n 19).

[34] The report in the *Tatler* ends with a paragraph printed in square brackets: "In laying before the reader the above sketches, with which a friend has fa-voured us, it is not to be concluded that we agree with all the opinions they advance; but our friend justly thought that the least fragments of the Sybilline Leaves of their author would be regarded as valuable."

LECTURE 10

DATE AND PLACE OF DELIVERY. Friday, 27 February 1818, in the Great Room of the London Philosophical Society, Fleur-de-Luce Court, Fleet Street.

SUBJECT. Dante and the *Divina Commedia* compared with *Paradise Lost*. In the Syllabus C had promised to speak "Of Donne, Dante, and Milton."

ADVERTISEMENTS AND ANNOUNCEMENTS. *Courier* Thurs, 26 Feb (announcement): "DANTE AND MILTON.—Mr. COLERIDGE's subjects for To-morrow Evening are, the Object, Plan, and characteristic Beauties; first, of DANTE's Hell, Purgatory and Paradise; and secondly of the *Paradise Lost*; with a sketch of the lives and moral grandeur of these two great masters of heroic song, as *Men*. By permission of the London Philosophical Society . . . at a quarter after Eight *precisely*, attention to which is particularly requested for *this* Lecture. Admission Five Shillings . . .". *The Times* Fri, 27 Feb (advertisement): "DANTE and MILTON:—Mr. COLERIDGE's SUBJECTS for THIS EVENING are, the Object, Plan and characteristic Beauties of Dante's divine Comedy and of the Paradise Lost, with a sketch of the lives and moral grandeur of these two Great masters as men and citizens, at the Great Room . . . at a quarter after eight precisely, attention to which is particularly requested for this lecture. Admission 5s." *M Chron* Fri, 27 Feb (advertisement): as in *The Times*, except for an alteration of phrasing as follows: ". . . with a comparative sketch of the lives and moral Grandeur of the Florentine and the English Poet. By permission of the London Philosophical Society, at their Great Room . . .".

TEXT. No notes have been found that can be related specifically to this lecture. In *LR* I 150–78 HNC published extended notes on Dante and Milton under the heading of this lecture, and these were reprinted in *Misc C* 145–65. However, HNC made no mention of the lectures of 1819 in *LR*, and it seems clear that the notes on Dante he edited were in fact those C prepared for Lect 5 in 1819, since they correspond so closely with C's ms notes in N 29 (*CN* III 4498). An additional piece of evidence is provided by C's reminder to himself to "pay a proper compliment to Mr Hallam" (*LR* I 158), alluding to Henry Hallam's *View of the State of Europe During the Middle Ages* (2 vols), published in Jun 1818, with a preface dated Apr of that year. Although Hallam seems to be first mentioned in C's letters in 1825, they were acquainted before 1818, since at one point Hallam printed a footnote stating that he had met four English authors who had read some Aquinas, one being C (II 577n), and in the 3-vol ed of his work issued in 1848 Hallam added a further note at this point beginning, "I leave this passage as it was written about 1814" (III 428n). So it is conceivable that C might have complimented Hallam in 1818, but there would have been little point in doing so publicly before the appearance of his book. The reference to Hallam therefore points to a date after Jun 1818 for the notes, which must belong to 1819. The puzzling aspect of this is that C headed his notes with the date "11 March, 1819", and HNC must have seen this if he used N 29. The explanation could be simply that HNC noticed "a good deal of overlapping" between the 1818 and 1819 series and decided "to make one good set of lectures out of them" (*CN* III 4501n), and his own omission of the 1819 series from *LR* could be taken as supporting this hypothesis. There are difficulties in accepting this view, as Kathleen Coburn goes on to observe in the note cited. However, in the case of the notes on Dante, the evidence for attaching these to Lect 5 in 1819, and by analogy the notes on Milton to Lect 4 in that series, seems overwhelming, and accordingly they are printed as part of the later series.

REPORTS. No reports of this lecture have been found.

BACKGROUND AND CIRCUMSTANCES. The Syllabus promised a lecture on Donne, Milton, and Dante, and the grouping of these three authors together was still very much in C's mind when he wrote to Cary on 2 Feb 1818 to say: "I am vain enough to set a more than usual value on the Critique, I have devoted to the names of Dante, Donne, and Milton (the middle name will, perhaps, puzzle you) and I mean to publish it singly, in the week following it's delivery". *CL* IV 827. C had long admired the poetry of Donne, which remained unfashionable and largely unknown; during the period when C was lecturing in Fleur-de-Luce Court, Hazlitt was giving his course of "Lectures on the English Poets" at the Surrey Institution, published under this title in 1818, without mentioning Donne. C had begun to notice Donne's poetry with enthusiasm as early as 1796 and left a record of his reactions in a large number of marginalia on a volume of Donne's poetry and on two sets of his sermons; see *CM (CC)* II 213–338. It is a pity, then, that C did not publish this lecture, though in fact there is no record of his speaking on Donne in it, and the connexions he saw with Dante and Milton remain as puzzling now as they must have been to Cary.

In the autumn of 1817 C arranged to spend some weeks by the sea for the sake of his health, and there, while walking on the beach at Littlehampton, he met H. F. Cary (*CL* IV 767, 778), who was Rector there, and became friendly with him. This encounter led to C's reading, in Oct, Cary's translation of *The Divine Comedy*, which had been published at the author's expense in 1814, after an edition of the *Inferno* in 1805 failed to win attention. In Nov C wrote to Cary warmly praising his translation (*CL* IV 782) and, soon after his return to London, began negotiations in Jan 1818 for Taylor and Hessey to bring out under their imprint the remaining copies of the 1814 ed (*CL* IV 823–4). According to Henry Cary, H. F. Cary's son, the results were startling: "The work, which had been published four years, but had remained in utter obscurity, was at once eagerly sought for. About a thousand copies of the first edition, that remained on hand, were immediately disposed of; in less than three months a new edition was called for . . . and henceforth the claims of the translator of Dante to literary distinction were universally admitted." *Memoir of the Rev. Henry Francis Cary* (2 vols 1847) II 28. The new edition appeared in the summer of 1819.

C had been presented with a copy of *La Divina Commedia* (Venice 1774) by Sir George Beaumont in 1804 (*CN* II 2014n), and in Feb 1812 had contemplated including Dante in the course of lectures to be given later that year (*CL* III 364), but changed this plan and lectured on drama instead. He studied Italian in connexion with his stay in Malta beginning in 1804 (see *CN* II Notes App A), when he thought of "Dante and a Dictionary" as comforts for the voyage (*CL* II 1059), and Henry Cary remembered that at Littlehampton in 1817 C was "able to recite whole passages of the version of Dante, and though he had not the original with him, repeated passages of that also, and commented on the translation." *Memoir of Cary* II 19; *C Talker* 126. However well C knew Dante's

185

poem in Italian, it seems likely that the encounter with Cary revived his interest. The notes C prepared for the lecture on Dante he gave in 1819 include a reminder to himself to praise Cary's translation (see below, ɪɪ 401), and there is little doubt that he spoke enthusiastically about Cary in his 1818 lecture. The 1819 notes probably represent a reworking of material used in 1818.

The linking of Dante with Milton is interesting. C had lectured on Milton in several earlier series, but is not known to have linked him with Dante, except perhaps in Lect 9 of the 1811–12 series (at n 35). Probably C found he had too much material for the lecture, which would account for his omission of any commentary on Donne; but even the restriction to Dante and Milton, announced in the advertisements immediately before the lecture, no doubt left him with too much to do, as is indicated by his allocation of a lecture each to Dante and Milton in 1819. Nevertheless, C's intention of comparing them (advertisement in the *M Chron*) may have been carried out; a few comparisons with Milton are made in the notes for the lecture on Dante given in 1819. In aiming at this, as in yoking Rabelais with Sterne in Lect 9, C contributed to the development of the comparative study of literature, and it may well be that the opening up of Europe to normal travel and intercourse after the Battle of Waterloo (1815) and the end of the Napoleonic wars generated a new interest in European literature and that C's courses in 1818 and 1819 in some measure reflect this. The lecture on Dante and Milton pleased HCR, who wrote in his Diary, "I took tea with Gurney and invited Mrs Gurney to accompany me to Coleridge's lecture. It was on Dante and Milton—one of his very best. He digressed less than usually and really gave information and ideas about the poets he professed to criticize." *CRB* ɪ 220. HCR's companion at the lecture was the wife of Hudson Gurney, MP (1775–1864), poet, translator, and antiquary.

LECTURE 11

DATE AND PLACE OF DELIVERY. Tuesday, 3 March 1818, in the Great Room of the London Philosophical Society, Fleur-de-Luce Court, Fleet Street.

SUBJECT. The best literature for children to read. This seems to be the common thread in the announcements of the lecture, which do not agree in the list of the works named, though all include the *Arabian Nights*, beginning with the Syllabus: "On the Arabian Nights Entertainments, and on the *romantic* Use of the Supernatural in Poetry, and in Works of Fiction not poetical. On the Conditions and Regulations under which such Books may be employed advantageously in the earlier Periods of Education."

ADVERTISEMENTS AND ANNOUNCEMENTS. *The Times* Tues, 3 Mar (advertisement): "MR. COLERIDGE'S ELEVENTH LECTURE, THIS EVENING, at a quarter after eight, in Flower-de-Luce court, Fleet-street; best entrance to the lecture room, from Fetter-lane. Subjects, Arabian Nights, Robinson Crusoe, etc. compared with novels, and in reference to the enquiry what are proper books for children. Admission 5s." *M Chron* Tues, 3 Mar (advertisement): "THIS EVENING, a quarter after eight, at the Great Room of the London Philosophical Society . . . MR. COLERIDGE lectures on the Arabian Nights, and other similar works, including Fictitious Travels, as Robinson Crusoe, Peter Wilkins, etc. Having shewn the laws prescribed by the nature of the subject in the use of the supernatural, and the especial merit of the Arabian Tales, as works of imagination, Mr. C. will attempt, as the moral of the Lectures, and his chief motive in the choice of the subjects, to settle the question, whether 'works of this kind, Tales of Enchanters, Genji, Fairies, etc.' can be safely and advantageously read at all during the period from childhood to early youth; and if so, under what conditions and regulations.—Admission, Five shillings. N.B. Best entrance for carriages from Fetter-lane." *Courier* Tues, 3 Mar (announcement): "ARABIAN NIGHTS, ROBINSON CRUSOE, NOVELS.—Mr. COLERIDGE'S Lecture of this evening, at a quarter after Eight precisely. Few questions are oftener or more anxiously asked by parents, than—what are the best books for children? And this again, is to all *practical* purposes, nearly tantamount to the inquiry: whether Fairy Tales, Stories of Enchanters, Genji, Imaginary Travels, etc. either (as in the Arabian Tales) *with*, or (as in *Robinson Crusoe*) *without*, the introduction of imaginary beings, are proper reading during the period from childhood to earliest youth: and under what regulations? To settle this point, and to contrast these Fictions of Imagination with Novels, both in kind and in the moral effects, gave an additional weight to the interest of the works themselves in determining Mr. COLERIDGE'S choice of them as subjects of his this Evening's Lecture.— N.B. The best passage to the Lecture Room in Fleur-de-Luce-Court, is from Fetter-lane."

TEXT. The elaborate advertisements, and the announcement in the *Courier*, all suggest a carefully thought-out lecture, but no notes have been found that specifically relate to it. In *LR* I 184–200 HNC printed some comments on the Samothracian mysteries, leading into brief remarks on the *Arabian Nights*, on Defoe, and notes on the education of children. These, he wrote, were partly from the notes of J. H. Green, without identifying which part or parts he meant. This suggests that only a part of these notes in fact relates to C's lecture, and that part cannot certainly be identified. The first note, on the Samothracian mysteries, has no connexion with the theme of the lecture as advertised and may well be drawn from marginalia or other sources; it is therefore not reprinted here. The brief paragraphs on the *Arabian Nights* and on Defoe may be from Green's notes. The notes on the education of children have much in common with the report by HCR of C's lecture on education in 1808 (Lect 12A) and with the report of Lect 7 at Bristol in 1813 and fit the topic of the lecture. Accordingly, these passages are reprinted below, from *LR* i 188–9 and 198–200. These and other notes printed by HNC, excluding the marginalia C wrote in 1830 in a copy of *Robinson Crusoe* and which HNC included in the material relating to this lecture, were reprinted in *Misc C* 191–6.

REPORTS. No reports of this lecture have been found.

BACKGROUND AND CIRCUMSTANCES. The announcement in the *Courier* reads more like a digest of the lecture than an advertisement, and the care C took over it and over the almost equally elaborate advertisement in the *M Chron* may reflect an anxiety about falling attendances. The lectures on education C gave in 1808 and in Bristol in 1813 had drawn large audiences, and by emphasising this element in the lecture of 3 Mar C perhaps hoped to attract numbers larger than the "scanty audiences" he complained of in a letter of 1 Mar (*CL* iv 927). What effect his advertising had is not known; there is no mention of this lecture in C's letters, and HCR did not attend it.

The theme of the lecture was one dear to C's heart. In the letters he wrote to Poole in 1797 describing his early life, there is a well-known account of his reading as a child of six years, where he couples together *Robinson Crusoe* and the *Arabian Nights*. One tale in the latter, he wrote, "made so deep an impression on me (I had read it in the evening while my mother was mending stockings) that I was haunted by spectres, whenever I was in the dark—and I distinctly remember the anxious & fearful eagerness, with which I used to watch the window, in which the books lay—& whenever the Sun lay upon them, I would seize it, carry it by the wall, & bask, & read—. My Father found out the effect, which these books had produced—and burnt them.—So I became a *dreamer* . . .". *CL* i 347. Writing a little later to Poole in continuation of his narrative, C went on, "from my early reading of Faery Tales, & Genii &c &c—my mind had been habituated *to the Vast*—& I never regarded *my senses* in any way as the criteria of my belief. I regulated all my creeds by my conceptions not by my *sight*—even at that age. Should children be permitted to read Romances, & Relations of Giants & Magicians, & Genii?—I know all that has been said against it; but I have formed my faith in the affirmative.— I know no other way of giving the mind a love of 'the Great', & 'the Whole'." *CL* i 354. C retained this "faith" formed by Oct 1797, and his love of the *Arabian Nights* especially, which he praised in conversation with John Payne Collier on 17 Oct 1811 (*C on Sh* 35) and again in Lect 5 of the 1811–12 series (at n 38). In that lecture he was echoing remarks he had made in his lecture on education in 1808, when he recommended giving children fairy-tales to read in preference to moral tales, and satirised books for children of the kind Maria Edgeworth wrote (see Lect. 12A, at n 38). He returned to the theme once more in Lect 7 at Bristol in 1813 (at n 13), again advising that children should be given books like fairy-tales rather than moral tales to make them forget themselves, so that the power of imagination might be developed, by which we are "enabled to anticipate the glories and honors of a future existence".

C's early reading of travel-books has been charted to some extent by J. L. Lowes (*RX*; see esp pp 312–30). C's proposed comparison of such "Fictions of Imagination" with novels, evidently to the disadvantage of the latter, recalls earlier occasions on which he had censured the habit of reading novels, in the lectures of 1808 (see Supplementary Records, at n 3), in Lect 1 of the 1811–12 series (at n 13), and in *BL* ch 3 (*CC*) I 48n–9. He regarded the routine novels of the circulating libraries as destructive of the powers of the mind, as merely a way of killing time. The advertisement in the *M Chron* included among the books of fictitious travels C was to discuss Robert Paltock's *Life and Adventures of Peter Wilkins* (1751), a narrative of a voyage in the manner of *Robinson Crusoe*, in which the eponymous hero is shipwrecked in the Antarctic. This was for a time a popular work, and C praised it in *TT* 5 Jul 1834 as a "work of uncommon beauty"; however, there do not appear to be any references to it in C's earlier writings or in his notebooks.

LECTURE 11

RECORDS OF THE LECTURE

COLERIDGE'S NOTES, AS EDITED BY
HENRY NELSON COLERIDGE
FROM *LR* I 188–9, 198–200

The three passages printed below, on the *Arabian Nights*, on Defoe, and on education, are taken from *LR* I, in which they form part of the material gathered by HNC as relating to this lecture. In *LR* they were printed as if parts of a whole, except that the last passage, on education, was separated by a line from the notes on Defoe that precede it. HNC heavily edited the notes, reports, and marginalia he found, cobbling them together with links of his own devising, which makes it difficult to determine what was the origin of many passages. Some of the notes for this lecture were contributed by J. H. Green, and either (*a*) or both (*a*) and (*b*) could have come from him; (*c*), on education, appears to have been copied from notes by C.

(a) On the Arabian Nights

The Asiatic supernatural beings are all produced by imagining an excessive magnitude, or an excessive smallness combined with great power; and the broken associations, which must have given rise to such conceptions, are the sources of the interest which they inspire, as exhibiting, through the working of the imagination, the idea of power in the will. This is delightfully exemplified in the Arabian Nights' Entertainments, and indeed, more or less, in other works of the same kind. In all these there is the same activity of mind as in dreaming, that is—an exertion of the fancy in the combination and recombination of familiar objects so as to produce novel and wonderful imagery. To this must be added that these tales cause no deep feeling of a moral kind—whether of religion or love; but an impulse of motion is communicated to the mind without excitement, and this is the reason of their being so generally read and admired.

I think it not unlikely that the Milesian Tales contained the germs of many of those now in the Arabian Nights; indeed it is scarcely possible to doubt that the Greek empire must have left deep impression on the Persian intellect. So also many of the Roman Catholic legends are taken from Apuleius.[1] In that exquisite story of Cupid and Psyche, the allegory is of no injury to the dramatic vividness of the tale. It is evidently a philosophic attempt to parry Christianity with a *quasi*-Platonic account of the fall and redemption of the soul.

(b) On Defoe

The charm of De Foe's works, especially of Robinson Crusoe, is founded on the same principle. It always interests, never agitates. Crusoe himself is merely a representative of humanity in general; neither his intellectual nor his moral qualities set him above the middle degree of mankind; his only prominent characteristic is the spirit of enterprise and wandering, which is, nevertheless, a very common disposition. You will observe that all that is wonderful in this tale is the result of external circumstances—of things which fortune brings to Crusoe's hand.

(c) On Education

In the education of children, love is first to be instilled, and out of love obedience is to be educed.[2] Then impulse and power should be given to the intellect, and the ends of a moral being be exhibited. For this object thus much is effected by works of imagination;—that they carry the mind out of self, and show the possible of the good and the great in the human character. The height, whatever it may be, of the imaginative standard will do no harm; we are commanded to imitate one who is inimitable. We should address ourselves to those faculties in a child's mind, which are first awakened by nature, and consequently first admit of cultivation, that is to say, the memory and the imagination.

---

[1] In Lect 8 F. Schlegel ascribed the more fabulous and fairy-tale elements of the *Arabian Nights* to Persian origin. *Geschichte* I 277 (Bohn 182). The *Milesian Tales* (to which C referred in Lect 2, above, at n 27), compiled or written by Aristides of Miletus about 100 B.C., are lost, but served as models for Petronius and Apuleius, whose *Golden Ass* contains a famous account of the legend of Cupid and Psyche. In this Psyche, successfully enduring the torments inflicted on her by the jealous Venus, and reunited finally with her lover Cupid, was often allegorised as the human soul or spirit. The idea that "Roman Catholic legends" stem from classical stories may distantly echo C's reading of Conyers Middleton's *A Letter from Rome* (1729), which attempts to show "an exact conformity between popery and paganism" and relates various "*Popish Legends*" (p 53) to fables of antiquity, but not specifically to Apuleius. See also *CN* II 2729 and *Misc C* 30–1.

[2] What follows has many links with C's lecture on education in 1808, and especially with Lect 7 of the Bristol series in 1813, when he also insisted on love as the guiding principle and on the importance of education through the imagination.

The comparing power, the judgement, is not at that age active, and ought not to be forcibly excited, as is too frequently and mistakenly done in the modern systems of education, which can only lead to selfish views, debtor and creditor principles of virtue, and an inflated sense of merit. In the imagination of man exist the seeds of all moral and scientific improvement; chemistry was first alchemy, and out of astrology sprang astronomy. In the childhood of those sciences the imagination opened a way, and furnished materials, on which the ratiocinative powers in a maturer state operated with success. The imagination is the distinguishing characteristic of man as a progressive being;[3] and I repeat that it ought to be carefully guided and strengthened as the indispensable means and instrument of continued amelioration and refinement. Men of genius and goodness are generally restless in their minds in the present, and this, because they are by a law of their nature unremittingly regarding themselves in the future, and contemplating the possible of moral and intellectual advance towards perfection. Thus we live by hope and faith; thus we are for the most part able to realize what we will, and thus we accomplish the end of our being. The contemplation of futurity inspires humility of soul in our judgement of the present.

I think the memory of children cannot, in reason, be too much stored with the objects and facts of natural history. God opens the images of nature, like the leaves of a book, before the eyes of his creature, Man— and teaches him all that is grand and beautiful in the foaming cataract, the glassy lake, and the floating mist.

The common modern novel,[4] in which there is no imagination, but a miserable struggle to excite and gratify mere curiosity, ought, in my judgment, to be wholly forbidden to children. Novel-reading of this sort is especially injurious to the growth of the imagination, the judgment, and the morals, especially to the latter, because it excites mere feelings without at the same time ministering an impulse to action. Women are good novelists, but indifferent poets; and this because they rarely or never thoroughly distinguish between fact and fiction. In the jumble of the two lies the secret of the modern novel, which is the *medium aliquid* between them, having just so much of fiction as to obscure the fact, and so much of fact as to render the fiction insipid. The perusal of a fashionable lady's novel is to me very much like looking

---

[3] For C's strongly held belief in the progressiveness of man and society, see Lect 8 of the 1811–12 series (at n 12) and Lect 7 of the 1813 series (at nn 3 and 17).

[4] C had attacked the novel and novel-reading in Lect 1 of the 1811–12 series (at n 13) and in *BL* ch 3 *(CC)* I 48n–9; see also *Friend (CC)* I 20–1.

at the scenery and decorations of a theatre by broad daylight. The source of the common fondnesss for novels of this sort rests in that dislike of vacancy and that love of sloth, which are inherent in the human mind; they afford excitement without producing reaction. By reaction I mean an activity of the intellectual faculties, which shows itself in consequent reasoning and observation, and originates action and conduct acccording to a principle. Thus, the act of thinking presents two sides for contemplation,—that of external causality, in which the train of thought may be considered as the result of outward impressions, of accidental combinations, of fancy, or the associations of the memory,—and on the other hand, that of internal causality, or of the energy of the will on the mind itself. Thought, therefore, might thus be regarded as passive or active; and the same faculties may in a popular sense be expressed as perception or observation, fancy or imagination, memory or recollection.

LECTURE 12

DATE AND PLACE OF DELIVERY. Friday, 6 March 1818, in the Great Room of the London Philosophical Society, Fleur-de-Luce Court, Fleet Street.

SUBJECT. Magic, witchcraft, and superstition. The Syllabus promised a lecture "On Tales of Witches, Apparitions, &c. as distinguished from the Magic and Magicians of Asiatic Origin. The probable Sources of the former, and of the Belief in them in certain Ages and Classes of Men. Criteria by which mistaken and exaggerated Facts may be distinguished from absolute Falsehood and Imposture. Lastly, the Causes of the Terror and Interest which Stories of Ghosts and Witches inspire, in early Life at least, whether believed or not."

ADVERTISEMENTS. *The Times* Fri, 6 Mar: "THIS EVENING, Quarter after Eight, Mr. COLERIDGE, on the HISTORY and PHILOSOPHY of MAGIC, Witchcraft, Dreams, Omens, Presentiments, Star-craft, etc. with a Theory of Superstition in general, at the Great Room, Flower-de-luce-court; entrance from Fetter-lane, Fleet-street. Admission 5s." *M Chron* Fri, 6 Mar: as in *The Times*, with the substitution of "Visions" for "Omens, Presentiments".

TEXT. A group of seven entries in N 22 appear to be notes prepared by C for this lecture, and the text of them printed below is based on that presented by Kathleen Coburn in *CN* III 4390–4396, omitting alterations, cancellations, etc. In *LR* I 201–16 HNC gathered together some notes taken from C's fragments, marginalia, and from memoranda contributed by J. H. Green, but did not use C's notes in N 22. Raysor identified part of the notes printed by HNC as from drafts of part of a lecture on stage-illusion, from what is now BM Add MS 34225 ff 54ᵛ, 56, written on paper watermarked 1805 and probably related to the lectures of 1808 (see Supplementary Records: C's notes *c*). In any case these notes, though on the subject of dreams, do not appear to have any connexion with the lectures of 1818. Consequently these, which Raysor printed in *Misc C* 197–9, and the marginalia included by HNC, which Raysor omitted, are not reprinted below. There remain two other items from *LR*, both of which were included in *Misc C* 199–203 and are reprinted below. One is a passage on apparitions, from C's notes, which may well belong to this lecture. The other is a note on alchemists contributed by Green; this relates to the subject of the lecture, although C's own notes do not mention alchemy.

REPORTS. No reports of this lecture have been found.

BACKGROUND AND CIRCUMSTANCES. In *The Friend* No 8 of 5 Oct 1809 C promised, in the course of remarks on apparitions, to "devote some future Numbers to the Subject of Dreams, Visions, Ghosts, Witchcraft, &c.". This promise was not fulfilled, but in the 1818 revision this passage was developed into an essay on ghosts and apparitions, and in it C wrote: "I have long wished to devote an entire work to the subject of Dreams, Visions, Ghosts, Witchcraft, &c. in which I might first give, and then endeavour to explain the most interesting and best attested fact of each, which has come within my knowledge, either from books or from personal testimony." *Friend (CC)* II 117, II 145. His lecture in 1818 was perhaps as close as he came to developing his wish, though many entries scattered in the notebooks, as well as marginalia in copies of J. H. Jung *Theorie der Geiste-Kunde* and *Apologie der Theorie der Geisterkunde* (Nuremberg 1808 and 1809), now in the BM, testify to his abiding interest in the subject. The memoranda C wrote in N 22 show that he used Aubrey's *Miscellanies* and read several works on witchcraft in preparation for this lecture, and he evidently had a lot of new material for it. One book he wanted but seems not to have obtained was John Webster's *The Displaying of Supposed Witchcraft* (1677), a copy of which, now in the BM, he annotated at some time, and which he probably read in 1810 (*CN* III 3886, 3887 and n), for he misremembered the name of the author in writing to Thomas Boosey, Jr, the bookseller, on 25 Feb 1818 to ask, "Do you happen to know where I can find Turner on Witch Craft, it is an old folio?" *CL* IV 844; VI 1045. The letters throw no further light on the lecture, and HCR does not mention it.

Perhaps this lecture impressed some, at any rate, of the audience, for it seems likely that T. L. Peacock is referring amusingly to it in ch 12 of *Nightmare Abbey* (1818) 179, in which Mr Flosky, the character based on C, speaks on ghosts, repeating one of his favourite remarks ("I have seen too many ghosts myself to believe in their external existence"; cf *Friend—CC—*I 146), and alluding to Pausanias, as C did in the lecture, apparently in mistake for Herodotus. Mr Flosky seems to be giving a kind of miniature parody of a lecture on ghosts and apparitions, and it suggests the possibility that Peacock, or someone close to him, attended C's lecture.

LECTURE 12

RECORDS OF THE LECTURE

COLERIDGE'S NOTES
CN III 4390–4396

*a*5 March, 1818 Highgate.

Aubrey's Miscellanies, p. 34. "Ex Chroᶠnicoˡ Saxonico," p. 112. Anno MCIV (1104)—conjuncti sunt quatuor circuli circa solem, albi coloris¹— &c

This is translated by Aubrey—Four Circles of a White color were seen TO ROLL IN CONJUNCTION around the Sun.—One of 10,000 instances of the manner, in which the extraordinary grows by superaccretion into the inexplicable Miraculous.—

So Pausanias's story of the miracle during the Oracle—Not indeed παλαιαι, but πελειαι—not winged old Women but really however there did take place a flight of Pigeons.—²

The march of an army across the breast of Blenkarthur, seen at Threlkeld near Keswick—on the entrance of the young Pretender—³

a CN III 4390

¹ C was quoting, as Kathleen Coburn noted in *CN* III 4390n, from John Aubrey *Miscellanies* (2nd ed 1721). On p 34, under the heading "Ostenta: Or, Portents", Aubrey cites the *Saxon Chronicle* in Latin and then translates the passage thus: "In the Year 1104, On the first Day of *Pentecost*, the sixth of *June*, and on the Day following being *Tuesday*, four Circles of a white Colour, were seen to roll in Conjunction round the Sun, each under the other regularly placed, as if they had been drawn by the Hand of a Painter."

² C seems to be recalling a story told in Herodotus 2.55, not Pausanias, though the Greek words, meaning "old women" and "doves", suggest grounds for his confusion, in that Pausanias also refers to the doves associated with the sacred grove at the oracle of Dodona. Herodotus writes of two holy women who were carried away from Thebes to be sold, one in Greece, one in Libya. Search was made for them, but neither could be found. "But the prophetesses at Dodona say thus, Two black doves flew up from Egyptian Thebes; and one of them went to Libya, but the other came thither and settling upon an oak-tree spake with a human voice and said there must needs be an Oracle of Zeus in that place." *CN* III 4390n.

³ Recalling further stories of apparitions from the folklore of the Lake District. The first, seen in Jun 1744, was

*b*Marriage the only doubtful or amphibion of Law & Religion—& yet these *Chief Justice Halites* made no bones about this—O the Puritans![4]

c[Co]nfirmation and discovery of Witchcraft &c
John Stearne, now of Lawshall near Burie [S] Edmonds in Suffolk, sometimes of Manning-tree in Essex. London, 1648.[5]—The 7 united States declared free and independent by the Treaty of Munster—Hobbes floruit—died 1679, æt. 91.—1649—Charles I beheaded.[6] N.B. This Stearne a Witch-finder, and Friend of Hopkin—"who was the Son of a godly Minister, and therefore without doubt within the Covenant" if as I supposed it be Hopkin, he alludes to—but affirms that he died at Manningtree of a Consumption with as quiet conscience—see p. 61. and that is the last page.[7]
    The argument from Scripture answered thus: None can really tell the fortunes of man; but does it follow, that there are no Fortune-tellers, or that such vagabonds are not rightly punished—11 et sequentia[8]— 14[9]—boy 9 years old[10]—**26**!!/[11] 43 the *marks* on the bodies of Witches—

b *CN* III 4391   *c* *CN* III 4392

reported by James Clarke in his *Survey of the Lakes* (1789) 55–6. The second refers to a vision, also seen at Threlkeld, at the very time the Young Pretender, Prince Charles Edward Stuart (1720–88), was landing in Scotland in 1745, anticipating by more than a year his arrival in Cumberland.
    [4] Sir Matthew Hale (1609–76) was the judge in the Suffolk witch-trials reported by Cotton Mather and by Francis Hutchinson, who treats his harsh sentence there as an error of judgement by a "great and good Man". *An Historical Essay Concerning Witchcraft* ch 8 (1718) 109–24. A Puritan, Hale was held in great respect by dissenters, whose cause he supported in various ways. Nearly all those accused as witches were women, but in the stories of them their husbands rarely figure, and their marital status seems to be ignored.
    [5] C quotes from the title-page of *A Confirmation and Discovery of Witchcraft* by John Stearne (1648); see *CN* III 4392 and n.
    [6] C registers presumably his amazement that during the same period when the Treaty of Munster marked the end of

the Thirty Years' War (1648) and the independence of the German states, when Hobbes the rationalist was about to bring out *Leviathan* (1651), and when Charles I was about to be executed, witch-hunting could still be taken so seriously.
    [7] C quotes from and summarises the last page of Stearne's book; Mathew Hopkins, the notorious witch-finder, was in fact hanged in 1647.
    [8] Pp 1–10 present the argument from the Bible for the existence of witches; p 11 introduces the argument that experience demonstrates their presence and that more are women than men.
    [9] P 14 contains the story of eighteen witches who refused to confess before their execution at Bury St Edmunds and joined in singing a psalm—evidence, for Stearne, of their guilt.
    [10] Pp 19–20 tell of a boy who confessed he had "suckled an Impe, and had it at command to do mischiefe, and nominated some, as the killing of some Chickings".
    [11] P 26 describes three "witches" who suckled imps: the first witch had imps in the form of a dove called Tib, a miller called Tom, a spider called Joan, and a

Too foul to be read/[12] skinless after *swoming* (i.e. swimming them) tho'
it had been *forewarned*—.[13] Horrible treatment of keeping them awake/
So denied as to be admitted—[14]

The Trial of Witchcraft, by John Cotta, Doctor in Physic.
London, 1616.

The Year in which Virginia was settled by Sir Walter Raleigh—&
Cape Horn first sailed round—[15]

The ordinary argument from Scripture facts, and ⌐. . .⌐ from Pliny,
Philostratus &c—but the fact related ⌐. . .⌐ Baptista Porta, Lib. II de
Magiâ Naturali is ⌐. . .⌐ reciting—as magnetic Torpor—See p. 35.[16]

[d]Poor John Aubry's Miscellanies—the probable original of Congreve's
Old omen-monger. 56. **58**, *60*[17] exquisite for the medical FACT that
follows—so like Animal Magnetism/.[18]

[d] *CN* III 4393

---

wasp called Nan; the second had three
imps like children; the third had four imps,
two like little boys, one like a lamb, and
the other like a buzzard.

[12] P 43 answers the question "How
shall they [the marks of witches] be dis-
cerned from natural marks?" The answer: sometimes they look like a teat,
"like the fingers of a glove" or "a little
red spot, much like . . . a flea-bite" and
so on.

[13] On pp 18–19 Stearne admits he
"swome" some suspected witches and
says that in this test by water "the free
person will presently be choaked, when
the other [i.e. witches] lye topling on the
water, striving to get their heads, or
themselves under the water, but cannot,
neither can they bring out water in their
mouthes, though they be foretold of it,
nor spit cleare water; for the water enters
them not when it will the other"; i.e.
witches float, while the innocent sink.
Stearne also says, p 18, that this test was
used as evidence during the period "from
March, or *May* 1645, to about the middle
of *August* next following; when Judge
Corbolt, that now is, forwarned it", i.e.
prohibited it.

[14] On p 13 Stearne says that he has
been accused of keeping suspects awake,
without food or drink, "and so made
them say what you would"; his equiv-

ocal reply in effect constitutes an admission that he did this, as C notes.

[15] As in the case of Stearne's book, C
points to events contemporary with Cotta's *The Triall of Witch-craft* and notes
that Cotta was a doctor, a man of scientific pretensions.

[16] Cotta, like Stearne, cites the Bible
and also numerous classical authorities,
including Pliny, but not, oddly, Philostratus (d A.D. 244), whose name C reasonably assumed would be listed as the
author of the life of the magician Apol-
lonius of Tyana. The story from Porta
concerns a witch who believed she had
spent a night riding in the air over mountains, when the author and others had
been watching her "within her chamber
profoundly sleeping; yea, had smitten her,
made her flesh blue with strokes, and
could not awake her". Cotta thinks of
this as showing "the juggling power of
the Devill", but C relates it to torpor
induced by animal magnetism; see *Friend
(CC)* I 59 and n.

[17] The page-references are to a section
on "Dreams", in which Aubrey reports
a series of stories of dreams that proved
to be instances of second sight. C was
evidently struck by Aubrey's gullibility
and connected him with Foresight in
Congreve's *Love for Love*.

[18] Aubrey went on to recount several

⟨Yet this very man relates the YEW DRENCH, p. 64.⟩[19]

Memory counterfeited by present impression, one great cause of the co-incidence of Dreams with the event—ἡ υητηϱ εμή.[20]

The story of Donne from Walton (p. **69**) from *about* the *very* hour—*about*)(*very*.—[21]

72, the counterpart of the famous story of Colonel Dennison's Cousin—[22]

78—the first story might puzzle; but luckily in comes the frisking Givenni Givanni[23]—& so much for Sir William Dugdale—

dreams in which sufferers dreamed that a particular fruit or syrup would cure their ailments and on taking the remedy found that it did indeed relieve their pain. C was fascinated by the idea of animal magnetism, or mesmerism, associated with the name of Friedrich Mesmer (1734–1815), and the reference here connects his interest in dreams and omens to his wider concern with the relation of mind to body, the workings of the subconscious mind, and the nature of volition. He rejected an unthinking belief in omens and dreams (as in witchcraft), but saw too the possible connexions of these with buried mental processes. So he noted in C. A. F. Kluge's *Versuch einer Darstellung des animalschen Magnetismus* ' (Berlin 1815): "Allowing the least possible to Fancy and Exaggeration, I can yet find nothing in the Cases collected by Dr Kluge that requires any other conclusion but this—that under certain conditions one human Being may so act on the body as well as on the mind of another as to produce a morbid Sleep, from which the Brain awakes while the organs of sense remain in stupor. I speak exclusively of the *intellectual* phænomena of An. Mag. That the same vis ab extra may act medically, there is no reason to doubt—any more than of the effects of Opium. . . ." *IS* 51. See also *P Lects* (1949) 45–7, 423–4.

[19] On p 64 of the *Miscellanies* is Aubrey's story of a woman who dreamed that her sick daughter would recover if given "a Drench of Yewgh pounded"; so she gave her the potion, and it killed her. Her chambermaid repeated the experiment and also died. Aubrey adds:

"This was about the Year 1670, or 1671. I knew the Family."

[20] Tr "my mother"—perhaps recalling the death of C's father, as narrated in a letter to Poole in Oct 1797: after dreaming that the figure of Death appeared to him, C's father returned home from a journey to Plymouth, went to bed in high spirits, and then "In a minute my mother heard a noise in his throat—and spoke to him—but he did not answer—& I said, 'Papa is dead.'—I did not know [of] my Father's return, but I knew that he was expected. How I came to think of his Death, I cannot tell; but so it was." *CL* I 355. See also below (at n 50).

[21] Another reference to Aubrey pp 69–71, the section on "Apparitions", reporting from Izaak Walton's *Life of Donne* the story of Donne's vision, when in France, of his wife with "*a dead Child in her Arms*" and of his learning subsequently that on the same day she had been delivered in London of a still-born baby, "about the *very* Hour that Mr. *Donne* affirmed he *saw her* pass by him in his *Chamber*".

[22] Aubrey reports two stories of apparitions on p 72, one of a "Hand with a bloody Sword", the other of a courtesan who, at the very moment that she killed herself in Italy, appeared to her lover in England. The story of Colonel Dennison's cousin has not been traced, but presumably is the counterpart of the second of these tales.

[23] The first story on p 78 of Aubrey relates to the phantom of Sir George Villiers appearing to a friend to announce three months in advance that the Duke

But more glorious than all—if Time allowed it—the Letter from the Reverend Mr Andrew Paschal, B.D. Rector of Chedzoy in Somersetshire to John Aubrey, Esqre at Gresham College, London—p. 149.[24]

Second Sight, p. 190—195^e.[25]
⌈. . .⌉ of Aubrey's Miscell.—a curious phrase. "The mistress somewhat ⌈nice⌉ and backward to give him Victuals, You need not (says he) *churle me in a piece of Meat*—"—So *rashed* for the noise & motion of Bed Curtains drawn back, by the Cross rings over the rod—
Several tracts of Second Sight correspond with Swedenborgh's Experience—[26]

^e Written in large letters and numbers

---

of Buckingham would be stabbed to death, and indeed it "might puzzle", but Aubrey reports that Sir William Dugdale affirms it to be true and goes on to narrate another story told to him by Dugdale. This one concerns the appearance of the ghost of Lord Bocconi to Lord Middleton when the latter lay in prison; the ghost "told him, that within three Days he should escape, and he did so, in his Wives Cloaths. When he had done his Message, he gave a Frisk, and said,

Givenni Givanni *tis very strange,*
In the World to see so sudden a
    Change.

And then gathered up and vanished." The second story quite undermines the authority of Dugdale as a witness, which is the point of C's reference.
[24] The reference is to pp 149–57 of Aubrey, in which the letter from Paschal is quoted. In it are reported the activities of a "discontented Daemon" in a Devonshire parish, which played all sorts of tricks on a young man named Fry, and of the poltergeist which carried out numerous "fantastical Freeks", "as the marching of a great Barrel full of Salt out of one Room into another", and the even more fantastic events involving a "Woman Spectre", who carried Fry through the air over a house and dumped him in a quagmire. There is no indication whether time allowed C to use any or all of this narrative, but evidently he enjoyed it as "glorious" entertainment and

was thinking of using it for humorous effect. See *CN* III 4393n, in which a long passage from Paschal's letter is quoted.
[25] The reference is to a section in Aubrey on "Second-Sighted Men in Scotland", in which various questions about the nature of second sight are asked and answered; e.g., do second-sighted men see visibly what they report? Answer, yes. May godly persons have the gift? Answer, no, only the vicious. Does it descend from parents to children? Answer, uncertain. How do men come by it? Answer, some say by compact with the Devil, others by converse with demons. The section also reports various stories of second sight, and C quotes from one occurring on p 198: ". . . a Traveller coming in to a certain House, desired some Meat: The Mistress being something nice and backward to give him Victuals; you need not, says he, churle me in a Piece of Meat; for before an Hour and Half be over, a young Man of such a Stature and Garb will come in with a great Salmon-fish on his Back, which I behold yonder on the Floor: And it came to pass within the said Time." The last phrase quoted relates to an anecdote in an earlier section of the *Miscellanies* on "Magic", p 147, about a haunted room in London in which "the Curtains would be rashed at Night". C was struck by the curious uses of "churl" = begrudge (the only example cited in *OED*) and "rash" to mean "dash violently".
[26] C possessed and annotated a copy

*f*The Wonders of the Invisible World—*g*
being an account of the Tryals of Several Witches lately executed in
New England &c—
by COTTON MATHER
Published by the special Command of his Excellency the Governor of
the Province of the Massachusetts Bay in New England/
Printed first at Bostun in N.E.—and reprinted at London, for John
Dunton, at the Raven in the Poultry. 1693.[27]
Well does C. M. call it storms of Witchcraft, that the Kingdoms of
Sweden, Denmark, Scotland, yea England itself have had/[28]
p. 8.—so p. 7.[29]
P. 57. Justice Hales & the INVISIBLE Mouse!![30]

*h*We hear of Witches among the Ancients fr ⌜. . . .⌝ chiefly who had
the best claim to them—the P⌜. . .⌝ in the decline & superannuation of
local Polytheism more as was to be expected/ but those in the central
parts of the Roman Empire either Poisoners, Charmers, or Manteis[31]—
the others are laid in Thrace, Thessaly—as well as in Africa—Witchery
being the abortion of the mind in the ⟨premature⟩ attempt to bring forth

f CN III 4394
g Title written in large letters
h CN III 4395

---

of Swedenborg's *De coelo et ejus mi-rabilibus, et de inferno, ex auditis & visis,*
i.e. "Of heaven and its marvels, and of
hell, from things heard and seen" (1758),
which is now in the BM. This contains
an account of Swedenborg's claim to have
been guided by angels, which C interpreted as symbolic visions. In *CN* III 3474
C commented at length on the nature of
Swedenborg's "memorable Experiences".

[27] C correctly sets out the title of the
edition he used of Cotton Mather's lurid
defence of witchcraft and account of the
Salem trials. This was the first London
printing of the book issued originally in
Boston, Mass in 1693.

[28] On p 8, in which Mather says, "The
Kingdoms of *Sweden, Denmark, Scotland,* yea, and *England* it self, as well
as the Province of *New-England,* have
had their Storms of *Witchcrafts* breaking
upon them, which have made most La-

mentable Devastations".

[29] This page concerns the special efforts of the Devil to "overturn" the colony of New England by witchcraft and
so recover what was formerly his own
territory, according to Mather.

[30] On pp 55–60 Mather reports a trial
of witches, borrowing his material from
*A Tryal of Witches at the Assizes Held
at Bury St. Edmonds for the County of
Suffolk; on the Tenth Day of March, 1644*
(1682). The judge was Sir Matthew Hale,
and in the course of the trial of two women
for bewitching a number of children, evidence was given of a child, p 57, that
"She one Day caught an Invisible *Mouse,*
and throwing it into the Fire, it Flush'd
like to Gun-Powder. None besides the
Child saw the *Mouse,* but every one saw
the *Flash.*"

[31] Diviners or prophets, plural of the
Greek μαντις.

a sacerdotal order—yet still the cases were few—till the 15th Century—. Joan of Arc, the poor Dutchess of Gloster & her agents[32]—& at the very beginning of the century, or rather in the very close of the preceding the University of Paris (1398) prefaced their rules for judging Witches with— Plus solito[33]—made use of by Richard 3[rd][34]—but in 1484 Pope Innocent the 8th sent forth his tremendous Bull ordering the search after Witches— & to burn them/[35]—The consequence was natural/ They multiplied as by miracle—turned against the Wadenses & other Predecessors of the Reformation/ One Inquisitor burnt a hundred in Piedmont, but as these were merely trying his hand, the People rose and chased him out of the country—[36]

1520—Danæus in his dialogue of Witches declares the number of Witches here infinitum tho' such Multitudes had been either burnt alive, or destroyed in the Trials—[37]

⌈1⌉523 Pope Adrian enforced his Predecessors Bull by a Bullcalf of his own, with power to excommunicate all tardy or sceptical Magistrates &c— in the next year a thousand burnt in the Diocese of Como alone/[38]

In 1541, toward the hideous close of Henry the 8[ths] reign the two acts, 1. against false Prophecies; the other against Conjuration, Witchcraft, Sorcery, &c—*and pulling down of Crosses*—This however was abrogated by the Reformers in the first year of Edward VI[ths][39]—whether on account of the last clause—? No!—They would have repealed that only—but alas!

---

[32] Here C began to select instances from Francis Hutchinson's *An Historical Essay Concerning Witchcraft* (1718), ch 2 of which consists of "A Chronological Table of the Executions, or Tryals of Supposed Witches and Conjurers"; examples from before the fifteenth century occupy pp 13–19, later instances down to 1701 continue to p 46. Joan of Arc and the Duchess of Gloucester, who was accused of seeking the death of Henry VI, and whose agent was burned as a witch, are listed on p 20.

[33] Hutchinson p 21: "the University of *Paris, Anno* 1398, in the Preface to their Rules for judging Witches, say, that that Crime was, *Plus solito in illa aetate*, more common in that Age than it had been before".

[34] "The same Year [1483], King *Richard*, being of the House of *York*, attainted for Sorcery several that supported the Line of *Lancaster*."

[35] Hutchinson pp 21–2 cites the Bull and adds: "From the Time of this superstitious Bull, observe how the Number of Executions increase, but chiefly in the Places where the *Waldenses* and *Protestants* were most numerous."

[36] "About this Time *Alciat*, a famous Lawyer, in his *Parerga*, says, One Inquisitor burnt a Hundred in *Piedmont*, and proceeded daily to burn more, till the *People rose* against the Inquisitor, and chased him out of the Country."

[37] Hutchinson p 24, referring to Lambert Daneau (1530–95), French Protestant divine, says: "About this Time, Multitudes were burnt in *France*", and cites a Latin phrase from Daneau or Danaeus, which includes the word "Infinitum", borrowed by C.

[38] Rephrasing passages in Hutchinson p 24.

[39] Based on Hutchinson p 25.

in this as throughout the reign of Elizabeth the Bishops were the *Burning Party*—Archbishop Cranmer's Articles of Visitation—& Elizabeth, induce to enact a Law—.[40]

Yet before the *Crash* came as if to leave the Witch-finders & their partizans without an excuse, several pretended *Possessed* who had charged others with bewitching them were *detected*—the gross absurdities—see Hutchinson p. 28[41]—Yet on such precious evidence Remigius burnt 900 in Lorrain from 1580 to 1595—a thousand fled the country to save their lives—15 destroyed themselves to escape—Towns were deserted—and all this is related in Triumph by Remigius himself in his Book De Dæmonolatriâ S[r]agarum[1].[42]

1603—King Solomon Stuart—& the Parliament in compliment repealed Elizabeth in order to enact a more merciless one—.[43] The consequences as might be expected—*Honor to Shakespear*—Middleton/ Ben Jonson, flattered—/

But the true Horrors commenced with the republican Parliament—too shocking to be detailed—confessions how extorted—Instance of the absurdity in Antoinetta Bourignon—50 poor Children at Lisle—p. 39[44]

Lord Chief Justice Holt set his face against it[45]—but Chief Justice Hale—his critique on Hales[46]—the Idol of our modern *Saints* in Parliament/ He, and his dear Friends Mather & Baxter the true causes of the New England Massacres/[47]

---

[40] Hutchinson pp 25–6: "*Item*, You shall enquire, whether you know of any that use Charms, Sorcery, Enchantments, Witchcraft, Soothsaying, or any like Craft, invented by the Devil. . . . In the Second Year of Queen *Elizabeth* was renew'd the same Article of Enquiry for Sorcerers".

[41] Here and on p 29 Hutchinson reports two cases of seventeenth-century convictions of people for witchcraft upon flimsy and absurd evidence.

[42] Based on Hutchinson pp 30–1. Remigius, or Nicolas Remi (1530–1612), a notorious suppressor of witches, was the author of *Daemonolatreiae libri tres* (Lyons 1595); the title as given by Hutchinson, "Of the Demonolatry of Witches", seems to be his own variant.

[43] Rewording Hutchinson p 34, "Solomon Stuart" was C's own name for James I, and he added the references to Shakespeare, Middleton, and Ben Jon-

son.

[44] On pp 37–8 Hutchinson lists many executions for witchcraft during the Commonwealth period. The story of Antonietta Bourignon is told on p 39: she ran a school for poor girls and described to them one day how "as she came into the School, she thought she saw a great Number of little black Children with Wings, flying about her Scholars Heads", with the result that most of the children shortly confessed to being witches.

[45] Hutchinson pp 44–5 reports four trials in 1694–6 at which Lord Chief Justice Sir John Holt (1642–1710) acquitted people accused of witchcraft.

[46] See above (at n 4). Hutchinson is not severe on Hale, who did, however, pass sentence of execution on the women tried in the notorious trial at Bury St Edmunds in 1664, reported by Cotton Mather and Hutchinson.

[47] In Hutchinson's ch 5, pp 72–94,

*i*Apparitions—The story of the Young woman from Birmingham/[48]—My converse with Faringdon/[49]

The mind never perhaps wholly uninformed of the circumstantia in Sleep—by means of the feeling, the temperature/ &c.—Persons will awake by removing Lights—how does sensation produce corresponding images?—My Father's dream[50]—ᴦfreᴸquent cause of the terror struck by apparitions ᴦisᴸ that in the first feeling the terror (as a bodily sensation) is the cause of the *Image*/ not vice versâ[51]—This illustrated & brought as a confutation of the reality of apparitions—"You are alive."—

2. Eternity, Infinity, ever negative, contemplated under the relations of Time/ the contradiction & consequent perplexity/ Hence the terrors of Conscience—

3. Lastly, and an overpowering answer to those who think Religion aided by Dæmonology, an apparent removal from God's protection, which is *for us* one with an established order of Cause and Effects—in Mechanism—and when the mind expands, Law in dynamics—: but Free Will to Powers ab extra, not subject to *human Love*—and supposed in rebellion to divine Law—would necessarily shelter itself in *Polytheism*—i.e. make the things themselves be sources of the Law/

i CN III 4396

---

which deals with the Salem trials and Cotton Mather's account of them, it is said: "Mr. *Mather* dispersed Mr. *Baxter's* Book in *New-England*, with the Character of it, as a Book that was *Ungainsayable.*" This was Richard Baxter's *The Certainty of the World of Spirits* (1691).

[48] Aubrey has a long section, pp 67–109, recording numerous stories of apparitions, but none relates to a young woman from Birmingham.

[49] In his diary entry for 25 Mar 1804 Joseph Farington records how Lady Beaumont prompted him to tell the story of the apparition to one Captain Wynyard of his brother, so that she could hear C's opinion of it. C said it was a deception created by a disordered imagination. Farington *Diary* II 210.

[50] In one of the autobiographical letters C wrote to Poole in 1797 he described how his father dreamt "that Death

had appeared to him", and died the following night. *CL* I 355. See above, n 20.

[51] In *Vorschule der Aesthetik* § 5 (1813) 37–8 (*Werke* v 45–6) Richter says that it is not the physical appearance of ghosts, but belief in them that paints the nightpiece of the world of spirits ("nicht das gemeine physische Wunder, sondern das Glauben daran malt das Nachtstück der Geisterwelt"). The point is roughly the same, and in a letter of 13 Dec 1817 C said that he had merely looked into Richter's book, but found one sentence "almost word for word the same as one written by myself in a fragment of an Essay on the Supernatural many years ago—viz. that *the presence* of a Ghost is the terror, not what he *does*". *CL* IV 793. The "Essay" was perhaps *The Friend* No 8 (5 Oct 1809), which contains the same idea differently expressed; see *Friend (CC)* II 117–19.

COLERIDGE'S NOTES, AS EDITED BY
HENRY NELSON COLERIDGE
FROM *LR* I 204–7

The fact really is, as to apparitions, that the terror produces the image instead of the contrary; for *in omnem actum perceptionis influit imaginatio*, as says Wolfe.[52]

O, strange is the self-power of the imagination—when painful sensations have made it their interpreter, or returning gladsomeness or convalescence has made its chilled and evanished figures and landscape bud, blossom, and live in scarlet, green, and snowy white (like the fire-screen inscribed with the nitrate and muriate of cobalt,)—strange is the power to represent the events and circumstances, even to the anguish or the triumph of the *quasi*-credent soul, while the necessary conditions, the only possible causes of such contingencies, are known to be in fact quite hopeless;—yea, when the pure mind would recoil from the eve-lengthened shadow of an approaching hope, as from a crime;—and yet the effect shall have place, and substance, and living energy, and, on a blue islet of ether, in a whole sky of blackest cloudage, shine like a firstling of creation!

To return, however to apparitions, and by way of an amusing illustration of the nature and value of even contemporary testimony upon such subjects, I will present you with a passage, literally translated by my friend, Mr. Southey, from the well known work of Bernal Dias, one of the companions of Cortes, in the conquest of Mexico:

Here it is that Gomara says, that Francisco de Morla rode forward on a dappled grey horse, before Cortes and the cavalry came up, and that the apostle St. Iago, or St. Peter, was there. I must say that all our works and victories are by the hand of our Lord Jesus Christ, and that in this battle there were for each of us so many Indians, that they could have covered us with handfuls of earth, if it had not been that the great mercy of God helped us in every thing. And it may be that he of whom Gomara speaks, was the glorious Santiago or San Pedro, and I, as a sinner, was not worthy to see him; but he whom I saw there and knew, was Francisco de Morla on a chestnut horse, who came up with Cortes. And it seems to me that now while I am writing this, the whole war is represented before these sinful eyes, just in the manner as we then went

---

[52] I.e. the imagination is involved in every act of perception. C wrote these words in a notebook entry of 1801 (*CN* I 905; see also *CN* III 3256n) and in the 1818 *Friend (CC)* I 146. W. Schrickx in *English Studies* XL (1959) 160–1 pointed out that the reference C gives in *CN* I 905, to "P I 76", is to Ernst Platner *Philosophische Aphorismen* (2 vols Leipzig 1793–1800) I 76, C's annotated copy of which is in the BM. Platner quotes from Christian von Wolff *Psychologia rationalis* 1.1.24: "imaginatio quoque in actum apperceptionis influit".

through it. And though I, as an unworthy sinner, might not deserve to see either of these glorious apostles, there were in our company above four hundred soldiers, and Cortes, and many other knights; and it would have been talked of and testified, and they would have made a church, when they peopled the town, which would have been called Santiago de la Vittoria, or San Pedro de la Vittoria, as it is now called, Santa Maria de la Vittoria. And if it was, as Gomara says, bad Christians must we have been, when our Lord God sent us his holy apostles, not to acknowledge his great mercy, and venerate his church daily. And would to God, it had been, as the Chronicler says!—but till I read his Chronicle, I never heard such a thing from any of the conquerors who were there.[53]

Now, what if the odd accident of such a man as Bernal Dias' writing a history had not taken place! Gomara's account, the account of a contemporary, which yet must have been read by scores who were present, would have remained uncontradicted. I remember the story of a man, whom the devil met and talked with, but left at a particular lane;—the man followed him with his eyes, and when the devil got to the turning or bend of the lane, he vanished! The devil was upon this occasion drest in a blue coat, plus waistcoat, leather breeches and boots, and talked and looked just like a common man, except as to a particular lock of hair which he had. "And how do you know then that it was the devil?"—"How do I know," replied the fellow,—"why, if it had not been the devil, being drest as he was, and looking as he did, why should I have been sore stricken with fright, when I first saw him? and why should I be in such a tremble all the while he talked? And, moreover, he had a particular sort of a kind of a lock, and when I groaned and said, upon every question he asked me, Lord have mercy upon me! or, Christ have mercy upon me! it was plain enough that he did not like it, and so he left me!"—The man was quite sober when he related this story; but as it happened to him on his return from market, it is probable that he was then muddled. As for myself, I was actually seen in Newgate in the winter of 1798;[54] the person who saw me there, said he had asked my name of Mr. A. B. a known acquaintance of mine, who told him that it was young Coleridge, who had married the eldest Miss———. "Will you go to Newgate, Sir?" said my friend; "for I

[53] Bernal Díaz del Castillo (1492–c 1581) *The True History of the Conquest of Mexico* (not published till 1632). The only translation available in print to C or to HNC before the publication of *LR* in 1836 was that by Maurice Keatinge (1800). The text of this, ch 3 pp 47–8, differs from that printed in *LR*, which may derive from RS. Francisco López de Gómara (1512–c 1557) published in 1552 a romanticised account of the conquest of Mexico. Francisco de Morla was one of Cortés' officers.

[54] C made a cryptic notebook entry in 1802 relating to this mistake; see *CN* I 1110 and n.

assure you that Mr. C. is now in Germany." "Very willingly," replied the other, and away they went to Newgate, and sent for A. B. "Coleridge," cried he, "in Newgate! God forbid!" I said, "young Col ——— who married the eldest Miss ———." The names were something similar. And yet this person had himself really seen me at one of my lectures.

I remember, upon the occasion of my inhaling the nitrous oxide at the Royal Institution, about five minutes afterwards, a gentleman came from the other side of the theatre and said to me,—"Was it not ravishingly delightful, Sir?"—"It was highly pleasurable, no doubt."—"Was it not very like sweet music?"—"I cannot say I perceived any analogy to it."—"Did you not say it was very like Mrs. Billington singing by your ear?"—"No, Sir, I said that while I was breathing the gas, there was a singing in my ears."[55]

REPORT BY JOSEPH HENRY GREEN
FROM *LR* I 208–10

Green's report relates to the subject of the lecture, although C's own notes do not mention alchemy, and there is nothing specifically to link this with Lect 12. First printed by HNC in *LR* I, it was included in *Misc C* 202–3.

There have been very strange and incredible stories told of and by the alchemists. Perhaps in some of them there may have been a specific form of mania,[56] originating in the constant intension of the mind on an imaginary end, associated with an immense variety of means, all of them substances not familiar to men in general, and in forms strange and unlike to those of ordinary nature.[57] Sometimes, it seems as if the alchemists wrote like the Pythagoreans on music, imagining a meta-

---

[55] C attended Humphry Davy's lectures on chemistry at the RI in Jan–Feb 1802 and may have inhaled nitrous oxide, or "laughing gas", then (see *CN* I 1098 f 25ᵛ and n). But he may have been confusing this occasion with his first meeting with Davy late in 1799 at Bristol, when Davy was full of his new discovery and all his friends, probably C among them, were trying its effects; see Cottle *Rem* 266–8 and *C Life* (EKC) 361. Elizabeth Billington (1768–1818) was the most distinguished English opera singer of the period; C attended a concert at her house in 1813. *CL* III 439. This anecdote

is a further illustration of the fallibility of reports based on what people say they see or hear and is linked with the Newgate story in notebook entries of 1802; see *CN* I 1107 and n.

[56] This paragraph consists of two passages to be found in *CN* III 4414 ff 9ᵛ and 10, dated May 1818 by Kathleen Coburn, who notes that C was extracting and condensing from Hermann Boerhaave's *A New Method of Chemistry* tr P. Shaw and E. Chambers (1727).

[57] Cf *CN* III 4414 f 9ᵛ, a similar passage, relating to the alchemist Helmont.

physical and inaudible music as the basis of the audible. It is clear that by sulphur they meant the solar rays or light, and by mercury the principle of ponderability, so that their theory was the same with that of the Heraclitic physics, or the modern German *Naturphilosophie*, which deduces all things from light and gravitation, each being bipolar; gravitation = north and south, or attraction and repulsion; light = east and west, or contraction and dilation; and gold being the tetrad, or interpenetration of both, as water was the dyad of light, and iron the dyad of gravitation.[58]

It is, probably, unjust to accuse the alchemists generally of dabbling with attempts at magic in the common sense of the term. The supposed exercise of magical power always involved some moral guilt, directly or indirectly, as in stealing a piece of meat to lay on warts, touching humours with the hand of an executed person, &c. Rites of this sort and other practices of sorcery have always been regarded with trembling abhorrence by all nations, even the most ignorant, as by the Africans, the Hudson's Bay people and others. The alchemists were, no doubt, often considered as dealers in art magic, and many of them were not unwilling that such a belief should be prevalent; and the more earnest among them evidently looked at their association of substances, fumigations, and other chemical operations as merely ceremonial, and seem, therefore, to have had a deeper meaning, that of evoking a latent power. It would be profitable to make a collection of all the cases of cures by magical charms and incantations; much useful information might, probably, be derived from it; for it is to be observed that such rites are the form in which medical knowledge would be preserved amongst a barbarous and ignorant people.

---

[58] Cf *CN* III 4414 f 10, almost word for word with the above passage from "Sometimes, it seems . . .". The reference is primarily to Schelling; for C's comment on *Einleitung zu seinem Entwurf eines Systems der Naturphilosophie* (1799) see *CN* III 4449; see also *BL* ch 9 (*CC*) I 160ff.

LECTURE 13

DATE AND PLACE OF DELIVERY. Tuesday, 10 March 1818, in the Great Room of the London Philosophical Society, Fleur-de-Luce Court, Fleet Street.

SUBJECT. The relation of genius to nature in the fine arts. The Syllabus proposed a lecture "On Colour, Sound, and Form, in Nature, as connected with POESY: the word 'Poesy' used as the *generic* or class term, including Poetry, Music, Painting, Statuary, and ideal Architecture, as its Species. The reciprocal Relations of Poetry and Philosophy to each other; and of both to Religion, and the Moral Sense."

ADVERTISEMENTS. *The Times* Tues, 10 Mar: "The Two concluding LECTURES of Mr COLERIDGE's COURSE on Tuesday and Friday evenings, March 6 and 10, at a quarter after Eight precisely: the first, on the relations of Genius to Nature in the Fine Arts, viz. Music, Painting, Statuary, and Architecture . . . at the Great Room Flower-de-luce-court, Fleet-street . . .". *M Chron* Tues, 10 Mar: as in *The Times*.

TEXT. The notes C prepared in N 22 for this lecture, headed with its number and date of delivery, were first printed, with omissions, additions, and rewriting, in *LR* I 216–30 under the title "On Poesy or Art". This version was reprinted in *NLS* (1849) II 157–71 and again in *BL* (1907) II 253–63. C's original notes were first published in *Misc C* 204–13, and a more detailed transcript of them has since been edited by Kathleen Coburn in *CN* III 4397. The text printed below is based on hers, but omits cancellations, alterations, etc. Raysor included at the end part of the next note in N 22 (*C* III 4398), but it is written in a different ink, and the connexion is not proved. Nevertheless, since this is a note on infancy, and could be an expansion of the heading "Childhood", which occurs towards the end of the preceding notes, it is also reprinted below.

REPORTS. No reports of this lecture have been found.

BACKGROUND AND CIRCUMSTANCES. Nothing is known of the success or otherwise of this lecture, which is not mentioned in C's letters or by HCR. Some of the notes, as Kathleen Coburn pointed out, are condensed transcriptions of the main headings of the first part of Schelling's lecture "Über das Verhältniss der bildenden Künste zu der Natur" (1807). C gave two page-references in his notes to the copy of *Philosophische Schriften* (Landshut 1809) he owned and annotated, which is now in the BM. C's debt to Schelling was pointed out by James Ferrier writing on "The Plagiarisms of Coleridge" in *Bl Mag* XLVII (Mar 1840) 287–99. The echoes of Schelling were further documented by SC in *NLS* (1849) II 363–9 and again by Shawcross in *BL* (1907) II 317–18 and Raysor in his footnotes in *Misc C*. The fullest account of the way C used Schelling's ideas, and material from other sources, is provided by Kathleen Coburn in her notes to *CN* III 4397, which are freely adapted in the sparer commentary provided below. As is so often the case with C, the notion of "plagiarism" falsifies; it is not merely that he did not publish the lecture, and can hardly be castigated for quoting Schelling in his notes, but rather that the whole matter is more complicated than a question of borrowing other people's ideas. What C took from Schelling, Schelling in turn had often derived from others, and, as Kathleen Coburn points out, "The seminal thinker in the whole range of problems here broached—nature as the object the artist 'imitates', nature as the universe of

214

which man is part, nature and its imitation in art distinguished and discussed in both anthropological and psychological terms—was Schiller, particularly the Schiller of 'Über naive und sentimentalische Dichtung' (first published 1795–6). Schelling's debt was marked; he added the dimension of neo-Platonic metaphysics, to which Coleridge, up to a point, responded.'' C's annotations record his disagreements with Schelling, whose work he was not slavishly echoing, but using, wherever he found it congenial, to develop and systematise his own theories, and perhaps also, as Shawcross suggests, to ''emancipate himself from Kantean limitations''. *BL* (1907) ɪɪ 317. Unfortunately, there is no evidence to show how, in the lecture–room, C developed his argument from the notes.

LECTURE 13

RECORDS OF THE LECTURE

COLERIDGE'S NOTES
CN III 4397–4398

*a*Thirteenth Lecture, Tuesday, 10 March, 1818.

Man communicates by articulation of Sounds,[1] and paramountly by the memory in the Ear—Nature by the impression of Surfaces and Bounds on the Eye, and thro' the Eye gives significance and appropriation, and thus the conditions of Memory (or the capability of being remembered) to Sounds, smells, &c. Now *Art* (I use the word collectively for Music, Painting, Statuary and Architecture) is the Mediatress, the reconciliator of Man and Nature.—

The primary Art is *Writing*, primary if we regard the purpose, abstracted from the different modes of realizing it—the *steps*, of which the instances are still presented to us in the lower degrees of civilization—gesticulation and rosaries or Wampum,[2] in the lowest—picture Language—Hieroglyphics—and finally, Alphabetic/ These all alike consist in the *translation*, as it were, of Man into Nature—the use of the visible in place of the Audible. The (so called) Music of Savage Tribes as little deserves the name of Art to the Understanding, as the Ear warrants it for Music—. Its lowest step is a mere expression of Passion by the sounds which the Passion itself necessitates—its highest, a voluntary re-production of those Sounds, in the absence of the occasioning Causes, so as to give the pleasure of *Contrast*—ex. gr. the various outcries of Battle in the song of Triumph, & Security.

---

a CN III 4397

[1] Kathleen Coburn noted the possible influence here of James Harris's *Three Treatises* (1744), a work praised by C in *BL* ch 16 (*CC*) II 36n. In the first two treatises, on "Art" and on "Music, Painting, and Poetry", C perhaps found "a congenial emphasis . . . on the activity of the mind in art, the passivity of the materials, and art as mediating between man and nature". *CN* III 4396 f 47ᵛn.

[2] Cylindrical beads used by North American Indians as currency, for symbolic purposes, and to convey messages by their colour and arrangement.

Poetry likewise is purely *human*—all its materials are *from* the mind, and all the products are *for* the mind. It is the Apotheosis of the former state—viz. Order and Passion—*N.b.* how by excitement of the Associative Power Passion itself imitates Order, and the *order* resulting produces a pleasurable *Passion* (whence Metre) and thus elevates the Mind by making its feelings the Objects of its reflection/ and how recalling the Sights and Sounds that had accompanied the occasions of the original passion it impregnates them with an interest not their own by means of the Passions, and yet tempers the passion by the calming power which all *distinct* images exert on the human soul. (This *illustrated.*)

In this way Poetry is the Preparation for Art: inasmuch as it avails itself of the forms of Nature to recall, to express, and to modify the thoughts and feelings of the mind—still however thro' the medium of *articulate Speech*, which is so peculiarly human that in all languages it is the ordinary phrase by which Man and Nature are contra-distinguished—it is the original force of the word *brute*[3]—and even now mute, and dumb do not convey the absence of sound, but the absence of articulate Sounds.

As soon as the human mind is intelligibly addressed by any outward medium, exclusive of articulate Speech, so soon does *Art* commence. But please to observe, that I have layed stress on the words, *human mind*—excluding thereby all results common to Man and all sentient creatures—and consequently, confining it to the effect produced by the congruity of the animal impression with the reflective Powers of the mind—so that not the Thing presented, but that which is *re*-presented, by the Thing, is the source of the Pleasure.—In this sense Nature itself is to a religious Observer the Art of God—and for the same cause Art itself might be defined, as of a middle nature between a Thought and a Thing, or, as before, the union and reconciliation of that which is Nature with that which is exclusively Human.—Exemplify this by a good Portrait, which becomes more and more like in proportion to its excellence as a Work of Art—While a real *Copy*, a Fac Simile, ends in shocking us.—[4]

Taking therefore *mute* as opposed not to sound but to articulate Speech, the oldest definition of Painting is in fact the true and the best definition of the Fine Arts in general—*muta Poesis*—mute Poesy[5]—and of course,

---

[3] In Latin *brutus* meant dull, heavy, or irrational, and "brute" in English basically refers to animals as wanting in reason or understanding, not in speech.

[4] Cf C's discussion of "copy" as opposed to "imitation" in Lect 3 of the 1811–12 series (at n 17).

[5] From this point C's notes become a

Poesy—/—(and as all Languages perfect themselves by a gradual process of desynonymizing words originally equivalent, as Propriety, Property—I, Me—Mister, Master—&c/[6] I have cherished the wish, to use the word, Poesy, as the generic or common term, distinguishing that species of Poesy, which is not *muta* Poesis, by its usual name, *Poetry*/) while of all the other species, which collectively form the *Fine Arts*, there would remain this as the common definition—that they all, like Poetry, are to express intellectual purposes, Thoughts, Conceptions, Sentiments that have their origin in the human Mind, but not, as Poetry, by means of articulate Speech, but as Nature, or the divine Art, does, by form, color magnitude, Sound, and proportion, silently or musically.—[7]

Well—it may be said—but who has ever thought otherwise. We all know, that Art is the imitatress of Nature.[8]—And doubtless, the Truths, I hope to convey, would be barren Truisms, if all men meant the same by the words, *imitate* and *nature*. But it would be flattering mankind

---

patchwork, incorporating or rewording passages from Schelling's "Über das Verhältniss der bildenden Künste zu der Natur" in *Philosophische Schriften* (1809) 341–96, but linking them with his own thoughts and converting Schelling's ideas to his own use in such a way as to make the whole Coleridgian, in spite of their obvious indebtedness, first pointed out by SC in *NLS* (1849). The phrase "*mute* Poesy" C took from Schelling pp 344–5: "Denn es soll die bildende Kunst, nach dem ältesten Ausdruck, eine stumme Dichtkunst seyn" (tr "For the imaging art, in the oldest form of expression, is said to be a mute poetry").

[6] C invented the word "desynonymise", according to *OED*; see *BL* ch 4 (*CC*) I 82–3 and C's n, on which his discussion here is based. He continually emphasised the need to make such distinctions, as in the 1808 series and in Lect 6 of the 1811–12 series (at n 28).

[7] This paragraph is developed from Schelling "Über das Verhältniss . . .", and the final passage is close to *Philosophische Schriften* 344–5, in which Schelling says that, like poetry, the arts are capable of expressing intellectual thoughts, conceptions originating in the mind, but not through speech, rather as silent nature does, through form, through

pattern, through sensuous works independent of herself ("geistige Gedanken, Begriffe, deren Ursprung die Seele ist, aber nicht durch die Sprache, sondern wie die schweigende Natur durch Gestalt, durch Form, durch sinnliche, von ihr unabhängige Werke ausdrücken").

[8] C here and in the next two paragraphs took as his starting-point a passage in Schelling: "ist nicht sogar alle Theorie neuerer Zeit von dem bestimmten Grundsatz ausgegangen, dass die Kunst sie Nachahmerin der Natur seyn solle? Wohl war dem so: aber was sollte dieser weite allgemeine Grundsatz dem Kunstler frommen bey der Vieldeutigkeit des Begriffs der Natur und da es von dieser fast so viele Vorstellungen als verschiedene Lebensweisen giebt"? (tr "has not every theory of recent times set out from the fixed principle that art should be the imitatress of nature? It has been so: but what did this broad general principle benefit the artist amid the many interpretations of the idea of nature, and when there were almost as many conceptions of it as there were different modes of life?") *Philosophische Schriften* 345–6. C began by developing his ideas on imitation and went on to discuss nature, giving the page-reference "346".

at large, to presume that this is the Fact. First, imitate—The impression on the wax is not an imitation but a *Copy* of the Seal—the Seal itself is an Imitation./[9] But farther—in order to form a philosophic conception, we must seek for the *kind*—as the *heat* in Ice—invisible Light—&c— but for practical purposes, we must have reference to the degree.

It is sufficient that philosophically we understand that in all Imitation two elements must exist, and not only exist but must be perceived as existing—Likeness and unlikeness, or Sameness and Difference. All Imitation in the Fine Arts is the union of Disparate Things.—Wax Image—Statues—Bronze—Pictures—the Artist may take his point where he likes—provided that the effect desired is produced—namely, that there should be a Likeness in Difference & a union of the two—*Tragic Dance*.

So Nature—*346.*[10]—i.e. natura naturata[11]—& hence the natural Question/ What *all* and every thing?—No, but the Beautiful.[12]—And what is the Beautiful?—The definition is at once undermined.—/ If the Artist painfully *copies* nature, what an idle rivalry! If he proceeds from a Form, that answers to the notion of Beauty, namely, the many seen as one[13]—what an emptiness, an unreality—as in Cypriani[14]—The *es-*

[9] C developed further here the distinction, vital to him, between an imitation and a copy, stressed in the 1808 and 1811–12 lectures (see also above, n 4). He was also making an important qualification to Schelling's argument.

[10] A page-reference to Schelling *Philosophische Schriften*; see n 8, above.

[11] As Kathleen Coburn notes, this is a reference to Schelling, who makes the distinction between *natura naturata*, nature as object or product, and *natura naturans*, nature as subject or essence, in *Einleitung zu seinem Entwurf eines Systems der Naturphilosophie* (Jena & Leipzig 1799) 22, a book C owned and annotated, his copy being now in Dr Williams's Library, London. The terms were given currency by Spinoza *Ethics* pt 1 scholium 29, but were in use much earlier. See *CN* III 4397 and n, also Lect 7, above (at n 6).

[12] This is condensed from Schelling *Philosophische Schriften* p 347: "Und sollte denn der Schüler der Natur alles in ihr ohne Unterschied und von jedem jedes nachahmen? Nur schöne Gegenstande und auch von diesen nur das

Schöne und Vollkommne soll er wiedergeben" (tr "And should the pupil of nature then imitate all and everything in it without discrimination? He ought to reproduce only beautiful objects, and even of these only the most beautiful and perfect").

[13] Cf C's definition of beauty in "On the Principles of Genial Criticism", "Multëity in Unity". *BL* (1907) II 232. In a letter to Sotheby [13 Jul 1829] he noted St Francis of Sales' "brief and happy definition of the Beautiful", "il piu nel uno". *CL* VI 799n. Cf *TT* 27 Dec 1831. The thought, though not the actual words, appear in St Francis *Traité de l'amour de Dieu* bk I ch 1, and C's Italian is probably his condensation of the sentence in his Italian translation of the work, *Il Teotima o sia il trattato dell' amor di Dio* (2 vols Padua 1790–1), which he owned and annotated; see *CM (CC)* II 792. Cf "God, then, bent on bestowing beauty on all things, transforms their multiplicity and diversity into perfect unity . . .". Tr Vincent Kerns (1962) 4. Cf also *IS* 106, *CL* V 99–100.

[14] Giovanni Battista Cipriani (1727–

sence must be mastered—the natura naturans, & this presupposes *a bond* between *Nature* in this higher sense and the soul of Man—.—

Sir Joshua Reynolds—/ 350—[15]

Far be it from me, to intend a censure—Sacred be his memory as that of a Benefactor of the Race in that which is its highest destination—&c—

The wisdom in Nature distinguished from Man by the coinstantaneity[16] of the Plan & the Execution, the Thought and the Production—In nature there is no reflex act—but the same powers without reflection, and consequently without Morality.[17] (Hence *Man* the *Head* of the visible Creation—*Genesis.*) Every step antecedent to full consciousness found in Nature—so to place them as for some one effect, totalized & fitted to the limits of a human Mind, as to elicit and as it were superinduce *into* the forms the reflection, to which they approximate—this is the Mystery of Genius in the Fine Arts—Dare I say that the Genius must act on the feeling, that *Body* is but a striving to become Mind—that it is *mind*, in its essence—?

As in every work of *Art* the Conscious is so impressed on the Unconscious, as to appear *in* it[18] (ex. gr. Letters on a Tomb compared with Figures constituting a Tomb)—so is the Man of Genius the Link that combines the two—but for that reason, he must partake of both—

---

85), Italian painter who moved to London in 1755, and whose decorative painting of artificial subjects, such as nymphs and cupids, was much admired.

[15] Here C adapted a passage from Schelling p 350, substituting Reynolds for Winckelmann: "Ferne sey es von uns, hiemit den Geist des vollendeten Mannes selbst tadeln zu wollen, dessen ewige Lehre und Offenbarung das Schönen mehr die veranlassende wurde! Heilig wie das Gedächtniss allgemeiner Wohlthäter bleibe uns sein Andenken!" (tr "Far be it from us to intend by this a censure of the spirit of that accomplished man whose immortal theory and revelation of the beautiful was more the occasion than the effective cause of this tendency in art. May his memory remain sacred, as that of a universal benefactor!").

[16] This is cited by *OED*, from *LR*, as the earliest use of the word.

[17] Cf Schelling p 352: "Die Wissenschaft, durch welche die Natur wirkt, ist freylich keine der menschlichen gleiche, die mit der Reflexion ihrer selbst verknüpft wäre: in ihr ist der Begriff nicht von der That, noch der Entwurf von der Ausführung verschieden" (tr "The wisdom through which nature works is certainly not like human knowledge, which is bound up with reflection on itself; in it thought is not separate from action, nor a plan from its realisation").

[18] Cf Schelling p 353: "Schon längst ist eingesehen worden, dass in der Kunst nicht alles mit dem Bewusstseyn ausgerichtet wird, dass mit der bewussten Thätigkeit eine bewustlose Kraft sich verbinden muss, und dass die vollkommne Einigkeit und gegenseitige Durchdringung dieser beyden das Höchste der Kunst erzeugt" (tr "It has long been observed that in art all things are not carried out consciously; that an unconscious power must combine with conscious activity, and that perfect union and reciprocal interpenetration of both produces the highest in art").

Hence, there is in Genius itself an unconscious activity—nay, that is *the* Genius in the man of Genius.—

This is the true Exposition of the Rule, that the Artist must first *eloign* himself[19] from Nature in order to return to her with full effect.—Why this?—Because—if he began by mere painful copying, he would produce Masks only, not forms breathing Life[20]—he must out of his own mind create forms according to the several Laws of the Intellect, in order to produce in himself that co-ordination of Freedom & Law, that involution of the Obedience in the Prescript, and of the Prescript in the impulse to obey, which assimilates him to Nature—enables him to understand her—. He absents himself from her only in his own Spirit, which has the same ground with Nature, to learn her unspoken language, in its main radicals, before he approaches to her endless compositions of those radicals—Not to acquire cold notions, lifeless technical Rules, but living and life-producing Ideas, which contain their own evidence/ and in that evidence the certainty that they are essentially one with the germinal causes in Nature, his Consciousness being the focus and mirror of both—for this does he for a time abandon the external *real*, in order to return to it with a full sympathy with its internal & actual—. Of all, we see, hear, or touch, the substance is and must be in ourselves—and therefore there is no alternative *in reason* between the dreary (& thank heaven! almost impossible) belief that every thing around us is but a phantom, or that the Life which is in us is in them likewise—and that to know is to *resemble*. When we speak of Objects out of ourselves, even as within ourselves to learn is, according to Plato, only to *recollect*.[21]—The only effective Answer to which (that I have been fortunate enough to meet with) is that which Mr Pope has consecrated for future use in the Line—

And Coxcombs vanquish Berkley with a *Grin*.[22]

[19] I.e. withdraw, retire to a distance. C noted in *CN* iii 3624 his finding of this word in a letter written by Queen Elizabeth, commenting "no word equivalent to it"; see also *CN* iii 4166. C is again referring to Schelling p 354: "Die Lage des Künstlers gegen die Natur sollte oft durch den Anspruch klar gemacht werden, dass die Kunst um dieses zu seyn sich erst von der Natur entsernen müsse, und nur in der letzten Vollendung zu ihr zurückkehre" (tr "The position of the artist in relation to nature should be frequently made clear by the claim that art in order to be art must first withdraw itself from nature, and only return to her in the final achievement").

[20] Cf Schelling p 354: "Wollte er sich aber mit Bewusstseyn dem Wirklichen ganz unterordnen, und das Vorhandene mit knechtischer Treue wiedergeben: so würde er wohl Larven hervorbringen, aber keine Kunstwerke" (tr "If he wished consciously to subordinate himself altogether to reality, and to reproduce what exists with slavish fidelity, he would produce masks indeed, but no works of art").

[21] See e.g. *Phaedo* 72c, 75e, and 76a, "learning is simply recollection". *CN* iii 3962n cites also *Meno* 81d, 85d, 98a.

[22] The line is from *An Essay on Satire, Occasioned by the Death of Mr. Pope*

To that within the thing, active thro' Form and Figure as by symbols [?discoursing/discovering/discerning]^b *Natur-geist*^{23} must the Artist imitate, as we unconsciously imitate those we love—So only can he produce any work truly *natural*, in the Object, and truly *human* in the Effect.—The Idea that puts the forms together, can not be itself form—It is above Form, is its Essence, the Universal in the Individual, Individuality itself—the Glance and the Exponent of the indwelling Power—

Each thing, that lives, has its moment of *self-exposition*, and each period of *each* thing—if we remove the disturbing forces of accident—and this is the business of ideal Art.—Childhood—Youth—Age—Man—Woman/—And each thing, that appears not to live, has its possible position & relation to Life/ & so it is in Nature—where she cannot *be*, she *prophecies* in the tree-like forms of ores &c/^{24}

^{b} Kathleen Coburn's conjectural readings

(1745) II 224. This poem, by John Brown (1715–66), was included in Warburton's and later editions of Pope's *Works* as an appendix to the *Moral Essays*. Cf *BL* ch 8 (*CC*) I 139 (C's n).

^{23} Nature-spirit; the word is Schelling's, and C developed this paragraph from Schelling pp 354–5: "Jenem in Innern der Dinge wirksamen durch Form und Gestalt nur wie durch Sinnbilder redenden Naturgeist soll der Künstler allerdings nacheisern, und nur insofern er diesen lebendig nachahmend ergreift, hat er selbst etwas Wahrhaftes erschaffen. Denn Werke, die aus einer Zusammensetzung auch übrigens schöner Formen entstünden, wären doch ohne alle Schönheit, indem das, wodurch nun eigentlich das Werk oder das Ganze schön ist, nicht mehr Form seyn kann. Es ist über die Form, ist Wesen, Allgemeines ist Blick und Ausdruck des inwohnenden Naturgeistes" (tr "The artist should certainly emulate that spirit of nature active in the soul of things, speaking through form and shape only, as through symbols, and only insofar as he seizes this by vitally imitating it has he himself created anything truthful. For works that originate merely in a combination of beautiful forms may nevertheless be without any beauty, because that by means of which the work or the whole now is beautiful cannot any longer be form. It is beyond form; it is the essential, the universal; it is the vision and expression of the indwelling spirit of nature").

^{24} This passage rearranges Schelling's comment on art as transcending time, p 356: "Wenn sie den schnellen Lauf menschlicher Jahre anhält wenn sie die Kraft entwickelter Männlichkeit mit dem sanften Reitz früher Jugend verbindet, oder eine Mutter erwachsener Söhne und Tochter in dem vollen Bestand kräftiger Schönheit zeigt: was thut sie anders, als dass sie auflet, was unwesentlich ist, die Zeit? Hat nach der Bemerkung des trefflichen Kenners ein jedes Gewächs der Natur nur einer Augenblick der wahren vollendenten Schönheit: so dürfen wir sagen, dass es auch nur einen Augenblick des vollen Daseyns habe. In diesem Augenblick ist es, was es in der ganzen Ewigkeit ist: ausser diesem kommt ihr nur ein Werden und ein Vergehen zu" (tr "If it detains the fleeting course of years, if it unites the energy of full-developed manhood with the grace of early youth, or presents a mother, grown-up sons, and daughters, in the full possession of energetic beauty, what does it but dissolve that which is inessential—time? If in accordance with the remark of the discerning critic, every growth of nature has but one moment of perfect beauty, we may also say that it has but one moment of full existence. In this

Difference of Form as proceeding and Shape as superinduced[25]—the latter either the Death or the imprisonment of the Thing; the former, its self-witnessing, and self-effected sphere of agency—

Art would or should be the Abridgment of Nature.[26] Now the Fullness of Nature is without character as Water is purest when without taste, smell or color[27]—but this is the Highest, the Apex, not the whole—& Art is to give *the whole* ad hominem/ hence each step of Nature has its Ideal, & hence too the possibility of a climax up to the perfect Form, of harmonized Chaos—

To the idea of Life Victory or Strife is necessary—As Virtue not in the absence of vicious Impulses but in the overcoming of them/ so Beauty not in the absence of the Passions, but on the contrary—it is heightened by the sight of what is conquered—this *in* the [? figure/ fugue],[c] or *out* by contrast—

[d]N.b.[28] The seeming Identity of Body and Mind in Infants, and thence the loveliness of the former—the commencing separation in Boyhood— the *struggle* of equilibrium in youth—from thence onward the Body first indifferent, then demanding the translucency of the mind not to be

[c] Kathleen Coburn's conjectural readings
[d] *CN* III 4398

moment it is what it is in eternity; besides this, there is but an approach to it and a falling away therefrom'').

[25] What follows, down to C's ''N.b.'' about infants, is condensed from Schelling pp 357–62; he there argues that art that portrays the empty husk or appearance of the individual would be dead art, and that art should aim at a sublime beauty in which fulness of form would do away with form itself. C's distinction between form and shape is much more sharply formulated and may in any case antedate his reading of Schelling; cf *CN* III 4066, ''all form as body, i.e. as shape, & not as forma efformans, is dead'', and Kathleen Coburn's note on this passage.

[26] In other words, the epitome of nature. What C meant is perhaps made clearer by a passage in HNC's version of this lecture, the essay ''On Poesy or Art'' (*LR* I 219, *BL*—1907—II 255), which adds that art ''is . . . distin-

guished from nature by the unity of all the parts in one thought or idea. Hence nature itself would give us the impression of a work of art, if we could see the thought which is present at once in the whole and in every part''.

[27] Cf Schelling p 360: ''Winckelmann vergleichet die Schönheit mit dem Wasser, das, aus dem Schooss der Quelle geschöpft, je weniger Geschmack es hat, desto gesunder geachtet wird'' (tr ''Winckelmann compares beauty to water, which, drawn from the bosom of the spring, is esteemed as more pure the less taste it has'').

[28] This note and the final memorandum are written, as Kathleen Coburn points out, ''in a different ink, pen, and slope of the hand'', and were probably added later. The note, but not the memorandum, was built into the final paragraph of the essay ''On Poesy or Art'' as its conclusion.

worse than indifferent—and finally, all that presents the Body as Body almost of a *recremental* (εξ) nature.—[29]

Mem. Mater juxta Hospitium Sancti Bartholomaei [30]—interrupting an earnest talk with a Sister Gossip with a nudge and a—Look! how pretty it does *ca* for one of *its* age—(her child about 2 years old)—

[29] C showed by the addition of the Greek prefix that he meant "excremental"; "recremental", current in the seventeenth century, was probably obsolete by C's time.

[30] "Mother near St Bartholomew's Hospital". Dr Gillman's assistant, J. H. B. Williams, was going to the hospital at this time (*CL* III 840–1). This anecdote does not appear in the essay "On Poesy or Art".

LECTURE 14

DATE AND PLACE OF DELIVERY. Friday, 13 March 1818, in the Great Room of the London Philosophical Society, Fleur-de-Luce Court, Fleet Street.

SUBJECT. History of style in relation to good and bad writing. The Syllabus promised a lecture "On the Corruptions of the English Language since the reign of Queen Anne, in our Style of writing Prose. A few easy Rules for the Attainment of a manly, unaffected, and pure Language, in our genuine Mother-Tongue, whether for the purposes of Writing, Oratory, or Conversation. Concluding Address." In fact C took off from ancient Greece, not from the reign of Queen Anne.

ADVERTISEMENTS. *The Times* Tues, 10 Mar: Lect 13, "the first", and Lect 14 were both announced in this composite advertisement, the last being described as follows: "the second, on the Correspondence of Language to Good Sense, in Conversation, Writing, and Public Speaking, with Mr. Coleridge's Address to the attendants on his Course . . .". *M Chron* Tues, 10 Mar: as in *The Times*.

TEXT. Under the heading "On Style" HNC printed in *LR* I 230–41 what appears to be an edited version of C's notes for this lecture. The two long quotations he incorporated, one from Chaucer and one from Hooker, HNC probably added himself. C is not likely to have written them out, and they are not mentioned in the report of this lecture published some years later. Raysor included these notes in *Misc C* 214–21, they were printed also in *C 17th C* 413–19, and they are reprinted below.

REPORT. A report of this lecture was contributed to the *Tatler* II No 224 (23 May 1831) 893–4 by "a Correspondent" who claimed to be one of C's audience, and who also attended Lect 9, sending in a report of that for publication on 24 May (see Lect 9 headnote: Report). This report was noticed by JDC, who reprinted it in "Coleridge's Lectures in 1818" *Athenaeum* 16 Mar 1889 pp 345–6. The report was included in *Misc C* 221–6 and in *C 17th C* and is reprinted below. It seems to have been made by an attentive member of the audience, who noted down references to many of C's numerous quotations illustrating his argument. There is sufficient correspondence between the report and the notes published in *LR* to confirm that both relate pretty closely to the lecture.

BACKGROUND AND CIRCUMSTANCES. The notes and the report both indicate a well-prepared lecture, with many illustrative quotations, which was much more a history of style in English prose and verse than the advertisement for it suggests, and which went back much further than the reign of Queen Anne, the starting-point announced in the Syllabus. The notes from which HNC drew the material he printed in *LR* appear to have been edited by him with his customary freedom. The correspondent who wrote the *Tatler* report lists many passages cited by C, but these do not include the quotations from Chaucer and Hooker, which are the only illustrative passages cited by HNC. It may well be that HNC added these himself, to expand the outline of the lecture provided by the notes he found; to judge from the report, he found no indications of C's intended quotations and so supplied a couple himself, knowing C's liking for Chaucer and Hooker. This is speculative, but such an interpretation would make sense of the one major discrepancy between the notes and the report. C ranged pretty widely in this lecture, but included quotations from favourite authors like Jeremy Taylor and Sir Thomas Browne and illustrated bad writing by a comparison between Dryden and Dr Johnson he had used several times before. C's "Address to the attendants on his Course", promised in the advertisement, remains a mystery. The report states that "a few brief observations" brought the lecture to an end. Perhaps he reminded his audience of the extra lecture he had promised, to consist of readings from poetry of the Middle Ages. There is no evidence that he gave this, but his intention to do so was very much alive still in Mar, and the lecture was eventually advertised for 26 May (see Lect 2 headnote: Background and Circumstances). Nothing is known about the success of C's last lecture of the course; it is not mentioned in his letters, and HCR did not attend it.

LECTURE 14

RECORDS OF THE LECTURE

COLERIDGE'S NOTES, AS EDITED BY
HENRY NELSON COLERIDGE
FROM *LR* I 230–41 (HEADED "ON STYLE")

I have, I believe, formerly observed[1] with regard to the character of the governments of the East, that their tendency was despotic, that is, towards unity; whilst that of the Greek governments, on the other hand, leaned to the manifold and the popular, the unity in them being purely ideal, namely of all as an identification of the whole. In the northern or Gothic nations the aim and purpose of the government were the preservation of the rights and interests of the individual in conjunction with those of the whole. The individual interest was sacred. In the character and tendency of the Greek and Gothic languages there is precisely the same relative difference. In Greek the sentences are long, and structure architectural, so that each part or clause is insignificant when compared with the whole. The result is every thing, the steps and processes nothing. But in the Gothic and, generally, in what we call the modern, languages, the structure is short, simple, and complete in each part, and the connexion of the parts with the sum total of the discourse is maintained by the sequency of the logic, or the community of feelings excited between the writer and his readers. As an instance equally delightful and complete, of what may be called the Gothic structure as contra-distinguished from that of the Greeks, let me cite a part of our famous Chaucer's character of a parish priest as he should be. Can it ever be quoted too often?

> A good man thér was of religiöun
> That was a pouré Parsone of a toun,
> But riche he was of holy thought and werk;
> He was alsó a lerned man, a clerk,

[1] C was thinking, presumably, of Lect 2; see above (sentence containing n 15 and sentences after n 34).

That Cristés gospel trewély wolde preche;
His párishens devoutly wolde he teche;
Benigne he was, and wonder diligent,
And in adversite ful patient,
And swiche he was ypreved often sithes;
Ful loth were him to cursen for his tithes,
But rather wolde he yeven out of doute
Unto his pouré párishens aboute
Of his offring, and eke of his substánce;
He coude in litel thing have suffisance:
Wide was his parish, and houses fer asonder,
But he ne left nought for no rain ne thonder,
In sikenesse and in mischief to visite
The ferrest in his parish moche and lite
Upon his fete, and in his hand a staf:
This noble ensample to his shepe he yaf,
That first he wrought, and afterward he taught,
Out of the gospel he the wordés caught,
And this figúre he added yet thereto,
That if gold rusté, what should iren do.
   He setté not his benefice to hire;
And lette his shepe accombred in the mire,
And ran untó London untó Seint Poules,
To seken him a chantérie for soules,
Or with a brotherhede to be withold,
But dwelt at home, and kepté wel his fold,
So that the wolf ne made it not miscarie:
He was a shepherd and no mercenarie;
And though he holy were and vertuous,
He was to sinful men not dispitous,
Ne of his speché dangerous ne digne,
But in his teching discrete and benigne,
To drawen folk to heven with fairénesse,
By good ensample was his besinesse;
But it were any persone obstinat,
What so he were of high or low estat,
Him wolde he snibben sharply for the nones:
A better preest I trowe that no wher non is;
He waited after no pompe ne reverence,
He maked him no spiced conscience,
But Cristés love and his apostles' twelve
He taught, but first he folwed it himselve.[2]

Such change as really took place in the style of our literature after
Chaucer's time is with difficulty perceptible, on account of the dearth
of writers, during the civil wars of the fifteenth century. But the tran-

[2] Prologue to *The Canterbury Tales*   editions provide a much improved text.
lines 477–528, omitting 501–6; modern

sition was not very great; and accordingly we find in Latimer[3] and our other venerable authors about the time of Edward VI. as in Luther, the general characteristics of the earliest manner;—that is, every part popular, and the discourse addressed to all degrees of intellect;—the sentences short, the tone vehement, and the connexion of the whole produced by honesty and singleness of purpose, intensity of passion, and pervading importance of the subject.

Another and a very different species of style is that which was derived from, and founded on, the admiration and cultivation of the classical writers, and which was more exclusively addressed to the learned class in society. I have previously mentioned Boccaccio as the original Italian introducer of this manner,[4] and the great models of it in English are Hooker, Bacon, Milton, and Taylor, although it may be traced in many other authors of that age. In all these the language is dignified but plain, genuine English, although elevated and brightened by superiority of intellect in the writer. Individual words themselves are always used by them in their precise meaning, without either affectation or slipslop. The letters and state papers of Sir Francis Walsingham are remarkable for excellence in style of this description.[5] In Jeremy Taylor the sentences are often extremely long, and yet are generally so perspicuous in consequence of their logical structure, that they require no reperusal to be understood; and it is for the most part the same in Milton and Hooker.

Take the following sentence as a specimen of the sort of style to which I have been alluding:—

Concerning Faith, the principal object whereof is that eternal verity which hath discovered the treasures of hidden wisdom in Christ; concerning Hope, the highest object whereof is that everlasting goodness which in Christ doth quicken the dead; concerning Charity, the final object whereof is that incomprehensible beauty which shineth in the countenance of Christ, the Son of the living God: concerning these virtues, the first of which beginning here with a weak apprehension of things not seen, endeth with the intuitive vision of God in the world to come; the second beginning here with a trembling expectation of things far removed, and as yet but only heard of, endeth with real and actual fruition of that which no tongue can express; the third beginning here with a weak inclination of heart towards him unto whom we are not able to approach, endeth with endless union, the mystery whereof is higher than the reach of the thoughts of men; concerning that Faith, Hope, and Charity, without which there can be no salvation, was there ever any mention made saving only in that Law which God himself hath from Heaven revealed? There is not in the world a syllable

---

[3] Hugh Latimer, bp of Worcester (c 1485–1555), whose sermons are notable for the qualities C lists, was a contemporary of Martin Luther (1483–1546).

[4] See Lect 3, above (from n 7 to n 8).

[5] See below (at n 19).

muttered with certain truth concerning any of these three, more than hath been supernaturally received from the mouth of the eternal God.

Eccles. Pol. I.s.II.[6]

The unity in these writers is produced by the unity of the subject, and the perpetual growth and evolution of the thoughts, one generating, and explaining, and justifying, the place of another, not, as it is in Seneca, where the thoughts, striking as they are, are merely strung together like beads, without any causation or progression. The words are selected because they are the most appropriate, regard being had to the dignity of the total impression, and no merely big phrases are used where plain ones would have sufficed, even in the most learned of their works.

There is some truth in a remark, which I believe was made by Sir Joshua Reynolds, that the greatest man is he who forms the taste of a nation, and that the next greatest is he who corrupts it.[7] The true classical style of Hooker and his fellows was easily open to corruption; and Sir Thomas Brown it was, who, though a writer of great genius, first effectually injured the literary taste of the nation by his introduction of learned words, merely because they were learned. It would be difficult to describe Brown adequately;[8] exuberant in conception and conceit, dignified, hyperlatinistic,[9] a quiet and sublime enthusiast; yet a fantast, a humourist, a brain with a twist; egotistic like Montaigne, yet with a feeling heart and an active curiosity, which, however, too often degenerates into a hunting after oddities. In his *Hydriotaphia* and, indeed, almost all his works the entireness of his mental action is very observable; he metamorphoses every thing, be it what it may, into the subject under consideration. But Sir Thomas Brown with all his faults had a genuine idiom; and it is the existence of an individual idiom in each, that makes the principal writers before the Restoration the great patterns or integers of English style. In them the precise intended meaning of a word can never be mistaken; whereas in the later writers, as especially in Pope, the use of words is for the most part purely arbitrary, so that the context will rarely show the true specific sense, but only that some-

[6] From *The Laws of Ecclesiastical Polity* I xi 6. *Works* (1682) 94. C had quoted from this part of Hooker's work in Lect 8 of the 1811–12 series (at nn 9 and 10).

[7] Source untraced. A variant of this remark was cited by C in *BL* ch 2 (*CC*) I 40n.

[8] The description of Browne that fol-lows is condensed from C's annotation in the form of a letter to SH dated 10 Mar 1804 with a copy of Sir Thomas Browne's *Works* (1658–9): *CM* (*CC*) I 762–3.

[9] C's coinage, first used in his 1804 annotation on Browne: *CM* (*CC*) I 762. Not recorded in *OED*.

thing of the sort is designed. A perusal of the authorities cited by Johnson in his dictionary under any leading word, will give you a lively sense of this declension in etymological truth of expression in the writers after the Restoration, or perhaps, strictly, after the middle of the reign of Charles II.

The general characteristic of the style of our literature down to the period which I have just mentioned, was gravity, and in Milton and some other writers of his day there are perceptible traces of the sternness of republicanism. Soon after the Restoration a material change took place, and the cause of royalism was graced, sometimes disgraced, by every shade of lightness of manner. A free and easy style was considered as a test of loyalty, or at all events, as a badge of the cavalier party; you may detect it occasionally even in Barrow,[10] who is, however, in general remarkable for dignity and logical sequency of expression; but in L'Estrange, Collyer, and the writers of that class,[11] this easy manner was carried out to the utmost extreme of slang and ribaldry. Yet still the works, even of these last authors, have considerable merit in one point of view; their language is level to the understandings of all men; it is an actual transcript of the colloquialism of the day, and is accordingly full of life and reality. Roger North's life of his brother the Lord Keeper, is the most valuable specimen of this class of our literature;[12] it is delightful, and much beyond any other of the writings of his contemporaries.

From the common opinion that the English style attained its greatest perfection in and about Queen Anne's reign I altogether dissent; not only because it is in one species alone in which it can be pretended that the writers of that age excelled their predecessors, but also because the specimens themselves are not equal, upon sound principles of judgment, to much that had been produced before. The classical structure of Hooker— the impetuous, thought-agglomerating, flood of Taylor[13]—to these there

---

[10] See below (at n 22).

[11] Sir Roger L'Estrange (1616–1704), journalist and translator, best known for his *Fables of Aesop*; C owned a copy of the 7th ed of this (1724); see *CN* III 3487 and n. "Collyer" is Jeremy Collier (1650–1726), as the *Tatler* report makes clear, best known as the author of *A Short View of the Immorality of the English Stage* (1698). C made a similar remark about these two writers in *Friend (CC)* I 359, in which he also praised Roger North. For C's views on these writers see *CM*

(CC) I 156–7, 182 and, below (at n 23).

[12] *The Life of the Right Honourable Francis North, Baron of Guildford, Lord Keeper of the Great Seal*, by Roger North (1653–1734), was published in 1742. In the revised *Friend* (1818) C praised North and introduced a long quotation from this work. *Friend (CC)* I 359–62.

[13] Cf C's letter to the Rev Joseph Hughes of 24 Nov 1819: "my thoughts . . . communicate their own continuity, and (to use a phrase of Jeremy Taylor's) *agglomeration* to my conversa-

is no pretence of a parallel; and for mere ease and grace, is Cowley inferior to Addison, being as he is so much more thoughtful and full of fancy? Cowley, with the omission of a quaintness here and there, is probably the best model of style for modern imitation in general. Taylor's periods have been frequently attempted by his admirers; you may, perhaps, just catch the turn of a simile or single image, but to write in the real manner of Jeremy Taylor would require as mighty a mind as his. Many parts of Algernon Sidney's treatises afford excellent exemplars of a good modern practical style;[14] and Dryden in his prose works, is a still better model, if you add a stricter and purer grammar. It is, indeed, worthy of remark that all our great poets have been good prose writers, as Chaucer, Spenser, Milton; and this probably arose from their just sense of metre. For a true poet will never confound verse and prose; whereas it is almost characteristic of indifferent prose writers that they should be constantly slipping into scraps of metre. Swift's style is, in its line, perfect; the manner is a complete expression of the matter, the terms appropriate, and the artifice concealed. It is simplicity in the true sense of the word.

After the Revolution, the spirit of the nation became much more commercial, than it had been before; a learned body, or clerisy,[15] as such, gradually disappeared, and literature in general began to be addressed to the common miscellaneous public. That public had become accustomed to, and required, a strong stimulus; and to meet the requisitions of the public taste, a style was produced which by combining triteness of thought with singularity and excess of manner of expression, was calculated at once to soothe ignorance and to flatter vanity. The thought was carefully kept down to the immediate apprehension of the commonest understanding, and the dress was as anxiously arranged for the purpose of making the thought appear something very profound. The essence of this style consisted in a mock antithesis, that is, an opposition of mere sounds, in a rage for personification, the abstract

---

tion". *Friend (CC)* ii 503, *CL* vi 1049. Cf also "Taylor, eminently discursive, *accumulative*, and (to use one of his own words) agglomerative . . .". "Apologetic Preface to *Fire, Famine, and Slaughter*" (1817): *PW* (EHC) ii 1106.

[14] Algernon Sidney (1622–83), whose *Discourses Concerning Government* was published posthumously in 1698; C quoted from it in *CN* ii 3118–19 and annotated several passages in it in *Works* (1772).

[15] If HNC did not introduce the word here, it may be C's earliest recorded use of it. In his *Lay Sermons* (1816, 1817) he was still working out his concept of a body of "men of *clerkly* acquirements", later characterised in a letter of 1821 as the "*Clerisy*" (a word coined by him) and fully developed in *C&S* (1830) ch 5. See *SM (CC)* 36, *CL* v 138, and *C&S (CC)* 42–7.

made animate, far-fetched metaphors, strange phrases, metrical scraps, in every thing, in short, but genuine prose. Style is, of course, nothing else but the art of conveying the meaning appropriately and with perspicuity, whatever that meaning may be, and one criterion of style is that it shall not be translateable without injury to the meaning.[16] Johnson's style has pleased many from the very fault of being perpetually translateable; he creates an impression of cleverness by never saying any thing in a common way. The best specimen of this manner is in Junius, because his antithesis is less merely verbal than Johnson's.[17] Gibbon's manner is the worst of all; it has every fault of which this peculiar style is capable.[18] Tacitus is an example of it in Latin; in coming from Cicero you feel the *falsetto* immediately.

In order to form a good style, the primary rule and condition is, not to attempt to express ourselves in language before we thoroughly know our own meaning;—when a man perfectly understands himself, appropriate diction will generally be at his command either in writing or speaking. In such cases the thoughts and the words are associated. In the next place preciseness in the use of terms is required, and the test is whether you can translate the phrase adequately into simpler terms, regard being had to the feeling of the whole passage. Try this upon Shakspeare, or Milton, and see if you can substitute other simpler words in any given passage without a violation of the meaning or tone. The source of bad writing is the desire to be something more than a man of sense,—the straining to be thought a genius; and it is just the same in speech making. If men would only say what they have to say in plain terms, how much more eloquent they would be! Another rule is to avoid converting mere abstractions into persons. I believe you will very rarely find in any great writer before the Revolution the possessive case of an inanimate noun used in prose instead of the dependent case, as "the

[16] C had put this more strongly in *BL* ch 22 (*CC*) II 142 as "the infallible test of a blameless style; namely, its *untranslatableness* in words of the same language without injury to the meaning".

[17] The letters of Junius, attacking political repression and corruption, appeared in the *London Public Advertiser* in 1769–72, were published in 2 vols in 1772, and were often reprinted. Their authorship remains a mystery, but Sir Philip Francis (1740–1818) may have written them. The irony of their invective often turns upon a neat antithesis,

as in this comment on the Duke of Grafton (Letter XII): "it is not that you do wrong by design, but that you should never do right by mistake". C annotated a copy of *The Letters of Junius* (1797), observing on pp 10–11 against Letter I that "the antitheses stand the test of analysis much better than Johnson's". *CM* (*CC*) III, *Misc C* 315–16. Cf *CN* III 3634.

[18] Cf "Gibbon's style is detestable"—*TT* 15 Aug 1833, in which C developed a more general critique of the *Decline and Fall*.

watch's hand," for "the hand of the watch." The possessive or Saxon genitive was confined to persons, or at least to animated subjects. And I cannot conclude this Lecture without insisting on the importance of accuracy of style as being near akin to veracity and truthful habits of mind; he who thinks loosely will write loosely, and, perhaps, there is some moral inconvenience in the common forms of our grammars which give children so many obscure terms for material distinctions. Let me also exhort you to careful examination of what you read, if it be worth any perusal at all; such examination will be a safeguard from fanaticism, the universal origin of which is in the contemplation of phenomena without investigation into their causes.

REPORT IN THE *TATLER* II NO 224
(23 MAY 1831) 893–4

Progressive Changes in English Prose Writing

[About thirteen years ago, Mr Coleridge delivered a series of Lectures on various subjects, at the room of the Philosophical Society in Fetter lane. The following are recollections of one of them, from a few notes made at the time, by one of his auditors, who felt too highly gratified with what he heard, not to be desirous of preserving something for future reflection. This sketch conveys a very inadequate idea of the Lecture itself, and is offered to the reader as the crude and imperfect attempt of an unprofessional and unpractised hand. It is to be regretted that the series has never been published by the author.]

The influence of national character on language is exemplified in the literature of the eastern nations, in that of the Greeks, of our own, and of the northern nations.

The Greek writings are distinguished by long sentences, formed, as it were, architecturally; each part is built on the preceding; and the whole sentence would lose by changing the arrangement. The modern construction among ourselves is more simple. The sentences are short, but preserve a consistency with each other. Such is the prose writing of Chaucer.

A more popular style followed; but the confusion resulting from the civil wars prevents us from seeing the transition. In Luther we have a striking example of the popular style, popular in the highest sense of the term, addressing the intellect of the reader, and readily understood wherever good sense is the habit of the mind. A similar style, with less genius, may be found in Latimer and other writers of Edward the Sixth's time and the preceding reign.

After the restoration came the classic style. A true relish of this style presupposed a taste and cultivation in the reader somewhat corresponding to it; for it was too learned to be popular. Boccaccio, it is true, was popular; but we can account for the exception in him, by the fascination of his subjects. Hooker, Bacon, Milton, and Jeremy Taylor are distinguished ornaments of the classic style.

[The Lecturer here read an extract from Sir Francis Walsingham, Minister in Queen Elizabeth's time. He characterized it as plain, sober language, but distinguished by talent; void of affectation, and of clear meaning. It bore evidence that the writer had thought before he attempted to communicate. The subject was Honesty.][19]

Jeremy Taylor reconciles the architectural and the classic styles. His sentences are of great length, yet do not require review in order to understand them; the words are judiciously chosen, and the sentence grows with the importance of the subject. [Two admirable extracts were read in illustration,—the first on Original Sin, the other on the Progress of Disputes.][20]

The style next in succession was of a very different nature. The new stylists resembled a person who tries to recollect all the good things he had heard during the last three months, that he may give utterance to them all together. They strung together sparkling points, unrelieved by intermediate plainness. Their writings bear marks of recollection, not of reflection. In the writings of Taylor, &c, uncommon and foreign words are not unfrequently used; but they are used only when no others could be found so expressive of the author's meaning. Sir Thomas Browne appears to be the first who used uncommon words for their own sake. Mr C. confessed that Sir Thomas, with all his imperfections,

[19] This extract from Walsingham's essay on honesty, written in 1590 and first printed in *Cottoni Posthuma: Divers Choice Pieces of That Renowned Antiquary Sir Robert Cotton* ed James Howell (1651), C copied into a notebook in 1804 from the 1679 ed of this work. The passage, printed in *CN* II 1880, begins: "Honesty is a quiet passing over the days of a man's life without doing injury to another man. There is required in an honest man not so much to do everything as he would be done unto; as to forbear any thing which he would not be content to suffer; for the essence of Honesty consists in forbearing to do ill."

[20] C probably quoted from one of his favourite books, Jeremy Taylor's Σύμβολον Θεολογικόν: *or a Collection of Polemicall Discourses*; he owned and annotated a copy of the 3rd ed (1674). The extracts he read may well have been those he included in the 1818 *Friend*, the first from *Unum Necessarium, or, The Doctrine and Practice of Repentance*, the second from *A Dissuasive from Popery* pt 2 bk II § 7: *Polemicall Discourses* 711, 459–61. These can be found in *Friend (CC)* I 433–4 and 283–7.

was a favourite of his. He described him as a sublime and quiet enthusiast; as bearing some resemblance to Montaigne, but entering into his speculations with more intenseness of purpose than the French writer. His writings bear the stamp of an original and amiable mind. The only imitable quality of them is their entireness, or plenitude of illustration. [A passage from Sir T. B.'s "Treatise on Urn-Burial" was read.][21]

Barrow and his contemporaries next come under consideration. Their predecessors offended by pedantry. It now became a mark of loyalty to pass into the other extreme, and everything must appear free and unlaboured. Hence proceeded occasional quaintness, and sometimes even ludicrousness. For instance, in Barrow's "Sermon on Spiritual Monarchy," the action of St Peter, in cutting off the ear of the High Priest's servant, is thus stated,—"Up rose his blood, and out popped his sword."[22] Sir Roger L'Estrange and Jeremy Collier carried this plainness to excess. The style of this period was infected with a sort of slang or blackguardism.[23] Notwithstanding these defects, there is much to approve in the writers in question. Their style is purely English, full of idioms, and partakes of the passions of man in general. An extract from Roger North's "Life of his Brother, the Lord Keeper," followed in illustration.[24] The liveliness of the thoughts were well conveyed by the words. It was the opinion of some, that the first perfect models of good writing were produced after the Revolution. We had, however, perfect models before,—of the architectural style in Hooker, of the impetuous in Taylor, of elegant simplicity in Cowley: with some abatement, Algernon Sydney and Dryden were also good models. [Here Cowley's account of Oliver Cromwell's funeral was in part extracted.][25]

[21] C had recently been reading Sir Thomas Browne's *Hydriotaphia, or Urn-Burial* (1656) and made a series of notebook entries based on or copied from it, mainly from ch 5, one of which he may have used here. See *CN* III 4368, 4372, 4375.

[22] In fact C's reference was to *A Treatise of the Pope's Supremacy* (1680) 43 by Isaac Barrow (1630–77), in which Supposition 1, "That Saint Peter had a Primacy over the Apostles", includes the sentence, "When our Lord was apprehended by the Souldiers, presently up was his spirit, and out went his Sword in defence of him." A marginal note refers to John 17.10, in which it is said that Peter "smote the high priest's servant, and cut off his right ear". C cited the same passage from Barrow in *CN* I

1655 and commented on the "LE-STRANGEism of his Style" in *CN* I 1660; see also above (at n 10).

[23] C thought the translation of *The Mythological Picture of Cebes the Theban* by Jeremy Collier "a Masterpiece of the *Black-guard Slang*" and linked it with Sir Roger L'Estrange (1616–1704), author of numerous political works, as "the Introducer of this Thames-Waterman's Language". See *CM (CC)* I 182, *CN* I 1655.

[24] See above (at n 12).

[25] Commonly known since 1668 as *A Discourse by Way of Vision, Concerning the Government of Oliver Cromwell*, this essay, on which C commented in *BL* ch 22 (*CC*) II 121 on its mixture of prose and verse, was printed in C's edition of Cowley *Works* (1681) vi 52–78.

The style of Cowley is most fitted for imitation; it is distinguished by variety of excellence.

Our great poets, Chaucer, Spenser, Milton, Dryden, &c. were all good prose-writers: they seemed to have kept their thoughts on separate shelves, so as to avoid that injudicious mixture of poetry with prose which disgusts us in less skilful writers. The style of Swift may be considered perfect: by no defects it reminds us of itself.

After the Revolution, we became commercial; and our style suffered considerably. It was not learned, nor plain, nor popular; the thoughts were commonplace, but the manner was strange. The first object seemed to be,—*not* to speak naturally. [Mr C. illustrated this part of his subject by extracts from Mr. Phillips's speech, in the case of Guthrie v. Sterne, and exposed the absurdities and false eloquence contained in it. The instances he selected, were of false antithesis, confusion of metaphor, bathos and sheer nonsense.][26]

Mr Coleridge then gave a few instructions which he conceived might be usefully adopted in order to write and talk respectably.—We should not express ourselves till we feel that we know clearly what we mean to express. The want of previous reflection is the cause of much incoherent and unconnected writing and talking.

Adverting to the opinion of a Greek writer (Strabo, I believe), that none but a good man could be a great poet,[27] the Lecturer concurred with him, and thought, moreover, that moral excellence was necessary to the perfection of the understanding and the taste. The good writer

[26] Charles Phillips (1787–1859) had by this time established a reputation as a fervently eloquent pleader in the Dublin lawcourts. His florid speech for the plaintiff in the case of adultery, Guthrie v Sterne, which won damages of £5000 for his client, published in 1815, reached a 15th ed within a year. Some extracts C may have read to his audience: "He has thought, perhaps, that truth needed no set phrase of speech, that misfortunes should not veil the furrows which its tears had burned, or hide, under the decorations of an artful drapery, the heart-rent heavings with which its bosom throbbed." "She [Ireland] saw it [the nuptial contract] the gift of heaven, the charm of earth, the joy of the present, the promise of the future, the innocence of enjoyment, the chastity of passion, the sacrament of love—the slender curtain that shades the sanctuary of the marriage bed, has in its purity the splendour of the mountain snow, and for its protection the texture of the mountain adamant." "Better, far better, their little feet had followed in her funeral, than that the hour which taught her value should reveal her vice; mourning her loss, they might have blessed her memory, and shame need not have rolled its fires into the fountain of their sorrow." *The Speech, of Mr. Phillips, in the Court of Common Pleas, Dublin, in the Case of Guthrie v. W. P. B. D. Sterne, for Crim. Con.* (1815) 3, 3–4, 9–10.

[27] Strabo *Geography* 1.2.5: ". . . the excellence of a poet is inseparably associated with the excellence of the man himself, and it is impossible for one to become a good poet unless he has previously become a good man". Tr H. L. Jones (LCL).

should be a lover of what is common to all his fellow-creatures, rather than of what makes them unequal; he should desire the esteem of good men; he should look to fame rather than to reputation. Fame is the approbation of the wise of successive generations; reputation is often no more than the echo of hastily-formed opinions.[28] Many contemptible works have had great reputation; few works greatly reputed at first, have afterwards ripened into fame.

We should use no words nor sentences which can be translated into simpler words with the same meaning.

Shakspeare and Milton are distinguished by their appropriate use of words. You cannot change a word without injury to the effect. The first two lines of Dryden's translation of Juvenal's Tenth Satire were contrasted with Johnson's imitation of the same passage.[29] Johnson takes up six lines, and does not well express his meaning after all.

Dryden's two lines are,—

> Look round the habitable globe: how few
> Know their own good, or knowing it, pursue.

Johnson's six are,—

> Let observation, with extensive view,
> Survey mankind, from China to Peru;
> Remark each anxious toil, each eager strife,
> And watch the busy scenes of crowded life;
> Then say how hope and fear, desire and hate,
> O'erspread with snares, the clouded maze of fate,
> Where wavering man, etc.

The great source of bad writing is a desire in the writers to be thought something more than men of sense. Language is made a sort of leap-frog. Our poetry runs after something more than human; our prose runs after our poetry; and even our conversation follows in the pursuit. At a dinner of twenty persons, when your health is proposed, you are expected to return thanks in a set speech. Metaphors are used, not to illustrate, but as substitutes for plain speaking. The frequent rendering of abstractions into persons is also a growing evil, as in the following line:—

> Come, I shed compassion's tear.[30]

which is the same as saying that Mrs A. sheds Mrs B.'s tear.

---

[28] On C's distinction between fame and reputation see Lect 2 of the 1811–12 series (at n 22).

[29] A comparison C liked to make; see Lect 6 of the 1811–12 series (at nn 21–2).

[30] Source untraced; C may have simply invented the line.

Sound sense and sound feeling are necessary to a good writer. Accuracy is akin to veracity.[31] They who are accustomed to weigh the meaning of words before they utter them are much less likely to disregard truth in greater matters, than those who, from neglecting accuracy, lose the sense of its importance. We should habituate ourselves to see the relation of our thoughts to each other; we should consider pleasure derived without any effort as enervating, and therefore undesirable. That only is permanent which appeals to something permanent in our natures.—[A few brief observations concluded the Lecture.]—*From a Correspondent.*

[31] The distinction was an important one to C, and he explained it in his essay "On the Communication of Truth", summing up his argument there in the phrase "Veracity, therefore, not mere accuracy; to convey truth, not merely to say it . . .". See *Friend (CC)* I 42–3.

GENERAL COMMENTS AND REPORTS

(1) JOHN PAYNE COLLIER IN HIS EDITION OF
THE WORKS OF WILLIAM SHAKESPEARE
(8 VOLS 1842–4)

In this ed Collier frequently quotes from *LR* but sometimes adds brief notes that he says he recorded when attending C's lectures in 1818 or 1815. C is not known to have lectured in 1815, and the brief comments recorded by Collier on a range of plays, including several comedies, fit best the four general lectures on Shakespeare C gave as part of the 1818 course in Feb of that year.

Vol I p 7, on *The Tempest*: Collier notes that C said of this play: " 'It is a species of drama, which owes no allegiance to time or space, and in which, therefore, errors of chronology and geography—no mortal sin in any species—are venial faults, and count for nothing: it addresses itself entirely to the imaginative faculty.' This opinion was delivered in 1818; and three years earlier Coleridge had spoken of 'The Tempest', as certainly one of Shakespeare's latest works, judging from the language only . . .".

Vol II p 5, on *Measure for Measure*: Collier says that C "pointed especially to the artifice of Isabella, and her seeming consent to the suit of Angelo, as the circumstances which tended to lower the character of the female sex. He then called 'Measure for Measure' only the 'least agreeable' of Shakespeare's dramas."

Vol II p 111: Collier says that C "passed over 'The Comedy of Errors' without any particular or separate observation . . .".

Vol II p 279: According to Collier, C was convinced that *The Comedy of Errors* was one of Shakespeare's earliest plays, and that "the internal evidence was indisputable".

Vol III p 5, on *As You Like It*: "In his Lectures in 1818, Coleridge eloquently and justly praised the pastoral beauty and simplicity of 'As You Like It'; but he did not attempt to compare it with Lodge's 'Rosalynde', where the descriptions of persons and of scenery are comparatively forced and artificial:—'Shakespeare', said Coleridge, 'never gives a description of rustic scenery merely for its own sake, or to show how well he can paint natural objects: he is never tedious or elaborate, but while he now and then displays marvellous accuracy and minuteness of knowledge, he usually touches upon the larger features and broader characteristics, leaving the fillings up to the imagination. Thus in ''As You Like It'' he describes an oak of many centuries growth in a single line:—

> Under an oak whose antique root peeps out.

Other and inferior writers would have dwelt on this description, and worked it out with all the pettiness and impertinence of detail. In Shakespeare the ''antique root'' furnishes the whole picture.'

''These expressions are copied from notes made at the time . . . [goes on to cite *LR* ii 115].''

Vol iii p 203, on *All's Well That Ends Well*: ''It was the opinion of Coleridge, an opinion which he first delivered in 1813, and again in 1818, though it is not found in his 'Literary Remains', that 'All's Well that Ends Well', as it has come down to us, was written at two different, and rather distant periods of the poet's life. He pointed out very clearly two distinct styles, not only of thought, but of expression.''

Vol iii p 323, on *Twelfth Night*: ''It was an opinion, confidently stated by Coleridge in his lectures in 1818, that the passage in Act. ii. sc. 4. beginning

> Too old, by heaven: let still the woman take
> An elder than herself, &c.

had a direct application to the circumstances of his own marriage with Anne Hathaway, who was so much senior to the poet. Some of Shakespeare's biographers had previously enforced this notion, and others have since followed it up; but Coleridge took the opportunity of enlarging eloquently on the manner in which young poets have frequently connected themselves with women of very ordinary personal and mental attractions, the imagination supplying all deficiencies, clothing the object of affection with grace and beauty, and furnishing her with every accomplishment.''

Vol iii p 427, on *The Winter's Tale* and *Othello*: ''In his lectures in 1815, Coleridge dwelt on the 'not easily jealous' frame of Othello's mind, and on the art of the great poet in working upon his generous and unsuspecting nature: he contrasted the characters of Othello and Leontes in this respect, the latter from predisposition requiring no such malignant instigator as Iago.''

Vol v p 5, on *1 Henry VI*: Collier says that ''in his Lectures in 1815,

Coleridge adduced many lines which he believed must have been written by Shakespeare''.

Vol vi pp 501–2, on *Timon of Athens*: ''Coleridge said, in 1815, that he saw the same vigorous hand at work throughout, and gave no countenance to the notion, that any parts of a previously existing play had been retained in 'Timon of Athens', as it has come down to us. It was Shakespeare's throughout; and, as originally written, he apprehended that it was one of the author's most complete performances: the players, however, he felt convinced, had done the poet much injustice; and he especially instanced (as indeed he did in 1818) the clumsy 'clap-trap' blow at the Puritans in Act iii. sc. 3, as an interpolation by the actor of the part of Timon's servant. Coleridge accounted for the ruggedness and inequality of the versification upon the same principle, and he was persuaded that only a corrupt and imperfect copy had come into the hands of the player-editors of the folio of 1623. Why the manuscript of 'Timon of Athens' should have been more mutilated, than that from which other dramas were printed for the first time in the same volume, was a question into which he did not enter. His admiration of some parts of the tragedy was unbounded; but he maintained that it was, on the whole, a painful and disagreeable production, because it gave only a disadvantageous picture of human nature, very inconsistent with what, he firmly believed, was our great poet's real view of the characters of his fellow creatures. He said that the whole piece was a bitter dramatic satire, a species of writing in which Shakespeare had shown, as in all other kinds, that he could reach the very highest point of excellence. Coleridge could not help suspecting that the subject might have been taken up under some temporary feeling of vexation and disappointment.''

Vol vii p 96, on *Macbeth*: Collier cites *LR* ii 235, C's avowal that the ''disgusting passage of the Porter'' was ''an interpolation of the actors'', and comments: ''This notion was not new to him in 1818; for three years earlier he had publicly declared it in a lecture devoted to 'Macbeth', although he admitted that there was something of Shakespeare in 'the primrose way to the everlasting bonfire'.'' Collier could not have known that HNC was quoting in *LR* notes relating to the course C gave at Bristol in 1813; see above, Lect 2 of the 1813 course (C's notes, first paragraph).

Vol vii p 193, on *Hamlet*: Collier cites *LR* ii 205, a passage again relating to the 1813 lectures at Bristol, but which Collier seems to have thought was from the 1818 lectures. Here C commented on the lack of balance in Hamlet, his "enormous intellectual activity, and a consequent proportionate aversion to real action" (see Lect 3 of the 1813 series, last sentence of first paragraph of C's notes). Collier asserts that C said this "after vindicating himself from the accusation that he had derived his ideas of Hamlet from Schlegel, (and we heard him broach then some years before the Lectures *Ueber Dramatische Kunst und Litteratur* were published)".

(2) WILLIAM MUDFORD IN

"THE LATE S. T. COLERIDGE, ESQ."

CANTERBURY MAGAZINE I

(SEPTEMBER 1834) 121–31

These recollections were by "Geoffrey Oldcastle", a pseudonym of William Mudford, the editor of the *Courier* in 1818. It is not clear whether Mudford himself attended many of the lectures, but he claims to have been intimate with C from 1817, and C advertised his courses in Mudford's newspaper. Mudford seems to have been an exception among newspaper editors this time in having literary interests, and his comments on the lectures show his sympathy for C. For further comment on Mudford see *EOT* (*CC*) I clxxivff. The passages quoted below are from pp 123, 125, 127, and 128 of the article in the *Canterbury Magazine*, which incorporates the Prospectus of the 1818 course and quotations from several letters written by C to Mudford, all of which are printed in full in *CL* IV.

About this period (1818) he projected a course of "Lectures", on Philosophy and Literature, embracing a wide range of inquiry and illustration, but every portion of which he was abundantly qualified to elucidate. . . .

It will be seen, that it formed a part of the above course, to give a critical and philosophical analysis of some of Shakspeare's characters; and well do I remember his magnificent developement of the bard's conceptions, in those of Lear, Macbeth, the Weird Sisters, Othello, Hamlet, Romeo and Juliet, &c. No man living, no man perhaps, among all those who have at any time undertaken to analyze and expound the writings of Shakespeare, ever studied him so profoundly, or was so thoroughly imbued with his mighty spirit, as Coleridge. No one could follow his daring flights with an eye so piercing and steady; and it may be doubted whether Shakspeare himself, was so intimately acquainted with all he had written, as Coleridge, who had worshipped him for years, with the deep devotion of idolatry. Warming, as he frequently would, with his theme, he poured forth such a full tide of mind in tracing the course of the mind of Shakspeare—pourtrayed, with such a glowing mixture of passion, philosophy, and poetry, its great crea-tions—that surely, could Shakspeare himself have listened to the rev-elation of his own imaginings, he would have exclaimed "Yes! it was thus I intended!" . . .

These lectures, so eminently worthy of every encouragement, at-tracted but scanty audiences. If, instead of deep philosophy, various erudition, eloquent disquisition, and the stores of an exuberant imagi-nation, Coleridge had invited the intellectual people of London to see a man swallow a sword, or toss about brass balls, he would have put money in his pocket. As it was, he gained nothing; if indeed he were not absolutely a loser by the experiment. His anxieties and disappoint-ments formed the theme of most of the letters I received from him at that time. . . .

I ventured to suggest to him, that he made his lectures too long for a mixed auditory, more especially as their matter was not of that flimsy, superficial character, that would admit of the attention being withdrawn and brought back at pleasure, without sustaining any intermediate loss. His reasonings were so close and subtle, and the series of his illustrations and demonstrations so beautifully connected, that like a problem in mathematics, if you missed any one of the propositions there was an end of the interest you felt in the deductions. But Coleridge, full of his subject, and his mind teeming with images, and facts, and illustrations, went on, without once considering, (though his delivery was not rapid,) how exhausting it was to those who really listened with a desire to follow him through the whole. In reply to this suggestion, he says, "I thank you for your kind and in all points judicious letter. In my last night's lecture I had pre-determined to avail himself of it—yet, still exceeded. I will try hard that my next Monday's shall be within the limits, which, I fully agree with you, is the utmost that a lecturer ought to inflict on a subject demanding any *catenation* of thought."

(3) JAMES GILLMAN IN *THE LIFE OF SAMUEL*
TAYLOR COLERIDGE (1838) 335–6

Gillman, the doctor who befriended C and with whom C lodged from 1816 onwards, attended the course C gave in 1818. Gillman had not previously heard C lecture, and his sympathetic response is perhaps more to be trusted than HCR's somewhat sour comments on the ten lectures he attended. After giving his account of this series, Gillman went on to describe an occasion when C lectured on the "Growth of the Individual Mind" at the London Philosophical Society. According to Gillman, C received the request to lecture in the morning, and the lecture was scheduled for the evening of the same day; he goes on to say (p 357): "The lecture was quite new to me, and I believe quite new to himself at least so far as the arrangement of his words were concerned. The floating thoughts were most beautifully arranged, and delivered on the spur of the moment." Gillman shows here his admiration for C as an impromptu speaker, but he emphasises that C had carefully prepared notes for the 1818 course.

These lectures, from his own account, were the most profitable of any he had given before, though delivered in an unfavorable situation; but being near the Temple, many of the students were his auditors. It was the first time I had ever heard him in public. He lectured from notes, which he had carefully made; yet it was obvious, that his audience was more delighted when, putting his notes aside, he spoke extempore;— many of these notes were preserved in, and have lately been printed in the Literary Remains. In his lectures he was brilliant, fluent, and rapid; his words seemed to flow as from a person repeating with grace and energy some delightful poem. If, however, he sometimes paused, it was not for the want of words, but that he was seeking the most appropriate, or their most logical arrangement.

The attempts to copy his lectures verbatim have failed, they are but comments. Scarcely in anything could he be said to be a mannerist, his mode of lecturing was his own. Coleridge's eloquence, when he gave utterance to his rich thoughts, flowing like some great river, which winds its way majestically at its own "sweet will," though occasionally slightly impeded by a dam formed from its crumbling banks, but over which the accumulated waters pass onward with increased force, so arrested his listeners, as at times to make them feel almost breathless. Such seemed the movement of Coleridge's words in lecture or in earnest discourse, and his countenance retained the same charms of benignity, gentleness, and intelligence, though his expression varied with the thoughts he uttered, and was much modified by his sensitive nature. His quotations from the poets, of high character, were most feelingly and most luminously given, as by one inspired with the subject. In my early intimacy with this great man, I was especially struck with the store of knowledge he possessed, and on which I ever found one might safely rely.

1818–1819
LECTURES ON SHAKESPEARE
(ALTERNATING WITH
PHILOSOPHICAL LECTURES)
(CROWN AND ANCHOR,
STRAND)

INTRODUCTION

The wide-ranging course on European literature and various other topics, designed, according to the Prospectus, to promote the "principles of sound judgment", given by Coleridge from January to March 1818 went so well that, after a two-month spell of busy journalistic activity, he planned another, shorter, course on Shakespeare. This was advertised towards the end of May, but was then cancelled, possibly because few subscriptions were forthcoming for a course likely to run on into the summer.[1] In a letter written early in June 1818 Coleridge remarked:

After due advice and consideration I have abandoned all thought of giving any further Lectures for the present season. Perhaps, I may prove hazardous enough to renew the attempt in November or December next—by which time the New Auditorium of the London Philosophical Society who rising rapidly into notice and respectability are about to remove from Fleur de lis Court to the vicinity of Charing Cross.[2]

At this point Coleridge cannot have heard of the strange events of 27 May, when, at a meeting of the Society, attended presumably by relatively few and especially interested members, an effective vote of no confidence was passed against Coleridge's friend, T. J. Pettigrew, the Treasurer of the Society.[3] When news of this circulated, a majority of members, including patrons drawn from the royal family and the aristocracy, resigned; among these was Coleridge, whose letter of resignation was written on 8 June.[4] The consequent decline in membership led to the dissolution of the Society in 1820.[5] Nothing more is heard of the "New Auditorium", and when Coleridge did in fact decide to attempt another course of lectures in November 1818 he had to find another location for them, hiring a room for the purpose in the Crown and Anchor Tavern in the Strand, which had a large room measuring eighty-four by thirty-five feet, much used for political and other meetings.[6]

---

[1] See above, conclusion of Introduction to the 1818 series (after n 58).

[2] To unknown correspondent: *CL* IV 865.

[3] See above, Introduction to the 1818 series (at n 12).

[4] *CL* IV 865.

[5] Fannie E. Ratchford "S. T. Coleridge and the London Philosophical Society" *MLR* XX (1965) 79–80.

[6] The Crown and Anchor was located on the east side of Arundel Street, south of the Strand, but with an alley providing an entrance from the Strand. It was well

The course advertised in May 1818 was to have included discussion of *Richard II, King Lear, Macbeth, Antony and Cleopatra, Henry VI, Richard III*, and *Twelfth Night*, with perhaps some reference also to *Pericles* and *Two Gentlemen of Verona*. The course of six lectures announced for December 1818 and January 1819 was less adventurous, and, except for Lecture 6, on *King Lear*, the first of Coleridge's lectures devoted wholly to this play, all were to be on plays dealt with in earlier courses, namely *The Tempest, Richard II, Hamlet, Macbeth,* and *Othello*. It may be that Coleridge's return, on the whole, to familiar and favourite plays was prompted by a desire to restrict the amount of preparation he would need to make, for this course was to run alternately with a course of fourteen lectures on the history of philosophy, which involved a very wide range of reading and reference. The Prospectus for the two courses was proof-read by Coleridge and returned to the printer on Tuesday, 17 November, but had apparently not been sent out by the following Friday, when Coleridge ordered 750 to be printed, and mailed so that copies could be "dispersed" by his friends.[7] By 24 November he was able to enclose some copies in a letter to Tulk. During the next two weeks he was writing to friends and relatives, sending tickets and batches of prospectuses for distribution. The first advertisement, in the *Courier* on 2 December, took the form of a reprinting of the Prospectus, which appeared also in the *New Times* on 5 December. The prospectuses for distribution were in the form of a four-page hand-out, with an elaborate announcement of the philosophical lectures, to begin on Monday, 7 December, and continue weekly, occupying two and a half pages. The announcement of the Shakespeare lectures, on the lower half of the third page, runs as follows:

ALTERNATE COURSE OF LECTURES.

On the Thursday Evenings, in the same room, Mr. COLERIDGE will give a Course of Six Lectures, each having for its subject some one Play of Shakespear's, scene by scene, for the purpose of illustrating the conduct of the plot, and the peculiar force, beauty, and propriety, of the language, in the particular passages, as well as the intention of the great Philosophic Poet in the prominent characters of each play, and the unity of interest in the whole and in the apparent contrast of the component parts.

---

established as a meeting-place, and provided good facilities, for the building had been reconstructed in 1790. When C lectured there it had radical associations (in contrast to the fashionable Willis's Rooms, frequented by the nobility and gentry, where C had lectured in 1812), and it was here that preliminary meetings were held in 1823, chaired by Dr George

Birkbeck of the Glasgow Mechanics' Institution, which led to the founding of Birkbeck College; see A. L. Macfie *The Crown and Anchor Tavern the Birthplace of Birkbeck College* (1973) and William Kent *An Encyclopedia of London* (1937, rev ed 1951) 542–3.

[7] *CL* iv 882.

Thursday, December 10, 1818.—The TEMPEST, as a specimen of the Romantic or Poetical Drama of Shakespear.—17. RICHARD THE SECOND, of his Dramatic Histories.—Thursday, January 7, 1819, HAMLET.—14, MACBETH.— 21. OTHELLO.—28, LEAR.

Double Ticket, admitting a Lady and Gentleman, *Two Guineas*. Single Ticket, *One Pound Five Shillings*. Admission to each Lecture, *Five Shillings*.—Tickets and Prospectuses to be had, as above.

Coleridge was unlucky in his timing. Queen Charlotte died on 17 November 1818, and a state funeral took place on 2 December, moving Coleridge to draft a piece on "The Character of Queen Charlotte" for the *Courier*.[8] Because of the period of national mourning consequent upon this, Coleridge postponed the commencement of both courses by a week. A copy of the Prospectus in the Berg Collection of the New York Public Library has a note apparently in Coleridge's hand below the announcement of the Shakespeare course that reads, "Courses postponed to the 14th and 17th". The Prospectus was reprinted pretty accurately in the *Courier* and *New Times* from the hand-out, but with a printer's fist at the bottom drawing attention to the note, "The Courses are Postponed to the 14th and 17th in consequence of the late public event." Further general advertisements appeared in *The Times* (7, 10, 14 December), and *Courier* (7, 9, 11, 14 December), for the two courses, the literary one being described as "the latter, or Critical Course, on Six of Shakespeare's Plays, each forming the subject of one Lecture". At the suggestion of his friend Thomas Allsop, Coleridge also decided to "send Prospectuses and Admission Tickets to the Literary Gazette, to some of the more serious Magazines, &c",[9] and he placed general advertisements in the Sunday *Observer* on 6 December and in the *Literary Gazette* on 12 December.

This general advertising of the course was followed up by separate advertisements in four or five newspapers for each individual lecture, but whether this produced the audiences Coleridge hoped for is doubtful. The course extended over Christmas and the new year, and the seasonal holidays and festivities affected attendance, as is clear from Coleridge's lament about Lecture 3 that the audience "were scarcely enough to pay the Rooms".[10] However, if the course had been financially disastrous, it seems unlikely that Coleridge would have planned another course of literary lectures to follow hard on this one. This course was advertised in the *Morning Chronicle* of 28 January as beginning on 4 February, the week following Coleridge's final lecture on *King Lear*. It seems he had some sort of fever or "ague-fit" commencing the day before he

---

[8] *EOT (CC)* III 251–6.
[9] To Allsop 2 Dec 1818: *CL* IV 889.
[10] To Mudford [8 Jan 1819]: *CL* IV 910.

was due to lecture on *King Lear*,[11] and the continuance of this illness led him to postpone the new course by a week. This lecture was nevertheless duly given on the advertised date, 28 January, and Coleridge asked William Mudford to notice it in the *Courier*: "If you could mention my LEAR in two or three lines, it would be of important service to my fresh Cause".[12] Mudford duly obliged him with a brief but enthusiastic report. Apart from the contemptuous reference to Coleridge in the *Champion* in relation to Lecture 3, the only reports of lectures in this course are those relating to Lectures 1 and 6.

This is a pity, for Coleridge's claim in his opening lecture that he would be commenting on Shakespeare "in a somewhat different and . . . in a more instructive form"[13] was not an empty promise. The Prospectus announced a scene-by-scene analysis of the plays to be considered, attending to plot, language, and character, a way of proceeding that looks conventional enough now, but was more unusual at a time when popular lecturers were likely to offer generalities or describe the characters of the plays. So William Hazlitt's *Characters of Shakespear's Plays* (1817, second edition 1818) was an immediate success, was hailed in the *Champion* as "the only work written on Shakespeare that can be deemed worthy of Shakespeare",[14] and seems to have been the immediate cause of his appointment as dramatic critic of *The Times*; and yet this book has not unfairly been summed up as follows:

> [Hazlitt] makes little attempt to divine the principal theme of each play; nor does he write with reference to dramatic production. By concentrating on the characters rather than the plays themselves he too often ignores the whole in favour of the part. He does not, indeed, analyse any of the characters in detail— as Maurice Morgann and others had begun to do in the previous century. What he does is to quote liberally from each play and discuss it in general terms. If the result sometimes reminds us of a collection of *Beauties of Shakespeare*, we must in justice remember that Hazlitt was reacting against the eighteenth century's tendency to condemn Shakespeare for violating rules which have in fact no relevance to his plays.[15]

Crabb Robinson was reading Hazlitt's book at the beginning of 1818 and, after reacting pretty sourly to Coleridge's course in January and February of that year, did not attend the 1818–19 course, but went instead to the lectures on the English comic writers that Hazlitt gave from November 1818 onwards at the Surrey Institution.[16] No doubt he supposed he had heard all Coleridge's ideas on Shakespeare before.

---

[11] To RS [31 Jan 1819]: *CL* IV 916.
[12] 26 Jan 1819: *CL* IV 915.
[13] See below, Lect 1 (opening sentence of C's notes).

[14] See *H Life* (H) 211–19.
[15] Ian Jack *English Literature 1815–1832* (Oxford 1963) 262.
[16] *CRB* I 225–6.

The reports of the first lecture show that, before going on to speak in detail about *The Tempest*, Coleridge rehearsed some of his familiar arguments about Shakespeare's judgement being equal to his genius, about the difference between a copy and an imitation, and so on, and these more general comments rather than his detailed criticism of the play form the substance of the accounts in the *Courier* and the *Champion*. Coleridge's design, however, is perhaps best illustrated by the draft notice of the course as he first outlined it in May 1818, proposing "six lectures of particular and practical Criticism".[17] He gave currency to the phrase "practical criticism" in *Biographia Literaria*,[18] and there, as here, seems to be using the term "practical" in its original sense, as opposed to the speculative or theoretical. His notes for the lectures of this course consist mainly of prefatory essays written on blank leaves in his interleaved copy of *The Dramatic Works of William Shakespeare* edited by Samuel Ayscough for John Stockdale and annotations to the text. Evidently he took these volumes with him into the lecture-room and developed his lectures from these notes, so that for the most part he was offering close readings of the text. In his notes Coleridge frequently referred to the text in Ayscough by page, column, or line-number or some combination of these. The text in Ayscough's edition is printed in double columns, and each page has its separate line-numbers centred between the columns. Coleridge's habit was to refer to the left column as "α" and the right as "β", and this notation is kept in the presentation of his notes below. Each note is given a standard act, scene, and line-reference as well as the relevant page-reference in Ayscough (that is, normally to the page facing the interleaves on which Coleridge wrote his notes), and Coleridge's own references are included. References to the Ayscough edition are expanded into the volume, page, and, where appropriate, column and line-numbers (for example, "Ayscough I 413 α 14"). Cancellations are not recorded; they will be printed in full in *Marginalia (CC)*.

The first lecture of the new course that began on 11 February 1819 was, according to the advertisements, to be devoted to a continuation of Lecture 3 of the 1818–19 course, dealing with "the third, fourth, and last acts" of *Hamlet*.[19] This advertisement implies that in Lecture 3 of the 1818–19 course Coleridge did not proceed beyond Act II. This extended treatment may be contrasted with Hazlitt's brief account of

---

[17] See above, Introduction to the 1818 series (at n 59).

[18] *BL* ch 15 (*CC*) II 19. Its wide use in the twentieth century is owing to

I. A. Richards, who borrowed it from C for the title of his *Practical Criticism* (1929).

[19] See below, Lect 1 of the 1819 series

the play in *Characters of Shakespear's Plays*, which is largely a sketch of Hamlet himself as a philosophical speculator whose ruling passion is to think, not act, followed by a sentence each on Ophelia, the Queen, Laertes and Polonius, and a paragraph of advice to actors on how to play the prince.

It must, then, have been galling to Coleridge to find the reporter in the *Champion* suggesting that Coleridge had perhaps "availed himself of the opinions of Hazlitt", or even of Thelwall,[20] when he justly felt he was doing something new in avoiding generalities and concentrating in detail on individual plays. The review of his first lecture in the *Champion* had attacked Coleridge for inconsistency in his political views and implied that a similar deficiency affected all his work. In addition, Coleridge's reassertion in this lecture of his claim to have been the first to demonstrate "to the full extent of the position" that Shakespeare's judgement equalled his genius provoked a retort in the *Morning Chronicle* assigning priority to Schlegel. Coleridge was sufficiently put out by this to respond privately, in a statement written in his copy of the Ayscough (Stockdale) Shakespeare he was using for the course, and he let off steam also in a letter to a friend, John Britton.[21] In spite of these irritations, the course went according to plan, and Coleridge was sufficiently encouraged by it to follow it almost immediately with another course that included three more lectures on Shakespeare.

(headnote: Advertisements).

[20] See below, Lect 3 (at nn 28 and 29). The *Champion* report implies that C might have borrowed ideas from a lecturer whose account of the character of Hamlet "during the last season, excited very popular attention". The reference is almost certainly to John Thelwall, whose lectures on Shakespeare were praised in the *Champion* 22 Feb 1818, and who probably wrote this report, as he had the report on Lect 1.

[21] See Lect 1, below (headnote: Reports). For the general issue of C's relation to Schlegel, see also Editor's Introduction, above (from n 61 onwards).

LECTURE 1

DATE AND PLACE OF DELIVERY. Thursday, 17 December 1818, at the Crown and Anchor Tavern, Strand, London.

SUBJECT. *The Tempest.*

ADVERTISEMENTS. *Courier* Wed, 16 Dec: "TO-MORROW EVENING, Eight o'Clock, Crown and Anchor, Strand, Mr. COLERIDGE's LECTURE on Shakespear's Tempest, scene by scene. On Thursday, Dec. 31, Richard the Second, and successively on the following Thursdays, Hamlet, Macbeth, Othello, and Lear. Admission Five Shillings . . ." (the rest as in the general advertisements for the course). *M Post, The Times, New Times* Thurs, 17 Dec: as in the *Courier*, all printing "TO-MORROW EVENING" in error for "THIS EVENING". *M Chron* Thurs, 17 Dec: as in the *Courier*, with the alteration to "THIS EVENING".

TEXT. Some notes made by C for this lecture begin on a single small sheet of paper now BM MS Egerton 2800 f 25. The leaf is headed "1" and "2", and C's writing fills both sides, the sentence at the end of "2" being finished down the side of the leaf. These notes then continue on three blank pages before the text of *The Tempest* in *Sh* (Ayscough). The first two pages were numbered "1" and "2" by C, and the third page is unnumbered. The notes on this page end in mid-sentence, and C returned to two further small leaves of paper, BM MS Egerton 2800 ff 26–7, to complete the sentence and the remainder of his "introduction" to the lecture. These two leaves are cut to the same size as f 25 and are drawn from the same stock of paper; one leaf, f 26, bears a watermark date 1817. The sides are numbered 4, 5, 6, and 7, and the notes end four lines down on 7, at the point where C began to analyse the opening scene. The newspaper reports of the lecture help to confirm that the notes were prepared for this occasion. Some of the notes, revised and rearranged, were printed by HNC in *LR* II 92–5, in which they are tied in with some further comments on the early scenes of the play and then on the play in general (*LR* II 95–102, reprinted in *Sh C* I 118–23 [131–7]). The source of these is untraced, except for two passages culled from note 12 of the notes for Lects 4 and 6 in the series C gave at Bristol in 1813; one is a sentence about Shakespeare's women, the other a general comment on Shakespeare's powers of characterisation. HNC wove these into his text with no indication of his sources, and other passages in the notes may have been drawn from materials not relating to the 1818–19 series. However, C is known to have lectured on *The Tempest* only in the 1811–12 series, Lect 9, of which a full report exists, and the notes do not relate to this. He may have lectured on this play in 1808, and he planned to do so in a second course at Bristol beginning in Dec 1813, but was taken ill a week before the starting date, and although he advertised the course again in Jan 1814, there is no evidence that he gave these lectures. It is possible that he prepared notes for the first one, which was to begin from *The Tempest*, and that these are the source of most of HNC's additional material on the play. The known copies of Shakespeare C used throw no light on the matter. There are no further annotations to *The Tempest* in *Sh* (Ayscough), and only two very brief ones in *Sh* (Rann), the ed C used in Bristol. Possibly he lectured impromptu from an unmarked text in 1818–19, or he had some additional notes, which might have been written in the copy of *The Tempest* he sought to borrow from Mrs Milne (see below, under "Background and Circumstances"). It does not seem very likely that when he was ill in the winter of 1813–14 he managed to prepare notes for the lectures he never gave, and so the balance of probabilities is that most of HNC's material relates to this lecture. This material is accordingly given below, following C's ms notes, which were first printed in their correct order in *Sh C* I 113–18. The text of these is based partly on a fresh transcript of BM MS Egerton 2800 ff 25, 26, and 27 and partly on the transcript of the notes in C's copy of *Sh* (Ayscough); the cancellations in the latter are, however, not given.

REPORTS. Several reports of this lecture were published. The first appeared in the *Courier* Fri, 18 Dec 1818 and was reprinted in the *M Post* 19 Dec. On the same day a slightly abbreviated version of this report was printed in the *New Times*, omitting all comment on the alternate course of lectures on the history of philosophy that C was giving during this period and leaving out also the final sentence. This report is reprinted below as it appeared in the *Courier* and *M Post*. A more elaborate report was published in the *Champion* Sun, 20 Dec. This begins with some sharply critical general observations on C and provides a more incisive, if less complimentary, account of the lecture than the previous reports, while still finding much to praise in it. This report was reprinted in the *Champion* Mon, 21 Dec, with some corrections in the text and the addition of the initials ''A. S.'' at the end. These initials probably disguise John Thelwall, editor of the *Champion* in 1819, a radical with whom C had been on friendly terms during the late 1790s. The criticism of C's change in his political views in the first part of the report in the *Champion* refers to his early correspondence with ''an individual'' who endured ''sufferings'' on account of his radicalism, and Thelwall was imprisoned and tried for treason in 1794. The introduction to the report also includes a quotation of some lines from C's sonnet *To John Thelwall*, first published from ms by EHC in *PW* (1912). There would seem, then, to be reasons enough to identify ''A. S.'' with Thelwall himself.

Finally, in the *M Chron* Tues, 29 Dec, a note was published with the heading ''MR. COLERIDGE'' as a sequel to the report printed in the *Courier* 18 Dec. This report accurately represented C as claiming to have been the first to maintain that Shakespeare's judgement was equal to his genius; his notes for the lecture confirm that he did so. The anonymous contributor to the *M Chron* took issue with C on this point and assigned priority to Schlegel. C was by this time very sensitive on this issue. The publication of John Black's translation of Schlegel's lectures in 1815 had made these more widely available. Hazlitt had reviewed the translation in the *Ed Rev* XXVI (Feb 1816), writing that Schlegel provided ''by far the best account'' of Shakespeare ever given by any writer. *H Works* XVI 59. In a letter to James Perry of Feb 1818 (*CL* IV 831), C referred to this review, which hurt him by its omission of any mention of his own lectures on Shakespeare, especially as he recalled Hazlitt as at one time defending him from the charge that he had borrowed his opinions from Schlegel. The comment in the *M Chron* rubbed salt in an old wound and no doubt prompted C to enter another statement, dated 7 Jan 1819, of his claim to priority over Schlegel— on a flyleaf of vol II of his set of *Sh* (Ayscough); see below, Lect 3 (from nn 1–5). He reasserted his claim yet again in a letter to John Britton on 28 Feb 1819 (*CL* IV 923–4), but does not seem to have responded to the comment in the *M Chron* by publishing a rebuttal in a newspaper at the time. The report in the *Champion*, included in *Sh C* II 257–9 (321–3), is reprinted below from the issue of 21 Dec. The note in the *M Chron* was reprinted in *P Lects* (1949) 467–8 and in *CL* IV 899–900; although not strictly a report, it is included with the other reports here, since it relates both to them and to C's lecture.

BACKGROUND AND CIRCUMSTANCES. The mistake in the advertisements in *The Times*, *M Post*, and *New Times*, all of which announced the lecture for Fri, 18 Dec, instead of Thurs, was blamed by C on the "young man" who copied out for him the advertisement he wrote for the *Courier*, in order to send it to these other newspapers. In a letter to Tulk written after the lecture C observed, "I must have lost a number of Auditors. Still however the audience was respectable in numbers, and most respectable in character—and I have reason to believe, went away more than usually satisfied". *CL* IV 898.

A few days before the course was due to begin, C wrote to some Highgate friends, neighbours of the Gillmans, with whom he had recently become intimate, Mr and Mrs Milne, enclosing tickets for the course and also asking, "If you have a small tolerably *pocketable* Edition of Shakspere, be so good as to lend me the Volume containing THE TEMPEST." *CL* IV 898. Evidently he succeeded at some point in borrowing an edition of Shakespeare from the Milnes, and annotated some plays in it, since in the marginalia in *Sh* (Ayscough) he twice provided cross-references to notes in Mrs Milne's edition, once in relation to *Hamlet* (Lect 3 of this series, at n 17) and once in relation to *Romeo and Juliet* (Lect 2 of the 1819 series, at n 2). This edition of Shakespeare, with C's annotations, has not been found, and there is no way of establishing whether he obtained the volume containing *The Tempest* and annotated it for this lecture. The absence of notes against the text of the play in *Sh* (Ayscough) might be taken as evidence that he did; the notes HNC published in *LR* as connected with this lecture could include notes copied from this source, but might equally well be from ms fragments.

Because C started the course late on 17 Dec, he had to allow a break for the Christmas holiday after Lect 1, and the second lecture was not given until 31 Dec.

LECTURE 1

RECORDS OF THE LECTURE

COLERIDGE'S NOTES
BM MS EGERTON 2800 FF 25–25ᵛ,
ANNOTATIONS ON THE INTERLEAVES OF *SH*
(AYSCOUGH) I, BM MS EGERTON 2800 FF 26–27ᵛ

a"Once more, tho' in a somewhat different and I would fain believe in a more instructive form I have undertaken the task of criticizing the works of that great Dramatist, whose own Name has become their best and most expressive Epithet. The Task will be genial in proportion as the criticism is reverential. Assuredly, the Englishman, who without reverence, who without a proud and affectionate Reverence can utter the name of Shakespear, stands disqualified for the office. He wants one at least of the very Senses, the language of which he is to employ, and will discourse at best, [like a blind man,]*b* while the whole harmonious creation of Light and Shade with all its subtle interchange of deepening and dissolving Colors rises in silence to the silent Fiat of the uprising Apollo. However inferior in ability to *c*some who have followed me, I am proud that I was the first in time who publicly demonstrated to the full extent of the position, that the supposed Irregularity and Extravagances of Shakespear ~~was~~ were the mere Dreams of a Pedantry that arraigned the Eagle because it had not the Dimensions of the Swan. In all the successive Courses, delivered by me, since my first attempt at the Royal Institution, it has been and it still remains my Object to prove that in all points from the most important to the most minutes, the Judgement of Shakespear is commensurate with his Genius[1]—nay,

---

a Egerton 2800 f 25
b Words supplied by the editor
c f 25ᵛ

[1] C was no doubt thinking of Schlegel's lectures, and, although not formulated in these precise terms, his claim can be substantiated from the 1808 series (Lect 4, at n 10) and the 1811–12 series (Lect 2, paragraphs following n 29), de-

that his Genius reveals itself in ~~its~~ his Judgement, as in its most exalted Form. And the more gladly do I recur to the subject, from the clear conviction that to judge aright and ~~in~~ with the distinct consciousness of the grounds of our Judgement, concerning the works of Shakespear implies the power & the means of judging rightly of all other works, those of abstract Science *d*alone excepted.*e*

*f*THE TEMPEST

⟨We commence with the Tempest, as a specimen of the Romantic Drama. But⟩ Whatever Play of Shakspere's we had selected, there is one preliminary point to be first settled, as the indispensable Condition not only of just and genial criticism, but of all consistency in our opinions.— This point is contained in the words, probable, natural. We are all in the habit of praising Shakespear or of hearing him extolled for his fidelity to Nature. Now what are we to understand by these words, in their application to the Drama? Assuredly, not the ordinary meaning of them. Farquhar ⟨the⟩ most ably and if we except a few sentences in one of Dryden's Prefaces (written for a partic. purp. and in contrad. to the opinions elsewhere supported by him) first exposed the ludicrous absurdities involved in the supposition, and demolished as with the single sweep of careless hand the whole Edifice of French Criticism respecting the so called Unities of Time and Place.[2]—But a moment's reflection suffices to make every man conscious of what every man must have before felt, that the Drama is an *imitation* of reality not a *Copy*—and that Imitation is contra-distinguished from Copy by this, that a certain quantum of Difference is essential to the former, and an indispensable condition and cause of the pleasure, we derive from it; while in a Copy it is a defect, contravening its name and purpose.[3] If illustration were

---

d-e Written up the leaf in the right margin, for want of space at the foot
f From the unnumbered blank leaves before *The Tempest*, the first play in *Sh* (Ayscough) 1

---

livered before he saw *DKL*. But see also, below (at n 30, also comment in the *M Chron* 29 Dec 1818).

[2] Farquhar dismissed the unities in *A Discourse upon Comedy*, published first in *Love and Business* (1702). Dryden was generally in favour of them, but at several points in his writings argued that the rules were "too strict" (Preface to his translation of C.A. du Fresnoy's *Art of Painting*, 1695), and "better a mechanic rule were stretched or broken, than a great beauty were omitted" (address to the Earl of Mulgrave prefixed to his translation of *The Works of Virgil*, 1697). See *Essays of John Dryden* ed Ker II 131, 158.

[3] C never tired of insisting upon this distinction; see e.g. Lect 4 of the 1808 series (at n 30) and Lect 3 of the 1811–12 series (at n 20).

needed, it would be sufficient to ask—why we prefer a Fruit Piece of Vanhuysen's to a marble Peach on a mantle piece[4]—or why we prefer an historical picture of West's to M[rs] Salmon's Wax-figure Gallery.[5] Not only that we ought, but that we actually do, all of us judge of the Drama under this impression, we need no other proof than the impassive slumber of our sense of Probability when we hear an Actor announce himself a Greek, Roman, Venetian or Persian in good Mother English. And how little our great Dramatist feared awakening on it we have a lively instance in proof in Portia's Answer to Neæra's[g] question, What say you then to Falconbridge, the young Baron of England?—to which she replies—You know, I say nothing to him: for he understands not me nor I him. He hath neither Latin, French or Italian: and you will come into the Court and swear that I have a poor Penny-worth in the English.[6]

Still, however, there is a sort of Improb[y] with which we are shocked in dramatic repres[n] no less than in the narration of real Life—Consequently, there must be Rules respecting it, and as Rules are nothing but Means to an end previously ascertained (the inattention to which simple truth has been the occasion of all the pedantry of the French School) we must first ascertain what the immediate End or object of the Drama is—Here I find two extremes in critical decision—The French, which evidently presupposes that a perfect Delusion is to be aimed at— an Opinion which now needs no fresh confutation—The opposite, supported by D[r] Johnson, supposes the auditors throughout as in the full and positive reflective knowlege of the contrary. In evincing the impossibility of Delusion he makes no sufficient allowance for an inter-

---

[g] A slip for "Nerissa's"

[4] Jan van Huysum (1682–1749), a Dutch artist famous for his paintings of flowers and fruit. C made the same point in a letter to Charles Mathews of 30 May 1814, in relation to acting, contrasting a "marble peach" as a copy with "a fruit-piece of Vanhuysen's" as an imitation. *CL* III 501. The general idea C had found in Adam Smith's essay "Of the Nature of That Imitation Which Takes Place in What Are Called the Imitative Arts": "Artificial Fruits and Flowers sometimes imitate so exactly the natural objects which they represent, that they frequently deceive us. We soon grow weary of them, however . . . But we do not grow weary of a good flower and fruit painting". *Essays on Philosophical Subjects* (1795) 141. See also Lect 4 of the 1808 series (at n 30) and the Supplementary Records of that series (at n 28).

[5] Benjamin West (1738–1820), the American artist who settled in London in 1763 and became President of the Royal Academy after Reynolds died; he was well known for his large-scale historical paintings like *The Death of Wolfe* (1771). Mrs Salmon died in 1760, but her name remained attached to the gallery of wax-figures housed in Fleet Street from 1795 to 1812, a popular attraction in London, the Mme Tussaud's of the day, until 1827.

[6] Nerissa's question, *Merchant of Venice* I ii 66ff.

mediate State, which we distinguish by the term, Illusion. In what this consists, I cannot better explain, than by referring you to the highest degree of it, namely, Dreaming. It is laxly said, that during Sleep we take our Dreams for Realities; but this is irreconcilable with the nature of Sleep, which consists in a suspension of the voluntary and therefore of the comparative power. The fact is, that we pass no judgement either way—we simply do *not* judge them to be ⟨un⟩ real—in conseq. of which the Images act on our minds, as far as they act at all, by their own force as images.[7] Our state while we are dreaming differs from that in which we are in the perusal of a deeply interesting Novel, in the degree rather than in the Kind, and from three causes—First, from the exclusion of all outward impressions on our senses the images in sleep become proportionally more vivid, than they can be when the organs of Sense are in their active state. Secondly, in sleep the sensations, and with these the Emotions & Passions which they counterfeit, are the causes of our Dream-images, while in our waking hours our emotions are the effects of the Images presented to us—*(apparitions so detectible)*[8] Lastly, in sleep we pass at once by a sudden collapse into this suspension of Will and the Comparative power: whereas in an interesting Play, read or represented, we are brought up to this point, as far as it is requisite or desirable gradually, by the Art of the Poet and the Actors, and with the consent and positive Aidance of our own Will. We *chuse* to be deceived.—The rule therefore may be easily inferred. What ever tends to prevent the mind from placing it[self][h] or from being gradually placed, in this state in which the Images have a negative reality, [i]must be a defect, and consequently any thing that must force itself on the Auditors' minds as improbable—not because it *is* improbable (for that the whole play is foreknown to be) but because ~~it probably~~ it can not but *appear* as such.

[h] C wrote "it"
[i] Egerton 2800 f 26

[7] In his Preface to Shakespeare Dr Johnson, attacking the veneration for the dramatic unities derived from Corneille, argued that the audience is never deluded, but "know, from the first act to the last, that the stage is only a stage, and that the players are only players". *Works* vii 77. This passage echoes some notes on dramatic illusion C made probably for the 1808 lectures, in which he also related it to dreaming (see Supplementary Records, at nn 17–19 and 26–8). He also spoke on "delusion" to much the same effect in Lect 3 of the 1811–12 series (at n 29). The issue was important to him, and relates both to his distinction between copy and imitation and to his concept of "that willing suspension of disbelief for the moment, which constitutes poetic faith"; see *BL* ch 14 (*CC*) ii 6.

[8] See C's notes for Lect 12 of the 1818 series (at n 51), in which he said of apparitions, "the terror . . . is the cause of the *Image!* not vice versâ".

But this again depends on the degree of excitement, in which the mind is supposed to be. Many things would be intolerable in the first scene of a Play, that would not at all interrupt our enjoyment in the height of the interest—The narrow ~~stage~~ Cockpit may hold

> The vasty field of France: or we may cram
> Within its wooden O the very casques
> That did affright the Air at Agincourt/[9]

And again on the other hand many obvious improbabilities will be endured as belonging to the groundwork of the story rather than to the Drama, in the first scenes which would disturb or disentrance us from all illusion in ~~our~~ the acme of our excitement—as for instance Lear's division of his Realm & banishment of Cordelia/ But besides this dramatic probability [j]all the other excellencies of the Drama, as unity of Interest,[10] with distinctness and subordination of the Characters, appropriateness of Style/ nay, and the charm of Language and Sentiment for their own sakes, yet still as far as they tend to increase the ⟨inward⟩ excitement, are all means to this chief end—that of producing and supporting this willing Illusion.

I have but one point more to add—namely, that tho' ~~these~~ excellencies above mentioned are means to this end, they do not therefore ~~to~~ cease to be themselves *ends*—and as such carry their own justification with them as long as they do not contravene or interrupt the Illusion. It is not even always or of necessity an objection to them, that they prevent it from ~~being~~ rising to as great a height as it might otherwise have attained—it is enough, if they are compatible with as high a degree as is requisite ~~for the purpose of~~. If the Panorama[11] had been invented in the time of Leo X, Raphael would still have smiled at the regret, that ~~the~~ Broom-twigs &c. [k]at the back of his grand pictures were not as ~~most~~ probable Trees as those in the Panorama./—Let me venture to affirm, that certain obvious, & if not palpable, improbabilities may be

[j] f 26[v]
[k] f 27

[9] *Henry V* Prologue lines 11–14 (var).
[10] See Lect 3 of the 1811–12 series (at n 26).
[11] The word is first recorded in 1796 (*OED*) as the name for a device patented in 1787 by the painter Robert Barker (1739–1806) for displaying the entire view of a landscape or scene as it would appear to someone turning round in a complete circle. The painting was done either on the inside of a cylindrical surface with the spectator in the centre or on a long sheet unrolled so as to show each part of the scene in succession. Barker exhibited his first panorama, a view of Edinburgh, in that city in 1788. Views of cities became the vogue and, with the Napoleonic wars, panoramic scenes of sea fights and land battles.

hazarded in order to keep down a scene, [to keep it]^l merely instrumental, and to preserve it in its due proportion of interest.—

I now quit this subject, for the time—with less regret, because in my next lecture I shall have occasion to take it up again, in application to Shakespear's *historical* Dramas.—. THE TEMPEST, I repeat, has been selected as a specimen of the Romantic Drama[12]—i.e. of a Drama, the interests of which are independent of all historical facts and associations, and arise from their fitness to that faculty of our ~~hu~~ nature, the Imagination I mean, which ow~~es~~ns no ~~homage~~ allegiance to Time and Place/ ~~and in wh~~ a species of Drama therefore, in which errors in Chronology and Geography, no mortal sins in any species, are venial, or count for nothing.

^{m}The Romance opens with a busy lively scene, admirably appropriate to the *kind* of Drama, giving as it were the key-note^n

COLERIDGE'S NOTES, CONTINUED

AS EDITED BY HENRY NELSON COLERIDGE

FROM *LR* II 95–102

The following notes were included by HNC in *LR* as a continuation of the notes by C given above. They incorporate and complete the unfinished sentence with which C's ms ends. There is no other lecture on *The Tempest* with which they might reasonably be linked (see headnote: Text, above), and C made only one annotation on the play in his copy of *Sh* (Ayscough), the edition of Shakespeare used by him for this series. The notes probably, then, relate on the whole to this lecture, but need to be treated with caution because HNC often reworded and linked together materials from disparate sources as if they formed a connected whole. Towards the end of these notes he incorporated a passage from notes by C for Lect 6 of the 1813 series at Bristol, a lecture on *Richard III*, and it is possible that other passages were drawn from sources that have nothing to do with *The Tempest* or with C's lectures.

. . . It addresses itself entirely to the imaginative faculty; and although the illusion may be assisted by the effect on the senses of the complicated scenery and decorations of modern times, yet this sort of assistance is dangerous. For the principal and only genuine excitement ought to come

---

^{l} Words supplied by the editor

^{m} f 27^v

^{n} The text ends four lines from the top of the page, the rest of which is blank

[12] In Lect 5 of the first series he gave in 1812 (at n 4), C, following A. W. Schlegel, defined "Shakespearian Drama" in general as romantic, but in Lect 9 of the 1811–12 series he had treated *The Tempest* as a play that especially "appealed to the imagination" (sentence containing n 28).

from within,—from the moved and sympathetic imagination; whereas, where so much is addressed to the more external senses of seeing and hearing, the spiritual vision is apt to languish, and the attraction from without will withdraw the mind from the proper and only legitimate interest which is intended to spring from within.

The romance opens with a busy scene admirably appropriate to the kind of drama, and giving, as it were, the key-note to the whole harmony.[13] It prepares and initiates the excitement required for the entire piece, and yet does not demand any thing from the spectators, which their previous habits had not fitted them to understand. It is the bustle of a tempest, from which the real horrors are abstracted;—therefore it is poetical, though not in strictness natural—(the distinction to which I have so often alluded)—and is purposely restrained from concentering the interest on itself, but used merely as an induction or tuning for what is to follow.

In the second scene, Prospero's speeches, till the entrance of Ariel, contain the finest example, I remember, of retrospective narration for the purpose of exciting immediate interest, and putting the audience in possession of all the information necessary for the understanding of the plot. Observe, too, the perfect probability of the moment chosen by Prospero (the very Shakspeare himself, as it were, of the tempest) to open out the truth to his daughter, his own romantic bearing, and how completely any thing that might have been disagreeable to us in the magician, is reconciled and shaded in the humanity and natural feelings of the father. In the very first speech of Miranda the simplicity and tenderness of her character are at once laid open;—it would have been lost in direct contact with the agitation of the first scene. The opinion once prevailed, but, happily, is now abandoned, that Fletcher alone wrote for women;[14]—the truth is, that with very few, and those partial, exceptions, the female characters in the plays of Beaumont and Fletcher are, when of the light kind, not decent; when heroic, complete viragos. But in Shakspeare all the elements of womanhood are holy, and there is the sweet, yet dignified feeling of all that *continuates* society, as sense of ancestry and of sex, with a purity unassailable by sophistry, because it rests not in the analytic processes, but in that sane equipoise of the faculties, during which the feelings are representative of all past experience,—not of the individual only, but of all those by whom she has been educated, and their predecessors even up to the first mother

---

[13] This completes the sentence C left incomplete on BM MS Egerton 2800 f 27ᵛ, above.

[14] The "opinion" was Dryden's, and C had argued against it in Lect 6 of the 1811–12 series (at n 36).

that lived.[15] Shakespeare saw that the want of prominence, which Pope notices for sarcasm,[16] was the blessed beauty of the woman's character, and knew that it arose not from any deficiency, but from the more exquisite harmony of all the parts of the moral being constituting one living total of head and heart. He has drawn it, indeed, in all its distinctive energies of faith, patience, constancy, fortitude,—shown in all of them as following the heart, which gives its results by a nice tact and happy intuition, without the intervention of the discursive faculty,—sees all things in and by the light of the affections, and errs, if it ever err, in the exaggerations of love alone. In all the Shakspearian women there is essentially the same foundation and principle; the distinct individuality and variety are merely the result of the modification of circumstances, whether in Miranda the maiden, in Imogen the wife, or in Katharine the queen.

But to return. The appearance and characters of the super or ultra-natural servants are finely contrasted. Ariel has in every thing the airy tint which gives the name; and it is worthy of remark that Miranda is never directly brought into comparison with Ariel, lest the natural and human of the one and the supernatural of the other should tend to neutralize each other; Caliban, on the other hand, is all earth, all condensed and gross in feelings and images;[17] he has the dawnings of understanding without reason or the moral sense,[18] and in him, as in some brute animals, this advance to the intellectual faculties, without the moral sense, is marked by the appearance of vice. For it is in the primacy of the moral being only that man is truly human; in his intellectual powers he is certainly approached by the brutes, and, man's whole system duly considered, those powers cannot be considered other than means to an end, that is, to morality.

In this scene, as it proceeds, is displayed the impression made by Ferdinand and Miranda on each other; it is love at first sight;—

[15] This sentence HNC took from notes made by C (and copied by EHC) for Lect 4 of the 1813 series at Bristol (second paragraph after n 22).

[16] The allusion is to Pope's "Of the Characters of Women" in the *Moral Essays* Epistle II line 2, "Most Women have no Characters at all". According to the newspaper report, C had quoted this in Lect 4 of the 1813 series at Bristol (at n 26), and HNC may again be borrowing material from C's notes for those lectures. On the general point, see also C's comments on Ophelia in Lect 1 of the 1819 series (clauses after n 2).

[17] C had begun from the same point, derived from Schlegel, that Ariel is of the air, Caliban of the earth, in contrasting these figures in Lect 9 of the 1811–12 series (at n 44), but here he develops the argument along different lines.

[18] For a full account of C's distinction between understanding and reason, see *Friend (CC)* I 153–61.

at the first sight,
They have chang'd eyes:—[19]

and it appears to me, that in all cases of real love, it is at one moment that it takes place. That moment may have been prepared by previous esteem, admiration, or even affection,—yet love seems to require a momentary act of volition, by which a tacit bond of devotion is imposed—a bond not to be thereafter broken without violating what should be sacred in our nature. How finely is the true Shakspearian scene contrasted with Dryden's vulgar alteration of it, in which a mere ludicrous psychological experiment, as it were, is tried—displaying nothing but indelicacy without passion.[20] Prospero's interruption of the courtship has often seemed to me to have no sufficient motive; still his alleged reason—

lest too light winning
Make the prize light—[21]

is enough for the ethereal connexions of the romantic imagination, although it would not be so for the historical. The whole courting scene, indeed, in the beginning of the third act, between the lovers is a masterpiece; and the first dawn of disobedience in the mind of Miranda to the command of her father is very finely drawn, so as to seem the working of the Scriptural command, *Thou shalt leave father and mother*, &c.[22] O! with what exquisite purity this scene is conceived and executed! Shakspeare may sometimes be gross, but I boldly say that he is always moral and modest. Alas! in this our day decency of manners is preserved at the expense of morality of heart, and delicacies for vice are allowed, whilst grossness against it is hypocritically, or at least morbidly, condemned.

In this play are admirably sketched the vices generally accompanying a low degree of civilization; and in the first scene of the second act Shakspeare has, as in many other places, shown the tendency in bad men to indulge in scorn and contemptuous expressions, as a mode of getting rid of their own uneasy feelings of inferiority to the good, and

[19] *The Tempest* I ii 441–2.
[20] In Dryden's reworking of *The Tempest, or The Enchanted Island* (1670), he gives Miranda a sister, Dorinda, and invents a youth, Hippolito, who has never seen a woman until he falls in love with Dorinda. Prospero "tests" Ferdinand in IV i by sending Miranda to him to beg him to love Hippolito, who he has at this point come to believe is his rival for Miranda's affections.
[21] *The Tempest* I ii 452–3.
[22] "Therefore shall a man leave his father and his mother, and shall cleave unto his wife: and they shall be one flesh." Gen 2.24; cf Matt 19.5, etc.

also, by making the good ridiculous, of rendering the transition of others to wickedness easy. Shakspeare never puts habitual scorn into the mouths of other than bad men,[23] as here in the instances of Antonio and Sebastian. The scene of the intended assassination of Alonzo and Gonzalo is an exact counterpart of the scene between Macbeth and his lady,[24] only pitched in a lower key throughout, as designed to be frustrated and concealed, and exhibiting the same profound management in the manner of familiarizing a mind, not immediately recipient, to the suggestion of guilt, by associating the proposed crime with something ludicrous or out of place,—something not habitually matter of reverence. By this kind of sophistry the imagination and fancy are first bribed to contemplate the suggested act, and at length to become acquainted with it. Observe how the effect of this scene is heightened by contrast with another counterpart of it in low life—that between the conspirators Stephano, Caliban, and Trinculo in the second scene of the third act, in which there are the same essential characteristics.

In this play and in this scene of it are also shown the springs of the vulgar in politics,—of that kind of politics which is inwoven with human nature. In his treatment of this subject, wherever it occurs, Shakspeare is quite peculiar. In other writers we find the particular opinions of the individual; in Massinger it is rank republicanism; in Beaumont and Fletcher even *jure divino* principles are carried to excess;[25]—but Shakspeare never promulgates any party tenets. He is always the philosopher and the moralist, but at the same time with a profound veneration for all the established institutions of society, and for those classes which form the permanent elements of the state—especially never introducing a professional character, as such, otherwise than as respectable.[26] If he must have any name, he should be styled a philosophical aristocrat, delighting in those hereditary institutions which have a tendency to bind one age to another, and in that distinction of ranks, of which, although few may be in possession, all enjoy the advantages. Hence, again, you will observe the good nature with which he seems always to make sport with the passions and follies of a mob, as with an irrational animal. He is never angry with it, but hugely content with holding up its absurdities

---

[23] C had made this point in Lect 4 of the 1818 series (at n 49).

[24] *The Tempest* II i is compared with *Macbeth* I vii, in which Macbeth determines finally on the murder of Duncan.

[25] This closely relates to comments C made when, probably in the period 1817–19, he annotated a set of *The Dramatic*

Works of Ben Jonson and Beaumont and Fletcher (4 vols 1811); see *CM (CC)* I 380, 389.

[26] C had made this point before, as in Lect 7 of the 1811–12 series (at n 34), and again in Lect 1 of the 1813 series (at n 4).

to its face; and sometimes you may trace a tone of almost affectionate superiority, something like that in which a father speaks of the rogueries of a child. See the good-humoured way in which he describes Stephano passing from the most licentious freedom to absolute despotism over Trinculo and Caliban. The truth is, Shakspeare's characters are all *genera* intensely individualized; the results of meditation, of which observation supplied the drapery and the colors necessary to combine them with each other. He had virtually surveyed all the great component powers and impulses of human nature,—had seen that their different combinations and subordinations were in fact the individualizers of men, and showed how their harmony was produced by reciprocal disproportions of excess or deficiency.[27] The language in which these truths are expressed was not drawn from any set fashion, but from the profoundest depths of his moral being, and is therefore for all ages.

NEWSPAPER REPORTS

(1) FROM THE *COURIER* FRIDAY, 18 DECEMBER 1818, AND THE *MORNING POST* SATURDAY, 19 DECEMBER

The report is headed "*MR. COLERIDGE'S LECTURES*". An abbreviated version of the same report was printed in the *New Times* Sat, 19 Dec.

This Gentleman commenced a double series of Lectures; one, on the origin and progress of Philosophy; the other, on certain select plays of Shakspeare. The introductory lecture of the former course was given on Monday last, at the Crown and Anchor Tavern, and though it could only be considered as a sort of rapid developement, a summary exposition, of the range which he intended to take, yet it was by no means deficient in interest or instruction. He commenced with the philosophy of THALES,[28] whose system, if so it may be called, he explained and illustrated with great felicity. Like a skilful, or rather, perhaps, like an honest disputant, he commenced with defining the terms he was to employ, particularly that ill-used word philosophy, which is so laxly

---

[27] This passage (from "the results of meditation . . . ") is taken from C's notes for Lect 6 of the 1813 series in Bristol, when he was speaking on Richard III and Falstaff; see above (§ 12, after n 3). As originally written, it has no connexion with *The Tempest*, and its presence here exemplifies HNC's casual and free treatment in *LR* of C's notes.

[28] C's opening lecture in the philosophical series, delivered on 14 Dec 1818, included an account of the "opinions of Thales". *P Lects* (1949) 85.

employed in popular language, that, as MR. COLERIDGE justly observed, he saw no reason why we might not talk of philosophical cobblers.

We were much pleased with the manner in which MR. COLERIDGE pressed upon the attention of his auditors the fact, so likely to be neglected, that the first attempt of the ancient philosophers, to penetrate the origin of things by the operation of their own minds, was, in itself, a most gigantic step. The more this position is analyzed, the more forcibly its truth will strike us.

The subject of MR. COLERIDGE's next Lecture upon Philosophy will be the life and doctrines of PYTHAGORAS.[29]

His Lectures upon SHAKSPEARE commenced on Thursday night with an examination of the *Tempest*; and Mr. COLERIDGE, with becoming zeal, asserted his claim, as the first person who taught the undoubted truth, that the judgment of SHAKSPEARE was, in all his writings, equally, if not more conspicuous, than his genius. This doctrine has since been maintained by eminent critics, both abroad and at home; but as far as our own knowledge qualifies us to speak, we believe MR. COLERIDGE's claim to priority of discovery cannot be denied.[30]

We have not space to follow MR. COLERIDGE through all the delightful course of reasoning and illustration which he pursued upon this subject. The enthusiasm which he brought to his task, was the proof of his ability to discharge it. SHAKSPEARE never had a more eloquent expositor; the fervid touches of his glowing pen, were never discoursed with more congenial feelings. There was frequently the finest poetry in his criticisms, as if he had caught inspiration from his subject. We allude particularly to the beautiful manner in which MR. COLERIDGE, when descanting upon the character of *Miranda*, described the influence of a first love upon a pure and susceptible heart, conscious only of its emotions, but timidly ignorant of their cause and object.[31] The same praise may be bestowed upon his closing observations upon the metre and rhythm of SHAKSPEARE's Language, which, to an ear properly attuned to their harmony, were of themselves sufficient to decide what parts of the disputed plays of SHAKSPEARE were really the production of his pen. MR. COLERIDGE justly observed, also, that this melody of diction was not the result of any laborious effort. It was wholly unpremeditated, and was as perceptible in his earliest as in his latest dramas. His thoughts

---

[29] Pythagoras was the central theme of C's second lecture in the philosophical series, delivered on 28 Dec 1818.

[30] See above (at n 1).

[31] C's emphasis in this lecture seems to have been different from that in Lect 9 of the 1811–12 series (paragraph containing n 31 and following), when he talked at length about the introduction of Miranda and her relation with Prospero.

were harmony itself, and they naturally created a language suitable to themselves.—But we cannot extend our observations any further at present, though we shall certainly take future opportunities of returning to these lectures as MR. COLERIDGE proceeds in them.

(2) FROM THE *CHAMPION*
MONDAY, 21 DECEMBER 1818

This report is a corrected version of that printed in the *Champion* on 20 Dec, with the addition of the initials "A. S." at the end, which probably conceal the authorship of John Thelwall, editor of this journal. The report is headed *"Mr. COLERIDGE's alternate Lectures on the History of Philosophy; and on Six Plays of Shakespeare"*.

The name Coleridge has a charm in it, which we should be sorry to see dissolved. His great learning—the known extent of his out-of-the-way reading, the torrent of fine, and of *extraordinary* ideas, which he can occasionally pour forth,—his original, though unorganised genius— nay, his very eccentricities, cast a sort of mysterious spell around him, that transports us out of the ordinary present, and makes him live in our imaginations as a sort of being of another generation, or another sphere: and, perhaps, it is well that he should be so considered. For our own part, at least, we are ready to confess, that we should otherwise have for him some of those feelings which we should be sorry to cherish for so extraordinary a man. Not that we mean to insinuate that moral character is necessarily impeached by changes, however great, of po- litical opinion or profession; but (those excepted which take place in the first age of boyhood, when the inculcated opinions of the nursery, like the shell upon the head of a new-hatched chick, may necessarily be expected not to have been shaken off;) they somewhat diminish our feelings of respect, in disturbing that clear perception of identity (in the past and the present man) which forms the associating link of personal attachment and esteem, and, demonstrating, at any rate, that either at one or the other period of his life (and who shall decide at which) the understanding, or the moral feeling of the individual, was obviously sophisticated, and delusive. But great changes of opinion upon such subjects, are apt to be *violent* also; and violence is, in our estimation, but an indifferent proof of their deep-felt and conscientious sincerity: while oblivion, or *misrecollection* of the past, is certainly not very demonstrative of that precision and sanity of mind, that should induce an implicit confidence in the present. We allude (and it is a painful allusion) to some passages in Mr. C's "Biographia Literaria." When he deliberately asserted that it was *always* a part of his political creed, that ["]*whoever ceased to act as an individual, by making himself a member of any society not sanctioned by his Government, forfeited the rights of a citizen;*"[32] how extraordinary that he should have forgotten his still producible correspondence with an individual, then one of the most conspicuous members of the societies thus stigmatized, whose friendship Mr. C. at that time courted, for *no other obvious reason, than for his intrepidity, and his sufferings on that very account.* Does Mr. C. recollect these lines—

> "Some ******** to the patriot's need aspire,
> Who, at safe distance, without wound or scar,
> Round pictur'd strong walls waging mimic war
> Closet their valour: you, 'midst thickest fire,
> Leap on the perilous wall. Therefore, I choose
> Ungaudy flowers that chastest odours breathe,
> To weave for thy young locks the civic wreathe"—etc. etc.[33]

Alas! poor Coleridge!—a seraph! and a worm! At least, a seraph he would have been, had there but been so much of the nerve of any one concentrating principle whatever, in his composition, as might have given consistency to the splendid but disjointed materials of his mind. This, only this, was wanting to his fame!—and it is in vain that the visions of mysticism and the unintelligibilities of metaphysics and Psychology are applied to, to supply its place. Every production of his genius, every effort of his mind, whether oral or written, bears some stamp and evidence,—some obscuring blot from this primitive deficiency. Let us not, however, be mistaken as though we wished to depreciate these lectures;—the very atoms and fragments of such a mind, have a value beyond the perfect coinages of the ordinary class of lecturers. That affluence of fine ideas—that power of expressive language, in which he frequently abounds—that store of miscellaneous knowledge, he has so elaborately attained, and which, occasionally, he so happily

---

[32] The quotation is from *BL* ch 10 *(CC)* I 187.

[33] Quoting C's sonnet *To John Thelwall*, which dates from the period 1795–7 (see Woodring 116–17), in a variant version. The sonnet was first published in *PW* (EHC) II 1090, the lines running as follows:

Some, Thelwall! to the Patriot's meed aspire,
Who, in safe rage, without or rent or scar,
Round pictur'd strongholds sketching mimic war
Closet their valour—Thou mid thickest fire
Leapst on the wall: therefore shall Freedom choose
Ungaudy flowers that chastest odours breathe,
And weave for thy young locks a Mural wreath . . .

imparts, entitle him to more than all the patronage that can crown his efforts; and we cannot conclude these remarks without recommending both the proposed courses to the attention of our readers.

The Lecture of Monday, if it did not satisfy us on all the doctrinal points it involved, furnished much curious information, and suggested many important reflections. It was rich in materials for serious meditation: food for the mind—matter of deliberate digestion; and we know not where so much information, upon subjects so erudite and abstract, could have been so easily, or so agreeably obtained. The company was numerous and respectable.

Mr. Coleridge commenced his Lecture on the Tempest, as a specimen of the Romantic or Poetical Drama of Shakespeare, on Thursday, by investigating the true nature and foundation of poetic probability. To give a *rule*, it is necessary first to investigate the end, to which it is to be subservient. The end of Dramatic Poetry is not to present a copy, but an *imitation* of real life. Copy is imperfect if the resemblance be not, in every circumstance, exact; but an imitation essentially implies some difference. The mind of the spectator, or the reader, therefore, is not to be deceived into any idea of reality, as the French Critics absurdly suppose; neither, on the other hand, is it to retain a perfect consciousness of the falsehood of the presentation. There is a state of mind between the two, which may be properly called allusion,[34] in which the comparative powers of the mind are completely suspended; as in a dream, the judgment is neither beguiled, nor conscious of the fraud, but remains passive. Whatever disturbs this repose of the judgment by its harshness, abruptness and improbability, offends against dramatic propriety.

Observing this distinction, Mr. C. proceeded to show that many natural improbabilities were innocent in the groundwork or outset of the play, which would break the illusion afterwards; and the contrary. The temper of mind in the spectator must be considered[;] a strong improbability in the story founded on some known tradition, does not offend, in the outset of a play; but the interest and plot must not depend upon that improbability. Again, violent emotions must not be excited at the very commencement; for if the mind is not prepared, the judgment is awakened and the illusion vanishes at once.

Mr. C proceeded to apply those principles to the *Tempest*, a romantic drama, in which the interest depends on the imagination, rather than the feelings. The plot has little intricacy, and its interest ceases in the 3d act, in which the conclusion becomes evident.[35]

---

[34] An error for "illusion"; see above (third sentence before n 7).

[35] C was perhaps recalling Schlegel's comments on *The Tempest* as a play with

It would be endless to refer to all the beautiful illustrations of his theory, which Mr. C. drew from the successive scenes of this play; the truth, the harmony which he made apparent, and the softening touches that he produced, to show how this great master tempered every thing (the wonderful and the terrible) to the feelings of his audience. This was illustrated in the circumstances of the shipwreck, and in the character of the magician *Prospero*. Criticism of this kind cannot be abridged; but it would be doing injustice to Mr. C. to pass over the beautiful manner in which he commented on the scene of the intended murder. Contempt, he remarked, is never attributed in Shakespeare, but to characters deep in villany, as *Edmund, Iago; Antonio* and *Sebastian*, in the play before us.[36] The sophistry of guilt diminishing the crime in its own eyes, by contempt for the object of its purpose, and by veiling in metaphor and mild language, the horrors from which the mind would revolt; all which was admirably exposed in comments upon this scene.

Mr. C. concluded with some beautiful observations on the versification of Shakespeare; which he compared to the sinuous and over-varied lapses of a serpent, writhing in every direction, but still progressive, and in every posture beautiful.[37] The connection between the character of the versification and of the language; and between the metre and the sense: one elucidating and assisting the other, were demonstrated with a truth and beauty which he only can arrive at who unites profound philosophy with exquisite taste and depth of poetic feeling.

(3) COMMENT IN THE *MORNING CHRONICLE*
TUESDAY, 29 DECEMBER 1818

The contributor is anonymous, and the comment is headed "*MR. COLERIDGE*".

In an account of Mr. Coleridge's Lectures, which appeared in *The Courier*, some days ago, it is said—

Mr. Coleridge, with becoming zeal, asserted his claim, as the first

---

little action. *DKL* II ii 126–7 (Black II 178–9). But Schlegel also said that it required considerable attention to see that the end is anticipated in the opening, and C's argument, as in Lect 9 of the 1811–12 series (paragraphs after n 28), seems to have been designed to illustrate the connexion.

[36] C made the same point in Lect 4 of the 1818 series (at n 49).

[37] C was probably echoing *BL* ch 14 (*CC*) II 14: "The reader should be carried forward, not merely or chiefly by the mechanical impulse of curiosity, or by a restless desire to arrive at the final solution; but by the pleasurable activity of mind excited by the attractions of the journey itself. Like the motion of a serpent . . .".

person who taught the undoubted truth, that the *judgment* of Shakspeare was, in all his writings, equally, if not more conspicuous, than his genius. This doctrine has since been maintained by eminent critics, both abroad and at home; but, as far as our own knowledge qualifies us to speak, we believe Mr. Coleridge's claim to priority of discovery cannot be denied.

As Mr. Coleridge seems to attach great importance to *this discovery*, let us see how the fact really stands with respect to it.

William Schlegel is evidently one of the foreign critics here alluded to. In his Dramatic Lectures which were delivered in 1808, but not published till 1809 and 1811, doctrines respecting Shakspeare, similar to those of Mr. Coleridge, are to be found. Now Mr. Coleridge contends that as early as 1806, he delivered to various audiences the substance of his present Lectures, and that as Schlegel's Lectures were not delivered till 1808, the priority *in this discovery*, is due to himself.

In Schlegel's Lectures it is said, "In an Essay on *Romeo and Juliet written a number of years ago*, I went through the whole of the scenes in their order, and demonstrated the inward necessity of each with reference to the whole; I shewed why such a particular circle of characters and relations was placed around the two lovers; I explained the signification of the mirth here and there scattered, and justified the use of the occasional heightening given to the poetical colours.—From all this it seemed to follow unquestionably, that with the exception of a few plays of wit, now become unintelligible or foreign to the present taste (imitations of the tone of society that day), nothing could be taken away, nothing added, nothing otherwise arranged, without mutilating and disfiguring the perfect work."[38] The Essay here described appeared in the first volume of *Charakteristiken und Kritiken*, published by William and Frederick Schlegel, at Konigsberg, in 1801.

Thus it appears that M. Schlegel, so early as 1801, threw down the gauntlet in defence of the judgment displayed by Shakspeare in the composition of his works. He confined his examination to one play,

---

[38] The quotation is from Black's translation of Schlegel's lectures (1815) II 127. There Black, following Schlegel (*DKL* II ii 53–4), gives the reference to *Charakteristiken und Kritiken*. Schlegel's essay first appeared in *Die Horen* ed J. C. F. von Schiller x pt 6 (1797) 18–48. The main part of the essay consists of a description in turn of each of the main characters, which does not justify the claim that the play shows a miraculous unity (the Nurse is seen as silly, and Capulet as merely ridiculous), and Schlegel's insistence on the overriding unity of impression conveyed by the play is not quite the same as C's claim about Shakespeare's judgement, which allowed for the imperfections of *Romeo and Juliet*; see Lect 7 of the 1811–12 series (paragraphs following n 6).

indeed, but the principles on which he conducted that examination are the same with those which run through his Lectures, and which Mr. Coleridge says were discovered by himself. Though Mr. Coleridge was long in Germany, and is well acquainted with German literature, it does not follow that he is indebted to Schlegel for any part of his ideas; but unless he can shew that in Lectures or publications of so early a date as 1801, he advocated the judgment displayed by Shakspeare in the composition of his works, it will be somewhat difficult for him to establish the claim to the title of a *discoverer*.

LECTURE 2

DATE AND PLACE OF DELIVERY. Thursday, 31 December 1818, at the Crown and Anchor Tavern, Strand, London.

SUBJECT. *Richard II*.

ADVERTISEMENTS AND ANNOUNCEMENTS. *Courier* Sat, 26 Dec (announcement, being an addendum to a long announcement of the philosophical lecture of 28 Dec): "On the Thursday Evening following, SHAKSPEARE's *Richard the Second*". *Courier* Wed, 30 Dec (announcement): "To-morrow Evening, December 31, eight o'clock, at the Crown and Anchor, Strand—Mr. COLERIDGE's Lecture on *Richard the Second*, as example and illustration of SHAKESPEARE's Historic Drama, its scheme, objects, and distinctive character. Admission 5s." (This continues with an announcement of the philosophical lecture of Mon, 4 Jan 1819). *New Times* Wed, 30 Dec (advertisement): substantially as in the *Courier* of 30 Dec, with the substitution of "instance" for "example". *The Times* Thurs, 31 Dec (advertisement): as in the *New Times*, but omitting the word "objects". *M Chron* Thurs, 31 Dec (advertisement): as in the *New Times*.

TEXT. C was using for this series his interleaved set of *Sh* (Ayscough) and seems to have lectured from the text with the help of the annotations he had made on the interleaves. These were first printed in *LR* I 164–78 and were included in *Sh C* I 128–37 (142–52), in which, following HNC, Raysor intermingled them with notes from other sources, without indicating when or where C wrote them. The text printed below is based on a fresh transcript of C's annotations, except that cancellations are not printed.

REPORTS. No reports of the lecture have been found.

BACKGROUND AND CIRCUMSTANCES. C had made a detailed analysis of *Richard II* for Lect 5 of the 1813 series, but the notes for that have page-references to his copy of *Sh* (Rann), and he did not use them again for the present lecture. However, if he relied on the marginalia in his *Sh* (Ayscough), he would have confined himself pretty well to the early part of the play. It may be that he also used for this lecture the edition he borrowed from Mrs Milne (*CL* IV 898, and see Lect 1 headnote: Background and Circumstances), and made notes also in this, as he did in relation to *Hamlet* and *Romeo and Juliet*, but this has not been traced. He knew the play well, and it is also possible that he developed critical points directly from the text, but his letters throw no light on the lecture, and nothing further is known about it.

LECTURE 2

RECORDS OF THE LECTURE

COLERIDGE'S NOTES
FROM HIS ANNOTATIONS ON THE INTERLEAVES
OF *SH* (AYSCOUGH) I 413–39

Some of the annotations are in pencil and could have been entered at a different time from the others, and all but one relate to Acts I and II. These notes were included amongst other marginalia and fragments in *Sh C* I 128–37 (142–52).

General Notes Prefacing Richard II

The transitional state between the Epic and the Drama is the Historic Drama. In the Epic a pre-announced Fate gradually adjusts and employs the will and the Incidents as its instruments—επομαι sequor;[1] while the Drama places Fate & Will in opposition, then most perfect when the victory of fate is obtained in consequence of imperfections in the opposing Will, so as to leave the final impression, that the Fate itself is but a higher and more intelligent Will.

[a]But this Richard the IInd—O God forbid that however unsuited for the Stage yet even there it should fall dead on the hearts of Jacobinized Englishmen—then indeed Præteriit gloria mundi[2]—The Spirit of patriotic reminiscence is the all-permeating Spirit of this Drama[b]

Richard III I i l-6, Sh *(Ayscough) 1413: On the opening lines of the play*

[a–b] Added in pencil

[1] Greek and Latin for "follow". C was thinking of the sequences of events as preordained in epic, and alluding to the then assumed etymological link between the Greek ἔπος and ἔπομαι? He had related *Richard II* to epic in Lect 5 of the 1813 series (at n1), but there his argument is different and starts from Schlegel.

[2] "The glory of the world has passed away"; a variant of "Sic transit gloria mundi", from Thomas à Kempis *Imitation of Christ* 3.6, which in turn echoes biblical phrases from the Vulgate, 1 Cor 7.31, etc.

The six opening Lines of this Play, each closing at the tenth syllable, to be compared with the rhythmless Metre of the verse in Henry 6th and Titus Andronicus—in order, that the difference, yea, heterogenëity, may be felt, etiam in simillimis primâ superficie.[3] Here the weight of each *word* supplies all the relief afforded by intercurrent verse:[4] while the whole represents the *Mood.*

I i 8, Sh *(Ayscough)* II *413* α *14: On "Tell me moreover, hast thou sounded him"*, *compared with* The Tempest *I ii 53*

L. 14. Compare with l. 30, 2nd Col. p. 2. of the *Tempest*—"Twelve years since, Miranda! twelve years since"[5]—examp. of the involved instructions to the actors how to pronounce the line.

I i 30–46, Sh *(Ayscough) I 414* α *10: On Bolingbroke's challenge to Mowbray, "First, heaven be the record to my speech . . ."*

10. I remember even in the Sophoclean Drama no more striking example of (the) το πρεπον, και σεμνον.[6] Yea, the rhymes in the 6 last lines well express the *preconcertedness*[7] of Bolingbrook's Scheme, so beautifully contrasted with the vehemence and sincere irritation of Mowbray.

I i 39–40, Sh *(Ayscough) I 414* α *19: On Bolingbroke's accusation, "Thou art a traitor, and a miscreant; | Too good to be so, and too bad to live"*

19. The passion that carries off its excess by play on words as naturally and therefore as appropriately to drama as by gesticulations, looks or tones. This belonging to human nature as *human*, independent of associations and habits from any particular rank of Life or mode of employment—and in this consists Sh.'s vulgarisms, as in Macbeth, (The Devil damn thee black, thou cream-faced Loon! &c)[8] it is (to play on Dante's words) in truth the *Nobile* vulgare eloquenza[9]*.—

* Defer this to p. 420, interview with old Gaunt/[c][10]

[c] Note added in pencil as an afterthought

[3] "Even those most alike, in external appearance".

[4] Literally "verse that comes between or intervenes". C seems to mean verse consisting of end-stopped lines.

[5] *Sh* (Ayscough) I 2 β 31, referring to Prospero's line at I ii 53.

[6] "The fitting and majestic".

[7] *OED* cites this passage, from *LR* II 168, for the earliest instance of the word.

[8] *Macbeth* V iii 11.

[9] Tr "the *noble* eloquence of the vernacular". C used an ed of Dante's *Opera* (5 vols Venice 1793) that gave a Latin and an Italian version of his treatise *De vulgari eloquentia*, which C referred to as "his admirable treatise on the Lingua Volgare Nobile"; see *CN* II 3011, III 3611, and nn.

[10] C referred his discussion of word-play to II i, especially Gaunt's punning on his name, II i 73ff; see the note to this passage, below.

I i 104–18, Sh (Ayscough) I 414 β 19: On Richard's reaction to Bolingbroke's accusation that Mowbray plotted the Duke of Gloucester's death: "Which blood, like sacrificing Abel's, cries | Even from the tongueless caverns of the earth, | To me for justice and rough chastisement . . ."

26.—The δεινον[11] "*to me*", & so felt by Richard—"How *high* a pitch &c." and the *effect* As he is but my Father's Brother's Son.

I i 148–51, Sh (Ayscough) I 415 α 10: On Mowbray's challenge in reply to Bolingbroke, specifically, "I pray | Your highness to assign our trial day"

10. Q<u>y</u> The occasional interspersion of rhymes and the more frequent winding up of a Speech therewith—what purpose was this to answer? In the earnest Drama, I mean.—Deliberateness? An attempt as in Mowbray to collect himself and *be cool* at the close? I can see that in the following Speeches the rhyme answers the purposes of the Greek Chorus, and distinguish[es][d] the *general* truths from the passions of the Dialogue—but this is not exactly to *justify* the practice which is unfrequent in proportion to the excellence of Sh's Plays—. One thing, however, is to be observed—they are *historical, known*, & so far *formal* Characters, the reality of which is already a *fact*.—*eThis dwelt upon* as predominant in Richard, the purest Historic Play—indeed, John & Henry VIIIth excepted, the only *puref*

I ii 37–41. Sh (Ayscough) I 415 β 55: On Gaunt's refusal to revenge his brother's death and lift his arm against the king: "God's substitute | His deputy anointed in His sight" (Ayscough has "heaven's substitute")

55. Without the hollow extravagance of Beaum. and Fletch's Ultra-royalism, how carefully does Shakspear acknowlege and reverence the eternal distinction between the mere Individual, and the Symbolic or representative: on which all genial Law no less than Patriotism depends![12]

I ii, I iii, Sh (Ayscough) I 416: General notes on Scenes ii and iii

This second Scene quite commencing and anticipative of, the tone and character of the Play at large.

---

[d] Ms reads "distinguish"
[e-f] An incomplete note written in pencil

[11] "Terrible"; the reference is to Bolingbroke's image of the Duke of Gloucester's blood crying for vengeance.

[12] See Lect 1, above (at n 25).

Scene III, compared with any of Shakespear's fictitious dramas, or those founded [on]*ᵍ* a History as unknown to his Auditors generally as Fiction: & no where this violent violation of the succession of Time.—Proof that the pure *historic* Drama had its own Laws.

I iii 69–72, Sh *(Ayscough) I 416 β 55: On Bolingbroke's appeal to Gaunt for his blessing as he is about to enter the lists: "O thou, the earthly author of my blood".*

55. Boling's Ambition.

I iii 144–75, Sh *(Ayscough) I 417 β 20: On the differing reactions of Bolingbroke and Mowbray to the sentence of banishment, beginning from Bolingbroke's "That sun that warms you here shall shine on me"*

20. Bolingbroke's ambitious hope, not yet shaped into definite plan, beautifully contrasted with Mowbray's desolation

I iii 156–8, Sh *(Ayscough) I 417 β 31: On Mowbray's lines, "A dearer merit, not so deep a maim . . . Have I deserved"*

31. "A dearer *Merit*" Shakespear's *instinctive* propriety in the choice of Words.

I iii 184–90, Sh *(Ayscough) I 418 α 5: On Richard's demand that Bolingbroke and Mowbray take an oath never to plot against him, "Nor never by advised purpose meet"*

5. Already the selfish Weakness of Richard's character opens. Nothing which such minds so readily embrace, as indirect ways softened down to their quasi Consciences by *Policy*, expedience &c—

I iii 206–7, Sh *(Ayscough) I 418 α 25: On Mowbray's lines, "Now no way can I stray;* | *Save back to England, all the world's my way"*

25. "The World was all before them" Milton.¹³

I iii 211–15, Sh *(Ayscough) I 418 α 31–5: On Bolingbroke's reaction to Richard's reduction of his banishment from 10 to 6 years, "How long a time lies in one little word!"*

31–35. admirable anticipation.

I iv 54–64, Sh *(Ayscough) I 419: On Richard's callous reception of the news of old Gaunt's sickness*

ᵍ Word supplied by the editor

¹³ Milton *Paradise Lost* XII 646.

*h*A striking conclusion of a first Act—letting the reader into the secret—⟨having before⟩ impressed the dignified & kingly manners of Richard, yet by well managed anticipations, leading to the full gratification of the Auditor's pleasure in his own penetration—*i*

II i 73–83, Sh *(Ayscough)* I 420: *On Gaunt's word-play on his name, referring back to C's note on word-play at* I i 39–40, *above*

*j*Turn back to p. 414 (Blank Mss page)—and here the death-bed feeling in which all things appear but as *puns* and equivocations—*k*

II i 141–6, Sh *(Ayscough)* I 421 α 35: *On York's appeal to Richard to forgive Gaunt's anger, and Richard's response,* ''As Hereford's love, so his, | As theirs, so mine, and all be as it is'', *compared to Richard's earlier reaction to Hereford (Bolingbroke) at* I i 104–18, Sh *(Ayscough)* I 414, *above*

*l*35. The depth of this—compared with the first scene, 414.''How high a pitch''.*m*

II ii 5–13, Sh *(Ayscough)* I 422: *On the Queen's speech of foreboding and fear of being parted from her* ''sweet Richard''

*n*It is clear, that Sh. never meant to represent Richard II*d* as a vulgar Debauchee/ but merely a wantonness in feminine shew, feminine *friend-ism*,[14] intensely Woman-like love of those immediately about him—mistaking the delight of being loved by him for a love for him—*o*

II ii 20–4, Sh *(Ayscough)* I 423: *On Bushy's attempt to comfort the Queen, saying her fears are* ''nought but shadows | Of what it is not''

*p*Tender Superstitions encouraged by S.—Terra incognita of the Human Mind—*q*

V v 76–92, Sh *(Ayscough)* I 439: *On Richard's reaction to the news that Bolingbroke rode on Richard's horse Roan Barbary to his coronation*

*r*The affecting Incident of the very Horse, as *realizing*[s15]

---

h–i In pencil	*j–k* In pencil
l–m In pencil	*n–o* In pencil
p–q In pencil	*r–s* In pencil

[14] C's coinage; *OED* cites this passage, from *LR* II 174.

[15] I.e. bringing vividly before us, making real; C was thinking perhaps both of Bolingbroke's new identity as king and Richard's final eclipse.

LECTURE 3

DATE AND PLACE OF DELIVERY. Thursday, 7 January 1819, at the Crown and Anchor Tavern, Strand, London.

SUBJECT. *Hamlet.*

ADVERTISEMENTS AND ANNOUNCEMENTS. *New Times* Wed, 6 Jan (advertisement): "TO-MORROW EVENING. Eight o'clock, Crown and Anchor, Strand, Mr. COLERIDGE's LECTURE on HAMLET. Admission, Five Shillings.—On the Thursdays following, Macbeth, Othello, and Lear, successively. Admission 5s." *Courier* Wed, 6 Jan (announcement): as in the *New Times*, with minor variants. *The Times, M Chron, M Post* Thurs, 7 Jan (advertisements): as in the *New Times*, with the alteration to "THIS EVENING".

TEXT. C used his interleaved copy of *Sh* (Ayscough) for the series and appears to have lectured from the text, with the help of the annotations he had made on the interleaves. First printed in *LR* I 202–26, they were included in *Sh C* I 16–26 (18–28), in which Raysor followed HNC in intermingling them with notes from other sources, without indicating where or when C wrote them. The text given below is based on a fresh transcript of C's annotations.

REPORT. The *Champion* of 10 Jan carried a brief and unsympathetic comment on this lecture, which was included in *Sh C* II 259 (323). It is reprinted, below, from the original.

BACKGROUND AND CIRCUMSTANCES. On the day he gave this lecture C entered on the interleaf facing the opening of *Hamlet* in his copy of *Sh* (Ayscough) a statement asserting that he came to his conclusions about Shakespeare independently of Schlegel and denying the charge of plagiarism. C was responding to a comment printed in the *M Chron* 29 Dec 1819, which in turn had been provoked by C's claim made in Lect 1 that he was the first to maintain that Shakespeare's judgement was equal to his genius. His motives for making the statement at this particular time are discussed above, in relation to Lect 1 (see headnote: Reports). It is interesting that C says in this statement: "Hamlet was the Play, or rather Hamlet himself was the Character, in the intuition and exposition of which I first made my turn for Philosophical criticism, and especially for the insight into the genius of Shakespear, *noticed* first among my Acquaintances . . .". Certainly it was the play to which he returned again and again and found especially congenial. He probably lectured on it at the RI in 1808, and certainly spoke on it in the course of lectures he gave in 1811–12, in the second course at Willis's Rooms in 1812, at the Surrey Institution in 1812–13, in the first course at Bristol in 1813, and in the course in London in 1818. For his lecture on *Hamlet* in Jan 1819 he made notes in his interleaved copy of *Sh* (Ayscough) and developed a commentary on the play from these and the text. It is evident from the advertisements to Lect 1 in the 1819 series (see headnote) that he reached no further than the end of *Hamlet* Act II in the current Lect 3, and must have expanded his commentary well beyond what pointers his notes supply. They show that he offered, as in earlier lectures on the play, an analysis of Hamlet's character, but the lecture seems to have been largely based on a detailed "particular Criticism" of the text (see the note on II ii 576–634, below). He gave a recapitulation of this lecture in Lect 1 of the 1819 series, before completing his account of the play by commenting on Acts

III to V. It is a pity that more is not known about it, for C was pleased with it, although the audience was thin, and he wrote to William Mudford, editor of the *Courier*, on the following day to say: "I was very sorry to miss you last night, because my Lecture gave, and, I believe, would have given *you*, more than ordinary satisfaction. But alas! the Audience (excluding free Tickets) were scarcely enough to pay the Rooms—. Perhaps, the Christmas Parties are inauspicious; but I must derive my best consolation (for the Heart tho' not the Purse) that this scant of Attendants has evidently not been occasioned by any disappointment of those who *have* attended." *CL* IV 910. If the report in the *Champion* can be trusted in its statement that C spent a lot of time on "apologies for belief in ghosts and goblins", he may have recalled some of the materials he prepared for Lect 12 in the 1818 series, when he spoke about witches, dreams, and apparitions.

LECTURE 3

RECORDS OF THE LECTURE

COLERIDGE'S NOTES
FROM HIS ANNOTATIONS ON THE INTERLEAVES
OF *SH* (AYSCOUGH) II 999–1016

A few of the notes on *Hamlet* Acts I to III, which are lexical and not likely to have been used in the lecture, are omitted here. For the continuation of C's use of his notes on the remaining acts, see Lect 1 of the 1819 series.

General Notes Prefacing Hamlet: Sh *(Ayscough) II 999–1000*

Hamlet was the Play, or rather Hamlet himself was the Character, in the intuition and exposition of which I first made my turn for Philosophical criticism, and especially for the insight into the genius of Shakespear, *noticed* first among my Acquaintances, as Sir G. Beaumont will bear witness, and as Mr Wordsworth knows, tho' from motives which I do not know or impulses which I *cannot* know, he has thought proper to assert that Schlegel and the German Critics *first* taught Englishmen to admire their own great Countryman intelligently[1]—and secondly, long before Schlegel had given at Vienna the Lectures on Shakespear which he afterwards published, I had given eighteen Lectures on the same subject,[2] *substantially* the same, proceeding from the same, the *very* same, point of view, and deducing the same conclusions, as far as I either then or now agree with him/

I gave them at the Royal Institution, before from six to seven hundred

[1] In WW's "Essay, Supplementary to the Preface" prefixed to his *Poems* (1815), in which he wrote: "The Germans only, of foreign nations, are approaching towards a knowledge and feeling of what he [Shakspeare] is. In some respects they have acquired a superiority over the fellow-countrymen of the Poet: for among us it is . . . an established opinion, that Shakspeare is justly praised when he is pronounced to be 'a wild irregular genius, in whom great faults are compensated by great beauties'. " *W Prose* III 69. C made a similar complaint in a letter to Mudford of 18 Feb 1818: *CL* IV 839.

[2] The number C actually gave at the RI in 1808 is not known for certain, and they were not all on Shakespeare, for he gave at least two on Milton and others possibly on later poets; see above, Introduction to the 1808 series.

293

Auditors of rank and eminence, in the spring of the same year in which Sir H. Davy, a fellow-lecturer, made his great revolutionary Discoveries in Chemistry.[3] Even in detail the coincidence of Schlegel with my Lectures was so extra-ordinary, that all ⟨at a later period⟩ who heard the same *words* (taken from my Royal Instit. Notes) concluded a borrowing on my part from Schlegel.—M[r] Hazlitt, whose hatred of me is in such an inverse ratio to my zealous Kindness toward him as to be defended by his warmest Admirer, C. Lamb who (besides his characteristic obstinacy of adherence to old friends, as long at least as they are at all down in the World,) is linked as by a charm to Hazlitt's conversation, only under the epithet of *"frantic"*[4]—M[r] Hazlitt himself replied to an assertion of my plagiarism from Schlegel in these words— "That is a Lie; for I myself heard the very same character of Hamlet from Coleridge before he went to Germany and when he had neither read or could read a page of German." Now Hazlitt was on a visit to my Cottage at Nether Stowey, Somerset, in the summer of the year 1798, in the September of which (see my Literary Life) I first was out of sight of the Shores of Great Britain.—[5]

Recorded by me, S. T. Coleridge, Jan[y] 7, 1819. Highgate.

Compare the easy language of common life, in which this Drama opens, with the wild wayward Lyric of the opening of Macbeth. The Language is familiar: no poetic descriptions of Night, no elaborate information conveyed by one speaker to another of what both had before their immediate perceptions (such as the first Distich in Addison's Cato, which is a translation into poetry of Past 4 o'clock, and a damp morning)[6]—

---

[3] It was in Nov 1807 that Davy announced the isolation of potassium and sodium in his Bakerian lecture; soon afterwards he fell ill and did not lecture again until March 1808. C's lectures began in Jan 1808, but were also interrupted by illness and resumed in Mar, so his account here is roughly correct.

[4] C was still smarting from Hazlitt's hostile reviews of *Christabel*, *SM*, and *BL* in 1816 and 1817 (*CH* 248–324). Lamb had an ambivalent attitude to Hazlitt's attacks on WW and C and retained an affection for him. HCR records Lamb as saying of him: "Hazlitt does bad actions without being a bad man". *CRB* I 200, 202; *H Life* (H) 191–6. C had quoted Hazlitt on his plagiarism in a letter of 5 Feb 1818: *CL* IV 831; see Lect 1, above (headnote: Reports).

[5] In the first of "Satyrane's Letters" C described sailing from Yarmouth for Germany on 16 Sept 1798. *BL* (*CC*) II 160. Hazlitt stayed with C in Nether Stowey for about three weeks in late May and early Jun 1798 and travelled with him to Bristol on 11 Jun; see *CL* I 411–13 and *H Life* (H) 38–43.

[6] The opening lines of Addison's tragedy, *Cato*, a great success when performed and published in 1712, are:

The dawn is overcast, the morning lowers,
And heavily in clouds brings on the day . . .

yet nothing bordering on the comic on the one hand, and no striving of the Intellect on the other. It is the language of *sensation* among Men who feared no charge of effeminacy for feeling what they felt no want of resolution to bear.—Yet the armour, the dead silence, the watchfulness that first interrupts it, the welcome relief of guard, the Cold—the broken expressions as of a man's compelled attention to bodily feelings allowed no man, all excellently accord with and prepare for the after gradual rise into Tragedy—but above all into a Tragedy the interest of which is emi[n]ently*a* ad et apud *intra*—as Macbeth e contra is ad extra.[7]

Hamlet I i 20–9, Sh *(Ayscough)* II *1000* β *20: On Horatio's initial scepticism about the Ghost*

20. The preparation *informative* of the Audience, just as much as was precisely necessary—how gradual first, and with the uncertainty appertaining to a question, What? has *this* THING appeared *again* to-night? (even the word *again* has its credibilizing[8] effect [)]*b*.—Then the representative of the ignorance of the Audience, Horatio (not himself but Marcellus to Bernardo) anticipates the common solution—"'tis but our phantasy"—but Marc. rises 2ndly into dreaded Sight—Then this "thing" becomes at once an APPARITION, and that too an intelligent Spirit that is to be *spoken* to.—

I i 30–6, Sh *(Ayscough)* II *1000* β *2: On the preparation for the appearance of the Ghost*

1000.—Tush, tush! twill not appear.—Then the shivery feeling, at such a time, with two eye-witnesses, of sitting down to hear a story of a Ghost—and this too a ghost that had appeared two nights before about this very time—the effort of the narrator to master his own imaginative terrors—the consequent elevation of the style, itself a continuation of this effort—the turning off to an *outward* Object "yon same Star"— O heaven!—words are wasted to those that feel and to those who do not feel the exquisite judgement of Sh—

I i 70–2, Sh *(Ayscough)* II *1000* α *55: On the passage beginning with Marcellus saying, "Good now, sit down", and Horatio's report of recent events*

---

a Letter supplied by the editor
b Closing bracket supplied by the editor

[7] I.e. directed towards and in what is *internal*, as *Macbeth* on the other hand is related to what is external.

[8] Cited in *OED* in this passage, from *LR* II 211, as C's coinage.

*c*55. α. The exquisitely natural transit into the narration retrospective.*d*

I i 76–110, Sh (Ayscough) II 1000 β 5–40): On the portentous circumstances connected with the appearance of the Ghost, from "Does not divide the Sunday from the week" to "Comes armed through our watch so like the King"

*e*1000. β 5–40. "of mine own eyes."[9]—Hume himself could not but have faith in *this* Ghost dramatically, let his anti-ghostism be as strong as Samson against Ghosts less powerfully raised—*f*[10]

I i 126–46, Sh (Ayscough) II 1001 α: On reactions to the re-entry of the Ghost, beginning from Horatio's "I'll cross it though it blast me"

1001. α. Horatio's increased Courage from having translated the late individual Spect[r]um*g*[11] into Thought & past experience, and Marcellus' & Bernardo's Sympathy with it, in daring to strike—while yet the former feeling returns in "We do it wrong &c."[12]

I i 151–66, Sh (Ayscough) II 1001 α 30–45: On the comments of Horatio and Marcellus after the departure of the Ghost, beginning from "The cock, that is the trumpet to the morn, | Doth with his lofty and shrill-sounding throat | Awake the god of day . . ."

*h*30–45.α. No Addison more careful to be poetical in diction than Shakespear in providing the grounds and sources of its propriety.—But *how* to elevate a thing almost mean by its familiarity, young Poets may learn in the Cock-crow.*i*

I i 169–71, Sh (Ayscough) II 1001 α 50: On Horatio's recommendation that "young Hamlet" be informed about the Ghost, "This spirit, dumb to us, will speak to him"

50α. the unobtrusive and yet fully adequate mode of introducing the

---

c–d Written on the interleaf facing p 1001
e–f Written on the interleaf facing p 1001
g Letter supplied by the editor
h–i The note runs on without a break from the previous one

[9] Horatio's "I might not this believe | Without the sensible and true avouch | Of mine own eyes."

[10] C had used this phrase in Lect 3 of the 1811–12 series (at n 26), but not in *ing* § x pts 1 and 2, in which Hume sets out to disprove the existence of miracles and prodigies and to offer "an everlasting check to all kinds of superstitious delusion".

[11] I.e. spectre, apparition.

[12] On Marcellus's lines, "We do it wrong, being so majestical, | To offer it the show of violence."

main Character, *Young* Hamlet, upon whom transfers itself all the interest excited for the acts & concerns of the King, his Father.

1 ii, Sh (Ayscough) II 1001 β 5: On the opening of Scene ii, headed by Ayscough "A Room of State"

5β. Relief by change of Scene to the Royal Court—this on any occasion; but how judicious that Hamlet should not have to take up the Leavings of Exhaustion.—The set pedantically antithetic form of the King's Speech—yet tho' in the concerns that galled the heels of Conscience, rhetorical below a King, yet in what follows not without Majesty. Was he not a Royal Brother?

1 ii 42, Sh (Ayscough) II 1001 β 50: On the introduction of Laertes, from the King's line, "And now, Laertes, what's the news with you?"

50β.—Shakespear's art in introduce[j] a most important but still subordinate character first—Milton's Beelzebub[13]—So Laertes—who is yet thus graciously treated from the assistance given to the election of the King's Brother instead of Son by Polonius—

1 ii 65, Sh (Ayscough) II 1002 α 22: On Hamlet's quibbling aside 1002.

22α. A little more than kin yet less than kind—Play on words—either [due][k] to 1. exuberant activity of mind, as in Shakespear's higher Comedy. 2. Imitation of it as a fashion which has this to say for it—why is not this now better than groaning?[14]—or 3 contemptuous Exultation in minds vulgarized and overset by their success—Milton's Devils[15]—Or 4 as the language of resentment, in order to express Contempt—most common among the lower orders, & origin of Nick-names—or lastly as the language of suppressed passion, especially of hardly smothered dislike.—3 of these combine in the present instance.—and doubtless Farmer is right in supposing the equivocation carried on into too much in the *Son*.[16]

[j] A slip for "introducing"
[k] Word supplied by the editor

[13] Beelzebub is the first of the fallen angels to be named in *Paradise Lost* I 79–81, although Satan has already been "introduced".

[14] Quoting *Romeo and Juliet* II iv 88–9 (var), in which Mercutio welcomes Romeo's involvement in witty word-play as better than "groaning for love".

[15] Alluding to the "ambiguous words" of Satan and Belial when they mock their adversaries before and after firing their new-invented guns at them in the battle in heaven, *Paradise Lost* VI 558–629.

[16] Referring to I ii 67. *Sh* (Ayscough) has a note on II 1002, keyed to this line: "Mr. Farmer questions whether a quib-

I ii 74, Sh (Ayscough) II 1002 α 35: On Hamlet's repetition of Gertrude's phrase referring to the death of old Hamlet, "Thou know'st 'tis common", in his line "Ay, madam, it is common"

35α. Suppression prepares for overflow—

I ii 120, Sh (Ayscough) II 1002 β 33: On Hamlet's "I shall in all my best obey you, madam"

33.β Hamlet's Silence to the long speech of the King, & general answer to his Mother.

I ii 129–58, Sh (Ayscough) II 1002 β 45: On Hamlet's first soliloquy, "O that this too, too solid flesh would melt"

45β.—See & transcribe from MSS*. & in Mrs Milne's Vol.[17]

I iii 117, Sh (Ayscough) II 1005 β 7: On Polonius's line "Lends the tongue vows. These blazes, daughter"

Line 7. 2nd Column—a spondee has, I doubt not, dropt out of the text. After "vows": insert either Gō tō! or "Mārk you!" If the latter be preferred, it might end the line—"Lends the tongue vows.—Go to!—these Blazes, Daughter" or "Lends the tongue vows.—These Blazes, Daughter—mark you—"

N.B. Shakespear never introduces a catalectic line without intending an equivalent to the foot omitted in the pauses, or the dwelling emphasis, or the diffused retardation. I do not, however, deny, that a good actor might by employing the last mentioned, viz. the retardation or solemn knowing drawl, supply the missing Spondee with good effect. But I do not believe, that in this or the foregoing Speeches Shakespear meant to bring out the senility or weakness of Polonius's mind. In the great ever-recurring dangers and duties of Life, where ⟨to distinguish⟩ the fit objects for the application of the maxims collected by the experience of a long life requires no fineness of tact as in the admonitions to his Son and Daughter. Polonius is always made respectable—But if the Actor were capable of catching these shades in the character, the Pit and Gallery would be malcontent.—[18]

---

ble between *sun* and *son* be not here intended." Richard Farmer (1735–97) was the author of the well-known *Essay on the Learning of Shakespeare* (1767).

[17] The "MSS" may refer to C's notes for Lect 3 of the 1813 series at Bristol (at n 5), as transcribed by EHC; see "260.5. The first Soliloquy . . ." and the report of that lecture in the *Bristol*

Gazette (at n 16). Mrs Milne's volumes have not been traced. C borrowed an edition of Shakespeare from Mrs Milne, a neighbour of the Gillmans, for his opening lecture on *The Tempest* (see Lect 1 headnote: Background and Circumstances) and evidently wrote annotations on it.

[18] Here, according to HNC in *LR* II

I iv 8–57, Sh (Ayscough) II 1006: On Hamlet's speech on the King's drinking and on Hamlet's reaction to the entry of the Ghost

1006.—In addition to the other excellencies of Hamlet's Speech concerning the *Wassel*[19] Music, so finely revealing the predominant idealism, ⟨the ratiocinative meditativeness,⟩ of his character, it has the advantage of giving nature and probability to the impassioned continuity of the Speech instantly directed to the Ghost. The momentum had been given to his mental Activity—the full current of the thoughts & words had set in—and the very forgetfulness, in the fervor of his Argumentation, of the purpose for which he was there, aided in preventing the Appearance from benumming the mind—Consequently, it acted as a new impulse, a sudden Stroke which increased the velocity of the body already in motion while it altered the direction.—The co-presence of Horatio, Marcellus and Bernardo[20] is most judiciously contrived—for it renders the courage of Hamlet and his impetuous eloquence perfectly intelligible/. The knowlege, the *unthought-of* consciousness, the *Sensation*, of human Auditors, of Flesh and Blood Sympathists,[21] acts as a support, a stimulation *a tergo*,[22] while the *front* of the Mind, the whole Consciousness of the Speaker, is filled by the solemn Apparition. Add too, that the Apparition itself has by its frequent previous appearances been brought nearer to a Thing of this World. This accrescence[23] of Objectivity in a Ghost that yet retains all its ghostly attributes & fearful Subjectivity, is truly wonderful.

I v 92–109, Sh (Ayscough) II 1007 β 27: On Hamlet's speech on the exit of the Ghost, beginning "O all you host of heaven!"

1007.—O all you Host of Heaven! &c

I remember nothing equal to this burst unless it be the first speech of Prometheus, after the exit of Vulcan & the two Afrites, in Eschylus.[24]

218, C developed further the analysis of Polonius he had made in Lect 1 of the 1813 series (paragraph containing n 31), in which he criticised actors for representing Polonius as a buffoon.

[19] This is the spelling in *Sh* (Ayscough) II 1005 β 45 (I iv 9).

[20] Bernardo is not present in I iv; C was perhaps confusing it momentarily with I i.

[21] According to *OED*, citing *LR* II 220, a word coined by C in this passage.

[22] I.e. from the rear.

[23] Continuous growth. C's coinage, according to *OED*, citing *SM*, which dates from 1816: *SM (CC)* 108.

[24] Referring to the speech of Prometheus, lines 89ff, following the exit of Hephaestos and Strength and Might, who shackle and pin him to a desolate rock at the orders of Zeus, in the *Prometheus Bound* of Aeschylus. In calling them "Afrites" C was using a term of Arabic origin for a demon or monster, drawn from Islamic mythology; the first example cited in *OED* under "Afreet" is from RS *Thalaba* (1801) XII 296, "Fit warden of the sorcery-gate, | A rebel Afreet lay".

But Shakespear alone could have produced the Vow of Hamlet to make his memory a blank of all maxims & generalized truths, that Observation had copied there, followed by the immediate noting down the generalized fact, that one may smile and smile and be a villain.

II i, Sh (Ayscough) II 1009: On the exchanges between Polonius and Reynaldo and then Polonius and Ophelia

In all things dependent on or rather made up of fine Address, the *manner* is no more or otherwise rememberable than the light motions, steps, and gestures of Youth and Health.—But this is almost every thing—no wonder therefore, if that which can be *put down by rule* in the memory should appear mere poring, maudlin-eyed Cunning, slyness blinking thro' the watry eye of superannuation. So in this admirable Scene. Polonius, who is throughout the Skeleton of his own former Skill and State-craft, hunts the trail of policy at a dead scent, supplied by the weak fever-smell in his own nostrils.—

II ii 173–82, Sh (Ayscough) II 1011 β 50: On Hamlet's greeting to Polonius, "You are a fishmonger", and his image of "a god, kissing carrion"

50, β.—i.e. You are sent to *fish* out the secret./ This is Hamlet's Meaning. The purposely obscure lines—For if the Sun &c. I rather think refers to some thought in Hamlet's mind contrasting the lovely daughter with such a tedious old fool, her Father: as *he* represents Polonius to himself.—"Why, fool as he is, he is some degrees in rank above a dead dog's carcase—and if the Sun, being a God that kisses carrion can raise life out of a dead Dog, why may good fortune, that favors fools, have raised a lovely Girl out of this dead-alive old fool.—"

II ii 217, Sh (Ayscough) II 1012 α 40: On Hamlet's words as Polonius takes leave of him, "You cannot, sir, take from me any thing that I will more willingly part withal; except my life, except my life, except my life"

1012. 40, α. The repetition of "*except my life*" is most admirable—

II ii 450–518, Sh (Ayscough) II 1015 α 10 to β 22: On the First Player's speech, "The rugged Pyrrhus, like th' Hyrcanian beast . . ."

10, α to 22, β.

This admirable substitution of the Epic for the Dramatic, giving such a *reality* to the impassioned Dramatic Diction of Shakspear's own Dialogue, and authorized too by the actual style of the Tragedies before Shakspeare (Porrex and Ferrex, Titus Andronicus &c)[25] is worthy of notice. The fancy, that Burlesque was intended, sinks below criticism. The lines, as *epic* narrative, are superb.

II ii 550ff, Sh (Ayscough) II 1015 β 55: On Hamlet's soliloquy "O, what a rogue and peasant slave am I"

55, β. Here after the recap. and charact. of Hamlet recommence the particular Criticism—as these lines contain Sh's own attestation of the truth of the Idea, I have started.—

II ii 601, Sh (Ayscough) II 1016 β 25: On Hamlet's line, "Out of my weakness and my melancholy", and his suggestion that the Ghost may be a devil tempting him

25, β.—Sir T. Brown These apparitions and ghosts of departed persons are not the wandering souls of men but the unquiet walks of Devils, prompting and suggesting us unto mischief, blood and villainy &c. Relig. Medici: sect. 37 ad finem.[26]

III i 5, Sh (Ayscough) II 1016 α 5 (of Act III): On Rosencrantz's remark about Hamlet: "He does confess, he feels himself distracted . . ."

5, α—Turn likewise to 1028, as Ham.'s Ch. self-attested.[27]

REPORT IN THE *CHAMPION*
10 JANUARY 1819

Coleridge's Lecture on Thursday was, as we expected, a splendid and ingenious display of metaphysical criticism and poetic enthusiasm. Many

---

[25] *Ferrex and Porrex, or Gorboduc* (1562), by Thomas Sackville and Thomas Norton, is written in stiff, elaborately rhetorical set speeches. The leading Shakespearian scholars of the eighteenth century, from Theobald to Malone, all thought *Titus Andronicus* was not written by Shakespeare; see the Introduction by J. C. Maxwell to the New Arden edition (1953) xix–xx.

[26] C was quoting here from Sir Thomas Browne *Religio Medici* (1643) i § 37: *Works* (1658–9) ii 16. The passage continues to the end of the section: "instill-

ing and stealing into our hearts, that the blessed Spirits are not at rest in their graves, but wander solicitous of the affaires of the world; but that those Phantasmes appear often, and do frequent Cimiteries, charnall houses & Churches, it is because those are the dormitories of the dead where the Divil like an insolent Champion beholds with pride the Spoyles and Trophies of his Victory in *Adam*."

[27] Referring to Hamlet's soliloquy, "How all occasions do inform against me", at the end of IV iv.

of his ideas were as just as they were beautiful; but we wish that he had given some portion of the time consumed by the almost unintelligibly ambiguous apologies for belief in ghosts and goblins, to the elucidation of the yet obscure traits of the character of Hamlet. In many particulars Mr. C. at least accords with, if he has not availed himself of the opinions of Hazlitt,[28] and of another Lecturer, whose discussion on the character of Hamlet, during the last season, excited very popular attention.[29] But we are still of opinion that he has not gone into the entire depths of this extraordinary delineation of physical, moral, and intellectual peculiarity of human character.

[28] Hazlitt's *Characters of Shakespear's Plays* (1817) contained a Preface quoting Schlegel at some length; Hazlitt said that no English writer since Dr Johnson had shown such admiration of Shakespeare or acuteness in pointing out his excellences. He ignored C in this work, no doubt intending the snub to be felt. If C saw this comment in the *Champion*, the implication that he might have borrowed Hazlitt's opinions would have added insult to injury.

[29] Probably Thelwall himself, editor of the *Champion*, and no friend of C at this time (see Lect 1 headnote: Reports), who had given a series of lectures on Shakespeare and Dr Johnson at an institution in Lincoln's Inn Fields in the winter of 1817–18.

LECTURE 4

DATE AND PLACE OF DELIVERY. Thursday, 14 January 1819, at the Crown and Anchor Tavern, Strand, London.

SUBJECT. *Macbeth* compared with *Hamlet*.

ADVERTISEMENTS AND ANNOUNCEMENTS. In the advertisements for the previous lecture on *Hamlet*, and in the advertisements for the philosophical lecture on Plato given Mon, 11 Jan, this lecture was announced as on *Macbeth*. *Courier* Wed, 13 Jan (announcement): "MR. COLERIDGE's Lectures.—Tomorrow evening, eight o'clock, Crown and Anchor Tavern, Strand: Mr. COLERIDGE's Lecture on SHAKESPEARE's *Macbeth*, compared with the Hamlet . . .". *New Times* Wed, 13 Jan (advertisement): "TO-MORROW EVENING, Eight o'-clock, CROWN and ANCHOR, Strand, Mr. COLERIDGE's LECTURE on Shakespeare's MACBETH, compared and contrasted with his HAMLET . . .". *The Times, M Post,* and *M Chron* Thurs, 14 Jan (advertisements): "THIS EVENING . . . Mr. COLERIDGE's LECTURE on MACBETH, illustrated by comparison with the Hamlet of Shakespeare . . .".

TEXT. Again C used his interleaved copy of *Sh* (Ayscough) and appears to have lectured from the text, with the help of annotations made on the interleaves. The annotations, first printed in *LR* I 235–48, were included by Raysor in *Sh C* I 60–9 (67–77), who followed HNC in interspersing them among notes from other sources without indicating where or when C wrote them. The text printed below is based on a fresh transcript of C's notes.

REPORTS. No reports of this lecture have been found.

BACKGROUND AND CIRCUMSTANCES. C announced Lect 4 at first as on *Macbeth* and then, closer to the date, as on *Macbeth* compared with *Hamlet*. In Lects 2 and 3 of the series he gave in Bristol in 1813, he had made some comparisons between the two plays, so that the theme was familiar to him, but he is not likely in 1819 to have gone back to his old notes because they give page-references to his copy of *Sh* (Rann) and he was now using his copy of *Sh* (Ayscough). On the interleaves before *Macbeth*, and continuing through much of Act I, is a long running note in C's hand beginning, "The opening of Macbeth contrasted with that of Hamlet". There are a further fifteen brief annotations on *Macbeth*, which may have been enough to guide C in a largely impromptu lecture on a familiar play, which included a good deal of commentary on the text in front of him. The long first annotation relates back to C's opening remarks on *Hamlet* in Lect 3, when he contrasted the style of the opening scenes in the two plays; evidently he started from this point again in his lecture on *Macbeth*.

During this series C continued to rely on the friendship of William Mudford of the *Courier*, who printed announcements of the lectures for him in the news pages of his evening paper, and a letter survives that was written to him about 12 Jan, suggesting that attendances at the lectures, though still low, were picking up a little after the Christmas period (*CL* IV 911). Otherwise nothing further is known about this lecture.

LECTURE 4

RECORDS OF THE LECTURE

COLERIDGE'S NOTES
FROM HIS ANNOTATIONS ON THE INTERLEAVES
OF *SH* (AYSCOUGH) I 363–85

General comments on the opening scenes of Macbeth *to* I v 28, *on the interleaves facing* Sh *(Ayscough)* I 363–6

The opening of Macbeth contrasted with that of Hamlet—. In the latter the gradual ascent from the simplest forms of conversation to the language of impassioned Intellect, yet still the Intellect remaining the *seat* of Passion—in the Macbeth the invocation is made at once to the Imagination, and the emotions connected therewith. A Superstition in both; yet in each not merely different but opposite. The Wierd Sisters, as true a *Creation* of Shakespear's as his Ariel and Caliban—the Fates, the Furies, and the *materializing* Witches being the elements.—

The II Scene illustrated by reference to the Play in Hamlet, in which the Epic is substituted for the Tragic[1] in order to make the latter be felt as the *real-Life* Diction.

Scene III. That I have assigned the true reason for the first appearance of the Weird Sisters, as the Key-note of the character of the whole Play is proved by the re-entrance of the Sisters—after such an order of the King's as establishes their supernatural* powers of information.

The wish that in Macbeth the attempt might be made to introduce the flexible character-mask of the Ancient Pantomime—that a Flaxman might contribute his Genius to the embodying of Shakspear's.[2]

---

* yet still information/

[1] C was thinking presumably of the bleeding Captain's speeches reporting Macbeth's victory over Macdonwald, I ii 7–42; cf his comments on the play within the play in *Hamlet*, in Lect 3,

above (sentence containing n 25).

[2] John Flaxman (1755–1826) became well known through his illustrations to Homer's *Iliad* and *Odyssey* (first published in England in 1795), and C was

King hereafter was still contingent[3]—still in Macbeth's moral will—tho' if he yielded to the temptation & thus forfeited his free-agency, then the link of *cause* and *effect more physico*[4] would commence—& thus the prophetic Vision afterwards. I surely need not say, that the *general* Idea is all that can be required from the Poet—not a scholastic logical consistency in all the parts so as to meet metaphysical Objections.

But O how truly Shakspearian is the opening of Macbeth's character given in the *unpossessedness*[5] of Banquo's mind, wholly present to the present Object—an unsullied un-scarified[6] Mirror—& in strict truth of Nature that he and not Macbeth himself directs our notice to the effect produced on Macbeth's Mind, rendered *temptible* by ⟨previous⟩ dalliance of the Fancy with ambitious Thoughts. (See Wallenstein's Soliloquy, Part I.)[7]

> Good Sir, why do you start?—and seem to fear
> Things that do sound so fair?[8]

And then again, still unintröitive,[9] addresses the appearances—[10]

The questions of Banquo those of natural Curiosity—such as a Girl would make after she had heard a Gypsey tell her School-fellow's Fortune—all perfectly general—or rather *planless*. But Macbeth, lost in thought, rouses himself to Speech only by their being about to depart—STAY, you imperfect Speakers[11]—and all that follows is reasoning on a problem already discussed in his mind—on a hope which he welcomes, and the doubts concerning its attainment he wishes to have cleared up—. His eagerness—the eager eye with which he had pursued

---

probably thinking of his drawings and sculpture in a neo-classical style. The *pantomimi* in ancient Rome were actors who performed entirely in gesture and actions, without words.

[3] Referring to *Macbeth* I iii 50.

[4] The phrase is Latin, *more physico*, meaning "in a natural manner".

[5] I.e. lacking prejudice, not possessing any prior knowledge or opinion. C's coinage, according to *OED*, which cites this passage (from *LR* II 239).

[6] Another word coined by C, according to *OED*, which cites this passage (from *LR*).

[7] Referring to his own translation of Schiller's *The Piccolomini, or, The First Part of Wallenstein* IV iv 1–92, in which Wallenstein says:

> I
> Must do the deed, because I thought of it,
> And fed this heart here with a dream?

PW (EHC) II 690–2.

[8] Banquo's words, addressed to Macbeth, I iii 51–2.

[9] C's coinage, and the only instance listed in *OED*, which cites this passage, literally "not entering", not being possessed by the utterance of the Witches, as Macbeth is.

[10] With the words, I iii 52ff,

> I' th' name of truth
> Are ye fantastical, or that indeed
> Which outwardly ye show?

[11] *Macbeth* I iii 70.

their evanition, compared with the easily satisfied mind of the self-uninterested Banquo

> The Earth hath bubbles—
>   Whither are they vanished?
> M. Into the Air—and what seem'd corporal melted
> As Breath into the wind—WOULD THEY HAD STAY'D[12]

Is it too minute to notice the appropriateness of the Simile "As Breath" in a cold Climate?

Still again Banquo's wonder that of any Spectator "Were such things here"[13] and Macbeth's recurrence to the *self-concerning*—Your Children shall be Kings—.[14] So truly is the guilt in its Germ anterior to the supposed cause & immediate temptation—Before he can cool, the *confirmation* of the tempting half of the Prophecy—and the *catenating* tendency fostered by the sudden coincidence.

Glamis and Thane of Cawdor—The greatest is behind[15]—⚹[16] Banquo's what can the Devil speak true—[17]

I doubt whether *enkindle* has not another sense than that of *stimulating*—whether the Kind, & Kin—as in Rabbits *kindle*[18]—However, Macbeth hears no more *ab extra*. "Two truths &c"[19] And (p. 365) the necessity of recollecting himself—I thank you, Gentlemen!—in the third line of his speech.—[20]

30–49, Col. β.[21]—confirm. of the remark on the birth-date of guilt.—And then the warning of the Conscience—& the mode of lulling it—If chance will have me King, why &c[22]—and the suspicion that others might see what was passing in his mind, all prospective, by the LIE—wrought with *Things forgotten*—and instantly the *promising Courtesies* of a Usurper in intention.—

And O the affecting beauty of the Death of Cawdor,[23] and the King's presentimental[24] remark, interrupted by the "Worthiest Cousin"! on the entrance of the deeper Traitor to whom Cawdor had made way—and here in contrast with Duncan's "plenteous Joys"[25] Macbeth has nothing but the common-places of Loyalty, in which he hides himself

---

[12] I iii 79-82, omitting after "bubbles", line 79, "as the water has, | And these are of them".

[13] I iii 83.

[14] I iii 86.

[15] I iii 116–17.

[16] C's sign for "as contrasted with".

[17] I iii 107.

[18] I.e. give birth. C's comment relates to the footnote in the edition he was us-

ing: "*Enkindle*, for to stimulate you to seek".

[19] *Macbeth* I iii 127.

[20] I iii 129, *Sh* (Ayscough) I 365 β 32.

[21] I iii 127–44.

[22] I iii 143.

[23] Reported in I iv 1–11.

[24] C's coinage: this passage is cited in *OED*, from *LR*.

[25] I iv 33.

in the "our".[26]—and in the same language of *effort* "The REST is Labor" &c[27]—at the moment that a new difficulty suggests a new crime. This, however, seems the first distinct notion, as to the *plan* of realizing his wishes—and here therefore with great propriety Macbeth's Cowardice of his own Conscience discloses itself.[28]

Macbeth described by Lady M. so as at the same time to describe her own character[29]—intellectually considered, he is powerful in all, but has strength in none[30]—morally, *selfish* i.e. as far as his weakness will permit him. Could he have every thing, he wanted, he would *rather* have it innocently—ignorant, as alas! how many are! that he who wishes a temporal end for itself does in truth will the *means*—hence the danger of indulging in fancies—

"Lady Macbeth—with the valor of my Tongue."[31] Day-dreamer's valiance.

I v 41–74, Sh (Ayscough) I 367: On Lady Macbeth's reception of her husband on his return home

All the false efforts of a mind accustomed only to the Shadows of the Imagination, vivid enough to throw the every day realities into shadows but not yet compared with their own correspondent realities.

No womanly, no wifely Joy at the return of her Husband—no retrospection on the dangers, he had escaped—✕ ⟨Macbeth's⟩[32] My dearest Love[33]—and his shrinking from the boldness with which she presents his own thoughts to him—We shall speak further—[34]

I vi 14–20, Sh (Ayscough) I 367 β 25: On Lady Macbeth's speech of welcome to Duncan at his arrival at Inverness: "All our service | In

---

[26] I iv 23–5:

> Your Highness' part
> Is to receive our duties; and our duties
> Are to your throne . . .

[27] I iv 44: "The rest is labour, which is not us'd for you."

[28] In the lines (I iv 49ff) beginning:

> The Prince of Cumberland! that is a step
> On which I must fall down, or else o'erleap.

[29] I v 15–30.

[30] In a letter of 1804 (*CL* II 1102) C distinguished between intellectual power and moral strength in relation to himself

in terms relevant here; he also applied the distinction in political terms to nations in *Friend* (*CC*) I 224 and *EOT* (*CC*) III 101.

[31] I v 27, Lady Macbeth's lines:

> And chastise with the valour of my tongue
> All that impedes thee from the golden round . . .

[32] C's sign for "in contrast to Macbeth's".

[33] I v 58.

[34] I v 71; Macbeth says: "We will speak further."

*every point twice done, and then done double, | Were poor and single
business to contend | Against those honours deep and broad, wherewith
| Your majesty loads our house . . ."*

25β. The very rhythm expresses the conscious over-much in Lady M.'s
Answer to the King.

*I vii 1–38, Sh (Ayscough) I 368: On Macbeth's soliloquy: "If it were
done when 'tis done . . ."*

The inward pangs & warnings of Conscience interpreted into *prudential*
reasonings.—

*II i 4ff, Sh (Ayscough) I 369 α 10: On Banquo's lines beginning "Hold,
take my sword . . ."*

10. α The disturbance of an innocent soul by painful suspicions of
another's guilty intentions & wishes—and fear of the *cursed thoughts.*

*II ii 9–11, Sh (Ayscough) I 369 β 40: On Lady Macbeth's first expression
of anxiety: "Alack! I am afraid they have awak'd . . ."*

40. β.—The very first reality, L. M. shrinks.

*II ii 70–1, Sh (Ayscough) I 370: On the last lines of the scene, Macbeth's
"To know my deed,—Twere best not know myself"*

Need I say, contrast with Soliloquy, p. 368.[35]

III i 74ff, Sh (Ayscough) I 373: On Macbeth's scene with the two Murderers

The Mistake of Schiller in his Wallenstein respecting the Assassins—[36]

*III ii 13ff, Sh (Ayscough) I 374: On Macbeth's speech beginning "We
have scotch'd the snake, not kill'd it . . ."*

Ever & ever mistaking the anguish of Conscience for Fears of Selfish-

---

[35] *Sh* (Ayscough) I 368 α: Macbeth's
soliloquy, I vii 1–38, "If it were done
when 'tis done . . .".

[36] C's annotations in a copy of his
translation of the two parts of *Wallenstein* include the comment: "The assassins talk ludicrously. This is a most egre-
gious misimitation of Shakespere—
Schiller should not have attempted trag-
ico-comedy, and none but Shakespere
has succeeded. It is wonderful, however,
that Schiller, who had studied Shakespere, should not have perceived his divine judgment in the management of his
assassins, as in Macbeth. They are fearful and almost pitiable Beings—not
loathsome, ludicrous miscreants." The
reference is to Butler, Macdonald, and
Devereux, who plot the murder of Wallenstein in Pt 2, *The Death of Wallenstein*
Acts III and IV. See *PW (EHC)* II 599,
776–85.

ness, and thus as a punishment of that Selfishness, plunging deeper in guilt & ruin.

III ii 44–5, Sh *(Ayscough)* I 374: *On Lady Macbeth's "What's to be done?" and Macbeth's response, "Be innocent of the knowledge, dearest chuck"*

Sympathy with his own state of feelings—& mistaking his Wife's opposite state—

III iv, Sh *(Ayscough)* I 376: *On the appearance of Banquo's ghost*

Tell the story of the *Portrait* that frightened every one—[37]

IV i 144–55, Sh *(Ayscough)* I 379: *On Macbeth's sudden decision to slaughter the family of Macduff*

Acme of the avenging Conscience—

IV iii 50–99, Sh *(Ayscough)* I 381: *On Malcolm's denigration of himself*

Moral—of the dreadful effects even on the best minds by the soul-sickening sense of Insecurity—

IV iii 207–35, Sh *(Ayscough)* I 382: *On Macduff's reception of the news of the slaughter of his family*

The manliness of the Pathos in harmony with the Play—it rends, not dissolves the heart—"the tune goes manly".[38]

V iii, Sh *(Ayscough)* I 384: *On Macbeth's dialogue with the Doctor at the end of this scene*

Now all is *inward*—no more prudential prospective reasonings—

V v 19–28, Sh *(Ayscough)* I 385: *On Macbeth's soliloquy: "To-morrow, and to-morrow, and to-morrow . . ."*

Despondency the final wretched Heart-armour—

---

[37] John Taylor Coleridge recorded the story of the "Phantom Portrait" in *TT* 1 May 1823. It told of a portrait in a merchant's house in Lübeck that frightened a guest staying overnight. The host told the guest that the portrait had been painted by an Italian artist who had murdered his patron. Wherever the artist went, he saw his victim's face glaring at him, and finally painted the portrait from memory with that frightening look. The painter gave the portrait to the merchant's father.

[38] Misquoting Malcolm's phrase at IV iii 235, "This tune goes manly", referring to preparations for war against Macbeth.

LECTURE 5

DATE AND PLACE OF DELIVERY. Thursday, 21 January 1819, at the Crown and Anchor Tavern, Strand, London.

SUBJECT. *Othello.*

ADVERTISEMENTS AND ANNOUNCEMENTS. *Courier* Wed, 20 Jan (announcement): "MR. COLERIDGE'S LECTURES—Tomorrow evening, eight o'-clock, Crown and Anchor, Strand; Mr. COLERIDGE's Lecture on OTHELLO, as the consummate perfection of Character, and as the Drama in which Shakespeare shines forth in his collective excellence as the Philosopher, the Poet, and the Man. On the Thursday following the present Critical Course finishes with the tragedy of Lear. Admission 5s." *New Times* Wed, 20 Jan (advertisement): as in the *Courier*, with minor variants and the substitution of "combined" for "collective". *The Times* Thurs, 21 Jan (advertisement): as in the *Courier*, with some omissions and the alteration to "THIS EVENING . . .". *M Post* Thurs, 21 Jan (advertisement): as in *The Times*, with minor variants. *M Chron* Thurs, 21 Jan (advertisement): as in the *Courier*, with minor variants and some additions, as follows: "the consummate Perfection of Plan, Character, and genuine Pathos, and the Drama, in which, more than in any other even of his own immortal writings, our Shakespeare shines forth . . .".

TEXT. As for the other lectures in this series, C used his interleaved copy of *Sh* (Ayscough). He appears to have lectured from the text of *Othello*, with the help of annotations made on the interleaves. These were printed by HNC in *LR* I 255–67, and Raysor included them in *Sh C* I 40–9 (44–54); he followed HNC in intermingling them among notes from other sources and in giving no indication as to where or when C wrote them. The text printed below is based upon a fresh transcript of C's annotations.

REPORTS. No reports of this lecture have been found.

BACKGROUND AND CIRCUMSTANCES. In several earlier courses C had lectured on *Othello*, but usually in association with some other play. In Lect 9 of the 1812–13 series he linked it with *Macbeth*, in Lect 4 of the 1813 series in Bristol with *The Winter's Tale*, and in Lect 6 in 1818 with *Hamlet*. So this was probably the first lecture he devoted entirely to *Othello*. Once again, as for Lects 3 and 4, he took his copy of *Sh* (Ayscough) into the lecture-room and developed his lecture from the text and the notes he made in Vol II of this set. As with *Hamlet* and *Macbeth*, he used the preliminary leaves before the text of *Othello* to write a long note, which was probably designed to start the lecture, beginning "The admirable preparation, so characteristic of Shakspeare". Raysor made it impossible to interpret this correctly in *Sh C* I 40–2 (44–7) by interpolating in it marginalia and notes from other sources, but it is printed below as C wrote it. There is another long note at the end of Act I, in which C takes issue with Dr Johnson over the application of rules and the three unities to drama. He had dealt with this question in earlier lectures, as in Lect 3 of the 1811–12 series (at n 26), and his return to this familiar theme here was sparked off by the transfer of the action from Venice to Cyprus in Act II of *Othello*. The remaining eighteen annotations to this play are brief, but could have served as pointers in the lecture-room. After using the fairly substantial introductory note, C probably developed the lecture impromptu from the text. His letters throw no light on this lecture, and nothing further is known about it.

312

LECTURE 5

RECORDS OF THE LECTURE

COLERIDGE'S NOTES
FROM HIS ANNOTATIONS ON THE INTERLEAVES
OF *SH* (AYSCOUGH) II 1042–76

General notes on Othello I i, *Sh (Ayscough) II 1042*

Othello. Act I. Scene I.

The admirable preparation, so characteristic of Shakspeare—/ in the introduction of Roderigo as the Dupe on whom Iago first exercises his art, and in so doing displays his own character.—Roderigo, already fitted & predisposed by his own passions—without any fixed principle or strength of character (The want of character and the power of the passions, like the wind loudest in empty houses, forms his character) but yet not without the moral notions and sympathies with honor, which his rank, connections had hung upon him. The very 3 first lines happily state the nature and foundation of the friendship—the purse—as well [as]*a* the contrast of R's intemperance of mind with Iago's coolness, the coolness of a preconceiving *Experimenter*.—The mere langue of protestation in "If ever—abhor me."[1] which fixing the associative link that determines Roderigo's continuation of complaint—in thy hate[2]—elicits a true feeling of Iago's—the dread of contempt fatal to those who encourage in themselves & have their keenest pleasure in the feeling & expression of contempt in others.—His high self-opinion—& how a wicked man employs his real feelings as well as assumes those most alien from his own, as instruments of his purposes.—

The necessity of Tyrwhytt's alteration of "wife" into life[3]—as contempt for whatever did not display power, & that intellectual—What

---

a Word supplied by the editor

[1] Iago's words, I i 5–6:

If ever I did dream of such a matter,
Abhor me.
[2] Roderigo's line, I i 7: "Thou toldst

me thou didst hold him in thy hate."
[3] In *Sh* (Ayscough) II 1043 β 9, a note is keyed to I i 21, "A fellow almost damn'd in a fair wife", and C was re-

follows, let the Reader *feel*—how by & thro' the glass of two passions, disappointed Passion & Envy, the very vices, he is complaining of, are made to act upon him as so many excellences—& the more appropriately, because Cunning is always admired & wished for by minds conscious of inward weakness—and yet it is but *half*—it acts like music on an inattentive auditor, *swelling* the thoughts which prevented him from listening to it. Roderigo—turns off to Othello—& here comes the one if not the only justification of the Blackamoor Othello, namely as a Negro—who is not a *Moor* at all—. Even if we supposed this an uninterrupted Tradition of the Theatre, and that Sh. himself from want of scenes & the experience that nothing could be made too *marked* for the senses of his Audience—would this prove aught concerning his own intentions as a Poet for all ages?—Can we suppose him so utterly ignorant as to make a barbarous *Negro* plead Royal Birth—Were Negros then known but as Slaves—on the contrary were not the Moors the warriors &c—

Iago's Speech to Brabantio implies merely that he was *a Moor*—i.e. black. Tho' I think the rivalry of Roderigo sufficient to account for his wilful confusion of Moor & Negro—yet tho' compelled to give this up, I should yet think it only adapted for the then *Acting*—& should complain of an enormity built only on one single word—in direct contradiction to Iago's "*Barbary* horse"[4]—If we can in good earnest believe Sh. ignorant of the distinction, still why take one against 10—as Oth. cannot be both—?—

"This accident is not unlike my dream"[5]—the old *careful* Senator who caught careless transfers his Caution to his *Dreaming* Power at least—

The forced praise of Othello—followed by the bitter hatred— — Iago—

and Brabantio's recurrence to philtres, so prepared [for][b] by the Dream— & both so prepared for the carrying on of the Plot by the arraig[n]ment[c] of Othello on *this ground—/*

[b] Word supplied by the editor
[c] Letter supplied by the editor

---

ferring to this. It reads: "Mr. Tyrwhitt ingeniously proposes to read 'damn'd in a fair *life*;' and is of opinion, that 'Shakspeare alludes to the judgement denounced in the Gospel against those *of whom all men speak well*'." Thomas Tyrwhitt (1730–86) was the author of *Observations and Conjectures upon Some Passages of Shakespeare* (1766).

[4] I i 111: "you'll have your daughter cover'd with a Barbary horse".

[5] Citing I i 142 and alluding to I i 171–3:

Is there not charms
By which the property of youth and maidhood
May be abus'd?

I ii 6–33, Sh (Ayscough) II 1045: Citing lines 6, 23, and 33 and referring to "not easily jealous, but being wrought" in Othello's last speech, V ii 345

Scene II.

" 'Tis better as it is.—" "not easily wrought" above all low passions—"unbonnetted" without the symbol of a petitioning inferior.—*By Janus*—in Iago's mouth—

I iii 293–6, Sh (Ayscough) II 1050 α 30: On Brabantio's "She has deceiv'd her father, and may thee"

30, α. In real life how do we look back to little speeches, either as presentimental[6] or most contrasted with an affecting Event. Shak. as secure of being read over and over, of becoming a family friend, how he provides this for *his readers*—& leaves it to them.

I iii 320–61, Sh (Ayscough) II 1050 β 5: On Iago's lines beginning "Our bodies are our gardens, to the which our wills are gardeners . . ."

5, β.—Iago's passionless character, all *will* in Intellect—therefore a bold partizan here of a truth, but yet of a truth converted into falsehood by absence of all the modifications by the frail nature of man—and the LAST SENTIMENT—there lies the Iago-ism of how many![7] And the repetition, Go, make money!—a pride in it, of an anticipated Dupe stronger than the love of Lucre—

I iii 380–404, Sh (Ayscough) II 1051 α 12: On Iago's farewell to Roderigo: "Go to, farewell. Put money enough in your purse", and his soliloquy beginning "Thus do I ever make my fool my purse . . ."

12, α. The triumph! again, *put money*[8] after the effect has been fully produced.—The last Speech, the motive-hunting of motiveless Malignity—how awful! In itself fiendish—while yet he was allowed to bear the divine image, too fiendish for his own steady View.—A being next to Devil—only *not* quite Devil—& this Shakespear has attempted—executed—without disgust, without Scandal!—[d]

Act I, Sh (Ayscough) II 1043, 1044: On Dr Johnson's comments on Act I and the dramatic unities

---

[d] C here added a direction to himself: "(then turn back to the blank fronting the first page)", referring to the note facing p 1043

[6] See above, Lect 4 (at n 24).
[7] Iago's "Seek thou rather to be hang'd in compassing thy joy than to be drown'd and go without her", III i 359–61.

[8] Iago's final repetition of "Put money enough in thy purse", III i 380–1, found only in the Quarto, but included in *Sh* (Ayscough).

*e*Dʳ Johnson has remarked that little or nothing is wanting to render the Othello a regular Tragedy but to have opened the play with the arrival of Othello in Cyprus, and to have thrown the preceding Act into the form of narration.⁹ Here then is the place to determine, whether such a change would or would not be an improvement, nay (to throw down the glove with a full challenge) whether or no the Tragedy would by such an arrangement become *more regular*, i.e. more consonant with the rules dictated by universal reason or the true Common Sense of mankind in its application to the particular case. *ᶠ*For surely we may safely leave to it to common sense whether to reply to or laugh at such a remark—as: for instance—Suppose a man had described a rhomboid or parallelogram, and a Critic were with great gravity to observe—if the lines had only been in true right-angles, or if the horizontal parallels had been but of the same length as the two perpendicular parallels that form the sides, the diagram would have been according to the strictest rules of Geometry.ᵍ—For ⟨in all acts of judgement⟩ it never [can]ʰ be too often recollected and scarcely too often repeated, that rules are means to ends, consequently, that the End must be determined and understood before it can be known what the rules are or ought to be. Now from a certain species of Drama, proposing to itself the accomplishment of certain Ends, these partly arising from the Idea of the Species itself but in part likewise forced upon the Dramatist by accidental circumstances beyond his power to remove or controll three rules have been abstracted—in other words, the means most conducive to the attainment of the proposed ends have been generalized and prescribed under the names of the three Unities, the unity of Time, the unity of Place, and the unity of Action, which last would perhaps have been appropriately as well as more intelligibly entitled the Unity of Interest.¹⁰ With this the present Question has no immediate concern. ⟨In fact its conjunction with the two former is a mere delusion of *words*.⟩ It is not properly *a rule*; but in itself the great End, not only of the

---

ᵉ Above this, C added a direction to himself: "(After the first act)"
ᶠ⁻ᵍ C drew a wavy line down the margin here and wrote against it: "N.B. *Very awkwardly expressed*."
ʰ Word supplied by the editor

⁹ He wrote, "Had the scene opened in Cyprus, and the preceding incidents been occasionally related, there had been little wanting to a drama of the most exact and scrupulous regularity." *Works* VIII 1048.

¹⁰ C had used this phrase in Lect 3 of the 1811–12 series (at n 26), but not in preference to "unity of action". It was Schlegel who, following Antoine de la Motte, proposed "unity of interest" as a better alternative, and C seems here to be recalling *DKL* II 95 (Black I 335–6). See also C's comments on the unities in Lect 1 of the 1813 series at Bristol (at nn 8 and 9 and 23–5).

Drama but of the Epic, Lyric, even to the Candle-flame Cone of an Epigram—not only of Poetry, but of Poesy in general, as the proper generic term inclusive of all the fine Arts, as its Species.[11] But of the unities of Time and Place which alone are entitled to the name of Rules, the history of their origin will be their best criterion.—Chorus[12]—you may take people to a place, but only by a palpable equivoque can you bring Birnam Wood to Macbeth at Dunsinane.[13] The same in a less degree as to the unity of Time—the positive fact, not for a moment removed from the Senses, the presence, I mean, of the very same persons is a continued measure of Time—and tho' the imagination may supersede perception, yet it must be granted an imperfection (tho' even here how easily do we not tolerate it?) to place the two in broad contradiction to each other./ Yet—dark scenes—*asides*—&c.—. But in truth it is a mere accident of Terms in the first place—(the Trilogy = Acts)[14]—and notwithstanding this, the strange contrivances as to place, as in THE FROGS[15]— and there is no lack of instances in the Greek Tragedies—the allowance extorted of 24 hours—as if perception once violated, it was more difficult to imagine 3 hours 3 years, or a whole day & night.—Fine instance in Eschylus—Agamemnon.[16]

The danger of introducing into a situation of great *interest* one for whom you had no previous Interest—φϱϛφϱϱ Ιωαν.[17]

Act II, Sh (Ayscough) II 1051: General note on the presentation of Othello

Act II

Confirmation of my reason—in how many ways is not Othello made, first, our acquaintance—then friend—then object of anxiety—before the deep interest is to be approached—so the storm &c—

---

[11] For C's effort to "desynonimize" Poesy and Poetry, see above, Lect 13 of the 1818 series (between nn 5 and 6).

[12] See Lect 1 of the 1813 series (sentence before n 23), in which C argued that "the chorus was always before the audience . . . *change of place* was impossible".

[13] *Macbeth* v v 30–7 and v vi.

[14] C elaborated on this, with reference to the *Oresteia*, in Lect 1 of the 1813 series (sentences after n 25).

[15] In Aristophanes' play, Dionysos travels from this world to visit the palace of Pluto in the underworld, which strains the notion of a unity of place.

[16] The play begins with a Watchman observing the firing of a beacon announcing the fall of Troy, but in the course of the action Agamemnon arrives, having sailed back from Troy to Argos, implying the lapse of much more than twenty-four hours. C had made this point, using the same illustration, borrowed from A. W. Schlegel, in Lect 1 of the 1813 series (at n 25).

[17] The sentence and C's cipher are unexplained. The Greek transliterated is "*Phrsphrr Joan*", possibly John Thelwall, who reviewed the opening lecture of this series in the *Champion*.

ɪɪ i 61–5, Sh *(Ayscough) ɪɪ 1052 α 15: On Cassio's praise of Desdemona, who, "in the essential vesture of creation | Does tire the ingener" (Ayscough has "Does bear all excellency")*

15, α. Cassio's warm-hearted yet perfectly disengaged praise of Desdemona—& sympathy with the "most fortunately" wived Othello—& yet an enthusiastic *Admirer*, almost Worshipper, of Desdemona.—Again, I must touch the detestable code that excellence can not be loved in *any* form/ that because it is female, it must needs be selfish—. The Venus de Medici/—[18]

ɪɪ i 74–124, Sh *(Ayscough) ɪɪ 1052 α 30: On Cassio's reference to "bold Iago" (line 75), his greeting of Emilia by kissing her (line 99), Iago's slander of women, and Desdemona's pretence of being merry*

30, α./ N.B.—it is Othello's *honest*, Cassio's *bold* Iago[19]—& Cassio's full-gui[le]less*ⁱ*-hearted Wishes!—But again the exquisite Circumstance of kissing Iago's Wife—as if it ought to be impossible that the dullest Auditor should not feel Cassio's religious Awe of Desdemona's purity—
Say, something a fair moral Critic ought to do on the sneers which a proud bad intellect feels towards woman, & expresses to a wife—
The struggle of courtesy in Desdemona to abstract her attention—

ɪɪ i 168–71, Sh *(Ayscough) ɪɪ 1053 α 25: On Iago's observation of Cassio as he takes Desdemona by the hand: "With as little a web as this will I ensnare as great a fly as Cassio"*

25, α. O excellent. The importance given to fertile trifles, made fertile by the villainy of the observer—

ɪɪ i 222–45, Sh *(Ayscough) ɪɪ 1053 β 30–55: On Iago's attempt to persuade Roderigo that Desdemona loves Cassio; from "Mark me with what violence she first lov'd the Moor" to "a devilish knave! Besides, the knave is handsome"*

30–55—Iago's rehearsing on the Dupe Roderigo his intentions on Othello—

ⁱ Letters supplied by the editor

[18] The Medici *Aphrodite*, a famous sculpture of the goddess as a nude standing figure, dating from the third century B.C., is in the Uffizi Gallery in Florence, which C visited in 1806 (see *CN* ɪɪ 2853), but numerous copies of this statue also survive.

[19] Othello begins to speak of "Honest Iago" at ɪ iii 294, and cf ɪɪ iii 6, on which C comments below.

II i 294–6, Sh (Ayscough) II 1054 α 50: On Iago's explanation of his hatred for Othello: "But partly led to diet my revenge, | For that I do suspect the lusty Moor | Hath leap'd into my seat"

50, α. The thought at first by his own confession a mere suspicion—now ripening—Tho' perhaps Shak. *compromised*

II iii 4–6, Sh (Ayscough) II 1054: On Othello's charge to Cassio to look to the guard

Oth. Iago is most honest—/ here perhaps the time for Othello's *not* jealous character—& the proofs—

II iii 246–7, Sh (Ayscough) II 1057: On Othello's "I know, Iago, | Thy honesty and love doth mince this matter"

Thy Honesty & Love—

II iii 336ff, Sh (Ayscough) II 1058 α 15: On Iago's soliloquy: "And what's he then that says I play the villain, | When this advice is free I give, and honest, | Probal to thinking, and indeed the course | To win the Moor again?" (Ayscough in line 3 has "probable to thinking")

15. Not absolute fiend—at least, he wishes to think himself [not]^{j} so

III iii 20, Sh (Ayscough) II 1059 β 20: On Desdemona's eager support of Cassio's cause: "I give thee warrant of thy place . . ."

20, β.
The overzeal of Innocence in Desdemona

III iii 213–17, Sh (Ayscough) II 1061: On Othello's response to Iago's "I see, this hath a little dash'd your spirits"

Not a jot, not a jot

III iii 278, Sh (Ayscough) II 1062 β 20: On Desdemona's entry summoning Othello to dinner on his line: "If she be false, O, then heaven mocks itself!"

20, β
Divine! the effect of innocence & the [bitter/better?]^{k} [? genius]^{k}

v ii 17ff, Sh (Ayscough) II 1076: On the dialogue between Othello and Desdemona before he smothers her

Is this jealousy?

^{j} Word supplied by the editor
^{k} Conjectural readings

LECTURE 6

DATE AND PLACE OF DELIVERY. Thursday, 28 January 1819, at the Crown and Anchor Tavern, Strand, London.

SUBJECT. *King Lear*.

ADVERTISEMENTS AND ANNOUNCEMENTS. *Courier* Wed, 27 Jan (announcement): "MR. COLERIDGE'S LECTURES.—To-morrow evening at the Crown and Anchor, Strand, Mr. COLERIDGE's First Critical Course concludes with the tragedy of *Lear*, as most evincing the sublimity, the depth, and the terrific energy of SHAKESPEARE's tragic and poetic genius. Admission 5s." (This goes on to describe C's proposals for a new course to begin on 4 Feb.) *The Times*, *M Chron*, *New Times*, *M Post* Thurs, 28 Jan (advertisements): as in the *Courier*, with the alteration to "THIS EVENING . . .".

TEXT. C again used his interleaved copy of *Sh* (Ayscough), lecturing from the text with the help of annotations he had made on the interleaves. A version of these annotations was printed in *LR* I 185–202, and Raysor included them in *Sh C* I 49–59 (54–67); like HNC, he intermingled them among other marginalia on *King Lear*, without indicating where or when C had written them. The text printed below is based on a fresh transcript of C's notes.

REPORTS. A report summarising the qualities of the course, attacking Hazlitt as a critic of Shakespeare, and ending with a brief account of the lecture on *King Lear* was published in the *Courier* Mon, 1 Feb 1819, and in the *M Post* the following day. This is reprinted below from the *Courier* text.

BACKGROUND AND CIRCUMSTANCES. On 26 Jan C wrote to C. A. Tulk, who had evidently attended some of the lectures, and drew his attention to this one: "On Thursday the LEAR, the Δεινότης, La Terribilitá of Shakspeare's tragic Might—
Lie, great TRAGEDIAN, Shakspeare! lie alone."
CL IV 915. The line of verse may have been a deliberate misquotation of the line "Sleep, rare Tragedian Shakespeare, sleep alone" from a sonnet by William Basse (1602–53) written on the death of the dramatist, which was printed for the first time in the *Poems* of John Donne (1633) and appeared over the initials "W. B." in Shakespear's *Poems* (1640). The comment is notable because it suggests that C regarded *King Lear* as the most terrible or awe-inspiring of Shakespeare's tragedies. In earlier courses he had rather neglected this play, mentioning it in Lect 2 of the 1811–12 series and commenting on it at greater length in Lect 14, but still in a lecture largely concerned with Dr Johnson's Preface to Shakespeare and with *Othello*. This is the first lecture C is known to have devoted wholly to the play. As for his lectures on *Hamlet*, *Macbeth*, and *Othello*, he seems to have worked from the text of the play in his copy of *Sh* (Ayscough). On the interleaves at the beginning of the play he wrote a long note that takes off from the division of Lear's kingdom announced in the opening lines and develops into a critical analysis of Edmund, Goneril, and Regan. There are twenty-three other annotations to *King Lear* in this text, all of them brief, but some, like those on Cordelia, Kent, Oswald, and the Fool, giving rapid pointers to their characterisation, could well have sufficed to prompt C in the lecture-room. Once again it seems likely that, with the help of an elaborate note to start him off, he proceeded to develop his lecture impromptu from the

text, helped by some of his other short notes. Although he had not given much attention to the play in previous lectures, he had studied it and had written a few annotations on it in two other editions of Shakespeare, one of them dated Jan 1813.

On the same day that he wrote to Tulk C also wrote to Mudford, asking him to mention the lecture "in two or three lines", as it would "be of important service to my fresh Cause". *CL* IV 915. The announcement of the lecture that appeared 27 Jan in the *Courier*, the newspaper Mudford edited, went on to advertise a new course of seven literary lectures beginning on 4 Feb, as did also the advertisements in all the other newspapers listed above. So presumably C was asking, in effect, for a report of the lecture, and the *Courier* obliged with one on 1 Feb, which begins by mentioning the proposed new course. The first part of this report reads like a riposte to the brief account of Lect 3 in the *Champion*. In this the reviewer insinuated that C borrowed opinions from Hazlitt, whereas the *Courier* review commented that C had "none of the glib nonsense of Mr. Hazlitt". The very favourable account of the course as a whole, and of the lecture on *King Lear*, pleased C, who wrote to thank Mudford on 9 Jan for "the very kind notice" (*CL* IV 918); he went on to comment on Hazlitt's "frantic hatred" towards him. Hazlitt, who could not forgive C's departure from his early radical views in politics, attacked what he regarded as C's apostasy in a series of articles and reviews of C's works, beginning with his review of *Christabel; Kubla Khan, A Vision; The Pains of Sleep* in Jun 1816. Indeed, Hazlitt's brilliantly clever essays are vitiated by his inability to resist an opportunity to sneer, and C felt bitterly the various attacks upon himself as a political turncoat and as a writer made by one who had been a friend and disciple. A more detailed account of their relationship may be found in Herschel Baker *William Hazlitt* (Cambridge, Mass 1962) 356–64; see also *CL* IV 668 and *BL* (*CC*) II 238–42. The report in the *Courier*, a newspaper attacked by Hazlitt in the *Examiner* in Mar 1817 and again in 1823 (see *H Works* XVI 228–9), must have been especially welcome to C. Unfortunately, it did not have a beneficial effect by swelling the audience for his new course, since he was already ill when he "contrived to get thro' the Thursday's Lecture as successfully as the subject (Lear) would allow" him (*CL* IV 916), and by the advice of his doctors he postponed the commencement of it for a week.

LECTURE 6

RECORDS OF THE LECTURE

COLERIDGE'S NOTES
FROM HIS ANNOTATIONS ON THE INTERLEAVES
OF *SH* (AYSCOUGH) II 928–60

General note on King Lear *I i, Sh (Ayscough) II 929–32 (C's specific reference is to II 929 α 5–10, the opening exchange between Kent and Gloucester:* "Kent. *I thought the King had more affected the Duke of Albany than Cornwall. Gloucester. It did always seem so to us; but now in the division of the kingdom, it appears not which of the Dukes he values most, for equalities are so weigh'd, that curiosity in neither can make choice of either's moiety."*)

*a*Line. Column
5–10. α.

It was [not]*b* without forethought, and it is not without its due significance, that the triple division is stated here as already determin'd, and in all its particulars, previously to the Trial of Professions, as the relative rewards of which the Daughters were to be made to consider their several portions. The strange yet by no means unnatural, mixture of Selfishness, Sensibility, and Habit of Feeling derived from & fostered by the particular rank and usages of the Individual—the intense desire to be intensely beloved, selfish and yet characteristic of the Selfishness of a loving and kindly nature—a feeble Selfishness, self-supportless and Leaning for all pleasure on another's Breast—the selfish Craving after a sympathy with a prodigal Disinterestedness, contradicted by its own ostentation and the mode and nature of its Claims—the anxiety, the distrust, the jealousy, which more or less accompany all selfish Affections, and are among the surest contradictions of mere fondness from Love, and which originate Lear's eager wish to enjoy his Daughter's violent Professions, while the inveterate habits of Sovereignty

---

a Headed by C: "LEAR, 1ˢᵗ page of the Notes."
b Word supplied by the editor

325

convert the wish into claim and positive Right, and the incompliance with it into crime and treason—these facts, these passions, these moral verities, on which the whole Tragedy is founded, ⟨are⟩ all prepared for, and will to the retrospect be found implied in, these first 4 or 5 lines of the Play.—They let us know that the Trial is but a Trick—and that the grossness of the old King's rage is in part the natural result of a silly Trick suddenly and most unexpectedly baffled, and disappointed. ⟨*Here* notice the improbability and nursery-tale character of the tale./ prefixed as the *Porch* of the Edifice, not laid as its foundation—So Shylock's Lb of Flesh—item, an old popular Ballad[1]—with how great judgement what still remains is combatable⟩[2] This having been provided in the fewest words, in a natural reply to as natural [a]*c* question, which yet answers a secondary purpose*d* of attracting our attention to the difference or diversity between the characters of Cornwall and Albany, the premises and *Data*, as it were, having been thus afforded for our after-insight into the mind and mood of the Person, whose character, passions and sufferings are the main *subject-matter* of the Play—from Lear, the Persona PATIENS[3] of his Drama Shaksp. passes without delay to the second in importance, to the main Agent, and prime Mover—introduces Edmund to our acquaintance, and with the same felicity of Judgement, in the same easy, natural way prepares us for his character in the seemingly casual communication of its origin and occasion.—From the first drawing up of the Curtain he has stood before us in the united strength and beauty of earliest Manhood. Our eyes have been questioning him. Gifted thus with high advantages of *person*, and further endowed by Nature with a powerful intellect and a strong energetic Will, even without any concurrence of circumstances and accident, Pride will be the Sin that most easily besets him/. But he is the known, and acknowleged Son of the princely Gloster—Edmund therefore has both the germ ⟨of Pride⟩ and the conditions best fitted to evolve and ripen it into a predominant feeling. Yet hitherto no reason appears why it should be other than the not unusual pride of Person, Talent and Birth, a pride auxiliary if not akin to many Virtues, and the natural ally of honorable

---

c Word supplied by the editor

d Here C added a direction to himself: "(overleaf, backwards)", then at the top of the previous page: "LEAR Notes on 2nd page, continued from over-leaf"

[1] C was thinking of the ballad of *Gernutus the Jew of Venice*, first noted as a possible source for *The Merchant of Venice* in Joseph Warton *Observations on the Faerie Queene* (1754) I 128, and printed by Thomas Percy in his *Reliques* of *Ancient English Poetry* (1765) bk II no XI.

[2] Capable of being opposed; C's coinage, the first use recorded in *OED* being in 1824.

[3] I.e. the character who suffers.

[impulses.]*ᵉ* *ᶠ*But, alas! in his own presence his own father takes shame to himself for the frank avowal—that he is his Father—has blushed so often to acknowlege him that he is now braz'd to it.[4] He hears his Mother and the circumstances of his Birth spoken of with a most degrading and licentious Levity—described as a Wanton by her own Paramour, and the remembrance of the animal sting, the low criminal gratifications connected with her Wantonness and prostituted Beauty assigned as the reason, why "the Whoreson must be acknowleged."[5]— This and the consciousness of its notoriety—the gnawing conviction that every shew of respect is an effort of courtesy which recalls while it represses a contrary feeling—this is the ever-trickling flow of Wormwood and Gall into the wounds of Pride—the corrosive Virus which inoculates Pride with a venom not its own, with Envy, Hatred, a lust of that Power which in its blaze of radiance would hide the dark spots on his disk—pangs of shame, personally undeserved, and therefore felt as wrongs—and a blind ferment of vindictive workings towards the occasions and causes, especially towards a Brother whose stainless Birth and lawful Honors were the constant remembrancers of *his* debasement, and were ever in the way to prevent all chance of its being unknown or overlooked—&—forgotten. Add to this that with excellent Judgement, and provident for the claims of the moral sense, for that which relatively to the Drama is called Poetic Justice; and as the fittest means for reconciling the feelings of the Spectators to the horrors of Gloster's after Sufferings—at least, of rendering them somewhat less unendurable—(for I will not disguise my conviction, that in this one point the Tragic has been urged beyond the outermost Mark and Ne plus Ultra of the Dramatic)—Shakspeare has precluded all excuse and palliation of the guilt incurred by both the Parents of the base-born Edmund by Gloster's confession, that he was at the time a married man and already blest with a lawful Heir of his fortunes. The mournful alienation of brotherly Love occasioned by Primogeniture in noble families, or rather by the unnecessary distinctions engrafted thereon, and this in Children of the same Stock, is still almost proverbial on the continent—especially as I know from my own observation in the South of Europe, and appears to have been scarcely less common in our own Island, before the Revolution of 1688, if we may judge from the characters and sentiments so frequent in our elder Comedies—the younger Brother, for instance,

ᵉ Word supplied by the editor
ᶠ Headed by C: "LEAR: Notes on, p. 3ʳᵈ"

[4] *King Lear* I i 10–11.   [5] I i 24.

in B. and F's Scornful Lady, on one side, and the Oliver in Sh's own As you like it, on the other.[6] Need it be said how heavy an aggravation the stain of Bastardy must have been—were it only, that the younger Brother was liable to hear his own dishonor and his Mother's infamy related by his Father with an excusing shrug of the shoulders, and in a tone betwixt waggery and Shame.

By the circumstances here enumerated, as so many predisposing causes, Edmund's Character might well be deem'd already sufficiently explained and prepared for. But in this Tragedy the story or fable constrained Shakespear to introduce wickedness in an outrageous form, in Regan and Gonerill. He had read Nature too heedfully not to know, that Courage, Intellect, and strength of Character were the most impressive Forms of Power: and that to Power in itself, without reference to any moral end, an inevitable Admiration & Complacency appertains, whether it be displayed in the conquests of a Napoleon or Tamurlane, or in the foam and thunder of a Cataract. But in the display of such a character it was of the highest importance to prevent the guilt from passing into utter *monstrosity*—which again depends on the presence or absence of causes and temptations sufficient to *account* for the wickedness, without the necessity of recurring to a thorough fiendishness of nature for its origination—For such are the appointed relations of intellectual Power to Truth, and of Truth to Goodness, that it becomes both morally and poetic[g] unsafe to present what is admirable—what our nature compels to admire—in the mind, and what is most detestable in the Heart, as co-existing in the same individual without any apparent connection, or any modification of the one by the other. That Shakspeare has in one instance, that of Iago, approached to this, and that he has done it successfully, is perhaps the most astonishing proof of his genius, and the opulence of its resources.—But in the present Tragedy, in which he [was][h] compelled to present a Goneril & Regan, it was most carefully to be avoided—and therefore the one only conceivable addition to the inauspicious influences on the preformation of Edmund's character is given in the information, that all the kindly counteractions to the mischievous feelings of Shame that might have been derived from co-domestication with Edgard & their common father, had been cut off by an absence from home and a foreign education from Boyhood to the

---

[g] A slip for "poetically"
[h] Word supplied by the editor

[6] Young Loveless, the wild and spendthrift younger brother in Beaumont and Fletcher's play *The Scornful Lady*, is contrasted with Oliver, the harsh elder brother who drives Orlando from his house in *As You Like It*.

present time—and the prospect of its continuance, as if to preclude all risk of his interference with the Father's Views for the elder and legitimate Son. "He hath been out nine years, and away he shall again"—[7]

1 i 85–93, Sh (Ayscough) II 930 α 45: On Lear's question: "What can you say, to draw | A third more opulent than your sister's?" and Cordelia's reply: "Nothing, my lord"

P. 930. 1. 45, α.—Something of Disgust at the ruthless hypocrisy of her Sisters, some little faulty admixture of pride and sullenness in Cordelia's—Nothing—well contrived to lessen the glaring absurdity of Lear—but the surest plan that of forcing away the attention from the nursery-tale the moment, it has answered its purpose that of supplying the canvas to paint on. This done by Kent—and displaying Lear's *moral* incapability of resigning the Sovereign power in the very moment of disposing of it.

1 i 150ff, Sh (Ayscough) II 931 α: On Kent's rebuke of Lear: "And in thy best consideration check | This hideous rashness"

931. α.—KENT—the nearest to perfect goodness of all Sh's Characters—and yet the most *individualized/* his passionate affection & fidelity to LEAR acts on our feelings in Lear's own favor—Virtue itself seems to be in company with him—

1 ii 103–34, Sh (Ayscough) II 933 β 30–934 α 7: On Edmund's scorn for Gloucester's belief in portents; the passage begins: "These late eclipses in the sun and moon portend no good to us", and ends with the entrance of Edgar, "Pat he comes, like the catastrophe of the old comedy"

933. 30, β–934, 7 α.—Scorn and misanthropy often the anticipations and mouth-pieces of Wisdom in the detection of superstitions. Both individuals and Nations may be free from superstitions by being below it as well as by rising above it.

1 iii 11ff, Sh (Ayscough) II 934 β 20: On the first appearance of Goneril's steward, Oswald, and his line, referring to Lear: "He's coming, madam, I hear him"

934. 20, β.—The Steward (⚹ Kent)[8] the only character of utter unredeemable *Bas[e]ness*[i] in Shakespear—even in this the judgment & in-

---

[i] Letter supplied by the editor

[7] *King Lear* I i 32–3.   [8] I.e. as opposed to Kent.

vention. What could the willing Tool of Goneril be/ Not a vice but this of Baseness was left open for him—

I iv, Sh (Ayscough) II 935: On Lear at the court of Goneril

Old age, like Infancy, is itself a character—in Lear the natural imperfections increased by life-long habits of being promptly obeyed—. Any addition of Individuality unnecessary & painful—The relations of others to him of wondrous fidelity and frightful ingratitude, sufficiently distinguish him—thus he is the open and ample Play-Room of *Nature's* Passions.

I iv 73–4, Sh (Ayscough) II 935 β 15: On the first mention of the Fool: "Since my young lady's going into France, sir, the fool hath much pined away"

935. 15, β. The Fool no comic Buffoon to make the groundlings laugh, no forced condescension of Shakspeare's Genius to the taste of his Audiences. Accordingly, he is *prepared* for—brought into living connection with the pathos of the play, with the sufferings.—Since my young Lady's &c—

I iv 94, Sh (Ayscough) II 935 β 40: On the first entrance of the Fool

40, β.—THE FOOL as wonderful a creation as the Caliban—an inspired Idcot—

I iv 201ff, Sh (Ayscough) II 937: On Goneril picking a quarrel with her father

937

The Monster, Goneril, performs what is *necessary*—while the character of Albany renders a still more madning grievance possible, viz—Regan & Cornwall in perfect Sympathy of Monstrosity.—Not a sentiment, not an image, that can give pleasure on its own account, admitted—Pure Horror when they are introduced—& brought forward as little as possible.

I iv 261ff, Sh (Ayscough) II 937 β 5: On Lear's outburst against Goneril: "Albany. Pray, sir, be patient. Lear (to Goneril). Detested kite, thou liest . . ."

5, β.—The *one* general sentiment, as the main spring of the Feelings throughout, in Lear's first speeches—in the early stage the outward Object is the Pressure—not yet sufficiently familiarized with the anguish for the imagination to work upon it.

I iv 310ff, Sh *(Ayscough)* II *938* α *8: On Goneril's attempt to sway Albany: "Do you mark that, my lord?"*

938

8, α. The baffled endeavor of Goneril to act on the fears of Albany— and yet his passiveness, inertia—not convinced, yet afraid of looking into the thing. Such characters yield to those who will take the trouble of governing them or for them. Σιϱ T. B. + Σ.Γ.B.⁹—The influence of a Princess whose choice of him had so royalized his state, some little excuse for Albany.

I v 46–7, Sh *(Ayscough)* II *938* β *50: On Lear's "O, let me not be mad, not mad, sweet heaven! . . . I would not be mad!"*

50, β.—The mind's own anticipation of madness—

II i 67ff, Sh *(Ayscough)* II *939* β *31: On Edmund's report of what he claims Edgar said to him, and Gloucester's credulity in believing Edgar to be a "strange and fasten'd villain"*

31, β. *Thou unpossessing Bastard* = the secret poison in Edmund's heart—and then poor Gloster's

II i 84, Sh *(Ayscough)* II *939* β *50: On Gloucester's praise of Edmund as "Loyal and natural"*

50, β. Loyal and *natural* Boy, as if praising the *crime* of his Birth?—

II i 89–91, Sh *(Ayscough)* II *940* α *6: On Regan's receipt of the "strange news", fabricated by Edmund, that Edgar has fled: "Regan. If it be true, all vengeance comes too short, | Which can pursue the offender. How does my lord?" Gloucester. O, madam, my old heart is crack'd, is crack'd! | Regan. What, did my father's godson seek your life?"*

6, α—Incomparable!—What, did *my father's* &c—compared with the unfeminine violence of the "all vengeance comes too short"—& yet no reference to the guilt but to the accident &c

II ii 98ff, Sh *(Ayscough)* II *941* β *10: On Cornwall's generalisations about the craft often concealed by "bluntness" such as Kent's:*

⁹ The Greek transliterated is "Sir T. B. + S. G. B.", signifying Sir Thomas Bernard and Sir George Beaumont. The philanthropist Bernard was one of the founders of the RI, where C lectured in 1808; C's friendship with the artist and patron of the arts, Sir George Beaumont, began in 1803. Both had helped him and acted as patrons of his course of lectures at Willis's Rooms in 1812.

"He cannot flatter, he! | An honest mind, and plain,—he must speak truth: | An they will take it, so; if not, he's plain . . ."

10, β.—In thus placing these profound general Truths in such mouths, as Cornwalls, Edmunds, Iagos &c. Sh. at once gives them & yet shews how indefinite their application—

II iii, Sh *(Ayscough)* II *942: On Edgar's soliloquy transforming himself into Poor Tom*

Edgar's false Madness taking off part of the Shock from the true, as well as displaying the profound difference—Modern light-headedness—in Otway &c[10]

II iv 101–5, Sh *(Ayscough)* II *943* β *40: On Lear's arrival at the court of Regan, in hope of a better welcome, "the dear father | Would with his daughter speak"*

40, β

The strong interest now felt by Lear to try to find excuses for his Daughter—most pathetic.

II iv 139ff, Sh *(Ayscough)* II *944* α *30: On Regan's defence of Goneril's behaviour: "You less know how to value her desert, | Than she to scant her duty", leading to Regan's speech: "O, Sir, you are old; | Nature in you stands on the very verge | Of her confine: you should be rul'd, and led | By some discretion, that discerns your state | Better than you yourself. Therefore, I pray you, | That to our sister you do make return; | Say you have wrong'd her, sir."*

30, α. Nothing so heart-cutting as a cold unexpected defence &c of a cruelty complained of passionately—or so expressive of hard-heartedness—

And the horror of—O Sir, you are old—and then drawing from that universal object of reverence and indulgence the reason for—Say, you have wronged her.

All Lear's faults increase our pity—we refuse to know them otherwise

---

[10] C no doubt had in mind Belvedera's "Light-headedness" in *Venice Preserved*, as expressed notably in the line "Lutes, Laurels, Seas of Milk, and ships of Amber" (act v line 369). HCR records C as calling this "fanciful delirium" and saying, "The excess of folly is delirium, of imagination mania". *CRD* I 196, entry for 15 Nov 1810. This distinction is developed also in relation to imagination and fancy in *BL* ch 4 (*CC*) I 84–5, in which C cites the same line from Otway's play in contrast to *King Lear* III iv 63, "What! have his daughters brought him to this pass?"

than as means and aggravations of his Sufferings & his Daughters' ingratitude—

II iv 263–86, Sh (Ayscough) II 945 β 10–35: On Lear's response to Regan's question, "What need one?" "O, reason not the need! our basest beggars | Are in the poorest thing superfluous. | Allow not nature more than nature needs, | Man's life is cheap as beast's . . ."

10–35, β.—The tranquillity from the first *stun* permitting Lear to REASON—recite this—

III iv, Sh (Ayscough) II 948: On Lear's breakdown into madness in the storm, and his encounter with Edgar as Poor Tom and then with Gloucester

915[j] What a World's *Convention* of Agonies—surely, never was such a scene conceived before or since—Take it but as a picture, for the eye only, it is more terrific than any a Michael Angelo inspired by a Dante could have conceived, and which none but a Michael Angelo could have executed—Or let it have been uttered to the Blind, the howlings of ⟨convulsed⟩ Nature would seem concerted in the voice of conscious Humanity—

III v, Sh (Ayscough) II 949: On the short scene between Edmund and Cornwall that precedes Lear's "full madness" in III vi

Scene V.
    The scene ends with the first symptoms of positive derangement— here how judiciously interrupted in order to allow an interval for Lear in full madness to appear.

III vii 27ff, Sh (Ayscough) II 951 β 25: On the blinding of Gloucester, from the point where he is brought on, and Cornwall asks: "Who's there? The traitor?"

Scene VII
    25, β—What can I say of this scene? My reluctance to think Sh. wrong—and yet—[k]necessary to harmonise their cruelty to their father[l]

IV vi 80ff, Sh (Ayscough) II 957: On the scene in which the mad Lear encounters the blind Gloucester

The Thunder recurs, but still at a greater distance from our feelings

---

[j] An error for "948"; the number on the facing page is poorly printed and could be misread as "915"

[k-l] Added in pencil as an afterthought

IV vii, Sh *(Ayscough)* II *960: On Lear's awakening to find himself in the presence of Cordelia*

The affecting return of Lear to reason, and the mild pathos preparing the mind for the last sad yet sweet consolation of his Death—

REPORT IN THE *COURIER*
MONDAY, FEBRUARY 1819 (REPRINTED IN THE
MORNING POST 2 FEBRUARY)

MR. COLERIDGE'S LECTURES

We are happy to find that the success which has attended this Gentleman's Lectures upon Shakspeare has induced him to undertake another series upon nearly the same subject. Notwithstanding all that has been written upon Shakspeare, both by his countrymen and by foreign critics, we will venture to say, that no person, even though he had read all that has thus been written, could attend the Lectures of Mr. Coleridge, without acquiring new perceptions of the mighty genius whose productions he has so forcibly and so eloquently expounded. Each Lecture constitutes a fine philosophical analysis of those characters, passions, and principles which Shakspeare alone could delineate, express and develope. He appears to us, to have studied our great Bard with an intensity of the reasoning faculties, and at the same time with a fervor and sensibility of poetical feeling which rarely unite in the same person. He has opened to himself an entirely new path. Great names undoubtedly appear upon the list of Shakspeare's illustrators; but with few exceptions, they have confined themselves to verbal and emendatory criticism; and even the exceptions do not array themselves against Mr. Coleridge's claims to perfect originality. In the present day he leaves competition far behind him. He has none of the glib nonsense of Mr. Hazlitt; no tinkling sentences of pretty phraseology, where big words rumble along without meaning, till the reader stares and wonders what it can be that is so utterly unintelligible. Mr. Hazlitt evidently never read a play of Shakspeare through, and the style in which he criticises him, always reminds us of Bradbury, the clown, dancing upon stilts, where a great clatter, ungainly labour, and violent distortion, are substituted for agility, ease, and elegance.[11]

---

[11] Alluding perhaps both to Hazlitt's *Characters of Shakespear's Plays* (1817, 2nd ed 1818) and to his lectures at the Surrey Institution in 1818. The criticism is unjust, but reflects the radical difference between his and C's method. Robert Bradbury (1777–1831), an acrobatic clown who did feats on high ladders: "He was a tumbling Clown rather than a humorous one, and would perform many

The subject with which Mr. Coleridge closed his first series of Lectures upon Shakespeare, last Thursday, was *Lear*; and we appeal to a numerous and delighted auditory for the impression which he produced. We shall not attempt to follow him through his admirable illustrations of that beautiful and most affecting drama. The manner in which he explained the motives of *Edmund's* baseness towards his brother, was at once original and profound; while the moral truths which he deduced from the opening lines of his first soliloquy, "Thou nature art my Goddess", &c.[12] supplied a practical test applicable to many "bold fac'd villains" of the present day. Nor were we less pleased with his analysis of the *Fool's* Character, which he considered as inferior, in all the qualities of invention, only to *Caliban*. His wild and incoherent language, still "babbling the food of anguish to the mind of *Lear*" (to use the happy expression of Mr. Coleridge himself), his half mysterious, yet always shrewd, rhapsodics, and his fond attachment to his master, were skilfully displayed. The same praise may be bestowed upon his touching elucidations of *Lear's* character. But we cannot better express our opinion of Mr. Coleridge's Lectures upon Shakspeare, than by saying, which we do with great sincerity, that they were every way worthy of their subject. We only regret, that they should be given to the world through so fleeting and transitory a medium, as extemporaneous delivery. The mind of the auditor feels that it carries away too little of what delighted him, while he listened, and wishes, but in vain, that he could convey to others what he remembers with a consciousness of pleasure, unfortunately as vague as it is intense.

---

wonderful and dangerous feats." Charles Dickens *Memoirs of Joseph Grimaldi* (1st pub 1838; 1969) 181. Cf Horace and James Smith *Rejected Addresses: Playhouse Musings* (a parody of C's *Religious Musings*):

Among the freaks that modern fashion sanctions,
It grieves me most to see live animals
Brought on the stage. Grimaldi has his rabbit,
Laurent his cat, and Bradbury his pig.

[12] *King Lear* I ii 1.

GENERAL COMMENT

C.R. LESLIE IN *AUTOBIOGRAPHICAL RECOLLECTIONS* EDITED BY TOM TAYLOR (BOSTON 1860) 29–32

Leslie attended three lectures given by C in Clifton in 1813 and may have made C's acquaintance then. C's letters show that they were on familiar terms in 1818–19, when Leslie made sketches of him, one of which was included in the *New Monthly Magazine* on 1 Apr 1819 (see *CL* IV 878, 893, and 927). In his memoirs Leslie referred to C's sole extant letter to him of this period, dated 1 Mar 1819, as marking the period of the late course of lectures he attended, but his comments, referring mainly to *Hamlet* and *Othello*, almost certainly relate to the 1818–19 course, which ran from 17 Dec 1818 to 28 Jan 1819.

I had frequent opportunities of seeing and hearing Coleridge. He delivered a course of lectures on Shakespeare, to which he gave me tickets, but I was sorry to see his London audiences much smaller than those at Bristol. . . . It is not the lot of any one, twice in his life, to meet with so extraordinary a man. I now read over and over again what his nephew has recorded of his conversation, and I can vouch for the exactness with which his manner is preserved in those precious little volumes. The remarks there given on "Othello" and "Hamlet", formed parts of his lectures on Shakespeare:—

"The clue to the inconsistencies of *Hamlet* might be found", he said, "in the undue predominance of the inner over the outer man."

Coleridge did not consider that the *passion* of jealousy was the subject of the tragedy of "Othello", but that Shakespeare had displayed it fully and truly in the "Winter's Tale". "*Othello* is anything but jealous in his nature, and made so only by the machinations of *Iago*, while *Leontes* requires no prompter but his own suspicious mind." He observed, that the difficulty was great in imagining an expression adequate to the feelings of *Othello* when he first sees *Iago* after having discovered his villany, and he thought it a master stroke of Shakespeare to surmount it as he has done:

> "I look down towards his feet; but that's a fable.
> If that thou be'st a devil I cannot kill thee."[1]

[1] *Othello* v ii 268–7.

He pointed out the great dramatic beauty of the opening scenes of "Hamlet", and the admirable skill with which the ghost is introduced. Although *Marcellus* and *Bernardo* are expecting its appearance, and *Horatio* has joined their watch with the same expectation, and they are even talking about it, its entrance is startling, and every succeeding appearance alike thrilling. In reading passages from the first scenes of the play, Coleridge noticed Shakespeare's respect even for the *superstitions* connected with the mysteries of Christianity, a beautiful instance of which occurs in the lines,

> "It faded on the crowing of the cock . . .
>
> . . . .
>
> So hallow'd and so gracious is the time."

He said the reply of *Horatio* was, he believed, exactly that which Shakespeare himself would have made:

> "So have I heard, and do in part believe it."[2]

He could never read, he said, any of those scenes in which children are introduced, "without laying the book down and *loving Shakespeare over again.*" He said the anachronisms noticed by Shakespeare's critics would not, perhaps, have given the poet himself any great uneasiness had they been pointed out to him, as possibly they were; and this may have given rise to that curious intentional anachronism in the third act of "Lear", where the fool, after fourteen lines of a burlesque prediction, says:

> "This prophecy Merlin shall make, for *I live before his time.*"[3]

I wish I could recollect what Coleridge said of the character of *Falstaff*. I only remember, with certainty, his opinion that Shakespeare, in the "Merry Wives of Windsor", had departed from the original conception of the character, and that the *Falstaff* in that play, though very amusing, was much below the *Falstaff* of the two parts of "Henry the Fourth." . . .

A most interesting portion of Coleridge's lectures consisted in his pointing out the truth and refinement of Shakespeare's women, beyond those of all other dramatists; and how purified his imagination was from every thing gross, in comparison with those of his contemporaries.

Coleridge's lectures were, unfortunately, extemporaneous. He now and then took up scraps of paper on which he had noted the leading points of his subject, and he had books about him for quotation. On turning to one of these (a work of his own), he said, "As this is a secret

---

[2] *Hamlet* I i 157–65. [3] *King Lear* III ii 95.

which I confided to the public a year or two ago, and which, to do the public justice, has been very faithfully kept, I may be permitted to read you a passage from it.''[4]

His voice was deep and musical, and his words followed each other in an unbroken flow, yet free from monotony. There was indeed a peculiar charm in his utterance. His pronunciation was remarkably correct: in some respects pedantically so. He gave the full sound of the *l* in *talk*, and *should* and *would*.

Sir James Mackintosh attended the whole course of lectures, and listened with the greatest interest. . . .

[4] Perhaps *BL* (1817). C seems to have quoted from *BL* at the end of Lect 1 of the 1818–19 series (see n 37) and may well have done so again in Lect 6.

1819
LECTURES ON SHAKESPEARE,
MILTON, DANTE, SPENSER,
ARIOSTO, AND CERVANTES
(ALTERNATING WITH
PHILOSOPHICAL LECTURES)
(CROWN AND ANCHOR,
STRAND)

INTRODUCTION

The advertisements Coleridge placed in five newspapers on 20 and 21 January 1819 for Lecture 5 of the 1818–19 series all announced both that lecture, on *Othello*, and the last one of the course, on *King Lear*.[1] Two of these advertisements, those in the *Courier* and the *New Times*, continued with an announcement of a new course:

But on Thursday, February 4th, Mr. COLERIDGE enters on a fresh course, similar in kind to the present, the subjects of which will be announced; and, at the particular request of numerous friends and auditors, he will commence with a Second Lecture on *Hamlet*, in which after a brief recapitulation of the substance of the former, the Criticism will be continued through the Third, Fourth, and Last Acts.

This is the first indication of Coleridge's plan to follow up the 1818–19 course on Shakespeare with another literary series, and it may well be that he had not decided at this time what the subjects of the lectures, other than the first, should be. On 26 January he wrote to Mudford of the *Courier*, asking him to mention the lecture on *King Lear*, to be given on 28 January, because it would "be of important service to my fresh Cause",[2] and the *Courier* duly obliged him on 1 February—with a congratulatory notice beginning, "We are happy to find that the success which has attended this Gentleman's Lectures upon Shakspeare has induced him to undertake another series upon nearly the same subject."[3] Meanwhile the advertisements for Lecture 6 in the *Courier* on 27 January, and in *The Times*, the *Morning Chronicle*, the *New Times*, and the *Morning Post* on 28 January gave further details:

On the Thursday following, 4th of February, Mr. COLERIDGE proposes to commence a fresh Course, similar in kind to the present, consisting of seven Lectures; three of which will be on SHAKSPEARE, and the remaining four on MILTON; DANTE and PETRARCH; SPENCER and ARIOSTO; and Don QUIXOTE, with the life, character, and genius of CERVANTES. Single Tickets for the Course, £1.5s.; and double Tickets, £2. May be procured at the Lecture Room on Monday and Thursday evenings, and at the Booksellers' as before.

[1] See Lect 5 of the 1818–19 series (headnote).

[2] *CL* IV 915.

[3] See Lect 6 of the 1818–19 series (report in the *Courier*).

This continued with a further announcement of the second lecture on *Hamlet*, as in the advertisement of 20 and 21 January, cited above. About the time he was to give his lecture on *King Lear*, Coleridge fell ill, and, according to a letter written to Southey on 31 January, it was at the "medical commands" of his doctors, Gillman and Green, that he "announced a week's intermission".[4] Further advertisements, in the *Courier, The Times*, the *Morning Chronicle*, and *New Times* on 1 February, and in the *Morning Post* on 2 February, informed subscribers and friends that "the LECTURES are intermitted during the present Week, previously to the commencement of a fresh Critical Course". The new course, now to begin on Thursday, 11 February, would thus run for the same seven weeks as the second half of the philosophical course Coleridge was giving on Mondays. The day before the first lecture, 10 February, the *Courier* printed the following general announcement (with advertisements with minor variants in *The Times*, the *Morning Chronicle*, and the *New Times* on the same day):

MR. COLERIDGE'S LECTURES.—Tomorrow Evening, Eight o'Clock, Crown and Anchor, Strand, Mr. COLERIDGE will commence a new Course of Critical Dissertations, and, at the particular request of his Friends, with a Second Lecture on *Hamlet*, in which, after a brief recapitulation of the sum and substance of the former, the criticism will be continued through the third, fourth, and last acts. On the Thursday following, February 18th, the Tragedy of *Romeo and Juliet*, with the Characters of *Antony* and *Cleopatra*. On February 25th, the Growth of SHAKSPEARE'S Genius traced through *all* his Plays; the probable order, in which they were composed, determined; and a compressed Character of each Play given (those excepted which have been already lectured on). The four Lectures following will have for their several subjects, MILTON; DANTE and PETRARCH; SPENSER, and his relation to CHAUCER and ARIOSTO; and lastly, DON QUIXOTE, and the genius of CERVANTES.—Admission to each single lecture, 5s.; Tickets for the Course, single 1*l*,5s., and double 2*l*.; may be procured at the Lecture Room; or at the Booksellers, as already advertised.

Each individual lecture was separately advertised, but they do not seem to have been well attended. Some time after the first lecture, Coleridge lamented that the week's intermission had been "unfortunate", and on 25 February, before his final Shakespeare lecture, he wrote to Mudford to say "scanty are my audiences!"[5] C. R. Leslie recorded in his memoirs his attendance at these lectures, or those of the 1818–19 course, when he was "sorry to see his London audiences much smaller than those at Bristol",[6] and Mrs Coleridge had reason to

[4] *CL* IV 916.
[5] *CL* IV 921.
[6] *Autobiographical Recollections* 29. Leslie says that he attended "a course of lectures on Shakespeare" and cites

C's letter to him of 1 Mar 1819 (*CL* IV 927) as marking the date of the course. It is possible that he attended both the literary courses that ran from Dec 1818 to Mar 1819.

think the course was unprofitable.[7] For the first two lectures, mainly on *Hamlet* and *Romeo and Juliet*, Coleridge continued to use his interleaved copy of the Ayscough edition of Shakespeare, taking it with him into the lecture-room. This edition omitted *Pericles*, and for Lecture 3 he wrote out notes on the chronology of Shakespeare's plays which show that he had not only the Ayscough edition, but Volume XII of another edition, in twelve volumes, published by Vernor, Hood and Sharpe and Taylor and Hessey in 1809.[8]

The last four lectures also contain new material, and for each of them Coleridge prepared elaborate notes. The first, on Milton, was announced in the *New Times* in an unusually long paragraph, which may have been inserted in the hope of increasing his audiences. The notes show that, as in the Shakespeare lectures, he took a text with him into the lecture-room and developed critical points from it. In Lecture 5, on Dante and his age, he paid a compliment to Henry Hallam, whose *View of the State of Europe During the Middle Ages*, published in June 1818, he used for background material. In Lecture 6, on Spenser, he cited comparisons from *Antar, a Bedoueen Romance*, published in 1819, so that right to the end he was rethinking his lectures and bringing to bear on them his current reading. As for his 1818 lectures on European literature, he also resorted to F. Schlegel's *Geschichte der alten und neuen Litteratur*, but largely to take issue with some of his points.[9] He also referred again to Henry Francis Cary's translation of Dante, and it seems that Cary was among his audiences for the series.[10]

Even if this course was not very rewarding in financial terms, it cannot have harmed Coleridge's reputation as a lecturer, for he was approached in February by John Britton about a possible course of literary lectures to be given at the Russell Institution in Great Coram Street on the pattern of those given at the Surrey Institution in 1812–13.[11] A long letter survives in which he expresses his willingness to

---

[7] *Minnow* 73. In Apr 1819 she wrote, "I am afraid his lectures were not very profitable, as he has not made me any remittance in consequence". C repeated his complaint about "scanty audiences" in a letter of 1 Mar: *CL* IV 927.

[8] See below, Lect 3 (at n 3).

[9] See e.g. Lect 4 (n 11) and Lect 5 (nn 1, 6, 7, 12, 14).

[10] R. W. King *The Translator of Dante. The Life, Work and Friendships of Henry Francis Cary* (1925) 115 and n records a series of entries in Cary's account-book marking payment for "Mr. Coleridge's

lectures", beginning in Dec 1818 and ending in Mar 1819.

[11] The Russell Literary and Scientific Institution, founded in 1808, was established in a building bought at the time but erected earlier as a speculation and intended for balls and assemblies. It contained a library and reading-rooms and was similar in its aims and activities to the other institutions founded in London at the beginning of the nineteenth century. It is briefly described in E. Walford *Old and New London* (6 vols 1891) IV 574.

give a "course of six or eight lectures", on subjects chosen from "English, Italian, or German literature" or the fine arts; his more detailed suggestions, which follow, cover most of the subjects of his previous courses on English literature:

I have learnt, what I might easily have anticipated, that the *Lear* of Shakspeare is not a good subject for a whole lecture, in *my* style; with that exception, any of the plays of Shakspeare, the *Twelfth Night*, or the *Tempest*, the *Henry IVth's, Richard II*, with the character of *Richard III., Romeo and Juliet, Antony and Cleopatra, Macbeth, Hamlet, Othello*, &c. &c.; the *Paradise Lost*, with the character of Milton, (which I appear to remember was the favourite lecture of those given at the Surrey Institution); Spencer, Dante, old English ballads and metrical romances; on the uses of poetry in the process of the mind's education, especially on the supernatural; the comparison of English poetry from Chaucer to Milton, with the period from Dryden (inclusive) to the Wartons:—of all these, and of any other congenerous subjects, the committee might take their choice . . .[12]

The comment on *King Lear* is interesting, as suggesting a dissatisfaction with his only lecture on this play, Lecture 6 of the 1818–19 series, but the rest reads like a résumé of previous courses. It seems probable that Britton asked Coleridge if he had by him the lectures he had given at the Surrey Institution, for the first part of Coleridge's letter of reply is devoted largely to explaining why he could not repeat those lectures and to a description of his method of preparing them. A passage of some importance, it is worth quoting in full:

The fact is this: during a course of lectures, I faithfully employ *all* the intervening days in collecting and digesting the materials, whether I have or have not lectured on the same subject before, making no difference. The day of the lecture, till the hour of commencement, I devote to the consideration, what of the mass before me is best fitted to answer the purposes of a lecture—*i.e.* to keep the audience awake and interested during the delivery, and to leave a *sting* behind—*i.e.* a disposition to study the subject anew, under the light of a new principle. Several times, however, partly from apprehension respecting my health and animal spirits, partly from the wish to possess copies that might afterwards be marketable among the publishers, I have previously written the lecture; but before I had proceeded twenty minutes, I have been obliged to push the MSS. away, and give the subject a new turn. Nay, this was so notorious, that many of my auditors used to threaten me, when they saw any number of written papers on my desk, to steal them away; declaring they never felt so secure of a good lecture as when they perceived that I had not a single scrap of writing before me. I take far, far more pains than would go to the set composition of a lecture, both by varied reading and by meditation; but for the words, illustrations, &c. I know almost as little as any one of my audience (*i.e.* those of

<hr/>

[12] This letter, from which two long quotations are cited, may be found in *CL*   IV 923–5 and *Sh C* II 261–4 (324–7).

any thing like the same education with myself) what they will be five minutes before the lecture begins. Such is *my way*, for such is *my nature*; and in attempting any other, I should only torment myself in order to disappoint my auditors—torment myself during the delivery, I mean; for in all other respects it would be a much shorter and easier task to deliver them from writing.

This account is informative, but it should not be taken as an accurate representation of Coleridge's normal habits. The notes he prepared for the 1819 lectures show what by this time seems to have been his characteristic procedure, namely a careful setting out in some detail of the introductory part of each lecture, with the rest developed from sketchy notes or marginalia that provided references to particular points in the text he wished to discuss. So he certainly listed the illustrations he intended to use, and although he liked to let it be known that he lectured extempore, it seems rather that, in common with many other good lecturers, he relied upon a mixture of prepared material that he could, if necessary, read and the impromptu development of arguments as he went along. There is no evidence that he did give a course at the Russell Institution or that negotiations proceeded any further. Perhaps this is as well, for the notes relating to the last lecture of the philosophical course on 29 March 1819 are headed with a cry of weariness, "O pray Heaven, that it may indeed be the Last".[13] He had already completed the literary course on 25 March and, as far is known, after this he offered no further courses of lectures.

[13] *CN* III 4504.

LECTURE 1

DATE AND PLACE OF DELIVERY. Thursday, 11 February 1819, at the Crown and Anchor Tavern, Strand, London.

SUBJECT. *Hamlet.*

ANNOUNCEMENTS AND ADVERTISEMENTS. The general advertisements for the course, described above (Introduction to the 1819 series, first paragraph), promised a discussion of the last three acts of *Hamlet. Courier* Wed, 10 Feb (announcement): "MR. COLERIDGE'S LECTURES.—Tomorrow Evening, Eight o'Clock, Crown and Anchor, Strand, Mr. COLERIDGE will commence a new Course of Critical Dissertations, and, at the particular request of his Friends, with a Second Lecture on Hamlet, in which, after a brief recapitulation of the sum and substance of the former, the criticism will be continued through the third, fourth, and last acts . . .". (This continues with a description of the rest of the course.) *The Times, M Chron*, and *New Times* Wed, 10 Feb (advertisements): as in the *Courier*, except that the heading, "MR. COLERIDGE'S LECTURES", was omitted in the *M Chron*.

TEXT. Once again C seems to have lectured from his interleaved copy of *Sh* (Ayscough), with the help of the annotations he had made on the interleaves. These notes, on Acts III to V of *Hamlet*, were printed by HNC in *LR* I 226–34, and Raysor included them in *Sh C* I 26–34 (29–37); following HNC, he intermingled them among notes from other sources, without indicating where or when C wrote them. The text printed below is based on a fresh transcript of C's notes. A few notes on metre are omitted, also lexical notes, which are unlikely to have been of use for a lecture.

REPORTS. No reports of this lecture have been found.

BACKGROUND AND CIRCUMSTANCES. The advertisements imply that C did not proceed beyond Act II of *Hamlet* in the lecture he gave on 7 Jan. For that lecture he relied for guidance upon the annotations he made on the text of it in his copy of *Sh* (Ayscough). The play is unusually heavily annotated, and twenty-eight of these annotations, all brief, relate to Acts III, IV, and V. When lecturing on the tragedies in his previous course, however, C provided himself with a long introductory note on each of the plays, and there is nothing of this sort to start off his follow-up lecture on *Hamlet*. It is likely, then, that after summarising what he had said earlier, he spoke impromptu, from the text of the play, developing points also from some of his annotations. His illness at the end of the previous course led him to postpone the opening of his new course from 4 to 11 Feb, and the week's break he thought responsible for a drop in attendance at this lecture (*CL* IV 921). He went on to complain of ill-health and despondency as barely enabling him to give his lectures "respectably", and the sense of failure registered here shows his disappointment with his performance on this occasion. Nothing else is known about this lecture.

LECTURE 1

RECORDS OF THE LECTURE

COLERIDGE'S NOTES
FROM HIS ANNOTATIONS ON THE INTERLEAVES
OF *SH* (AYSCOUGH) II 1017–36

III i 55–87, Sh (Ayscough) II 1017 α 30: On Hamlet's soliloquy, "To be or not to be"

30, α.
Of such universal interest, and yet to which of all Shakspear's other characters could it have *appropriately* [been]^a given but to Hamlet? For Jaques it would have been too deep: for Iago too habitual a communion with the *Heart*, that belongs or ought to belong, to all mankind.

III i 102ff, Sh (Ayscough) II 1017 β 27: On Hamlet's questioning of Ophelia: "Ha, ha! are you honest?"

27, β.—Hamlet here discovers that he is watched, and Ophelia a Decoy.—Even this in a mood so anxious and irritable accounts for a certain harshness in him; and yet a wild upworking[1] of Love sporting with opposites with a wilful self-tormenting Irony is perceptible throughout—ex. gr. I *did* love you[2]—& the faults of the sex from which Oph. is so charact. free, that the freedom therefrom constitutes her Character.—Here again Shakespear's Charm of constituting female character by absences of characters, = outjuttings—[3]

---

^a Word supplied by the editor

[1] C's coinage; this passage is cited in *OED* under "Up-", *prefix*, 7.(b).
[2] Hamlet says, "I did love you once", III i 114.
[3] C seems to mean absence of outjuttings, or projections, as it were to relieve and define a smooth surface. This passage helps to explain his comments elsewhere on the absence of character in the women in Shakespeare's plays, as in Lect 6 of the 1813 series (at n 2) and in Lect 1 of the 1818–19 series (at n 16).

III i 128–49, Sh *(Ayscough)* II *1018* α *1–25: On Hamlet's harshness to Ophelia, from "Go thy ways to a nunnery. Where's your father?" to "Those that are married already (all but one) shall live, the rest shall keep as they are. To a nunnery, go."*

1–25, α. The dallying with the inward purpose that of one who had not brought his mind to the steady acting point—would fain *sting* the Uncle's Mind, but—to stab the body!—

III i 150ff, Sh *(Ayscough)* II *1018: On Ophelia's soliloquy, "O what a noble mind is here o'erthrown!"*

The soliloquy of Ophelia is the perfection of Love/ so exquisitely unselfish.

III ii, Sh *(Ayscough)* II *1018: On Hamlet's advice to the Players*

Scene II. one and among the happiest of Shaks' power of diversifying the scene while he is carrying on the plot.

III ii 98ff, Sh *(Ayscough)* II *1019* β*: On Hamlet's retort when Polonius says he once acted the part of Caesar and was killed by Brutus in the Capitol: "It was a brute part of him, to kill so capital a calf there."*

β. in any direct form to have kept Hamlet's Love for Ophelia before the Audience, would have made a breach in the unity of the interest; but yet to the thoughtful reader it is suggested by *his* spite to poor Polonius whom he cannot let rest.

III ii 155ff, Sh *(Ayscough)* II *1020: On the dialogue of the play within the play*

As in the first interview with the Players by *epic* verse, so here by rhyme.[4]

III ii 387ff, Sh *(Ayscough)* II *1022* β *10: On Hamlet's soliloquy at the end of the scene, " 'Tis now the very witching time of night"*

10, β. The Utmost Hamlet arrives to, is a disposition, a mood, to do *something*. *What* is still left undecided—while every word, he utters, tends to betray his disguise.

III ii 390ff, Sh *(Ayscough)* II *1022: On Hamlet's lines: "Now could I drink hot blood, | And do such bitter business as the day | Would quake*

---

[4] See Lect 3 of the 1818–19 series (paragraph containing n 25). C's point is that the rhyme of the dialogue in the play within the play gives greater reality to the rest of the scene.

to look on. Soft, now to my mother.'' (Ayscough in line 2 has ''such business as the bitter day''.)

*ᵇ*The perfect equal to any call of the moment in Hamlet, let it only not be for a Future*ᶜ*

III iii 11ff, Sh (Ayscough) II 1022 β 40: On Rosencrantz's speech about protecting the life of the King: ''The single and peculiar life is bound | With all the strength and armour of the kind | To keep itself from noyance, but much more | That spirit upon whose weal depends and rests | The lives of many . . .''

40, β.—To bring all possible good out of evil, yet how characteristically is this just sentiment placed in the mouth of Rosencrantz.

III iii 27–9, Sh (Ayscough) II 1023: On Polonius volunteering to hide behind the arras and listen to Hamlet's conversation with his mother

Polonius's volunteer obtrusion of himself into this business while it is appropriate to his character still letching[5] after former importance removes all likelihood that Hamlet should suspect his presence, and prevents us from making his death injure Hamlet in our opinion.

III iii 36–72, Sh (Ayscough) II 1023: On Claudius's soliloquy, ''O, my offence is rank . . .''

The King's Speech well marks the difference between Crime and Guilt of Habit. The Conscience is still admitted to Audience. Nay, even as an audible soliloquy, it is far less improbable than is supposed by such as have watched men only in the beaten road of their feelings.—But it deserves to be dwelt on, that final ''All may be well''!—a degree of Merit attributed by the self-flattering Soul to its own struggle, tho' baffled—and to the indefinite half-promise, half-command, to persevere in religious Duties. The divine Medium of the Christian Doctrine of Expiation—in the—Not what you have done, but what you *are*, must determine—Metanoia[6]

III iii 75–98, Sh (Ayscough) II 1023 α 55: On Hamlet's reluctance to kill Claudius at prayer: ''That would be scann'd | A villain kills my father, and for that | I, his sole son, do this same villain send | To heaven . . .''

ᵇ⁻ᶜ Written in pencil below the next note

[5] ''Lechering'' was the usual form, according to *OED*.

[6] Greek for ''repentance'' or ''change of heart''. The contrast is between works and faith, as exemplified in St Paul's injunction against ''laying again the foundation of repentance from dead works''; see Heb 6.1, 6.

55, α. Dr Johnson's mistaking of the marks of reluctance & procrastination for impetuous, horror-striking fiendishness![7] Of such importance is it to understand the *Germ* of a character. But the interval taken up by Hamlet's Speech is truly aweful! And then—''My words fly up''— O what a lesson concerning the essential difference between Wishing & Willing: and the folly of all motive-mongering, while the individual Self remains.

III iv 27–34, Sh *(Ayscough)* II *1024: On Gertrude's response to the death of Polonius:* "Queen. *O, what a rash and bloody deed is this!* Hamlet. *A bloody deed;—almost as bad, good mother,* | *As kill a king and marry with his brother.* Queen. *As kill a king?*"

I confess, that Sh. has left the character of the Queen in an unpleasant perplexity—was she or was she not conscious of the fratricide.

IV ii 14–23, Sh *(Ayscough)* II *1026: On Hamlet calling Rosencrantz a sponge "that soaks up the king's countenance, his rewards, his authorities"*

Hamlet's madness is made to consist in the full utterance of all the thoughts that had past thro' his mind before—in telling home truths.—

IV v 20ff, Sh *(Ayscough)* II *1028: On Ophelia's appearance, mad, and singing "How should I your true love know?"*

The conjunction here of those two thoughts that had never subsisted in disjunction, the Love for Hamlet and her filial Love, and the guile[le]ss^d floating on the surface of her pure imagination of the cautions so lately expressed and the fears not too delicately avowed by her Father and Brother concerning the danger to which her honor lay exposed—. Thought and Affliction, Passion, Murder itself She runs to favor and to prettiness.[8]—This play of association is sweetly instanced in the close. ''My brother shall know of it: and I thank you for your good COUNSEL.''[9]

IV v 124, Sh *(Ayscough)* II *1029* β *25: On Claudius's "There's such divinity doth hedge a king . . ."*

---

^d Letters supplied by the editor

[7] Dr Johnson said, "This speech, in which Hamlet, represented as a virtuous character, is not content with taking blood for blood, but contrives damnation for the man that he would punish, is too horrible to be read or to be uttered." *Works* VIII 990.

[8] Laertes' comment, IV v 188–9, substituting "Murder" for "hell".

[9] IV v 70–1, just before Ophelia's first exit with the words "Good night, ladies" etc.

25, β. Proof, as indeed all else is, that Sh. never intended us to see the King with Hamlet's Eyes—tho' I suspect, the Managers have long done so.

IV v 155ff, Sh (Ayscough) II 1030: On Laertes' response to the madness of Ophelia: "O heat, dry up my brains . . ."

Shakspeare evidently wishes as much as possible to spare the character of Laertes, to break the extreme turpitude of his consent to become an Agent and Accomplice of the King's treacherous[e]—and to this end works the re-introduction of Ophelia—

IV vi 13ff, Sh (Ayscough) II 1031: On the capture of Hamlet by pirates, as described in his letter

Almost the only play of Shakespeare, in which mere accidents independent of all will form an essential part of the plot; but here how judiciously in keeping with the Character of the over-meditative Hamlet ever at last determined by accident or by a fit of passion—

IV vii 82ff, Sh (Ayscough) II 1032 α 15: On Claudius praising Laertes for his skill in fencing on the basis of a "report" by "a gentleman of Normandy", and so prompting him to match with Hamlet

15, α

First awakens Laertes' Vanity by the praises of the Report[f]—then gratifies it by the report itself—and then. "Did Hamlet so envenom with his envy.—"

IV vii, Sh (Ayscough) II 1033: On the end of Act IV, the report of the death of Ophelia

And that Laertes might be excused in some degree for not cooling the Act concluding with the affecting Death of Ophelia—who does not[g] seem like a little projection of Land into a Lake or Stream, covered with spring-flowers lay quietly reflected in the great waters but at length undermined and loosened becomes a floating Faery Isle, and after a brief vagrancy sinks almost without an eddy.

V i, Sh (Ayscough) II 1033: On the dialogue between Hamlet and the Clowns, or gravediggers

---

[e] So in ms; C left the sentence incomplete
[f] A slip for "Reporter"?
[g] A slip for "now"?

The contrast between the Clowns and Hamlet as two extremes—the mockery of Logic, the traditional wit valued like truth for its Antiquity, and treasured up like a Tune for use—

v i 179–91, Sh *(Ayscough)* II *1035: On the First Clown's description of Yorick: "A pestilence on him for a mad rogue! he pour'd a flagon of Rhenish on my head once . . ."*

Shall I tell the story of the fierce Methodist & my Answer?[10]

v i 238ff, Sh *(Ayscough)* II *1036: On the burial of Ophelia, and Hamlet's "towering passion" in leaping into the grave, continuing with notes on Hamlet's encounters with Horatio and then Osric in* v ii

Sh. seems to mean *all Hamlet's* character to be brought together before his final disappearance from the scene—his med. excess[11] in the grave-digging—his yielding to passion—his Love for Ophelia blazing out—his tendency to generalize on all occasions in the dialogue with Horatio—his fine gentlemanly manners with Osrick—

v ii 219, Sh *(Ayscough)* II *1039: On Hamlet's "We defy augury"*

and his & Shakespear's fondness for presentiment—O my prophetic Soul[12]—and his "Most generous & free from all contriving"[13] in his Fencing-Duel—and all at last done by shock[h] & accident at the conclusion.

---

[h] Doubtful reading

[10] C was perhaps recalling the story he told in *BL* ch 10 about an evening spent with a minister and his friends when canvassing for *The Watchman.* C arrived dizzy after smoking, and to relieve his embarrassment someone asked him if he had seen that day's newspaper: "Sir! (I replied, rubbing my eyes,) 'I am far from convinced, that a christian is permitted to read either newspapers or any other works of merely political and temporary interest.' This remark so ludicrously inapposite to, or rather, incongruous with, the purpose, for which I was known to have visited Birmingham, and to assist me in which they were all then met, produced an involuntary and general burst of laughter . . .". *BL (CC)* I 183. This anecdote follows immediately on another relating to a "rigid Calvinist" (I 180). C was probably illustrating the effect of comic incongruity in the grave-digger's remarks.

[11] Presumably excess of meditation.

[12] I v 40.

[13] Claudius describes Hamlet when plotting the fencing-match with Laertes, IV vii 135.

LECTURE 2

DATE AND PLACE OF DELIVERY. Thursday, 18 February 1819, at the Crown and Anchor Tavern, Strand, London.

SUBJECT. *Romeo and Juliet* and *Antony and Cleopatra*.

ANNOUNCEMENTS AND ADVERTISEMENTS. The subjects of all the lectures for this course were announced in the advertisements for Lect 1. *Courier*, Wed, 17 Feb (announcement): "MR COLERIDGE'S LECTURES.—To-morrow evening, Crown and Anchor, Strand. Mr. COLERIDGE's Lecture on the Tragedy of *Romeo and Juliet*, with the characters of *Antony* and *Cleopatra*: or, SHAKESPEARE'S Twin Portraits of The Passion of Love, as displayed in Youth and in Maturity.—Admission, Five Shillings." *The Times* Thurs, 18 Feb (advertisement): as in the *Courier*, with the alteration to "THIS EVENING". *New Times* Thurs, 18 Feb (advertisement): as in the *Courier*, with the alteration to "THIS EVENING" and the addition of an advertisement for Lect 3. *M Chron* Thurs, 18 Feb (advertisement): "THIS EVENING, Eight o'clock—CROWN and ANCHOR, Strand—Mr. COLERIDGE will deliver a LECTURE on the Tragedy of ROMEO and JULIET, with the Characters of ANTONY and CLEOPATRA; or Shakspeare's double Portrait of Love, as it displays itself in Youth and in Manhood . . ." (the rest as in the *New Times*).

TEXT. Probably C used for this lecture annotations made in his copy of *Sh* (Ayscough). The annotations on *Romeo and Juliet* were first printed in *LR* I 149–58, on *Antony and Cleopatra* in *LR* I 143–4; Raysor included them in *Sh C* I 4–11 (4–12) and 77 (86) and followed HNC in intermingling them with marginalia from other sources, without indicating where or when C wrote them. The text printed below is based on a fresh transcript of C's notes.

REPORTS. No reports of this lecture have been found.

BACKGROUND AND CIRCUMSTANCES. In the annotations to *Othello* in his interleaved copy of *Sh* (Ayscough), C had been prompted, by the transfer of the action at the beginning of Act II from Venice to Cyprus, to write a long note on the dramatic unities, which he apparently developed in the lecture he gave on this play 21 Jan. This theme is picked up in another long note at the opening of *Romeo and Juliet* in this edition, which begins: "We have had occasion to speak at large on the subject of the three Unities, Time, Place, and Action, as applied to the Drama in abstract . . .". C used this as a starting-point for an appraisal of the kind of dramatic unity to be found in *Romeo and Juliet*, and it is virtually certain that he wrote the note to provide part of an introduction for this lecture. Of the twenty-seven further annotations to this play, several of those relating to the early scenes, and especially those commenting on the characters of the Nurse and Mercutio, could have been used as lecture-notes. Many of the others are very brief, but this was one of C's favourite plays, to which he devoted two lectures in the 1811–12 series (Lects 7 and 8), and he could well have gone on from the introductory note to speak impromptu from the text, with the help of the annotations. For the first part of his introduction to this lecture, however, he seems to have relied on other notes, for he began from "Memoranda on Pathos", which have not been identified, and went on to use notes in the untraced edition of Shakespeare belonging to "Mrs Milne" (see above, Lect 1 of the 1818–19 series, headnote: Background and Circumstances). He then attacked sentimental domestic tragedies and novels, a favourite target (cf Lect 1 of the 1811–12 series), before launching into his introduction of the play, which dealt with the three unities.

After the disappointment of his first lecture, C was pleased with this one: "The Romeo and Juliet pleased even beyond my anticipation; but alas! scanty are my audiences!" *CL* iv 921. If he was thinking of it in retrospect as a lecture on this one play, it could well be that he did not fulfil the promise of the advertisements that he would speak also on *Antony and Cleopatra*. In his *Sh* (Ayscough) he has just one brief general note prefacing the play, beginning "But of all perhaps of Shakespeare's plays the most wonderful is the Antony and Cleopatra . . ." and ending with a page-reference to the death-scene of Cleopatra and a reminder to himself to take this as a "specimen" of Shakespeare's strength in the play. This suggests that he prepared for a lecture mainly on *Romeo and Juliet*, and that if he commented at all on *Antony and Cleopatra* it was chiefly in relation to her death by the bite of the asp. He is not otherwise known to have lectured on this play.

LECTURE 2

RECORDS OF THE LECTURE

COLERIDGE'S NOTES
FROM HIS ANNOTATIONS ON THE INTERLEAVES
OF *SH* (AYSCOUGH) II 966–97, 767

General prefatory note to Romeo and Juliet, Sh *(Ayscough)* II 966

*a*Memoranda on Pathos—introductory to Romeo and Juliet.

The Gamester, Fatal Marriage, liable to the same Objections, as Novels*b1*—*c*(transcribe from the marble leaf of M*rs* Milne's Sh V. VIII.)*d* 2

Introductory note to Romeo and Juliet, Sh *(Ayscough)* II 966–7

Romeo and Juliet

We have had occasion to speak at large on the subject of the three Unities, Time, Place, and Action,[3] as applied to the Drama in abstract,

---

a–b Added in pencil as an afterthought
c–d Added in pencil as a further postscript

---

[1] Two domestic tragedies, *The Gamester*, by Edward Moore, first acted in 1753, and *The Fatal Marriage* (1694), by Thomas Southerne, both retained an appeal on the stage in C's time. C saw Miss Smith, who became principal dramatic actress at Drury Lane in 1812, perform as Isabella in Southerne's play in Dec 1812 (*CL* VI 1028), in anticipation of her part as the heroine Teresa in his own *Remorse*, which opened there in Jan 1813. He criticised *The Gamester* in a conversation with John Payne Collier in 1811, saying "there was nothing in it to improve the heart, or enlighten the understanding. To be sure, it produced tears, and so would a blunt razor on shaving the upper lip". *C on Sh* 32. C attacked popular novels in similar terms in Lect 1 of the 1811–12 series; and cf *BL* ch 3

(*CC*) I 48n–9.
[2] This set of Shakespeare has not been traced, but the reference may be to *The Plays of William Shakespeare . . . from the Text of . . . Steevens* (8 vols 1797) or the reprint (8 vols 1811), in which *Romeo and Juliet* is printed in vol VIII, preceded by *King Lear* and followed by *Hamlet* and *Othello*. It is a "*pocketable* Edition" (12m°), which C had requested in his letter to the Milnes concerning *The Tempest* (*CL* IV 898), and has marbled leaves. C also used the Milnes's set for his lecture on *Hamlet* in Jan 1819; see above, Lect 3 of the 1818–19 series (at n 17).

[3] C had spoken of them in Lect 1 of the 1818–19 series (at n 2) and more elaborately in Lect 5 on *Othello* (at nn 10–16).

and to the particular stage for which Shakspeare wrote as far as he can be said to have written for any stage but that of the universal Mind. We succeeded in demonstrating that the two former instead of being Rules were mere inconveniences attached to the local peculiarities of the Athenian Drama; that the last alone deserved the name of a Principle, and that in this Shakspear stood pre-eminent.

Yet instead of Unity of Action I should great*e* prefer the more appropriate tho' scholastic and uncouth words—Homogeneity, proportionateness and totality of Interest.—The distinction or rather the essential difference betwixt the Shaping skill of mechanical Talent, and the creative Life-power of inspired Genius.[4] In the former each part [is]*f* separately conceived and then by a succeeding Act put together—not as Watches are made for wholesale—for here each part supposes a preconception of the Whole in *some* mind—but as the Pictures on a motley Screen—(N.b. I must seek for a happier illustration.)

Whence the Harmony that strikes us in the wildest natural landscapes? In the relative shapes of rocks, the harmony of colors in the Heath, Ferns, and Lichens, the Leaves of the Beech, and Oak, the stems and rich choc[ol]ate-brown*g* Branches of the Birch, and other mountain Trees, varying from varying Autumn to returning Spring—compared with the visual effect from the greater number of artificial Plantations?—The former are effected by a single energy, modified ab intra[5] in each component part—. Now as this is the particular excellence of the Shakspearian Dramas generally, so is it especially characteristic of the Romeo and Juliet.—First, the groundwork of the Tale is altogether in family Life, and the events of the Play have their first origin in family-feuds—Filmy as are the eyes of Party-spirit, at once dim and truculent, still there is commonly some real or supposed Object in view, or Principle to be maintained—and tho but = the twisted Wires on the Plate of rosin in the preparation for electrical pictures,[6] it is still a guide in some

---

e A slip for "greatly"
f Word supplied by the editor
g Letters supplied by the editor

[4] This was one of C's favourite distinctions; see Lect 6 of the 1811–12 series (at nn 7 and 30).
[5] I.e. from within.
[6] I.e. the necessary components that, when charged, would produce the action. In the early nineteenth century "electricians" experimented with electrical machines to produce a variety of effects—stars, dancing images, electric figures. John Culbertson e.g. passed an electric current through a machine on to a resinous plate "to produce two figures of different but most beautiful colours", an experiment "very striking . . . and much admired". See "To prepare a resinous Plate for electrical Figures" in his *Practical Electricity, or Galvanism* (1807, 2nd ed 1821) 125–9. Two illustrations of such electrical pictures, "surprisingly

degree, an assimilation to an Outline; but in family quarrels, which have proved scarcely less injurious to States, wilfulness and precipitancy and passion from the mere habit and custom can alone be expected— With his accustomed Judgement Shak. has begun by placing before us a lively picture of all the impulses of the Play, like a prelude/ and human folly ever presents two sides, one for Heraclitus & one for Democritus,[7] he has first given the laughable absurdity of the Evil in the contagion of the Servants—The domestic Tale begins with Domestics that have so little to do that they are under the necessity of letting the superfluity of sensorial power[8] fly off thro' the escape-valve of Wit-combats and Quarreling with Weapons of sharper-edge—all in humble imitation of their Masters—Yet there is a sort of unhired fidelity, an *our* ishness[9] about it that makes it rest pleasant on one's feelings—and all that follows to p. 968, 55, β[10]—is a motley dance of all ranks and ages to one Tune, as if the Horn of Huon had been playing—[11]

I i 118ff, Sh *(Ayscough)* II *968* β *56: On the descriptions of the lovesick Romeo by Benvolio and Montague*

56, β. This but far more strikingly the following speech of old Montague, first, proves that Sh. meant it to approach to a Poem—which and its early date proved likewise by the multitude of rhyming Couplets—

I i 155ff, Sh *(Ayscough)* II *969: On the entrance of Romeo, confessing his love for Rosaline; at* I i *125 Benvolio had reported that the lovesick Romeo "stole into the covert of the wood"*

beautiful'' (p 231)—one purplish-grey from charging gold wire, the other yellow and grey from charging copper wire— are reproduced in George John Singer *Elements of Electricity* (1814) Plates 5 and 6. True electrical pictures, of coins, medals, etc, using similar but more complex apparatuses, were not produced till the 1840s. See G. Karsten "On Impressions or Pictures Produced by Electricity" *Electrical Magazine* I (1843) 8–16.

[7] The emphasis of Heraclitus in his philosophy on the fleeting nature of all things led to his being associated with melancholy; Democritus, by contrast, maintained his cheerfulness in spite of blindness. The two became associated through contrast as the "weeping" and the "laughing" philosopher.

[8] A phrase C may have borrowed from Erasmus Darwin *Zoonomia* (1794) I 75, "The sensorial power, or spirit of animation", meaning nervous energy (so *OED*).

[9] C's coinage; *OED* cites this passage (from *LR* II 151). C seems to mean that the scene is faithful to common human feelings and connects readily with our sympathies, and was trying for an English equivalent to the German *Gemütlichkeit*.

[10] *Sh* (Ayscough) II 968 β 55. C's reference is to the dialogue from the entry of Tybalt at I i 65 to Lady Montague's line, "Right glad I am he was not at this fray".

[11] Referring to the magic horn given by Oberon to Huon of Bordeaux in the French romance best known in the translation by Lord Berners (1534).

If, as I believe from the internal evidence, this was one of Sh. early Dramas, it marks strongly the fineness of his insight into the nature of the Passions, that Romeo is introduced already love-bewildered—The necessity of loving creating an Object for itself &c[12]—and yet a difference there is, tho' to be known only by the perception—. The difference in this respect between Men & Women—it would have displeased us that Juliet had been in love or fancied herself so—

R. running away from his Rosaline to woods & Nature, in which she indeed alone existed, as the name for his yearning—contrast this with his Rushing to Juliet—[13]

I i 234ff, Sh (Ayscough) II 970: On Romeo's boast: "Show me a mistress that is passing fair, | What doth her beauty serve but as a note | Where I may read who pass'd that passing fair?"

The POSITIVENESS of Romeo in a Love of his own making—and the boastfulness, never shewn of what's near the heart—
    again shewn 45, β.[14]

I iii, Sh (Ayscough) II 971: On the character of the Nurse, who first appears in this scene

The character of the Nurse, the nearest of any thing in Shakespear to borrowing Observation—the reason is, that as in infancy & childhood the individual in Nature is a representative—Like Larch Trees, in describing one you generalize a grove— the garrulity of Age strengthened by the long-trusted Servant, whose sympathy with the Mother's affections gives her privileges & rank in the House—the mode of connecting by accidents of Time & Place and the childlike fondness of repetition in her child age—and that happy humble ducking under yet resurgence against the check, Yes, Madam!—*yet* I can not chuse but laugh[15]

I iv, Sh (Ayscough) II 972: On the introduction of Mercutio

Scene IV introduces Mercutio to us—O how shall I describe that exquisite ebullience and overflow of youthful Life, wafted on over the laughing Wavelets of Pleasure & Prosperity, Waves of the Sea like a

---

[12] C probably here developed his commentary on Romeo's passion for Rosaline along the lines of his argument in Lect 8 of the 1811–12 series (at n 20).
[13] Romeo "rushes" to Juliet in II i, immediately after meeting her in the dance at Capulet's house.
[14] Referring to line 45, second col-

umn, in *Sh* (Ayscough), the passage in which Romeo strongly protests the "devout religion" of his love in response to Benvolio's, "Compare her face with some that I shall show . . ." (I ii 88ff). See also C's note on II ii, below.
[15] Citing the Nurse's line, I iii 50.

wanton Beauty that distorted a face on which she saw her lover gazing enraptured, had wrinkled her surface in the Triumph of its smoothness— Wit, ⟨ever wakeful, Fancy ⟨busy &⟩ procreative as Insects,⟩ Courage, an easy mind that without cares of its own was at once disposed to laugh away those of others & yet be interested in them/ these and all congenial qualities, melting into the common copula of all, the man of quality and the Gentleman, with all its excellencies & all its foibles—/

I v 77ff, Sh *(Ayscough)* II *974 α 15: On old Capulet's anger with Tybalt, who wants to quarrel with Romeo at his feast:* "Tybalt. *I'll not endure him.* Capulet. *He shall be endur'd.* | *What, goodman boy? I say he shall, go to!"*

15, α—The old man's impetuosity at once contrasting, yet harmonized with, the young Tybalt's/ but this it would be endless to repeat.—Every leaf is different on an Oak: but still we can only say, our Tongues defrauding our Eyes, this is another Oak Leaf—

II ii, Sh *(Ayscough)* II *975: On the balcony scene*

The contrast with Romeo's former boastful positiveness—.[16] Skill in justifying Romeo from inconstancy by making us feel the difference of the passion/—

Yet this too is a Love in, not merely of, the Imagination: as in R. & J.'s Language

II ii 62ff, Sh *(Ayscough)* II *976: On Juliet's concern for Romeo's safety:* "*How cam'st thou hither, tell me . . .*"

With Love, pure Love, the anxiety for the safety of the Object—the disinterestedness by which it is distinguished from the counterfeits of its name—

II ii 85ff, Sh *(Ayscough)* II *976 α 40: On Juliet's speech,* "*Thou know'st, the mask of night is on my face . . .*"

40, α

compared with Miranda & Ferdinand—how fine the variety on the same Air/[17]

and the truly sweet girlish Lingering & *Busy*ness[18]

---

[16] Cf C's note on I i 232–7, above.
[17] *The Tempest* III i.
[18] C's coinage, recovering the original meaning of "business"; the earliest instance given in *OED* dates from 1868.

II iii, Sh *(Ayscough) II 977: On the scene between Friar Laurence and Romeo*

The reverend Character of the Friar as always in Sh.[19] & yet no digression but carrying on the Plot—

II iv 36, Sh *(Ayscough) II 978: On Romeo jesting with Mercutio*

Romeo's half-exerted, half real ease of mind—here again compared with Rosaline—his Will had come to the clenching point—

II vi 6–14, Sh *(Ayscough) II 981 β 5: On Romeo's haste in marrying Juliet, "Do thou but close our hands with holy words", and the Friar's anxiety, "These violent delights have violent ends"*

5, β—The precipitation which is the character of the Play, so well marked in both the Speakers—

III i 96ff, Sh *(Ayscough) II 982: On Mercutio's joking even as he is dying, "Ask for me to-morrow, and you shall find a grave man", in relation to Romeo's attempt to stop the fight with Tybalt*

The wit and raillery habitual to Mercutio struggling with the pain giving so fine an effect to Romeo's Speech, & the whole so completely justifying him—

III i 152ff, Sh *(Ayscough) II 983: On Benvolio's report to the Prince of the death of Mercutio, putting the blame on Tybalt ("but that he tilts . . . at bold Mercutio's breast"), when in fact Mercutio was the first to draw his sword*

The *small* portion of untruth in Benvolio's Narration finely conceived—''but that he tilts'' &c

III ii 18ff, Sh *(Ayscough) II 983 β 50: On Juliet's soliloquy summoning the night that will bring Romeo to her: "For thou wilt lie upon the wings of night | Whiter than new snow upon a raven's back . . ."*

50, β.—The imaginative sustained to the highest—what an effe⟨c⟩t on the *purity* of the mind—think what Dryden & W. of C. II.[20] would have made—/

---

[19] C never tired of emphasising Shakespeare's respectful treatment of priests; see esp Lect 7 of the 1811–12 series (at n 34).

[20] Presumably Dryden and Wycherley of the reign of Charles II; in other words, Restoration comedy.

III ii 85ff, Sh (Ayscough) II 984: On the Nurse's readiness to go along with Juliet's complaint against Romeo for killing Tybalt, and Juliet's sharp retort: "Nurse. Shame come to Romeo! Juliet. *Blister'd be thy tongue | For such a wish! he was not born to shame . . ."*

The Nurse's mistake of the Minds audible struggles with *itself* for its decision in toto—

III iii 29ff, Sh (Ayscough) II 985: On Romeo's reaction to his banishment: " 'Tis torture and not mercy: heaven is here, | Where Juliet lives . . ."

All deep Passions a sort of Atheists, that believe no Future—

III v 127ff, Sh (Ayscough) II 988: On Capulet's anger with Juliet for refusing to marry Paris

A noble scene—Don't I see it? with my own eyes? Yes! but not with Juliet's.—

III v 177ff, Sh (Ayscough) II 989: On Capulet's explanation for his anger: "still my care hath been | To have her match'd"

and the mistake as if Love's causes were generalizable—

IV iii 55, Sh (Ayscough) II 991: On Juliet drinking the potion as she thinks she sees Tybalt's ghost

The taking the poison in a fit of fright! how S. provides for the finest decencies!—a Girl of 15[21]—too bold for her but for—

IV v, Sh (Ayscough) II 992: On the lamentation of her family over Juliet, supposed dead

Something I must say on this Scene—yet without it the Pathos would have been anticipated—

V i 1ff, Sh (Ayscough) II 993: On Romeo's hopefulness: "My dreams presage some joyful news at hand . . ."

Fondness for presentiments and as if aware—yet reconciling with the superstition all-reconciling of opposites—of any thing unusual as un-lucky/[22]

---

[21] Juliet's age is just under fourteen, according to her mother at I iii 12.

[22] Romeo treats as a presentiment of joyful news a dream that Juliet found him dead and revived him with kisses, so reconciling the unlucky with good fortune.

v i 34ff, Sh *(Ayscough)* II 994 α 30: *On Romeo seeking the aid of the Apothecary in his desire to join Juliet:* "*Well, Juliet, I will lie with thee to-night.* | *Let's see for means.* O *mischief, thou art swift* | *To enter in the thoughts of desperate men!*"

30, α

So beautiful as to have been self-justified—yet what a fine preparation for the Tomb scene—

v iii 59ff, Sh *(Ayscough)* II 995: *On Romeo's attempt to avoid a fight with Paris*

The gentleness of Romeo shewn before as softened by Love; but now by Love & Sorrow & the Awe of the Place—

v iii 88–96, Sh *(Ayscough)* II 995 β 45: *On Romeo in the tomb looking at Juliet:* "*How oft when men are at the point of death* | *Have they been merry . . .*"

45, β

Here, here, is the master-example how Beauty can at once increase & modify Passion—like the subtle net of Vulcan—[23]

v iii 208ff, Sh *(Ayscough)* II 997: *On the entry of Montague and the end of the play*

a beautiful Close—*poetic* Justice indeed! all are punished!—

The Spring & Winter meet, & Winter assumes the character of Spring, Spring the sadness of Winter—

General note on Antony and Cleopatra, Sh *(Ayscough)* II 767

But of all perhaps of Shakspeare's Plays the most wonderful is the Antony & Cleopatra—scarcely any in which he has followed history more minutely, and yet few even of his own in which he impresses the notion of giant strength, so much, perhaps none in which he impresses it more strongly.—This owing to the manner in which it is sustained throughout—that he *lives* in & through the Play—to the numerous momentary flashes of Nature counteracting the historic abstraction—in short take as a specimen the 801 ad finem.—[24]

---

[23] Vulcan's unfaithful wife, Venus, was seen in the act of love with Mars by Apollo, who at once told Vulcan. Vulcan made a cunningly contrived net to trap them and exposed the lovers to the mockery of the gods. The story is told in Homer *Odyssey* 8.265ff.

[24] The last two pages of *Antony and Cleopatra* in *Sh* (Ayscough) II 801–2, beginning at 801 β 7 (v ii 280): "Give me my robe, put on my crown, I have | Immortal longings . . .".

LECTURE 3

DATE AND PLACE OF DELIVERY. Thursday, 25 February 1819, at the Crown and Anchor Tavern, Strand, London.

SUBJECT. The development of Shakespeare's genius.

ANNOUNCEMENTS AND ADVERTISEMENTS. The general advertisements for the course, described above (Introduction to the 1819 series, first paragraph), promised "the Growth of SHAKSPEARE's Genius traced through *all* his Plays; the probable order, in which they were composed, determined; and a compressed Character of each Play given (those excepted which have been already lectured on)". *New Times* Thurs, 18 Feb (continuing from an advertisement for Lect 2): "On Thursday next, the concluding Lecture on Shakspeare, tracing the gradual ascent and expansion of his Genius, with the probable order in which his several Dramas were composed . . .". *M Chron* Thurs, 18 Feb (continuing from the advertisement for Lect 2): "On Thursday sennight, the concluding Lecture on Shakspeare, tracing the ascent of his Genius from its Rise to its Zenith . . .". *Courier* Wed, 24 Feb (announcement): MR. COLERIDGE's LEC- TURES.—Mr. COLERIDGE will deliver, TO-MORROW EVENING, his last Shak- sperian Lecture, in which he will characterize the Genius of SHAKSPEARE, and trace its growth through his several compositions . . .". *M Chron* Wed, 24 Feb, and *The Times* Thurs, 25 Feb (advertisements): "MR. COLERIDGE's CON- CLUDING LECTURE on SHAKSPEARE, tracing the growth and characteristics of his genius through his several works. THIS EVENING, Crown and Anchor, Strand . . .". *New Times* Thurs, 25 Feb (advertisement): substantially as in *The Times* of this date, with the alteration, "the growth and distinctive character of . . .".

TEXT. C made some notes for this lecture under the heading of the date, 25 Feb, in N 24, now in the BM. They consist of eight numbered notes and end with a list of titles of plays with page-references to them in *Sh* (Ayscough). These notes, without the page-references, were included in *Sh* C I 212 14 (240– 2) and have since been printed in full in *CN* III 4486. The text printed below is based on that in *CN*, omitting cancellations. The report in the *New Times* shows that C also used annotations in his interleaved copy of *Sh* (Ayscough). These notes, on *Love's Labour's Lost* and *Troilus and Cressida*, first printed inaccurately in *LR* II 102–3 and 130–4, were included in *Sh* C I 83 and 98– 100 (92 and 108–11). The text printed below is based on a fresh transcript of C's notes.

REPORT. An "extract" from this lecture, headed "TROILUS AND CRESSIDA", was printed in the *New Times* Mon, 1 Mar 1819. It appears to have been taken down more or less verbatim, since it is an expansion of part of two annotations in C's copy of *Sh* (Ayscough), which he used for the last two courses of literary lectures. The report has not been reprinted since it appeared.

BACKGROUND AND CIRCUMSTANCES. For his previous lectures in this series C seems to have relied on his familiarity with the texts of the plays he discussed and his ability to develop annotations in his copy of *Sh* (Ayscough). His last lecture on Shakespeare was of a different kind, a survey of the dramatist's career, and he sketched out a plan for it in N 24 in a series of numbered notes. These show that he began by quoting from *BL* ch 15, in which he had analysed *Venus and Adonis* and *The Rape of Lucrece* as exemplifying Shakespeare's poetic power but also his immaturity (the notes refer to *BL* vol I, but this must be an error for vol II). They also show that in the course of the lecture he used notes on *Love's Labour's Lost* and *Troilus and Cressida* in his copy of *Sh* (Ayscough). In addition, there is a reference to *Pericles* in "Sharpe's edition", published in twelve volumes in 1809; C had recourse to vol XII of this edition, the one containing this play, because it was omitted from *Sh* (Ayscough). Presumably C took *BL*, vol XII of Sharpe's edition, and the set of *Sh* (Ayscough) with him into the lecture-room. His notes end with a list of sixteen plays, with references to the page numbers at which each of them begins in *Sh* (Ayscough). He had lectured on two of the plays named in the list (*Romeo and Juliet* in Lect 2 of this series and *Richard II* in Lect 2 of the course that immediately preceded it, given on 31 Dec 1818). There are no annotations against most of the others in his copy of *Sh* (Ayscough), and he presumably provided himself with the list of page-references so that he would be able to turn to any of these plays if he wished to do so in commenting on the chronology of Shakespeare's work.

The chronology C proposed in his division of Shakespeare's career into five "Æras" now looks peculiar. However, the first scholarly *Attempt to Ascertain the Order in Which the Plays Attributed to Shakespeare Were Written* was that so titled by Edmund Malone and included in the edition of Shakespeare by Samuel Johnson and George Steevens (1778). The external evidence known to Malone was still scanty enough to make much of his dating little more than guesswork, so that, for example, he assigned *The Winter's Tale*, now thought to have been composed about 1610, to 1594, whereas *Twelfth Night*, now generally attributed to about 1600, he thought was Shakespeare's last play, written in 1614. So it is not surprising that C should have felt free to criticise sharply attempts to order the plays by external evidence, as he did in Lect 4 of the 1811–12 series (at nn 1–6 and the first eight paragraphs of Tomalin's notes), in which he referred to Malone's essay. In the absence of convincing external evidence, C proposed there to use internal evidence supplemented by "the few certain data that were known of an external kind which tended to corroborate the internal testimony". His assessment of the internal "evidence", i.e. his estimate of the relative quality and maturity of Shakespeare's plays, did not remain constant, and the chronology he proposed in 1811 differs from that recorded by HNC, from some source now lost, in *LR* II 86–8 and dated by him 1802; this list is remarkably like, though not identical with, a classification of the plays in BM Add MS 34225 ff 52–3, printed in *Sh C* I 209–11 (237-9). The ordering of the plays C put forward in this lecture of 1819 differs again from both the earlier ones, most notably perhaps in his revised conception of the last of the five divisions of Shakespeare's career, which suggests that he was continually revising his evaluation of plays like *Troilus and Cressida* and *Measure for Measure*.

Although much of the lecture was probably concerned with Shakespeare's career, C used notes relating to *Love's Labour's Lost* and *Troilus and Cressida*. The note prefacing *Love's Labour's Lost* is a short one reaffirming his argument that the play was the earliest of Shakespeare's to be written. The report of the lecture published in the *New Times* on 1 Mar shows that he did not merely read the long preliminary annotations to *Troilus and Cressida*, but expanded and played some variations on them. This report confirms that he did indeed use

371

the notes written for this lecture, and since the annotations to these two plays are the only marginalia connected with them in *Sh* (Ayscough) apart from a brief textual comment on Act IV of *Troilus and Cressida*, it is probable that they were written as part of his preparation for it. His procedure was different from that outlined in a letter written to John Britton on 28 Feb 1819 in response to an invitation to lecture at the Russell Institution (see Introduction to the 1819 series, extract following n 12), in which he said, ''for the words, illustrations, &c. I know almost as little as any one of my audience (*i.e.* those of any thing like the same education with myself) what they will be five minutes before the lecture begins''. *CL* IV 924. Lect 3 of this course was his final lecture on Shakespeare, the ninth in an almost continuous series, and he went to a lot more trouble over it than this letter suggests. He had lectured on *Love's Labour's Lost* in Lect 5 of the 1811–12 series and again in Lect 4 of the 1812 series, first course, at Willis's Rooms, but he is not known to have spoken previously on *Troilus and Cressida*.

LECTURE 3

RECORDS OF THE LECTURE

COLERIDGE'S NOTES
(1) *CN* III 4486

Thursday, 25 Feb? 1819.
Crown and Anchor.

1—Shakspear's Poems as prophetic of his Dramas: from the Lit. Life. Vol. I.[1]

2. But if we are to be guided by internal evidence—and how little weight the external ought to have, I have shewn—his earliest dramatic attempt, prior in its first sketch at least to his Venus and Adonis, and probably planned before he had left Stratford, is the Love's Labor Lost, Quart. 1598. Page (in Stockdales of 1807) 147.[2]

3. Shortly after, I suppose the Pericles to have been first produced: from the *Pericles*, in Sharpe's Edition—blank Leaf to the Tit. Andron.—[3]

4. And certain scenes in Jeronymo.[4]

5. And in the same æra ⟨the Winter's Tale, &⟩ the Cymbeline, different from the Pericles by the entire Rifacciamento when Shak's celebrity as Poet and his Interest no less than his Influence as Manager enabled him to bring forward his laid-by Labor of Youth.—The example

---

[1] A slip for vol II: *BL* ch 15 (*CC*) II 19–28.

[2] *Sh* (Ayscough) I 147; for C's note on *Love's Labour's Lost*, see below (at n 9).

[3] *The Plays of William Shakespeare, from the correct edition of Isaac Reed, Esq* . . . Printed for Vernor, Hood and Sharpe, Poultry; and Taylor and Hessey, Fleet Street (12 vols 1809) XII 278 (so Raysor and Kathleen Coburn). The copy that C evidently annotated on the blank leaf between *Titus Andronicus* and *Pericles* has not been traced.

[4] In 1809 C apparently told RS he "had

proved those mad scenes in Jeronymo to be Shakespeare's". See *Friend* (*CC*) II 495. C was thinking of Kyd's *Spanish Tragedy*; Lamb had included the mad scenes from this play in his *Specimens of English Dramatic Poets* (1808) 6–12, with a note, derived from *Sh* (Reed), that Ben Jonson had been paid for these scenes as additions to the play, and indicating his own preference for Webster as the putative author of them. In *TT* 5 Apr 1833, C rejected the ascription to Jonson in favour of Shakespeare. See also *CN* III 4486n.

of Tit. Andron. most popular as well as Jeronymo in Shakspere's first Æra, but after by words of contempt, had led the young Dramatist to the lawless mixture of Dates & Manners—

6. As included in this æra I should place, 1. the Comedy of Errors (remarkable as being the only specimen of *poetical Farce* in our Language, that is, intentionally such. That all the distinct *kinds* of Drama, that might be educed a priori, have their representatives in his Works— Too many of B. and Fletcher's Com, Trag. & Tragi Comedies, and the greater number of Jonson's Comedies are Farce-plots.) 2. the All's well that ends well, originally intended as the Counterpart of L. Lab. Lost, and accordingly entitled, Love's Labor Won—3. The Taming of the Shrew.—and The Midsummer Night's Dream.

7. As concluding the Æra, the Much Ado about Nothing, and the Romeo and Juliet.

Second Æra.

8. The Richard the Second.

The King John.

The rifacciamento of the three parts of Henry VI—(reasons for refusing this to Sh.)

and the Richard the Third—

The Third Æra

The Two Parts of Henry the IV.

Henry the 5.

The Merry Wives of Windsor

and, as a sort of Historical Mask or Shew Play, Henry the 8th—

Fourth Æra

gives all the graces and facilities of a genius in full possession and habit of power—peculiarly of the femine,[5] *Lady*, character

The Tempest

The As you like it.

The Merchant of Venice.

The Twelfth Night—

and finally as its Summit, the Lear, the Hamlet, the Macbeth and the Othello.

Fifth and last Æra

when the Energies of Intellect in the cycle of Genius were tho' in a richer and potenziated[6] form becoming predominant over Passion and

---

[5] An obsolete form of "feminine", current in the sixteenth century, according to *OED*.

[6] C's coinage, first used in *BL* ch 12 *(CC)* 1 287: ". . . I have even hazarded the new verb potenziate with its derivatives in order to express the combination or transfer of powers".

creative Self-modification—I am inclined to place ⟨Meas. for Meas. Timon of Ath. (see Tr. and Cr.*)⟩ the Coriolanus, the Julius Cæsar, Antony and Cleopatra, wth the Troilus and Cressida.

Second Volume begins at p.	543—[8]	
Cymbeline Vol. 2. p.	893	
Winter's Tale Vol. 1.	333.	
Comedy of Errors V. 1.	103	
All's Well that ends well 1	277	
Taming of the Shrew	251	
Midsummer	175.	
Much Ado about N.	121.	
Romeo and Juliet	967	
Rich. II	Vol. 1	413
John		387
Hen. VI.—begins Vol. 2nd		2 543
Rich. III.		633
Henry IV.		441
—— V		509
Merry Wives of W.		45
Henry VIII.		671

(2) FROM HIS ANNOTATIONS ON THE INTERLEAVES OF *SH* (AYSCOUGH) I 147, II 857–8

General note on Love's Labour's Lost, Sh *(Ayscough)* I 147[9]

According to internal evidence the earliest of Shakspear's dramas, probably prior to the V. and A. and sketched out before he left Stratford.— Characters either impersonated out of his own multiformity, by imaginative Self-position, or of such as a Country Town and a School-boys Observation might supply—the Curate, School-master, the Armado (which even in my time was not extinct in the cheaper Inns of N. Wales)—the Satire too on follies of *Words*—Add too that the characters of Byron and Rosaline are evidently the pre-existent state of his Beatrice and

---

*—Timon compared with Lear, in the blank Leaves before Troilus and Cressida.[7]

[7] See below (sentences after n 10).

[8] This and the following references are to vols I or II of *Sh* (Ayscough).

[9] This note summarises what C had said about the play in Lect 5 of the 1811– 12 series (paragraphs containing nn 27– 35) and Lect 4 of the 1812 series (at n 13). He always thought of this play as the earliest of Shakespeare's and associated it with his Stratford life.

Benedict—. Add too the number of the rhymes, and the sweetness as well as smoothness of the metre—and the number of acute and fancifully illustrated Aphorisms. Just as it ought to be. True Genius begins by generalizing, and condensing;—it ends in realizing, and expanding— It first collects the seeds—

Yet if this juvenile Drama had been the only one extant of our Shakspeare, and we possessed the tradition only of his riper works or from Writers who had not even mentioned the Love's Labor Lost—how many of S's characteristic Features might we not discover, tho' as in a portrait taken of him in his Boyhood.—

General notes on Troilus and Cressida, Sh *(Ayscough)* II 857–8[a]

The Troil: and Cressida of Sh. can scarcely be classed with his Gr. and Rom. *History* Dramas; but it forms an intermediate Link between the fictitious ⟨G. & R.⟩ Histories, which we may call Legendary Dramas and the proper ancient Histories: ex. gr. between the Pericles or Tit. Andron. and the Coriolanus, Julius Cæsar &c. Cymbeline is congener[10] with Pericles—distinguished from Lear by not having any declared prominent Object. But where shall we class the Timon of Athens? Immediately, below Lear. It is a Lear of the satirical Drama, a Lear of domestic or ordinary Life—a local Eddy of Passion on the High Road of Society while all around is the week-day Goings on of Wind and Weather a Lear therefore without its soul-scorching flashes, its ear-cleaving Thunder Claps, its meteoric splendors, without the contagion & fearful sympathies of Nature, the Fates, the Furies the frenzied Elements dance in and out, now breaking thro' and scattering, now hand in hand, with the fierce or fantastic group of Human Passions, Crimes and Anguishes, reeling ⟨on the unsteady ground⟩ in a wild harmony to the Swell and Sink of the Earthquake.—But my present Subject was Troilus & Cressida: and I suppose that scarcely knowing what to say of it I by a cunning of instinct ran off to Subjects on which I should find it difficult not to say too much, tho' certain after all I should still leave the better part unsaid, and the gleaning for others richer than my own harvest. Indeed, there is none of Sh's Plays harder to characterize. The name & the remembrances connected with it, prepare us for the representation of attachment no less faithful than fervent on the side of the youth, and of sudden and shameless inconstancy on the part of the

---

[a] First paragraph—on the naming of Lollius in footnote in *Sh* (Ayscough) to the title of the play—omitted

[10] I.e. of the same kind as, a term used in classifying plants and animals; the first   more general use cited in *OED* is dated 1837.

Lady. And this indeed is the gold thread on which the scenes are strung, tho' often kept out of sight and out of mind by gems of greater value than itself. But as Sh. calls-forth nothing from the Mausoleum of Hist. or the Catacombs of Tradition without giving or eliciting some permanent and general interest, brings forward no subject which he does not moralize or intellectualize, so here he has drawn in Cressida the Portrait of a vehement *Passion* that having its true origin and proper cause in warmth of temperament fastens on, rather than fixes to, some one Object by *Liking* and temporary Preference/ ⟨881, 40, β.[11] This he has contrasted⟩ with the profound Affection represented in Troilus, and alone worthy the name of Love, Affection, passionate indeed, swoln from the confluence of youthful instincts and youthful Fancy, glowing in the radiance of Hope newly risen, in short enlarged by the collective sympathies of Nature; but still having a depth of calmer element, in a will stronger than Desire, more entire than Choice, and which gives permanence to its own act by converting it into Faith and Duty.—Hence with excellent Judgement and with an excellence higher than mere Judgement can give, at the close of the Play, when Cressida has sunk into infamy below retrieval and beneath a hope, the same Will, which had been the substance and the basis of his Love, while the restless Pleasures and Passionate Longings, like Sea-waves, had tossed but on its surface, the same moral energy snatches him ⟨aloof⟩ from all neighbourhood with her Dishonor, from all lingering Fondness and languishing Regrets while it rushes with him into other and nobler Duties, and deepens the Channel, which his heroic Brother's Death had left empty for its collected Flood.—Yet another, secondary and subordinate purpose he has inwoven with the two characters, that of opposing the inferior civilization but purer morals of the Trojans to the refinements, deep policy, but duplicity and sensual corruptions of the Greeks.

To all this,[12] however, there is so little comparative projection given, nay, the masterly Group of Agamemnon, Nestor, Ulysses, and still more in advance, of Achilles, Ajax and Thersites so manifestly occupy the foreground, that the subservience and vassalage of Strength and animal Courage to Intellect and Policy seem to be the Lesson most often in our Poet's View, and which he has taken little pains to connect with the former more interesting Moral impersonated in the titular Hero

---

[11] *Sh* (Ayscough) II 881 β 40, on *Troilus and Cressida* IV v 54–5, Ulysses' attack on Cressida: "Fie, fie upon her! | There's language in her eye, her cheek, her lip . . .". Cf the report in the *New Times*

[12] The report in the *New Times* (extract at n 18) quotes C's words in the lecture, showing how he used the rest of these notes on *Troilus and Cressida*.

& Heroine of the Drama. But I am half inclined to believe, that Shakspeare's main object, or shall I rather say that his ruling impulse was to translate the ⟨poetic⟩ Heroes [of]*ᵇ* Paganism into the not less rude but more intellectually vigorous, more *featurely*¹³ Warriors of Christian Chivalry, to substantiate the distinct and graceful Profiles or Outlines of the Homeric Epic into the flesh and blood of the Romantic Drama—in short, to give a grand History-piece in the robust style of Albert Durer.—¹⁴

The character of Thersites¹⁵ well deserves a more particular attention—as the Caliban of Demagogues—the admirable Portrait of intellectual power deserted by all grace, all moral principle, all not momentary purpose, just wise enough to detect the weak head and fool enough to provoke the armed fist of his Betters, whom Malcontent Achilles can inveigle from Malcontent Ajax, under the one condition, that he shall be called on to do nothing but to abuse and slander and that he shall be allowed to abuse as much and as purulently as he likes—that is, aᶜ can—in short, a mule—⟨quarrelsome by the original discord of its Nature,⟩ a slave by tenure of his own baseness made to bray and be brayed [at],*ᵈ* to despise and be despicable—

Aye, Sir! but say what you will, he is a devilish clever fellow: tho'—the best friends will fall out; but there was a time when Ajax thought, he deserved to have a statue of Gold erected to him, and handsome Achilles, ⟨at⟩ the head of the Myrmidons, gave no little credit to his "friend, Thersites."

REPORT IN THE *NEW TIMES*
MONDAY, 1 MARCH 1819

TROILUS AND CRESSIDA

The following extract from Mr. Coleridge's last Shakspearian Lecture will highly gratify the admirers of philosophical criticism. It is seldom

---

ᵇ Word supplied by the editor; C wrote "Heroic age of Paganism", cancelled "age of", inserted "poetic" above the line, and altered "Heroic" to "Heroes"
ᶜ So in ms; a slip for "he"?
ᵈ Word supplied by the editor

¹³ I.e. having strongly marked features. C's coinage, according to *OED*, citing this passage from *LR* I 117.
¹⁴ No earlier reference to Dürer in C's writings has been found. The linking of the Greek and Trojan warriors with Christian chivalry may have recalled for C his reading in F. Schlegel's *Geschichte* for the early lectures of the 1818 series; Schlegel mentions Dürer in Lect 10, but in the context of the Reformation.
¹⁵ Cf the report in the *New Times* (from

that the eagle flight of genius is so much as attempted to be pursued by the keen glance of a just philosophy.

In contrasting the *passion* of Cressida with the *affection* of Troilus, the Lecturer dwelt particularly on the observant remarks of Ulysses (Act 4, s. 4)

> "———fie! fie upon her!
> There's language in her eye, her cheek, her lip;
> Nay, her foot speaks. Her wanton spirits look out
> At every joint of her body.—Set such down
> For sluttish spoils of opportunity
> And daughters of the game."—[16]

"Cressida's passion",[17] said he, "originates in constitutional temperament, and fastens on, rather than fixes to one object, by mere *liking*; whilst the profound affection of Troilus alone deserves the name of love."

The succeeding passage may be called truly eloquent, and is in the present state of the world peculiarly instructive:—

To all this,[18] however, there is so little comparative projection given, nay, the masterly group of the Greek warriors and statesmen, Agamemnon, Nestor, Ulysses, and, still more in advance, Ajax, Achilles, and Thersites, so manifestly occupy the foreground, that the moral uppermost in the poet's intentions seems to be the natural vassalage of strength and courage to superior intellect. Nor has Shakespeare taken any pains to connect this truth with the more interesting moral embodied in the titular hero and heroine of the play. In fact, I am half inclined to believe, that in this piece Shakespeare gratified a fancy of his own, that he amused himself by translating the heroes of Greek tradition into the more intellectual, more complex, charactered, more featurely Knights of Christian Chivalry, the distinct yet lightly pencilled profiles of the Epic and Homeric muse into the substantial, robust individualities of the romantic drama. I mean that the Troilus and Cressida is and was meant to be a bold, broad picture, the subject being the Tale of Troy, but the figures all Gothic faces, and in Gothic drapery, each intensely filling the space it occupies, or recalling the wild fig or yew-tree, which as if by some strange metempsychosis, the spirit of the hero below, had passed into it, splits the solid marble of the ancient tomb, out of which it rises. In short, it is a grand history piece, in the style of Albert Durer. I regret that I must leave Thersites without a more particular notice; for verily he is the CALIBAN of DEMAGOGUES, who hates all his betters so sincerely, that he needs no end or motive for his malignity, but its own cordial and comforting virulence! Just shrewd enough to detect the weak brain, and sufficiently fool

---

the sentence before n 19), which shows how C used this note on Thersites in his lecture.

[16] From IV v 54–63, omitting several lines; see above (at n 11).

[17] Cf C's notes (sentences before and after n 11).

[18] For C's notes on Thersites, see above (at n 15).

to provoke "the armed fist"[19] of his superiors—he will shift at an hour's notice from one faction to its opposite, and enlist for a fresh bounty into a malcontent corps, with no other condition but that he shall be required to do nothing but *abuse*, and be allowed to abuse as much, and as *purulently* as he likes—i.e., as he can. Briefly, Thersites is—I say, is, for he is one of the Immortals, and independently of his apotheosis and canonization by Homer and Shakespeare, survives by successive transmigrations. Our Thersites is a mule, quarrelsome by the original discord of his parentage, and contradictory in embryo, a slave by tenure of his own baseness, made to kick and be cudgeled, to bray and be brayed, to hate and despise, and to sink below hatred by being utterly despicable.

Aye, aye! but he is devilish clever fellow, for all that. The handsome Achilles, at the head of the myrmidons, he who will trust neither party, and scorns both Greek and Trojan, yet gave no little credit, we know, to his good friend, Thersites, and even Ajax, the champion of his country in a perilous time, declared publicly, that this very Thersites ought to have a statue of gold raised to his honour. True! and as far as relates to the latter instance, strange; but, as true! Since an ass once spoke like an angel,[20] a wise man, and with almost an angel's tongue, may perhaps be forgiven for having once in his life uttered sounds too near to those of an ass.

---

[19] C was recalling the words of Ajax when, puffed with pride, he threatens Achilles: "with my armed fist | I'll pash him o'er the face", II iii 202–3.

[20] Alluding to the story of Balaam and his ass, as told in Num 22.28–30, and cf 2 Pet 2.16, "the dumb ass speaking with man's voice forbad the madness of the prophet".

LECTURE 4

DATE AND PLACE OF DELIVERY. Thursday, 4 March 1819, at the Crown and Anchor Tavern, Strand, London.

SUBJECT. *Paradise Lost* and the character of Milton.

ANNOUNCEMENTS AND ADVERTISEMENTS. An unusually elaborate announcement of this lecture appeared in the *New Times* Thurs, 4 Mar, under the heading "Critical Lectures": "It [is] a novel entertainment, in the present day, which is afforded by the Critical Lectures delivered in the metropolis, on the works of our own Poets. A taste is thus diffused through society, which cannot but be ultimately favourable to the general cause of mental and moral improvement; for the great English Bards are no less remarkable for loftiness of moral feeling than for sterling weight of intellect. Milton, in these respects, stands 'proudly eminent;' and we are happy to perceive that his great work, the *Paradise Lost*, has been taken as a subject for illustration, by so accomplished a critic as Mr. Coleridge. We remember having been present, in the year 1814, at the very popular course of criticism, which that gentleman delivered at the Royal Institution, when the Lecture on Milton was unanimously considered as the most splendid and most interesting of the whole. If Mr. Coleridge's continued study of our great elder Poet since that time should be found to have added to his Lecture of this evening, compared with the former, as much as it is allowed to have achieved for his late Shakespearean Course, his auditors may confidently anticipate a genial pleasure that will remain in the memory; as well as a gratification of no vulgar kind during the passing hour." *Courier* Wed, 3 Mar (announcement): "Mr. COLERIDGE's Lecture for To-morrow Evening is, the *Paradise Lost*, and the Character of MILTON.—Eight o'Clock, Crown and Anchor, Strand." *The Times, New Times, M Chron* Thurs, 4 Mar (advertisement): as in the *Courier*, with minor variants.

TEXT. C prepared full notes for the introduction to this lecture, and a further list of "Quotations and Passages referred to" in *Paradise Lost*, under the date 4 Mar 1819, in N 29. These notes, without the list of references and with some editorial reworking, were printed by HNC in *LR* I 166–72. Raysor reprinted the text given in *LR*, associating it with Lect 10 of the 1818 series, in *Misc C* 157–61. They were first printed in full by R. F. Brinkley in *C 17th C* 572–6 and were included in the sequence of C's notebook material in *CN* III 4494–4495. The text printed below is based on that of *CN*, omitting cancellations. In *LR* the notebook entry is linked with other material on Milton's superiority to Klopstock, and on the object and style of *Paradise Lost*, to form a continuous prose commentary. The source of this additional material has not been traced, and there is no reason to connect it with this lecture. It may relate to Lect 10 in the 1818 series, and for further comment on it, see the headnote to that lecture.

REPORTS. No reports of this lecture have been found.

BACKGROUND AND CIRCUMSTANCES. C's notebook entry giving references to passages he intended to quote begins on a fresh page, and the page before it (f 142) is blank, so that it could have been written while the other surrounding pages were blank and might just possibly have been made earlier, in connexion with Lect 10 in the 1818 series (see *CN* III 4495n). C was using an edition of

Milton identified by Kathleen Coburn as *Paradise Lost. A Poem in Twelve Books*, reprinted from Jacob Tonson's text of 1711 and issued for a group of publishers in 1804, but his copy has not been traced. He evidently began by characterising the age in which Milton wrote, in relation to the earlier period of Queen Elizabeth and King James I. This was a favourite theme, which he developed e.g. in Lect 6 of the 1811–12 series (at n 10; see also *C 17th C* 3–13), and it was closely related to the topic of his eleventh philosophical lecture, on the age of Queen Elizabeth, delivered on Mon, 8 Mar. Probably much of the lecture echoed previous comments on Milton, for C had lectured on *Paradise Lost* in 1808, 1811–12, 1813, 1814 at Bristol (where he devoted four lectures to Milton and his poetry), and again in Lect 10 in 1818. However, the trouble he went to to write an introduction and select passages as examples shows that he was not content simply to rely on experience or old notes. In a letter of 1 Mar 1819, he was still complaining that his audiences were "scanty" (*CL* IV 927), though it is not clear whether he was referring to the literary lectures, the philosophical lectures, or both courses. The announcement in the *New Times* may have done something to improve attendance at this lecture, but the author of it had a muddled memory, for C had lectured at the RI in 1808, not 1814.

LECTURE 4

RECORDS OF THE LECTURE

COLERIDGE'S NOTES
CN III 4494–4495

^aLecture on Milton
and the
Paradise Lost.
4 March, 1819.

If we divide the period from the ascension of Elizabeth to the Protectorate of Cromwell into two unequal portions, the first ending with the Death of James the First, the other comprehending the reign of Charles and the brief glories of the Republic, we are forcibly struck with a difference in the character of the illustrious Actors, by whom each period is severally memorable.[1] Or rather, the difference in the characters of the great men in each leads us to make this division. Eminent as the intellectual Powers were, that were displayed in both, yet in the number of great men, in the various sorts of excellence, and not merely the variety but almost diversity of talents united in the same Individual, the age of Charles falls short of its predecessor, and the Stars of the Parliament, keen as their radiance was, yet in fullness and richness of lustre yield to the constellation at the Court of Elizabeth. To be equalled only by Greece at time of her Epaminondases, Pericles, Xenophon, Thucydides, when the Poet, Philosopher, Historian, Statesman, and General formed a garland round the same head—Sir W. Ralegh[2]—But on the other hand, there is a vehemence of Will, an enthusiasm of principle,

a CN III 4494

[1] This is a sophisticated variation on a favourite theme, developing more subtly contrasts and connexions C discussed elsewhere, as in Lect 6 of the 1811–12 series (at n 10). In that lecture C also mentioned Sir Walter Raleigh specifically as one of the "great men" of the age of Elizabeth. He had read Raleigh's *History of the World* in 1807; see *CN* II 3079–91.

[2] Epaminondas of Thebes (c 412–363 B.C.) and Pericles of Athens (d 429 B.C.)

a depth and an earnestness of Spirit, which the charm of individual fame and personal aggrandizement could not pacify, an aspiration after reality, permanence, and General Good—in short, a moral Grandeur in the latter æra, with which the low intrigues, Macchiavelian maxims, and the selfish and servile ambition of the former stand in painful contrast.

The causes of this it belongs not to the present occasion to detail at full—the quick succession of Revolutions in Religion, breeding a political indifference in the mass of men to Religion itself, the enormous increase of the Royal Power from the humiliation of the Nobility & the Clergy, and the transference of the Papal Power to the Crown, and especially the unfixed state of Elizabeth's Opinions, whose inclinations were as Papal as her interests were Protestant, and the controversial extravagance and practical imbecillity of her successor,[3] explain the *former* period—. And the persecutions that had given a life and such interest to the Disputes imprudently fostered by James, the ardour of a conscious increase of Power in the minority and the greater austerity of manners & maxims which is the natural product and the most formidable weapon of religious Minorities, not merely in conjunction, but in closest combination with new-awakened political and republican Zeal—these account for the latter.—

In the close of the former period and during the bloom of the latter the Poet, Milton, was educated and formed—survived the latter and all the fond hopes & aspirations which had been its life, and in evil days standing as the representative of the combined excellence of both produced the Paradise Lost, as by an after-throe of Nature.—

"There are some persons" (observes a Divine, a Contemporary of Milton's) "of whom the Grace of God takes early hold, and the good Spirit inhabiting them carries them on in an even constancy thro' innocence into virtue: their christianity bearing equal date with their manhood, and reason and religion like warp and woof running together, make up one web of a wise and exemplary life. This (he adds) is a most happy case, where ever it happens—for besides that there is no more sweeter or more lovely thing on earth than the early Buds of

---

were noted generals and statesmen; Xenophon (c 444–359 B.C.) and Thucydides (471–c 401 B.C.) were historians who both had experience as commanders in battle. Raleigh, as soldier, poet, thinker, and historian, exemplified C's sense of the age of Elizabeth; see Lect 6 of the 1811–12 series (at n 10). This passage was added by C as a footnote and marked for insertion here.

[3] For C's low opinion of James I, whom he elsewhere called a "loathsome lackwit", see *C 17th C* 7–8.

Piety—which drew from our Savior signal affection to the beloved Disciple, it is better to have no wound than to experience the most sovereign Balsam, which if it work a cure yet usually leaves a scar behind.—[4]

Tho' it was and is my intention to defer the consideration of Milton's own character to the conclusion of this Address, yet I could not prevail on myself to approach to the Paradise without impressing on your minds the *conditions* under which such a work was producible, the original Genius having been assumed as the immediate agent and efficient cause— and these conditions I was to find in the character of his times and in his own character. The age, in which the foundations of his mind were laid, was congenial to it, as our golden æra of profound Erudition and original Genius—that in which its superstructure was carried up, no less congenial by a sterness of its discipline and a shew of self-control highly flattering to the imaginative dignity of "an heir of Fame"[5]— and which won him over from the dear-loved delights of academic groves, and Cathedral aisles, to the Anti-prelatic Party—and it acted on him, no doubt, and modified his studies by its characteristic contro- versial spirit, no less busy ⟨indeed⟩ in political than in theological & ecclesiastical dispute, but the former always more or less in the guise of the latter—and as far as Pope's censure of our Poet, that he makes God the Father a School-divine is just,[6] we must attribute it to the character of his Age, from which the men of genius, who escaped, escaped by a worse disease, the licentiousness of the French court—. —Such were the nidus or soil in which he was, in the strict sense of the word, the circumstances of his mind.[7]—in the mind itself purity, piety, an imagination to which neither the Past nor the Present were interesting except as far as they called forth and embraced the great Ideal, in which and for which he lived, a keen love of Truth which after many weary pursuits found an harbour in a sublime listening to the low still voice in his own spirit, and as keen a love of his Country which after disappointment, still more depressive at once expanded and sobered into a love of Man as the Probationer of Immortality, these

[4] Source untraced.

[5] Recalling Milton's sonnet *On Shake- spear* line 5: "Dear son of memory, great heir of fame". C quoted this in Lect 4 of the 1818 series (at n 3).

[6] In Pope *Imitations of Horace* bk II ep 1 lines 101–2:

In Quibbles, Angel and Archangel join,

And God the Father turns a School- Divine.

C referred to Pope's censure again in *TT* 4 Sept 1833.

[7] C seems to mean that Milton was formed by himself; "nidus" means nest, hence fostering source, and in the strict sense "circumstances" means the con- ditions prevailing at the time.

were, these alone could be, the conditions under which such a work could be conceived, and accomplished. By a life-long study he had known

> what was of use to know,
> What best to say could say, to do had done—
> His actions to his words agreed, his words
> To his large Heart gave utterance due, his heart
> Contain'd of good, wise, fair, the perfect shape—[8]

and left the imperishable Total, as a bequest to Ages, in the PARADISE LOST.

(Not perhaps, *here*, but towards or as the conclusion to chastise the fashionable notion, that Poetry is a relaxation, amusement, one of the superfluous Toys & Luxuries of the Intellect!)

Difficult as I shall find it to turn over these Leaves without catching some passage which would tempt one,[9] I propose to consider first, the general plan and arrangement of the work—2nd the subject with its difficulties and advantages—3rd the Poet's *Object*, the Spirit in the Letter, the επιμυθιον εν μυθω[10]—the true School-*divinity*, and lastly, the characteristic excellences, of the poem, & in what they consist and by what means they are produced.

First then, the plan and ordonnance/

1. compared with the Iliad, many of the books of which might change placcs without any injury to the thread of the story—and 2ndly—with both the Iliad and more or less in all epic Poems whose subjects are from History, they have no *rounded* conclusion—they remain after all but a single chapter from the volume of History tho' an ornamented Chapter—. In Homer too the importance of his subject, namely, as the first effort of confederated Greece, an after thought of the critics—& the interest, such as it is, derived from the event as distinguished from the manner of representing these, languid to all but Greeks—The superiority of the Paradise Lost is obvious, but not dwelt on because it may be attributed to Christianity itself, tho' in this instance it comprehends the whole Mahometan World as well as Xtndom[11]—and as the origin of evil, and the combat of Evil and Good, a matter of such interest

---

[8] Adapting *Paradise Regained* III 7–11.

[9] C was presumably holding the copy of *Paradise Lost* from which he quoted later in the lecture; see above, headnote (Background and Circumstances), and n 14, below.

[10] I.e. moral in the tale.

[11] In his Lect 12 F. Schlegel spoke dismissively of *Paradise Lost* as lacking unity and having only occasional passages of beauty. C's view is very different, but he may have picked up Schlegel's comment that Milton used fables taken from the Talmud and the Koran. *Geschichte* II 142–3 (Bohn 278).

to all mankind as to form the basis of all religions, and the true occasion of all Philosophy.

—Next the exquisite simplicity. It and it alone really possesses the Beginning, Middle, and End—the totality of a Poem or circle as distinguished from the ab ovo birth, parentage, &c or strait line of History—an exquisite Propriety in the narrations by Rafael & Adam[12]—et artis est celare artem,[13] the propriety of beginning as he does.—

^bQuotations and Passages referred to.

P. 4—to 5. "thus began"—in proof of fore figure preserved foremost—L. 26 to 83 and of *ascent*[14]

P. 11 "He scarce had ceased" to 12. of Hell resounded. L. 283 to 315.[15]

364 to 520—judgement in humanizing the Spirits to the imagination.[16]

P. 20 (587) further proof—and of the increased humanity of Satan[17]

P. 48—l. 666.—of allegory, and the difference of Poetry from Painting.[18]

P. 63. Beginning of the Third Book—its utility in the construction of the poem, as a connecting link, in addition to its beauty—besides the whole objective character of the Poem.

78. Limbo very *entertaining* but out of character.[19]

^b *CN* III 4495

[12] C seems to mean the long narration by Raphael of the war in heaven and the creation of the world in *Paradise Lost* bks v–vii, and Adam's account of his own memories to Raphael in bk viii.

[13] "And the essence of art is to conceal art", varying the more usual and proverbial "ars est celare artem".

[14] The page-references show that C was using the small octavo edition of *Paradise Lost. A Poem in Twelve Books* printed for a consortium of publishers (1804), from Jacob Tonson's text of 1711. The passage referred to here is I 27–83, from "Say first, for Heav'n hides nothing from thy view" to "Breaking the horrid silence thus began". The "fore figure" here is Satan, whose fall from heaven is here described.

[15] I 283–315, in which Satan emerges from the burning lake to stand on the shore.

[16] Pp 14–18: I 364–520, in which the fallen angels are identified by the "var-

ious names" by which they were later to be known to men.

[17] I 587, in which the description of Satan begins:

Thus far these beyond
Compare of mortal prowess, yet observ'd
Their dread commander . . .

[18] II 666, in which Satan encounters Death and Sin, and Death is described as

The other shape,
If shape it might be call'd that shape had none . . .

C had defined allegory in Lect 3 of the 1818 series (from nn 37 onwards).

[19] III 444–97, in which the future home "Of all things transitorie and vain" is described, that limbo which, in Milton's vision, will be largely peopled by monks and friars.

91. Minute Landscape of Paradise—no attempt to describe Heaven! Judgement.[20]

95. (B. IV. 270) Judicious conclusion with fables of *human forms* prior to the introduction of the first human Pair—[21]

P. 304. Book XI. 248. (Michael finally contrasted with Rafael)[22]

P. 274 (⟨1.⟩ 425. B. X—& ⟨1.⟩ 505.)[23]

96. She as a veil—*Dress*. So 101. 1. 492.—So p. 235 (B. IX. 425)— and again of the Angel (Book V. 276) P. 127.[24]

108.—Love in Paradise—No Rosicrucianism,[25] but far removed as Heaven from Hell, from Dryden's degradation[26]—Explain. The difference in the Like, or correspondent opposites—all the images which preclude passions collected & last the Prayer—[27]

Book VI.

P. 173. 824. After the justification of the Book VI. on the grounds stated by Raphael—(Book V. 1. 560) P. 135—and the philos. p. 133.[28]

---

[20] C was referring to the extended description of Eden, IV 131ff.

[21] Referring to Milton's use of the legend of Proserpine:

Her self a fairer flow'r by gloomy Dis
Was gather'd, which cost Ceres all that pain
To seek her through the world.

[22] Here Eve sees Michael descend, not "sociably mild" like Raphael, but "sublime" as "Satan's dire dread, and in his hand the spear" (line 248).

[23] The page-reference and line-reference do not match: if C meant the first, p 274, then he was thinking of the return of Satan in triumph to hell, x 455ff, but if the line-reference is right, then he referred to the splendour of pandemonium (x 424–5):

citie proud seate
Of *Lucifer* . . .

He contrasted one of these passages with the transformation of the fallen angels to serpents (x 504ff).

[24] C linked various passages describing dress: the first is the appearance of Eve, IV 304ff, in which she, as a veil, "Her unadorned golden tresses wore"; the second, IV 492, refers again to Eve's hair; the third, IX 425, relates to Satan's finding of Eve "Veil'd in a cloud of fra-

grance", and the fourth describes Raphael's appearance as he lands in Eden:

to his proper shape returns
A Seraph wing'd; six wings he wore, to shade
His lineaments divine.

C's argument here was probably about the "metaphysics of dress", as indicated in notes that may relate to this lecture, but were printed by HNC as part of Lect 10 of the 1818 series; see below, App A (at n 6).

[25] Referring to IV 736–57, in which the "connubial love" of Adam and Eve is described, with no implications of mystery or secret knowledge or special powers, which is what C seems to mean by "Rosicrucianism".

[26] Presumably in his opera, *The State of Innocence and Fall of Man* (1677), based on *Paradise Lost*, which turns the story of Adam and Eve into a divertissement; see Lect 4 of the 1811–12 series (at n 46).

[27] The morning prayer of Adam and Eve, V 153–208.

[28] At VI 824ff the Son launches his chariot at the rebel angels and drives them out of heaven; this follows after Raphael's comments in V 560ff on the difficulty in narrating to human ears the "invisible exploits" and "secrets of an-

Book IX. What could not be escaped, how well overcome in the *fall* before the *fall*—and still more magnificently, p. 237. 1. 495.

Book X. The pathos of p. 287. 1. 915.[29]

Why the XIth and the XIIth Books are less interesting, owing in great measure to the habit of reading Poetry for the Story—. If read in connection as the History of mankind nothing can be finer—.

The Beauty of the two last Lines, as presenting *a picture*—and so representative of the state of Man, at best, in the fallen World.—[30]

---

other world''. P 133 contains v 476–505, Raphael's account of the nature of man and the possibility that human bodies

> may at last turn all to spirit,
> Improv'd by tract of time, and wing'd
> ascend
> Ethereal, as we, or may at choice
> Here or in heav'nly paradises dwell.

[29] The fall before the fall is Eve's in IX 494ff; C seems to have been commenting on the problems of treating the fall of man, and the more magnificent

passage, X 914ff, is Eve's plea to Adam not to forsake her:

> Forsake me not thus, Adam, witness
> Heaven
> What love sincere, and reverence in
> my heart
> I bear thee, and unweeting have of-
> fended . . .

[30] XII 648–9:

> They hand in hand with wand'ring
> steps and slow
> Through Eden took their solitary way.

LECTURE 5

DATE AND PLACE OF DELIVERY. Thursday, 11 March 1819, at the Crown and Anchor Tavern, Strand, London.

SUBJECT. Dante and his age.

ADVERTISEMENTS AND ANNOUNCEMENTS. *Courier* Wed, 10 Mar (announcement): "Mr. COLERIDGE'S LECTURES.—Tomorrow Evening, 8 o'clock, on DANTE and the Age of DANTE; the Lecture following, SPENSER'S *Faery Queen*, etc.; and on Thursday, 25th March, Mr. COLERIDGE will deliver his last lecture, the subject being the *Don Quixote*." *The Times* and *M Chron* Thurs, 11 Mar (advertisements): "Mr. COLERIDGE'S LECTURE for THIS EVENING DANTE . . ." (the rest a variant of the *Courier* announcement). *New Times* Thurs, 11 Mar (advertisement): "MR. COLERIDGE'S LECTURE for THIS EVENING:—DANTE'S DIVINA COMOEDIA, and the AGE OF DANTE . . ." (the rest as in the *Courier* announcement).

TEXT. Under the heading of the title and date, C wrote notes for this lecture in N 29. A heavily edited and reworked version of these notes, leaving out the opening and final paragraphs, was printed in *LR* I 150–66 by HNC as relating to Lect 10 in the 1818 series. Raysor, who did not have access to N 29, reprinted in *Misc C* 145–57 what he found in *LR*. The notes were printed for the first time in full and as C set them down by Kathleen Coburn in *CN* III 4498. The text printed below is based on that of *CN*, but omits the first paragraph and cancellations, with the exception of the last paragraph, which is scored through with three lines to cancel it. However, it reflects something of C's mood and so is included here in square brackets. The opening paragraph is given, below, under "Background." A further brief note, written on the facing page opposite the list of Dante's "excellencies" at the end of the notes on this poet, also seems to be connected with Lect 5 and is reprinted below from the text in *CN* III 4500. Like the notes on Dante, this refers to F. Schlegel's *Geschichte der alten und neuen Litteratur* and touches upon the crusades and chivalry, which C talked about in the first part of his lecture.

REPORTS. No reports of this lecture have been found.

BACKGROUND AND CIRCUMSTANCES. C's notes for this lecture begin with a "splenetic joke" about the thin attendance at his lectures: "Dante and the Age of Dante, Thursday Evening, 11 March, 1819, 1/4 after 8, Crown and Anchor, Strand. Admission, Five Shillings, excepting Subscribers to the Course, and Franks presented by the Lecturer, S. T. Coleridge. Call these 3 classes A. B. & C. and the proportion will be—A = 1/50 B. ½/50 C 48½/50—.—This is a mere splenetic joke; but the spleen is not removed tho' the joke is by the real truth and matter of fact—viz. that the Lecture Room, Advertisements, and Coach hire amount to 5£ each evening, and that the Receipts very often fall short of 3£, and once of 2£!—But Poverty and I are a match made in heaven— and whom God hath united, let no man put asunder—say the Public. O 'tis a very religious Age!" The cancelled concluding paragraph of the notes contains a further reminder about his expectation of a small audience. His letters during this period also contain several complaints of this kind, but little otherwise is known about the circumstances in which the lectures were given.

In this lecture, as in his previous one on Milton, he seems to have begun with general comments on the age of Dante and then developed his lecture from the text he had with him, using his notes, which include a number of page-references as pointers. The page-references are to H. F. Cary's translation of *The Vision; or Hell, Purgatory, and Paradise, of Dante Alighieri* (3 vols 1814). C was instrumental in arranging for the remaining copies of the 1814 edition to be issued by Taylor and Hessey in 1818, and he no doubt referred to Cary in Lect 10 of the 1818 series, which was on Dante and Milton (see the headnote to that lecture: Background and Circumstances). The thousand or so copies remaining were quickly sold, and a new edition appeared in 1819, with a preface dated Jul of that year, which included an expanded version of the "Chronological View of the Age of Dante" Cary provided in the 1814 edition and a complimentary acknowledgement in the preface of C's "strenuous exertions" in recommending the translation "to public notice". In the course of this lecture, as C reminded himself in his notes, he spoke, presumably with enthusiasm, about Cary's translation. He also included in the notes a reminder that he was to pay a "compliment to Hallam", i.e. Henry Hallam, whose *View of the State of Europe During the Middle Ages* (2 vols) had appeared in Jun 1818. He borrowed material from this work for the lecture, though the notes also show that he was taking issue with F. Schlegel's historical account of mediaeval poetry and allegory in his *Geschichte der alten und neuen Litteratur* and incorporating and modifying ideas from A. W. Schlegel and from Schiller. The notes indicate that C had prepared for the lecture and that it was not simply a repetition of Lect 10 of 1818. At the same time, the two lectures may have had much in common, and the poor attendance C expected may have been in part owing to this, that the course, with its lectures on Milton, Dante, Spenser, and Cervantes, looked too much like the course he had given only a year previously in Fleet Street. The additional note, *CN* III 4500, printed below in connexion with this lecture, has a reference in it to *Antar, a Bedoueen Romance*, which he was reading in the early months of 1819. This was inserted by him probably as a later addition, but he used this translation from the Arabic in his next literary lecture, a week later, and quoted from it when discussing Spenser; see Lect 6, below (at nn 7 and 8).

LECTURE 5

RECORDS OF THE LECTURE

COLERIDGE'S NOTES
CN III 4498 AND 4500

*a*1. As remarked in a former Lecture on a different subject (for the most diverse have tangents)[1] the Gothic character and its good & evil fruits apppear less in Italy than in any other part of European Christendom— / Less *Romance* or rather a Romance instead of Chivalry—earlier imitation of the Latin Literature,—above all, far less of that singular chain of independents interdependent—in short, an afterbirth of eldest Greece— and of Italy itself under the Kings & first Consuls of Rome—free as *little Republics*[2]—& as a necessary counter-balance a far greater uniformity of Religion, common to all—Just as in Greece—

2. In the height of this DANTE born and flourished—at the acme of Scholastic Philosophy even *in itself*; far more in Italy where it never had the predominance as Northward—⟨Dante's works *read* as a Philosophy—John of Ravenna⟩[3] Dante the Link of Christian poetry and

---

a *CN* III 4498, omitting the first paragraph

[1] C was referring to Lect 3 of the 1818 series (at n 17), as his note on Petrarch in *CN* III 4388 shows. The source of the comment is F. Schlegel *Geschichte* II 4 (Bohn 197). "The Chivalry of the North, the genuine Chivalry, was less felt in Italy than in any other part of Europe."

[2] C perhaps here developed his notes from Henry Hallam *View of the State of Europe During the Middle Ages* (2 vols 1818) I 237–46, in which Hallam describes the election of Conrad II of Germany as King of the Romans in 1024, and the rise of city-states in Lombardy and Tuscany during the following century, and comments on "the love of freedom" of "these little republics" (I 246). He also reports their wars and mutual hostilities, which C does not seem to

have touched on.

[3] The idea of treating Dante as a philosopher may have been suggested by Hallam *View* II 597–8, in which he says that we read Dante for his "moral wisdom", and that in Italy his "abstruse philosophy" was more highly regarded than his poetry. Hallam does not there mention John of Ravenna (c 1346–1417), the scholar and teacher who provided a link between Petrarch and the later humanists. The argument of this paragraph is close to that developed at length in Lects 9 and 10 of the lectures on the history of philosophy: *P Lects* (1949) 283– 94. There C argued (p 291) that as scholastic philosophy lost its utility, it was replaced by superstition, "the other part of the Gothic mind".

Christianized Philosophy, and in this union, the Link again of the Platonic, christianized into the Mystic, and the *Aristot*otelean,[4] by the numerous minute articles of Faith & Ceremony & converted into Hairsplitting—.—Impossible to understand the genius of Dante, difficult to understand the Poem, without dwelling on the SCHOOL MEN, in reference to the preceding & following centuries—i.e. X.[5] degraded into complex Fetisch Worship by its divorce from Philosophy—.

Philosophy revived under condition of defending this Superstition and in so doing necessarily leading to its subversion, in exact proportion to the influence of the Schools—ex. gr. Most in Germany—next in England—then in France—then in Spain—least of all in Italy—. We have therefore to take Poetry as *simply* christianized, but without the further or gothic accession of proper Chivalry—at a somewhat later Period the importations from the East, thro' Venice & the Crusades, strongest in Italy.—[6]

3. We have therefore to seek for the differences produced by Xtnty itself—*First*, Allegory as the substitute of Polytheism; but this I defer to my next Lecture ⟨for I differ from *Schlegel* & his Ritter-ged.-Minne. & *allegories*⟩—[7]

---

[4] Punning on the Latin "toto" (all), explained by C's comments in Lects 5 and 10 of the lectures on the history of philosophy: "Aristotle . . . affirmed that all our knowledge had begun in experience", and "The tyranny of Aristotle and the Aristotelian philosophy called forth the visionaries and the mystics." *P Lects* (1949) 187, 282.

[5] I.e. Christianity.

[6] C may have drawn here on F. Schlegel's account, in Lect 8, of the influence on Europe of oriental poetry as a result of the crusades (*Geschichte* I 275–81, Bohn 180–4), and also on Lect 9 (*Geschichte* II 20, Bohn 206), in which Schlegel said that the arts and manners of the Venetians were copied from those of the East.

[7] For C narrative allegory was a Christian development, and he noted in 1818 how "among the classics" there were "of narrative or epic allegories scarce any, the multiplicity of their Gods and Goddesses precluding it" (see Lect 3 of the 1818 series, at n 43), which explains the contrast with "Polytheism". He did not disagree with Schlegel on the nature

of allegory as chiefly a Christian genre. His reference is to Schlegel's Lect 9 (*Geschichte* II 6–7, Bohn 198), in which Schlegel says that in the Middle Ages three main genres of poetry were most important, poetry of chivalry, love poems, and allegory, by which he meant poems in which the inward disposition and the outward form were allegorical, as in the works of Dante ("so würde man drey Hauptgattungen als die wesentlichsten finden, das Rittergedicht, den Minnegesang und die Allegorie. Solche Gedichte nähmlich, in denen der Zweck und Gegenstand, die innere Einrichtung des Ganzen, ja auch die äussere Form schon allegorische ist, wie in dem Werke des Dante"). C's disagreements may have been, as Kathleen Coburn suggests in *CN* III 4498n, firstly that Schlegel placed a high valuation on allegory, and C a low one (cf Lect 7, below, n 9), and secondly that C rejected the notion that Dante's poem was essentially an allegory, which is the point of his § 6. If the notes HNC printed as belonging to Lect 3 of the 1818 series really belong to Lect 6 in 1819, then C did indeed go

Secondly & mainly—the opposition to the Spirit of Pagan Greece which receiving the very names of their Gods from Egypt yet soon deprived them of all the universal/[8] To interest, the Ideas must be turned into Finites, and these into Finites anthropomorphic—Their Religion, their Poetry, their very pictures, statues &c &c/[9]

The reverse in Christianity—Finites, even the human Form, must be brought into connection with the Infinite—must be thought of in some shadowy, or enduring relation—Soul, Futurity &c and—⟨3⟩ Hence two great Effects—a combination of Poetry with *Doctrines*[10]—and ⟨4.⟩ (by turning the mind inward on its own *essence* instead of its circumstances and communities) with *sentiment.*—The re-action of the Poet's general reflections on any Act or Image more *fore-grounded* than the act itself—. The change of arms between Diomed & the Trojan Prince in Homer with the two Knights, Saracen and Christian, in Ariosto—[11]

on to discuss allegory further; see Lect 6 headnote (Text). He commented on the polytheism of the Greeks also in Lect 1 of the 1813 series (sentence containing n 21).

[8] C's information came from Herodotus 2.50, as is shown by his discussion in Lect 2 of the lectures on the history of philosophy; see *P Lects* (1949) 88–9.

[9] Here C was rehearsing familiar points recalled from his reading of A. W. Schlegel's Lect 1, in which a contrast is drawn between ancient art as finite and plastic and modern or romantic art as infinite and picturesque. *DKL* I 14, 23 (Black I 9, 15). C was also using Schlegel's source in Schiller's "Über naive und sentimentalische Dichtung", first published in *Die Horen* in 1795–6, from which he culled the comparison that follows between Homer and Ariosto (see n 11, below). For a detailed account of the differences and connexions between Schiller and Schlegel, and of C's use of Schiller here, see *CN* III 4498 f 139n. As Kathleen Coburn notes, the words "pictures, statues" are casually scrawled, and another reading is possible; so HNC has "Hence their religion, their poetry, nay, their very pictures, become statuesque", which he may owe to Schiller. See Lect 1 of the 1813 series (at n 21).

[10] See § 7, below (and n 14). The im-

mediate source seems to be F. Schlegel, but Kathleen Coburn traces an echo here of Schiller; see *CN* III 4498 f 139n.

[11] The examples C found in Schiller's "Über naive and sentimentalische Dichtung": *Kleinere prosaische Schriften* (Leipzig 1800) II 52–5. The references are firstly to the incident in *Iliad* 6.212–31, in which Diomedes, on discovering that their grandfathers were friends, refuses to fight with Glaucus and exchanges armour with him; and secondly to Ariosto's *Orlando furioso* I xxii 1–6 ("le" in line 5 and "h" in "haversi" in line 6 are intrusive), in which the action is presented through Ariosto's commentary:

Oh! the great bounty of each ancient knight!
Rivals they were, and of a faith diverse,
As yet they felt of the sharp strokes the might,
Sore in their bodies from their strife perverse;
Thro' paths oblique, dark woods they take their flight,
Nor of each other least suspicion nurse.

Tr William Huggins (1757). C seems to have coined the verb "fore-grounded", which is not in *OED*.

O gran bontà de cavalieri antiqui
Eran rivali, eran di fè diversi,
E si sentian degli aspri colpi iniqui
Per tutta la persona anco dolersi
E pur per le selve oscure e calli obliqui
Insieme van senza sospetto haversi—

5. The different mode in which the imagination is acted on/ Pantheon, the whole perceived in *perceived* harmony with the parts that compose it—where the Parts preserve their distinct individuality, this is Beauty simply—where they melt undistinguished into the Whole, it is Majestic Beauty—in Chr. the parts are in themselves sharply distinct, and this distinction counterbalanced only by their multitude & variety—while the Whole, and that there is a Whole produced, is altogether a Feeling, in which all the thousand several impressions lose themselves as in a universal Solvent.—[12]

6. I have deferred the consideration of Allegory;[13] but I must not defer my reason—as respects Dante's Poem—. The Poem is a system of moral political, and theological Truths with arbitrary personal exemplifications—⟨the punishments indeed allegorical *perhaps*—⟩

7. The comb. of Poetry with Doctrines one of the charac. of Xtn Poetry—but in this Dante has failed,[14] far more than Milton—

8.—But to all these we must add the modification from the state of N. Italy, intensely represented in Dante's own Life—. Importance attached to Individuals by democratic faction—vast field for the passions, when envy &c can assume the form of patriotism even for the individuals—

9 Aggravated as well as colored by the Guelf and Ghibelline factions—here & in 8 an *historical movement* with compliment to Hallam/[15] n.b. the Pope had been[b] recently *territorialized* his authority—

[b] A slip for "but"?

[12] This is a particularly interesting formulation of a contrast C made at least as early as 1810 (see *CN* III 4021). He was no doubt influenced here by F. Schlegel's glowing account of the manifold variety of Gothic architecture as contributing to a feeling of unity and conveying the idea of eternity. *Geschichte* I 292–3 (Bohn 190–1).

[13] To the next lecture; see C's § 3, above.

[14] C is echoing Schlegel's Lect 9, in which he says that poetry and Christian doctrine "are not harmoniously wedded in his poem, of which some passages do not rise higher than didactic theology" ("die Poesie und das Christenthum auch bei ihm nicht in volkomner Harmonie sind, und dass sein Werk zwar nicht im Ganzen, aber doch Stellenweise nur ein theologisches behrgedicht sei"). *Geschichte* II 13 (Bohn 202).

[15] C's §§ 8 and 9 read like a digest of passages in Hallam *View* I 258–61. Hallam describes there how Pope Innocent III extended his authority, gaining "temporal sovereignty" over Rome, and how cities gladly "put themselves under the

the increase of which would not be to the citizens of Free Republics what it was to the Vassals oppressed by the proud Barons—/—

Dante's excellencies—

1. Style—why superior to Milton's—The passion and miracle of Words after a slumber in Barbarism, which of itself gives a romantic somewhat not felt by the original Classics themselves.—*P. 3.—& 53.*[16]

2. Images not only taken from obvious Nature & all intelligible to all; but ever conjoined with the universal feeling received from them—opposed to the idiosyncracies of some meritorious modern Poets—P. 8. As Florets—and here of Mr Carey's Translation—[17]

3. The wonderful sublimity of the (p. 10)[18] explained from the true nature of RELIGION. The Reason + Understanding—[19]

4. Picturesque beyond all, modern or ancient—more in the stern style of Pindar than of any other—p. 12, 13. 95—‖ p. 27, *præterpictur*—[20]

---

protection of the Holy See, which held out the prospect of securing them from . . . rapacious partizans''. He then goes on to say that it was the Pope's interest to ''maintain the freedom of the Italian republics'', and that the independent cities of Tuscany formed a union for the aggrandisement of the Papacy. There follows, on p 260, an account of the Guelf and Ghibelline factions, their jealousies and animosities, and of the way these affected individuals, stirring passions so that, ''From this time, every city, and almost every citizen, gloried in one of these barbarous denominations''. C's phrase ''here & in 8 an *historical movement*'' suggests that he developed at this point a more elaborate sketch of Italian history relative to Dante's time than is included in his notes, and he may well have borrowed more largely from Hallam.

[16] The page-references are to *The Vision; or Hell, Purgatory, and Paradise, of Dante Alighieri* tr H. F. Cary (3 vols 1814) vol I, or ''Hell''. P 3 contains canto I 63–98, Dante's meeting with Virgil; p 53 refers to canto XIII 1–29, the description of the ''drear mystic wood'' in which those who have done violence to themselves are turned into trees.

[17] Canto II 127ff:

As florets, by the frosty air of night

Bent down and clos'd, when day has
   blanch'd their leaves,
Rise all unfolded on their spiry stems;
So was my fainting vigour new re-
   stor'd . . .

On C's compliment to Cary, see above, headnote to this lecture (Background and Circumstances).

[18] Referring to the opening of canto III, the famous inscription on Hell-gate, ending ''All hope, abandon, ye who enter here''.

[19] For C's distinction between reason and understanding, see also Lect 1 of the 1818–19 series (at n 18) and *Friend (CC)* I 153–61.

[20] Canto III 95–126, which contains the vivid account of Charon, ''demoniac form, | With eyes of burning coal'', set against p 27, the opening of canto VII, in which Plutus, the god of riches, is encountered in the shape of a fiend, who collapses at Virgil's command.

As sails, full spread and bellying with
   the wind,

Drop suddenly collaps'd, if the mast split;
So to the ground down dropp'd the cruel
   fiend.

''Præterpictur'' suggests that C is groping for a word to express ''picturesque beyond the picturesque'' (so *CN* III 4498n). There may be an echo here of

5. P. 19—Giotto? or Dante—[21]

6. p. 21. Francesca—*Pathos*—and p. 145. Ugolino—[22]

7. p. 30—Topographic REALITY[23]—Dwell on this as Dante's Charm, and that which makes him indeed a *Poet*—Nature worse than Chaos, a thousand delusive forms having reality *only* for the Passions, they excite: the Poet compels them into the service of the Permanent/—

8—such endless subtle beauties in Dante—as ex. gr. p. 126, the 3 *first* lines of Canto XXIX.[24]

Comparison with Milton—?? if so, p. 150, 151, Canto 34th & last.—[25]

[N.B. At the conclusion of this Lecture to announce the Monday nexts fully if the Audience do not make it (as I suspect) useless by its paucity—][c]

[d]There[26] is to the best of my knowlege—no reason to suppose that during the period from the first to the last Crusade or in the century following any oriental work of Fiction, or poetized History was *translated* into any of the European Languages: whatever may have been

[c] Brackets added by the editor; the note was cancelled by C
[d] *CN* III 4500

A. W. Schlegel's labelling, in his first lecture, of modern art as picturesque; for him the picturesque work represented things brought together by accident but somehow blended into a whole and conveying a unity of impression. *DKL* II ii 16–17 (Black II 100–1). But see Lect 9 of the 1811–12 series (at n 35).

[21] This refers to the opening of canto V, in which Dante descends to the second circle of Hell and sees Minos sentencing carnal sinners. In describing Minos as "Grinning with ghastly feature" (v 5), Cary consciously echoed Milton's image of Death (Death "grinn'd horrible a ghastly smile": *Paradise Lost* II 845), reminding C of the figure of Death in the frescoes of the Campo Santo in Pisa, once attributed to Giotto; see Lect 1 of the 1818 series (at nn 13 and 23).

[22] Canto V 73ff, in which Dante and Virgil meet the gentle lovers Paolo and Francesca, contrasted with the opening of canto XXXIII, in which they encounter Ugolino, cruelly murdered with his children by imprisonment and starvation.

[23] The end of canto VII, in which the Stygian lake is described, at the foot of "grey wither'd cliffs", and full of miry figures sunk in the marsh and brutally slashing at one another.

[24]
So were mine eyes inebriate with the view
Of the vast multitude, whom various wounds
Disfigur'd, that they long'd to stay and weep.

[25] *Canto* XXXIV, the last in Hell, beginning with the description of "Hell's Monarch", the terrifying three-faced giant C intended to compare with Milton's description of Satan, probably *Paradise Lost* IV 114ff. There is no record to show whether he did in fact make this comparison.

[26] This note is written immediately below the notes on Dante, *CN* III 4498, and seems to belong to Lect 5. C perhaps used it to develop his account of the "importations from the East" in § 2 of his main lecture-notes (at n 6, above).

transferred—The Arab. nights evidently persian—and Ferdusi[27]—when first translated, as far as the latter can be said to have been translated at all?—Therefore it must have been from the Story-tellers in the Levant Coffee-houses—if so, Schlegel is in an error with regard to the *Persian* Character of the Round Table Allegorical Romances,[28] & the Italian Chivalries—⟨*Antar*⟩[29]

[27] C was once again, as for Lect 2 of the 1818 series, using F. Schlegel's lectures on the history of literature, and he begins by repeating a point made in 1818 (see Lect 2 of that series, at nn 27 and 28), that the influence of oriental literature on Europe was not great and such influence as existed was Persian rather than Arabian. *Geschichte* I 275 (Bohn 180). Schlegel goes on to say that the *Thousand and One Nights* is of Persian origin, and comments at length on the epic of Ferdusi, the spelling C takes from him. *Geschichte* I 277, 275–82 (Bohn 182, 180–4). Firdausi, regarded as the greatest Persian poet for his huge *Shahnama* or *Book of Kings*, died c 1020; a translation of part of it into English was published in Calcutta in 1785, and of selections in London in 1815, but the whole was not translated until much later; see *CN* III 4500n.

[28] C seems to have misunderstood Schlegel, and to have thought he was establishing a connexion where, in Lect 8, he was passing from an account of the Arthurian tales as peculiarly allegorical, and as enriched by material from the East afforded by the crusades, to a general discussion of the influence of the East on European poetry, in which he says that the crusades brought to bear a Persian rather than an Arabian influence.

[29] C had been reading *Antar, a Bedoueen Romance* tr Terrick Hamilton, published in Jan 1819, and used it in Lect 6 (see headnote to that lecture and nn 7 and 8). The Introduction, p vi, contains the following sentence, which may be the point of the reference here: "whether from the frequent intercourse between the Eastern and Western Kingdoms of the Roman world, in the 8th, 9th and 10th centuries, our Romance writers imbibed their taste for the adventures of Chivalry from this singular Tale, is a question, to the Solution of which we may look forward, when the whole of it shall be before the public". See also *CN* III 4500n.

LECTURE 6

DATE AND PLACE OF DELIVERY. Thursday, 18 March 1819, at the Crown and Anchor Tavern, Strand, London.

SUBJECT. Spenser's *Faerie Queene.*

ADVERTISEMENTS AND ANNOUNCEMENTS. The general advertisements described above (Introduction to the 1819 series, first paragraph), listed this lecture as on "SPENSER, and his relation to CHAUCER and ARIOSTO". The advertisements for Lect 5 went on to announce the subject of this lecture as "SPENSER" or "SPENSER's *Faery Queen*, etc.". *Courier* Wed, 17 Mar (announcement): "MR. COLERIDGE'S LECTURE FOR THURSDAY EVENING.—On the *Fairy Queen* of SPENSER, the *Italian School of Poetry*, and the nature of Allegory . . ." (this continues with an announcement of the next philosophical lecture). *The Times, M Chron*, and *New Times* Thurs, 18 Mar (advertisements): as in the *Courier*, with the alteration to "THIS EVENING".

TEXT. C entered a series of eight numbered notes for this lecture under the heading "Spenser" in N 29 ff 136–136ᵛ, with a cross reference to a further brief note on f 137. These notes, reworked and reduced in number to six, appear to be the source of the notes HNC printed in *LR* I 91–7 (reprinted in *Misc C*), though these do not contain C's reference to *Remorse*, his play from which he quoted in the lecture, or his reference in the footnote on f 137 to *Antar, a Bedoueen Romance* tr from the Arabic by Terrick Hamilton and published in Jan 1819. HNC associated these notes with Lect 3 of the 1818 series and printed them as part of a longer piece on Spenser, combining them with material from other sources. His omission of the reference to *Antar* may have been deliberate, but raises at least the possibility that he had access to notes for the 1818 lecture, now lost, and did not see N 29 (see *CN* III 4501 f 136ᵛn). The notes in *LR* are close enough in matter and sequence to those in N 29 to make this improbable; in any case, the notes printed by Kathleen Coburn in the form in which C wrote them in *CN* III 4501 clearly relate to the lecture of 1819. The text printed below is based on that of *CN*, but omits cancellations. Advertisements for this lecture announced that C would speak on allegory, but a note on this subject, now BM MS Egerton 2800 ff 48–9, fits more clearly into the sequence of Lect 3 of 1818 and is accordingly given there (see also the headnote to that lecture), though C may have reused those notes for Lect 6 of 1819. If C included comments on "the *Italian School of Poetry*", as the advertisements promised, he may again have used notes he made for Lect 3 in 1818 (see headnote to that lecture: Text). No notes on this subject specifically associated with the 1819 series have been found.

REPORTS. No reports of this lecture have been found.

BACKGROUND AND CIRCUMSTANCES. Nothing is known about this lecture apart from what C's notes show. The page- and column-references C provided in his notes were to *The Works of the English Poets, from Chaucer to Cowper* ed Alexander Chalmers (21 vols 1810), in which Spenser's poems appear in vol III. C probably received a set on its publication (see *CN* III 3653n), but there is no evidence that he used this edition for lectures before 1819, even if he may well have done so in 1818. No marginalia on Spenser in a set of Chalmers have been recorded, although he annotated Spenser in two sets of *B*

Poets. He also quoted from *Antar*, which he had begun to read almost as soon as it was published, according to a letter of 31 Jan 1819 (*CL* IV 917). W. R. Hamilton, brother of the translator, Terrick Hamilton, was attending C's lectures, and apologised at the lecture on *King Lear* given on 28 Jan for not having sent him "a Copy of his Brother's work". In the Introduction to *Antar* C found a comment on the *Arabian Nights* that prompted him to add a reference to *Antar* in an entry in N 29 written immediately below his notes for his lecture on Dante (Lect 5), and he added a cross reference to *Antar* in his notes for Lect 6, with page-numbers for quotations. It seems likely, then, that he was reading or re-reading *Antar* immediately before he gave this lecture. He also quoted some lines from his own play *Remorse*, staged at Drury Lane Theatre in 1813, and paid a compliment to Walter Scott, as a writer who glorified his country, but whether with reference to his novels, the authorship of which remained anonymous at this time, or to the poems, is not certain. In a letter to Thomas Allsop of Apr 1820, by which time the anonymity was broken, C praised the novels but was more critical of the poems (*CL* V 32–4). Once again, as for the other lectures in this series, C seems to have brought his recent reading to bear on Lect 6 and to have given fresh thought to what he was to say.

LECTURE 6

RECORD OF THE LECTURE

COLERIDGE'S NOTES
CN III 4501

Spenser.

1 The indescribable sweetness of his verse distinguished from Shakspear & Milton/ p. 51. Stanza. 3, β.—and p. 387, s! 4, β.[1]

2 The scientific construction of his metre, 52. S. 3, α.[2]

3. The harmony of his description with the allegorical and activity of the Poem, p. 53, 4, β—and p. 64, St. 2, α.[3]

4. The quintessential Spirit of christian Chivalry in all his characters, but more especially in those of Women—. The ancients knew no way of making their women interesting but by unsexualizing them, Medea, Electra—contrast Una, 5 C. I, α.—[4]

5. The exceeding *vividness* of his descriptions ⟨not picturesque; but a wondrous *series* as in certain Dreams—⟩ P. 73, His haughty Helmet.[5]

6. The marvellous independence or true imaginative absence of all particular place & time—it is neither in the domains of History or Geography, is ignorant of all artificial boundary—truly in the Land of

---

[1] The references are to vol III of *The Works of the English Poets, from Chaucer to Cowper* ed Alexander Chalmers (21 vols 1810), the letters "α" and "β" indicating the first and second columns on the page. C here cited *The Faerie Queene* bk I canto 1 st 27, "His lady seeing all, that chaunst, from farre . . .", and *Astrophel* st 4, "A gentle shepheard borne in Arcady . . .".

[2] Chalmers III 52 col 1: *The Faerie Queene* bk I canto 1 st 34, "A little lowly hermitage it was . . .".

[3] *The Faerie Queene bk* I canto 2 st

1, "By this the northerne wagoner had set", and bk I canto 5 st 2, "At last, the golden orientall gate . . .".

[4] C seems to have meant p 50, canto 1 col 1, i.e. bk I canto 1 sts 4 and 5, "A lovely ladie rode him faire beside . . ." and "So pure and innocent, as the same lambe . . .".

[5] C may have read to his audience several stanzas, beginning with bk I canto 7 st 31, "His haughtie helmet, horrid all with gold", describing Prince Arthur's armour.

409

Faery—i.e. in mental space—Reminds me of Alhadra's wish—Would to Alla!⁶[*]

> The Raven or the Sea-mew were appointed
> To bring me food—or rather that my soul
> Might draw in life from the universal air—
> It were a blesséd lot in some small skiff
> Along some ocean's boundless solitude
> To float forever with a careless course
> And think myself the only Being alive!—

Indeed, Spenser himself uses almost the same image, his *symbolizing* purpose being *his* mariner's compass in P. 116, last St. β—& two first St. of p. 117.⁹

7. Nationality, eminent in Spenser: tho' a common characteristic of our elder poets.— To *glorify their country*—this was the great Object—and how much it tells, let Spain & her Cid declare—.¹⁰ Here a deserved compliment to Walter Scott/¹¹ and the Judgement no less than the just feelings.—/ The very names in an E. India victory—what a damper to all interest—. Illustrated in Spenser's Chronicle of British Kings, p.

* Spenser—Satyrane compared with Antar, SAT. p. 69, I, β.—Antar, ANTAR, p. 28. 29. *30.* & **p. 49.**⁷
The descriptions of Spenser—p. 53 of Antar—& p. 144 of Spenser, Eftsoones/ War-Song. 59.⁸

⁶ Alhadra's lines in C's *Remorse* IV iii 13–20; *PW* (EHC) II 868 (var).
⁷ *The Faerie Queen* bk I canto 6 sts 23ff, describing the birth and upbringing of Satyrane,

> in life and maners wilde
Emongst wild beastes and woods, from lawes of men exilde.

This is to be compared with passages in *Antar* describing how the warrior Shedad lies with a black woman who tends flocks in the fields; she gives birth to Antar, a shaggy-haired, wild child, who kills a wolf with his bare hands, subdues herds of camels, and is quite fearless. On p 49 he fights a lion, overcomes it, then roasts and eats its four legs, before going to sleep with its head for a pillow.
⁸ Bk II canto 12 st 70, "Eftsoones they heard a most melodious sound", the harmonious music of the Bower of Bliss; C related it to the description (*Antar* 53) of a feast at which Antar watches a group of "damsels" take off their robes and

dance to the music made by servants. The feast is interrupted by marauding horsemen who carry off the women, but Antar rescues them, and on p 59 Semeeah, wife of Antar's father, sings a song celebrating the rescue effected by Antar.
⁹ Guyon, having lost the Palmer, his guide, rides on alone, and Spenser compares him to a mariner steering his boat through cloud and darkness by "card and compass"; C thinks of his purpose, or quest for "praise-worthy deeds", as his guide or compass.
¹⁰ C had recently been reading F. Schlegel's account of the mediaeval *Poema del Cid* as the great national epic of Spain, but he knew RS's version, *The Chronicle of the Cid* (1808); see *CN* III 3708 and n and *BL* ch 3 (*CC*) I 59n–60.
¹¹ C thought less well of Scott's poems than of his novels, but well enough to find in them "*true picturesque Unity*", and Scott certainly glorified his country in verse. See *CL* v 33.

130 (Book II. Canto X.)[12] and the marriage of the Thames to the Medway, p. 235. (Book IV. Canto XI.)[13] Quote his sweet reference to Ireland, p. 238. I, α with 380. Colin Clout β. One day, quoth he—[14]

⟨add the prejudices of Chivalry, sometimes dear to *impermanent* permanence-loving Man (299.)⟩[15]

8.—Spenser's great character of mind, Fancy under the conditions of Imagination, with a feminine tenderness & almost maidenly purity— above all, deep moral earnestness—. The conception of Talus is, per- haps, the boldest effort of imaginative Power[16]—as if no substance so untractable to which the Poet would not give Life, as in a Swedenborg World.—[17]

---

[12] The phrase is from the preliminary quatrain to canto 10.

[13] The account of the marriage begins in st 8 and includes the roll-call of guests, among them Neptune, Amphitrite, Phor- cys, and many more.

[14] *The Faerie Queene* bk IV canto 11 st 41, "There was the Liffy rolling downe the lea . . .", and *Colin Clouts Come Home Again* lines 56ff. Both passages celebrate the river Mulla as Spenser's own favourite.

[15] *The Faerie Queene* bk VI canto 4 sts 33ff, in which Matilda laments the lack of children to continue the line of the good Sir Bruin and defend his lands from the giant Cormoraunt.

[16] Talus, the iron man who attends on Artegal in *The Faerie Queene* bk V.

[17] "Swedenborg" replaced the can- celled "Dream", which suggests some- thing of what C had in mind. See *CN* III 3474, in which C comments on Swe- denborg's visionary experiences, by which he created a mystical "world" quite distinct from that known by "impressions from the outward Senses", and *CN* IV 4689.

LECTURE 7

DATE AND PLACE OF DELIVERY. Thursday, 25 March 1819, at the Crown and Anchor Tavern, Strand, London.

SUBJECT. Cervantes and *Don Quixote*.

ADVERTISEMENTS AND ANNOUNCEMENTS. The advertisements for the lecture on German philosophy C gave on Mon, 22 Mar, all announced the subject of this lecture as *Don Quixote*. *Courier* Wed, 24 Mar (announcement): "Tomorrow Evening Mr. COLERIDGE concludes his Thursday Evening's Course, with a Lecture on *Don Quixote* and CERVANTES . . ." (this continues as an announcement of the last of the philosophical lectures on Mon, 29 Mar). *The Times, New Times, M Chron* Thurs, 25 Mar (advertisements): as in the *Courier*, with the alteration to "THIS EVENING . . .".

REPORTS. No reports of this lecture have been found.

TEXT. Again C used N 29 and made notes for this lecture under the heading of the date and title "Don Quixote" on ff 135ᵛ–133. The notes consist of a long introduction on the distinction between wit and humour, which is based on the first part of Lect 9 of the 1818 series. The remaining notes are headings for development in the lecture-room, with page-references to the edition of *Don Quixote* C had used for Lect 8 in 1818, the translation by Charles Jarvis (4 vols 1809). HNC printed notes closely related to those in N 29 as connected with Lect 8 (*LR* I 113–21) and Lect 9 (*LR* I 131–8) of the 1818 series. The first group, relating to Cervantes, were reprinted in *Misc C* 98–103, but Raysor was able to substitute for the second group C's ms notes in BM Add MS 34225 ff 63, 74–80. It looks as though C reused materials from two lectures of the 1818 series, with changes and additions, and in a new order, for his last literary lecture. The notes for this lecture in N 29 were printed by Kathleen Coburn in *CN* III 4503, and the text given below is based on that, but omits cancellations.

BACKGROUND AND CIRCUMSTANCES. C's lecture on Cervantes in his 1818 series had been well attended and successful, and in 1819 he seems to have settled for a reworking of that, supplemented by an introduction beginning from "general principles" and largely refashioned from ideas used in Lect 9 in 1818. Probably he was weary of the course and glad to bring it to an end, for he headed his notes for the philosophical lecture on 29 Mar "the Last (O pray Heaven, that it may indeed be the Last) of All". *CN* III 4504. Nevertheless, he went to the trouble of preparing a fresh outline in notes for the lecture, which followed the common pattern of his lectures in his last two literary courses, those of 1818–19 and 1819, in starting from a general introduction and going on to a critical commentary on a text, developed from brief headings, with much use of quotation.

LECTURE 7

RECORD OF THE LECTURE

COLERIDGE'S NOTES
CN III 4503

Thursday, 25 March, 1819.—Don Quixote—
⟨In the critical course, which I am to conclude, on this the 13ᵗʰ Evening, I have usually introduced & as it were laid the foundation of each Lecture by the enunciation of the general principles, from which the particular subject was to receive and at the same time to give illustration—and this I consider as not the least valuable, tho' it may most often have been felt both by the Audience and myself as the heaviest portion, for with it you must have foregone &c—the being interested during the delivery, & the carrying away with you—⟩

Humour and the distinction of the humorous from the Witty, the Droll and the Odd;[1]

Madness and its different sorts—(considered without pretension to medical science);

and the nature and eminence of Symbolical Writing;—[2]

to each of these three, ⟨or at least to my own notions respecting it,⟩ I must devote a few words of explanation in order to render the after Critique on this Master-work of Cervantes' and his Country's genius easily and throughout intelligible. This is not the least valuable tho' it may most often be felt by us both as the heaviest & least entertaining portion of these Critical Disquisitions: for without it I must ⟨have⟩ foregone one at least of the two appropriate objects of a Lecture, that of interesting you during its delivery, and of leaving behind the germs of after thought, the materials of future enjoyment. To have been assured by several of my intelligent Auditors that they have reperused the Hamlet or the Othello with increased satisfaction in consequence of the new points of view in which I had placed these characters is the highest

---

[1] These were topics discussed in Lect 9 of the 1818 series.

[2] On symbolic writing, see below (sentences following n 8), and on madness, below (paragraph containing n 10).

415

compliment, I could receive or desire; and should the address of this Evening open out a new source of pleasure, or enlarge the former, in the perusal of Don Quixote, it will compensate for the failure of any personal and temporary object.—

Humour and (&c)

Wit consists in presenting thoughts or images in an unus⟨u⟩al connection with each other, for the purpose of exciting pleasure by the surprize—this connection may be real & there is in fact a scientific Wit, tho' when the conscious object is truth not amusement, we commonly give it some higher name—or it may be apparent only & transitory—& this again by ⟨Thoughts, or by⟩ words or by images—the first is our Butler's eminence, the second Voltaire's,[3] the third which we oftener call Fancy, constitutes the larger & more peculiar part of the Wit of Shakespear. You can scarce turn to a single speech of Falstaff's without instances of it.—Nor does Wit cease always to deserve the name by being transient or incapable of analysis. Compare it to Fire flies—

Where the Laughable is its own end, and neither inference or Moral is intended, or where at least the Writer would wish it to appear as such, there arises what we call *Drollery*—and lastly when words or images are placed in unusual juxta-position rather than connection, merely because it is unusual, we have the *Odd* or the Grotesque—the occasional use of which in the minor ornaments of architecture is an interesting problem for a student in ⟨the⟩ psychology of the Fine Arts.

Humor is of more difficult definition—I must try to describe it in the first place by its points of diversity from the former. Humour does not, like the different species of Wit, consist wholly in the Understanding and the Senses—no combination of Thoughts, Images, or Words will of itself constitute HUMOUR, unless some peculiarity of character be indicated thereby, as the cause of the same. Compare the Comedies of Congreve with the Falstaff in Henry IV, or with Sterne's Corporal Trim, Uncle Toby and Mr Shandy,[4] & you will feel the difference better than I can express it.—Thus again (to take an instance from the different works of the same writer) in Smollett's Strap, his Lieutenant Bowling, his Morgan, the honest Welshman, and his Matthew Bramble, we have exquisite Humor—while in his Peregrine Pickle we find an abundance

---

[3] As in Lect 9 of the 1818 series (see at nn 7 and 26), C drew his examples from Richter's *Vorschule*, though he liked Butler's *Hudibras* and in *CN* II 2112 cited it as exemplifying the "conjunction disjunctive of Wit".

[4] In Lect 9 of the 1818 series C commented on Falstaff (second paragraph of the *Tatler* report) and on *Tristram Shandy*, noting there "The moral *good* of Sterne in the characters of Trim &c" (at n 22), but the comparison with Congreve is new.

of Drollery, which too often degenerates into mere oddity[5]—in short, we feel that a number of things are put together to counterfeit Humor, not a growth from within—. And this indeed is the origin of the word—derived from Humoral Pathology and excellently put by Ben Jonson.[6]—Hence we may explain the congeniality of Humour with Pathos, so exquisite in Sterne & Smollett—and this would be enough, & indeed less than this has passed for a sufficient account of Humor if we did recollect, that not every pre-dominance of character, even where not precluded by the moral sense as in criminal dispositions, constitutes what we mean by a Humorist, or the presentation of it produce Humor—What then is it? Is it manifold? Or is there some one *humorific* point common to all that can be called *humorous?* I am not prepared to answer this at full even if my Time permitted; but I think, there is—& that it consists in a certain reference to the General, and the Universal, by which the finite great is brought into identity with the Little, or the Little with the ⟨Finite⟩ Great, so as to make both *nothing* by comparison with the Infinite.[7] "It is not without reason, Brother Toby! that Learned Men write dialogues on long Noses."[8] In the highest Humor at least there is always a reference to, a connection with, some general Power not finite in the form of some Finite ridiculously disproportionate in our feelings to that of which it is nevertheless representative/ or by which it is to be displayed.—The *not finite* or *infinite explained*—the Mind, the *idea* of the World, &c is *sine finibus*—subjectively infinite—and this leads us at once to the Symbolical, which cannot perhaps be better defined, in distinction from the Allegorical,[9] than that it is always

---

[5] The first three are characters in *Roderick Random* (1748), whereas Matthew Bramble belongs to *Humphry Clinker* (1771); *Peregrine Pickle* was published in 1751.

[6] In the Prologue to *Every Man Out of His Humour* (acted 1599), in which Jonson applies the four humours (choler, melancholy, phlegm, and blood) by metaphor

Unto the general disposition:
As when some one peculiar quality
Doth so possess a man, that it doth
    draw
All his affects, his spirits, and his
    powers,
In their confluxions, all to run one
    way,

This may be truly said to be a humour.

[7] In this attempt to relate humour to the "General" and the "Infinite" C was recalling Richter's *Vorschule*. What he meant is perhaps clarified by his notes for Lect 9 in the 1818 series (at nn 8 and 27); see also *CN* III 4503 and n, in which Kathleen Coburn discusses in detail the use of Jean Paul here.

[8] *Tristram Shandy* bk III ch 37, "Learned men, brother Toby, don't write dialogues upon long noses for nothing". C was quoting incorrectly, no doubt from memory, a passage cited more accurately in Lect 9 of the 1818 series (at n 21).

[9] The distinction was a vital one for C, who thought of allegory as "but a translation of abstract notions into a pic-

itself a *part* of that of the whole of which it is representative—Here comes a *Sail*—that is, a Ship, is a symbolical Expression—Behold our Lion, when we speak of some gallant Soldier, is allegorical—of most importance to our own present subject, that the latter cannot be other than spoken consciously/ while in the former it is very possible that *the general truth* represented may be working unconsciously in the Poet's mind during the construction of the symbol—yet proves itself by being produced out of his own mind, as the Don Quixote out of the perfectly sane mind of Cervantes—& not by outward observation or historically—/. ⟨The advantage of symbolical writing over allegory, that it presumes no disjunction of Faculty—simple *predomination*⟩

Lastly, Madness—1 Hypochondriasis, or out of his *senses*—2. Derangement of the Understanding, or out of his Wits—3 & Loss of Reason—4. Frenzy—or derangement of *the Sensations*—[10]

Sheet 2.—P. 3.—P. 5. (the non-repetition of the Exper. with the Helmet.)[11] Even the long deliberation about the Horse's name is full of meaning[12]—for in these day-dreams the greater part of the History passes & is carried on *in Words* & look forward to *Words* as what will be said of them—

The advent. with the galley slaves, Vol. I. p. 192—? p. 195 as the only passage in which C. seems C. & not Q. ⟨and yet!⟩[13]

P. 7. Don Quixote's praises of himself only praises of the imaginary Being, he is *acting*—[14]

---

ture-language which is itself nothing but an abstraction from objects of the senses", i.e. as mechanical, whereas symbol was characterised by "a translucence of the Eternal through and in the Temporal"; see *SM* (*CC*) 30 and *CN* III 4498n.

[10] These headings recall the fivefold division of madness in C's little essay on "The Soul and its organs of Sense" ,contributed as entry No 174 in *Omniana* (1812), in which the order is different and includes as a fourth category a combination of the first three. There too he comments on Don Quixote as having lost his wits but not his reason or the use of his senses, "and, therefore, we love and reverence him". *Omniana* II 15.

[11] "Sheet 2" may refer to a lost sheet on which C wrote out passages; the page-references are to *Don Quixote* pt I bk I ch 1 tr Charles Jarvis (4 vols 1809) vol I, in which Don Quixote loses his wits

through reading romances of chivalry, and decides to turn knight-errant, making a pasteboard helmet, which falls apart when he tries his sword on it; so he refurbishes it, but "without caring to make a fresh experiment on it" regards it as a "most excellent helmet".

[12] Jarvis tr I 5–6, pt I bk I ch 1, in which Don Quixote, after much thought, names his horse "Rozinante", i.e. formerly (ante) an ordinary horse (rozin), a name "lofty and sonorous, and at the same time expressive of what he had been, when he was but a common steed".

[13] In pt I bk I ch 22, in which Don Quixote questions some prisoners and is told that they have been chained, tortured, and sent to the galleys for petty thefts, pimping, etc. C evidently felt that Cervantes was speaking in his own voice here.

[14] Jarvis tr I 7, the end of pt I bk I ch

P. 9.—. how happily already is the abstraction from the senses, from observation, and the consequent confusion of the Judgement, marked in this description—. The Knight is describing objects *immediate* to his senses & sensations without borrowing a single trait from either.[15] Would it be difficult to find parallel descriptions in Dryden's Plays—& his successors?—

The story of the Goats in Vol. I. p. 169.[16]—O how admirable a symbol of the dependence of all *copula* on the higher powers of the mind, with the single exception of the succession in time & the accidental relations of Space.—

The contrast between the Madness of Imagination and that of Passion, p. 227, 228, 229.—[17]

Sancho's proverbs (specimen of) 232. ⟨Vol. I.⟩[18]

Vol. III. Adventure of the Lions, 134[19]

P. 194 Don Q's account of his adventures in the cave of *Montesino*[20]

1, in which Don Quixote imagines himself the heroic conqueror of a giant named Caraculiambro.

[15] Jarvis tr I 9, pt I bk I ch 2, in which Don Quixote's first sally forth is described; as he travels he invents stories about himself, incorporating the actual scene around him into them.

[16] Jarvis tr I 169, pt I bk I ch 20. So as to prevent Don Quixote from going off to investigate a dreadful noise at night, Sancho, in order to pass the time till dawn, promises to tell him a story. This concerns a shepherd who has 300 goats which have to be ferried across a river one by one. Sancho tells Don Quixote to keep an account of the goats, but does not give him the information to make this possible, and Sancho makes this a pretext for ending the tale: " 'How many are passed already?' said Sancho. 'How the devil should I know?' answered Don Quixote. 'See there now; did I not tell you to keep an exact account? Before God, there is an end of the story; I can go no further' " (p 170).

[17] In pt I bk I ch 24, Don Quixote interrupts the tale of Cardenio's love for Lucinda at the moment when she asks Cardenio to lend her *Amadis de Gaul*, in order to praise her for reading books of chivalry. This prompts Cardenio to say

that he's certain Elizabat in *Amadis de Gaul* lay with Queen Madasima. When Don Quixote in anger says this is not true, Cardenio flies into a rage, attacking and beating Sancho and Don Quixote. In the romance, Elizabat, a surgeon, and Madasima, wife of Gantasi, travel together, but there is no hint that they behave dishonourably.

[18] When Don Quixote continues to defend Queen Madasima (see n 17, above), Sancho evades agreeing with him by citing a string of proverbs, ". . . I come from my vineyard; I know nothing; I am no friend to inquiring into other men's lives; for he that buys and lies shall find the lie left in his purse behind: besides, naked was I born, and naked I remain; I neither win nor lose; if they were guilty, what is that to me? . . .", and so on.

[19] Pt II ch 17, in which Don Quixote stops two wagons carrying lions to the King of Spain and insists on fighting them, causing all those accompanying the wagons to flee in fright; but when the cage is opened, the lion yawns, washes, turns round, and lies down with its back towards Don Quixote, who nevertheless is taken as proving his valour by this adventure (III 134–43).

[20] Vol III p 194 (pt II ch 23); Don Quixote spends only an hour or so in the

Vol. IV. p. 39. Sancho's Counterpart to the Cave of Montesino in *his* style—[21]

---

cave of Montesino (p 202), but reports having a series of marvellous adventures that he thinks occupied three days.

[21] Pt II ch 41, in which Sancho describes his imaginary journey on the wooden horse Clavileno, as taking him to heaven, where he finds green, blue, carnation, and motley-coloured she-goats, which remind him of his childhood when he was a goatherd, and so, he says, "I slipped down fair and softly from Clavileno, and played with those she-goats, which are like so many violets, about the space of three quarters of an hour." This shows how earthy and limited Sancho's imagined horizons are compared with those of his master.

APPENDIXES

APPENDIX A
UNASSIGNED LECTURE NOTES

UNASSIGNED LECTURE NOTES

(1) MILTON AND PARADISE LOST

The notes on *Paradise Lost* reprinted below were first published by HNC in *LR* I 172–8, in which they form the later part of the notes he associated with Lect 10 of the 1818 series. The first part of these notes is now known to belong to Lect 4 of the 1819 series, but there is no reason to connect the rest with this lecture or with the 1818 series, in which C compared Milton with Dante. As elsewhere in *LR*, HNC seems to have cobbled together unrelated notes as if they formed a coherent unity. The second part of the notes, with their echoes of Schiller, their comparisons of Milton and Klopstock, and their reference to Napoleon, might well relate rather to one of the earlier lectures C gave on Milton, in 1808, 1811–12, 1812–13, or 1814. There is, however, no evidence to connect them specifically with any one of these. Raysor followed HNC in printing these notes under the heading of Lect 10 in the 1818 series in *Misc C* 161–5.

The Fall of Man is the subject; Satan is the cause; man's blissful state the immediate object of his enmity and attack; man is warned by an angel who gives him an account of all that was requisite to be known, to make the warning at once intelligible and awful; then the temptation ensues, and the Fall; then the immediate sensible consequence; then the consolation, wherein an angel presents a vision of the history of men with the ultimate triumph of the Redeemer. Nothing is touched in this vision but what is of general interest in religion; any thing else would have been improper.

The inferiority of Klopstock's Messiah is inexpressible.[1] I admit the prerogative of poetic feeling, and poetic faith; but I cannot suspend the judgment even for a moment. A poem may in one sense be a dream, but it must be a waking dream. In Milton you have a religious faith

---

[1] On going to Germany in 1798 C and WW called on Klopstock in Hamburg, a visit recorded in *CN* I 339 and in "Satyrane's Letters" in *Friend* (*CC*) II 239–47. C's admiration of the "splendid era" to which Klopstock belonged (*BL* ch 10— *CC*—I 211) did not prevent him from being sharply critical of the *Messias* (finished 1773), inspired by Milton's *Paradise Lost*. In 1802 he recorded on the first page of his copy that he found it boring; see *CL* II 811.

combined with the moral nature; it is an efflux; you go along with it. In Klopstock there is a wilfulness; he makes things so and so. The feigned speeches and events in the Messiah shock us like falsehoods; but nothing of that sort is felt in the Paradise Lost, in which no particulars, at least very few indeed, are touched which can come into collision or juxta-position with recorded matter.

But notwithstanding the advantages in Milton's subject, there were concomitant insuperable difficulties, and Milton has exhibited marvellous skill in keeping most of them out of sight. High poetry is the translation of reality into the ideal under the predicament of succession of time only. The poet is an historian, upon condition of moral power being the only force in the universe. The very grandeur of his subject ministered a difficulty to Milton. The statement of a being of high intellect, warring against the supreme Being, seems to contradict the idea of a supreme Being. Milton precludes our feeling this, as much as possible, by keeping the peculiar attributes of divinity less in sight, making them to a certain extent allegorical only. Again, poetry implies the language of excitement; yet how to reconcile such language with God? Hence Milton confines the poetic passion in God's speeches to the language of scripture; and once only allows the *passio vera*, or *quasi-humana*[2] to appear, in the passage, where the Father contemplates his own likeness in the Son before the battle:—

> Go then, thou Mightiest, in thy Father's might,
> Ascend my chariot, guide the rapid wheels
> That shake Heaven's basis, bring forth all my war,
> My bow and thunder; my almighty arms
> Gird on, and sword upon thy puissant thigh;
> Pursue these sons of darkness, drive them out
> From all Heaven's bounds into the utter deep:
> There let them learn, as likes them, to despise
> God and Messiah his anointed king.
>
> B. VI. v. 710.

3. As to Milton's object:—

It was to justify the ways of God to man![3] The controversial spirit observable in many parts of the poem, especially in God's speeches, is immediately attributable to the great controversy of that age, the origination of evil. The Arminians considered it a mere calamity. The Calvinists took away all human will. Milton asserted the will, but declared for the enslavement of the will out of an act of the will itself.

---

[2] I.e. true or, as it were, human emotion.   [3] *Paradise Lost* bk I line 26 (var).

There are three powers in us, which distinguish us from the beasts that perish;—1, reason; 2, the power of viewing universal truth; and 3, the power of contracting universal truth into particulars. Religion is the will in the reason, and love in the will.

The character of Satan is pride and sensual indulgence, finding in self the sole motive of action. It is the character so often seen *in little* on the political stage. It exhibits all the restlessness, temerity, and cunning which have marked the mighty hunters of mankind from Nimrod to Napoleon.[4] The common fascination of men is, that these great men, as they are called, must act from some great motive. Milton has carefully marked in his Satan the intense selfishness, the alcohol of egotism, which would rather reign in hell than serve in heaven. To place this lust of self in opposition to denial of self or duty, and to show what exertions it would make, and what pains endure to accomplish its end, is Milton's particular object in the character of Satan. But around this character he has thrown a singularity of daring, a grandeur of sufferance, and a ruined splendour, which constitute the very height of poetic sublimity.

Lastly, as to the execution:—

The language and versification of the Paradise Lost are peculiar in being so much more necessarily correspondent to each than those in any other poem or poet. The connexion of the sentences and the position of the words are exquisitely artificial; but the position is rather according to the logic of passion or universal logic, than to the logic of grammar. Milton attempted to make the English language obey the logic of passion as perfectly as the Greek and Latin. Hence the occasional harshness in the construction.

Sublimity is the pre-eminent characteristic of the Paradise Lost. It is not an arithmetical sublime like Klopstock's, whose rule always is to treat what we might think large as contemptibly small. Klopstock mistakes bigness for greatness. There is a greatness arising from images of effort and daring, and also from those of moral endurance; in Milton both are united. The fallen angels are human passions, invested with a dramatic reality.

The apostrophe to light at the commencement of the third book is particularly beautiful as an intermediate link between Hell and Heaven; and observe, how the second and third book support the subjective character of the poem. In all modern poetry in Christendom there is an under consciousness of a sinful nature, a fleeting away of external things,

---

[4] This paragraph is very close to C's characterisation of "commanding genius" in *SM* (*CC*) 65–6.

the mind or subject greater than the object, the reflective character predominant. In the Paradise Lost the sublimest parts are the revelations of Milton's own mind, producing itself and evolving its own greatness; and this is so truly so, that when that which is merely entertaining for its objective beauty is introduced, it at first seems a discord.

In the description of Paradise itself you have Milton's sunny side as a man; here his descriptive powers are exercised to the utmost, and he draws deep upon his Italian resources.[5] In the description of Eve, and throughout this part of the poem, the poet is predominant over the theologian. Dress is the symbol of the Fall, but the mark of intellect; and the metaphysics of dress are, the hiding what is not symbolic and displaying by discrimination what is.[6] The love of Adam and Eve in Paradise is of the highest merit—not phantomatic,[7] and yet removed from every thing degrading. It is the sentiment of one rational being towards another made tender by a specific difference in that which is essentially the same in both; it is a union of opposites, a giving and receiving mutually of the permanent in either, a completion of each in the other.

Milton is not a picturesque, but a musical, poet;[8] although he has this merit that the object chosen by him for any particular foreground always remains prominent to the end, enriched, but not incumbered, by the opulence of descriptive details furnished by an exhaustless imagination. I wish the Paradise Lost were more carefully read and studied than I can see any ground for believing it is, especially those parts which, from the habit of always looking for a story in poetry, are scarcely read at all,—as for example, Adam's vision of future events in the 11th and 12th books. No one can rise from the perusal of this immortal poem without a deep sense of the grandeur and the purity of Milton's soul, or without feeling how susceptible of domestic enjoyments he really was, notwithstanding the discomforts which actually resulted from an apparently unhappy choice in marriage. He was, as every truly great

[5] Bk IV lines 132ff.

[6] Cf Lect 4 of the 1819 series (at n 24).

[7] Unreal, phantom-like. C's coinage, according to *OED*, which cites this passage, from *LR* I 177.

[8] The implied contrast is with Shakespeare as a "picturesque" poet (see Lect 4, at n 13, and Lect 9, at nn 9 and 35, of the 1811–12 series). Schlegel had opposed ancient art as plastic, or in C's term statuesque, to modern art as pic-turesque (*DKL* I 15, Black I 9), but C was probably recalling too Schiller's description of Klopstock's *Messias* as musical rather than plastic (so Raysor, *Misc C* 165). If C took up Schiller's distinction here, then he was pointing to the abstract nature of the figures in *Paradise Lost*, conceived as ideas rather than as living persons. See Schiller "Über naive und sentimentalische Dichtung" *Kleinere prosaische Schriften* (4 vols Leipzig 1792–1802) II 103–6.

poet has ever been, a good man; but finding it impossible to realize his own aspirations, either in religion, or politics, or society, he gave up his heart to the living spirit and light within him, and avenged himself on the world by enriching it with this record of his own transcendent ideal.

(2) AN ANNOTATION IN *THE WORKS OF SHAKESPEARE* EDITED BY LEWIS THEOBALD (8 VOLS 1773) vi

The ten headings printed below C jotted down in *Sh* (Theobald) vi⁺1. This set belonged to his friend John Morgan and seems to have been used by him in the period from 1808 to 1813, probably in the preparation of lectures. In fact there is little or no evidence to connect the generally brief notes he made on no fewer than twenty-seven of the plays with specific lectures, although they illustrate the range of his reading in Shakespeare during this period. It is useful to bear this in mind in relation to HCR's comments on C's indolence in connexion with the 1811–12 lectures, when he said that C *"will not* look into Shakespear the Morgans are continually laying the book in his way; But as if spell-bound, he canᵗ prepare ⟨himself for his⟩ lecture'' (see Lect 8 of the 1811–12 series, at n 33). The longest note in this set, on *King Lear*, on the front flyleaves of Vol vi, is dated 1 Jan 1813, when C was giving the 1812–13 course at the Surrey Institution. But his lecture on 5 Jan 1813 seems to have been on *Macbeth* and *Othello*, and there is no certain evidence that he spoke on *Lear* during this series. The note, which is largely on Shakespeare's superiority to Beaumont and Fletcher, could, however, have been used in the general lecture on Shakespeare as a dramatic poet given on 19 Jan 1813. Further on in this volume, after the last play in it, *Coriolanus*, C set out on a back flyleaf what appear to be headings for a lecture. In *C Talker* pp 55–9, Armour and Howes argued that these headings relate to Lect 7 of the 1811–12 series, ostensibly on *Romeo and Juliet*, and they were able to show a general connexion between the headings and the shape of that lecture as shown in Collier's report of it (they were using the 1856 text). However, this lecture, in spite of its digressiveness, constantly returns to the characters of *Romeo and Juliet* and the nature of love, which is especially relevant to this play. There is no specific connexion between the headings and this lecture; the text of *Romeo and Juliet* is in another volume of *Sh* (Theobald)—viii—and these notes read like a variant of other lists of headings C prepared for general lectures on Shakespeare, such as those for Lect 1 of the 1813 series at Bristol. They could have been drawn up in relation to any of the general lectures in his early courses, but if there is any connexion between them and the dated note on *King Lear* in the same volume, then they might with more probability be regarded as belonging to his preparations for Lect 11 of the 1812–13 series, when HCR found him "very eloquent and popular on the general character of Shakespeare". The text given here is based on a transcript of C's annotation, omitting cancellations.

1. Drawn from the fontal faculties of the Human Mind, the Idea always a priori, tho' incarnated by Observation a posteriori et ab extra—

2. No appeals to appetites; but to the Passions.

3. In the high road of nature.

4. The only Poet, except Milton's Eve, who drew women as they are in their uncorrupted Nature—

5. The only modern English Poet who was both a poet & at the same time a dramatic Poet—

6. The only one who supplied all the beauties of the observant Chorus without its defects ⟨&⟩ limitations, first by the exquisite Lyric Intermixtures, & 2—by making general Truths the outbursts of Passion—

7. Reverence for all the Professions & established Ranks & Usages of Society—Friar—Physician—&c

8.—In very few Instances mere Monsters introduced, as in Gonerill— & then with what Judgement—

9 Moral & prudential Wisdom.

10. Comparative Purity

APPENDIX B
JOHN PAYNE COLLIER'S SHORTHAND NOTES OF LECTURES 9 AND 12 OF THE 1811–12 SERIES

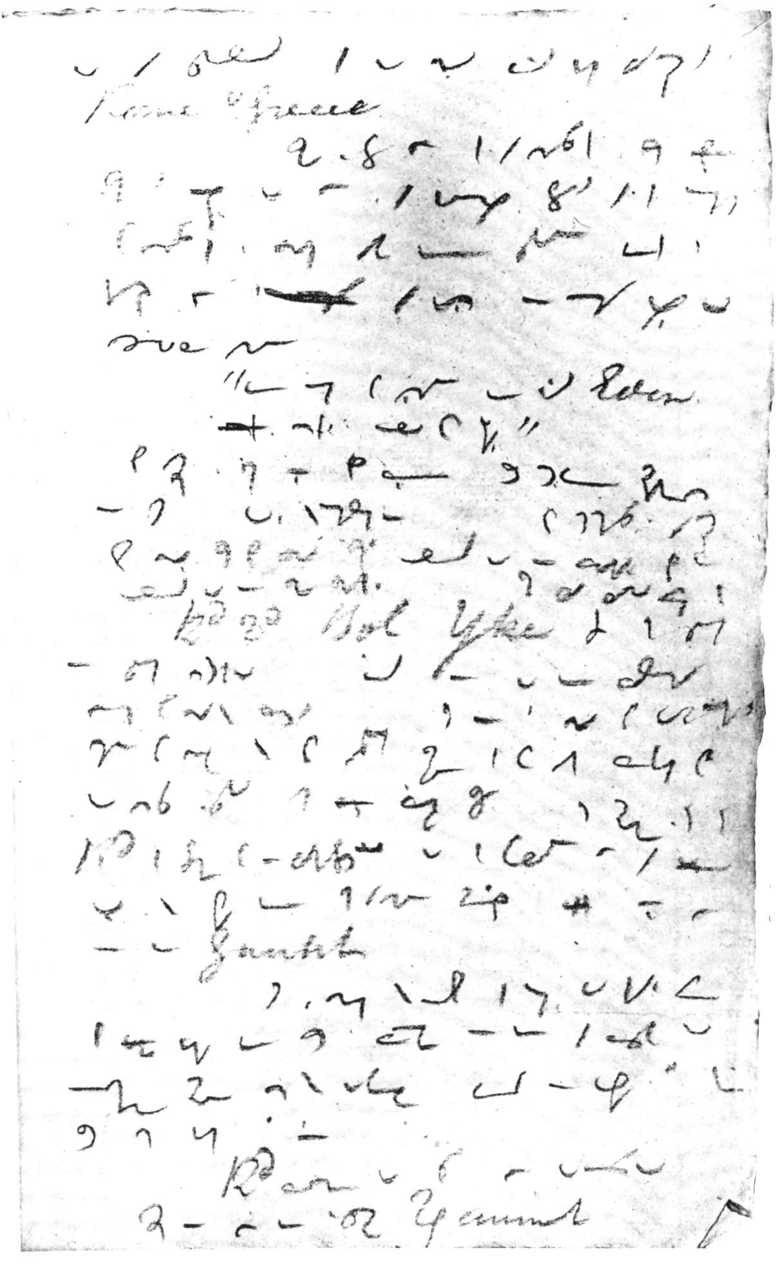

5. A page, f 2, from John Payne Collier's shorthand notes taken at Lecture 12 of the 1811–12 series.
The Furness Shakespeare Library of the University of Pennsylvania reproduced by kind permission

JOHN PAYNE COLLIER'S
SHORTHAND NOTES OF
LECTURES 9 AND 12
OF THE 1811–12
SERIES

The original shorthand notes taken down by Collier at Lects 9 and 12 of C's 1811–12 course have recently been found in the Furness Shakespeare Library of the University of Pennsylvania in Philadelphia.[1] They were once in the possession of Paul Kaufman of Seattle, who offered them for sale to the Folger Shakespeare Library in Washington, D.C., in 1937. His offer was declined, but two sets of photostats were made at that time, and deposited, one in the Folger Library, and one in the Library of Congress. Those in the Folger Library were bound in two volumes, each containing a note in the hand of J. Q. Adams dated 30 Mar 1937 stating that they had been presented to the Folger by Dr Jameson of the Library of Congress. Mr. Kaufman later sold the originals, but kept no records, and all trace of them was lost until 1982, when they were discovered in a package with some other Collier items in the Furness Library; it appears that the then Librarian of the University of Pennsylvania, C. Seymour Thompson, bought the documents in April 1940, and put them aside without cataloguing them. Paul Kaufman told him that he acquired them from Collier's granddaughter in London in 1924.

The notes were written in two unbound gatherings, or what Collier called "brochures," similar to those in which he transcribed the longhand notes for seven lectures of the 1811–12 series, but not from the same stock of paper. The brochures containing the longhand transcripts have pages measuring about 7¼ by 4 inches, and the paper bears watermarks dated 1806, 1807, and 1811. The pages in the brochures containing shorthand notes measure about 8 by 5 inches, and the paper is watermarked with the initials MJL and the date 1809. Each brochure consists of 32 pages. For Lect 9, Collier began taking notes on the first recto, and when he reached the end of the brochure, he turned it round, and worked back through the versos, the notes ending on f 9^v, leaving eight blank sides. He followed a similar procedure for Lect 12, starting a new brochure on the first recto, but the notes for this lecture are much shorter, and end on f 12; the last four rectos and the versos contain no notes. Each brochure was marked in ink on the first verso with the letters G (Lect 9) and H (Lect 12),

---

[1] See Georgianna Ziegler's essay, "A Victorian Reputation: John Payne Col- lier and His Contemporaries" in *Shakespeare Studies* (1984).

and a note signed "Wm Clark a Comm^ss r", showing that Collier submitted them on 8 Jan 1856 to the Court of Queen's Bench in support of an affidavit designed to establish that an anonymous pamphlet called *Literary Cookery with Reference to Matters Attributed to Coleridge and Shakespeare* (1855) was libellous. In this the author, now known to be A. E. Brae, insinuated that Collier had fabricated or misrepresented the evidence in the announcement he made in four issues of *N&Q* in 1854 of his "discovery" of notes relating to C's 1811–12 lectures.[2] Collier sought to repudiate the charge by means of an application in the High Court, and he subsequently printed the text of the affidavit in the Preface to his edition of *Seven Lectures*.[3]

Collier's shorthand notes are in pencil, and on f 6 of the notes for the 1812 lecture is a large pencilled letter "A" at a point roughly corresponding to the words "See shorthand note A" written in his longhand transcript of this lecture, which confirms that the transcripts are based on these shorthand notes. The opening rectos of both brochures are worn and rubbed, and f 16^v, the last page of the brochure containing Lect 9, is so worn that I have not been able to decipher all the notes on it. On the first page of Lect 9 the numbers "1.2.6.7.8.9.12." are written in ink in Collier's hand, these being the numbers of all the lectures at which he took notes. The first page of this brochure also has a pencilled "G" in the top right-hand corner, and the brochure containing Lect 12 has a corresponding pencilled "H", in the hand of William Clark. Collier filled the pages with his notes, leaving no margins, and added a number of pencilled asterisks to the left of his markings, usually where a line of signs is indented at the start of a paragraph, but not always. These may be connected with Collier's transcription of his notes into longhand, like the pencilled "done" scrawled in large letters across the first page of Lect 9. Elsewhere in his notes occasional ink lines or scrawls through part of a page, and brackets at the end of a sentence or paragraph, seem to mark points where he paused in transcribing from shorthand into longhand. The word "Done" is also written in ink across f 12 of Lect 9. These asterisks, scrawls, and brackets are not recorded in the textual notes.

According to Collier, he learned shorthand from his father, a reporter for *The Times* and the *M Chron*, "at an early age",[4] and he seems to have developed a personal variant of the system worked out by John Byrom in the eighteenth century and popularized in books like T. Molineux's *An Introduction to Mr. Byrom's Universal English Short Hand* (1804). Like a great many modern systems, including Pitman's, introduced in 1837, Byrom's starts from a primary system of signs for consonants. It may be that Collier picked up these, together with a few special signs for common prepositions and word-endings like "ant" and "ing", but never mastered the placing of marks for vowels. At any rate,

[2] Brae subsequently developed his critique in *Collier, Coleridge and Shakespeare* (1860). Collier published his account of finding notes relating to the 1811–12 lectures in *N&Q* x (Jul–Aug 1854) 1–2, 21–3, 57–8, and 117–19. For fuller comment on this affair, see *C on Shakespeare* 6–9 and Dewey Ganzel *Fortune and Men's Eyes: The Career of John Payne Collier* Oxford 1982) 200–3. Ganzel's version is biased in favour of Collier and dismisses Brae's criticisms as merely "outrageous".

[3] In 1856; pp ii–v. Collier stated here, pp iii–iv, that he had destroyed his shorthand notes of the 1811–12 lectures, with the exception of these two brochures.

[4] *Seven Lectures* v.

in taking down C's lectures he indicated few vowels and almost no punctuation. This in itself might suggest that he was never a really expert shorthand writer, and though his skill was probably adequate for routine journalism, it did not enable him to take down fully or accurately everything C said in his lectures. This is hardly surprising, since a noted expert, Joseph Gurney, is said to have given up the attempt, finding it impossible to predict from the beginning of C's sentences what the end would be.[5]

It has proved possible to decipher almost all of Collier's shorthand notes, although a number of readings must remain dubious, if only because it is not always possible to be certain what word is meant by a particular group of consonants, as, for instance, "pnt" may represent "paint" or "point", or "fct" can signify "fact" or "effect", and the context does not always show which is intended. What a transcription of the notes shows is that Collier's skill in shorthand enabled him to take down only part of a lecture, about 4800 words in respect of Lect 9 and only 2500 words in respect of Lect 12. Both reports contain garbled or incomprehensible passages, in which Collier seems to have lost the thread of the argument, and both show that he often resorted to registering the main words but not the whole of sentences. At one point in Lect 9 C quoted most or all of a long poem, and Collier gradually lost track of this, so that he twice simply omitted a number of lines.[6] He must also have omitted passages elsewhere, especially in Lect 12, and there is little doubt that he relied upon his ability to fill out his shorthand notes from memory when transcribing them. In the Preface to his *Seven Lectures* in 1856, Collier acknowledged that the text was "full of omissions, owing in some degree to want of facility" on his part, and also said he had been sometimes so "engrossed, and absorbed by the almost inspired look and manner of the speaker" that he was rendered incapable of taking notes.[7]

The shorthand notes therefore provide at best a rather inaccurate and incomplete skeleton of C's lectures, which Collier fleshed out from memory and corrected in his longhand transcripts; these provide a fuller text and on balance may be regarded as the best version of the lectures. At the same time, Collier took some licenses in transcribing the notes, as a comparison between the texts shows. He inevitably expanded the shorthand notes, filling in gaps or making sense of abbreviations, from memory, but this passes into and overlaps with an inclination to revise or reword as he went along. He seems to have been intent on shaping a coherent and lucid report and was more concerned with clarity and tidiness than with fidelity to what C said. He sometimes substituted a more common word for a more unusual but characteristic usage by C, changing "transplaces" to "transports", or "simulacrum" to "similarity", "cadenza" to "piece". There are many more rather arbitrary substitutions, which tend to smooth out the style and render it anonymous, so that something, at times a great deal, of the individuality of C's phraseology is lost. Sometimes, too, when defeated by his shorthand, either because it made no sense or he could

---

[5] Gurney invented his own system, and was eminent enough as a legal and parliamentary reporter to earn a mention in Byron's *Don Juan*; see *C Talker* 145 and the Editor's Introduction, above, I lxxxiii.

[6] See paragraph 27, below, and compare Collier's transcript, Lect 9 of the 1811–12 series (at n 26).

[7] *Seven Lectures* xiii.

not decipher it, Collier simply omitted words or sentences from his own transcription. A few omissions are not explicable in this way, but, like many of his substitutions, appear to be casual oversights or arbitrary changes.

The shorthand notes deserve to be studied because, in spite of their obscurities, omissions, and other inadequacies, and the uncertainties involved in transcribing them now, they take us as close as we can get to C in the lecture-room. The changes Collier made when he transcribed them can readily be seen by comparing the text printed here with Lects 9 and 12 of the 1811–12 series as printed above in the sequence of lectures. The textual notes attempt to provide only two kinds of information. They draw attention to some doubtful readings and indecipherable passages and also indicate those words other than proper names written out in longhand in the ms. It was Collier's general habit to write out proper names in longhand, often in an abbreviated form, as he invariably wrote "Sh" for "Shakespeare", but sometimes in full, when the name was less familiar, like "Pindar". There seems little point in documenting this general characteristic of the ms, but the other words Collier felt it necessary to write out in longhand are interesting because they illustrate the limitations of his shorthand, as in the case of words like "eye" or "gnome", or perhaps moments when he simply lost his touch, since there seems no obvious reason for him to write out "organic" or "Planet". All such words are indicated by being underlined. The textual notes draw attention to the main words and phrases Collier omitted from his transcription. The list is inevitably incomplete, since the point where omission shades into alteration or substitution cannot easily be determined. However, these passages are perhaps most immediately interesting to the student of C because they add a little to the known records of these lectures. On one occasion it has proved possible to fill a blank space Collier left in his transcript with the word "individual". Passages in which the text seems obscure or makes little sense may reflect the difficulties of a modern transcriber, but I believe it has proved possible to recover most of what Collier noted down. The notes contain almost no punctuation and no indication other than an inconsistent and intermittent use of spacing to show where sentences end; in transcribing them I have marked what seem to be the beginnings of sentences by a space and an initial capital letter. I have not recorded Collier's false starts or cancellations, none of which seem to be of any consequence. There are many blanks on one page of Lect 9, f 16ᵛ, the last page of the brochure, which is badly worn. A fuller account of Collier's shorthand may be found in *C on Sh* 157–62, and a more detailed comparison of the shorthand notes and Collier's transcript is made in "What Did Coleridge Say? John Payne Collier and the Reports of the 1811–12 Lectures" in *Reading Coleridge: Approaches and Applications* ed Walter B. Crawford (Ithaca, NY 1979) 191–210.

ᵃ9th Lecture

It is a known and at present unexplained phenomenon that among the ancients statuary rose to such a degree of perfection as so to leave the very hope ⟨if hoping then mingle it with despair⟩ baffled of ever imitating

---

ᵃ f 1; in the top left-hand corner are the numbers "1.2.6.7.8.9.12."

it   at the same time painting praise the pictures <u>Pliny</u> &c have given pictures of <u>Apelles</u> has been proved to be not only much greater excellence but at the same time to have fallen off here from statuary.

Remember some ones pointing to sign post observed that could not have been effected if <u>Titian</u> had not existed and his colours even here was certain richness of representation by colour which employed in those imperfections at pre-existence of some eminent mind   It seems that perspective remain to discoveries of Herculaneum and the palace of <u>Nero</u> such blunders as would render some evidence those who maintained the ancients were ignorant of it   This is confuted by <u>Vitruvius</u> in the introduction to his second book

Something same kind appears to have been the case with regard to their dramas early taken notice greek drama imitated by the French and by the [b]more shabby[c] writers of England since the reign of <u>Ch 2</u>[d] who allowed nothing more than variation same note of admitting nothing of that which is the true principle of life by attaining the same end by infinite variety of means

It is true that writings of <u>Sh</u> are not likeness of the Greeks they are analogous because by very different means they produce the same end whereas the greater part of the French tragedies offered and the English tragedies on the same plan cannot call them so changed but may be defined perhaps failing same end by adopting the same means in most inappropriate circumstances

This has led him to realise the [d]fitness at roots[e] of that ancient drama meaning really the writings of <u>Esch Eurip</u> and <u>Soph</u> for the miserable rhetorical works by the Romans are scarcely to be [f]mentioned as dramatic poems consider that the ancient drama might be contrasted with the <u>Sh</u>[n] call that <u>Sh</u>[n] because knew no other author who so realised the same idea though told <u>Cald</u>[n] has done that

They might be compared to the others and in the same manner as painting to statuary   The figures must be few because the very essence of statuary is great abstraction and prevent great many being combined into one effect   Consider a grand group of <u>Niobe</u> or an old heroic subject   Suppose the old <u>Nurse</u> were introduced that would be disgusting   The numbers must be circumscribed and nothing undignified must be brought into company with what is dignified and no one of the group can be known but what is abstraction and nothing by the <u>eye</u> and figure which gives the effect of multitude without introducing anything

[b-c] Not transcribed by Collier
[d-e] Not transcribed by Collier
[f] f 2

discordant   This compare the picture of <u>Rap</u>[l] or <u>Titian</u> where immense number of figures may be introduced the dog cat and beggar and by the very circumstance less degree of labour and by less degree of abstraction effect is produced equally harmonious to the mind more true to nature and in all but one respect superior to statuary   A man to effect the perfect of satisfaction in a thing as a work of art

He wholly felt it that exquisite feeling in imperfect being mighty preface of his future existence being holy is often that object presented to him

What the reason conceives possible gives momentary reality to it

Stated before the circumstances which permitted <u>Sh</u> to make an alteration so suitable to his age and so necessitated by the circumstances of the age   In the ancient theatres the plays were composed for the whole stage the voice distorted by it

[g]This distinction between imitation and likeness is the mixture of a greater number of dissimilarities with the similarities   An imitation differs from a copy precisely as sameness differs from likeness in that sense of the word in which we imply a difference conjoined with that sameness

<u>Sh</u> had many advantages   The great then instead of throwing the <u>Chev de frise</u> round them of mere manners endeavoured to distinguish themselves by attainments and powers of mind

The poet was obliged to appeal to the imagination and not to the senses and that gave him a power of space and time which in the ancient theatre would have been absurd simply because it was contradictory

The advantage is vast indeed on the side of the modern   He appeals to the imagination to the reason and to the noblest powers of the human heart above the iron compulsion of space and time   He appeals to that which we most want to be when we are most worthy of being while the other binds us often to the meanest part of our nature and its chief compensation is a simple cold acquiescence of the mind that what the poet has represented might possibly have taken place   A poor compliment to the poet who is to be a creator to tell him he has all the excellences of a historian   But in dramatic that so narrows the space of action so impoverishes the state of art that of all the Ath[n] dramas scarcely no one which has not fallen into absurdity by aiming at the thing and failing or incurred greater absurdity by bringing things into the same space of time that could not have occurred   Not to mention that the grandest effect of the dramatic poet to be the mirror of life is completely lost   The passing in 6 or 12 hours though this depicted 24 hours though in fact we might have supposed that as easily 20 months as 20 hours because it has become an object of imagination and when *h*once the bound is passed there is no limit which can be appointed it

Above all things in order to read Sh it is important we must determine too in which plays he means to appeal to our reason and imagination which have no relation to time or place excepting as in the one case they imply succession of cause and effect and in the imagination they form a harmonious picture so that the impulses we feel by reason are be carried on by imagination

The sentimental arises out of this thing which consists only in taking some very affecting incidents which at the highest only aspired to the genius of a onion that of drawing tears *i*into the eye*j* and in which the author acting like a ventriloquist distributed his own insipidity   Seen some plays seen translated ⟨and written⟩ so well acted that could have drugged man if he produced an artificial deafness in which have done whole in pantomime

Sh characters from Macbeth down to Dogberry are ideal they are not the things but abstracts of the things which great mind may take into itself and naturalise to its own happiness   The Dogberry strikes at some folly reigning at the day and which must forever reign

Enlightened readers are two one those who read with feeling and understanding are ⟨two⟩ those who without affecting to understand or criticise merely feel and are the recipients of the poet's power that between the 2 find no medium endurable

In the plays of Sh almost every man sees himself without knowing that he sees himself as in the phenomena of nature a man sees in the mountains projected into *k*mist not the same indeed but knows it so that is the same by trust in a glory round the head which distinguishes it from vulgar copy

Or as travellers in the north of Germ*y* when the sun rise at the immense tops askance the mountain they see figure gigantic of dimensions so distant and mighty so great in size that they scarce think it credible *l*but which corresponds with their own simulacrum so we may compare them with the famous phata Morgana*m* at Messina in which all forms at determined distances are represented in the mist which is invisible all in the gorgeous colours of prismatic imagination with magic harmony producing whole in the mind of the spectator

h f 4
i-j Not transcribed by Collier
k f 5   *l-m* Not transcribed by Collier

Rather humiliating to find that since <u>Sh</u> time there seems to be no one of the critics who enters into his peculiarities not dwell as intend to devote lecture to <u>Pope</u> and <u>J</u>ⁿ

Some of his contemporaries seem to have understood him and in way that does him no small honour when we give him all praise prefaces ⁿprefer him to the modernsᵒ but when they come to the notes treat him like schoolboy and exercise the vulgarest of all feeling that of wonderment

<u>C</u> went on to ridicule further the idea of <u>Sh</u> being an irregular poet ᵖnow a man and now a god now the wonder and now the abhorrenceᵠ and they were reconciled to it by saying he wrote for the mob   But no man of genius ever felt so   He never would write that which is below himself   Careless he might be he might even ʳwrite at time when his better genius did not attend him but he never wrote to produce that which had to impress and degrade himself so   If man were to attempt to act for beast or a <u>Cat</u>ⁱ only because she did not feel in a mood to sing begin to bray

Yesterday friend had left for him a work by German writer and of course had only time to read small part ˢof the volumesᵗ and would praise that with much greater warmth were it not that he would praise himself were it not that the sentiments coincided with his own at the <u>R</u> <u>I</u>   But others there were who heard but wonder that various ages had elapsed since the birth of <u>Sh</u> that should remain for foreigners first to feel truly and to appreciate properly his mighty genius   The solution of the fact must be sought in the history of nation we have become busy commercial people and derived many advantages moral and physical we have become mighty nation too one of the giant nations whom the moral superiority still enables to struggle with the other the evil genius of the <u>Planet</u>

The Germans unable to act at all have now by race driven into speculation all the feelings have been forced back into the thinking and the reasoning mind to do was impossible but what ought to be done they perhaps have exceeded all other nations on earth   They first rationally recalled the ancient philosophy incapable of acting outwardly have acted upon their own spirits with an energy which <u>Eng</u>ᵈ produces no example since the truly heroic times in soul and ᵘthe time of <u>Eliz</u>

ⁿ⁻ᵒ Not transcribed by Collier
ᵖ⁻ᵠ Not transcribed by Collier
ʳ f 6
ˢ⁻ᵗ Not transcribed by Collier
ᵘ f 7

If ½ of what has been written by <u>Eng</u> on <u>Sh</u> were burnt for want of candles to read his works this would advantage to England   By giving us the greatest man providence has thrown a sop to <u>Envy</u> by giving the worst possible critics of him

His contemporaries were not so poem addressed to him truly poetical order on him and he knew nowhere where he could find a fuller but more contradistinguishing description of great genius than contained

A mind reflecting ages past whose full and clear surface can make things appear distant a thousand years and represent them in their lively colours just extent to outrun hasty time retrieve the fates roll back the heavens blow ope the iron gates of death and <u>Lethe</u> litter confused lie great heaps of ruinous mortality in that deep dusky dungeon to discern a royal ghost from churls by art to learn the <u>phi</u> of shades and give them sudden birth wondering how oft they lived what story coldly tell what poet feign at second hand and picture without brain senseless with all

To raise our ancient sovereigns from their hearse make kings his subjects by exchanging verse enlive their pale trunk that the present age ⱽjoys in their joys and trembles at their rage yet so to temper passion that our ears take pleasure at their pain and <u>eyes</u> in tears both weep and smile fearful at plots so sad then laughing at our fear abused and glad to be abused affected with that truth which we perceive is false pleased in that ruth

At which we start this and much more which cannot be expressed but by himself his tongue and his own breast was <u>Sh free</u> which his cunning brain improved by favour of the sevenfold train ʷthe buskinned muse the comic queen the grand and louder tone of <u>Clio</u> nimble hand and nimbler foot of the melodious pair   The silver voiced lady the most fair <u>Cal</u>ᵉ whose speaking silence daunts and she whose praise the heavenly body chants   These finely moving''ˣ never was more happily expressed the characteristic of <u>Sh</u> mind

It is a mistake to suppose that any of <u>Sh</u> characters strike us as portraits   They have the union of reason perceivingʸ generality the judgment recording actual facts the imagination which diffuses over all these a magic glory and while it records the ᶻpast it projects the spirits in a wonderful degree future and makes us feel however dimly the state of being in which there is neither past nor future but which is permanent which is the energy of nature

ⱽ f 8
ʷ⁻ˣ Not transcribed by Collier
ʸ Written twice in ms   ᶻ f 9

Yet though had affirmed and this truly that all <u>Sh</u> people [a]are real and all idealised[b] there might be just division made of those where the ideal is more prominent to the mind brought forward more intentionally to its consciousness as ideal though in reality not more or less real 2nd is of those speakers who though equally idealised the delusion put upon the mind is that of their being real

Divide <u>Sh</u> plays into those where the real[c] is disguised in the real and those in which the ideal is hidden from us in the real   The difference is made by the powers of the mind which the poet chiefly appeals to

At present speak only of those plays where the ideal is predominant and chiefly for this reason that those plays are the performances of <u>Sh</u> which have occasioned most the great objection which is not the growth of our own country but the growth of France the judgment of monkies by some wonderful disease given to men

We are told by these <u>Sh</u> sort of wonderful monster in whom sort of heterogeneous [d]components were thrown together into one mass with genius of proportions

Among the ideal plays was the <u>Tempest</u> he could mention many others but it is impossible to go through every separate play of <u>Sh</u> and what he says to this will apply to most of them

In this play <u>Sh</u> has appealed to the imagination and he has constructed a plan according to this   Have said before that the very scheme of his drama did not appeal to the <u>sensuous</u> impression ⟨of time and space⟩ (authorised by Milton) but to the imagination

In the first scene ⟨he has⟩ introduced a mere confusion on board ship   The lowest persons are brought together with the highest and with what excellence   Great part of his genius was the combination of the highest and the lowest in true combination   Neither he has droll nor he has sad scene but that the laughter we relish increases the tears and throws as it were a poetic light into them   In the tears he mixes tenderness with the laughter which follows

In the first scene he has shown that power which more than any other of all other men he possessed that of introducing the profoundest sentiments of wisdom just where you would least expect them and yet where with the truly natural and the admirable secret [e]of his drama is that separate speeches do not appear to be produced the one by the former but from the peculiar character of the speaker

[a–b] Not transcribed by Collier
[c] So in ms   [d] f 10
[e] f 11; "of" written twice

He explained difference between the mechanic and the <u>organic</u> life

Explain this by the different kinds of trees what life and principle it is that is in what form it is grown must be considered

It was the case with <u>Sh</u> he shows the life and principle of the being when the storm is seen as the infernal danger and the latest proof of destruction has thrown off the bonds off[f] to which are in reverence gives loose to his feelings of vulgar mind hence . . . counsellor

Hence what care these roarers for the name of King   Hence trouble us not <u>Gn</u>[g]   Yet remember whom thou has aboard   None that I more love than myself you are counsellor if you can so to end

An ordinary dramatist would have introduced through moralising [h]or imagining some connection with it about having boat saved[i] for these are not men of genius they connect their ideas by association or logical connection whereas the vital writer in the moment transplaces himself into the very being of each character and instead of diffusing all the play to making artificial little puppets [j]which he has to play he allows being to realise being before you

<u>Gon</u> says I have great comfort from this fellow methinks he hath no drowning mark upon him his complexion is perfect gallows stand fast good fate to his hanging make the rope of his destiny our cable if he be not born to be hanged the case is miserable

It is the true sailor proud of the contempt of danger and the high feeling of the old man who instead of condescending to words addressed to him turns off and meditates in himself and draws some feeling of solid estimation in own mind by the trifling with the man's face and drawing species of hope from his looks

<u>Sh</u> had determined to make the plot of the play such as to involve certain number of low characters and he has done so admirably   At the beginning he has pitched the note as it were of the whole   This was evidently introduced as a lively mode of telling a story you are prepared for something to be developed and in the next scene he introduces [k]<u>P</u> and <u>M</u>[l]

And how does it   By first introducing the favourite character [m]<u>the frightened</u>[n] Miranda which at once expresses the vehemence of the storm such as it might appear to witness from the land and tenderness of her feelings

[f] So in ms
[g] I.e. "Gonzalo"
[h-i] Not transcribed by Collier
[j] f 12
[k-l] I.e. "Prospero and Miranda"
[m-n] Not transcribed by Collier

^oThe exquisite feelings of a female brought up in a desert yet with the advantages of excellent^p education all that could be given by wise learned and affectionate father   With all the powers of mind which ^qnever rotting with the combats of life only revealed themselves thus to excite from her the glorification of good in exposed feelings^r

"Oh I have suffered with those I saw suffer &c"^s

The doubt which could have occurred to no mind but Miranda's who had been bred up with her father and a monster only that like one's knowing what was in a rumour   Thus he never have brought it in as a conjecture but he is displaying the vast excellence never fails to introduce some touch or other which not only makes it characteristic particular person but combines the two the person and circumstances that acted upon the person

"Oh the cry did knock against my very heart &c freighting souls within her"

Still dwelling on that which was most wanting in her nature these fellow creatures from who she had appeared banished with only one relict to keep them alive not in her memory but (in her) imagination

Another instance of excellent judgment for of this he speaking principally ^tdirect presentation is the preparation   Pros is in[troduced]^u first in his magic robes bids his daughter pull off the magic robes which is the first time you know him as being possessing supernatural power

He then instructs his daughter answer to understand the story and does it thus so that no reader conjectures the technical use the poet has made of it <u>viz</u> informing the audience of the story

The next step is he gives you warning beforehand he meant for particular purpose to lull her asleep ensuring thereby double effect

Not like vulgar plays where person is introduced to tell you something he thereby gives you first proof of his magical powers   First <u>Pros</u> is introduced as magician by his robes then in the mildest manner he lulls her to sleep and develops the story and by the effects of the sleep stops at the very moment when it was necessary to poet to stop in order to excite the curiosity and yet to fill in understanding and memory with what has passed so as to carry it on uninterruptedly

In this scene was fine touch of <u>Sh</u> knowledge of human nature and

---

^o f 13
^p Not transcribed by Collier
^{q-r} Not transcribed by Collier
^s "&c" written twice, the second one cancelled; closing quotation marks supplied by the editor
^t f 14
^u End of word concealed by turned-down corner of the leaf

generally of the great laws of the mind <u>vid</u> Miranda's infant remembrance of all her recollections for nothing beyond the island

Canst thou remember a time &c ᵛwomen that tended me

This is exquisite in general our early remembrances of life are those of vivid colours especially if they have been seen in motion persons will remember for instance a bright green door ʷfor moving colours are the first ways to conceive visionˣ

But in Miranda who was somewhat older than this to remember 4 or 5 women ʸher sight ⟨fully⟩ formedᶻ   Her father might be the man and the remembrance of the past might be worn out by the present object but she had only then herself in the fountain and yet she recalled to her mind what had been   It is not that she saw such and such grandees or such peeresses but had seen something like a reflection of herself which was not herself and brought back to her mind what was most like herself   Constant yearning of fancy reproducing the past of what she had only seen in herself and could only see in herself

Picturesque power of <u>Sh</u> nothing like but <u>Pindar</u>ᵃ and <u>Dante</u> who were the most picturesque poets that ever existed

The power of genius was not in elaborating picture of which many specimens were given in late poems where throughout so many minute touches so dutchified that you ask why the poet did not refer ᵇto one to paint it young lady reading versifications of works of travellers and observing that if not know have no eyes but when they look round for coloured prints

The power of the poet was by a single word to produce the picture in the imagination   So when <u>Pros</u>

Whereon fated to the purpose (conᵗ open the gates of Milan &c[)]ᶜ

By introducing the simple <u>Epithet</u> me and thy <u>crying</u>ᵈ self this produces figure in the mind ᵉby the single use of a present participleᶠ and in this the power of true poetry consists

Next mention the <u>preparation</u>ᵍ first by the storm before mentioned

The introduction of all that preceded the tale in a manner not only the tale that completely but to develop the main character which ap-

---

ᵛ f 15
ʷ⁻ˣ Not transcribed by Collier
ʸ⁻ᶻ Not transcribed by Collier
ᵃ Collier substituted "Milton" in his transcription
ᵇ f 16
ᶜ Closing bracket supplied by the editor
ᵈ Underlined twice in the ms
ᵉ⁻ᶠ Not transcribed by Collier
ᵍ Underlined twice in the ms

peared finally in the intentions of Prospero [h]who was grandly introduced by a Supernatural being   If Sh had been busy working he would have produced that first which was most object in his mind to chaste character[i] but before he introduces Ariel he has prepared [j]our particular belief[k] by our moral feeling by Mir[a] when she interrupted her father with the sweet words ''alack what trouble was I then to you''   And not only prepared for [l]supernatural being [   ]
for a being so lovely [   ]
to the thought
 This state of mind comprehended what he call poetic faith [
        ] poet induces historic faith   You have first
[   ] some digressive in order to lead
to future lectures Paradise Lost of Milton
 Many scriptural poems were written [   ]
not scripture [m][   ] of Lear to put to silence all
objections [   ] It is idle to say that [   ]
says fact is so [   ] Story of Milton so far is taken from
scriptures and [   ] contained in 4 or 5 lines [   ]
renewed by the impulse of the mind regard what would otherwise have appeared absurdity
 Return to the subject the introduction of Ariel [ ] prepared
[   ]
 If ever there could be doubt that Sh was [n]acting without laws or acting by laws that arise out of his nature this would be from Character of Ariel the very first words of Ariel's introduce not as the angel above men not as gnome or a fiend but while he grants him all the advantages all the faculties of the reason he divests him of all moral character not positively but negatively   In air he lives from air he derives his being his colours and all his effects seem to be brought from the clouds
 There is nothing in him which the mind could not conceive in the sun set or sun rise hence all that belongs to Ariel is all that belongs to the delight the mind can receive from external appearances abstracted from any inborn or individual[o] purpose   His answers to Prospero are either directly to the question nothing beyond or if he expatiates which he does frequently it is report his own delights and the unnatural situation

[h-i] Not transcribed by Collier
[j-k] Not transcribed by Collier
[l] f 16[v], the outer page of the last leaf of the brochure, rubbed, soiled, and often indecipherable, as indicated by the spaces in brackets
[m] Several lines here are not deciphered; they include ''Sh'' in longhand
[n] f 15[v]
[o] Not transcribed by Collier, who left a blank in his longhand here

in which he finds himself though in good power and employed to good ends   Hence Sh has made his very first demand introduced him as discontented from his confinement that he was bound to obey anything which he orders him   We feel it almost unnatural and yet delightful of him to be employed so   As if we were to command one of the winds to [   ]^p ^{q}one of the waves dying away or now rising ^{r}can move in this way or go to this or that vessel^s

But when Sh contrasted the treatment of P with the ^{t}miserable precedent^u from Sic^v instead of producing curses and discontent ^{w}in case of Sic^x Ari immediately assumes the airy being with a mind when the moment one feeling has passed away leaves not a relict of his feeling behind

If there be anything in nature from which Sh has caught the idea of Ar it must be from the child to whom supernatural powers given neither born of heaven or earth but borne perpetually between both like a may blossom kept up by blast of the air

Thus is not only kept up throughout the whole the aversion of the sylph ^{y}to be tied down to any definite doing who seems to require a mortal to compel him to do anything but when compelled he loves spies^z into it^a By this admirable judgment Sh has availed himself of this fact to produce an admirable effect he has given Ariel interest in the play looking forward to that moment when he was to gain his last and only reward simple liberty

Another instance of judgment is admirable ^{b}preparation of the contrast of Ariel Cal

Described by Pros so as to expect monstrous unnatural being   You do not see Cal at once but you hear his voice   It is following nature that we do not receive disgust so great from sight   Therefore it is prepared for by the sound

Still Cal does not appear but Ar comes in as a water nymph   All the strength in which the contrast is thus secured without any of the shock of abruptness or of unpleasant feelings which surprise awakes when the object of it is a being in any way hateful to our sense

^{p} Several words undeciphered where the leaf is soiled and crumpled
^{q} f 14^v
$^{r-s}$ Not transcribed by Collier; several readings in this passage are doubtful
$^{t-u}$ Not transcribed by Collier
^{v} I.e. "Sycorax"
$^{w-x}$ Not transcribed by Collier
$^{y-a}$ Not transcribed by Collier
^{z} Collier wrote signs for "spsd", cancelled them, and substituted "sps"
^{b} f 13 ^{v}

The dour^c character of Cal is admirably conceived a sort of creature of the earth partaking of the quality of the brute is distinguished from them in 2 ways   1 by having mere understanding without moral reason 2^d not having the instincts which show themselves in mere animals

But still he has noble being a man in the sense of imagination all the images he utters are drawn from nature and are all highly poetical they fit in with the images of Ariel

Ariel gives you pictures of the air Cal all the pictures of the earth

Difficulty of finding fresh water ^dall the circumstances which the brute intellect not possessing reason could command   No mean image is brought forward and no mean passion but the animal passions and the sense of being commanded.

The manner in which lovers are introduced is the last he could mention in the wonderful play except in every scene you might point out the same judgment still preparing and still recalling like a lively cadenza in music   Therefore though a perfection that he would mention the admirable appearance of the Conspirators caught notice then how Sh has prepared the feeling of their plot to execute the most detestable of all crimes which ^ehe has finely called^f his murder of sleep

These men ^gwere first introduced^h have no such notion suggested only by the magical sleep thrown on Alon and Gonz but he introduced them as scoffing and scorning ^iand marring^j all said without any forbearance of age with regard to excess and without any feeling of the excellence of the truths and admiration but giving themselves up entirely to the malignant and unsocial feeling that of listening to everything said not to understand but to find something that may gratify belief that the person speaking is inferior to themselves

^kThe grand ^lprinciple and^m characteristic of a villain and it would be not a presentiment but anticipation of Hell ^nif a man to be wicked seeks solely by this^o to believe that all mankind were not only wicked as themselves but would be if they were not too great fools to be so

Pope objected to this passage but it would leave a blank if it were omitted   The grandeur of the language of Pros where Pros leaves his magic   But mention one passage noted by Pope and Arb^p as ⟨gross⟩ bombast

---

^c Not transcribed by Collier

^d f 12^v

^e–f Not transcribed by Collier

^g–h Not transcribed by Collier

^i–j Not transcribed by Collier

^k f 11^v

^l–m Not transcribed by Collier

^n–o Not transcribed by Collier

^p I.e. "Arbuthnot"

''Advance the fringed curtain of thine eyes and say what comes yond''

Putting this as paraphrase of look at such a person it would appear ridiculous and seems to fall under the rule that whatever is translatable into other language in simple terms ought to be so in the original or it is not good

The difference arose from the difference of situation and education Blackguard might express that very differently *q*to rest*r* as a threat of half-brute who has neither respect for himself or others

But he would try this by the introduction how does <u>Pros</u> introduce it   He has told <u>M</u>ᵃ a story which affects her most*s* deeply and has *ᵗ*lulled her into sleep and the actress *u*ought to have represented it*v* with her <u>eye</u>lids sunk down and living in her dreams   He sees and he wishes to point out to his daughter not with great but almost scenic solemnity himself present to her and to the spectators and auditors as magician Therefore in that state is something which was to appear on sudden which was no more expected that we should at first great actor when the curtain is drawn up

Then *w*is driven or forced to say*x* curtain of the <u>eye</u> &c

Thus to him mind is completely in character which <u>Pros</u> is assuming a magician whose very art seems to cause all the objects of nature in some mysterious character and controlled the impression on <u>M</u>ᵃ at first then with the unexpected being

It is much easier to find fault with writer merely by reference to former notions and experience than to sit down and read him and to connect the one feeling with the other and to judge of words and phrases in proportion as they convey those feelings together

In <u>M</u>ᵃ be able to point out in what found at play ideal powers of <u>Sh</u> not object to point out the exquisite poet but the exquisite judgment *y*about female characters*z*   Introduced in all in which to describe the one is almost to describe the whole in which they invested   *a*Effects *b*of which one of the greatest excellences of <u>Sh</u> and yet more than all in other nature*c* of his works*c* and yet with all splendours*c* has character of great saints who felt himself to have facts and appearance of life only as means of realising and giving thus replica feelings of human*c* creatures that of individual which could not but be found without them

q–r Not transcribed by Collier

s Not transcribed by Collier

. *t* f 10ᵛ

u–v Not transcribed by Collier

w–x Not transcribed by Collier

y–z Not transcribed by Collier

a–d Most of this passage was not transcribed, or radically altered in transcription, by Collier

b f 9ᵛ   *c* Doubtful readings

But always we must recollect this is Sh the wonder certainly among ignorant and the more so because the more he is tried the more he proves to be so in long pleasing them more with enthusiasm now[d] another instance that profundity of thought a prophet and yet with all the wonderful powers making us feel as if he were unconscious of himself in his own powers and disguise the half-god in the character of child or affectionate companion

[e]*12 Lecture*

In last lecture endeavoured to point out where the pride of intellect was supposed to be the ruling impulse [f]which was exemplified[g] by characters of Iago R[d] 3 and Falstaff

In R[d] 3[d] ambition was first [h]the means and[i] channel in which the character directed himself Sh has not only given us the character but explained his reasons as to source and generation

The inferiority of body induced him to seek comfort by his sense of superiority in mind   He has displayed this most beautifully by causing R[d] bring his very deformities as a boast   Is not unfounded in nature so Wilkes said that the best formed man in the world had but 10 minutes advantage of him [j]in the company of females[k]

He then talked of R[d] II from its connection with it In R[d] 3[d] Sh has painted a character in whom ambition was only the channel in which a ruling impulse flows   He has here given us in the character of Bol or H 4 a character where ambition mingled with great talents is the uppermost feeling

The object is to point out the difference between Sh and other dramatists and know no greater than taking 2 characters which appear at first to be the same and drawing them distinct also apparently the same

Contains at once the most magnificent and truest eul[l] on our native country [m]in our language or in any other not excepting Rome and Greece

When I feel that upon our morality was owing safety and that our national feelings are the support of morality I cannot read these lines without a triumph that our enemy is superior only in mechanic means

"This seat of Mars this other Eden
envious siege of watery"

[e] f 1
[f-g] Not transcribed by Collier
[h-i] Not transcribed by Collier
[j-k] Not transcribed by Collier
[l] I.e. "eulogy"
[m] f 2

Every motive he sees every cause which produces patriotism is here
No abstraction   If properly repeated every man would have gone away
secure in his country if secure in his own virtue   [n]He means examine
first[o] the R[d] 2[d] Bol Yk and take the last as least important   There is
in this character most admirable keeping   He is a man of ordinary[p]
strong powers of mind but of latent wishes to do right content if in
himself alone he acted well   He points out to R[d] the effects of his
extravagance and the dangers that R is in but after this he remains
passive   So it is with <u>Gaunt</u>

Here I must observe the beauty and true force of nature with which
conceits as they are called and sometimes puns may be introduced
There was never an abuse which had not a use

R[d] comes in royal with insolence

"How is it with aged <u>Gaunt</u>"

[q]G[t] replies "Within a tedious and who abstains from meat that is not
G[t] R[d] can sick men play so nicely with their names G[t] no misery makes
sport to mock itself ⟨mock my name⟩ great King &c

He who knows the state of deep passion by this must knows[r] it
approaches to that state of madness not frenzy or delirium but [s]to trance[r]
idea modelling all to rest still to depart from the main subject of grievance   The abruptness of thought is true to nature   In a poem called
the <u>Mad Mother</u> she says The breeze I see is in yon tree   It comes to
cool my babe and me

If this be admired in images can we suppose those to be unnatural
in works which are in fact part of our life   We find these plays upon
words in the best of ancients and the most beautiful parts of <u>Sh</u> and
because these have been [cri]ticised[u] we confound all in a general censure   When it disgusts us we should inquire is it rightly or wrongly
used   Is it in its right place [v]I should not detain you on this point did
I not know that[w] it was on this point that all the abuse of <u>Sh</u> was
founded   D[r] J[n] says he loses the world for a toy and can no more
withstand them <u>Ant</u>[y] could <u>Cleop</u>[a]   He has [x]condensed and[y] has gained
far more by the figures of speech than the moderns have by abandoning
them

[n-o] Not transcribed by Collier
[p] Not transcribed by Collier
[q] f 3
[r] So in ms
[s-t] Not transcribed by Collier
[u] Collier omitted the sign for "cr"
[v-w] Not transcribed by Collier
[x-y] Not transcribed by Collier

[z]Passed to the character of R̲ᵈ 2 [who is][a] not deficient in immediate courage as appears by [the last][a] assassination or in powers of mind as is [shown][a] by his foresight throughout the play   The feelings which amiable as they would have been in a woman become misplaced in a man and altogether improper in a King   He is insolent and presumptious Quotes D̲ʳ J̲ⁿ [   ] adversity[b] [c]wise patient and passive fortitude[d] The latter part I object to as the same character goes on throughout the play   [e]He does not yield in a moment[f]   The first misfortune overwhelmed him but so far from being any taming any subduing of feelings the returning glance of hope lifts him to a strange degree of elevation

He asks for his old followers G̲r̲e̲e̲n̲ dangerous enemy measures our confines   Terrible hell make war upon their souls   Those whom you curse have felt the worst of death   On receiving an equivocal answer he takes it in the worst sense   He looks out for new hope and at last makes a merit of resigning himself and at last by a cloud of his own thoughts [g]one pressing on the others[h] endeavours to shelter himself from that which is around him   Throughout the play the progression from insolence to despair from love to the very[i] agonies of resentment and this joined with capaciousness of thought and expression and if there were an actor capable of representing it would delight us more than any other character exception K̲ L̲e̲a̲r̲

[j]Knew no other character where he has preserved a character so perfectly as in this

The next character is B̲o̲l̲ his rival great courage ambition equal [k]to the throne[l] and yet the similarity drawn between B̲o̲l̲ and R̲ᵈ 3ᵈ yet R̲ᵈ is no vulgar tyrant no N̲e̲r̲o̲ or C̲a̲l̲i̲g̲u̲l̲a̲   In B̲o̲l̲ on the contrary we find a man in the first instance sorely injured next encouraged by the grievance of his country and the strange mismanagement of government scarcely daring to look at his own views   Coming home to claim his dukedom and keeping it up in the play in which at last letting out his design to the full extent of which he was unconscious in the first stage of it   This is shown in so many passages that I will only select one among a great number and I select it because in the 2̲1̲ volumes of notes on S̲h̲ this empty[m] page seems to be the only one left quite naked

---

[a] Conjectural readings; the corner of the leaf is torn off
[b] Inserted in the margin; two or three words indecipherable
[c-d] Not transcribed by Collier
[e-f] Not transcribed by Collier
[g-h] Not transcribed by Collier
[i] Not transcribed by Collier   [j] f 5
[k-l] Not transcribed by Collier
[m] Not transcribed by Collier

This is where <u>Bol</u> approaches the castle in which the unfortunate King has taken shelter and <u>Yk</u> is with him the noble <u>Y</u> who is still contented with saying the truth and then drawing back and becoming passive

(North^d R^d not far from hence <u>Yk</u> beseem <u>N^d</u> to say King <u>R^d</u> <u>N^d</u> only to be brief to shorten for taking so the head lest you mistake it)

ⁿThere a play of words is perfectly in character   He meant not only answer to regent but the tone of passion

''But who comes here noble lord go to the rude ribs of that ancient castle and thus deliver—''

The reason why <u>Sh</u> uses his is because although <u>Bol</u> was only speaking of the castle he meant <u>R^d</u>

In Milton he uses the word <u>her</u> in relation to the word <u>form Bol</u> had a equivocation ^oin his mind^p and was dwelling on the king in his mind ''noble lord go & <u>Harry Bolinbbroke</u>['']^q is the only line denoting his own importance

''to lay my arms and powers that lands restored again be freely granted the summers dust with blood''

then checked [by]^r the <u>eye</u> of <u>Yk</u> proceeds ^sA my [stoop]ing^t duty tenderly will show ^uanother example in <u>Macbeth</u> where <u>Sh</u> gives him the most natural rhodomontade^v   <u>Bol</u> checked passes into the very contrary when broken off yet does not sink greatly by flow of the subject

This passage direct attention ''lets march without the noise of threatening drum   Me thinks King Richard and myself

Tears the cloudy cheeks of heaven''

<u>Yk</u> again checks him ^wthe ''yield[ing]^x water rain on the earth and not on him''

Throughout the play with the exception of some of the last scenes though written with exquisite beauty <u>Sh</u> seems to have raised to the summit the presentation of character

In order to obviate the general prejudice against <u>Sh</u> he had to speak of the character of <u>Hamlet</u> where so much has been objected to that ought to be praised and where so many beauties have been hidden of the highest kind

The first question is what meant <u>Sh</u> by the character of <u>Hamlet</u>   I

ⁿ f 6
^{o–p} Not transcribed by Collier
^q Collier omitted the closing quotation marks
^r Word obscured by a smudge
^s Here a large ''A'', linked to the left margin by a double line, refers to Collier's longhand transcript, 1 385 and n 20, above
^t Word partly obscured by a smudge
^{u–v} Not transcribed by Collier
^w f 7
^x End of word supplied by the editor

believe he regarded his stories little more than a painter does his canvas
*y*as the circumstances on which he was to write his plays*z*   What is
the point to which S̲h̲ directed himself   In H̲ he meant to show us a
being whose *a*dizzying intellectual circumstances*b* a man in whom all
we have when we shut our e̲y̲e̲s̲ *c*was more strong more vivid than is
consistent with that perfect balance of our being in which the outward
impressions have throughout day force to be corrected by our uneven
circumstances*d*   But in H̲ he meant to describe a character in whom
the play's external world and all its incidents are comparatively dim of
no interest in themselves but commencing to interest as soon as they
are recollected in causes *e*and thus as soon as they have formed a part
of that other world in which a man of vivid imagination exists

He places him in the most stimulating circumstances from that in
which a human being can be placed   He is the heir apparent to the
throne father dies suspiciously his mother excludes him by marrying
the uncle from the throne   This is not enough but he is induced by
ghost of the murdered father *f*to declare he was murdered in the most
infamous circumstances*g*   What is the result endless reasoning perpetual solicitation of the mind to act but as constant escapes from
action   Reproaches of himself for his sloth yet the whole energy
passing away in these reproaches   But not from cowardice he is made
one of the bravest not from want of forethought he sees through the
soul of those who come near them but merely from the aversion to
action of those who have a world within themselves

*h*Admirable is the judgment of the speaker*i* his own fancy has not
conjured up the ghost that is seen first by others   He is prepared to
witness this and when he does he is not brought forward as having long
brooded on the subject   The moment when the ghost enters he speaks
of other matters to *j*relieve the weight on his mind*k*

"cold night bitter strikes it is struck*l* honoured in the breach than the
observance"

Roused from his casual state of mind he breaks out into moral re-

y-z Not transcribed by Collier

a-b Not transcribed by Collier

c-d Not transcribed by Collier

e f 8

f-g Not transcribed by Collier

h Collier cancelled several words before this paragraph

i Collier first wrote and cancelled the signs for "play"

j f 9

k Collier cancelled several words here

l Collier added quotation marks after "struck"

flections   Then the ghost enters "look my lord it comes angels and ministers of grace defend us"

The same occurs in <u>Macbeth</u> in the dagger scene the moment before he has his mind drawn off to some indifferent things so that the mind[m] has all the effect of abruptness so as to remove from the mind of the reader any idea that this proceeds from the figure in the imagination of the person beholding

Here <u>Sh</u> is so admirable that his language though poetry is made the language of nature   No words can occur to us associated with such feelings but those which we have employed on the highest the most august the [gra]ndest[n] subjects of our maker of being in the sentient world   That this is no fancy of mine will show by <u>Sh</u> himself   After the players come on he expresses the notion I have been expressing when <u>H1</u> remains [o]after the players have spoken these lines which presents some early verses of his own writing[p] <u>Hamlet</u> says "God be with ye so good bye now I am alone [q]Hecuba like a very <u>drab</u>"

The very same feeling in an after part of the play "How all occasions do inform against me &c   What is a man if his chief good and market of his time cause will and strength and means to do it"

And yet with all cause nothing is done   The admirable character observing deeply acquainted with his own feelings and pointing them out yet still yielding to the same retiring from all reality which is the result of having a world within himself

Such a mind as this is <u>akin</u> to madness   <u>Dryden</u> said great wit to madness nearly is allied   He is right if he means by wit great genius

Yet still there is sense of imperfection even in moralising on the <u>skull</u> which wants something to make it perfect   He is therefore described as attached to <u>Ophelia</u>

His madness is assumed when he finds witnesses are placed to hear him behind the <u>Arras</u> when <u>Oph</u> is placed as a <u>decoy</u> and when they want to know what he says

There is another objection which <u>D[r] J[n]</u> has spoken of very severely

Seeing his [r]<u>Unkle</u> praying not to kill him when he was praying that would [   ][s] but take him when in the height iniquity   This has said to be sentiment so atrocious and horrible as to be unfit to be placed in the mouth of a human being

---

[m] So in ms
[n] Word completed by the editor
[o-p] Not transcribed by Collier
[q] f 10
[r] f 11
[s] Undeciphered; Collier wrote the signs for one or two words, apparently "rlts rd"

This was meant as a part of the same irresolute character Hamlet seizes hold of that as a pretext for not acting [t]If he had seen him feasting the same feeling would have induced him to see cause why be sympathy not revenge[u]

Dr Jn says his journey to Engd that Sh was merely following a novel Sh never followed the novel but where he saw the story telling some great truth perpetual in human nature [v]with whom would destiny with whom would the contingencies of fortune be connected if not with the man who[w] still resolving and still refusing [x]gives himself up at last to groans[y]

Even when Osrick comes in he cannot mocking but only that and runs away from his duty again [z]at last King himself King has name and his Unkle by circumstances[a]

Draw moral impossible to state that action is the great end that no faculties of intellect however grand can be counted as valuable or otherwise than misfortunes if they [b]draw us from action and bid us to think and think of doing when the time has wasted in which he ought to act Sh has shown in this the fulness of his powers All that is amiable in nature is combined in Hamlet but in one article The man living in meditation does no action independent of all meditation

[t–u] Not transcribed by Collier; "sympathy" is a doubtful reading
[v–w] Not transcribed by Collier
[x–y] Not transcribed by Collier
[z–a] Not transcribed by Collier
[b] f 12; Collier wrote signs for "draw" twice

APPENDIX C

THE TEXT OF LECTURES
1, 2, 6, 7, 8, 9, AND 12
OF THE 1811–12 SERIES
AS PUBLISHED BY
JOHN PAYNE COLLIER
IN *SEVEN LECTURES*
ON SHAKESPEARE
AND MILTON (1856)

THE TEXT OF LECTURES
1, 2, 6, 7, 8, 9, AND 12
OF THE 1811–12 SERIES
AS PUBLISHED BY
JOHN PAYNE COLLIER
IN *SEVEN LECTURES*
ON SHAKESPEARE
AND MILTON (1856)

Collier's text gained general acceptance as a more or less authentic report of what C said in seven of the 1811–12 series of lectures and was reprinted in all subsequent editions of the lectures up to and including *Sh C*. The relationship between this printed text and Collier's ms has been described above (Introduction to the 1811–12 series: Textual Introduction) and is analysed at greater length in *C on Sh* pp 22–6. It is now clear that the text Collier printed in 1856 is a radically revised version of the notes he took at the lectures. He rewrote almost every sentence, sometimes omitting or curtailing, more often expanding and elaborating in a way that subtly affects the sense of the earlier version without adding anything significant. There are some more substantial expansions and additions, which generally do not introduce any fresh ideas, but it is possible that Collier was incorporating fragmentary recollections of the 1811–12 lectures, or material from the 1818 course, which he also attended. These more substantial additions are underlined in the text as given below, which is otherwise reprinted as it appeared in *Seven Lectures*. Most of Collier's alterations in 1856 take the form of modifications of his original notes, and in order to appreciate the extent and pervasiveness of these it is necessary to compare the different versions. He also made a number of cuts, removing proper names and references he perhaps could not trace, and occasionally omitting a phrase or sentence for no apparent reason.

Although this text has no authority, unless some of the additions Collier introduced are authentic, its inclusion here will enable the reader to make his own comparisons between the various texts of these lectures. Collier's ms notes are printed in Vol I among the materials relating to this course, and a transcript of his shorthand notes taken at Lects 9 and 12 can be found in App B.

THE FIRST LECTURE

I cannot avoid the acknowledgment of the difficulty of the task I have undertaken; yet I have undertaken it voluntarily, and I shall discharge it to the best of my abilities, requesting those who hear me to allow for deficiencies, and to bear in mind the wide extent of my subject. The field is almost boundless as the sea, yet full of beauty and variety as the land: I feel in some sort oppressed by abundance; *inopem me copia fecit.*

What I most rely upon is your sympathy; and, as I proceed, I trust that I shall interest you: sympathy and interest are to a lecturer like the sun and the showers to nature—absolutely necessary to the production of blossoms and fruit.

May I venture to observe that my own life has been employed more in reading and conversation—in collecting and reflecting, than in printing and publishing; for I never felt the desire, so often experienced by others, of becoming an author. It was accident made me an author in the first instance: I was called a poet almost before I knew I could write poetry. In what I have to offer I shall speak freely, whether of myself or of my contemporaries, when it is necessary: conscious superiority, if indeed it be superior, need not fear to have its self-love or its pride wounded; and contempt, the most absurd and debasing feeling that can actuate the human mind, must be far below the sphere in which lofty intellects live and move and have their being.

On the first examination of a work, especially a work of fiction and fancy, it is right to inquire to what feeling or passion it addresses itself— to the benevolent, or to the vindictive? whether it is calculated to excite emulation, or to produce envy, under the common mask of scorn? and, in the next place, whether the pleasure we receive from it has a tendency to keep us good, to make us better, or to reward us for being good.

It will be expected of me, as my prospectus indicates, that I should say something of the causes of false criticism, particularly as regards poetry, though I do not mean to confine myself to that only: in doing so, it will be necessary for me to point out some of the obstacles which impede, and possibly prevent, the formation of a correct judgment. These are either—

1. Accidental causes, arising out of the particular circumstances of the age in which we live; or—

2. Permanent causes, flowing out of the general principles of our nature.

Under the first head, accidental causes, may be classed—1. The events that have occurred in our own day, which, from their importance alone, have created a world of readers. 2. The practice of public speaking, which encourages a too great desire to be understood at once, and at the first blush. 3. The prevalence of reviews, magazines, newspapers, novels, &c.

Of the last, and of the perusal of them, I will run the risk of asserting, that where the reading of novels prevails as a habit, it occasions in time the entire destruction of the powers of the mind: it is such an utter loss to the reader, that it is not so much to be called pass-time as kill-time. It conveys no trustworthy information as to facts; it produces no improvement of the intellect, but fills the mind with a mawkish and morbid sensibility, which is directly hostile to the cultivation, invigoration, and enlargement of the nobler faculties of understanding.

Reviews are generally pernicious, because the writers determine without reference to fixed principles—because reviews are usually filled with personalities; and, above all, because they teach people rather to judge than to consider, to decide than to reflect: thus they encourage superficiality, and induce the thoughtless and the idle to adopt sentiments conveyed under the authoritative WE, and not, by the working and subsequent clearing of their own minds, to form just original opinions. In older times writers were looked up to almost as intermediate beings, between angels and men; afterwards they were regarded as venerable and, perhaps, inspired teachers; subsequently they descended to the level of learned and instructive friends; but in modern days they are deemed culprits more than benefactors: as culprits they are brought to the bar of self-erected and self-satisfied tribunals. If a person be now seen reading a new book, the most usual question is—"What trash have you there?" I admit that there is some reason for this difference in the estimate; for in these times, if a man fail as a tailor, or a shoemaker, and can read and write correctly (for spelling is still of some consequence) he becomes an author.*

The crying sin of modern criticism is that it is overloaded with personality. If an author commit an error, there is no wish to set him right for the sake of truth, but for the sake of triumph—that the reviewer may show how much wiser, or how much abler he is than the writer. Reviewers are usually people who would have been poets, historians, biographers, &c., if they could: they have tried their talents at one or

---

* Here my short-hand note informs me that Coleridge made a quotation from Jeremy Taylor, but from what work, or of what import, does not appear. He observed, that "although Jeremy Taylor wrote only in prose, according to some definitions of poetry he might be considered one of our noblest poets."—J. P. C.

at the other, and have failed; therefore they turn critics, and, like the Roman emperor, a critic most hates those who excel in the particular department in which he, the critic, has notoriously been defeated. This is an age of personality and political gossip, when insects, as in ancient Egypt, are worshipped in proportion to the venom of their stings—when poems, and especially satires, are valued according to the number of living names they contain; and where the notes, however, have this comparative excellence, that they are generally more poetical and pointed than the text. This style of criticism is at the present moment one of the chief pillars of the Scotch professorial court; and, as to personality in poems, I remember to have once seen an epic advertised, and strongly recommended, because it contained more than a hundred names of living characters.

How derogatory, how degrading, this is to true poetry I need not say. A very wise writer has maintained that there is more difference between one man and another, than between man and a beast: I can conceive of no lower state of human existence than that of a being who, insensible to the beauties of poetry himself, endeavours to reduce others to his own level. What Hooker so eloquently claims for law I say of poetry—''Her seat is the bosom of God, her voice the harmony of the world; all things in heaven and on earth do her homage.'' It is the language of heaven, and in the exquisite delight we derive from poetry we have, as it were, a type, a foretaste, and a prophecy of the joys of heaven.

Another cause of false criticism is the greater purity of morality in the present age, compared even with the last. Our notions upon this subject are sometimes carried to excess, particularly among those who in print affect to enforce the value of a high standard. Far be it from me to depreciate that value; but let me ask, who now will venture to read a number of the Spectator, or of the Tatler, to his wife and daughters, without first examining it to make sure that it contains no word which might, in our day, offend the delicacy of female ears, and shock feminine susceptibility? Even our theatres, the representations at which usually reflect the morals of the period, have taken a sort of domestic turn, and while the performances at them may be said, in some sense, to improve the heart, there is no doubt that they vitiate the taste. The effect is bad, however good the cause.

Attempts have been made to compose and adapt systems of education; but it appears to me something like putting Greek and Latin grammars into the hands of boys, before they understand a word of Greek or Latin. These grammars contain instructions on all the minutiæ and refinements of language, but of what use are they to persons who do not comprehend the first rudiments? Why are you to furnish the means of judging, before you give the capacity to judge? These seem to me to be among the principal accidental causes of false criticism.

Among the permanent causes, I may notice—

First, the great pleasure we feel in being told of the knowledge we possess, rather than of the ignorance we suffer. Let it be our first duty to teach thinking, and then what to think about. You cannot expect a person to be able to go through the arduous process of thinking, who has never exercised his faculties. In the Alps we see the Chamois hunter ascend the most perilous precipices without danger, and leap from crag to crag over vast chasms without dread or difficulty, and who but a fool, if unpractised, would attempt to follow him? it is not intrepidity alone that is necessary, but he who would imitate the hunter must have gone through the same process for the acquisition of strength, skill, and knowledge: he must exert, and be capable of exerting, the same muscular energies, and display the same perseverance and courage, or all his efforts will be worse than fruitless: they will lead not only to disappointment, but to destruction. Systems have been invented with the avowed object of teaching people how to think; but in my opinion the proper title for such a work ought to be "The Art of teaching how to think without thinking." Nobody endeavours to instruct a man how to leap, until he has first given him vigour and elasticity.

Nothing is more essential—nothing can be more important, than in every possible way to cultivate and improve the thinking powers: the mind as much requires exercise as the body, and no man can fully and adequately discharge the duties of whatever station he is placed in without the power of thought. I do not, of course, say that a man may not get through life without much thinking, or much power of thought; but if he be a carpenter, without thought a carpenter he must remain: if he be a weaver, without thought a weaver he must remain.—On man God has not only bestowed gifts, but the power of giving: he is not a creature born but to live and die: he has had faculties communicated to him, which, if he do his duty, he is bound to communicate and make beneficial to others. Man, in a secondary sense, may be looked upon in part as his own creator, for by the improvement of the faculties bestowed upon him by God, he not only enlarges them, but may be said to bring new ones into existence. The Almighty has thus condescended to communicate to man, in a high state of moral cultivation, a portion of his own great attributes.

A second permanent cause of false criticism is connected with the habit of not taking the trouble to think: it is the custom which some people have established of judging of books by books.—Hence to such the use and value of reviews. Why has nature given limbs, if they are not to be applied to motion and action; why abilities, if they are to lie asleep, while we avail ourselves of the eyes, ears, and understandings of others? As men often employ servants, to spare them the nuisance of rising from their seats and walking across a room, so men employ reviews in order to save themselves the trouble of exercising their own powers of judging: it is only mental slothfulness and sluggishness that induce so many to adopt, and take for granted the opinions of others.

I may illustrate this moral imbecility by a case which came within my own knowledge. A friend of mine had seen it stated somewhere, or had heard it said, that Shakespeare had not made Constance, in "King John," speak the language of nature, when she exclaims on the loss of Arthur,

> "Grief fills the room up of my absent child,
> Lies in his bed, walks up and down with me;
> Puts on his pretty looks, repeats his words,
> Remembers me of all his gracious parts,
> Stuffs out his vacant garments with his form:
> Then have I reason to be fond of grief."
>
> *King John*, Act iii., Scene 4.

Within three months after he had repeated the opinion, (not thinking for himself) that these lines were out of nature, my friend died. I called upon his mother, an affectionate, but ignorant woman, who had scarcely heard the name of Shakespeare, much less read any of his plays. Like Philip, I endeavoured to console her, and among other things I told her, in the anguish of her sorrow, that she seemed to be as fond of grief as she had been of her son. What was her reply? Almost a prose parody on the very language of Shakespeare—the same thoughts in nearly the same words, but with a different arrangement. An attestation like this is worth a thousand criticisms.

As a third permanent cause of false criticism we may notice the vague use of terms. And here I may take the liberty of impressing upon my hearers, the fitness, if not the necessity, of employing the most appropriate words and expressions, even in common conversation, and in the ordinary transactions of life. If you want a substantive do not take the first that comes into your head, but that which most distinctly and peculiarly conveys your meaning: if an adjective, remember the grammatical use of that part of speech, and be careful that it expresses some quality in the substantive that you wish to impress upon your hearer. Reflect for a moment on the vague and uncertain manner in which the word "taste" has been often employed; and how such epithets as "sublime," "majestic," "grand," "striking," "picturesque" &c. have been misapplied, and how they have been used on the most unworthy and inappropriate occasions.

I was one day admiring one of the falls of the Clyde; and ruminating upon what descriptive term could be most fitly applied to it, I came to the conclusion that the epithet "majestic" was the most appropriate. While I was still contemplating the scene a gentleman and a lady came up, neither of whose faces bore much of the stamp of superior intelligence, and the first words the gentleman uttered were "It is very majestic." I was pleased to find such a confirmation of my opinion, and I complimented the spectator upon the choice of his epithet, saying that he had used the best word that could have been selected from our language: "Yes, sir," replied the gentleman, "I say it is very majestic: it is sublime, it is beautiful, it is grand, it is picturesque."—"Ay (added the lady), it is the prettiest thing I ever saw." I own that I was not a little disconcerted.

You will see, by the terms of my prospectus, that I intend my lectures to be, not only "in illustration of the principles of poetry," but to include a statement of the application of those principles, "as grounds of criticism on the most popular works of later English poets, those of the living included." If I had thought this task presumptuous on my part, I should not have voluntarily undertaken it; and in examining the merits, whether positive or comparative, of my contemporaries, I shall dismiss all feelings and associations which might lead me from the formation of a right estimate. I shall give talent and genius its due praise, and only bestow censure where, as it seems to me, truth and justice demand it. I shall, of course, carefully avoid falling into that system of false criticism, which I condemn in others; and, above all, whether I speak of those whom I know, or of those whom I do not know, of friends or of enemies, of the dead or of the living, my great aim will be to be strictly impartial. No man can truly apply principles, who displays the slightest bias in the application of them; and I shall have much greater pleasure in pointing out the good, than in exposing the bad. I fear no accusation of arrogance from the amiable and the wise: I shall pity the weak, and despise the malevolent.

END OF THE FIRST LECTURE.

THE SECOND LECTURE

Readers may be divided into four classes:

1. Sponges, who absorb all they read, and return it nearly in the same state, only a little dirtied.

2. Sand-glasses, who retain nothing, and are content to get through a book for the sake of getting through the time.

3. Strain-bags, who retain merely the dregs of what they read.

4. Mogul diamonds, equally rare and valuable, who profit by what they read, and enable others to profit by it also.*

I adverted in my last lecture to the prevailing laxity in the use of terms: this is the principal complaint to which the moderns are exposed; but it is a grievous one, inasmuch as it inevitably tends to the misapplication of words, and to the corruption of language. I mentioned the word "taste," but the remark applies not merely to substantives and adjectives, to things and their epithets, but to verbs: thus, how frequently is the verb "indorsed" strained from its true signification, as given by Milton in the expression—"And elephants indorsed with towers." Again, "virtue" has been equally perverted: originally it signified merely strength; it then became strength of mind and valour, and it has now been changed to the class term for moral excellence† in all its various species. I only introduce these as instances by the way, and nothing could be easier than to multiply them.

At the same time, while I recommend precision both of thought and expression, I am far from advocating a pedantic niceness in the choice of language: such a course would only render conversation stiff and

---

* In "Notes and Queries," July 22, 1854, I quoted this four-fold division of readers; and in a friendly letter to me, the Rev. S. R. Maitland pointed out the following passage in the Mishna (*Cap. Patrum*, v. § 15), which Coleridge clearly had in his mind, but to which my short-hand note does not state that he referred. It is very possible that I did not catch the reference; but more probable that he omitted it, thinking it not necessary, in an extemporaneous lecture, to quote chapter and verse for whatever he delivered. Had Coleridge previously written, or subsequently printed, his Lectures, he would, most likely, not have omitted the information:—"Quadruplices conditiones (inveniunt) in his qui sedent coram sapientibus (audiendi causa) videlicet conditio spongiæ, clepsydræ, sacci fecinacei, et cribri. Spongia sugendo attrahit omnia. Clepsydra, quod ex una parte attrahit, ex altera rursum effundit. Saccus fecinaceus effundit vinum, et colligit feces. Cribrum emittit farinam, et colligit similam."—J. P. C.

† My short-hand note of this part of the sentence strongly illustrates the point adverted to in the Preface, viz., how easy it is for a person, somewhat mechanically taking down words uttered *viva voce*, to mishear what is said. I am confident that Coleridge's words were "moral excellence"—there cannot be a doubt about it— but in my note it stands "*modern* excellence." My ear deceived me, and I thought he said *modern*, when in fact he said "moral."—J. P. C.

stilted. Dr. Johnson used to say that in the most unrestrained discourse he always sought for the properest word,—that which best and most exactly conveyed his meaning: to a certain point he was right, but because he carried it too far, he was often laborious where he ought to have been light, and formal where he ought to have been familiar. Men ought to endeavour to distinguish subtilely, that they may be able afterwards to assimilate truly.

I have often heard the question put whether Pope is a great poet, and it has been warmly debated on both sides, some positively maintaining the affirmative, and others dogmatically insisting upon the negative; but it never occurred to either party to make the necessary preliminary inquiry—What is meant by the words "poet" and "poetry?" Poetry is not merely invention: if it were, Gulliver's Travels would be poetry; and before you can arrive at a decision of the question, as to Pope's claim, it is absolutely necessary to ascertain what people intend by the words they use. Harmonious versification no more makes poetry than mere invention makes a poet; and to both these requisites there is much besides to be added. In morals, politics, and philosophy no useful discussion can be entered upon, unless we begin by explaining and understanding the terms we employ. It is therefore requisite that I should state to you what I mean by the word "poetry," before I commence any consideration of the comparative merits of those who are popularly called "poets."

Words are used in two ways:—

1. In a sense that comprises everything called by that name. For instance, the words "poetry" and "sense" are employed in this manner, when we say that such a line is bad poetry or bad sense, when in truth it is neither poetry nor sense. If it be bad poetry, it is not poetry; if it be bad sense, it is not sense. The same of "metre": bad metre is not metre.

2. In a philosophic sense, which must include a definition of what is essential to the thing. Nobody means mere metre by poetry; so, mere rhyme is not poetry. Something more is required, and what is that something? It is not wit, because we may have wit where we never dream of poetry. Is it the just observation of human life? Is it a peculiar and a felicitous selection of words? This, indeed, would come nearer to the taste of the present age, when sound is preferred to sense; but I am happy to think that this taste is not likely to last long.

The Greeks and Romans, in the best period of their literature, knew nothing of any such taste. High-flown epithets and violent metaphors, conveyed in inflated language, is not poetry. Simplicity is indispensable, and in Catullus it is often impossible that more simple language could be used; there is scarcely a word or a line, which a lamenting mother in a cottage might not have employed.* That I may be clearly understood, I will venture to give the following definition of poetry.

It is an art (or whatever better term our language may afford) of representing, in words, external nature and human thoughts and affections, both relatively to human affections, by the production of as much immediate pleasure in parts, as is compatible with the largest sum of pleasure in the whole.

Or, to vary the words, in order to make the abstract idea more intelligible:—

It is the art of communicating whatever we wish to communicate, so as both to express and produce excitement, but for the purpose of immediate pleasure; and each part is fitted to afford as much pleasure, as is compatible with the largest sum in the whole.

You will naturally ask my reasons for this definition of poetry, and they are these:—

"It is a representation of nature;" but that is not enough: the anatomist and the topographer give representations of nature; therefore I add:

"And of the human thoughts and affections." Here the metaphysician interferes: here our best novelists interfere likewise,—excepting that the latter describe with more minuteness, accuracy, and truth, than is consistent with poetry. Consequently I subjoin:

"It must be relative to the human affections." Here my chief point of difference is with the novel-writer, the historian, and all those who describe not only nature, and the human affections, but relatively to the human affections: therefore I must add:

"And it must be done for the purpose of immediate pleasure." In poetry the general good is to be accomplished through the pleasure, and if the poet do not do that, he ceases to be a poet to him to whom he gives it not. Still, it is not enough, because we may point out many prose writers to whom the whole of the definition hitherto furnished would apply. I add, therefore, that it is not only for the purpose of immediate pleasure, but—

"The work must be so constructed as to produce in each part that highest quantity of pleasure, or a high quantity of pleasure." There metre introduces its claim, where the feeling calls for it. Our language

---

* It appears by my short-hand note that Coleridge here named some particular poem by Catullus; but what it was is not stated, a blank having been left for the title. It would not be difficult to fill the chasm speculatively; but I prefer to give my memorandum as it stands.—J. P. C.

gives to expression a certain measure, and will, in a strong state of passion, admit of scansion from the very mouth. The very assumption that we are reading the work of a poet supposes that he is in a continuous state of excitement; and thereby arises a language in prose unnatural, but in poetry natural.

There is one error which ought to be peculiarly guarded against, which young poets are apt to fall into, and which old poets commit, from being no poets, but desirous of the end which true poets seek to attain. No: I revoke the words; they are not desirous of that of which their little minds can have no just conception. They have no desire of fame—that glorious immortality of true greatness—

> "That lives and spreads aloft by those pure eyes,
> And perfect witness of all judging Jove;"
>
> MILTON'S Lycidas.

but they struggle for reputation, that echo of an echo, in whose very etymon its signification is contained. Into this error the author of "The Botanic Garden" has fallen, through the whole of which work, I will venture to assert, there are not twenty images described as a man would describe them in a state of excitement. The poem is written with all the tawdry industry of a milliner anxious to dress up a doll in silks and satins. Dr. Darwin laboured to make his style fine and gaudy, by accumulating and applying all the sonorous and handsome-looking words in our language. This is not poetry, and I subjoin to my definition—

That a true poem must give "as much pleasure in each part as is compatible with the greatest sum of pleasure in the whole." We must not look to parts merely, but to the whole, and to the effect of that whole. In reading Milton, for instance, scarcely a line can be pointed out which, critically examined, could be called in itself good: the poet would not have attempted to produce merely what is in general understood by a good line; he sought to produce glorious paragraphs and systems of harmony, or, as he himself expresses it,

> "Many a winding bout
> Of linked sweetness long drawn out."
>
> L'Allegro.

Such, therefore, as I have now defined it, I shall consider the sense of the word "Poetry:" pleasurable excitement is its origin and object; pleasure is the magic circle out of which the poet must not dare to tread. Part of my definition, you will be aware, would apply equally to the arts of painting and music, as to poetry; but to the last are added words and metre, so that my definition is strictly and logically applicable to poetry, and to poetry only, which produces delight, the parent of so many virtues. When I was in Italy, a friend of mind, who pursued painting almost with the enthusiasm of madness, believing it superior to every other art, heard the definition I have given, acknowledged its correctness, and admitted the pre-eminence of poetry.

I never shall forget, when in Rome, the acute sensation of pain I experienced on beholding the frescoes of Raphael and Michael Angelo, and on reflecting that they were indebted for their preservation solely to the durable material upon which they were painted. There they are, the permanent monuments (permanent as long as walls and plaster last) of genius and skill, while many others of their mighty works have become the spoils of insatiate avarice, or the victims of wanton barbarism. How grateful ought mankind to be, that so many of the great literary productions of antiquity have come down to us—that the works of Homer, Euclid, and Plato, have been preserved—while we possess those of Bacon, Newton, Milton, Shakespeare, and of so many other living-dead men of our own island. These, fortunately, may be considered indestructible: they shall remain to us till the end of time itself— till time, in the words of a great poet of the age of Shakespeare, has thrown his last dart at death, and shall himself submit to the final and inevitable destruction of all created matter.*

A second irruption of the Goths and Vandals could not now endanger their existence, secured as they are by the wonders of modern invention, and by the affectionate admiration of myriads of human beings. It is as nearly two centuries as possible since Shakespeare ceased to write, but when shall he cease to be read? When shall he cease to give light and delight? Yet even at this moment he is only receiving the first-fruits of that glory, which must continue to augment as long as our language is spoken. English has given immortality to him, and he has given immortality to English. Shakespeare can never die, and the language in which he wrote must with him live for ever.

Yet, in spite of all this, some prejudices have attached themselves to the name of our illustrious countryman, which it will be necessary for me first to endeavour to overcome. On the continent, we may remark,

---

* Alluding, of course, to Ben Jonson's epitaph on the Countess of Pembroke:

> "Underneath this sable herse
> Lies the subject of all verse,
> Sidney's sister, Pembroke's mother.
> Death! ere thou hast slain another,
> Learn'd, and fair, and good as she,
> Time shall throw a dart at thee."
>   *Ben Jonson's Works; edit. Gifford*, viii. 337.—J. P. C.

the works of Shakespeare are honoured in a double way—by the admiration of the Germans, and by the contempt of the French.

Among other points of objection taken by the French, perhaps, the most noticeable is, that he has not observed the sacred unities, so hallowed by the practice of their own extolled tragedians. They hold, of course after Corneille and Racine, that Sophocles is the most perfect model for tragedy, and Aristotle its most infallible censor; and that as Hamlet, Lear, Macbeth, and other dramas by Shakespeare are not framed upon that model, and consequently not subject to the same laws, they maintain (not having impartiality enough to question the model, or to deny the rules of the Stagirite) that Shakespeare was a sort of irregular genius—that he is now and then tasteful and touching, but generally incorrect; and, in short, that he was a mere child of nature, who did not know any better than to write as he has written.

It is an old, and I have hitherto esteemed it a just, Latin maxim, *Oportet discentem credere, edoctum judicare*; but modern practice has inverted it, and it ought now rather to stand, *Oportet discentem judicare, edoctum credere*. To remedy this mistake there is but one course, namely the acquirement of knowledge. I have often run the risk of applying to the ignorant, who assumed the post and province of judges, a ludicrous, but not inapt simile: they remind me of a congregation of frogs, involved in darkness in a ditch, who keep an eternal croaking, until a lantern is brought near the scene of their disputation, when they instantly cease their discordant harangues. They may be more politely resembled to night-flies, which flutter round the glimmering of a feeble taper, but are overpowered by the dazzling splendour of noon-day. Nor can it be otherwise, until the prevalent notion is exploded, that knowledge is easily taught, and until the conviction is general, that the hardest thing learned is that people are ignorant. All are apt enough to discover and expose the ignorance of their friends, but their blind faith in their own sufficiency is something more than marvellous.

Some persons have contended that mathematics ought to be taught by making the illustrations obvious to the senses. Nothing can be more absurd or injurious: it ought to be our never-ceasing effort to make people think, not feel; and it is very much owing to this mistake that, to those who do not think, and have not been made to think, Shakespeare has been found so difficult of comprehension. The condition of the stage, and the character of the times in which our great poet flourished, must first of all be taken into account, in considering the question as to his judgment. If it were possible to say which of his great powers and qualifications is more admirable than the rest, it unquestionably appears to me that his judgment is the most wonderful; and at this conviction I have arrived after a careful comparison of his productions with those of his best and greatest contemporaries.

If indeed "King Lear" were to be tried by the laws which Aristotle established, and Sophocles obeyed, it must be at once admitted to be outrageously irregular; and supposing the rules regarding the unities to be founded on man and nature, Shakespeare must be condemned for arraying his works in charms with which they ought never to have been decorated. I have no doubt, however, that both were right in their divergent courses, and that they arrived at the same conclusion by a different process.

Without entering into matters which must be generally known to persons of education, respecting the origin of tragedy and comedy among the Greeks, it may be observed, that the unities grew mainly out of the size and construction of the ancient theatres: the plays represented were made to include within a short space of time events which it is impossible should have occurred in that short space. This fact alone establishes, that all dramatic performances were then looked upon merely as ideal. It is the same with us: nobody supposes that a tragedian suffers real pain when he is stabbed or tortured; or that a comedian is in fact transported with delight when successful in pretended love.

If we want to witness mere pain, we can visit the hospitals: if we seek the exhibition of mere pleasure, we can find it in ball-rooms. It is the representation of it, not the reality, that we require, the imitation, and not the thing itself; and we pronounce it good or bad in proportion as the representation is an incorrect, or a correct imitation. The true pleasure we derive from theatrical performances arises from the fact that they are unreal and fictitious. If dying agonies were unfeigned, who, in these days of civilisation, could derive gratification from beholding them?

Performances in a large theatre made it necessary that the human voice should be unnaturally and unmusically stretched; and hence the introduction of recitative, for the purpose of rendering pleasantly artificial the distortion of the face, and straining of the voice, occasioned by the magnitude of the building. The fact that the ancient choruses were always on the stage made it impossible that any change of place should be represented, or even supposed.

The origin of the English stage is less boastful than that of the Greek stage: like the constitution under which we live, though more barbarous in its derivation, it gives more genuine and more diffused liberty, than Athens in the zenith of her political glory ever possessed. Our earliest dramatic performances were religious, <u>founded chiefly upon Scripture</u> <u>history; and, although countenanced by the clergy,</u> they were filled with blasphemies and ribaldry, such as the most hardened and desperate of the present day would not dare to utter. In these representations vice and the principle of evil were personified; and hence the introduction of fools and clowns in dramas of a more advanced period.

While Shakespeare accommodated himself to the taste and spirit of the times in which he lived, his genius and his judgment taught him to use these characters with terrible effect, in aggravating the misery and agony of some of his most distressing scenes. This result is especially obvious in "King Lear": the contrast of the Fool wonderfully heightens the colouring of some of the most painful situations, where the old monarch in the depth and fury of his despair, complains to the warring elements of the ingratitude of his daughters.

> "————Spit, fire! spout, rain!
> Nor rain, wind, thunder, fire, are my daughters:
> I tax not you, you elements, with unkindness,
> I never gave you kingdom, call'd you children;
> You owe me no subscription: then, let fall
> Your horrible pleasure; here I stand, your slave,
> A poor, infirm, weak, and despis'd old man."
>
> *King Lear*, Act iii., Scene 2.

<u>Just afterwards, the Fool interposes, to heighten and inflame the</u> <u>passion of the scene.</u>

<u>In other dramas, though perhaps in a less degree, our great poet has</u> <u>evinced the same skill and felicity of treatment; and in no instance can</u> <u>it be justly alleged of him, as it may be of some of the ablest of his</u> <u>contemporaries, that he introduced his fool, or his clown, merely for</u> <u>the sake of exciting the laughter of his audiences. Shakespeare had a</u> <u>loftier and a better purpose, and in this respect availed himself of</u> <u>resources, which, it would almost seem, he alone possessed.*</u>

END OF THE SECOND LECTURE.

THE SIXTH LECTURE

<u>The recollection of what has been said by some of his biographers, on</u> <u>the supposed fact that Milton</u> received corporal punishment at college, induces me to express my entire dissent from the notion, that flogging or caning has a tendency to degrade and debase the minds of boys at

---

* <u>I most deeply regret, that I have not recovered any of my notes of the third,</u> <u>fourth, and fifth Lectures.</u>—J. P. C.

school. In my opinion it is an entire mistake; since this species of castigation has not only been inflicted time out of mind, but those who are subjected to it are well aware that the very highest persons in the realm, and those to whom people are accustomed to look up with most respect and reverence, such as the judges of the land, have quietly submitted to it in their pupilage.

I well remember, about twenty years ago, an advertisement from a schoolmaster, in which he assured tenderhearted and foolish parents, that corporal punishment was never inflicted, excepting in cases of absolute necessity; and that even then the rod was composed of lilies and roses, the latter, I conclude, stripped of their thorns. What, let me ask, has been the consequence, in many cases, of the abolition of flogging in schools? Reluctance to remove a pimple has not unfrequently transferred the disease to the vitals: sparing the rod, for the correction of minor faults, has ended in the commission of the highest crimes. A man of great reputation (I should rather say of great notoriety) sometimes punished the pupils under his care by suspending them from the ceiling in baskets, exposed to the derision of their school-fellows; at other times he pinned upon the clothes of the offender a number of last dying speeches and confessions, and employed another boy to walk before the culprit, making the usual monotonous lamentation and outcry.

On one occasion this absurd, and really degrading punishment was inflicted because a boy read with a tone, although, I may observe in passing, that reading with intonation is strictly natural, and therefore truly proper, excepting in the excess.*

Then, as to the character and effect of the punishment just noticed, what must a parent of well regulated and instructed mind think of the exhibition of his son in the manner I have described? Here, indeed, was debasement of the worst and lowest kind; for the feelings of a child were outraged, and made to associate and connect themselves with the sentence on an abandoned and shameless criminal. Who would not prefer the momentary, but useful, impression of flogging to this gross attack upon the moral feelings and self-respect of a boy? Again, as to the proper mode of reading: why is a tone in reading to be visited as a criminal offence, especially when the estimate of that offence arises out of the ignorance and incompetence of the master? Every man who reads

---

* This was the Lecturer's own mode of reading verse, and even in prose there was an approach to intonation. I have heard him read Spenser with such an excess (to use his own word) in this respect, that it almost amounted to a song. In blank verse it was less, but still apparent. Milton's "Liberty of unlicensed Printing" was a favourite piece of rhetorical writing, and portions of it I have heard Coleridge recite, never without a sort of habitual rise and fall of the voice.—J. P. C.

with true sensibility, especially poetry, must read with a tone, since it conveys, with additional effect, the harmony and rhythm of the verse, without in the slightest degree obscuring the meaning. That is the highest point of excellence in reading, which gives to every thing, whether of thought or language, its most just expression. There may be a wrong tone, as a right, and a wrong tone is of course to be avoided; but a poet writes in measure, and measure is best made apparent by reading with a tone, which heightens the verse, and does not in any respect lower the sense. I defy any man, who has a true relish of the beauty of versification, to read a canto of "the Fairy Queen," or a book of "Paradise Lost," without some species of intonation.

In various instances we are hardly sensible of its existence, but it does exist, and persons have not scrupled to say, and I believe it, that the tone of a good reader may be set to musical notation. If in these, and in other remarks that fall from me, I appear dogmatical, or dictatorial, it is to be borne in mind, that every man who takes upon himself to lecture, requires that he should be considered by his hearers capable of teaching something that is valuable, or of saying something that is worth hearing. In a mixed audience not a few are desirous of instruction, and some require it; but placed in my present situation I consider myself, not as a man who carries moveables into an empty house, but as a man who entering a generally well furnished dwelling, exhibits a light which enables the owner to see what is still wanting. I endeavour to introduce the means of ascertaining what is, and is not, in a man's own mind.

Not long since, when I lectured at the Royal Institution, I had the honour of sitting at the desk so ably occupied by Sir Humphry Davy, who may be said to have elevated the art of chemistry to the dignity of a science; who has discovered that one common law is applicable to the mind and to the body, and who has enabled us to give a full and perfect Amen to the great axiom of Lord Bacon, that knowledge is power. In the delivery of that course I carefully prepared my first essay, and received for it a cold suffrage of approbation: from accidental causes I was unable to study the exact form and language of my second lecture, and when it was at an end, I obtained universal and heart-felt applause. What a lesson was this to me not to elaborate my materials, nor to consider too nicely the expressions I should employ, but to trust mainly to the extemporaneous ebullition of my thoughts. In this conviction I have ventured to come before you here; and may I add a hope, that what I offer will be received in a similar spirit? It is true that my matter may not be so accurately arranged: it may not dovetail and fit at all times as nicely as could be wished; but you shall have my thoughts warm from my heart, and fresh from my understanding: you shall have the whole skeleton, although the bones may not be put together with the utmost anatomical skill.

The immense advantage possessed by men of genius over men of talents can be illustrated in no stronger manner, than by a comparison of the benefits resulting to mankind from the works of Homer and of Thucydides. The merits and claims of Thucydides, as a historian, are at once admitted; but what care we for the incidents of the Peloponnesian War? An individual may be ignorant of them, as far as regards the particular narrative of Thucydides; but woe to that statesman, or, I may say, woe to that man, who has not availed himself of the wisdom contained in "the tale of Troy divine!"

Lord Bacon has beautifully expressed this idea, where he talks of the instability and destruction of the monuments of the greatest heroes, and compares them with the everlasting writings of Homer, one word of which has never been lost since the days of Pisistratus. Like a mighty ship, they have passed over the sea of time, not leaving a mere ideal track, which soon altogether disappears, but leaving a train of glory in its wake, present and enduring, daily acting upon our minds, and ennobling us by grand thoughts and images: to this work, perhaps, the bravest of our soldiery may trace and attribute some of their heroic achievements. Just as the body is to the immortal mind, so are the actions of our bodily powers in proportion to those by which, independent of individual continuity,* we are governed for ever and ever; by which we call, not only the narrow circle of mankind (narrow comparatively) as they now exist, our brethren, but by which we carry our being into future ages, and call all who shall succeed us our brethren, until at length we arrive at that exalted state, when we shall welcome into Heaven thousands and thousands, who will exclaim—"To you I owe the first development of my imagination; to you I owe the withdrawing of my mind from the low brutal part of my nature, to the lofty, the pure, and the perpetual."

Adverting to the subject more immediately before us, I may observe that I have looked at the reign of Elizabeth, interesting on many accounts, with peculiar pleasure and satisfaction, because it furnished

---

* I give this passage exactly as I find it on my notes; but it strikes me that something explanatory must have been accidentally omitted, and perhaps that the word I have written "continuity" ought to be *contiguity*. I might have left out the whole from "Just as the body" down to "the pure and the perpetual," but I preferred showing my own imperfectness to omitting what may be clear to others, though, at this distance of time, not so evident to me. The general point and bearing of what Coleridge said will be easily understood.—J. P. C.

circumstances so favourable to the existence, and to the full development of the powers of Shakespeare. The Reformation, just completed, had occasioned unusual activity of mind, a passion, as it were, for thinking, and for the discovery and use of words capable of expressing the objects of thought and invention. It was, consequently, the age of many conceits, and an age when, for a time, the intellect stood superior to the moral sense.

The difference between the state of mind in the reign of Elizabeth, and in that of Charles I. is astonishing. In the former period there was an amazing development of power, but all connected with prudential purposes—an attempt to reconcile the moral feeling with the full exercise of the powers of the mind, and the accomplishment of certain practical ends. Then lived Bacon, Burghley, Sir Walter Raleigh, Sir Philip Sidney, and a galaxy of great men, statesmen, lawyers, politicians, philosophers, and poets; and it is lamentable that they should have degraded their mighty powers to such base designs and purposes, dissolving the rich pearls of their great faculties in a worthless acid, to be drunken by a harlot. What was seeking the favour of the Queen, to a man like Bacon, but the mere courtship of harlotry?

Compare this age with that of the republicans: that indeed was an awful age, as compared with our own. England may be said to have then overflowed from the fulness of grand principle—from the greatness which men felt in themselves, abstracted from the prudence with which they ought to have considered, whether their principles were, or were not, adapted to the condition of mankind at large. Compare the revolution then effected with that of a day not long past, when the bubbling-up and overflowing was occasioned by the elevation of the dregs— when there was a total absence of all principle, when the dregs had risen from the bottom to the top, and thus converted into scum, founded a monarchy to be the poisonous bane and misery of the rest of mankind.

It is absolutely necessary to recollect, that the age in which Shakespeare lived was one of great abilities applied to individual and prudential purposes, and not an age of high moral feeling and lofty principle, which gives a man of genius the power of thinking of all things in reference to all. If, then, we should find that Shakespeare took these materials as they were presented to him, and yet to all effectual purposes produced the same grand result as others attempted to produce in an age so much more favourable, shall we not feel and acknowledge the purity and holiness of genius—a light, which, however it might shine on a dunghill, was as pure as the divine effluence which created all the beauty of nature?

One of the consequences of the idea prevalent at the period when Shakespeare flourished, viz., that persons must be men of talents in proportion as they were gentlemen, renders certain characters in his dramas natural with reference to the date when they were drawn: when we read them we are aware that they are not of our age, and in one sense they may be said to be of no age. A friend of mine well remarked of Spenser, that he is out of space: the reader never knows where he is, but still he knows, from the consciousness within him, that all is as natural and proper, as if the country where the action is laid were distinctly pointed out, and marked down in a map. Shakespeare is as much out of time, as Spenser is out of space; yet we feel conscious, though we never knew that such characters existed, that they might exist, and are satisfied with the belief in their existence.

This circumstance enabled Shakespeare to paint truly, and according to the colouring of nature, a vast number of personages by the simple force of meditation: he had only to imitate certain parts of his own character, or to exaggerate such as existed in possibility, and they were at once true to nature, and fragments of the divine mind that drew them. Men who see the great luminary of our system through various optical instruments declare that it seems either square, triangular, or round, when in truth it is still the sun, unchanged in shape and proportion. So with the characters of our great poet: some may think them of one form, and some of another; but they are still nature, still Shakespeare, and the creatures of his meditation.

When I use the term meditation, I do not mean that our great dramatist was without observation of external circumstances: quite the reverse; but mere observation may be able to produce an accurate copy, and even to furnish to other men's minds more than the copyist professed; but what is produced can only consist of parts and fragments, according to the means and extent of observation. Meditation looks at every character with interest, only as it contains something generally true, and such as might be expressed in a philosophical problem.

Shakespeare's characters may be reduced to a few—that is to say, to a few classes of characters. If you take his gentlemen, for instance, Biron is seen again in Mercutio, in Benedick, and in several others. They are men who combine the politeness of the courtier with the faculties of high intellect—those powers of combination and severance which only belong to an intellectual mind. The wonder is how Shakespeare can thus disguise himself, and possess such miraculous powers of conveying what he means without betraying the poet, and without even producing the consciousness of him.

In the address of Mercutio regarding Queen Mab, which is so well known that it is unnecessary to repeat it, is to be noted all the fancy of the poet; and the language in which it is conveyed possesses such facility and felicity, that one would almost say that it was impossible for it to be thought, unless it were thought as naturally, and without effort, as Mercutio repeats it. This is the great art by which Shakespeare combines the poet and the gentleman throughout, borrowing from his most amiable nature that which alone could combine them, a perfect simplicity of mind, a delight in all that is excellent for its own sake, without reference to himself as causing it, and by that which distinguishes him from all other poets, alluded to by one of his admirers in a short poem, where he tells us that while Shakespeare possessed all the powers of a man, and more than a man, yet he had all the feelings, the sensibility, the purity, innocence, and delicacy of an affectionate girl of eighteen.

Before I enter upon the merits of the tragedy of "Romeo and Juliet," it will be necessary for me to say something of the language of our country. And here I beg leave to observe, that although I have announced these as lectures upon Milton and Shakespeare, they are in reality, as also stated in the prospectus, intended to illustrate the principles of poetry: therefore, all must not be regarded as mere digression which does not immediately and exclusively refer to those writers. I have chosen them, in order to bring under the notice of my hearers great general truths; in fact, whatever may aid myself, as well as others, in deciding upon the claims of all writers of all countries.

The language, that is to say the particular tongue, in which Shakespeare wrote, cannot be left out of consideration. It will not be disputed, that one language may possess advantages which another does not enjoy; and we may state with confidence, that English excels all other languages in the number of its practical words. The French may bear the palm in the names of trades, and in military and diplomatic terms. Of the German it may be said, that, exclusive of many mineralogical words, it is incomparable in its metaphysical and psychological force: in another respect it nearly rivals the Greek,

> "The learned Greek, rich in fit epithets,
> Blest in the lovely marriage of pure words;"*

I mean in its capability of composition—of forming compound words. Italian is the sweetest and softest language; Spanish the most majestic.

---

* From Act I., Scene 1, of "Lingua, or the Combat of the Tongue and the Five Senses." This drama is reprinted in Dodsley's Old Plays, vol. v., (last edition) and the lines may be found on p. 107 of that volume.

All these have their peculiar faults; but I never can agree that any language is unfit for poetry, although different languages, from the condition and circumstances of the people, may certainly be adapted to one species of poetry more than to another.

Take the French as an example. It is, perhaps, the most perspicuous and pointed language in the world, and therefore best fitted for conversation, for the expression of light and airy passion, attaining its object by peculiar and felicitous turns of phrase, which are evanescent, and, like the beautifully coloured dust on the wings of a butterfly, must not be judged by the test of touch. It appears as if it were all surface and had no substratum, and it constantly most dangerously tampers with morals, without positively offending decency. As the language for what is called modern genteel comedy all others must yield to French.

Italian can only be deemed second to Spanish, and Spanish to Greek, which contains all the excellences of all languages. Italian, though sweet and soft, is not deficient in force and dignity; and I may appeal to Ariosto, as a poet who displays to the utmost advantage the use of his native tongue for all purposes, whether of passion, sentiment, humour, or description.

But in English I find that which is possessed by no other modern language, and which, as it were, appropriates it to the drama. It is a language made out of many, and it has consequently many words, which originally had the same meaning; but in the progress of society those words have gradually assumed different shades of meaning. Take any homogeneous language, such as German, and try to translate into it the following lines:—

> "But not to one, in this benighted age,
>   Is that diviner inspiration given,
> That burns in Shakespeare's or in Milton's page,
>   The pomp and prodigality of heaven."
> GRAY's *Stanzas to Bentley.*

In German it would be necessary to say "the pomp and *spend-thriftness* of heaven,*" because the German has not, as we have, one word with two such distinct meanings, one expressing the nobler, the other the baser of the same action.

The monosyllabic character of English enables us, besides, to express more meaning in a shorter compass than can be done in any other language. In truth, English may be called the harvest of the unconscious wisdom of various nations, and was not the formation of any particular time, or assemblage of individuals. Hence the number of its passionate phrases—its metaphorical terms, not borrowed from poets, but adopted by them. Our commonest people, when excited by passion, constantly employ them: if a mother lose her child she is full of the wildest fancies, and the words she uses assume a tone of dignity; for the constant hearing and reading of the Bible and Liturgy clothes her thoughts not only in the most natural, but in the most beautiful forms of language.

I have been induced to offer these remarks, in order to obviate an objection often made against Shakespeare on the ground of the multitude of his conceits. I do not pretend to justify every conceit, and a vast number have been most unfairly imputed to him; for I am satisfied that many portions of scenes attributed to Shakespeare were never written by him. I admit, however, that even in those which bear the strongest characteristics of his mind, there are some conceits not strictly to be vindicated. The notion against which I declare war is, that whenever a conceit is met with it is unnatural. People who entertain this opinion forget, that had they lived in the age of Shakespeare, they would have deemed them natural. Dryden in his translation of Juvenal has used the words "Look round the world," which are a literal version of the original; but Dr. Johnson has swelled and expanded this expression into the following couplet:—

> "Let observation, with extensive view,
> Survey mankind from China to Peru;"
> *Vanity of Human Wishes.*

mere bombast and tautology; as much as to say, "Let observation with extensive observation observe mankind extensively."

Had Dr. Johnson lived in the time of Shakespeare, or even of Dryden, he would never have been guilty of such an outrage upon common sense and common language; and if people would, in idea, throw themselves back a couple of centuries, they would find that conceits, and even puns, were very allowable, because very natural. Puns often arise out of a mingled sense of injury, and contempt of the person inflicting it, and, as it seems to me, it is a natural way of expressing that mixed feeling. I could point out puns in Shakespeare, where they appear almost as if the first openings of the mouth of nature—where nothing else could so properly be said. This is not peculiar to puns, but is of much wider application: read any part of the works of our great dramatist, and the conviction comes upon you irresistibly, not only that what he puts into the mouths of his personages might have been said, but that it must have been said, because nothing so proper could have been said.

In a future lecture I will enter somewhat into the history of conceits, and shew the wise use that has heretofore been made of them. I will now, (and I hope it will be received with favour) attempt a defence of conceits and puns, taking my examples mainly from the poet under consideration. I admit, of course, that they may be misapplied; but throughout life, I may say, I never have discovered the wrong use of a thing, without having previously discovered the right use of it. To the young I would remark, that it is always unwise to judge of anything by its defects: the first attempt ought to be to discover its excellences. If a man come into my company and abuse a book, his invectives coming down like water from a shower bath, I never feel obliged to him: he probably tells me no news, for all works, even the best, have defects, and they are easily seen; but if a man show me beauties, I thank him for his information, because, in my time, I have unfortunately gone through so many volumes that have had little or nothing to recommend them. Always begin with the good—*à Jove principium*—and the bad will make itself evident enough, quite as soon as is desirable.

I will proceed to speak of Shakespeare's wit, in connexion with his much abused puns and conceits; because an excellent writer, who has done good service to the public taste by driving out the nonsense of the Italian school, has expressed his surprise, that all the other excellences of Shakespeare were, in a greater or less degree, possessed by his contemporaries: thus, Ben Jonson had one qualification, Massinger another, while he declares that Beaumont and Fletcher had equal knowledge of human nature, with more variety. The point in which none of them had approached Shakespeare, according to this writer, was his wit. I own, I was somewhat shocked to see it gravely said in print, that the quality by which Shakespeare was to be individualised from all others was, what is ordinarily called, wit. I had read his plays over and over, and it did not strike me that wit was his great and characteristic superiority. In reading Voltaire, or (to take a standard and most witty comedy as an example) in reading "The School for Scandal," I never experienced the same sort of feeling as in reading Shakespeare.

That Shakespeare has wit is indisputable, but it is not the same kind of wit as in other writers: his wit is blended with the other qualities of his works, and is, by its nature, capable of being so blended. It appears in all parts of his productions, in his tragedies, comedies, and histories: it is not like the wit of Voltaire, and of many modern writers, to whom the epithet "witty" has been properly applied, whose wit consists in a mere combination of words; but in at least nine times out of ten in Shakespeare, the wit is produced not by a combination of words, but by a combination of images.

It is not always easy to distinguish between wit and fancy. When the whole pleasure received is derived from surprise at an unexpected turn of expression, then I call it wit; but when the pleasure is produced not only by surprise, but also by an image which remains with us and gratifies for its own sake, then I call it fancy. I know of no mode so satisfactory of distinguishing between wit and fancy. I appeal to the recollection of those who hear me, whether the greater part of what passes for wit in Shakespeare, is not most exquisite humor, heightened by a figure, and attributed to a particular character? Take the instance of the flea on Bardolph's nose, which Falstaff compares to a soul suffering in purgatory. The images themselves, in cases like this, afford a great part of the pleasure.

These remarks are not without importance in forming a judgment of poets and writers in general: there is a wide difference between the talent which gives a sort of electric surprise by a mere turn of phrase, and that higher ability which produces surprise by a permanent medium, and always leaves something behind it, which satisfies the mind as well as tickles the hearing. The first belongs to men of cleverness, who, having been long in the world, have observed the turns of phrase which please in company, and which, passing away the moment, are passed in a moment, being no longer recollected than the time they take in utterance. We must all have seen and known such people; and I remember saying of one of them that he was like a man who squandered his estate in farthings: he gave away so many, that he must needs have been wealthy. This sort of talent by no means constitutes genius, although it has some affinity to it.

The wit of Shakespeare is, as it were, like the flourishing of a man's stick, when he is walking, in the full flow of animal spirits: it is a sort of exuberance of hilarity which disburdens, and it resembles a conductor, to distribute a portion of our gladness to the surrounding air. While, however, it disburdens, it leaves behind what is weightiest and most important, and what most contributes to some direct aim and purpose.

I will now touch upon a very serious charge against Shakespeare— that of indecency and immorality. Many have been those who have endeavoured to exculpate him by saying, that it was the vice of his age; but he was too great to require exculpation from the accidents of any age. These persons have appealed to Beaumont and Fletcher, to Massinger, and to other less eminent dramatists, to prove that what is complained of was common to them all. Oh! shame and sorrow, if it were so: there is nothing common to Shakespeare and to other writers of his day—not even the language they employed.

In order to form a proper judgment upon this point, it is necessary to make a distinction between manners and morals; and that distinction being once established, and clearly comprehended, Shakespeare will appear as pure a writer, in reference to all that we ought to feel, as he is wonderful in reference to his intellectual faculties.

By manners I mean what is dependent on the particular customs and fashions of the age. Even in a state of comparative barbarism as to manners, there may be, and there is, morality. But give me leave to say that we have seen much worse times than those—times when the mind was so enervated and degraded, that the most distinct associations, that could possibly connect our ideas with the basest feelings, immediately brought forward those base feelings, without reference to the nobler impulses; thus destroying the little remnant of humanity, excluding from the mind what is good, and introducing what is bad to keep the bestial nature company.

On looking through Shakespeare, offences against decency and manners may certainly be pointed out; but let us examine history minutely, and we shall find that this was the ordinary language of the time, and then let us ask, where is the offence? The offence, so to call it, was not committed wantonly, and for the sake of offending, but for the sake of merriment; for what is most observable in Shakespeare, in reference to this topic, is that what he says is always calculated to raise a gust of laughter, that would, as it were, blow alway all impure ideas, if it did not excite abhorrence of them.

Above all, let us compare him with some modern writers, the servile imitators of the French, and we shall receive a most instructive lesson. I may take the liberty of reading the following note, written by me after witnessing the performance of a modern play at Malta, about nine years ago:—"I went to the theatre, and came away without waiting for the entertainment. The longer I live, the more I am impressed with the exceeding immorality of modern plays: I can scarcely refrain from anger and laughter at the shamelessness, and the absurdity of the presumption which presents itself, when I think of their pretences to superior morality, compared with the plays of Shakespeare."

Here let me pause for one moment; for while reading my note I call to mind a novel, on the sofa or toilet of nearly every woman of quality, in which the author gravely warns parents against the indiscreet communication to their children of the contents of some parts of the Bible, as calculated to injure their morals. Another modern author, who has done his utmost to undermine the innocence of the young of both sexes, has the effrontery to protest against the exhibition of the bare leg of a Corinthian female. My note thus pursues the subject:—

"In Shakespeare there are a few gross speeches, but it is doubtful to me if they would produce any ill effect on an unsullied mind; while in some modern plays, as well as in some modern novels, there is a systematic undermining of all morality: they are written in the true cant of humanity, that has no object but to impose; where virtue is not placed in action, or in the habits that lead to action, but, like the title of a book I have heard of, they are 'a hot huddle of indefinite sensations.' In these the lowest incitements to piety are obtruded upon us; like an impudent rascal at a masquerade, who is well known in spite of his vizor, or known by it, and yet is allowed to be impudent in virtue of his disguise. In short, I appeal to the whole of Shakespeare's writings, whether his grossness is not the mere sport of fancy, dissipating low feelings by exciting the intellect, and only injuring while it offends? Modern dramas injure in consequence of not offending. Shakespeare's worst passages are grossnesses against the degradations of our nature: those of our modern plays are too often delicacies directly in favour of them."

Such was my note, made nine years ago, and I have since seen every reason to adhere firmly to the opinions it expresses.

In my next lecture I will proceed to an examination of "Romeo and Juliet;" and I take that tragedy, because in it are to be found all the crude materials of future excellence. The poet, the great dramatic poet, is throughout seen, but the various parts of the composition are not blended with such harmony as in some of his after writings. I am directed to it, more than all, for this reason,—because it affords me the best opportunity of introducing Shakespeare as a delineator of female character, and of love in all its forms, and with all the emotions which deserve that sweet and man-elevating name.

It has been remarked, I believe by Dryden, that Shakespeare wrote for men only, but Beaumont and Fletcher (or rather "the gentle Fletcher") for women. I wish to begin by shewing, not only that this is not true, but that, of all writers for the stage, he only has drawn the female character with that mixture of the real and of the ideal which belongs to it; and that there is no one female personage in the plays of all his contemporaries, of whom a man, seriously examining his heart and his good sense, can say "Let that woman be my companion through life: let her be the object of my suit, and the reward of my success."

END OF THE SIXTH LECTURE.

THE SEVENTH LECTURE

In a former lecture I endeavoured to point out the union of the Poet and the Philosopher, or rather the warm embrace between them, in the "Venus and Adonis" and "Lucrece" of Shakespeare. From thence I passed on to "Love's Labours Lost," as the link between his character as a Poet, and his art as a Dramatist; and I shewed that, although in that work the former was still predominant, yet that the germs of his subsequent dramatic power were easily discernible.

I will now, as I promised in my last, proceed to "Romeo and Juliet," not because it is the earliest, or among the earliest of Shakespeare's works of that kind, but because in it are to be found specimens, in degree, of all the excellences which he afterwards displayed in his more perfect dramas, but differing from them in being less forcibly evidenced, and less happily combined: all the parts are more or less present, but they are not united with the same harmony.

There are, however, in "Romeo and Juliet" passages where the poet's whole excellence is evinced, so that nothing superior to them can be met with in the productions of his after years. The main distinction between this play and others is, as I said, that the parts are less happily combined, or to borrow a phrase from the painter, the whole work is less in keeping. Grand portions are produced: we have limbs of giant growth; but the production, as a whole, in which each part gives delight for itself, and the whole, consisting of these delightful parts, communicates the highest intellectual pleasure and satisfaction, is the result of the application of judgment and taste. These are not to be attained but by painful study, and to the sacrifice of the stronger pleasures derived from the dazzling light which a man of genius throws over every circumstance, and where we are chiefly struck by vivid and distinct images. Taste is an attainment after a poet has been disciplined by experience, and has added to genius that talent by which he knows what part of his genius he can make acceptable, and intelligible to the portion of mankind for which he writes.

In my mind it would be a hopeless symptom, as regards genius, if I found a young man with anything like perfect taste. In the earlier works of Shakespeare we have a profusion of double epithets, and sometimes even the coarsest terms are employed, if they convey a more vivid image; but by degrees the associations are connected with the image they are designed to impress, and the poet descends from the ideal into the real world so far as to conjoin both—to give a sphere of active operations to the ideal, and to elevate and refine the real.

In "Romeo and Juliet" the principal characters may be divided into two classes: in one class passion—the passion of love—is drawn and drawn truly, as well as beautifully; but the persons are not individualised farther than as the actor appears on the stage. It is a very just description and development of love, without giving, if I may so express myself, the philosophical history of it—without shewing how the man became acted upon by that particular passion, but leading it through all the incidents of the drama, and rendering it predominant.

Tybalt is, in himself, a common-place personage. And here allow me to remark upon a great distinction between Shakespeare, and all who have written in imitation of him. I know no character in his plays, (unless indeed Pistol be an exception) which can be called the mere portrait of an individual: while the reader feels all the satisfaction arising from individuality, yet that very individual is a sort of class character, and this circumstance renders Shakespeare the poet of all ages.

Tybalt is a man abandoned to his passions—with all the pride of family, only because he thought it belonged to him as a member of that family, and valuing himself highly, simply because he does not care for death. This indifference to death is perhaps more common than any other feeling: men are apt to flatter themselves extravagantly, merely because they possess a quality which it is a disgrace not to have, but which a wise man never puts forward, but when it is necessary.

Jeremy Taylor in one part of his voluminous works, speaking of a great man, says that he was naturally a coward, as indeed most men are, knowing the value of life, but the power of his reason enabled him, when required, to conduct himself with uniform courage and hardihood. The good bishop, perhaps, had in mind a story, told by one of the ancients, of a Philosopher and a Coxcomb, on board the same ship during a storm: the Coxcomb reviled the Philosopher for betraying marks of fear: "Why are you so frightened? I am not afraid of being drowned: I do not care a farthing for my life."—"You are perfectly right," said the Philosopher, "for your life is not worth a farthing."

Shakespeare never takes pains to make his characters win your esteem, but leaves it to the general command of the passions, and to poetic justice. It is most beautiful to observe, in "Romeo and Juliet," that the characters principally engaged in the incidents are preserved innocent from all that could lower them in our opinion, while the rest of the personages, deserving little interest in themselves, derive it from being instrumental in those situations in which the more important personages develope their thoughts and passions.

Look at Capulet—a worthy, noble-minded old man of high rank, with all the impatience that is likely to accompany it. It is delightful to see all the sensibilities of our nature so exquisitely called forth; as if the poet had the hundred arms of the polypus, and had thrown them out in all directions to catch the predominant feeling. We may see in Capulet the manner in which anger seizes hold of everything that comes in its way, in order to express itself, as in the lines where he reproves Tybalt for his fierceness of behaviour, which led him to wish to insult a Montague, and disturb the merriment.—

> "Go to, go to;
> You are a saucy boy. Is't so, indeed?
> This trick may chance to scath you;—I know what.
> You must contrary me! marry, 'tis time.—
> Well said, my hearts!—You are a princox: go:
> Be quiet or—More light, more light!—For shame!
> I'll make you quiet.—What! cheerly, my hearts!"
>
> *Act I., Scene 5.*

The line

> "This trick may chance to scath you;—I know what,"

was an allusion to the legacy Tybalt might expect; and then, seeing the lights burn dimly, Capulet turns his anger against the servants. Thus we see that no one passion is so predominant, but that it includes all the parts of the character, and the reader never has a mere abstract of a passion, as of wrath or ambition, but the whole man is presented to him—the one predominant passion acting, if I may so say, as the leader of the band to the rest.

It could not be expected that the poet should introduce such a character as Hamlet into every play; but even in those personages, which are subordinate to a hero so eminently philosophical, the passion is at least rendered instructive, and induces the reader to look with a keener eye, and a finer judgment into human nature.

Shakespeare has this advantage over all other dramatists—that he has availed himself of his psychological genius to develope all the minutiæ of the human heart: shewing us the thing that, to common observers, he seems solely intent upon, he makes visible what we should not otherwise have seen: just as, after looking at distant objects through a telescope, when we behold them subsequently with the naked eye, we see them with greater distinctness, and in more detail, than we should otherwise have done.

Mercutio is one of our poet's truly Shakespearian characters; for throughout his plays, but especially in those of the highest order, it is plain that the personages were drawn rather from meditation than from observation, or to speak correctly, more from observation, the child of meditation. It is comparatively easy for a man to go about the world, as if with a pocket-book in his hand, carefully noting down what he sees and hears: by practice he acquires considerable facility in representing what he has observed, himself frequently unconscious of its worth, or its bearings. This is entirely different from the observation of a mind, which, having formed a theory and a system upon its own nature, remarks all things that are examples of its truth, confirming it in that truth, and, above all, enabling it to convey the truths of philosophy, as mere effects derived from, what we may call, the outward watchings of life.

Hence it is that Shakespeare's favourite characters are full of such lively intellect. Mercutio is a man possessing all the elements of a poet: the whole world was, as it were, subject to his law of association. Whenever he wishes to impress anything, all things become his servants for the purpose: all things tell the same tale, and sound in unison. This faculty, moreover, is combined with the manners and feelings of a perfect gentleman, himself utterly unconscious of his powers. By his loss it was contrived that the whole catastrophe of the tragedy should be brought about: it endears him to Romeo, and gives to the death of Mercutio an importance which it could not otherwise have acquired.

I have this in answer to an observation, I think by Dryden, (to which indeed Dr. Johnson has fully replied) that Shakespeare having carried the part of Mercutio as far as he could, till his genius was exhausted, had killed him in the third Act, to get him out of the way. <u>What shallow nonsense! As I have remarked,</u> upon the death of Mercutio the whole catastrophe depends; it is produced by it. The scene in which it occurs serves to show how indifference to any subject but one, and aversion to activity on the part of Romeo, may be overcome and roused to the most resolute and determined conduct. Had not Mercutio been rendered so amiable and so interesting, we could not have felt so strongly the necessity for Romeo's interference, connecting it immediately, and passionately, with the future fortunes of the lover and his mistress.

But what am I to say of the Nurse? We have been told that her character is the mere fruit of observation—that it is like Swift's "Polite Conversation," certainly the most stupendous work of human memory, and of unceasingly active attention to what passes around us, upon record. The Nurse in "Romeo and Juliet" has sometimes been compared to a portrait by Gerard Dow, in which every hair was so exquisitely painted, that it would bear the test of the microscope. Now, I appeal confidently to my hearers whether the closest observation of the manners of one or two old nurses would have enabled Shakespeare to draw this character of admirable generalisation? Surely not. Let any man conjure up in his mind all the qualities and peculiarities that can possibly belong to a nurse, and he will find them in Shakespeare's picture of the old woman: nothing is omitted. This effect is not produced by mere observation. The great prerogative of genius (and Shakespeare felt and availed himself of it) is now to swell itself to the dignity of a god, and now to subdue and keep dormant some part of that lofty nature, and to descend even to the lowest character—to become everything, in fact, but the vicious.

Thus, in the Nurse you have all the garrulity of old-age, and all its fondness; for the affection of old-age is one of the greatest consolations of humanity. I have often thought what a melancholy world this would be without children, and what an inhuman world without the aged.

You have also in the Nurse the arrogance of ignorance, with the pride of meanness at being connected with a great family. You have the grossness, too, which that situation never removes, though it sometimes suspends it; and, arising from that grossness, the little low vices attendant upon it, which, indeed, in such minds are scarcely vices.— Romeo at one time was the most delightful and excellent young man, and the Nurse all willingness to assist him; but her disposition soon turns in favour of Paris, for whom she professes precisely the same admiration. How wonderfully are these low peculiarities contrasted with a young and pure mind, educated under different circumstances!

Another point ought to be mentioned as characteristic of the ignorance of the Nurse:—it is, that in all her recollections, she assists herself by the remembrance of visual circumstances. The great difference, in this respect, between the cultivated and the uncultivated mind is this—that the cultivated mind will be found to recal the past by certain regular trains of cause and effect; whereas, with the uncultivated mind, the past is recalled wholly by coincident images, or facts which happened at the same time. This position is fully exemplified in the following passages put into the mouth of the Nurse:—

> "Even or odd, of all days in the year,
> Come Lammas eve at night shall she be fourteen.
> Susan and she—God rest all Christian souls.—
> Were of an age.—Well, Susan is with God;
> She was too good for me. But, as I said,
> On Lammas eve at night shall she be fourteen;
> That shall she, marry: I remember it well.
> 'Tis since the earthquake now eleven years;
> And she was wean'd,—I never shall forget it,—

Of all the days of the year, upon that day;
For I had then laid wormwood to my dug,
Sitting in the sun under the dove-house wall:
My lord and you were then at Mantua.—
Nay, I do bear a brain:—But, as I said,
When it did taste the wormwood on the nipple
Of my dug, and felt it bitter, pretty fool,
To see it tetchy, and fall out with the dug!
Shake, quoth the dove-house: 'twas no need, I trow,
To bid me trudge.
And since that time it is eleven years;
For then she could stand alone.''

Act I., Scene 3.

She afterwards goes on with similar visual impressions, so true to the character.—More is here brought into one portrait than could have been ascertained by one man's mere observation, and without the introduction of a single incongruous point.

I honour, I love, the works of Fielding as much, or perhaps more, than those of any other writer of fiction of that kind: take Fielding in his characters of postillions, landlords, and landladies, waiters, or indeed, of any-body who had come before his eye, and nothing can be more true, more happy, or more humorous; but in all his chief personages, Tom Jones for instance, where Fielding was not directed by observation, where he could not assist himself by the close copying of what he saw, where it is necessary that something should take place, some words be spoken, or some object described, which he could not have witnessed, (his soliloquies for example, or the interview between the hero and Sophia Western before the reconciliation) and I will venture to say, loving and honouring the man and his productions as I do, that nothing can be more forced and unnatural: the language is without vivacity or spirit, the whole matter is incongruous, and totally destitute of psychological truth.

On the other hand, look at Shakespeare: where can any character be produced that does not speak the language of nature? <u>where does he not put into the mouths of his *dramatis personæ*, be they high or low, Kings or Constables, precisely what they must have said?</u> Where, from observation, could he learn the language proper to Sovereigns, Queens, Noblemen or Generals? yet he invariably uses it.—Where, from observation, could he have learned such lines as these, which are put into the mouth of Othello, when he is talking to Iago of Brabantio?

''Let him do his spite:
My services, which I have done the signiory,
Shall out-tongue his complaints. 'Tis yet to know,

Which, when I know that boasting is an honour,
I shall promulgate, I fetch my life and being
From men of royal siege; and my demerits
May speak, unbonneted, to as proud a fortune
As this that I have reach'd: for know, Iago,
But that I love the gentle Desdemona,
I would not my unhoused free condition
Put into circumscription and confine
For the sea's worth.''

Act I., Scene 2.

I ask where was Shakespeare to observe such language as this? If he did observe it, it was with the inward eye of meditation upon his own nature: for the time, he became Othello, and spoke as Othello, in such circumstances, must have spoken.

Another remark I may make upon "Romeo and Juliet" is, that in this tragedy the poet is not, as I have hinted, entirely blended with the dramatist,—at least, not in the degree to be afterwards noticed in "Lear," "Hamlet," "Othello," or "Macbeth." Capulet and Montague not unfrequently talk a language only belonging to the poet, and not so characteristic of, and peculiar to, the passions of persons in the situations in which they are placed—a mistake, or rather an indistinctness, which many of our later dramatists have carried through the whole of their productions.

When I read the song of Deborah, I never think that she is a poet, although I think the song itself a sublime poem: it is as simple a dithyrambic production as exists in any language; but it is the proper and characteristic effusion of a woman highly elevated by triumph, by the natural hatred of oppressors, and resulting from a bitter sense of wrong: it is a song of exultation on deliverance from these evils, a deliverance accomplished by herself. When she exclaims, "The inhabitants of the villages ceased, they ceased in Israel, until that I, Deborah, arose, that I arose a mother in Israel," it is poetry in the highest sense: we have no reason, however, to suppose that if she had not been agitated by passion, and animated by victory, she would have been able so to express herself; or that if she had been placed in different circumstances, she would have used such language of truth and passion. We are to remember that Shakespeare, not placed under circumstances of excitement, and only wrought upon by his own vivid and vigorous imagination, writes a language that invariably, and intuitively becomes the condition and position of each character.

On the other hand, there is a language not descriptive of passion, nor uttered under the influence of it, which is at the same time poetic, and shows a high and active fancy, as when Capulet says to Paris,—

> "Such comfort as do lusty young men feel,
> When well-apparell'd April on the heel
> Of limping winter treads, even such delight
> Among fresh female buds, shall you this night
> Inherit at my house."
>
> *Act I., Scene 2.*

Here the poet may be said to speak, rather than the dramatist; and it would be easy to adduce other passages from this play, where Shakespeare, for a moment forgetting the character, utters his own words in his own person.

In my mind, what have often been censured as Shakespeare's conceits are completely justifiable, as belonging to the state, age, or feeling of the individual. Sometimes, when they cannot be vindicated on these grounds, they may well be excused by the taste of his own and of the preceding age; as for instance, in Romeo's speech,

> "Here's much to do with hate, but more with love:—
> Why then, O brawling love! O loving hate!
> O anything, of nothing first created!
> O heavy lightness! serious vanity!
> Misshapen chaos of well-seeming forms!
> Feather of lead, bright smoke, cold fire, sick health!
> Still-waking sleep, that is not what it is!"
>
> *Act I., Scene 1.*

I dare not pronounce such passages as these to be absolutely unnatural, not merely because I consider the author a much better judge than I can be, but because I can understand and allow for an effort of the mind, when it would describe what it cannot satisfy itself with the description of, to reconcile opposites and qualify contradictions, leaving a middle state of mind more strictly appropriate to the imagination than any other, when it is, as it were, hovering between images. As soon as it is fixed on one image, it becomes understanding; but while it is unfixed and wavering between them, attaching itself permanently to none, it is imagination. Such is the fine description of Death in Milton:—

> "The other shape,
> If shape it might be call'd, that shape had none
> Distinguishable in member, joint, or limb,
> Or substance might be call'd, that shadow seem'd,
> For each seem'd either: black it stood as night;
> Fierce as ten furies, terrible as hell,

And shook a dreadful dart: what seem'd his head
The likeness of a kingly crown had on.''

Paradise Lost, Book II.

The grandest efforts of poetry are where the imagination is called forth, not to produce a distinct form, but a strong working of the mind, still offering what is still repelled, and again creating what is again rejected; the result being what the poet wishes to impress, namely, the substitution of a sublime feeling of the unimaginable for a mere image. I have sometimes thought that the passage just read might be quoted as exhibiting the narrow limit of painting, as compared with the boundless power of poetry: painting cannot go beyond a certain point; poetry rejects all control, all confinement. Yet we know that sundry painters have attempted pictures of the meeting between Satan and Death at the gates of Hell; and how was Death represented? Not as Milton has described him, but by the most defined thing that can be imagined—a skeleton, the dryest and hardest image that it is possible to discover; which, instead of keeping the mind in a state of activity, reduces it to the merest passivity,—an image, compared with which a square, a triangle, or any other mathematical figure, is a luxuriant fancy.

It is a general but mistaken notion that, because some forms of writing, and some combinations of thought, are not usual, they are not natural; but we are to recollect that the dramatist represents his characters in every situation of life and in every state of mind, and there is no form of language that may not be introduced with effect by a great and judicious poet, and yet be most strictly according to nature. Take punning, for instance, which may be the lowest, but at all events is the most harmless, kind of wit, because it never excites envy. A pun may be a necessary consequence of association: one man, attempting to prove something that was resisted by another, might, when agitated by strong feeling, employ a term used by his adversary with a directly contrary meaning to that for which that adversary had resorted to it: it might come into his mind as one way, and sometimes the best, of replying to that adversary. This form of speech is generally produced by a mixture of anger and contempt, and punning is a natural mode of expressing them.

It is my intention to pass over none of the important so-called conceits of Shakespeare, not a few of which are introduced into his later productions with great propriety and effect. We are not to forget, that at the time he lived there was an attempt at, and an affectation of, quaintness and adornment, which emanated from the Court, and against which satire was directed by Shakespeare in the character of Osrick in Hamlet.

Among the schoolmen of that age, and earlier, nothing was more common than the use of conceits: it began with the revival of letters, and the bias thus given was very generally felt and acknowledged.

I have in my possession a dictionary of phrases, in which the epithets applied to love, hate, jealousy, and such abstract terms, are arranged; and they consist almost entirely of words taken from Seneca and his imitators, or from the schoolmen, showing perpetual antithesis, and describing the passions by the conjunction and combination of things absolutely irreconcileable. In treating the matter thus, I am aware that I am only palliating the practice in Shakespeare: he ought to have had nothing to do with merely temporary peculiarities: he wrote not for his own only, but for all ages, and so far I admit the use of some of his conceits to be a defect. They detract sometimes from his universality as to time, person, and situation.

If we were able to discover, and to point out the peculiar faults, as well as the peculiar beauties of Shakespeare, it would materially assist us in deciding what authority ought to be attached to certain portions of what are generally called his works. If we met with a play, or certain scenes of a play, in which we could trace neither his defects nor his excellences, we should have the strongest reason for believing that he had had no hand in it. In the case of scenes so circumstanced we might come to the conclusion that they were taken from the older plays, which, in some instances, he reformed or altered, or that they were inserted afterwards by some under-hand, in order to please the mob. If a drama by Shakespeare turned out to be too heavy for popular audiences, the clown might be called in to lighten the representation; and if it appeared that what was added was not in Shakespeare's manner, the conclusion would be inevitable, that it was not from Shakespeare's pen.

It remains for me to speak of the hero and heroine, of Romeo and Juliet themselves; and I shall do so with unaffected diffidence, not merely on account of the delicacy, but of the great importance of the subject. I feel that it is impossible to defend Shakespeare from the most cruel of all charges,—that he is an immoral writer—without entering fully into his mode of pourtraying female characters, and of displaying the passion of love. It seems to me, that he has done both with greater perfection than any other writer of the known world, perhaps with the single exception of Milton in his delineation of Eve.

When I have heard it said, or seen it stated, that Shakespeare wrote for man, but the gentle Fletcher for woman, it has always given me something like acute pain, because to me it seems to do the greatest injustice to Shakespeare: when, too, I remember how much character is formed by what we read, I cannot look upon it as a light question, to be passed over as a mere amusement, like a game of cards or chess. I never have been able to tame down my mind to think poetry a sport, or an occupation for idle hours.

Perhaps there is no more sure criterion of refinement in moral character, of the purity of intellectual intention, and of the deep conviction and perfect sense of what our own nature really is in all its combinations, than the different definitions different men would give of love. I will not detain you by stating the various known definitions, some of which it may be better not to repeat: I will rather give you one of my own, which, I apprehend, is equally free from the extravagance of pretended Platonism (which, like other things which super-moralise, is sure to demoralise) and from its grosser opposite.

Considering myself and my fellow-men as a sort of link between heaven and earth, being composed of body and soul, with power to reason and to will, and with that perpetual aspiration which tells us that this is ours for a while, but it is not ourselves; considering man, I say, in this two-fold character, yet united in one person, I conceive that there can be no correct definition of love which does not correspond with our being, and with that subordination of one part to another which constitutes our perfection. I would say therefore that—

"Love is a desire of the whole being to be united to some thing, or some being, felt necessary to its completenesss, by the most perfect means that nature permits, and reason dictates."

It is inevitable to every noble mind, whether man or woman, to feel itself, of itself, imperfect and insufficient, not as an animal only, but as a moral being. How wonderfully, then, has Providence contrived for us, by making that which is necessary to us a step in our exaltation to a higher and nobler state! The Creator has ordained that one should possess qualities which the other has not, and the union of both is the most complete ideal of human character. In everything the blending of the similar with the dissimilar is the secret of all pure delight. Who shall dare to stand alone, and vaunt himself, in himself, sufficient? In poetry it is the blending of passion with order that constitutes perfection: this is still more the case in morals, and more than all in the exclusive attachment of the sexes.

True it is, that the world and its business may be carried on without marriage; but it is so evident that Providence intended man (the only animal of all climates, and whose reason is pre-eminent over instinct) to be the master of the world, that marriage, or the knitting together of society by the tenderest, yet firmest ties, seems ordained to render him capable of maintaining his superiority over the brute creation. Man alone has been privileged to clothe himself, and to do all things so as to make him, as it were, a secondary creator of himself, and of his own happiness or misery: in this, as in all, the image of the Deity is impressed upon him.

Providence, then, has not left us to prudence only; for the power of calculation, which prudence implies, cannot have existed, but in a state which pre-supposes marriage. If God has done this, shall we suppose that he has given us no moral sense, no yearning, which is something more than animal, to secure that, without which man might form a herd, but could not be a society? The very idea seems to breathe absurdity.

From this union arise the paternal, filial, brotherly and sisterly relations of life; and every state is but a family magnified. All the operations of mind, in short, all that distinguishes us from brutes, originate in the more perfect state of domestic life.—One infallible criterion in forming an opinion of a man is the reverence in which he holds women. Plato has said, that in this way we rise from sensuality to affection, from affection to love, and from love to the pure intellectual delight by which we become worthy to conceive that infinite in ourselves, without which it is impossible for man to believe in a God. In a word, the grandest and most delightful of all promises has been expressed to us by this practical state—our marriage with the Redeemer of mankind.

I might safely appeal to every man who hears me, who in youth has been accustomed to abandon himself to his animal passions, whether when he first really fell in love, the earliest symptom was not a complete change in his manners, a contempt and hatred of himself for having excused his conduct by asserting, that he acted according to the dictates of nature, that his vices were the inevitable consequences of youth, and that his passions at that period of life could not be conquered? The surest friend of chastity is love: it leads us, not to sink the mind in the body, but to draw up the body to the mind—the immortal part of our nature. See how contrasted in this respect are some portions of the works of writers, whom I need not name, with other portions of the same works: the ebullitions of comic humour have at times, by a lamentable confusion, been made the means of debasing our nature, while at other times, even in the same volume, we are happy to notice the utmost purity, such as the purity of love, which above all other qualities renders us most pure and lovely.

Love is not, like hunger, a mere selfish appetite: it is an associative quality. The hungry savage is nothing but an animal, thinking only of the satisfaction of his stomach: what is the first effect of love, but to associate the feeling with every object in nature? the trees whisper, the roses exhale their perfumes, the nightingales sing, nay the very skies smile in unison with the feeling of true and pure love. It gives to every object in nature a power of the heart, without which it would indeed be spiritless.

Shakespeare has described this passion in various states and stages, beginning, as was most natural, with love in the young. Does he open his play by making Romeo and Juliet in love at first sight—at the first glimpse, as any ordinary thinker would do? Certainly not: he knew what he was about, and how he was to accomplish what he was about: he was to develope the whole passion, and he commences with the first elements—that sense of imperfection, that yearning to combine itself with something lovely. Romeo became enamoured of the idea he had formed in his own mind, and then, as it were, christened the first real being of the contrary sex as endowed with the perfections he desired. He appears to be in love with Rosaline; but, in truth, he is in love only with his own idea. He felt that necessity of being beloved which no noble mind can be without. Then our poet, our poet who so well knew human nature, introduces Romeo to Juliet, and makes it not only a violent, but a permanent love—a point for which Shakespeare has been ridiculed by the ignorant and unthinking. Romeo is first represented in a state most susceptible of love, and then, seeing Juliet, he took and retained the infection.

This brings me to observe upon a characteristic of Shakespeare, which belongs to a man of profound thought and high genius. It has been too much the custom, when anything that happened in his dramas could not easily be explained by the few words the poet has employed, to pass it idly over, and to say that it is beyond our reach, and beyond the power of philosophy—a sort of terra incognita for discoverers—a great ocean to be hereafter explored. Others have treated such passages as hints and glimpses of something now non-existent, as the sacred fragments of an ancient and ruined temple all the portions of which are beautiful, although their particular relation to each other is unknown. Shakespeare knew the human mind, and its most minute and intimate workings, and he never introduces a word, or a thought, in vain or out of place: if we do not understand him, it is our own fault or the fault of copyists and typographers; but study, and the possession of some small stock of the knowlege by which he worked, will enable us often to detect and explain his meaning. He never wrote at random, or hit upon points of character and conduct by chance; and the smallest fragment of his mind not unfrequently gives a clue to a most perfect, regular, and consistent whole.

As I may not have another opportunity, the introduction of Friar Laurence into this tragedy enables me to remark upon the different manner in which Shakespeare has treated the priestly character, as compared with other writers. In Beaumont and Fletcher priests are represented as a vulgar mockery; and, as in others of their dramatic personages, the errors of a few are mistaken for the demeanour of the many: but in Shakespeare they always carry with them our love and respect. He made no injurious abstracts: he took no copies from the worst parts of our nature; and, like the rest, his characters of priests are truly drawn from the general body.

It may strike some as singular, that throughout all his productions he has never introduced the passion of avarice. The truth is, that it belongs only to particular parts of our nature, and is prevalent only in particular states of society; hence it could not, and cannot, be permanent. The Miser of Molière and Plautus is now looked upon as a species of madman, and avarice as a species of madness. Elwes, of whom everybody has heard, was an individual influenced by an insane condition of mind; but, as a passion, avarice has disappeared. How admirably, then, did Shakespeare foresee, that if he drew such a character it could not be permanent! he drew characters which would always be natural, and therefore permanent, inasmuch as they were not dependent upon accidental circumstances.

There is not one of the plays of Shakespeare that is built upon anything but the best and surest foundation; the characters must be permanent—permanent while men continue men,—because they stand upon what is absolutely necessary to our existence. This cannot be said even of some of the most famous authors of antiquity. Take the capital tragedies of Orestes, or of the husband of Jocasta: great as was the genius of the writers, these dramas have an obvious fault, and the fault lies at the very root of the action. In Œdipus a man is represented oppressed by fate for a crime of which he was not morally guilty; and while we read we are obliged to say to ourselves, that in those days they considered actions without reference to the real guilt of the persons.

There is no character in Shakespeare in which envy is pourtrayed, with one solitary exception—Cassius, in "Julius Cæsar;" yet even there the vice is not hateful, inasmuch as it is counterbalanced by a number of excellent qualities and virtues. The poet leads the reader to suppose that it is rather something constitutional, something derived from his parents, something that he cannot avoid, and not something that he has himself acquired; thus throwing the blame from the will of man to some inevitable circumstance, and leading us to suppose that it is hardly to be looked upon as one of those passions that actually debase the mind.

Whenever love is described as of a serious nature, and much more when it is to lead to a tragical result, it depends upon a law of the mind, which, I believe, I shall hereafter be able to make intelligible, and which would not only justify Shakespeare, but show an analogy to all his other characters.

END OF THE SEVENTH LECTURE.

THE EIGHTH LECTURE

It is impossible to pay a higher compliment to poetry, than to consider the effects it produces in common with religion, yet distinct (as far as distinction can be, where there is no division) in those qualities which religion exercises and diffuses over all mankind, as far as they are subject to its influence.

I have often thought that religion (speaking of it only as it accords with poetry, without reference to its more serious impressions) is the poetry of mankind, both having for their objects:—

1. To generalise our notions; to prevent men from confining their attention solely, or chiefly, to their own narrow sphere of action, and to their own individual circumstances. By placing them in certain awful relations it merges the individual man in the whole species, and makes it impossible for any one man to think of his future lot, or indeed of his present condition, without at the same time comprising in his view his fellow-creatures.

2. That both poetry and religion throw the object of deepest interest to a distance from us, and thereby not only aid our imagination, but in a most important manner subserve the interest of our virtues; for that man is indeed a slave, who is a slave to his own senses, and whose mind and imagination cannot carry him beyond the distance which his hand can touch, or even his eye can reach.

3. The grandest point of resemblance between them is, that both have for their object (I hardly know whether the English language supplies an appropriate word) the perfecting, and the pointing out to us the indefinite improvement of our nature, and fixing our attention upon that. They bid us, while we are sitting in the dark at our little fire, look at the mountain-tops, struggling with darkness, and announcing that light which shall be common to all, in which individual interests shall resolve

into one common good, and every man shall find in his fellow man more than a brother.

Such being the case, we need not wonder that it has pleased Providence, that the divine truths of religion should have been revealed to us in the form of poetry; and that at all times poets, not the slaves of any particular sectarian opinions, should have joined to support all those delicate sentiments of the heart (often when they were most opposed to the reigning philosophy of the day) which may be called the feeding streams of religion.

I have heard it said that an undevout astronomer is mad. In the strict sense of the word, every being capable of understanding must be mad, who remains, as it were, fixed in the ground on which he treads—who, gifted with the divine faculties of indefinite hope and fear, born with them, yet settles his faith upon that, in which neither hope nor fear has any proper field for display. Much more truly, however, might it be said that, an undevout poet is mad: in the strict sense of the word, an undevout poet is an impossibility. I have heard of verse-makers (poets they are not, and never can be) who introduced into their works such questions as these:—Whether the world was made of atoms?—Whether there is a universe?—Whether there is a governing mind that supports it? As I have said, verse-makers are not poets: the poet is one who carries the simplicity of childhood into the powers of manhood; who, with a soul unsubdued by habit, unshackled by custom, contemplates all things with the freshness and the wonder of a child; and, connecting with it the inquisitive powers of riper years, adds, as far as he can find knowledge, admiration; and, where knowledge no longer permits admiration, gladly sinks back again into the childlike feeling of devout wonder.

The poet is not only the man made to solve the riddle of the universe, but he is also the man who feels where it is not solved. What is old and worn-out, not in itself, but from the dimness of the intellectual eye, produced by worldly passions and pursuits, he makes new: he pours upon it the dew that glistens, and blows round it the breeze that cooled us in our infancy. I hope, therefore, that if in this single lecture I make some demand on the attention of my hearers to a most important subject, upon which depends all sense of the worthiness or unworthiness of our nature, I shall obtain their pardon. If I afford them less amusement, I trust that their own reflections upon a few thoughts will be found to repay them.

I have been led to these observations by the tragedy of "Romeo and Juliet," and by some, perhaps, indiscreet expressions, certainly not well chosen, concerning falling in love at first sight. I have taken one of Shakespeare's earliest works, as I consider it, in order to show that he, of all his contemporaries (Sir Philip Sidney alone excepted), entertained a just conception of the female character. Unquestionably, that gentle-man of Europe—that all-accomplished man, and our beloved Shake-speare, were the only writers of that age, who pitched their ideas of female perfection according to the best researches of philosophy: com-pared with all who followed them, they stand as mighty mountains, the islands of a deluge, which has swallowed all the rest in the flood of oblivion.*

I certainly do not mean, as a general maxim, to justify so foolish a thing as what goes by the name of love at first sight; but, to express myself more accurately, I should say that there is, and has always existed, a deep emotion of the mind, which might be called love mo-mentaneous—not love at first sight, nor known by the subject of it to be or to have been such, but after many years of experience.†

I have to defend the existence of love, as a passion in itself fit and appropriate to human nature;—I say fit for human nature, and not only so, but peculiar to it, unshared either in degree or kind by any of our fellow creatures: it is a passion which it is impossible for any creature to feel, but a being endowed with reason, with the moral sense, and with the strong yearnings, which, like all other powerful effects in nature, prophesy some future effect.

If I were to address myself to the materialist, with reference to the human kind, and (admitting the three great laws common to all beings,—1, the law of self-preservation; 2, that of continuing the race; and 3, the care of the offspring till protection is no longer needed),—were to ask him, whether he thought any motives of prudence or duty enforced the simple necessity of preserving the race? or whether, after a course of serious reflection, he came to the conclusion, that it would be better

---

* I remember, in conversing on this very point at a subsequent period,—I cannot fix the date,—Coleridge made a willing exception in favour of Spenser; but he added that the notions of the author of the "Faery Queen" were often so romantic and heightened by fancy, that he could not look upon Spenser's females as creatures of our world; whereas the ladies of Shakespeare and Sidney were flesh and blood, with their very defects and qualifications giving evidence of their humanity: hence the lively interest taken regarding them.—J. P. C.

† Coleridge here made a reference to, and cited a passage from Hooker's "Ec-clesiastical Polity;" but my note contains only a hint regarding it; and the probability is, that I did not insert more of it, because I thought I should be able, at some future time, to procure the exact words, or a reference to them, from the Lecturer. Whether I did so or not I cannot remember, but I find no trace of anything of the kind.—J. P. C.

to have a posterity, from a sense of duty impelling us to seek that as our object?—if, I say, I were to ask a materialist, whether such was the real cause of the preservation of the species, he would laugh me to scorn; he would say that nature was too wise to trust any of her great designs to the mere cold calculations of fallible mortality.

Then the question comes to a short crisis:—Is, or is not, our moral nature a part of the end of Providence? or are we, or are we not, beings meant for society? Is that society, or is it not, meant to be progressive? I trust that none of my auditors would endure the putting of the question—Whether, independently of the progression of the race, every individual has it not in his power to be indefinitely progressive?—for, without marriage, without exclusive attachment, there could be no human society; herds, as I said, there might be, but society there could not be: there could be none of that delightful intercourse between father and child; none of the sacred affections; none of the charities of humanity; none of all those many and complex causes, which have raised us to the state we have already reached, could possibly have existence. All these effects are not found among the brutes; neither are they found among savages, whom strange accidents have sunk below the class of human beings, insomuch that a stop seems actually to have been put to their progressiveness.

We may, therefore, safely conclude that there is placed within us some element, if I may so say, of our nature—something which is as peculiar to our moral nature, as any other part can be conceived to be, name it what you will,—name it, I will say for illustration, devotion,— name it friendship, or a sense of duty; but something there is, peculiar to our nature, which answers the moral end; as we find everywhere in the ends of the moral world, that there are proportionate material and bodily means of accomplishing them.

We are born, and it is our nature and lot to be composed of body and mind; but when our heart leaps up on hearing of the victories of our country, or of the rescue of the virtuous, but unhappy, from the hands of an oppressor; when a parent is transported at the restoration of a beloved child from deadly sickness; when the pulse is quickened, from any of these or other causes, do we therefore say, because the body interprets the emotions of the mind and sympathises with them, asserting its claim to participation, that joy is not mental, or that it is not moral? Do we assert, that it was owing merely to fulness of blood that the heart throbbed, and the pulse played? Do we not rather say, that the regent, the mind, being glad, its slave, its willing slave, the body, responded to it, and obeyed the impulse? If we are possessed with a feeling of having done a wrong, or of having had wrong done to us, and it excites the blush of shame or the glow of anger, do we pretend to say that, by some accident, the blood suffused itself into veins unusually small, and therefore that the guilty seemed to evince shame, or the injured indignation? In these things we scorn such instruction; and shall it be deemed a sufficient excuse for the materialist to degrade that passion, on which not only many of our virtues depend, but upon which the whole frame, the whole structure of human society rests? Shall we pardon him this debasement of love, because our body has been united to mind by Providence, in order, not to reduce the high to the level of the low, but to elevate the low to the level of the high? We should be guilty of nothing less than an act of moral suicide, if we consented to degrade that which on every account is most noble, by merging it in what is most derogatory: as if an angel were to hold out to us the welcoming hand of brotherhood, and we turned away from it, to wallow, as it were, with the hog in the mire.

One of the most lofty and intellectual of the poets of the time of Shakespeare has described this degradation most wonderfully, where he speaks of a man, who, having been converted by the witchery of worldly pleasure and passion, into a hog, on being restored to his human shape still preferred his bestial condition:—

> "But one, above the rest in special,
> That had a hog been late, hight Grill by name,
> Repined greatly, and did him miscall,
> That from a hoggish form him brought to natural.
>
> "Said Guyon, See the mind of beastly man!
> That hath so soon forgot the excellence
> Of his creation, when he life began,
> That now he chooseth, with vile difference,
> To be a beast and lack intelligence.
> To whom the Palmer thus:—The dunghill kind
> Delights in filth and foul incontinence:
> Let Grill be Grill, and have his hoggish mind;
> But let us hence depart, whilst weather serves and wind."
>
> *Fairy Queen, Book II.,* c. 12.

The first feeling that would strike a reflecting mind, wishing to see mankind not only in an amiable but in a just light, would be that beautiful feeling in the moral world, the brotherly and sisterly affections,—the existence of strong affection greatly modified by the difference of sex; made more tender, more graceful, more soothing and conciliatory by the circumstance of difference, yet still remaining perfectly pure, perfectly spiritual. How glorious, we may say, would be the effect, if the instances were rare; but how much more glorious, when they are so frequent as to be only not universal. This species of affection is the object of religious veneration with all those who love their fellow men, or who know themselves.

The power of education over the human mind is herein exemplified, and data for hope are afforded of yet unrealised excellences, perhaps dormant in our nature. When we see so divine a moral effect spread through all classes, what may we not hope of other excellences, of unknown quality, still to be developed?

By dividing the sisterly and fraternal affections from the conjugal, we have, in truth, two loves, each of them as strong as any affection can be, or ought to be, consistently with the performance of our duty, and the love we should bear to our neighbour. Then, by the former preceding the latter, the latter is rendered more pure, more even, and more constant: the wife has already learned the discipline of pure love in the character of a sister. By the discipline of private life she has already learned how to yield, how to influence, how to command. To all this are to be added the beautiful gradations of attachment which distinguish human nature;—from sister to wife, from wife to child, to uncle, to cousin, to one of our kin, to one of our blood, to our near neighbour, to our county-man, and to our countryman.

The bad results of a want of this variety of orders, of this graceful subordination in the character of attachment, I have often observed in Italy in particular, as well as in other countries, where the young are kept secluded, not only from their neighbours, but from their own families—all closely imprisoned, until the hour when they are necessarily let out of their cages, without having had the opportunity of learning to fly—without experience, restrained by no kindly feeling, and detesting the control which so long kept them from enjoying the full hubbub of licence.

The question is, How have nature and Providence secured these blessings to us? In this way:—that in general the affections become those which urge us to leave the paternal nest. We arrive at a definite time of life, and feel passions that invite us to enter into the world; and this new feeling assuredly coalesces with a new object. Suppose we are under the influence of a vivid feeling that is new to us: that feeling will more firmly combine with an external object, which is likewise vivid from novelty, than with one that is familiar.

To this may be added the aversion, which seems to have acted very strongly in rude ages, concerning anything common to us and to the animal creation. <u>That which is done by beasts man feels a natural repugnance to imitate.</u> The desire to extend the bond of relationship, in families which had emigrated from the patriarchal seed, would likewise have its influence.

All these circumstances would render the marriage of brother and sister unfrequent, and in simple ages an ominous feeling to the contrary might easily prevail. Some tradition might aid the objections to such a union; and, for aught we know, some law might be preserved in the Temple of Isis, and from thence obtained by the patriarchs, which would augment the horror attached to such connexions. This horror once felt, and soon propagated, the present state of feeling on the subject can easily be explained.

Children begin as early to talk of marriage as of death, from attending a wedding, or following a funeral: a new young visitor is introduced into the family, and from association they soon think of the conjugal bond. If a boy tell his parent that he wishes to marry his sister, he is instantly checked by a stern look, and he is shewn the impossibility of such a union. The controlling glance of the parental eye is often more effectual, than any form of words that could be employed; and in mature years a mere look often prevails where exhortation would have failed. As to infants, they are told, without any reason assigned, that it could not be so; and perhaps the best security for moral rectitude arises from a supposed necessity. Ignorant persons recoil from the thought of doing anything that has not been done, and because they have always been informed that it must not be done.

The individual has by this time learned the greatest and best lesson of the human mind—that in ourselves we are imperfect; and another truth, of the next, if not of equal, importance—that there exists a possibility of uniting two beings, each identified in their nature, but distinguished in their separate qualities, so that each should retain what distinguishes them, and at the same time each acquire the qualities of that being which is contradistinguished. This is perhaps the most beautiful part of our nature: the man loses not his manly character: he does not become less brave or less resolved to go through fire and water, if necessary, for the object of his affections: rather say, that he becomes far more brave and resolute. He then feels the beginnings of his moral nature: he then is sensible of its imperfection, and of its perfectibility. All the grand and sublime thoughts of an improved state of being then dawn upon him: he can acquire the patience of woman, which in him is fortitude: the beauty and susceptibility of the female character in him becomes a desire to display all that is noble and dignified. In short, the only true resemblance to a couple thus united is the pure blue sky of heaven: the female unites the beautiful with the sublime, and the male the sublime with the beautiful.

Throughout the whole of his plays Shakespeare has evidently looked at the subject of love in this dignified light: he has conceived it not only with moral grandeur, but with philosophical penetration. The mind of man searches for something which shall add to his perfection—which shall assist him; and he also yearns to lend his aid in completing the moral nature of another. Thoughts like these will occupy many of his serious moments: imagination will accumulate on imagination, until at last some object attracts his attention, and to this object the whole weight and impulse of his feelings will be directed.

Who shall say this is not love? Here is system, but it is founded upon nature: here are associations; here are strong feelings, natural to us as men, and they are directed and finally attached to one object:—who shall say this is not love? Assuredly not the being who is the subject of these sensations.—If it be not love, it is only known that it is not by Him who knows all things. Shakespeare has therefore described Romeo as in love in the first instance with Rosaline, and so completely does he fancy himself in love that he declares, before he has seen Juliet,

> "When the devout religion of mine eye
> Maintains such falsehood, then turn tears to fires;
> And these, who, often drown'd, could never die,
> Transparent heretics, be burnt for liars.
> One fairer than my love? the all-seeing sun
> Ne'er saw her match since first the world begun."
>
> *Act I., Scene 1.*

This is in answer to Benvolio, who has asked Romeo to compare the supposed beauty of Rosaline with the actual beauty of other ladies; and in this full feeling of confidence Romeo is brought to Capulet's, as it were by accident: he sees Juliet, instantly becomes the heretic he has just before declared impossible, and then commences that completeness of attachment which forms the whole subject of the tragedy.

Surely Shakespeare, the poet, the philosopher, who combined truth with beauty and beauty with truth, never dreamed that he could interest his auditory in favour of Romeo, by representing him as a mere weathercock blown round by every woman's breath; who, having seen one, became the victim of melancholy, eating his own heart, concentrating all his hopes and fears in her, and yet, in an instant, changing, and falling madly in love with another. Shakespeare must have meant something more than this, for this was the way to make people despise, instead of admiring his hero. Romeo tells us what was Shakespeare's purpose: he shows us that he had looked at Rosaline with a different feeling from that with which he had looked at Juliet. Rosaline was the object to which his over-full heart had attached itself in the first instance: our imperfect nature, in proportion as our ideas are vivid, seeks after something in which those ideas may be realised.

So with the indiscreet friendships sometimes formed by men of genius: they are conscious of their own weakness, and are ready to believe others stronger than themselves, when, in truth, they are weaker: they have formed an ideal in their own minds, and they want to see it realised; they require more than shadowy thought. Their own sense of imperfection makes it impossible for them to fasten their attachment upon themselves, and hence the humility of men of true genius: in, perhaps, the first man they meet, they only see what is good; they have no sense of his deficiencies, and their friendship becomes so strong, that they almost fall down and worship one in every respect greatly their inferior.

What is true of friendship is true of love, with a person of ardent feelings and warm imagination. What took place in the mind of Romeo was merely natural; it is accordant with every day's experience. Amid such various events, such shifting scenes, such changing personages, we are often mistaken, and discover that he or she was not what we hoped and expected; we find that the individual first chosen will not complete our imperfection; we may have suffered unnecessary pangs, and have indulged idly-directed hopes, and then a being may arise before us, who has more resemblance to the ideal we have formed. We know that we loved the earlier object with ardour and purity, but it was not what we feel for the later object. Our own mind tells us, that in the first instance we merely yearned after an object, but in the last instance we know that we have found that object, and that it corresponds with the idea we had previously formed.

[Here my original notes abruptly break off: the brochure in which I had inserted them was full, and I took another for the conclusion of the Lecture, which is unfortunately lost.]

THE NINTH LECTURE

It is a known but unexplained phenomenon, that among the ancients statuary rose to such a degree of perfection, as almost to baffle the hope of imitating it, and to render the chance of excelling it absolutely impossible; yet painting, at the same period, notwithstanding the admiration bestowed upon it by Pliny and others, has been proved to be an art of much later growth, as it was also of far inferior quality. I remember a man of high rank, equally admirable for his talents and his taste, pointing to a common sign-post, and saying that had Titian never lived, the richness of representation by colour, even there, would never have been attained. In that mechanical branch of painting, perspective, it has been shown that the Romans were very deficient. The excavations and consequent discoveries, at Herculaneum and elsewhere, prove the Roman artists to have been guilty of such blunders, as to give plausibility to the assertions of those, who maintain that the ancients were wholly ignorant of perspective. However, that they knew something of it is established by Vitruvius in the introduction to his second book.

Something of the same kind, as I endeavoured to explain in a previous lecture, was the case with the drama of the ancients, which has been imitated by the French, Italians, and by various writers in England since the Restoration. All that is there represented seems to be, as it were, upon one flat surface: the theme,* if we may so call it in reference to music, admits of nothing more than the change of a single note, and excludes that which is the true principle of life—the attaining of the same result by an infinite variety of means.

The plays of Shakespeare are in no respect imitations of the Greeks: they may be called analogies, because by very different means they arrive at the same end; whereas the French and Italian tragedies I have read, and the English ones on the same model, are mere copies, though they cannot be called likenesses, seeking the same effect by adopting the same means, but under most inappropriate and adverse circumstances.

I have thus been led to consider, that the ancient drama (meaning the works of Æschylus, Euripides, and Sophocles, for the rhetorical productions of the same class by the Romans are scarcely to be treated as original theatrical poems) might be contrasted with the Shakespearean drama.—I call it the Shakespearean drama to distinguish it, because I know of no other writer who has realised the same idea, although I am told by some, that the Spanish poets, Lopez de Vega and Calderon, have been equally successful. The Shakespearean drama and the Greek drama may be compared to statuary and painting. In statuary, as in the Greek drama, the characters must be few, because the very essence of statuary is a high degree of abstraction, which prevents a great many

---

* Here occurs another evident mistake of mine, in my original short-hand note, in consequence of mishearing: I hastily wrote *scheme*, instead of "theme," which last must have been the word of the Lecturer.

figures being combined in the same effect. In a grand group of Niobe, or in any other ancient heroic subject, how disgusting even it would appear, if an old nurse were introduced. Not only the number of figures must be circumscribed, but nothing undignified must be placed in company with what is dignified: no one personage must be brought in that is not an abstraction: all the actors in the scene must not be presented at once to the eye; and the effect of multitude, if required, must be produced without the intermingling of anything discordant.

Compare this small group with a picture by Raphael or Titian, in which an immense number of figures may be introduced, a beggar, a cripple, a dog, or a cat; and by a less degree of labour, and a less degree of abstraction, an effect is produced equally harmonious to the mind, more true to nature with its varied colours, and, in all respects but one, superior to statuary. The man of taste feels satisfied, and to that which the reason conceives possible, a momentary reality is given by the aid of imagination.

I need not here repeat what I have said before, regarding the circumstances which permitted Shakespeare to make an alteration, not merely so suitable to the age in which he lived, but, in fact, so necessitated by the condition of that age. I need not again remind you of the difference I pointed out between imitation and likeness, in reference to the attempt to give reality to representations on the stage. The distinction between imitation and likeness depends upon the admixture of circumstances of dissimilarity; an imitation is not a copy, precisely as likeness is not sameness, in that sense of the word "likeness" which implies difference conjoined with sameness. <u>Shakespeare reflected manners in his plays, not by a cold formal copy, but by an imitation; that is to say, by an admixture of circumstances, not absolutely true in themselves, but true to the character and to the time represented.</u>

It is fair to own that he had many advantages. The great of that day, instead of surrounding themselves by the *chevaux de frise* of what is now called high breeding, endeavoured to distinguish themselves by attainment, by energy of thought, and consequent powers of mind. The stage, indeed, had nothing but curtains for its scenes, but this fact compelled the actor, as well as the author, to appeal to the imaginations, and not the senses of the audience: thus was obtained a power over space and time, which in an ancient theatre would have been absurd, because it would have been contradictory. The advantage is vastly in favour of our own early stage: the dramatic poet there relies upon the imagination, upon the reason, and upon the noblest powers of the human heart; he shakes off the iron bondage of space and time; he appeals to that which we most wish to be, when we are most worthy of being, while the ancient dramatist binds us down to the meanest part of our nature, and the chief compensation is a simple acquiescence of the mind in the position, that what is represented might possibly have occurred in the time and place required by the unities. It is a poor compliment to a poet to tell him, that he has only the qualifications of a historian.

In dramatic composition the observation of the unities of time and place so narrows the period of action, so impoverishes the sources of pleasure, that of all the Athenian dramas there is scarcely one in which the absurdity is not glaring, of aiming at an object, and utterly failing in the attainment of it: events are sometimes brought into a space in which it is impossible for them to have occurred, and in this way the grandest effort of the dramatist, that of making his play the mirror of life, is entirely defeated.

The limit allowed by the rules of the Greek stage was twenty-four hours; but, inasmuch as, even in this case, time must have become a subject of imagination, it was just as reasonable to allow twenty-four months, or even years. The mind is acted upon by such strong stimulants, that the period is indifferent; and when once the boundary of possibility is passed, no restriction can be assigned. In reading Shakespeare, we should first consider in which of his plays he means to appeal to the reason, and in which to the imagination, faculties which have no relation to time and place, excepting as in the one case they imply a succession of cause and effect, and in the other form a harmonious picture, so that the impulse given by the reason is carried on by the imagination.

We have often heard Shakespeare spoken of as a child of nature, and some of his modern imitators, without the genius to copy nature, by resorting to real incidents, and treating them in a certain way, have produced that stage-phenomenon which is neither tragic nor comic, nor tragi-comic, nor comi-tragic, but sentimental. This sort of writing depends upon some very affecting circumstances, and in its greatest excellence aspires no higher than the genius of an onion,—the power of drawing tears; while the author, acting the part of a ventriloquist, distributes his own insipidity <u>among the characters, if characters they can be called, which have no marked and distinguishing features.</u> I have seen dramas of this sort, some translated and some the growth of our own soil, so well acted, and so ill written, that if I could have been made for the time artificially deaf, I should have been pleased with that performance as a pantomime, which was intolerable as a play.

Shakespeare's characters, from Othello and Macbeth down to Dogberry and the Grave-digger, may be termed ideal realities. They are not the things themselves, so much as abstracts of the things, which a great mind takes into itself, and there naturalises them to its own conception. Take Dogberry: are no important truths there conveyed, no admirable lessons taught, and no valuable allusions made to reigning follies, which the poet saw must for ever reign? He is not the creature of the day, to disappear with the day, but the representative and abstract of truth which must ever be true, and of humour which must ever be humorous.

The readers of Shakespeare may be divided into two classes:—

1. Those who read his works with feeling and understanding;

2. Those who, without affecting to criticise, merely feel, and may be said to be the recipients of the poet's power.

Between the two no medium can be endured. The ordinary reader, who does not pretend to bring understanding to bear upon the subject, often feels that some real trait of his own has been caught, that some nerve has been touched; and he knows that it has been touched by the vibration he experiences—a thrill, which tells us that, by becoming better acquainted with the poet, we have become better acquainted with ourselves.

In the plays of Shakespeare every man sees himself, without knowing that he does so: as in some of the phenomena of nature, in the mist of the mountain, the traveller beholds his own figure, but the glory round the head distinguishes it from a mere vulgar copy. In traversing the Brocken, in the north of Germany, at sunrise, the brilliant beams are shot askance, and you see before you a being of gigantic proportions, and of such elevated dignity, that you only know it to be yourself by similarity of action. In the same way, near Messina, natural forms, at determined distances, are represented on an invisible mist, not as they really exist, but dressed in all the prismatic colours of the imagination. So in Shakespeare: every form is true, everything has reality for its foundation; we can all recognise the truth, but we see it decorated with such hues of beauty, and magnified to such proportions of grandeur, that, while we know the figure, we know also how much it has been refined and exalted by the poet.

It is humiliating to reflect that, as it were, because heaven has given us the greatest poet, it has inflicted upon that poet the most incompetent critics: none of them seem to understand even his language, much less the principles upon which he wrote, and the peculiarities which distinguish him from all rivals. I will not now dwell upon this point, because it is my intention to devote a lecture more immediately to the prefaces of Pope and Johnson. Some of Shakespeare's contemporaries appear to have understood him, and imitated him in a way that does the original no small honour; but modern preface-writers and commentators, while they praise him as a great genius, when they come to publish notes upon his plays, treat him like a schoolboy; <u>as if this great genius did not understand himself, was not aware of his own powers, and wrote without design or purpose.</u> Nearly all they can do is to express the most vulgar of all feelings, wonderment—wondering at what they term the irregularity of his genius, sometimes above all praise, and at other times, if they are to be trusted, below all contempt. They endeavour to reconcile the two opinions by asserting that he wrote for the mob; as if a man of real genius ever wrote for the mob. Shakespeare never consciously wrote what was below himself: careless he might be, and his better genius may not always have attended him; but I fearlessly say, that he never penned a line that he knew would degrade him. No man does anything equally well at all times; <u>but because Shakespeare could not always be the greatest of poets, was he therefore to condescend to make himself the least?</u>*

Yesterday afternoon a friend left a book for me by a German critic, of which I have only had time to read a small part; but what I did read I approved, and I should be disposed to applaud the work much more highly, were it not that in so doing I should, in a manner, applaud myself. The sentiments and opinions are coincident with those to which I gave utterance in my lectures at the Royal Institution. It is not a little wonderful, that so many ages have elapsed since the time of Shakespeare, and that it should remain for foreigners first to feel truly, and to appreciate justly, his mighty genius. The solution of this circumstance must be sought in the history of our nation: the English have become a busy commercial people, and they have unquestionably derived from this propensity many social and physical advantages: they have grown to be a mighty empire—one of the great nations of the world, whose moral superiority enables it to struggle successfully against him, who may be deemed the evil genius of our planet.

On the other hand, the Germans, unable to distinguish themselves in action, have been driven to speculation: all their feelings have been forced back into the thinking and reasoning mind. To do, with them is

---

* It is certain that my short-hand note in this place affords another instance of mishearing: it runs literally thus—"but because Shakespeare could not always be the greatest of poets, was he therefore to condescend to make himself a beast?" For "a beast," we must read *the least,* the antithesis being between "greatest" and "least", and not between "poet" and "beast." Yet "beast" may be reconciled with sense, as in *Macbeth*: "Notes and Emend." 420.

impossible, but in determining what ought to be done, they perhaps exceed every people of the globe. Incapable of acting outwardly, they have acted internally: they first rationally recalled the ancient philosophy, and set their spirits to work with an energy of which England produces no parallel, since those truly heroic times, heroic in body and soul, the days of Elizabeth.

If all that has been written upon Shakespeare by Englishmen were burned, in the want of candles, merely to enable us to read one half of what our dramatist produced, we should be great gainers. Providence has given England the greatest man that ever put on and put off mortality, and has thrown a sop to the envy of other nations, by inflicting upon his native country the most incompetent critics. I say nothing here of the state in which his text has come down to us, farther than that it is evidently very imperfect: in many places his sense has been perverted, in others, if not entirely obscured, so blunderingly represented, as to afford us only a glimpse of what he meant, without the power of restoring his own expressions. But whether his dreams have been perfectly or imperfectly printed, it is quite clear that modern inquiry and speculative ingenuity in this kingdom have done nothing; or I might say, without a solecism, less than nothing (for some editors have multiplied corruptions) to retrieve the genuine language of the poet. His critics among us, during the whole of the last century, have neither understood nor appreciated him; for how could they appreciate what they could not understand?

His contemporaries, and those who immediately followed him, were not so insensible of his merits, or so incapable of explaining them; and one of them, who might be Milton when a young man of four and twenty, printed, in the second folio of Shakespeare's works, a laudatory poem, which, in its kind, has no equal for justness and distinctness of description, in reference to the powers and qualities of lofty genius. It runs thus, and I hope that, when I have finished, I shall stand in need of no excuse for reading the whole of it.

> "A mind reflecting ages past, whose clear
> And equal surface can make things appear,
> Distant a thousand years, and represent
> Them in their lively colours, just extent:
> To outrun hasty time, retrieve the fates,
> Roll back the heavens, blow ope the iron gates
> Of death and Lethe, where confused lie
> Great heaps of ruinous mortality:
> In that deep dusky dungeon to discern
> A royal ghost from churls; by art to learn

The physiognomy of shades, and give
Them sudden birth, wondering how oft they live;
What story coldly tells, what poets feign
At second hand, and picture without brain,
Senseless and soul-less shows: to give a stage
(Ample and true with life) voice, action, age,
As Plato's year, and new scene of the world,
Them unto us, or us to them had hurl'd:
To raise our ancient sovereigns from their herse,
Make kings his subjects; by exchanging verse,
Enlive their pale trunks; that the present age
Joys at their joy, and trembles at their rage:
Yet so to temper passion, that our ears
Take pleasure in their pain, and eyes in tears
Both weep and smile; fearful at plots so sad,
Then laughing at our fear; abus'd, and glad
To be abus'd; affected with that truth
Which we perceive is false, pleas'd in that ruth
At which we start, and, by elaborate play,
Tortur'd and tickl'd; by a crab-like way
Time past made pastime, and in ugly sort
Disgorging up his ravin for our sport:—
—While the plebeian imp, from lofty throne,
Creates and rules a world, and works upon
Mankind by secret engines; now to move
A chilling pity, then a rigorous love;
To strike up and stroke down, both joy and ire
To steer th'affections; and by heavenly fire
Mold us anew, stol'n from ourselves:—
   This, and much more, which cannot be express'd
But by himself, his tongue, and his own breast,
Was Shakespeare's freehold; which his cunning brain
Improv'd by favour of the nine-fold train;
The buskin'd muse, the comick queen, the grand
And louder tone of Clio, nimble hand
And nimbler foot of the melodious pair,
The silver-voiced lady, the most fair
Calliope, whose speaking silence daunts,
And she whose praise the heavenly body chants;
These jointly woo'd him, envying one another;
(Obey'd by all as spouse, but lov'd as brother)
And wrought a curious robe, of sable grave,
Fresh green, and pleasant yellow, red most brave,
And constant blue, rich purple, guiltless white,
The lowly russet, and the scarlet bright;
Branch'd and embroider'd like the painted spring;
Each leaf match'd with a flower, and each string
Of golden wire, each line of silk: there run
Italian works, whose thread the sisters spun;

And these did sing, or seem to sing, the choice
Birds of a foreign note and various voice:
Here hangs a mossy rock; there plays a fair
But chiding fountain, purled: not the air,
Nor clouds, nor thunder, but were living drawn;
Not out of common tiffany or lawn,
But fine materials, which the Muses know,
And only know the countries where they grow.
   Now, when they could no longer him enjoy,
In mortal garments pent,—death may destroy,
They say, his body; but his verse shall live,
And more than nature takes our hands shall give:
In a less volume, but more strongly bound,
Shakespeare shall breathe and speak; with laurel crown'd,
Which never fades; fed with ambrosian meat,
In a well-lined vesture, rich, and neat.
So with this robe they clothe him, bid him wear it;
For time shall never strain, nor envy tear it."

This poem is subscribed J. M. S., meaning, as some have explained the initials, "John Milton, Student:" the internal evidence seems to me decisive, for there was, I think, no other man, of that particular day, capable of writing anything so characteristic of Shakespeare, so justly thought, and so happily expressed.

It is a mistake to say that any of Shakespeare's characters strike us as portraits: they have the union of reason perceiving, of judgment recording, and of imagination diffusing over all a magic glory. While the poet registers what is past, he projects the future in wonderful degree, and makes us feel, however slightly, and see, however dimly, that state of being in which there is neither past nor future, but all is permanent in the very energy of nature.

Although I have affirmed that all Shakespeare's characters are ideal, and the result of his own meditation, yet a just separation may be made of those in which the ideal is most prominent—where it is put forward more intensely—where we are made more conscious of the ideal, though in truth they possess no more nor less ideality; and of those which, though equally idealised, the delusion upon the mind is of their being real. The characters in the various plays may be separated into those where the real is disguised in the ideal, and those where the ideal is concealed from us by the real. The difference is made by the different powers of mind employed by the poet in the representation.

At present I shall only speak of dramas where the ideal is predominant; and chiefly for this reason—that those plays have been attacked with the greatest violence. The objections to them are not the growth of our own country, but of France—the judgment of monkeys, by some wonderful phenomenon, put into the mouths of people shaped like men. These creatures have informed us that Shakespeare is a miraculous monster, in whom many heterogeneous components were thrown together, producing a discordant mass of genius—an irregular and ill-assorted structure of gigantic proportions.

Among the ideal plays, I will take "The Tempest," by way of example. Various others might be mentioned, but it is impossible to go through every drama, and what I remark on "The Tempest" will apply to all Shakespeare's productions of the same class.

In this play Shakespeare has especially appealed to the imagination, and he has constructed a plot well adapted to the purpose. According to his scheme, he did not appeal to any sensuous impression (the word "sensuous" is authorised by Milton) of time and place, but to the imagination, and it is to be borne in mind, that of old, and as regards mere scenery, his works may be said to have been recited rather than acted—that is to say, description and narration supplied the place of visual exhibition: the audience was told to fancy that they saw what they only heard described; the painting was not in colours, but in words.

This is particularly to be noted in the first scene—a storm and its confusion on board the king's ship. The highest and the lowest characters are brought together, and with what excellence! Much of the genius of Shakespeare is displayed in these happy combinations—the highest and the lowest, the gayest and the saddest; he is not droll in one scene and melancholy in another, but often both the one and the other in the same scene. Laughter is made to swell the tear of sorrow, and to throw, as it were, a poetic light upon it, while the the tear mingles tenderness with the laughter. Shakespeare has evinced the power, which above all other men he possessed, that of introducing the profoundest sentiments of wisdom, where they would be least expected, yet where they are most truly natural. One admirable secret of his art is, that separate speeches frequently do not appear to have been occasioned by those which preceded, and which are consequent upon each other, but to have arisen out of the peculiar character of the speaker.

Before I go further, I may take the opportunity of explaining what is meant by mechanic and organic regularity. In the former the copy must appear as if it had come out of the same mould with the original; in the latter there is a law which all the parts obey, conforming themselves to the outward symbols and manifestations of the essential principle. If we look to the growth of trees, for instance, we shall observe that trees of the same kind vary considerably, according to the circumstances of soil, air, or position; yet we are able to decide at once whether they are oaks, elms, or poplars.

So with Shakespeare's characters: he shows us the life and principle of each being with organic regularity. The Boatswain, in the first scene of "The Tempest," when the bonds of reverence are thrown off as a sense of danger impresses all, gives a loose to his feelings, and thus pours forth his vulgar mind to the old Counsellor:—

"Hence! What care these roarers for the same name of King? To cabin: silence! trouble us not."

Gonzalo replies—"Good; yet remember whom thou hast aboard." To which the Boatswain answers—"None that I more love than myself. You are a counsellor: if you can command these elements to silence, and work the peace of the present, we will not hand a rope more; use your authority: if you cannot, give thanks that you have lived so long, and make yourself ready in your cabin for the mischance of the hour, if it so hap.—Cheerly, good hearts!—Out of our way, I say."

An ordinary dramatist would, after this speech, have represented Gonzalo as moralising, or saying something connected with the Boatswain's language; for ordinary dramatists are not men of genius: they combine their ideas by association, or by logical affinity; but the vital writer, who makes men on the stage what they are in nature, in a moment transports himself into the very being of each personage, and, instead of cutting out artificial puppets, he brings before us the men themselves. Therefore, Gonzalo soliloquises,—"I have great comfort from this fellow: methinks, he hath no drowning mark upon him; his complexion is perfect gallows. Stand fast, good fate, to his hanging! make the rope of his destiny our cable, for our own doth little advantage. If he be not born to be hanged, our case is miserable."

In this part of the scene we see the true sailor with his contempt of danger, and the old counsellor with his high feeling, who, instead of condescending to notice the words just addressed to him, turns off, meditating with himself, and drawing some comfort to his own mind, by trifling with the ill expression of the boatswain's face, founding upon it a hope of safety.

Shakespeare had pre-determined to make the plot of this play such as to involve a certain number of low characters, and at the beginning he pitched the note of the whole. The first scene was meant as a lively commencement of the story; the reader is prepared for something that is to be developed, and in the next scene he brings forward Prospero and Miranda. How is this done? By giving to his favourite character, Miranda, a sentence which at once expresses the violence and fury of the storm, such as it might appear to a witness on the land, and at the same time displays the tenderness of her feelings—the exquisite feelings of a female brought up in a desert, but with all the advantages of education, all that could be communicated by a wise and affectionate father. She possesses all the delicacy of innocence, yet with all the powers of her mind unweakened by the combats of life. Miranda exclaims:—

> "O! I have suffered
> With those that I saw suffer: a brave vessel,
> Who had, no doubt, some noble creatures in her,
> Dash'd all to pieces."

The doubt here intimated could have occurred to no mind but to that of Miranda, who had been bred up in the island with her father and a monster only: she did not know, as others do, what sort of creatures were in a ship; others never would have introduced it as a conjecture. This shows, that while Shakespeare is displaying his vast excellence, he never fails to insert some touch or other, which is not merely characteristic of the particular person, but combines two things—the person, and the circumstances acting upon the person. She proceeds:—

> "O! the cry did knock
> Against my very heart. Poor souls! they perish'd.
> Had I been any god of power, I would
> Have sunk the sea within the earth, or e'er
> It should the good ship so have swallow'd, and
> The fraughting souls within her."

She still dwells upon that which was most wanting to the completeness of her nature—these fellow creatures from whom she appeared banished, with only one relict to keep them alive, not in her memory, but in her imagination.

Another proof of excellent judgment in the poet, for I am now principally adverting to that point, is to be found in the preparation of the reader for what is to follow. Prospero is introduced, first in his magic robe, which, with the assistance of his daughter, he lays aside, and we then know him to be a being possessed of supernatural powers. He then instructs Miranda in the story of their arrival in the island, and this is conducted in such a manner, that the reader never conjectures the technical use the poet has made of the relation, by informing the auditor of what is necessary for him to know.

The next step is the warning by Prospero, that he means, for particular purposes, to lull his daughter to sleep; and here he exhibits the earliest and mildest proof of magical power. In ordinary and vulgar plays we should have had some person brought upon the stage, whom nobody knows or cares anything about, to let the audience into the secret. Prospero having cast a sleep upon his daughter, by that sleep stops the narrative at the very moment when it was necessary to break it off, in order to excite curiosity, and yet to give the memory and understanding sufficient to carry on the progress of the history uninterruptedly.

Here I cannot help noticing a fine touch of Shakespeare's knowledge of human nature, and generally of the great laws of the human mind: I mean Miranda's infant remembrance. Prospero asks her—

> "Canst thou remember
> A time before we came unto this cell?
> I do not think thou canst, for then thou wast not
> Out three years old."

Miranda answers,

> "Certainly, sir, I can."

Prospero inquires,

> "By what? by any other house or person?
> Of any thing the image tell me, that
> Hath kept with thy remembrance."

To which Miranda returns,

> "'Tis far off;
> And rather like a dream than an assurance
> That my remembrance warrants. Had I not
> Four or five women once, that tended me?"
>
> *Act I., Scene 2.*

This is exquisite! In general, our remembrances of early life arise from vivid colours, especially if we have seen them in motion: for instance, persons when grown up will remember a bright green door, seen when they were quite young; but Miranda, who was somewhat older, recollected four or five women who tended her. She might know men from her father, and her remembrance of the past might be worn out by the present object, but women she only knew by herself, by the contemplation of her own figure in the fountain, and she recalled to her mind what had been. It was not, that she had seen such and such grandees, or such and such peeresses, but she remembered to have seen something like the reflection of herself: it was not herself, and it brought back to her mind what she had seen most like herself.

In my opinion the picturesque power displayed by Shakespeare, of all the poets that ever lived, is only equalled, if equalled, by Milton and Dante. The presence of genius is not shown in elaborating a picture: we have had many specimens of this sort of work in modern poems, where all is so dutchified, if I may use the word, by the most minute touches, that the reader naturally asks why words, and not painting, are used? I know a young lady of much taste, who observed, that in reading recent versified accounts of voyages and travels, she, by a sort of instinct, cast her eyes on the opposite page, for coloured prints of what was so patiently and punctually described.

The power of poetry is, by a single word perhaps, to instil that energy into the mind, which compels the imagination to produce the picture. Prospero tells Miranda,

> "One midnight,
> Fated to the purpose,* did Antonio open
> The gates of Milan; and i' the dead of darkness,
> The ministers for the purpose hurried thence
> Me, and thy crying self."

Here, by introducing a single happy epithet, "crying," in the last line, a complete picture is presented to the mind, and in the production of such pictures the power of genius consists.

In reference to preparation, it will be observed that the storm, and all that precedes the tale, as well as the tale itself, serve to develope completely the main character of the drama, as well as the design of Prospero. The manner in which the heroine is charmed asleep fits us for what follows, goes beyond our ordinary belief, and gradually leads us to the appearance and disclosure of a being of the most fanciful and delicate texture, like Prospero, preternaturally gifted.

In this way the entrance of Ariel, if not absolutely forethought by the reader, was foreshewn by the writer: in addition, we may remark, that the moral feeling called forth by the sweet words of Miranda,

> "Alack, what trouble
> Was I then to you!"

in which she considered only the suffering and sorrows of her father, puts the reader in a frame of mind to exert his imagination in favour of an object so innocent and interesting. The poet makes him wish that, if supernatural agency were to be employed, it should be used for a being so young and lovely. "The wish is father to the thought," and

---

* Coleridge, of course, could only use the text of the day when he lectured; but, since that period, many plausible, and some indisputable, changes have been introduced into it: one of them occurs in reference to the word "purpose," for which *practice* has been proposed as the true reading: the change is not absolutely necessary, but still we can entertain little doubt that "purpose" is a corruption, arising perhaps out of the similarity of the appearance of the words "purpose" and *practice* in hastily written manuscript. The word "purpose" recurs in the very next line but one.—J. P. C.

Ariel is introduced. Here, what is called poetic faith is required and created, and our common notions of philosophy give away before it: this feeling may be said to be much stronger than historic faith, since for the exercise of poetic faith the mind is previously prepared. I make this remark, though somewhat digressive, in order to lead to a future subject of these lectures—the poems of Milton. When adverting to those, I shall have to explain farther the distinction between the two.

Many Scriptural poems have been written with so much of Scripture in them, that what is not Scripture appears to be not true, and like mingling lies with the most sacred revelations. Now Milton, on the other hand, has taken for his subject that one point of Scripture of which we have the mere fact recorded, and upon this he has most judiciously constructed his whole fable. So of Shakespeare's "King Lear:" we have little historic evidence to guide or confine us, and the few facts handed down to us, and admirably employed by the poet, are sufficient, while we read, to put an end to all doubts as to the credibility of the story. It is idle to say that this or that incident is improbable, because history, as far as it goes, tells us that the fact was so and so. Four or five lines in the Bible include the whole that is said of Milton's story, and the Poet has called up that poetic faith, that conviction of the mind, which is necessary to make that seem true, which otherwise might have been deemed almost fabulous.

But to return to "The Tempest," and to the wondrous creation of Ariel. If a doubt could ever be entertained whether Shakespeare was a great poet, acting upon laws arising out of his own nature, and not without law, as has sometimes been idly asserted, that doubt must be removed by the character of Ariel. The very first words uttered by this being introduce the spirit, not as an angel, above man; not a gnome, or a fiend, below man; but while the poet gives him the faculties and the advantages of reason, he divests him of all mortal character, not positively, it is true, but negatively. In air he lives, from air he derives his being, in air he acts; and all his colours and properties seem to have been obtained from the rainbow and the skies. There is nothing about Ariel that cannot be conceived to exist either at sun-rise or at sun-set: hence all that belongs to Ariel belongs to the delight the mind is capable of receiving from the most lovely external appearances. His answers to Prospero are directly to the question, and nothing beyond; or where he expatiates, which is not unfrequently, it is to himself and upon his own delights, or upon the unnatural situation in which he is placed, though under a kindly power and to good ends.

Shakespeare has properly made Ariel's very first speech characteristic of him. After he has described the manner in which he had raised the storm and produced its harmless consequences, we find that Ariel is discontented—that he has been freed, it is true, from a cruel confinement, but still that he is bound to obey Prospero, and to execute any commands imposed upon him. We feel that such a state of bondage is almost unnatural to him, yet we see that it is delightful for him to be so employed.—It is as if we were to command one of the winds in a different direction to that which nature dictates, or one of the waves, now rising and now sinking, to recede before it bursts upon the shore: such is the feeling we experience, when we learn that a being like Ariel is commanded to fulfil any mortal behest.

When, however, Shakespeare contrasts the treatment of Ariel by Prospero with that of Sycorax, we are sensible that the liberated spirit ought to be grateful, and Ariel does feel and acknowledge the obligation; he immediately assumes the airy being, with a mind so elastically correspondent, that when once a feeling has passed from it, not a trace is left behind.

Is there anything in nature from which Shakespeare caught the idea of this delicate and delightful being, with such child-like simplicity, yet with such preternatural powers? He is neither born of heaven, nor of earth; but, as it were, between both, like a May-blossom kept suspended in air by the fanning breeze, which prevents it from falling to the ground, and only finally, and by compulsion, touching earth. This reluctance of the Sylph to be under the command even of Prospero is kept up through the whole play, and in the exercise of his admirable judgment Shakespeare has availed himself of it, in order to give Ariel an interest in the event, looking forward to that moment when he was to gain his last and only reward—simple and eternal liberty.

Another instance of admirable judgment and excellent preparation is to be found in the creature contrasted with Ariel—Caliban; who is described in such a manner by Prospero, as to lead us to expect the appearance of a foul, unnatural monster. He is not seen at once: his voice is heard; this is the preparation; he was too offensive to be seen first in all his deformity, and in nature we do not receive so much disgust from sound as from sight. After we have heard Caliban's voice he does not enter, until Ariel has entered like a water-nymph. All the strength of contrast is thus acquired without any of the shock of abruptness, or of that unpleasant sensation, which we experience when the object presented is in any way hateful to our vision.

The character of Caliban is wonderfully conceived: he is a sort of creature of the earth, as Ariel is a sort of creature of the air. He partakes of the qualities of the brute, but is distinguished from brutes in two ways:—by having mere understanding without moral reason; and by not possessing the instincts which pertain to absolute animals. Still, Caliban is in some respects a noble being: the poet has raised him far above contempt: he is a man in the sense of the imagination: all the images he uses are drawn from nature, and are highly poetical; they fit in with the images of Ariel. Caliban gives us images from the earth, Ariel images from the air. Caliban talks of the difficulty of finding fresh water, of the situation of morasses, and of other circumstances which even brute instinct, without reason, could comprehend. No mean figure is employed, no mean passion displayed, beyond animal passion, and repugnance to command.

The manner in which the lovers are introduced is equally wonderful, and it is the last point I shall now mention in reference to this, almost miraculous, drama. The same judgment is observable in every scene, still preparing, still inviting, and still gratifying, like a finished piece of music. I have omitted to notice one thing, and you must give me leave to advert to it before I proceed: I mean the conspiracy against the life of Alonzo. I want to shew you how well the poet prepares the feelings of the reader for this plot, which was to execute the most detestable of all crimes, and which, in another play, Shakespeare has called "the murder of sleep."

Antonio and Sebastian at first had no such intention: it was suggested by the magical sleep cast on Alonzo and Gonzalo; but they are previously introduced scoffing and scorning at what was said by others, without regard to age or situation—without any sense of admiration for the excellent truths they heard delivered, but giving themselves up entirely to the malignant and unsocial feeling, which induced them to listen to everything that was said, not for the sake of profiting by the learning and experience of others, but of hearing something that might gratify vanity and self-love, by making them believe that the person speaking was inferior to themselves.

This, let me remark, is one of the grand characteristics of a villain; and it would not be so much a presentiment, as an anticipation of hell, for men to suppose that all mankind were as wicked as themselves, or might be so, if they were not too great fools. Pope, you are perhaps aware, objected to this conspiracy; but in my mind, if it could be omitted, the play would lose a charm which nothing could supply.

Many, indeed, innumerable, beautiful passages might be quoted <u>from this play, independently of the astonishing scheme of its construction.</u> <u>Every body will call to mind</u> the grandeur of the language of Prospero in that divine speech, where he takes leave of his magic art; and were I to indulge myself by repetitions of the kind, I should descend from the character of a lecturer to that of a mere reciter. Before I terminate, I may particularly recal one short passage, which has fallen under the very severe, but inconsiderate, censure of Pope and Arbuthnot, who pronounce it a piece of the grossest bombast. Prospero thus addresses his daughter, directing her attention to Ferdinand:

> "The fringed curtains of thine eye advance,
> And say what thou seest yond."
>
> *Act I., Scene 2.*

Taking these words as a periphrase of—"Look what is coming yonder," it certainly may to some appear to border on the ridiculous, and to fall under the rule I formerly laid down,—that whatever, without injury, can be translated into a foreign language in simple terms, ought to be in simple terms in the original language; but it is to be borne in mind, that different modes of expression frequently arise from difference of situation and education: a blackguard would use very different words, to express the same thing, to those a gentleman would employ, yet both would be natural and proper; difference of feeling gives rise to difference of language: a gentleman speaks in polished terms, with due regard to his own rank and position, while a blackguard, a person little better than half a brute, speaks like half a brute, showing no respect for himself, nor for others.

But I am content to try the lines I have just quoted by the introduction to them; and then, I think, you will admit, that nothing could be more fit and appropriate than such language. How does Prospero introduce them? He has just told Miranda a wonderful story, which deeply affected her, and filled her with surprise and astonishment, and for his own purposes he afterwards lulls her to sleep. When she awakes, Shakespeare has made her wholly inattentive to the present, but wrapped up in the past. An actress, who understands the character of Miranda, would have her eyes cast down, and her eyelids almost covering them, while she was, as it were, living in her dream. At this moment Prospero sees Ferdinand, and wishes to point him out to his daughter, not only with great, but with scenic solemnity, he standing before her, and before the spectator, in the dignified character of a great magician. Something was to appear to Miranda on the sudden, and as unexpectedly as if the hero of a drama were to be on the stage at the instant when the curtain is elevated. It is under such circumstances that Prospero says, in a tone calculated at once to arouse his daughter's attention,

> "The fringed curtains of thine eye advance,
> And say what thou seest yond."

<u>Turning from the sight of Ferdinand to his thoughtful daughter, his attention was first struck by the downcast appearance of her eyes and eyelids;</u> and, in my humble opinion, the solemnity of the phraseology assigned to Prospero is completely in character, recollecting his preternatural capacity, in which the most familiar objects in nature present themselves in a mysterious point of view. It is much easier to find fault with a writer by reference to former notions and experience, than to sit down and read him, recollecting his purpose, connecting one feeling with another, and judging of his words and phrases, in proportion as they convey the sentiments of the persons represented.

Of Miranda we may say, that she possesses in herself all the ideal beauties that could be imagined by the greatest poet of any age or country; but it is not my purpose now, so much to point out the high poetic powers of Shakespeare, as to illustrate his exquisite judgment, <u>and it is solely with this design that I have noticed a passage with which, it seems to me, some critics, and those among the best, have been unreasonably dissatisfied.</u> If Shakespeare be the wonder of the ignorant, he is, and ought to be, much more the wonder of the learned: not only from profundity of thought, <u>but from his astonishing and intuitive knowledge of what man must be at all times, and under all circumstances,</u> he is rather to be looked upon as a prophet than as a poet. Yet, with all these unbounded powers, with all this might and majesty of genius, he makes us feel as if he were unconscious of himself, and of his high destiny, disguising the half god in the simplicity of a child.

END OF THE NINTH LECTURE.

THE TWELFTH LECTURE

In the last lecture I endeavoured to point out in Shakespeare those characters in which pride of intellect, without moral feeling, is supposed to be the ruling impulse, such as Iago, Richard III., and even Falstaff. In Richard III., ambition is, as it were, the channel in which this impulse directs itself; the character is drawn with the greatest fulness and perfection; and the poet has not only given us that character, grown up and completed, but he has shown us its very source and generation. The inferiority of his person made the hero seek consolation and compensation in the superiority of his intellect; he thus endeavoured to counterbalance his deficiency. This striking feature is pourtrayed most admirably by Shakespeare, who represents Richard bringing forward his very defects and deformities as matters of boast. It was the same pride of intellect, or the assumption of it, that made John Wilkes vaunt that, although he was so ugly, he only wanted, with any lady, ten minutes' start of the handsomest man in England. This certainly was a high compliment to himself; but a higher to the female sex, <u>on the supposition that Wilkes possessed this superiority of intellect, and relied upon it for making a favourable impression, because ladies would know how to estimate his advantages.</u>

I will now proceed to offer some remarks upon the tragedy of "Richard II.," on account of its not very apparent, but still intimate, connection with "Richard III." As, in the last, Shakespeare has painted a man where ambition is the channel in which the ruling impulse runs, so, in the first, he has given us a character, under the name of Bolingbroke, or Henry IV., where ambition itself, conjoined unquestionably with great talents, is the ruling impulse. <u>In Richard III. the pride of intellect makes use of ambition as its means; in Bolingbroke the gratification of ambition is the end, and talents are the means.</u>

One main object of these lectures is to point out the superiority of Shakespeare to other dramatists, and no superiority can be more striking, than that this wonderful poet could take two characters, which at first sight seem so much alike, and yet, when carefully and minutely examined, are so totally distinct.

The popularity of "Richard II." is owing, in a great measure, to the masterly delineation of the principal character; but were there no other ground for admiring it, it would deserve the highest applause, from the fact that it contains the most magnificent, and, at the same time, the truest eulogium of our native country that the English language can boast, or which can be produced from any other tongue, not excepting the proud claims of Greece and Rome. When I feel, that upon the morality of Britain depends the safety of Britain, and that her morality is supported and illustrated by our national feeling, I cannot read these grand lines without joy and triumph. Let it be remembered, that while this country is proudly pre-eminent in morals, her enemy has only maintained his station by superiority in mechanical appliances. Many of those who hear me will, no doubt, anticipate the passage I refer to, and it runs as follows:—

> "This royal throne of kings, this sceptered isle,
> This earth of majesty, this seat of Mars,
> This other Eden, demi-paradise;
> This fortress, built by nature for herself

Against infection and the hand of war;
This happy breed of men, this little world,
This precious stone set in the silver sea,
Which serves it in the office of a wall,
Or as a moat defensive to a house,
Against the envy of less happier lands;
This blessed plot, this earth, this realm, this England,
This nurse, this teeming womb of royal kings,
Feared by their breed, and famous by their birth,
Renowned for their deeds as far from home,
For Christian service and true chivalry,
As is the Sepulchre in stubborn Jewry
Of the world's ransom, blessed Mary's son:
This land of such dear souls, this dear, dear land,
Dear for her reputation through the world,
Is now leas'd out, I die pronouncing it,
Like to a tenement, or pelting farm.
England, bound in with the triumphant sea,
Whose rocky shore beats back the envious siege
Of watery Neptune, is now bound in with shame,
With inky blots, and rotten parchment bonds.''

Act II., Scene 1.

Every motive to patriotism, every cause producing it, is here collected, without one of those cold abstractions so frequently substituted by modern poets. If this passage were recited <u>in a theatre with due energy and understanding, with a proper knowledge of the words, and a fit expression of their meaning,</u> every man would retire from it secure in his country's freedom, if secure in his own constant virtue.

The principal personages in this tragedy are Richard II., Bolingbroke, and York. I will speak of the last first, although it is the least important; but the keeping of all is most admirable. York is a man of no strong powers of mind, but of earnest wishes to do right, contented in himself alone, if he have acted well: he points out to Richard the effects of his thoughtless extravagance, and the dangers by which he is encompassed, but having done so, he is satisfied; there is no after action on his part; he does nothing; he remains passive. When old Gaunt is dying, York takes care to give his own opinion to the King, and that done he retires, as it were, into himself.

It has been stated, from the first, that one of my purposes in these lectures is, to meet and refute popular objections to particular points in the works of our great dramatic poet; and I cannot help observing here upon the beauty, and true force of nature, with which conceits, as they are called, and sometimes even puns, are introduced. What has been the reigning fault of an age must, at one time or another, have referred to something beautiful in the human mind; and, however conceits may have been misapplied, however they may have been disadvantageously multiplied, we should recollect that there never was an abuse of anything, but it previously has had its use. Gaunt, on his death-bed, sends for the young King, and Richard, entering, insolently and unfeelingly says to him:

> "What, comfort, man! how is't with aged Gaunt?"
>
> *Act II., Scene 1.*

and Gaunt replies:

> "O, how that name befits my composition!
> Old Gaunt, indeed; and gaunt in being old:
> Within me grief hath kept a tedious fast,
> And who abstains from meat, that is not gaunt?
> For sleeping England long time have I watched;
> Watching breeds leanness, leanness is all gaunt:
> The pleasure that some fathers feed upon
> Is my strict fast, I mean my children's looks;
> And therein fasting, thou hast made me gaunt.
> Gaunt am I for the grave, gaunt as a grave,
> Whose hollow womb inherits nought but bones."

Richard inquires,

> "Can sick men play so nicely with their names?"

To which Gaunt answers, <u>giving the true justification of conceits:</u>

> "No; misery makes sport to mock itself:
> Since thou dost seek to kill my name in me,
> I mock my name, great king, to flatter thee."

He that knows the state of the human mind in deep passion must know, that it approaches to that condition of madness, which is not absolute frenzy or delirium, but which models all things to one reigning idea; still it strays from the main subject of complaint, and still it returns to it, by a sort of irresistible impulse. Abruptness of thought, under such circumstances, is true to nature, and no man was more sensible of it than Shakespeare. In a modern poem a mad mother thus complains:

> "The breeze I see is in yon tree:
> It comes to cool my babe and me."

This is an instance of the abruptness of thought, so natural to the excitement and agony of grief; and if it be admired in images, can we say that it is unnatural in words, which are, as it were, a part of our life, of our very existence? In the Scriptures themselves these plays upon words are to be found, as well as in the best works of the ancients,

and in the most delightful parts of Shakespeare; and because this additional grace, not well understood, has in some instances been converted into a deformity—because it has been forced into places, where
it is evidently improper and unnatural, are we therefore to include the
whole application of it in one general condemnation? When it seems
objectionable, when it excites a feeling contrary to the situation, when
it perhaps disgusts, it is our business to enquire whether the conceit has
been rightly or wrongly used—whether it is in a right or in a wrong
place?

In order to decide this point, it is obviously necessary to consider
the state of mind, and the degree of passion, of the person using this
play upon words. Resort to this grace may, in some cases, deserve
censure, not because it is a play upon words, but because it is a play
upon words in a wrong place, and at a wrong time. What is right in
one state of mind is wrong in another, and much more depends upon
that, than upon the conceit (so to call it) itself. I feel the importance
of these remarks strongly, because the greater part of the abuse, I might
say filth, thrown out and heaped upon Shakespeare, has originated in
want of consideration. Dr. Johnson asserts that Shakespeare loses the
world for a toy, and can no more withstand a pun, or a play upon
words, than his Antony could resist Cleopatra. Certain it is, that Shakespeare gained more admiration in his day, and long afterwards, by the
use of speech in this way, than modern writers have acquired by the
abandonment of the practice: the latter, in adhering to, what they have
been pleased to call, the rules of art, have sacrificed nature.

Having said thus much on the, often falsely supposed, blemishes of
our poet—blemishes which are said to prevail in ''Richard II'' especially,—I will now advert to the character of the King. He is represented
as a man not deficient in immediate courage, which displays itself at
his assassination; or in powers of mind, as appears by the foresight he
exhibits throughout the play: still, he is weak, variable, and womanish,
and possesses feelings, which, amiable in a female, are misplaced in a
man, and altogether unfit for a king. In prosperity he is insolent and
presumptuous, and in adversity, if we are to believe Dr. Johnson, he
is humane and pious. I cannot admit the latter epithet, because I perceive
the utmost consistency of character in Richard: what he was at first, he
is at last, excepting as far as he yields to circumstances: what he shewed
himself at the commencement of the play, he shews himself at the end
of it. Dr. Johnson assigns to him rather the virtue of a confessor than
that of a king.

True it is, that he may be said to be overwhelmed by the earliest misfortune that befalls him; but, so far from his feelings or disposition being changed or subdued, the very first glimpse of the returning sunshine of hope reanimates his spirits, and exalts him to as strange and unbecoming a degree of elevation, as he was before sunk in mental depression: the mention of those in his misfortunes, who had contributed to his downfall, but who had before been his nearest friends and favourites, calls forth from him expressions of the bitterest hatred and revenge. Thus, where Richard asks:

> "Where is the Earl of Wiltshire? Where is Bagot?
> What is become of Bushy? Where is Green?
> That they have let the dangerous enemy
> Measure our confines with such peaceful steps?
> If we prevail, their heads shall pay for it.
> I warrant they have made peace with Bolingbroke."
> *Act III., Scene 2.*

Scroop answers:

> "Peace have they made with him, indeed, my lord."

Upon which Richard, without hearing more, breaks out:

> "O villains! vipers, damn'd without redemption!
> Dogs, easily won to fawn on any man!
> Snakes, in my heart-blood warm'd, that sting my heart!
> Three Judases, each one thrice worse than Judas!
> Would they make peace? terrible hell make war
> Upon their spotted souls for this offence!"

Scroop observes <u>upon this change, and tells the King how they had made their peace:</u>

> "Sweet love, I see, changing his property
> Turns to the sourest and most deadly hate.
> Again uncurse their souls: their peace is made
> With heads and not with hands: those whom you curse
> Have felt the worst of death's destroying wound,
> And lie full low, grav'd in the hollow ground."

Richard receiving at first an equivocal answer,—"Peace have they made with him, indeed, my lord,"—takes it in the worst sense: his promptness to suspect those who had been his friends turns his love to hate, and calls forth the most tremendous execrations.

From the beginning to the end of the play he pours out all the peculiarities and powers of his mind: he catches at new hope, and seeks new friends, is disappointed, despairs, and at length makes a merit of his resignation. He scatters himself into a multitude of images, and in conclusion endeavours to shelter himself from that which is around him by a cloud of his own thoughts. Throughout his whole career may be noticed the most rapid transitions—from the highest insolence to the lowest humility—from hope to despair, from the extravagance of love to the agonies of resentment, and from pretended resignation to the bitterest reproaches. The whole is joined with the utmost richness and copiousness of thought, and were there an actor capable of representing Richard, the part would delight us more than any other of Shakespeare's master-pieces,—with, perhaps, the single exception of King Lear. I know of no character drawn by our great poet with such unequalled skill as that of Richard II.

Next we come to Henry Bolingbroke, the rival of Richard II. He appears as a man of dauntless courage, and of ambition equal to that of Richard III.; but, as I have stated, the difference between the two is most admirably conceived and preserved. In Richard III. all that surrounds him is only dear as it feeds his inward sense of superiority: he is no vulgar tyrant—no Nero or Caligula: he has always an end in view, and vast fertility of means to accomplish that end. On the other hand, in Bolingbroke we find a man who in the outset has been sorely injured: then, we see him encouraged by the grievances of his country, and by the strange mismanagement of the government, yet at the same time scarcely daring to look at his own views, or to acknowledge them as designs. He comes home under the pretence of claiming his dukedom, and he professes that to be his object almost to the last; but, at the last, he avows his purpose to its full extent, of which he was himself unconscious in the earlier stages.

This is proved by so many passages, that I will only select one of them; and I take it the rather, because out of the many octavo volumes of text and notes, the page on which it occurs is, I believe, the only one left naked by the commentators. It is where Bolingbroke approaches the castle in which the unfortunate King has taken shelter: York is in Bolingbroke's company—the same York who is still contented with speaking the truth, but doing nothing for the sake of the truth,—drawing back after he has spoken, and becoming merely passive when he ought to display activity. Northumberland says,

> "The news is very fair and good, my lord:
> Richard not far from hence hath hid his head."
>
> *Act III., Scene 3.*

York rebukes him thus:

> "It would beseem the Lord Northumberland
> To say King Richard:—Alack, the heavy day,
> When such a sacred king should hide his head!"

Northumberland replies:

> "Your grace mistakes me: only to be brief
> Left I his title out."*

To which York rejoins:

> "The time hath been,
> Would you have been so brief with him, he would
> Have been so brief with you, to shorten you,
> For taking so the head, your whole head's length."

Bolingbroke observes,

> "Mistake not, uncle, farther than you should;"

And York answers, <u>with a play upon the words "take" and "mis-</u>
<u>take:"</u>

> "Take not, good cousin, farther than you should,
> Lest you mistake. The heavens are o'er our heads."

Here, give me leave to remark in passing, that the play upon words
is perfectly natural, and quite in character: the answer is in unison with
the tone of passion, and seems connected with some phrase then in
popular use.† Bolingbroke tells York:

> "I know it, uncle, and oppose not myself
> Against their will."

Just afterwards, Bolingbroke thus addresses himself to Northumberland:

> "Noble lord,
> Go to the rude ribs of that ancient castle;
> Through brazen trumpet send the breath of parle
> Into his ruin'd ears, and thus deliver."

Here, in the phrase, "into his ruin'd ears," I have no doubt that
Shakespeare purposely used the personal pronoun, "his," to shew, that
although Bolingbroke was only speaking of the castle, his thoughts
dwelt on the king. In Milton the pronoun, "her" is employed, in relation
to "form," in a manner somewhat similar. Bolingbroke had an equivocation in his mind, and was thinking of the king, <u>while speaking of</u>
<u>the castle.</u> He goes on <u>to tell Northumberland what to say beginning,</u>

> "Henry Bolingbroke,"

---

* <u>So Coleridge read the passage, his ear requiring the insertion of *me*, which is</u>
<u>one of the emendations in the corrected folio 1632, discovered many years after-</u>
<u>wards.</u>—J. P C.

† <u>Nicholas Breton wrote a "Dialogue between the Taker and Mistaker," but the</u>
<u>earliest known edition is dated 1603.</u>—J. P. C.

which is almost the only instance in which a name forms the whole line; Shakespeare meant it to convey Bolingbroke's opinion of his own importance:—

> "Henry Bolingbroke
> On both his knees doth kiss King Richard's hand,
> And sends allegiance and true faith of heart
> To his most royal person; hither come
> Even at his feet to lay my arms and power,
> Provided that, my banishment repealed,
> And lands restor'd again, be freely granted.
> If not, I'll use th'advantage of my power,
> And lay the summer's dust with showers of blood,
> Rain'd from the wounds of slaughter'd Englishmen."

At this point Bolingbroke seems to have been checked by the eye of York, and thus proceeds in consequence:

> "The which, how far off from the mind of Bolingbroke
> It is, such crimson tempest should bedrench
> The fresh green lap of fair King Richard's land,
> My stooping duty tenderly shall show."

He passes suddenly from insolence to humility, owing to the silent reproof he received from his uncle. This change of tone would not have taken place, had Bolingbroke been allowed to proceed according to the natural bent of his own mind, and the flow of the subject. Let me direct attention to the subsequent lines, for the same reason; they are part of the same speech:

> "Let's march without the noise of threat'ning drum,
> That from the castle's tatter'd battlements
> Our fair appointments may be well perused.
> Methinks, King Richard and myself should meet
> With no less terror than the elements
> Of fire and water, when their thundering shock
> At meeting tears the cloudy cheeks of heaven."

Having proceeded thus far with the exaggeration of his own importance, York again checks him, and Bolingbroke adds, in a very different strain,

> "He be the fire, I'll be the yielding water:
> The rage be his, while on the earth I rain
> My waters; on the earth, and not on him,"

I have thus adverted to the three great personages in this drama, Richard, Bolingbroke, and York; and of the whole play it may be asserted, that with the exception of some of the last scenes (though they have exquisite beauty) Shakespeare seems to have risen to the summit of excellence in the delineation and preservation of character.

We will now pass to "Hamlet," in order to obviate some of the general prejudices against the author, in reference to the character of the hero. Much has been objected to, which ought to have been praised, and many beauties of the highest kind have been neglected, because they are somewhat hidden.

The first question we should ask ourselves is—What did Shakespeare mean when he drew the character of Hamlet? He never wrote any thing without design, and what was his design when he sat down to produce this tragedy? My belief is, that he always regarded his story, before he began to write, much in the same light as a painter regards his canvas, before he begins to paint—as a mere vehicle for his thoughts—as the ground upon which he was to work. What then was the point to which Shakespeare directed himself in Hamlet? He intended to pourtray a person, in whose view the external world, and all its incidents and objects, were comparatively dim, and of no interest in themselves, and which began to interest only, when they were reflected in the mirror of his mind. Hamlet beheld external things in the same way that a man of vivid imagination, who shuts his eyes, sees what has previously made an impression on his organs.

The poet places him in the most stimulating circumstances that a human being can be placed in. He is the heir apparent of a throne; his father dies suspiciously; his mother excludes her son from his throne by marrying his uncle. This is not enough; but the Ghost of the murdered father is introduced, to assure the son that he was put to death by his own brother. What is the effect upon the son?—instant action and pursuit of revenge? No: endless reasoning and hesitating—constant urging and solicitation of the mind to act, and as constant an escape from action; ceaseless reproaches of himself for sloth and negligence, while the whole energy of his resolution evaporates in these reproaches. This, too, not from cowardice, for he is drawn as one of the bravest of his time—not from want of forethought or slowness of apprehension, for he sees through the very souls of all who surround him, but merely from that aversion to action, which prevails among such as have a world in themselves.

How admirable, too, is the judgment of the poet! Hamlet's own disordered fancy has not conjured up the spirit of his father; it has been seen by others: he is prepared by them to witness its re-appearance, and when he does see it, Hamlet is not brought forward as having long brooded on the subject. The moment before the Ghost enters, Hamlet speaks of other matters: he mentions the coldness of the night, and observes that he has not heard the clock strike, adding, in reference to the custom of drinking, that it is

> "More honour'd in the breach than the observance."
> *Act I., Scene 4.*

Owing to the tranquil state of his mind, he indulges in some moral reflections. Afterwards, the Ghost suddenly enters.

> "*Hor.*   Look, my lord! it comes.
> *Ham.* Angels and ministers of grace defend us!"

This same thing occurs in "Macbeth:" in the dagger-scene, the moment before the hero sees it, he has his mind applied to some indifferent matters; "Go, tell thy mistress," &c. Thus, in both cases, the preternatural appearance has all the effect of abruptness, and the reader is totally divested of the notion, that the figure is a vision of a highly wrought imagination.

Here Shakespeare adapts himself so admirably to the situation—in other words, so puts himself into it—that, though poetry, his language is the very language of nature. No terms, associated with such feelings, can occur to us so proper as those which he has employed, especially on the highest, the most august, and the most awful subjects that can interest a human being in this sentient world. That this is no mere fancy, I can undertake to establish from hundreds, I might say thousands, of passages. No character he has drawn, in the whole list of his plays, could so well and fitly express himself, as in the language Shakespeare has put into his mouth.

There is no indecision about Hamlet, as far as his own sense of duty is concerned; he knows well what he ought to do, and over and over again he makes up his mind to do it. The moment the players, and the two spies set upon him, have withdrawn, of whom he takes leave with a line so expressive of his contempt,

> "Ay so; good bye you.—Now I am alone,"

he breaks out into a delirium of rage against himself for neglecting to perform the solemn duty he had undertaken, and contrasts the factitious and artificial display of feeling by the player with his own apparent indifference;

> "What's Hecuba to him, or he to Hecuba,
> That he should weep for her?"

Yet the player did weep for her, and was in an agony of grief at her sufferings, while Hamlet is unable to rouse himself to action, in order that he may perform the command of his father, who had come from the grave to incite him to revenge:—

> "This is most brave!
> That I, the son of a dear father murder'd,
> Prompted to my revenge by heaven and hell,
> Must, like a whore, unpack my heart with words,
> And fall a cursing like a very drab,
> A scullion."
>
> *Act II., Scene 2.*

It is the same feeling, the same conviction of what is his duty, that makes Hamlet exclaim in a subsequent part of the tragedy:

> "How all occasions do inform against me,
> And spur my dull revenge! What is a man,
> If his chief good, and market of his time,
> Be but to sleep and feed? A beast, no more. * * *
> ————————I do not know
> Why yet I live to say—'this thing's to do,'
> Sith I have cause and will and strength and means
> To do't."
>
> *Act IV., Scene 4.*

Yet with all this strong conviction of duty, and with all this resolution arising out of strong conviction, nothing is done. This admirable and consistent character, deeply acquainted with his own feelings, painting them with such wonderful power and accuracy, and firmly persuaded that a moment ought not to be lost in executing the solemn charge committed to him, still yields to the same retiring from reality, which is the result of having, what we express by the terms, a world within himself.

Such a mind as Hamlet's is near akin to madness. Dryden has some-where said,

> "Great wit to madness nearly is allied,"

and he was right; for he means by "wit" that greatness of genius, which led Hamlet to a perfect knowledge of his own character, which, with all strength of motive, was so weak as to be unable to carry into act his own most obvious duty.

With all this he has a sense of imperfectness, which becomes apparent when he is moralising on the skull in the churchyard. Something is wanting to his completeness—something is deficient which remains to be supplied, and he is therefore described as attached to Ophelia. His madness is assumed, when he finds that witnesses have been placed behind the arras to listen to what passes, and when the heroine has been thrown in his way as a decoy.

Another objection has been taken by Dr. Johnson, and Shakespeare has been taxed very severely. I refer to the scene where Hamlet enters and finds his uncle praying, and refuses to take his life, excepting when he is in the height of his iniquity. To assail him at such a moment of confession and repentance, Hamlet declares,

> "Why, this is hire and salary, not revenge."
> *Act III., Scene 4.*

He therefore forbears, and postpones his uncle's death, until he can catch him in some act

> "That has no relish of salvation in't."

This conduct, and this sentiment, Dr. Johnson has pronounced to be so atrocious and horrible, as to be unfit to be put into the mouth of a human being.* The fact, however, is that Dr. Johnson did not understand the character of Hamlet, and censured accordingly: the determination to allow the guilty King to escape at such a moment is only part of the indecision and irresoluteness of the hero. Hamlet seizes hold of a pretext for not acting, when he might have acted so instantly and effectually: therefore, he again defers the revenge he was bound to seek, and declares his determination to accomplish it at some time,

> "When he is drunk, asleep, or in his rage,
> Or in th'incestuous pleasures of his bed."

This, allow me to impress upon you most emphatically, was merely the excuse Hamlet made to himself for not taking advantage of this particular and favourable moment for doing justice upon his guilty uncle, at the urgent instance of the spirit of his father.

Dr. Johnson farther states, that in the voyage to England, Shakespeare merely follows the novel as he found it, as if the poet had no other reason for adhering to his original; but Shakespeare never followed a novel, because he found such and such an incident in it, but because he saw that the story, as he read it, contributed to enforce, or to explain some great truth inherent in human nature. He never could lack invention to alter or improve a popular narrative; but he did not wantonly vary from it, when he knew that, as it was related, it would so well apply to his own great purpose. He saw at once how consistent it was with the character of Hamlet, that after still resolving, and still deferring,

---

* See Malone's Shakespeare by Boswell, vii., 382, for Johnson's note upon this part of the scene. J. P. C.

still determining to execute, and still postponing execution, he should finally, in the infirmity of his disposition, give himself up to his destiny, and hopelessly place himself in the power, and at the mercy of his enemies.

Even after the scene with Osrick, we see Hamlet still indulging in reflection, and hardly thinking of the task he has just undertaken: he is all dispatch and resolution, as far as words and present intentions are concerned, but all hesitation and irresolution, when called upon to carry his words and intentions into effect; so that, resolving to do everything, he does nothing. He is full of purpose, but void of that quality of mind which accomplishes purpose.

Anything finer than this conception, and working out of a great character, is merely impossible. Shakespeare wished to impress upon us the truth, that action is the chief end of existence—that no faculties of intellect, however brilliant, can be considered valuable, or indeed otherwise than as misfortunes, if they withdraw us from, or render us repugnant to action, and lead us to think and think of doing, until the time has elapsed when we can do anything effectually. In enforcing this moral truth, Shakespeare has shown the fulnesss and force of his powers: all that is amiable and excellent in nature is combined in Hamlet, with the exception of one quality. He is a man living in meditation, called upon to act by every motive human and divine, but the great object of his life is defeated by continually resolving to do, yet doing nothing but resolve.

END OF THE TWELFTH LECTURE.

INDEX

INDEX

* = Coleridge's footnotes   a = textual footnotes   tr = translated
n = editorial footnotes   q = quoted
superscript numbers = volume numbers (where there is none, the previous one applies)
C = Coleridge   S = Shakespeare
Textual misspellings or peculiarites, often Coleridge's, are sometimes indicated within parentheses.

All works appear under the author's name; anonymous works, newspapers, periodicals, are listed under titles. Translators and editors are usually listed under the author's name, with cross references giving birth and death dates.

Subentries are arranged alphabetically, sometimes in two parts, the first containing the general references, the second particular works. For example, under Dante, "age of", "as philosopher", precede *La Divina Commedia*. The arrangement of subentries under Coleridge, Lectures, and Shakespeare is indicated at the head of those entries.

Birth dates of persons now living are not given.

17; fashions of [1]295, [2]486; feudal [1]48; garrulity of old [1]308, [2]364, 492; guilt of a. past [1]64; heroic [2]50; incest in rude [1]333; of Milton [2]386–7; old [2]330 (*see also* garrulity, *above*); of personality and gossip [1]190, 190n, [2]464; present [1]191, 205, [2]464, 469; reading [1]125; reigning fault of [1]379, [2]530–1; republican [1]288, [2]479; S's *see* Shakespeare (3): age of; spirit of [2]114; of superstition [2]120; warlike [1]43; wars and neglect in all [2]58; in which we live [1]186, 189, [2]463 (*see also* present, *above*); wonder-loving [1]277

aged, world without [1]308, 319, [2]492

agency, invisible [2]160

agglomeration [2]235, 235n–6

aggregative, power [1]67, 67n

Agincourt [2]267

Agis *see* Catullus

agonies

dying [2]474; world's convention of [2]333

agreeable [1]36

definition of [1]31n; taste and [1]36

Aguecheek, Sir Andrew (*Twelfth Night*) [2]150

Aikin, Anne (Wakefield) (d 1821) [1]396

air

deity for [2]49; images from [1]365, [2]526

Ajax (*Troilus and Cressida*) [2]377, 378, 379, 380, 380n

Akenside, Mark (1721–70) [1]386n

The Pleasures of Imagination [1]272n

Albany (*Lear*) [2]325, 326, 330, 331

Albemarle St *see* London

Albizi family [2]96

Albuera [1]331n

alchemists

Bacon vs [2]49; and magic [2]211; and mania [2]210; stories told of [2]210; wrote like Pythagoreans [2]211

alchemy [2]48n, 53n, 196

chemistry and [2]193; of genius [2]111; mystical [2]56, 56n

Alciati, Andrea (1492–1550) *Parerga* [2]205n

alcohol, of egotism [2]427

Aldgate *see* London

Alexander the Great, King of Macedon (356–323 B.C.) [1]77n, [2]78n, 165

and conquest of India [1]44; history of conquests of [1]287; singing praise of Bacchus [1]44, 44n; son of Jupiter [1]44

Alexandrian philosophers [2]49n

Alfred the Great, King of the West Saxons (849–901) [2]56, 56n, 67, 75, 75n

character of [2]81, 81n; framing hymns to

Madonna [2]75; institution of trial by jury [2]81, 81n; translating Scriptures [2]75, 81, 81n

Algiers [2]163

Alhadra (C *Remorse*) [2]410, 410n

Alison, Archibald (1757–1839) *Essays on the Nature and Principles of Taste* q [1]lxx n

all

subordination of a. to one [2]137; thinking of a. in reference to a. [1]288; vs whole [1]430

Alla(h) [2]410

Allan, George A. T. *Christ's Hospital* q [1]584n

Allan Bank *see* Grasmere

allegoric(al)

personages [1]53, 53n, [2]102; romances [2]403; spirit [2]77, 77n; symbolical vs [2]417–18, 417n–18

allegory/-ies [2]86, 389, 389n, 395

of Bunyan *Pilgrim's Progress* [2]103; and *Divina Commedia* [2]398, 398n, 400; and fable [2]100–1; first modern [2]102; history of [2]99n; images in [2]99; living [2]162; meaning of [2]99; vs metaphor [2]99, 100, 101; most beautiful [2]102; narrative or epic [2]101–3, 398n; nature of [2]406; picture [2]101; and picture language [2]417n–18; Spenser and [2]409; substitute for polytheism [2]398, 398n; and understanding [2]172

Allsop, Thomas (1795–1880) [2]28n, 255, 255n, 407

Letters, Conversations and Recollections of S. T. Coleridge q [1]361n

Allston, Washington (1779–1843) [1]76n, 87n, 207–8, 208n

Lectures on Art and Poems [1]76n

Almack, William (d 1781) [1]416

Almack's (novel) [1]416

Almack's Room *see* London: Willis's Rooms

Almeida [1]331n

Almighty, communicating own attributes [2]465; *see also* God; Supreme Being

Alonzo (*Tempest*) [1]365, 369, [2]272, 450, 526

alphabetic, writing [2]217

Alpheus [1]85

Alps [1]191, [2]465

birth-place in [1]439, 439n

Alston, Aaron Burr (Gampillo) (1802–12) [1]263

COLERIDGE, SAMUEL TAYLOR (1772–1834)

I BIOGRAPHICAL AND GENERAL:
(1) Biographical (2) Characteristics
(3) Observations, opinions, ideas
(4) Relationships (5) Images (6) Word-coinages
II POETICAL WORKS   III PROSE WORKS   IV CONTRIBUTIONS TO
NEWSPAPERS AND PERIODICALS   V ESSAYS   VI LECTURES (by year)
VII MSS   VIII PROJECTED WORKS   IX COLLECTIONS AND SELECTIONS
X LETTERS   XI MARGINALIA   XII NOTEBOOKS

IV CONTRIBUTIONS TO NEWSPAPERS AND PERIODICALS

V ESSAYS

courtesy
offering of [1]37; spirit of [2]91
Courtier, Peter (b 1776) *The Pleasures of Solitude* [1]272n
courtiers
flings at [2]151; politeness of [1]290, [2]480; wit of [1]266
Courts of the Queen's Bench *see* London
Courts of Love [1]266, 276–7
Covent Garden *see* London
coward(s)
most men [1]305, [2]489; philosopher as [1]305, 305n
cowardice
courage and [2]174; terror and [1]138
Cowley, Abraham (1618–67)
prose style [2]236, 240–1
A Discourse by Way of Vision [2]240, 240n; *Works* [2]240n
Cowper, William (1731–1800) [1]120, 141
coxcomb, and philosopher [1]305, [2]489
Crabb, George (1778–1851) *English Synonymes Explained* [1]lxix n, 488
crabs, soldier [1]437
cramming [1]107
Crane Court *see* London
Cranford, Mr (fl 1812) [1]421n
Cranmer, Thomas, abp of Canterbury (1489–1556) [2]138, 138n
articles of visitation (witchcraft) [2]206, 206n
craving, for that which is not [1]544
Crawford, Walter Byron (ed) *Reading Coleridge* [1]lxxxiii n, 171n, [2]438
creation(s)
of arbitrary will [1]456; artistic [1]495n–6; firstling of [2]208; of genius [2]162; man head of visible [2]221; pock-freckled [1]401; of universe [1]401
creative
act [1]lxxv; joy [1]543; power [1]137, [2]116n
creator
man own [1]192, 315, [2]465, 499; poet as [1]350
Creator
and union of man and woman [1]314
creature(s)
born to die [1]192, [2]465; of day [2]514; sentient [2]218
credibilizing [2]295, 295n
Creed, H. H. "Coleridge on 'Taste' " [1]lxix n
Cressida (*Troilus and Cressida*) [2]377, 377n, 379
Crete, Jupiter King of [1]44, 54

crime(s)
association with [2]149; commission of [1]531; and early correction [2]476; guilt and [1]317, [2]353, 501; guilt diminishing [2]278; and ludicrous [2]272; most detestable of all [1]365, [2]526
criminal
dispositions [2]417; sentence on [1]286, [2]476
critic(s) [1]262
arguing from abuse of thing [1]564; C as [1]lxiv–lxxx; damning Milton [1]427; eighteenth-century [1]lviii, lviii n, lix, lxiii, lxvi, lxix; English [1]494; failed writers turn [2]463–4; French [1]135, 491, 494; as frog [1]138, 138n, 209, 209n, [2]473; and geniuses [1]511; hate those who excel [2]464; insolence of [1]268; like monkey [1]268, 268n; as night flies [1]209, [2]473; and pursuit of fly [1]402; readers and [1]187; and rule of reason [1]491; of S *see* Shakespeare (3); critics, 18th-century commentary on; and spirit of poetry [1]465; as springs and tanks [1]352n; superiority over author [1]268; as supreme judge [1]79–80
critical
principles [1]xxxix, lxv–lxvi, lxviii, lxxiii, lxxvi; synod [2]146; vocabulary [1]xxxix, lxvi, lxix, lxxv n
Critical Review [1]296n
criticism
beauty-and-blemish mode of [1]lxvii; commonplace vs philosophical [1]560; condition of genial [2]264; English [1]21, 368; false [1]179, 182, 186–8, 186n, 188–93, 194–5, 196–7, 564, [2]462–3, 464–6, 467; French [1]268n, 368, [2]264, 265, 277, 344; German [1]21, 105, 107, 107n, 113, 118, 368, [2]293, 293n; grounds of [1]179, 182, 193, [2]467; only nomenclature of [1]564; overloaded with personality [2]463; philosophical [1]560, [2]290, 293, 378; practical [1]lxiii, lxxv, lxxvn, lxxvii, [2]34, 34n, 35, 257; rules of [1]lxvi, lxviii; Shakespearian [1]xxxix, xl, lxvi, lxxv; technical [2]70; that binds poetry to one model [1]437
Crocker, Francis [1]525
Cromwell, Oliver (1599–1658) [2]240, 385
crosses, pulling down of [2]205
Crowe, William (1745–1829) [1]8, 8n, 16n
Lewesdon Hill [1]8, 8n
crown, transfer of papal power to [2]386
Crown and Anchor *see* London
Crown and Britannia (watermark) [1]452, 491

epithets—*continued*
1304, 304n, 2488; high-flown 2469; misuse of 2468
equality
of free men 254; perfect 1594; ridiculous notion of 1586; of women 254
Erasmus, Desiderius (Gerhard Gerhards) (c 1466–1536) 1270, 270n, 516, 516n
error(s)
author who commits 2463; of chronology and geography 2245; of few 1317, 2501; and laughter 2178; liability to 138
erudition 178
golden aera of 2387
Erzgebirge 256n
essayists, give account of selves 1124
Essays and Studies 1lxxv n
Essays in Criticism 1lxxiii n
essentials, and accidents 1511, 515
Essex 1159, 2200
Colne Priory 2109; County Record Office *see* Chelmsford
Estlin, John Prior (1747–1818) 11, 27, 7n, 11
eternal
of our nature 2119; and temporal 2418n; truths 1467
eternity, time and 184–5, 2207
ether 1401
blue islet of 2208
ethics, of Greece 1481
Etienne (tobacco) 124
etymon, of reputation 1206, 206n, 2471
Euclid (fl c 300 B.C.) 177, 208, 2472
Euripides (5th century B.C.) 152, 225, 227, 348, 348n, 444, 458, 458n, 2439, 511
Medea 1541, 541n; *Orestes* 1541n
Europe
after Waterloo 2186; christianized 1269; dark ages in 1xxxix, 241; feudal 250; gentleman of (Sidney) 1327, 327n, 2504; hierarchy and progress of 258; introduction of ancient literature into 148; languages of 1283, 410; Latin spoken in 289; liberation of 213; mediaeval 1424, 255n; modern 1424, 255; no dark age of 275, 75n; at peace 233; peopling of 278; primogeniture in south of 2327; progress of sciences in 1270; Reformation in 1516; representation of birth of Christ in south of 149, 49n; Sidney gentleman of 1327, 327n; travel in 1lxxvii
European
Christendom 240–1, 44, 49–50, 61, 397;

drama, C's lectures on 1413–71; history 224; literature 1xliii, lxxvii, 224, 33, 186, 253; literature influenced by Persian 278n, 402, 403n, 403n
Europeans, of Asia 272
evangelicals 1xlvix, 133n, 487, 489, 490, 497
Evans, Sir Hugh (*Merry Wives*) 1233
Evans, John (fl 1814) *The Picture of Bristol* q 1601, 601n, q 602, 602n
Evans, Mary *see* Todd
Evans, Thomas (fl 1790s) 191
Evans, Sir Hugh (*Merry Wives*) 1528, 2118n, 178, 178n
Eve (Bible) 150, 51n, 254, 254n, 554, 554n
Eve (*Paradise Lost*) 1313, 213, 390n, 390n, 391n, 428, 431, 497
Eve (*Sachs Kinder Eve*) 283, 83n
event(s)
of day 1189, 227, 40, 463; dreams coincident with 2202; germ of after 1lxxiv, 559; long since passed 1517; proceeding from passions 145; relating e. in simple states 145; of sacred history 149; stimulant power of 1186, 189; stimulus of political 1194–5; in tragicomedy 152; will has no share in 163
external vs internal 1lxxii, 239n, 240, 247, 2116, 371, 373
evil
combat of good and 2388–9; good from 148, 2353; impersonation of moral 153; nature of e. to beget 1398, 411; origin of 2388–9, 426; oscillation of good and 2174; restrained 254
Evil, in religious plays 2475
Evil Being/Prince of Hell
as Pluto 293, 93n; *see also* Devil; Satan
evolution
and assimilation 2147; of thoughts 2234
examination, of what you read 2238
Examiner 1273n, 2323
excellence
loved in any form 2318; moral 112, 2241, 468, 468*; prostrate before 1335n; virtue meaning 1204, 2468, 468*
excellencies/-ces
defects vs 1293, 2484; unrealized 1332, 2507; within 1505, 505n
excitement
and disease 1222n; from external objects 248; inanimate objects seen in 166; language of 1428, 2426; language natural in states of 1218, 221, 221a, 222, 230; in

faith(s)—*continued*
tions and half- [1]lv, lvii; temporary [1]130; we live by [2]193; will and [2]377; works and [2]353
falcon [1]87, 87n
Falconbridge (*Merchant of Venice*) [2]265
fall
before the f. [2]391, 391n; of man [2]391, 391n, 425, 428
fallibility, individual [1]37
falsehood
facts vs [2]42, 196; mind prepared for [1]106
falsetto, in prose style [2]237
Falstaff [1]lxvi, lxvii, lxvii n, lxxv, 167, 179, 294, 294n, 374, 377, 391, 502, 567, 570, 574, 574n, 575, 575n, 576, 576n, [2]126, 127, 130–1, 169, 178, 273n, 338, 416, 416n, 452, 485, 528
fame
charm of [2]386; desire of [1]206, [2]471; heir of [2]387, 387n; vs reputation [1]206, 206n, [2]242, 242n, 471; works of genuine [1]77
familiarity, thing mean by [2]296
family/-ies
bond of relationship in [1]333; British royal [2]75, 75n; feuds [2]362, 363; pride of [1]304, 308, [2]74, 489, 492; state f. magnified [1]315, [2]499; which had emigrated [1]333, [2]508
fanaticism, origin of [2]238
fancies
danger of indulging in [2]308; sensual [1]552
fanciful [2]41, 168
fancy [1]lxvi, 12, 30, 127, 290, 480, 480n, 492
and ambitious thoughts [2]306; of author [1]85, 274; and business [1]115; definition of [1]67, 67n, 81, 81n; and imagery [2]191; imagination vs [1]81n, 215, 217, 220, 245, 459, [2]113n, 194, 272, 332, 411; and ludicrous [2]171; nature of [1]319; reproducing past [1]361; sport of [1]297, [2]487; warblers of [2]113, 113n; wit vs [1]31n, 283, 294, 294n, [2]365, 416, 484–5
faquir, brooding [2]113, 113n
farce
plots [2]374; poetical [2]374; ridiculing ancient plays [1]227; of world [2]173
Farington, Joseph (1747–1821) [2]207, 207n
Diary ed James Greig [1]12n, 14n, q 76n, q 121, q 145, [2]207n
Farmer, Richard (1735–97) [2]297, 297n–8
Essay on the Learning of Shakespeare [2]298n

Farquhar, George (1678–1707)
on unities [2]264, 264n
A Discourse upon Comedy [1]lx, lx n, q 210n, [2]264n; *Love and Business* [2]264n; *Works* (1742) [1]210n
farthings, man who squandered estate in [1]295, [2]485
fashion(s)
accidents of [2]27, 40; of age [1]295, [2]486; men of rank and [1]266; punning as [2]297
fata morgana [1]352, 352–3, [2]441, 514
fate
in epic [2]283; free will and [1]559; in Greek tragedy [1]444, 448; as higher will [2]283; must conquer [1]448; oppressed by [1]317, [2]501; power of [1]448
Fates [1]531, 531n, [2]114n, 305, 376
father, child and [1]106, 330, [2]273, 505
fatuity, as species of madness [2]165
fault(s)
and beauties *see* beauty: defects/faults vs; moral [1]64; reigning f. of age [1]379, [2]530–1; *see also* defects
favour
promised [2]178; of queen harlotry [1]288
favourites, of fortune [2]151
Fazzerkeley, Mr (fl 1812) [1]421n
fear(s)
and child [1]588; from external dangers [1]529; faculty of [1]326, [2]503; hope becomes [1]137; obscure [1]492; pleasures of [1]272; of selfishness [2]309–10
featurely [2]378, 378n
feeling(s) [1]28, 36
aloofness of poet's [1]242; appeal to [1]55; balance and antithesis of [1]84; base [1]296, [2]486; of child [1]286, 581, [2]476; of childhood into manhood [1]326, 326n, 336–7; distinct truths and vivid [1]594; distortion of [1]586; domestic [1]249; exhaustion of bodily [1]540; and experience [1]554, [2]269; given to fellow men [1]492, 492n; of inferiority [2]271; intellectual [1]297; language and [1]366n; low [2]487; minutiae of [2]175; misplaced in man [1]381; of moment [1]588; moral [1]116–17, 195, 283, 288, 333, 377, 493, 553, 567, 593, [2]5, 14, 182, 479, 528; motives vs [1]106; national [1]378, [2]452, 529; necessary to future poet [1]585; nobler [1]296; notions and [1]107, 107n; objects of reflection [2]218; ordinary life master of our [1]187; overflow of [1]561; and past experience [1]554, [2]269; poetic [1]67, 251–2, [2]425; predominant [1]241, 249,

Gillman, James (1782–1839) [2]225n, 344
C patient of [1]xliii; on C's lectures [1]lii n,
liii, lxv; on 1818 lectures [2]28, 33, 134
Life of Samuel Taylor Coleridge q [1]lii n,
q liii, liii n, q lxv, lxv n, [2]28n, 249–50,
q 250
Gillmans [2]109, 262, 298n
C living with [1]xliii, lxxx, [2]23, 24
Giotto di Bondone (c 1276–c 1337) [1]lxxxiv,
[2]60, 402
frescoes in Pisa cemetery attributed to [2]60,
60n, 62–3, 62n, 402n
Triumph of Death see Traini
girls, education of [1]505, 592, 594–5
Giulio Romano (Giulio Pippi de' Gian-
nuzzi, c 1492–1546) [1]471
Givenni Givanni [2]202, 203n
giving, power of [1]192, 465
gladiators, [1]48
gladness, distribute portion of [2]485
gladsomeness, returning [2]208
Glamis (*Macbeth*) [1]531, 531n
Glasgow
Mechanics' Institution [2]254n; University
of [1]33n
glass, man made of [2]165
Glaucus (*Iliad*) [2]399, 399n
Globe Theatre *see* London
glory
round head of figure in mist [1]352, 352n,
[2]441, 514; spiritualized to state of [1]457;
of world [2]283, 283n
Gloucester [1]24
Gloucester, Eleanor Cobham, Duchess of
(d 1454) [2]205, 205n
Gloucester ("Gloster") (*King Lear*) [1]528,
[2]325, 326, 327, 329, 331, 333
Gloucester (*Richard II*) [1]560, 565, [2]285,
285n
Goat, Hymn/Song of the [1]44, 45, 45n, 225
goat, sacrifice of [1]517
goblet, cast by Myron [1]34
goblin(s) [2]56n, 291, 302
in nightmares [1]136
God
belief in [1]315, [2]499; bestowed gifts on
man [1]192, [2]465; good from [1]293n; grace
of [2]386; G's house [1]129, 132; and man
[2]426; and moral sense [1]315; nature art
of [2]218; protection of [2]207; School-Divine [2]387, 387n; soul absorbed into [2]60n;
a traditional hero [1]43; of the Vine [1]44;
and Word [2]97, 97n
God (*Paradise Lost*) [1]406, 407, [2]426

Godalming
Charterhouse [1]579
godhead, unity of [2]77n
godlike
power [1]44; within [2]173
gods
and destiny [1]562n; in fable [2]100; of Greece
from Egypt [2]399; Greek [1]448, 517, [2]56–
7, 57n, 80; in Greek tragedy [1]46, [2]120;
to heroes [2]56–7; intervention of [1]562n;
man on level with [1]448; ministers of destiny [1]448; multiplicity of [2]101, 398n
Godwin, William (1756–1836) [1]155n, 167,
263
attended 1808 lectures [1]18, 92, 93; and
1811–12 lectures [1]158, 158n, 262, 282,
394; and 1818 lectures [2]67, 163; and
perfectibility [1]334n
Mandeville [2]163, 163n
Godwin's Juvenile Library [1]180, 182
Goethe, Johann Wolfgang von (1749–1832)
[1]lxxvii
tr of Diderot [1]119n; on Voltaire [1]119, 119n
Sämtliche Werke [1]119n
Gog [2]49
Golconda [1]65n, 204n
gold
definition of [1]218; as tetrad [2]211
Goldsmith, Oliver (1728–74)
Essays and Criticisms [1]211n; *Miscellaneous Works* [1]211n; "On the Origin of
Poetry" [1]211, 211n; "On the Study of
the Belles Lettres. On Taste" [1]211n
Goliath (Bible) [1]201
Goneril (*Lear*) [2]322, 328, 329, 330, 331,
332, 431
Gonzalo (*Tempest*) [1]358–9, 365, [2]272, 445,
450, 520, 526
good
begin with [1]293, [2]484; combat of evil and
[2]388–9; from evil [1]48, [2]353; general [2]386;
from God [1]293n; made ridiculous [2]272;
one man can do [1]109; oscillation of g.
and evil [2]174; seeds of g. in man [1]117;
taste and [1]36; from work [1]189, [2]462
Goodfellow, Robin *see* Puck
goodness
teaching [1]108; and truth [2]328
good neighbours [2]56, 56n
goodyness [1]108, 108n
Gorée [2]73, 73n
Gospel
cathedral symbol of [2]74–5; preaching 586;
see also Bible: New Testament

LECTURES

I GENERAL AND BACKGROUND
lectures on education related to literary lectures [1]lxxix–lxxx; not published [1]liii, lxiv, lxxvi, lxxxx, 14, 100, 119–20; not systematic [1]lxv; preparations/notes for [1]xlvi–xlvii, xlvix–liii, liv, 65, 113, [2]250, 346–7 (*see also* notes *under individual lectures*); repetitions [1]xl, xlvix, reports [1]xl, lxxx–lxxxviii (*see also* comments and reports *under individual lectures*); reuse of lectures [1]xli; sources of lectures [1]liv–lviii; texts of lectures [1]lxxx–lxxxviii (*see also* texts *under individual lectures*); use of notes/speaking extempore [1]xlvi, xlvii, xlvii n, xlviii, lxiv, lxv, lxxx–lxxxviii; unassigned lecture notes [2]423–31

II LECTURES 1806 (PROPOSED)
proposed for RI [1]xl–xli, 3–8, 11, 12, 24, 123

III LECTURES 1808
(1) *General and Background* [1]9–149, 153, 157, 182, 190, 190n, 194, 194n, 196, 286, 354, 416, 417, [2]135, 260, 263, 266n, 290, 293–4, 331n, 382, 383, 442, 477, 515
auditors/audience [1]xlii, xlix–xlv, xlvii–xlviii, lxxxiii–lxxxiv, lxxxv, 141, 142, 143, 286, [2]293–4; background [1]24–5, 40–1, 61, 72, 90, 91–2, 96–104, 113–14, 116, 118–22; basic issues [1]lxviii–lxxxi; borrowings [1]lv; delivery [1]194; on education *see* (3), *below*, Lecture 12A; Godwin attended [1]18; last lecture [1]21; mainly on S and Milton [1]xxxix, xli, 19; main object of [1]78; on modern poetry [1]138–9; number [1]xli, xliv, 12, 15, 16, 17, 90, 122, 146, 146n, [2]293n; payment [1]xlii, 12, 16–17, 92, 122, 146, 146n; postponed by Davy's illness [1]12, 13n;

preparation [1]145, 147–8, 147n, 149, 286; and principles of poetry [1]xli, xlviii–xlvix, lxv, lxxiii; remarks on WW [1]13, 14–15; resignation from [1]xli, 15; HCR and [1]xlv, xlv n, lxxix n, 14, 14n, 18, 40, 54–5, 96, 105–9, 113–14, 114–16, 116–19, 155, 603; and A. W. Schlegel [1]lvi, lxii, lxiii, 113, 116n, 173, 175, [2]109–10; S's judgement [1]lx, lx n, 19, 20; on S's Sonnets [1]lx; subscribers [1]lxxxv; WW attended [1]lx, 18
(2) *Texts and Notes*
C's notes [1]xlvi–xlvii, xlviii, q [1]27–38, q 43–54, q 63–70, q 75–87, q 123–39; N 25 used [1]60–1, q 65–70, 72–3, q 75–82, 138, q 138–9, 214; texts [1]24, 40, 60–1, 72
(3) *Lectures (by number)*
Lect 1 [1]23–38, 182, 185, 186n, 193n, 286, 602, [2]14; Lect 2 [1]39–57, 60, 211n, 225n, 269n, 286, 345, 603, [2]67; Lect 3 [1]60–70, 72, 126, 200, 203n, 576n; Lect 4 [1]61, 65n, 72–87, 126, 187n, 208n, 210n, 221n; Lects 5–12 [1]89–93, 126; Lect 12A [1]xxxix, xli, lxxviii–lxxxix, 14, 14n, 15, 16, 96–109, 278n, 283, 285n, 504, 505, 578, 579, 584n, 585n, 586n, 587n, [2]189, 192n; Lects 13–20 [1]111–22, 134n, 407n, 521n
(4) *Comments and Reports*
comments by: Beaumont [1]xlviii, 13, 13n; C [1]xlvi–xlvii, 65, 141–3; De Q [1]18, 40, 56–7, 90, 145–8; Farington [1]145; Jerningham [1]143–5; HCR [1]xlv, xlvn, lxxix n, 14, 14n, 18, 40, 54–5, 96, 105–9, 113–14, 114–16, 116–19, 155, 603; Thomson [1]148–9
reports [1]40, q 54–7, 96, q 105–9, q 114–16, q 116–18, q 141–9
(5) *Supplementary Records*
C mss [1]123–39

society—*continued*
[2]498; ladder of privileged [1]589; man in [1]43; marriage and [1]330, [2]505; not sanctioned by government [2]276; order and gradations in [1]586; privileges in [2]163; progressive [1]330, 330n, [2]505; rests on love [1]331, [2]506; reverence for ranks of [2]431; structure of [1]331; welfare of [1]125
Society for Bettering the Conditions of the Poor [1]100
Socinian, Satan sceptical [2]7, 12
Socinians [1]107, 107n
Socrates (before 469–399 B.C.) [1]315n, 327n, 427, 455, 460, [2]55, 101n
and humour [2]173
sodium [1]12, [2]294n
soil
plant dependent on [1]511, 515, [2]111; poets drew aliment from [2]119
soldier(s)
crabs [1]437; in Jonson's plays [1]265, 275; lion allegorical for [2]418
soldiery, heroic deeds of [1]287, [2]478
soliloquies [2]151
solitude, bliss of [1]68
Somerset House *see* London
Somersetshire [2]203, 294
song(s)
choral s. of Greek drama [1]441, 441n; drinking [1]44; English [2]41, 44, 66; heroic [2]80, 184; in honour of deity [1]440; love-[2]61n, 67; of minerals [1]519; national [2]44, 66, 69; in S [2]118; of triumph [2]217
Song of Roland [2]76, 77n
soothsaying [2]206n
Sophia (Fielding *Tom Jones*) [1]309, [2]493
Sophia (Massinger *Picture*) [2]151n–2
Sophocles (c 496–406 B.C.) [1]52, 211n, 225, 227, 348, 348n, 444, 455, 466, [2]284, 439, 474, 511
model of tragedy [1]78, 209, [2]473; vs S [1]432, 432n, 517
Electra [1]317, 317n; *Oedipus Rex* [1]210, 317, 317n, [2]501
Sophron (5th century B.C.) [1]459–60, 459n
sorceresses [1]531, [2]114n
sorcery [2]206n
Act against [2]205; practices of s. regarded with abhorrence [2]211
sorrow, joy and [1]337
Sotheby, Mary (Isted) (1759–1834) [1]415
Sotheby, William (1757–1833) [1]7n, 17n, 19, 86n, 93, 113, 141, 142, 417, 424, 425, 432, 434

soul
absorbed into God [2]60n; battle of [2]102; and being in life [1]329n; body and [1]314, 457, [2]498; convergence of powers of [1]456; fall and redemption of [2]192; freedom of human [1]448; genial climate of [1]530; idea of [2]172; imperishable [1]492; passions which arise out of [1]457; quasi-credent [2]208; to realize its images [1]137; of romance language [2]89; self-flattering [2]353; unshackled by custom [1]326, [2]503
sound(s) [2]219
absence of articulate [2]218; attention to minute [2]138; combinations of [1]36; man communicates by [2]217; and memory [2]217; in nature [2]42, 214; passion and [2]217; preferred to sense [1]205, [2]469; richness and sweetness of [1]241, 248; vs sight [1]135n, 364, [2]218; taste vs [1]36–7
South, arts and philosophy of [2]111
Southampton, Earl of *see* Wriothesley
Southerne, Thomas (1660–1746) *The Fatal Marriage* [2]361, 361n
Southey, Robert (1774–1843) [1]5, 12, 16, 17n, 40, 60, 143, 147n, 154, 232, 417n, [2]47n, 256n, 344, 373n
and Bell [1]104n, 578; on Bell vs Lancaster [1]98, 99, 101–2; on bigotry of *Eclectic Review* [1]133n; and C [1]335n; and C's lecture on education (1808) [1]98, 101, 103, 578; and C's opium addiction [2]20; and 1811–12 lectures [1]160; offered to recite C's lectures [1]61; possesses his genius [1]244n; and proposed 1806 lectures [1]xl, 6, 7; review on new systems of education q [1]101–2, 102n, silhouette by Miers [1]208n
Madoc [1]263; *New Letters of Robert Southey* ed Kenneth Curry q [1]160, 160n; *The Origin, Nature, and Object of the New System of Education* [1]98, 98n, q 101–2, 102n, q 103, 103n, 504–5, 578, 579, 583n; *Thalaba* [1]263, 299n; tr of *Amadis de Gaula* [1]164n; tr of *Chronicle of the Cid* [2]410n; tr of Díaz del Castillo q [2]208–9, 209n
sovereign
attachment to [2]61; conqueror as [1]455
sovereignty, habits of [2]325–6
sow, wallow with [1]331, [2]506
space
accidental relations of [2]419; iron compulsion/bondage of [1]350, [2]512; mental [2]410; power over [1]350, [2]512; and reason

temple—*continued*
existence [2]47–8; palace and [2]74; for unseen angels [2]75
Temple *see* London
temporal, eternal and [2]418n
temptation, warfield of [1]128
tempters, of themselves [1]531
Ten Commandments [1]50
tenderness, S's [1]553, 565
Terence (Publius Terentius Afer) (c 190–159 B.C.) [2]82n
Teresa (C *Remorse*) [2]361n
term(s)
connected with taste [1]188; contemporary, an ambiguous [2]145; definition of [1]lix, lxix, 491; difficulty of defining [2]101; diplomatic [1]291; grotesque [1]544; laxity in use of *see* terms: vague use of; metaphorical [1]292, [2]482–3; military and diplomatic [1]291, [2]481; misuse of [1]34–5; in morals [2]469; nine meanings to same [1]487; obscure [2]238; in philosophy [1]204, [2]469; in politics [1]204, [2]469; precise meaning of [1]126; preciseness in [2]237; vague use of [1]187–8, 187n, 193, 197, 201–2, 204, 487, [2]466, 468
terminations, vocabulary of [1]594
terrible, and ludicrous [1]544–5
terror(s)
from apparitions [1]131; cause of image [2]207, 208, 266n; of conscience [2]207; and cowardice [1]138; in dreams [1]131; of ghosts [2]42, 196, 207n; laugh of [1]545; and ludicrous [1]541; of nature [1]127; to rage [1]529, 530; struck by apparitions [2]207
testimony, contemporary [2]208–10
tetrad, gold as [2]211
Teutonic
languages [2]89–90, 89n; nations [2]78; race [2]52; tribes [2]79
text, notes more poetical than [1]190, [2]464
Thales (fl 580 B.C.) [2]273, 273n
Thames [2]411
waterman's language [2]240n
theatre(s)
ancient [1]53, 350, 434, 439, [2]440, 512; beings in senses sitting in [1]83; blest he in public [1]529, 529n; church changed into [1]129, 132; definition of [1]129, 132; differences of modern and ancient [1]47; few frequenters of [1]247; Grecian [1]225; Greek v English [1]52; large [1]430; in Middle Ages [1]266; and morals [1]191; origin of English [1]211, [2]474–5; and public mind

[1]429; scenery seen in daylight [2]194; in S's age [1]228, 229; size of [1]211, 225, 231, 349, 563, [2]150, 474; and stage-illusion [1]128, [2]277; taken domestic turn [1]191, [2]464; voice for large [1]211, 225–6, 349; *see also* stage
theatrical
representations [1]211; scenery [1]46
Thebes [1]115n, 226, 226n, 518, [2]199n, 385n
Thelwall, John (1764–1834)
and C [1]lxx, 106n, 586, [2]28; on C as lecturer [1]lii; vs C as lecturer [2]302, 302n; lectures on S [2]28, 258, 258n; reports of C's lectures [2]28, 28n, 258, 261, 262, q 275–8, 317n; and uncultivated garden [1]106, 106n, 586, 586n
Theobald, Lewis (1688–1744)
on *Titus Andronicus* [2]301n
Preface to Shakespeare [1]lxvii; *see also* Shakespeare (6) *The Works*
Theocritus (c 310–250 B.C.) "Feast of Adonis" [1]459–60, 459n
Theodoret (Fletcher *Thierry*) [2]149n
Theodoric the Great, King of the Ostrogoths (c 454–526) [2]56, 56n, 74, 74n, 75, 75n, 80
Theodorus (d 826) [2]112n
Theodosius I (Flavius Theodosius) (c 346–395), the Great, Roman emperor [1]48n
theologians, 17th-century [1]lix
theological, philosophical and [1]lxxx
theory, mind having formed [1]306, [2]491
theosophy [2]56
Thersites (*Troilus and Cressida*) [2]377, 378, 378n, 379–80
thesis, illustration swallows up [1]64n
Thessaly [2]204
thing(s)
abstracts of [1]351, [2]441, 514; admired by mankind [1]271; contemplation of mind upon [1]225; each t. that lives [2]223; external [2]427; images symbol of [1]582; and language [1]429; mean by familiarity [2]296; notions and [1]85n; ocean of unknown [1]316; origin of [2]274; person degraded to [1]555; by power of imagination become [1]69; real nature of [1]29; remote from feelings [1]67; re-presented [2]218; thoughts and [1]366n, 540n, [2]218; union of disparate [2]220; word and [1]273
thinker
extraordinary [1]124; profound [1]583
thinking
act of [2]194; of all in reference to all [1]288,

voice, for large theatres [1]211, 225–6, 349, [2]440, 474
volition, nature of [2]202n
Voltaire (François Marie Arouet) (1694–1778) [1]107, 116, 116n, 119, 119n, 208n, 269n, 357n, [2]104
criticism of S [1]495, 495n; on Greek tragedy vs Italian opera [1]441n, [2]120n; insolent critic [1]268, 268n; wit [1]294, [2]168, 416, 484
Dissertation sur la tragédie ancienne et moderne [1]441n, q [2]120n; *Oeuvres complètes* [2]120n
Volterra, Daniel (1509–66) *Descent from the Cross* [1]77n
voluptuous, passion for [2]91
voyages
images from [1]249; versifications of [1]362, [2]523
Vulcan [2]49n, 368, 368n
vulgar, the
and appeal to feelings [1]55; love Bible [1]55; passions [1]68, 68n; in politics [2]272; and S [1]117n–18
vulgarisms
as human in human nature [2]284; in S [2]284
vulgarity
of bad passions [1]530; humour and cunning constitute [2]165; vehicle of profound truths [2]123

Wade, Josiah (fl 1796–1814) [1]502, [2]3, 4, 4n, 6, 7, 20
Wade, Launcelot (c 1796–c 1830) [1]594n
Wadman, Widow (Sterne *Tristram Shandy*) [1]338n, [2]175n
waking
dream [1]lvii; half w. and half-sleeping [1]lv; sleeping and [1]136
Waldenses [2]205, 205n
Wales [1]597, [2]375
Walford, Edward (1823–97) *Old and New London* [2]345n
Wallenstein (Schiller) [2]306, 306n, 309n
Walsingham, Sir Francis (c 1530–90) [2]233, 239, 239n
essay on honesty [2]239, 239n
Walter, John (1776–1847) [1]158, 183, 411, 411n
Walton, Izaak (1593–1683) *Life of Donne* [2]202, 202n; *Life of Hooker* [1]328n
wampum [2]217, 217n
war
against pedantry [2]116, 122; in all ages

[2]58; chivalry in [2]59; embrace [1]230, 230n; propensity to [2]54; Romans and [1]47, [2]48
warblers, of fancy [2]113, 113n
Warburton, William, bp of Gloucester (1698–1779) [2]175n
Divine Legation of Moses Demonstrated [2]77n; Preface to Shakespeare [1]lxvii; *see also* Pope *Works*
Wark, Robert Rodger *see* Reynolds
Warner, Ferdinando (1703–68) *Remarks on the History of Fingal* [1]563n
Warner, Sir George Frederic (1845–1936) q [1]164
warriors
of Christian chivalry [2]378, 378n, 379; Moors as [2]314; name of [1]44; tombs of [2]74; under protection of godlike power [1]43–4
Wartburg [2]81n
Warton, Joseph (1722–1800) [1]lv, lxviii, [2]346
Observations on the Faerie Queene [2]326n
Warton, Thomas (1728–90) [2]346
The History of English Poetry [1]48n, q 49n, 50n, q 53n, 211n, [2]90n, 92n; *The Pleasures of Melancholy* [1]272n
Washington, George (1732–99) [1]137n
Washington, D.C.
Folger Shakespeare Library [1]66n, 162–3, 166, 170, 178, 183, 215, 344, 503, 524, [2]34n, 435; Library of Congress [1]170, [2]435
wassailing [1]545
watches, made for wholesale [2]362
watchings, outward [1]306, [2]491
watchmaker [1]583
water
dyad of light [2]211; phial of w. and Niagara [1]79–80, 80n; from well [1]269; without taste, smell, colour [2]224
waterfall(s)
beauty of [1]34, 34n; and sublime [1]544
Waterloo [2]33, 186
wavelets, of pleasure [2]364
waves
before tide [1]439; command [1]364, [2]525; longings like sea [2]377; of sea [2]364–5
wax(en)
figures [2]265, 265n; image [1]224, [2]220; impression on w. vs seal [2]220
we, sentiments dictated under word [1]189, [2]463
weak, pity [1]194, [2]467
weakness
and cunning [2]314; from inaction [1]565; in-